EVIDENCE:
Materials for L

Peter Murphy MA, LLB

and

John Beaumont LLM

First published in Great Britain 1982 by Financial Training Publications Limited, Holland House, 140-144 Freston Road, London W10 6TR

© Financial Training Publications, 1982
Second Edition, 1987

ISBN: 0 906322 97 9

Typeset by Kerrypress Ltd, Luton
Printed by Redwood Burn Ltd, Trowbridge

Contents

Preface

In 1958 C.P. Harvey QC, in his excellent book *The Advocate's Devil*, wrote somewhat ungraciously of the law of evidence as follows:

> I suppose there never was a more slapdash, disjointed and inconsequent body of rules than that which we call the law of evidence. Founded apparently on the propositions that all jurymen are deaf to reason, that all witnesses are presumptively liars and that all documents are presumptively forgeries, it has been added to, subtracted from and tinkered with for two centuries until it has become less of a structure than a pile of builders' debris.

It would be comforting to suppose that the considerable volume of statutory and judicial blue-prints promulgated in the years since this pessimistic pronouncement would at least have invested the pile with a modicum of architectural merit. In some respects it may have done so. Yet the student is still today faced in his or her study of the law of evidence with a daunting variety of rules and a daunting array of cases.

When *Evidence: Cases and Argument*, the predecessor of this book, was published, the authors imagined that some structural form could be provided by supplying arguments of counsel as they might have been delivered at different stages of the proceedings in our hypothetical cases of *R* v *Coke; R* v *Littleton*, and *Blackstone* v *Coke*. To judge by the reaction of teachers and students, we succeeded to some extent. But that success was necessarily achieved at a high price. This price consisted in sacrificing space which might have been occupied by materials. With some reluctance, therefore, we have radically altered the format of the book. In place of the arguments we have included more authorities and have expanded the extracts from the more important cases. We have supplied more topics for tutorial discussion, which we hope will be both challenging and practical. Many of these, as before, are based on the hypothetical cases, but we have also included additional questions unrelated to these. The new title of the book reflects the changed emphasis, but will not, we hope, be taken as meaning that we have abandoned all continuity with what may still properly be called the first edition.

We have omitted some more formal topics, such as documentary and real evidence, in favour of an expanded treatment of key areas such as character, public policy, corroboration and hearsay, in which there have been significant changes since the publication of the first edition. In this we have been emboldened by the knowledge that many teachers have followed our recommendation that this book be used in conjunction with, and not as a substitute for, *A Practical Approach to Evidence* (second edition) by Peter Murphy, which provides a complete textbook treatment of the law based on the same hypothetical cases. This frees us to attempt to fulfil the true aspiration of a case-book, to challenge, stimulate and offer an introduction to in-depth thinking about the front-line areas of the subject.

The book has of course been thoroughly updated and includes treatment of the Police and Criminal Evidence Act 1984 as well as the most significant case law developments.

Our publishers, in particular Alistair MacQueen and Heather Saward, have as ever, been a model of friendly and cheerful efficiency and enthusiasm. Our debt to them is beyond repayment. The same is true of our respective wives, without whose encouragement we could not have contemplated this work. Thanks are also due to Uschi Gubser and to Alan Wharam; and, finally, a mention to Helen and Andrew, without whom no preface would be complete.

John Beaumont, Leeds
Peter Murphy, Houston
1987
Feast of St. Pius X

Table of Cases

Table of Statutes

Table of Statutory Instruments

1   The Science of Proof

A: RELEVANCE, ADMISSIBILITY AND WEIGHT

(Suggested preliminary reading: *A Practical Approach to Evidence*, pp. 1-15.)

Stephen's Digest of the Law of Evidence 12th ed, art 1

The word 'relevant' means that any two facts to which it is applied are so related to each other that according to the common course of events one either taken by itself or in connection with other facts proves or renders probable the past, present, or future existence or non-existence of the other.

Stephen: 'A General View of the Criminal Law of England', 1st ed

Any specific facts or set of facts, employed for the purpose of inferring therefrom the existence of any other fact, is said to be evidence of that fact. Suppose the question is whether John Smith is living or dead; A says, 'I knew John Smith, and I saw him die.' B says, 'I knew John Smith. I saw him in bed; he looked very ill. I shortly afterwards heard he was dead, and saw a funeral procession, which I attended, and which every one said was his funeral, leave his house and go to the churchyard, where I saw a coffin buried with his name on it.' C says, 'Z told me that he heard from X that John Smith was dead.' D says, 'I had a dream that John Smith was dead.' Each of these facts, if used for the purpose of supporting the inference that John Smith was really dead, would be evidence of his death. The assertions of A and B would, under ordinary circumstances, be convincing; that of C far from satisfactory, and that of D altogether idle, except to a very superstitious person. This would be usually expressed by saying that the assertions of A and B would be good evidence, that of C weak evidence, and that of D no evidence at all of the fact of the death. But this is not quite a correct way of speaking: whether one fact is evidence of another, depends on the way in which it is used. If people usually believed in dreams, the assertion that a man had dreamt of John Smith's death would be evidence of his death. Whether or not it would be wise to allow it to be evidence of his death, would depend on the further question, whether in point of fact the practice of inferring the truth of the dream from the fact of its occurrence, usually produced true belief.

The mode of testing this is by throwing the matter under discussion into the form of a syllogism, of which the evidence forms the minor, and by seeing whether the major which it implies is one, the truth of which the person drawing the conclusion is prepared to assert. The inverted syllogism in the case supposed would stand thus:

John Smith is dead (conclusion),
  for
D dreamed that he saw him dead (minor),
  and
Whenever one man dreams that another is dead, he is dead.

The major might also be, 'Whenever D dreams that another person is dead, that other person is dead;' or, 'Whenever D *under certain circumstances*,' etc. But unless the person engaged in considering whether Smith is dead or not, is prepared to make one or other of these general assertions, D's dream is no evidence to him. If he is prepared to do so, it would be evidence. To a person who believes in spirit-rapping, the noises which he hears are evidence of the truth of what he supposes them to assert. That this is the true view of the nature of evidence, appears from the consideration that otherwise there could be no such thing as evidence in favour of a false proposition. Two witnesses falsely swear that they saw A accept a bill of exchange. Are not their oaths evidence that he did accept it? Yet, as the assertion is false in fact, they must imply a false major usually believed, or they would not produce belief.

In the particular instance the false major would be, 'Probable stories affirmed by credible witnesses are true;' and the error would arise from not stating that one of the many exceptions to this rule which would adapt it to the particular instance.

These illustrations show the true nature of evidence. The general observations which men make on the world in which they live—the world of things, and the world of men—are embodied, more or less expressly and consciously, in a number of general assertions. These general assertions form the major propositions (tacit for the most part) of the conclusions which it is one great business of our lives to draw; and whatever is capable of being made into a minor corresponding to one of these general propositions, is evidence of the truth of the conclusion. The major propositions are of very different degrees of authenticity. Many of them are false. Few of them, except those which relate to comparatively simple phenomena, such as the relations of space and number, are perfectly explicit, and almost all require qualifications and reservations which are seldom expressed, and, indeed, are far from being clearly understood.

This may be illustrated by a few examples. The most important of all the major propositions referred to, in reference at least to the administration of justice, is, that men when put upon their oaths, usually speak the truth as to matters of fact within their knowledge. It is this general conviction which makes the explicit statement— 'I saw such a thing occur,'—evidence that the thing really did occur; but the qualifications to the general proposition in question are so numerous, so intricate, and of such vital importance, that few things are more difficult than to say what degree of credit ought to be attached to the bare assertion of an unknown person that such and such an event did occur. It is evidence of the truth of the event: that is, it is one of a class of facts usually connected in the way of cause and effect with such facts as the one alleged to exist; but that is all that can be said on the subject.

Contrast this with a major proposition of another kind. The question is, whether the moon had risen at a given time on a given night. An almanack is produced which affirms that it had. Here the conclusion is—the moon had then risen. The minor— the almanack, says that it had risen. The major—whatever the almanack says about the time of the moon's rising is true. The connection between the minor and the conclusion here is not more direct and explicit than in the case of the direct assertion of the eye-witness. But the major is affirmed with infinitely stronger conviction and with fewer qualifications, and hence the evidence is far more convincing than in the other case. It thus appears that the question, What is evidence? and the question, What is the probative force of evidence? are distinct, though nearly connected. Anything is evidence which is a particular case of a general rule which the judge of the question is prepared to affirm to be true. The probative force, or the weight of evidence, depends to a great extent upon the degree of confidence with which he is prepared to affirm the truth of the general rule, and the clearness and fulness with which it is expressed.

DPP v Kilbourne [1973] AC 729 (HL)

(For facts, see *post* p. 491.)

LORD SIMON OF GLAISDALE: 'Your Lordships have been concerned with four concepts in the law of evidence: (i) relevance; (ii) admissibility; (iii) corroboration; (iv) weight. The first two terms are frequently, and in many circumstances legitimately, used interchangeably; but I think it makes for clarity if they are kept separate, since some relevant evidence is inadmissible and some admissible evidence is irrelevant (in the senses that I shall shortly submit). Evidence is relevant if it is logically probative or disprobative of some matter which requires proof. I do not pause to analyse what is involved in 'logical probativeness', except to note that the term does not of itself express the element of experience which is so significant of its operation in law, and possibly elsewhere. It is sufficient to say, even at the risk of etymological tautology, that relevant (i.e., logically probative or disprobative) evidence is evidence which makes the matter which requires proof more or less probable. To link logical probativeness with relevance rather than admissibility (as was done in *R v Sims* [1946] KB 531) not only is, I hope, more appropriate conceptually, but also accords better with the explanation of *Sims* given in *Harris v Director of Public Prosecutions* [1952] AC 694, 710. Evidence is admissible if it may be lawfully adduced at a trial. "Weight" of evidence is the degree of probability (both intrinsically and inferentially) which is attached to it by the tribunal of fact once it is established to be relevant and admissible in law (though its relevance may exceptionally, as will appear, be dependent on its evaluation by the tribunal of fact).

Exceptionally evidence which is irrelevant to a fact which is in issue is admitted to lay the foundation for other, relevant, evidence (e.g., evidence of an unsuccessful search for a missing relevant document, in order to lay the foundation for secondary evidence of the document). Apart from such exceptional cases no evidence which is irrelevant to a fact in issue is admissible. But some relevant evidence is nevertheless inadmissible. To cite a famous passage from the opinion of Lord Herschell LC in *Makin v Attorney-General for New South Wales* [1894] AC 57, 65:

> It is undoubtedly not competent for the prosecution to adduce evidence tending to show that the accused has been guilty of criminal acts other than those covered in the indictment, for the purpose of leading to the conclusion that the accused is a person likely from his criminal conduct or character to have committed the offence for which he is being tried. On the other hand, the mere fact that the evidence adduced tends to show the commission of other crimes does not render it inadmissible if it is relevant to an issue before the jury and it may be so relevant if it bears upon the question whether the acts alleged to constitute the crime charged in the indictment were designed or accidental, or to rebut a defence which would otherwise be open to the accused.

That what was declared to be inadmissible in the first sentence of this passage is nevertheless relevant (i.e., logically probative) can be seen from numerous studies of offences in which recidivists are matched against first offenders, and by considering that it has never been doubted that evidence of motive (which can be viewed as propensity to commit the particular offence charged, in contradistinction to propensity to commit offences generally of the type charged) is relevant. All relevant evidence is *prima facie* admissible. The reason why the type of evidence referred to by Lord Herschell LC in the first sentence of the passage is inadmissible is, not because it is irrelevant, but because its logically probative significance is considered to be grossly outweighed by its prejudice to the accused, so that a fair trial is endangered if it is admitted; the law therefore exceptionally excludes this relevant evidence: whereas in the circumstances referred to in the second sentence the logically probative significance of the evidence is markedly greater. (See also Lord Moulton in *R v Christie* [1914] AC 545, 559, 560.)

Not all admissible evidence is universally relevant. Admissible evidence may be relevant to one count of an indictment and not to another. It may be admissible against one accused (or party) but not another. It may be admissible to rebut a defence but inadmissible to reinforce the case for the prosecution. The summing up of Scrutton J in *R v Smith* (*George Joseph*) (1915) 11 Cr App R 229 ("The Brides in the Bath" case: see the report in the *Notable British Trials* series, at pp 276-278) was a striking example; the jury was directed to consider the drowning of other newly-wedded and well-insured wives of the accused for the purpose only of rebutting a defence of accidental death by drowning, but not otherwise for the purpose of positive proof of the murder charged. (See also Lord Atkinson, Lord Parker concurring, in *R v Christie* [1914] AC 545, 553.)

Hart v Lancashire and Yorkshire Railway Co. (1869) 21 LT 261 (Exch)

A runaway engine ran into a stationary train on a branch line and the plaintiff, a passenger in one of the carriages, was injured. He sued the railway company for compensation, alleging negligence in that, *inter alia*, the company had since the accident made an alteration in the method of changing the points so that a runaway engine would pass on to a supplementary siding leading up to a 'dead end'. The jury found for the plaintiff. The company moved for a rule for a new trial.

BRAMWELL B: '. . .[P]eople do not furnish evidence against themselves simply by adopting a new plan in order to prevent the recurrence of an accident. I think that a proposition to the contrary would be barbarous. It would be, as I have often had occasion to tell juries, to hold that, because the world gets wiser as it gets older, therefore it was foolish before.'

CHANNELL B: 'With regard to the branch siding and its alteration since the accident, it is not because the defendants have become wiser and done something subsequently to the accident that their doing so is to be evidence of any antecedent negligence on their part in that respect.'

(KELLY CB and CLEASBY B delivered concurring judgments.)
Rule absolute.

Holcombe v Hewson *(NP)* (1810) 2 Camp 391

This was an action of assumpsit by a brewer against a publican, on an agreement whereby it was stipulated that the defendant should take all his beer of the plaintiff, and that if he did not, he should pay an advanced rent for the house which he occupied.

Garrow for the plaintiff allowed (which was confirmed by Lord Ellenborough) that if it should appear that the beer supplied by the plaintiff to the defendant, while they dealt together, was not of a fair merchantable quality, and such as ought to have given satisfaction to the defendant's customers, the present action could not be maintained. To prove its excellence, the plaintiff's foreman was called, and stated that it was made of malt and hops only.

Garrow then proposed to call several other publicans who dealt with the plaintiff at the same time as with the defendant, and since the latter had taken his beer of another brewer, to swear that they were supplied with an excellent commodity, which was highly approved of by their customers.

LORD ELLENBOROUGH: 'This is *res inter alios acta*. We cannot here enquire into the quality of different beer furnished to different persons. The plaintiff might deal well with one, and not with the others. Let him call some of those who frequented the defendant's house, and there drank the beer which he sent in; or let him give any other evidence of the quality of this beer; but I cannot admit witnesses to his general character and habits as a brewer.'

The defendant afterwards proved that the beer supplied to him by the plaintiff was very bad, and that he had lost almost the whole of his customers before he began to deal with another brewer; since which he has carried on a thriving trade.

The plaintiff submitted to be nonsuited.

Hollingham v Head (1858) 27 LJCP 241

The plaintiff was in the habit of travelling about to different market towns selling an artificial manure called 'Rival guano'. He met the defendant, a farmer, and persuaded him to buy a quantity of this guano which turned out to be worthless. The plaintiff sued for the price of the guano. The defence was that this guano was a new kind, which the plaintiff, being anxious to introduce onto the market, and in order to induce the defendant to become a purchaser, had sold to him at £7 a ton, on condition that if it was not equal to Peruvian guano, the price of which was £14 a ton, the defendant was not to pay for it. In order to establish this defence the defendant wished to call witnesses to prove that the plaintiff had made contracts with other persons for the sales of his guano upon the same evidence. The trial judge held this evidence to be inadmissible and the jury returned a verdict for the plaintiff. The defendant moved for a new trial.

WILLES J: 'I am of opinion that the evidence was properly disallowed, as not being relevant to the issue. It may be often difficult to decide upon the admissibility of evidence, where it is offered for the purpose of establishing probability, but to be admissible it must at least afford a reasonable inference as to the principal matter in dispute. No doubt the rule, confining evidence to that which is relevant, is one of great importance; not only with regard to the particular case in which it has to be applied, but with reference to saving the time of the Court, and preventing the minds of the jury being prejudiced, and distracted from the point in issue. The rule is nowhere more clearly laid down than in the very valuable work by Mr Best, on *Evidence*, (2nd ed, p. 319), where he says, "Of all rules of evidence the most universal and most obvious is this—that the evidence adduced should be alike directed and confined to the matters which are in dispute, or form the subject of investigation." And the same learned author, in another part of his book, speaks of the admissibility of evidence, which shows the affirmative of the issue to be more probable than the negative. It appears to me that the evidence, which was proposed to be given in this case, would not have shown that it was probable that the plaintiff had made the contract, which the defendant contended he had made; for I do not see how the fact, that a man has once or more in his life acted in a particular way, makes it probable that he so acted on a given occasion. The admission of such evidence would be fraught with the greatest inconvenience. Where, indeed, the question is one of guilty knowledge or intent, as in cases of uttering forged documents, or base coin, such evidence is admissible as tending to establish a necessary ingredient of the crime. But if the evidence were admissible in this case, it would be difficult to say that in any case, where the question was whether or not goods had been sold upon credit, the defendant might not call evidence to prove that other persons had received credit from the plaintiff; or in an action for an assault, that the plaintiff might not prove that the defendant had assaulted other persons generally, or persons of a particular class. To obviate the prejudice, the injustice, and the waste of time to which the admission of such evidence would lead, and bearing in mind the extent to which it might be carried, and that litigants are mortal, it is necessary not only to adhere to the rule, but to lay it down strictly. I think, therefore, the fact that the plaintiff had entered into contracts of a particular kind with other persons on other occasions could not properly be admitted in evidence, where no custom of trade to make such contracts, and no connexion between such and the one in question, was shown to exist.'

(BYLES J and WILLIAMS J gave concurring judgments.)

Rule refused.

Joy v Phillips, Mills and Co. Ltd [1916] 1 KB 849 (CA)

The father of the deceased claimed compensation for himself and other dependants under the Workmen's Compensation Act 1906. The deceased, who was employed as a stable boy by the respondents, was found in their stable in a dying condition, suffering from a kick behind the ear from one of their horses. There was no direct evidence as to how the accident happened. There was evidence that when the boy was found he was clutching in his hand a halter; that at the time when the accident happened the boy had nothing to do with the halter and had nothing to do in the stable; and that the horse was a quiet horse. There was also evidence that the foreman of the respondents' yard had some time previously had occasion to speak to the boy about hitting the horses with a halter and teasing them. The county court judge held that the boy must have done something to the horse, which was a quiet one, to make it kick out, and that at the time of the accident the boy's duties in the stable were over, and accordingly that the accident did not arise out of his employment. The father of the deceased appealed.

LORD COZENS-HARDY MR: 'It seems to me that in a case like this the habits of the deceased cannot be disregarded. It is utterly impossible to do so. If the question was whether a man was drowned in a stream in one circumstance or another, could you not ask whether the man was in the habit of going to his work by the side of the stream and then crossing over a bridge? It seems to me that you could. Otherwise you would be shutting your eyes altogether to facts necessary for drawing the proper inferences. So it is here. I cannot disregard the fact that this lad had on more than one occasion been remonstrated with for teasing the horses. On one occasion he was remonstrated with by the foreman for teasing the horses with a halter, and when his body was found a halter was found clutched in his hand, and that was close to the rear of a very quiet horse.

In my opinion we cannot say that the judge was not entitled to find as he did on a question of fact which was for him, and I think we cannot interfere with his finding.'

PHILLIMORE LJ: 'Wherever an inquiry has to be made into the cause of the death of a person, and, there being no direct evidence, recourse must be had to circumstantial evidence, any evidence as to the habits and ordinary doings of the deceased which may contribute to the circumstances by throwing light upon the probable cause of death is admissible, even in the case of a prosecution for murder. Especially in these cases under the Workmen's Compensation Act the books are full of cases where evidence as to the habits or practice of the deceased or even of his class has been admitted both in favour of the applicant and against him or her, both to contribute towards the conclusion that the accident to the deceased arose out of and in the course of the employment, and to contribute towards the opposite result.'

SARGANT J: 'In a case of this sort where an accident has happened, when no one but the deceased was present, the Court necessarily has to deal with an estimate of probabilities; but an estimate of probabilities is not necessarily the same as mere conjecture. Here in estimating the probabilities it seems to me as relevant to admit evidence that the boy was mischievous as to admit evidence that the horse was quiet.'

Woolf v *Woolf* [1931] P 134 (CA)

On an undefended petition by a wife for dissolution of marriage by reason of the adultery of her husband, the evidence was that the husband passed two nights in a bedroom at an hotel with a woman. He then informed his wife of the fact, but disclosed no name or address of the woman in question either to his wife or to her solicitors or to the King's Proctor to whom the papers in the case had been sent by the Court, although both the solicitors and the King's Proctor applied to him for these particulars. As the result of inquiries by the King's Proctor there was no evidence of any association of the husband with a woman other than his wife, still less of illicit association. The judge held that adultery was not proved and dismissed the petition. The wife appealed.

LORD HANWORTH MR: 'In *Loveden* v *Loveden* (1810) 2 Hagg Cons 1, Sir William Scott said that it was not necessary to prove the direct fact of adultery, for "if it were otherwise, there is not one case in a hundred in which that proof would be attainable: it is very rarely indeed that the parties are surprised in the direct fact of adultery. In every case almost the fact is inferred from circumstances that lead to it by fair inference as a necessary conclusion; and unless this were the case, and unless this were so held, no protection whatever could be given to marital rights." That passage has been quoted with approval in the Court of Appeal by Lopes LJ in *Allen* v *Allen* [1894] P 248, where he says: "To lay down any general rule, to attempt to define what circumstances would be sufficient and what insufficient upon which to infer the fact of adultery, is impossible. Each case must depend on its own particular circumstances."

It seems to me that, human nature being what it is, adultery must be inferred here. The husband was twenty-five, and no more, and he had been married, and there is no reason to assume that his sexual appetite was less than that of a normal healthy man. I think that to say that an adulterous inclination should be proved is to lay an unjustifiable burden on the petitioner. The case is one of an innocent woman proving opportunity for adultery, and the fact that the parties spent two nights in the same bedroom. In my opinion in this case the Court ought to be satisfied that adultery has been proved.'

(LAWRENCE LJ and ROMER LJ delivered concurring judgments.)

Appeal allowed and decree *nisi* granted.

B: EVIDENCE ILLEGALLY OR UNFAIRLY OBTAINED; JUDICIAL DISCRETION

(Suggested preliminary reading: *A Practical Approach to Evidence*, pp. 15-32.)

The materials contained in this section deal with criminal cases only. For civil cases see *A Practical Approach to Evidence*, pp. 20-21.

Kuruma, Son of Kaniu v The Queen [1955] AC 197 (PC)

The appellant was charged with the unlawful possession of two rounds of ammunition contrary to emergency regulations in Kenya. He had been stopped and searched illegally in that the searchers were not of the rank of assistant inspector or above. The ammunition was alleged to have been found during the search and evidence of this was given at the trial. The appellant was convicted and appealed on the ground that evidence of the finding was inadmissible because of the manner in which it was obtained.

LORD GODDARD LJ, delivering the judgment of their Lordships: 'In their Lordships' opinion the test to be applied in considering whether evidence is admissible is whether it is relevant to the matters in issue. If it is, it is admissible and the court is not concerned with how the evidence was obtained. While this proposition may not have been stated in so many words in any English case there are decisions which support it, and in their Lordships' opinion it is plainly right in principle. In *R* v *Leatham* (1861) 8 Cox CC 498, an information for penalties under the Corrupt Practices Act, objection was taken to the production of a letter written by the defendant because its existence only became known by answers he had given to the commissioners who held the inquiry under the Act, which provided that answers before that tribunal should not be admissible in evidence against him. The Court of Queen's Bench held that though his answers could not be used against the defendant, yet if a clue was thereby given to other evidence, in that case the letter, which would prove the case it was admissible. Crompton J said: "It matters not how you get it; if you steal it even, it would be admissible." *Lloyd* v *Mostyn* (1842) 10 M & W 478 was an action on a bond. The person in whose possession it was objected to produce it on the ground of privilege. The plaintiff's attorney, however, had got a copy of it and notice to produce the original being proved the court admitted the copy as secondary evidence. To the same effect was *Calcraft* v *Guest* [1898] 1 QB 759. There can be no difference in principle for this purpose between a civil and a criminal case. No doubt in a criminal case the judge always has a discretion to disallow evidence if the strict rules of admissibility would operate unfairly against an accused. This was emphasised in the case before this Board of *Noor Mohamed* v *The King* [1949] AC 182 and in the recent case in the House of Lords, *Harris* v *Director of Public Prosecutions* [1952] AC 694. If, for instance, some admission of some piece of evidence, e.g., a document, had been obtained from a defendant by a trick, no doubt the judge might properly rule it out. It was this discretion that lay at the root of the ruling of Lord Guthrie in *HM Advocate* v *Turnbull* [1951] SC(J) 96. The other cases from Scotland to which their Lordships' attention was drawn, *Rattray* v *Rattray* (1897) 25 Rettie 315, *Lawrie* v *Muir* [1950] SC(J) 19 and *Fairley* v *Fishmongers of London* [1951] SC(J)14, all support the view that if the evidence is relevant it is admissible and the court is not concerned with how it is obtained.

No doubt their Lordships in the Court of Justiciary appear at least to some extent to consider the question from the point of view whether the alleged illegality in the obtaining of the evidence could properly be excused, and it is true that Horridge J in *Elias* v *Passmore* [1934] 2 KB 164 used that expression. It is to be observed, however, that what the judge was there concerned with was an action of trespass, and he held that the trespass was excused. In their Lordships' opinion, when it is a question of the admission of evidence strictly it is not whether the method by which it was obtained in tortious but excusable but whether what has been obtained is relevant to the issue being tried. Their Lordships are not now concerned with whether an action for assault would lie against the police officers and express no opinion on that point. It is right, however, that it should be stated that the rule with regard to the admission of confessions, whether it be regarded as an exception to the general rule or not, is a rule of law which their Lordships are not qualifying in any degree whatsoever.'

Appeal dismissed.

Jeffrey v Black [1978] QB 490 (DC)

The defendant was arrested by two police officers of the drug squad for stealing a sandwich from a public house. The officers then quite improperly searched his home and found cannabis and cannabis resin. He was charged with possession of those drugs. The justices ruled that evidence obtained during the search was inadmissible and dismissed the informations. The prosecutor appealed.

LORD WIDGERY CJ: 'It is firmly established according to English law that the mere fact that evidence is obtained in an irregular fashion does not of itself prevent that evidence from being relevant and acceptable to a court. The authority for that is *Kuruma v The Queen* [1955] AC 197, and I need only refer to one passage to make good the proposition which I have already put forward, and that is at p. 203 and reads: "In their Lordships' opinion the test to be applied in considering whether evidence is admissible is whether it is relevant to the matters in issue. If it is, it is admissible and the court is not concerned with how the evidence was obtained. While this proposition may not have been stated in so many words in any English case there are decisions which support it, and in their Lordships' opinion it is plainly right in principle." There one has that pronouncement from the Privy Council, and I have not the least doubt that we must firmly accept the proposition that an irregularity in obtaining evidence does not render the evidence inadmissible. Whether or not the evidence is admissible depends on whether or not it is relevant to the issues in respect of which it is called.

At this point it would seem that the prosecutor ought to succeed in his appeal because at this point what he appears to have shown is that the justices were wrong in failing to recognise the law as stated in *Kuruma* v *The Queen* [1955] AC 197. But that is not in fact the end of the matter because the justices sitting in this case, like any other tribunal dealing with criminal matters in England and sitting under the English law, have a general discretion to decline to allow any evidence to be called by the prosecution if they think that it would be unfair or oppressive to allow that to be done. In getting an assessment of what this discretion means, justices ought, I think, to stress to themselves that the discretion is not a discretion which arises only in drug cases. It is not a discretion which arises only in cases where police can enter premises. It is a discretion which every judge has all the time in respect of all the evidence which is tendered by the prosecution. It would probably give justices some idea of the extent to which this discretion is used if one asks them whether they are appreciative of the fact that they have the discretion anyway, and it may well be that a number of experienced justices would be quite ignorant of the possession of this discretion. That gives them, I hope, some idea of how relatively rarely it is exercised in our courts. But if the case is exceptional, if the case is such that not only have the police officers entered without authority, but they have been guilty of trickery or they have misled someone, or they have been oppressive or they have been unfair, or in other respects they have behaved in a manner which is morally reprehensible, then it is open to the justices to apply their discretion and decline to allow the particular evidence to be let in as part of the trial. I cannot stress the point too strongly that this is a very exceptional situation, and the simple, unvarnished fact that evidence was obtained by police officers who had gone in without bothering to get a search warrant is not enough to justify the justices in exercising their discretion to keep the evidence out.'

(FORBES and CROOM-JOHNSON JJ agreed.)

Appeal allowed.

R v *Sang* [1980] AC 402 (HL)

Two defendants were charged with conspiracy to utter counterfeit United States banknotes. They alleged by counsel that they had been induced by an informer, acting on the instructions of the police to commit an offence that they would not have committed otherwise. As it was then clear law that the existence of entrapment, even if established, would not have been a ground to exclude evidence of the offence as a matter of law, counsel sought to investigate the issue in a trial within a trial, with a view to persuading the trial judge to exclude that evidence in his discretion. The trial judge, taking the view that he had no such discretion to exclude admissible prosecution evidence, ruled accordingly after hearing argument on the hypothetical basis that the defendants' allegations were true. The Court of Appeal dismissed an appeal against conviction, but certified the following point of law of general public importance: 'Does a trial judge have a discretion to refuse to allow evidence—being evidence other than evidence of admission—to be given in any circumstances in which such evidence is relevant and of more than minimal probative value.' One of the defendants appealed to the House of Lords.

LORD DIPLOCK: 'I understand this question as inquiring what are the circumstances, if there be any, in which such a discretion arises; and as not being confined to trials by jury. That the discretion, whatever be its limits, extended to whoever presides in a judicial capacity over a criminal trial, whether it be held in the Crown Court or in a magistrates' court, was expressly stated by Lord Widgery CJ in *Jeffrey* v *Black* [1978] QB 490, an appeal by the prosecution to a Divisional Court by way of case stated from magistrates who had exercised their discretion to exclude evidence of possession of drugs that had been obtained by an illegal search of the accused's room by the police. The Divisional Court held that the magistrates had exercised their discretion wrongly in the particular case; but Lord Widgery CJ, while stressing that the occasions on which the discretion ought to be exercised in favour of excluding admissible evidence would be exceptional, nevertheless referred to it as applying to "all the evidence which is tendered by the prosecution" and described its ambit in the widest terms, at p 498:

> . . . If the case is such that not only have the police officers entered without authority, but they have been guilty of trickery or they have misled someone, or they have been oppressive or they have been unfair, or in other respects they have behaved in a manner which is morally reprehensible, then it is open to the justices to apply their discretion and decline to allow the particular evidence to be let in as part of the trial.

One or other of the various dyslogistic terms which Lord Widgery uses to describe the kind of conduct on the part of the police that gives rise to judicial discretion to exclude particular pieces of evidence tendered by the prosecution can be found in earlier pronouncements by his predecessor Lord Parker CJ, notably in *Callis* v *Gunn* [1964] 1 QB 495, 502, where he adds to them false representations, threats and bribes; while unfairness and trickery are referred to in *dicta* to be found in a judgment of the Privy Council in *Kuruma* v *The Queen* [1955] AC 197, 204, the case which is generally regarded as having first suggested the existence of a wide judicial discretion of this kind. What is unfair, what is trickery in the context of the detection and prevention of crime, are questions which are liable to attract highly subjective answers. It will not have come as any great surprise to your Lordships to learn that those who preside over or appear as advocates in criminal trials are anxious for guidance as to whether the discretion really is so wide as these imprecise expressions would seem to suggest and, if not, what are its limits. So, although it may not be strictly necessary to answer the certified question in its full breadth in order to dispose of the instant appeal I think that your Lordships should endeavour to do so.

Before turning to that wider question, however, I will deal with the narrower point of law upon which this appeal actually turns. I can do so briefly. The decisions in *R* v *McEvilly* (1973) 60 Cr App R 150 and *R* v *Mealey and Sheridan* (1974) 60 Cr App R 59 that there is no defence of "entrapment" known to English law are clearly right. Many crimes are committed by one person at the instigation of others. From earliest times at common law those who counsel and procure the commission of the offence by the person by whom the *actus reus* itself is done have been guilty themselves of an offence, and since the abolition by the Criminal Law Act 1967 of the distinction between felonies and misdemeanours, can be tried, indicted and punished as principal offenders. The fact that the counsellor and procurer is a policeman or a police informer, although it may be of relevance in mitigation of penalty for the offence, cannot affect the guilt of the principal offender; both the physical element (*actus reus*) and the mental element (*mens rea*) of the offence with which he is charged are present in his case.

My Lords, this being the substantive law upon the matter, the suggestion that it can be evaded by the procedural device of preventing the prosecution from adducing evidence of the commission of the offence does not bear examination. Let me take first the summary offence prosecuted before magistrates where there is no practical distinction between a trial and a "trial within a trial." There are three examples of these in the books, *Brannan* v *Peek* [1948] 1 KB 68; *Browning* v *JWH Watson (Rochester) Ltd* [1953] 1 WLR 1172; *Sneddon* v *Stevenson* [1967] 1 WLR 1051. Here the magistrates in order to decide whether the crime had in fact been instigated by an agent provocateur acting upon police instructions would first have to hear evidence which *ex hypothesi* would involve proving that the crime had been committed by the accused. If they decided that it had been so instigated, then, despite the fact that they had already heard evidence which satisfied them that it had been committed, they would have a discretion to prevent the prosecution from relying on that evidence as proof of its commission. How does this differ from recognising entrapment as a defence— but a defence available only at the discretion of the magistrates?

Where the accused is charged upon indictment and there is a practical distinction between the trial and a "trial within a trial," the position, as it seems to me, would be even more anomalous if the judge were to have a discretion to prevent the prosecution from adducing evidence before the jury to prove the commission of the offence by the accused. If he exercised the discretion in favour of the accused he would then have to direct the jury to acquit. How does this differ from recognising entrapment as a defence—but a defence for which the necessary factual foundation is to be found not by the jury but by the judge and even where the factual foundation is so found, the defence is available only at the judge's discretion.

My Lords, this submission goes far beyond a claim to a judicial discretion to exclude *evidence* that has been obtained unfairly or by trickery; nor in any of the English cases on agents provocateurs that have come before appellate courts has it been suggested that it exists. What it really involves is a claim to a judicial discretion to acquit an accused of any offences in connection with which the conduct of the police incurs the disapproval of the judge. The conduct of the police where it has involved the use of an agent provocateur may well be a matter to be taken into consideration in mitigation of sentence; but under the English system of criminal justice, it does not give rise to any discretion on the part of the judge himself to acquit the accused or to direct the jury to do so, notwithstanding that he is guilty of the offence. Nevertheless the existence of such a discretion to exclude the evidence of an agent provocateur does appear to have been acknowledged by the Courts-Martial Appeal Court of Northern Ireland in *R* v *Murphy* [1965] NI 138. That was before the rejection of "entrapment" as a defence by the Court of Appeal in England; and Lord MacDermott CJ in delivering the judgment of the court relied upon the *dicta* as to the existence of a wide discretion which appeared in cases that did not involve an agent provocateur. In the result he held that the court-martial had been right in exercising its discretion in such a way as to admit the evidence.

I understand your Lordships to be agreed that whatever be the ambit of the judicial discretion to exclude admissible evidence it does not extend to excluding evidence of a crime because the crime was instigated by an agent provocateur. In so far as *R* v *Murphy* suggests the contrary it should no longer be regarded as good law.

I turn now to the wider question that has been certified. It does not purport to be concerned with self incriminatory admissions made by the accused himself after commission of the crime though in dealing with the question I will find it necessary to say something about these. What the question is concerned with is the discretion of the trial judge to exclude all other kinds of evidence that are of more than minimal probative value.

Recognition that there may be circumstances in which in a jury trial the judge has a discretion to prevent particular kinds of evidence that is admissible from being adduced before the jury, has grown up piecemeal. It appears first in cases arising under proviso (f) of section 1 of the Criminal Evidence Act 1898, which sets out the circumstances in which an accused may be cross-examined as to his previous convictions or bad character. The relevant cases starting in 1913 with *R* v *Watson* (1913) 109 LT 335 are conveniently cited in the speech of Lord Hodson in *R* v *Selvey* [1970] AC 304, a case in which this House accepted that in such cases the trial judge had a discretion to prevent such cross-examination, notwithstanding that it was strictly admissible under the statute, if he was of opinion that its prejudicial effect upon the jury was likely to outweigh its probative value.

Next the existence of a judicial discretion to exclude evidence of "similar facts," even where it was technically admissible, was recognised by Lord du Parcq, delivering the opinion of the Privy Council in *Noor Mohamed* v *The King* [1949] AC 182, 192. He put the grounds which justified its exercise rather more narrowly than they had been put in the "previous conviction" cases to which I have been referring; but in *Harris* v *Director of Public Prosecutions* [1952] AC 694, 707, Viscount Simon, with whose speech the other members of this House agreed, said that the discretion to exclude "similar facts" evidence should be exercised where the "probable effect" (sc. prejudicial to the accused) "would be out of proportion to its true evidential value."

That phrase was borrowed from the speech of Lord Moulton in *R* v *Christie* [1914] AC 545, 559. That was neither a "previous conviction" nor a "similar facts" case, but was one involving evidence of an accusation made in the presence of the accused by the child victim of an alleged indecent assault and the accused's failure to answer it, from which the prosecution sought to infer an admission by the accused that it was true. Lord Moulton's statement was not confined to evidence of inferential confessions but was general in its scope and has frequently been cited as applicable in cases of cross-examination as to bad character or previous convictions under the

Criminal Evidence Act 1898 and in "similar facts" cases. So I would hold that there has now developed a general rule of practice whereby in a trial by jury the judge has a discretion to exclude evidence which, though technically admissible, would probably have a prejudicial influence on the minds of the jury, which would be out of proportion to its true evidential value.

Ought your Lordships to go further and to hold that the discretion extends more widely than this, as the comparatively recent *dicta* to which I have already referred suggest? What has been regarded as the fountain head of all subsequent *dicta* on this topic is the statement by Lord Goddard delivering advice of the Privy Council in *Kuruma* v *The Queen* [1955] AC 197. That was a case in which the evidence of unlawful possession of ammunition by the accused was obtained as a result of an illegal search of his person. The Board held that this evidence was admissible and had rightly been admitted; but Lord Goddard although he had earlier said at p 203 that if evidence is admissible "the court is not concerned with how the evidence was obtained," nevertheless went on to say, at p 204:

> No doubt in a criminal case the judge always has a discretion to disallow evidence if the strict rules of admissibility would operate unfairly against an accused. This was emphasised in the case before this Board of *Noor Mohamed* v *The King* [1949] AC 182, and in the recent case in the House of Lords, *Harris* v *Director of Public Prosecutions* [1952] AC 694. *If, for instance, some admission of some piece of evidence, e.g., a document, had been obtained from a defendant by a trick, no doubt the judge might properly rule it out.*

Up to the sentence that I have italicised there is nothing in this passage to suggest that when Lord Goddard spoke of admissible evidence operating "unfairly" against the accused he intended to refer to any wider aspect of unfairness than the probable prejudicial effect of the evidence upon the minds of the jury outweighing its true evidential value; though he no doubt also had in mind the discretion that had long been exercised in England under the Judges' Rules to refuse to admit confessions by the accused made after the crime even though strictly they may be admissible. The instance given in the passage I have italicised appears to me to deal with a case which falls within the latter category since the document "obtained from a defendant by a trick" is clearly analogous to a confession which the defendant has been unfairly induced to make, and had, indeed, been so treated in *R* v *Barker* [1941] 2 KB 381 where an incriminating document obtained from the defendant by a promise of favours was held to be inadmissible.

It is interesting in this connection to observe that the only case that has been brought to your Lordships' attention in which an appellate court has actually excluded evidence on the ground that it had been unfairly obtained (*R* v *Payne* [1963] 1 WLR 637) would appear to fall into this category. The defendant, charged with drunken driving, had been induced to submit himself to examination by a doctor to see if he was suffering from any illness or disability, upon the understanding that the doctor would not examine him for the purpose of seeing whether he were fit to drive. The doctor in fact gave evidence of the defendant's unfitness to drive based upon his symptoms and behaviour in the course of that examination. The Court of Criminal Appeal quashed the conviction on the ground that the trial judge ought to have exercised his discretion to exclude the doctor's evidence. This again, as it seems to me, is analogous to unfairly inducing a defendant to confess to an offence, and the short judgment of the Court of Criminal Appeal is clearly based upon the maxim *nemo debet prodere se ipsum*.

In no other case to which your Lordships' attention has been drawn has either the Court of Criminal Appeal or the Court of Appeal allowed an appeal upon the ground that either magistrates in summary proceedings or the judge in a trial upon indictment ought to have exercised a discretion to exclude admissible evidence upon the ground that it has been obtained unfairly or by trickery or in some other way that is morally reprehensible; though they cover a wide gamut of apparent improprieties from illegal searches, as in *Kuruma* v *The Queen* itself and in *Jeffrey* v *Black* [1978] QB 490 (which must be the high water mark of this kind of illegality) to the clearest cases of evidence obtained by the use of agents provocateur. Of the latter an outstanding example is to be found in *Browning* v *JWH Watson* (*Rochester*) *Ltd* [1953] 1 WLR 1172 where Lord Goddard CJ remitted the case to the magistrates *with a direction that the offence had been proved*, but pointedly reminded them that it was open to them to give the defendant an absolute discharge and to award no costs to the prosecution.

Nevertheless it has to be recognised that there is an unbroken series of *dicta* in judgments of appellate courts to the effect that there is a judicial discretion to exclude admissible evidence which has been "obtained" unfairly or by trickery or oppressively, although except in *R* v *Payne* [1963] 1 WLR 637, there never has been a case in which those courts have come across conduct so unfair, so tricky or so oppressive as to justify them in holding that the discretion ought to have been exercised in favour of exclusion. In every one of the cases to which your Lordships have been referred where such *dicta* appear, the source from which the evidence sought to be excluded had been obtained has been the defendant himself or (in some of the search cases) premises occupied by him; and the dicta can be traced to a common ancestor in Lord Goddard's statement in *Kuruma* v *The Queen* [1955] AC 197 which I have already cited. That statement was not, in my view, ever intended to acknowledge the existence of any wider discretion than to exclude (1) admissible evidence which would probably have a prejudicial influence upon the minds of the jury that would be out of proportion to its true evidential value; and (2) evidence tantamount to a self-incriminatory admission which was obtained from the defendant, after the offence had been committed, by means which would justify a judge in excluding an actual confession which had the like self-incriminating effect. As a matter of language, although not as a matter of application, the subsequent *dicta* go much further than this; but in so far as they do so they have never yet been considered by this House.

My Lords, I propose to exclude, as the certified question does, detailed consideration of the role of the trial judge in relation to confessions and evidence obtained from the defendant after commission of the offence that is tantamount to a confession. It has a long history dating back to the days before the existence of a disciplined police force, when a prisoner on a charge of felony could not be represented by counsel and was not entitled to give evidence in his own defence either to deny that he had made the confession, which was generally oral, or to deny that its contents were true. The underlying rationale of this branch of the criminal law, though it may originally have been based upon ensuring the reliability of confessions is, in my view, now to be found in the maxim *nemo debet prodere se ipsum*, no one can be required to be his own betrayer or in its popular English mistranslation "the right to silence." That is why there is no discretion to exclude evidence discovered as the result of an illegal search but there is discretion to exclude evidence which the accused has been induced to produce voluntarily if the method of inducement was unfair.

Outside this limited field in which for historical reasons the function of the trial judge extended to imposing sanctions for improper conduct on the part of the prosecution before the commencement of the proceedings in inducing the accused by threats, favour or trickery to provide evidence against himself, your Lordships should, I think, make it clear that the function of the judge at a criminal trial as respects the admission of evidence is to ensure that the accused has a fair trial according to law. It is no part of a judge's function to exercise disciplinary powers over the police or prosecution as respects the way in which evidence to be used at the trial is obtained by them. If it was obtained illegally there will be a remedy in civil law; if it was obtained legally but in breach of the rules of conduct for the police, this is a matter for the appropriate disciplinary authority to deal with. What the judge at the trial is concerned with is not how the evidence sought to be adduced by the prosecution has been obtained, but with how it is used by the prosecution at the trial.

A fair trial according to law involves, in the case of a trial upon indictment, that it should take place before a judge and a jury; that the case against the accused should be proved to the satisfaction of the jury beyond all reasonable doubt upon evidence that is admissible in law; and, as a corollary to this, that there should be excluded from the jury information about the accused which is likely to have an influence on their minds prejudicial to the accused which is out of proportion to the true probative value of admissible evidence conveying that information. If these conditions are fulfilled and the jury receive correct instructions from the judge as to the law applicable to the case, the requirement that the accused should have a fair trial according to law is, in my view, satisfied; for the fairness of a trial according to law is not all one-sided; it requires that those who are undoubtedly guilty should be convicted as well as that those about whose guilt there is any reasonable doubt should be acquitted. However much the judge may dislike the way in which a particular piece of evidence was obtained before proceedings were commenced, if it is admissible evidence probative of the accused's guilt it is no part of his judicial function to exclude it for this reason. If your Lordships so hold you will be reverting to the law as it was laid down by Lord Moulton in *R* v *Christie* [1914] AC 545, Lord du Parcq in *Noor Mohamed* v *The King* [1949] AC 182 and Viscount Simon in *Harris* v *Director of Public Prosecutions* [1952] AC 694 before the growth of what I believe to have been a misunderstanding of Lord Goddard's *dictum* in *Kuruma* v *The Queen* [1955] AC 197.

I would accordingly answer the question certified in terms which have been suggested by my noble and learned friend, Viscount Dilhorne, in the course of our deliberations on this case. (1) A trial judge in a criminal trial has always a discretion to refuse to admit evidence if in his opinion its prejudicial effect outweighs its probative value. (2) Save with regard to admissions and confessions and generally with regard to evidence obtained from the accused after commission of the offence, he has no discretion to refuse to admit relevant admissible evidence on the ground that it was obtained by improper or unfair means. The court is not concerned with how it was obtained. It is no ground for the exercise of discretion to exclude that the evidence was obtained as the result of the activities of an agent provocateur.'

(VISCOUNT DILHORNE, LORDS SALMON, FRASER of TULLYBELTON and SCARMAN delivered judgments agreeing with LORD DIPLOCK's answer to the certified question.)

Appeal dismissed.

Police and Criminal Evidence Act 1984

78(1) In any proceedings the court may refuse to allow evidence on which the prosecution proposes to rely to be given if it appears to the court that, having regard to all the circumstances, including the circumstances in which the evidence was obtained, the admission of the evidence would have such an adverse effect on the fairness of the proceedings that the court ought not to admit it.

(2) Nothing in this section shall prejudice any rule of law requiring a court to exclude evidence.

82(3) Nothing in this part of this Act shall prejudice any power of a court to exclude evidence (whether by preventing questions from being put or otherwise) at its discretion.

(On the application of s. 78 see also the unreported cases of *R* v *Mason* (1987) *The Times*, 23 May; and *Matto* v *Wolverhampton Crown Court* (1987) *The Times*, 27 May.)

Questions for Discussion

1 D is charged with the rape of V. Which of the following facts is relevant and why?

  (a) D and V were living together until shortly before the alleged rape.
  (b) V was working as a prostitute at the time of the alleged rape.
  (c) D has a previous conviction for rape.
  (d) D has a previous conviction for indecent assault on a male.
  (e) D refused to answer questions put to him by the police and demanded to see a solicitor.
  (f) D refused to testify at his trial.
  (g) At the time of his arrest, D was in possession of a copy of *Playboy*.
  (h) Statistics show that rape is on the increase.
  (i) V has a previous conviction for shop-lifting.
  (j) Traces of a fibre identified as coming from D's sweater were found on V's dress.

2 What is the distinction between the terms relevance, admissibility and weight when used in the law of evidence?

3 'A room is searched against the law, and the body of a murdered man is found. If the place of discovery may not be proved, the other circumstances may be insufficient to connect the defendant with the crime. The privacy of the home has been infringed and the murderer goes free.' (*The People* v *Defoe* 242 NY 413 (1926), per Cardozo J.) Does this justify the English approach to the question of the admissibility of improperly obtained evidence?

4 How, if at all, does section 78 of the Police and Criminal Evidence Act 1984, differ from the rule developed in *R* v *Sang* [1980] AC 402.

Further reading

Eggleston, *Evidence, Proof and Probability*, 2nd ed (1983), Ch. 6.
Hoffman, 'Those dogs again' (1974) 91 South African Law Journal 237.

2 The Queen v Coke; The Queen v Littleton; Blackstone v Coke

A: THE QUEEN V COKE; THE QUEEN V LITTLETON

BRIEF FOR THE PROSECUTION

Instructions to Counsel

Counsel is instructed in the prosecution of these two defendants, who are due to stand trial at the Oxbridge Crown Court upon the indictment sent with these papers. Counsel also has the statements of witnesses tendered in the committal proceedings on behalf of the prosecution, and a letter from solicitors representing the defendant Littleton, giving notice of alibi as required by s. 11 of the Criminal Justice Act 1967.

There are a number of matters of evidence which Counsel will no doubt wish to consider. Both complainants are under the age of eighteen. The elder sister, Margaret, has been in trouble for shoplifting. On the other hand, the defendant Coke has a previous conviction for rape, said to have been committed under very similar circumstances. In the case of Littleton, the evidence of identification will be of crucial importance, especially in view of his defence of alibi.

The fact of sexual intercourse between Coke and Margaret Blackstone seems to be undisputed, but is in any event supported by the forensic evidence suggesting that the girl had had recent sexual intercourse. There is also the fact which appears to be strongly disputed, that the same defendant was probably the author of the questioned written exhibit, which may assist in the question of his state of mind at the relevant time. Counsel will no doubt wish to consider the state of the expert evidence.

Certain issues arise from the evidence of the police officers, in respect of the search of Coke's flat, apparently without a search warrant, and from the circumstances in which Coke subsequently made his incriminating statement under caution. Counsel's attention is also drawn to the admission of guilt said to be contained in the tape-recorded conversation at the police station between Littleton and his wife.

Counsel is instructed to consider and advise on these and any other points of evidence which may arise.

Indictment

IN THE CROWN COURT AT OXBRIDGE

THE QUEEN v HENRY EDWARD COKE and
                    MARTIN STEPHEN LITTLETON

Charged as follows:

COUNT 1

Statement of Offence

Rape contrary to section 1(1) of the Sexual Offences Act 1956.

Particulars of Offence

Henry Edward Coke on the 8th day of July 1984 raped Margaret Ann Blackstone.

COUNT 2

Statement of Offence

Indecent Assault contrary to section 14(1) of the Sexual Offences Act 1956.

Particulars of Offence

Martin Stephen Littleton on the 8th day of July 1984 indecently assaulted Angela Hazel Blackstone.

W. RUSSELL COX

Officer of the Court

Depositions

STATEMENT OF WITNESS

(Criminal Justice Act 1967, s. 9; Magistrates' Courts Act 1980, s. 102; Magistrates' Courts Rules 1981, r. 70)

Statement of: Margaret Ann Blackstone

Age of Witness   17 (born 3 May 1976)

Occupation of Witness   Schoolgirl

Address of Witness   4 The Hyde, Oxbridge.

This statement, consisting of 2 pages, each signed by me, is true to the best of my knowledge and belief, and I make it knowing that if it is tendered in evidence, I shall be liable to prosecution if I have wilfully stated in it anything which I know to be false or do not believe to be true.

Dated the 12th day of July 1984.

Signed: M.A. Blackstone

Witnessed: Dennis Bracton D/S

Helen Blackstone (mother)

I am a schoolgirl aged seventeen and live with my parents and my sister Angela at the above address. I have known Henry Coke for quite a long time, because he goes to a youth club which my friends and I go to at weekends. I think he lives in Plowden Drive in Oxbridge. From time to time he has approached me at the club and asked me to go to bed with him, but I have always refused.

On Sunday, 8 July, I was walking after lunch in the park with Angela, when I saw Henry Coke coming towards us with another man who looked rather older, whom I did not know. We all started talking, and Henry said he had a new album by a band we liked and invited us to his flat to listen to it. I did not really want to go, but Angela was very excited about the idea and so we did. When we got there, Henry put the record on and made us all some coffee. I was sitting on the divan and Henry came and sat next to me. Angela was sitting on the window-ledge next to a large armchair where the other man was sitting.

After a while, Henry started making suggestions to me that we should have sexual intercourse. I told him to stop and that I did not want him even saying such things while my sister was around. At first he seemed to accept this, but then he got very persistent and started trying to hold my hand and put his arm round my shoulder. I pushed him away. All of a sudden, he pushed me backwards very hard, so that I fell on my back on the divan. I was so taken by surprise that I did not try to get up straight away, and then Henry put his hand up my skirt and pulled my pants down to my ankles. I was very frightened and just lay there. It was only when I saw that he was unzipping his trousers that I started to scream and fight. I was expecting the other man to stop him, but he did nothing. Henry was far too strong for me and he had sexual intercourse with me. I understand what this means, and that is what happened. I did not consent to it, and did nothing to lead Henry to think that I might consent.

When it was over, I got up quickly. I was terribly distressed. To my horror, I saw that Angela was sitting on the other man's lap and that he had his hand up her skirt. I shouted at her to come with me, and we both ran out of the flat and home. Neither of them made any effort to stop us.

When we got home, I could not bring myself to say anything to my mother, and ran straight upstairs, but Angela said something, and shortly afterwards, my mother came up and asked me what had happened. I didn't want to say anything, but after some time my mother more or less dragged the truth out of me, and then called the police. I then went to bed until a bit later, when a lady doctor came and examined me.

I didn't see what was happening to Angela while Henry was having intercourse with me. It was only afterwards that I noticed that she was sitting with the other man. I think I would recognise the other man if I saw him again.

Signed: M.A. Blackstone   Witnessed: Dennis Bracton D/S
                                                 Helen Blackstone (mother)

STATEMENT OF WITNESS

(Criminal Justice Act 1967, s. 9; Magistrates' Courts Act 1980, s. 102; Magistrates' Courts Rules 1981, r. 70)

Statement of: Angela Hazel Blackstone

Age of Witness   13 (born 4 June 1971)

Occupation of Witness   Schoolgirl

Address of Witness   4 The Hyde, Oxbridge.

This statement, consisting of 2 pages, each signed by me, is true to the best of my knowledge and belief, and I make it knowing that if it is tendered in evidence, I shall be liable to prosecution if I have wilfully stated in it anything which I know to be false or do not believe to be true.

Dated the 12th day of July 1984.

Signed: Angela H. Blackstone

Witnessed: Dennis Bracton D/S
Helen Blackstone (mother)

I am a schoolgirl aged thirteen and live with my parents and my sister Margaret at 4 The Hyde, Oxbridge. On Sunday after lunch, Margaret and I went for a walk in the park. We quite often do that. While we were walking, we met two men who I didn't know. One was a bit older than Margaret, and the other was even older, about the same as my uncle Paul, who is about thirty, I think. The older man didn't say much, but the younger one said he had the Least's new album and said we could listen to it. So we went home with him, and the older man came as well.

When we got there, I sat on the window ledge drinking some coffee and listening to the record, which was great. The younger man was sitting next to Margaret on the sofa. They were talking and messing about. Then they seemed to be having an argument and I saw Margaret fall backwards and the man fall on top of her. Margaret was shouting to the man to stop. I didn't understand what was going on, and I was frightened. The older man who was sitting in an armchair by the window told me not to worry, they were only playing. He lifted me off the window ledge and sat me on his lap. He didn't want me to watch Margaret, and asked me if I liked boys. I wanted to listen to the music, which was very good. Then he put his hand up my skirt and asked me if I liked it. I said I didn't, but he still kept on, and he was rubbing his leg against me.

After one or two minutes, Margaret got up off the sofa. She was crying a lot and shouted to me to come home with her, which I did. Margaret was crying all the way home but she wouldn't tell me what was the matter, and she went straight to her room when we got home. I thought I had better tell mummy in case anything was the matter with Margaret, so I told her everything that had happened.

Later on Sunday afternoon, a policeman came round with a lady police officer and I told them what had happened. Then we went out in the police car, and drove round the streets near the park. While we were doing this, I saw the older man walking along. I am sure it was the same man. We got out and went up with the police to the man, and I pointed at him and said it was the same man who had been sitting in the armchair. Then mummy took me back home while the police spoke to the man. Later on, a lady doctor came and examined me.

Signed: Angela H. Blackstone   Witnessed: Dennis Bracton D/S
                                                      Helen Blackstone (mother)

STATEMENT OF WITNESS

(Criminal Justice Act 1967, s. 9; Magistrates' Courts Act 1980, s. 102; Magistrates' Courts Rules 1981, r. 70)

Statement of: Helen Blackstone

Age of Witness   Over 21

Occupation of Witness   Housewife

Address of Witness   4 The Hyde, Oxbridge.

This statement, consisting of 1 page, signed by me, is true to the best of my knowledge and belief, and I make it knowing that if it is tendered in evidence, I shall be liable to prosecution if I have wilfully stated in it anything which I know to be false or do not believe to be true.

Dated the 12th day of July 1984.

Signed: Helen Blackstone

Witnessed: Dennis Bracton D/S

I live with my husband and two children, Margaret Ann (aged seventeen, born on 3 May 1967) and Angela Hazel (aged thirteen, born on 4 June 1971) at the above address. I now produce copies of the certificates of birth of both my children, marked 'HB1' and 'HB2' respectively.

On Sunday 8th July, the children went for a walk together after lunch round the park, as they quite often do. They left the house at about 2 o'clock. They are usually back by 3 o'clock to half past, and on this occasion, I noticed that it was a little after 4 o'clock. I heard Margaret running upstairs, and Angela went into the kitchen very quietly, which is unusual. I went into the kitchen and asked Angela if everything was all right. She told me that she and Margaret had been with two men at a flat, and that one of the men had done something to Margaret which upset her. They seemed to be fighting. Angela also said that the other man had sat her on his lap and put his hand up her skirt and kept rubbing his leg against her. She said she didn't like it.

I was very alarmed by all this, and I went up to Margaret's bedroom, where I found her on the bed sobbing violently. She did not want to talk about it, but being sure by now that something terrible had just happened, I shouted at her and slapped her. She then told me that she had been raped by Henry Coke at his flat. I at once went and called the police, and when they came some time later, they talked to both children. They said that Margaret should go to bed until a doctor came to look at her. Angela and I were asked to go out in the police car with them to have a look around.

As we were driving in Plowden Drive, which is not far from the park, Angela suddenly pointed to a man walking towards the police car, and said that it was the man who had touched her while they were sitting in the chair. The car stopped, and the officers and I and Angela approached the man. Angela pointed to the man and said: 'That's him.' The man said he didn't know what she was talking about, or words to that effect, and the officers told me to take Angela home, which I did.

Shortly after we got back home, a doctor arrived from the police and examined both children in my presence.

Signed: Helen Blackstone   Witnessed: Dennis Bracton D/S

STATEMENT OF WITNESS

(Criminal Justice Act 1967, s. 9; Magistrates' Courts Act 1980, s. 102; Magistrates' Courts Rules 1981, r. 70)

<u>Statement of:</u>   Dr Susan Geraldine Vesey

<u>Age of Witness</u>   Over 21

<u>Occupation of Witness</u>   Medical Practitioner

<u>Address of Witness</u>   27 Random Cuttings, Oxbridge.

This statement; consisting of 1 page, signed by me, is true to the best of my knowledge and belief, and I make it knowing that if it is tendered in evidence, I shall be liable to prosecution if I have wilfully stated in it anything which I know to be false or do not believe to be true.

<u>Dated the</u> 16th day of July 1984.

<u>Signed:</u>   Susan Vesey

<u>Witnessed:</u>   Dennis Bracton D/S

I am a medical practitioner in general practice at the above address. I also act as one of the surgeons to the Oxbridge Constabulary. On Sunday 8 July 1984, I was on call as duty police surgeon when as a result of a call from D/I Glanvil, I went to 4 The Hyde, Oxbridge, where I examined Margaret Ann Blackstone (D.O.B. 3 May 1967) and Angela Hazel Blackstone (D.O.B. 4 June 1971) who were identified to me by their mother, Mrs Helen Blackstone.

RESULTS OF EXAMINATION

Margaret Ann Blackstone

This girl was evidently distressed and crying at the time of my visit, though not hysterical. She was generally in excellent health. Examination of the genital area showed signs of recent sexual intercourse. There were traces of what appeared to be semen, and some reddening of the vaginal region. There were no bruising of or damage to the genitals. I took a vaginal swab which I placed in a sealed polythene bag and labelled 'SGV1'. I later handed this to D/S Bracton.

Angela Hazel Blackstone

This girl was composed and able to tell me what had happened to her. She was in excellent general health and examination revealed nothing of relevance to the inquiry.

<u>Signed:</u>   Susan Vesey   <u>Witnessed:</u>   Dennis Bracton D/S

STATEMENT OF WITNESS

(Criminal Justice Act 1967, s. 9; Magistrates' Courts Act 1980, s. 102; Magistrates' Courts Rules 1981, r. 70)

Statement of: Geoffrey Glanvil

Age of Witness   Over 21

Occupation of Witness   Detective Inspector

Address of Witness   Oxbridge Police Station

This statement, consisting of 2 pages, each signed by me, is true to the best of my knowledge and belief, and I make it knowing that if it is tendered in evidence, I shall be liable to prosecution if I have wilfully stated in it anything which I know to be false or do not believe to be true.

Dated the 16th day of July 1984.

Signed: Geoffrey Glanvil D/I

Witnessed: Dennis Bracton D/S

On Sunday 8 July 1984, at about 4.15 p.m., I was on duty in plain clothes when as a result of information received, I went in an unmarked police car with D/S Bracton and WPC Raymond to 4 The Hyde, Oxbridge. I there saw a Mrs Helen Blackstone and her two daughters, Miss Margaret Ann Blackstone aged seventeen and Miss Angela Hazel Blackstone aged thirteen. As a result of what they told me, I advised Margaret Blackstone to go to bed at once and I called for the duty police surgeon to attend. WPC Raymond remained with Margaret at my request.

Together with D/S Bracton, Mrs Blackstone and Angela I then drove the police car slowly through a number of streets around the public park near The Hyde. As we were driving along Plowden Drive, I noticed a man walking towards us, tall, slightly built, about thirty to thirty-five, dark hair, wearing a light shirt and blue jeans. Angela pointed out this man at once as the man who had assaulted her. I stopped the car, and with the other occupants got out and approached the man. Angela looked at him, pointed at him and said: 'That's him.' The man replied: 'What on earth is she talking about?' I then asked Mrs Blackstone to take Angela home.

I said to the man: 'What is your name?' He said: 'Martin Littleton. Why?' I said: 'We are police officers. It is alleged that earlier this afternoon you assaulted that girl indecently.' He said: 'Rubbish. I've never seen her before in my life.' I said: 'Have you been at Henry Coke's flat today?' Littleton said: 'I know Henry Coke, but I haven't been there today. I've been at home on my own. In fact, I've only just got up. This must be some sort of mistake.' I said: 'Where do you live?' Littleton said: 'Eldon Villas, number 17.' I then arrested Littleton for indecent assault and cautioned him, and he replied: 'You've got the wrong man, I tell you.' We then conveyed him to Oxbridge police station where he was detained.

At about 5.30 p.m. the same afternoon with D/S Bracton, I went to a first floor flat at 52 Plowden Drive, where the door was opened by a youth of about eighteen years of age, medium build, fair hair and casually dressed. I said: 'Henry Edward Coke?' He said: 'Yes.' I said: 'We are police officers. You are under arrest for raping Margaret Blackstone earlier this afternoon,' and cautioned Coke, who replied: 'Yes, all right, I was expecting you.' While D/S Bracton sat with Coke, I then searched the flat. In a drawer of the bedside cabinet I found several sheets of notepaper upon which were written in ink references to Margaret Blackstone. I took possession of these sheets, which I now produce marked 'GG1'. We then conveyed Coke to Oxbridge Police Station, where he too was detained.

Later, at 7 p.m. the same day, with D/S Bracton, I interviewed Littleton at the police station in the CID office. I reminded him of the caution, and said: 'Now, what about it, Mr Littleton?' Littleton said: 'I'm not answering any questions. I want to see my solicitor.' I said: 'You can see a solicitor at a time convenient to me. I am investigating a serious offence.' Littleton said: 'Nothing to say.' I said: 'Very well, you will be detained over night and I will see you in the morning.' Littleton said: 'No. Please give me bail. My wife will be so worried.' I said: 'Bail is not on at the moment, but I will make sure your wife knows where you are.'

At 7.20 p.m. the same day, with D/S Bracton, I interviewed Henry Coke in the CID office. I said: 'You are still under caution. Do you want to tell me about it?' Coke said: 'Yes, I may as well. With form for the same thing, I reckon I'm going down for a while. Will you write a statement for me?' I said: 'Certainly.' I then wrote at Coke's dictation a statement under caution, between 7.30 and 8 p.m. without any break. I now produce this statement marked 'GG2'. After completing this statement, I said to Coke: 'You have not mentioned the sheets of paper referring to Margaret which I found in your room.' Coke said: 'No. Actually, those are not mine. Lots of my mates fancy Margaret.' I said: 'How do they come to be in your room on this particular day when you rape her?' Coke said: 'They may have been there for months.' I said: 'Will you supply me with specimens of your handwriting so that I can have a scientific comparison made?' He said: 'Yes, all right.' Coke then wrote at my dictation on a piece of paper which I now produce marked 'GG3'. I then handed exhibits 'GG1' and 'GG3' to D/S Bracton for transmission to the forensic science laboratory.

At about 8.45 p.m. the same day, Mrs Davina Littleton arrived at the police station, and was allowed to see her husband in a cell. I positioned myself nearby, so that I could hear clearly what was said, and recorded the conversation using a pocket cassette recorder. After some general conversation, Mrs Littleton asked: 'Martin, tell me the truth. Is there any truth in what the police say?' Littleton replied: 'Yes, I'm afraid so. I don't know what came over me. I just felt her up. I couldn't help myself. I can't explain it.' I now produce the cassette as exhibit 'GG4'.

The next morning at about 9 a.m. I formally charged Coke with rape and Littleton with indecent assault. They were cautioned and neither made any reply.

Signed: Geoffrey Glanvil D/I   Witnessed: Dennis Bracton D/S

STATEMENT UNDER CAUTION

<u>GG2</u>

Oxbridge Police Station

Date: 8 July 1984

Time: 7.30 p.m.

<u>Statement of:</u>   Henry Edward Coke

<u>Address:</u>   52 Plowden Drive, Oxbridge

<u>Age:</u>   18

<u>Occupation:</u>   Apprentice Tailor.

    I, Henry Edward Coke, wish to make a statement. I want someone to write down what I say. I have been told that I need not say anything unless I wish to do so and that whatever I say may be given in evidence.

<u>Signed:</u>   H.E. Coke

<u>Witnessed:</u>   Geoffrey Glanvil D/I

It's difficult to know where to start really. I've known Margaret for years from the club and seeing her around. I've always fancied her. She's really lovely. I saw her down the club last night wearing one of those see-through blouses. I went home and thought about it a lot, and decided to do something about it. My mate Martin Littleton came round this morning and he had a couple of drinks with me at lunchtime. I told him that Margaret and her sister always went for a stroll in the park after lunch and I was telling him how much I fancied Margaret. We agreed we would meet them if we could and find some reason to take them back to my place. I was really only going to chat Margaret up a bit. Martin said he would look after the little girl for me. So we went up the park, and it went all right. They said they would come back with us to listen to a new record which is very popular down the club at the moment. I put the record on and started chatting Margaret up, while Martin talked to the little girl. Margaret didn't want to know. She was giving me no joy at all. I suddenly came over all funny. I felt I had to have her at all costs. It wasn't difficult. She was sitting next to me on my divan bed. I pushed her backwards on to the bed. She looked rather surprised more than anything else. She had taken her shoes off and she wasn't wearing tights, so I had her pants off quite easily. It was only then she started struggling. It was no trouble. I had it off with her. Then she started crying, which was a bit silly, because she would have enjoyed it if she'd thought about it. She called over to her sister and dragged her off. She was carrying her shoes. I don't think she remembered her pants. I threw them out afterwards.

    After she went I was worried. Obviously, I knew you would probably come for me, but actually, I was more worried about Martin. It was only when I had finished with Margaret that I saw what he was up to with the little girl. He was touching her up and fondling her. I know I was a bit forceful with Margaret, but at least she is old enough. Doing that to a kiddy is really sick. No way was I involved with that. I want to make that clear. That is down to Martin on his own. Once I discovered what was going on, I gave Martin a mouthful. We had quite an argument and I threw him out. I don't know what happened to him after that.

I would like to say I'm sorry for what happened. I really like Margaret and I didn't want to hurt her. It's all very silly. Why can't girls say yes sometimes and just enjoy it?

<u>Signed:</u>　H.E. Coke

<u>Witnessed:</u>　Geoffrey Glanvil D/I

I have read the above statement and I have been told that I can correct, alter or add anything I wish. This statement is true. I have made it of my own free will.

<u>Signed:</u>　H.E. Coke

<u>Witnessed:</u>　Geoffrey Glanvil D/I

Statement taken by me Geoffrey Glanvil between 7.30 p.m. and 8 p.m. No breaks for refreshments.

<u>Signed:</u>　Geoffrey Glanvil D/I

STATEMENT OF WITNESS

(Criminal Justice Act 1967, s. 9; Magistrates' Courts Act 1980, s. 102; Magistrates' Courts Rules 1981, r. 70)

<u>Statement of:</u>   Dennis Bracton

<u>Age of Witness</u>   Over 21

<u>Occupation of Witness</u>   Detective Sergeant

<u>Address of Witness</u>   Oxbridge Police Station.

This statement, consisting of 2 pages, each signed by me, is true to the best of my knowledge and belief, and I make it knowing that if it is tendered in evidence, I shall be liable to prosecution if I have wilfully stated in it anything which I know to be false or do not believe to be true.

<u>Dated the</u> 16th day of July 1984.

<u>Signed:</u>   Dennis Bracton D/S

<u>Witnessed:</u>   Geoffrey Glanvil D/I

On Sunday 8 July 1984 at about 4.15 p.m. I was on duty in plain clothes when as a result of information received, I went in an unmarked police car with D/I Glanvil and WPC Raymond to 4 The Hyde, Oxbridge. I there saw a Mrs Helen Blackstone and her two daughters, Miss Margaret Blackstone aged seventeen and Miss Angela Blackstone aged thirteen. As a result of what they said, D/I Glanvil advised Margaret Blackstone to go to bed and await the arrival of a doctor. D/I Glanvil then called for the duty police surgeon, Dr Vesey, to attend. WPC Raymond remained at the house with Margaret.

Together with D/I Glanvil, Mrs Blackstone and Angela, I then drove in the police car slowly around various streets near the park just by The Hyde. As we were driving along Plowden Drive, I saw Angela point to a man walking towards us, tall, slightly built, about thirty to thirty-five, dark hair, wearing a light shirt and blue jeans. D/I Glanvil stopped the car, and we all got out and approached the man. Angela looked at him, pointed to him and said: 'That's him.' The man replied: 'What on earth is she talking about?' D/I Glanvil then asked Mrs Blackstone to take Angela home.

D/I Glanvil said to the man: 'What is your name?' He said: 'Martin Littleton. Why?' D/I Glanvil said: 'We are police officers. It is alleged that earlier this afternoon you assaulted that girl indecently.' He said: 'Rubbish. I've never seen her before in my life.' D/I Glanvil said: 'Have you been at Henry Coke's flat today?' Littleton said: 'I know Henry Coke, but I haven't been there today. I've been at home on my own. In fact, I've only just got up. This must be some sort of mistake.' D/I Glanvil said: 'Where do you live?' Littleton said: 'Eldon Villas. Number 17.' D/I Glanvil then arrested Littleton for indecent assault and cautioned him, and Littleton replied: 'You've got the wrong man, I tell you.' We then conveyed Littleton to Oxbridge police station where he was detained.

At about 5.30 p.m. the same day, with D/I Glanvil, I went to a first-floor flat at 52 Plowden Drive, where the door was opened by a youth of about eighteen years, medium build, fair hair and casually dressed. D/I Glanvil said: 'Henry Edward Coke?' He said: 'Yes'. D/I Glanvil said: 'We are police officers. You are under arrest for raping Margaret Blackstone earlier this afternoon' and cautioned Coke, who said: 'Yes, all right, I was expecting you.' I then sat with Coke while D/I Glanvil searched the flat. In a drawer in a bedside cabinet I saw D/I Glanvil find a number of sheets of notepaper, of which he took possession. Coke was then detained at Oxbridge police station.

Later the same day at 7 p.m. with D/I Glanvil I interviewed Littleton in the CID office at Oxbridge police station. D/I Glanvil reminded Littleton of the caution and said: 'Now, what about it, Mr Littleton?' Littleton said: 'I'm not answering any questions. I want to see my solicitor.' D/I Glanvil said: 'You can see a solicitor at a time convenient to me. I am investigating a serious offence.' Littleton said: 'Nothing to say.' D/I Glanvil said: 'Very well, you will be detained overnight and I will see you in the morning.' Littleton said: 'No. Please give me bail. My wife will be so worried.' D/I Glanvil said: 'Bail is not on at the moment, but I will make sure your wife knows where you are.'

At 7.20 p.m. the same day, with D/I Glanvil I interviewed Henry Coke in the CID office. D/I Glanvil said: 'You are still under caution. Do you want to tell me about it?' Coke said: 'Yes, I may as well. With form for the same thing, I reckon I'm going down for a while. Will you write a statement for me?' D/I Glanvil said: 'Certainly.' D/I Glanvil then took a statement under caution from Coke, and while this was being done, I left the room to attend to other matters.

The next morning at about 9 a.m. I was present when D/I Glanvil formally charged Coke and Littleton with rape and indecent assault respectively. They were cautioned and made no reply.

During the evening of 8 July, I had taken possession from D/I Glanvil of exhibits GG1 and GG3. After the defendants had been charged, I took these exhibits from the police station to the surgery of Dr Susan Vesey at 27 Random Cuttings, Oxbridge. I there collected from the doctor a swab contained in a polythene bag marked 'SGV1'. I then conveyed these exhibits personally to the appropriate departments of the Oxbridge forensic science laboratory.

<u>Signed:</u>   Dennis Bracton D/S   <u>Witnessed:</u>   Geoffrey Glanvil D/I

STATEMENT OF WITNESS

(Criminal Justice Act 1967, s. 9; Magistrates' Courts Act 1980, s. 102; Magistrates' Courts Rules 1981, r. 70)

Statement of: Lorraine Raymond

Age of Witness   Over 21

Occupation of Witness   Police Constable 24

Address of Witness   Oxbridge Police Station.

This statement, consisting of 1 page, signed by me, is true to the best of my knowledge and belief, and I make it knowing that if it is tendered in evidence, I shall be liable to prosecution if I have wilfully stated in it anything which I know to be false or do not believe to be true.

Dated the 16th day of July 1984.

Signed: Lorraine Raymond WPC24

Witnessed: Dennis Bracton D/S

On Sunday 8 July 1984, at about 4.15 p.m. I was on duty in uniform at Oxbridge Police Station, when as a result of information received, I went with D/I Glanvil and D/S Bracton, to 4 The Hyde, Oxbridge, where I saw a Mrs Helen Blackstone and her two daughters, Miss Margaret Blackstone aged seventeen and Miss Angela Blackstone aged thirteen. As a result of what they said, D/I Glanvil advised Margaret Blackstone to go to bed and await the arrival of the police surgeon. At D/I Glanvil's request, I remained in the bedroom with Margaret while the other officers went out in the police car with Mrs Blackstone and Angela.

While we were together, Margaret was initially upset but recovered her composure rapidly. I asked her various questions, in reply to which she gave me an account of her having been raped by a young man known to her called Henry Coke.

At about 5.40 p.m. just after Mrs Blackstone and Angela had returned to the house, the duty police surgeon, Dr Susan Vesey, arrived and I then left and returned to the police station.

Signed: Lorraine Raymond WCP24   Witnessed: Dennis Bracton D/S

STATEMENT OF WITNESS

(Criminal Justice Act 1967, s. 9; Magistrates' Courts Act 1980, s. 102; Magistrates' Courts Rules 1981, r. 70)

<u>Statement of:</u>   Philip Hale BSc

<u>Age of Witness</u>   Over 21

<u>Occupation of Witness</u>   Higher Scientific Officer

<u>Address of Witness</u>   Forensic Science Laboratory, Portland Road, Oxbridge.

This statement, consisting of 1 page, signed by me, is true to the best of my knowledge and belief, and I make it knowing that if it is tendered in evidence, I shall be liable to prosecution if I have wilfully stated in it anything which I know to be false or do not believe to be true.

<u>Dated the</u> 20th day of July 1984.

<u>Signed:</u>   Philip Hale

<u>Witnessed:</u>   Dennis Bracton D/S

I have specialised for the last seven years in the scientific examination of documents and comparison of handwriting. On Monday, 9 July 1984, I received from D/S Bracton exhibits GG1 and GG3 which were identified by means of labels.

Exhibit GG1

This was a bundle of four sheets of lined white notepaper containing various short passages in cursive handwriting in blue ball-point ink. The passages contained references in a sexual context to someone called Margaret Blackstone. I took this to be questioned writing.

Exhibit GG3

This was a single sheet of plain notepaper containing the following words in cursive handwriting in blue ball-point ink: 'Margaret. Margaret Blackstone. I want you. I need you. I must have you. I think about Margaret all the time.'
I took this to be the known handwriting of Henry Edward Coke.
I examined and compared these exhibits.

RESULTS OF EXAMINATION

I found a high probability that the writer of exhibit GG3 also wrote the text of exhibit GG1. I cannot wholly exclude the possibility that the writer of GG1 was a different person from the writer of GG3 but in my opinion this is unlikely.
After examination, I returned the exhibits to Oxbridge police station where I handed them to D/S Bracton.
I have prepared a chart of comparison of the two exhibits which I can use to illustrate my conclusions if necessary.

<u>Signed:</u>   Philip Hale   <u>Witnessed:</u>   Dennis Bracton D/S

STATEMENT OF WITNESS

(Criminal Justice Act 1967, s. 9; Magistrates' Courts Act 1980, s. 102; Magistrates' Courts Rules 1981, r. 70)

Statement of:　Ernest Espinasse MSc PhD

Age of Witness　Over 21

Occupation of Witness　Higher Scientific Officer

Address of Witness　Forensic Science Laboratory, Portland Road, Oxbridge

This statement, consisting of 1 page, signed by me, is true to the best of my knowledge and belief, and I make it knowing that if it is tendered in evidence, I shall be liable to prosecution if I have wilfully stated in it anything which I know to be false or do not believe to be true.

Dated the 16th day of July 1984.

Signed:　Ernest Espinasse

Witnessed:　Dennis Bracton D/S

On Monday 9 July 1984, I received from D/S Bracton a polythene bag bearing an identifying label marked 'SGV1' and containing a sterilised cotton swab.

I specialise in the detection and identification of traces of blood, semen and other biological matter and in the scientific examination of specimens and exhibits within these fields. I examined exhibit SGV1.

RESULTS OF EXAMINATION

This exhibit yielded positive and readily detectable evidence of human spermatozoa, seminal acid phosphatase and seminal blood-group antigens. From the presence of these factors and the high level at which they were detected, I am able to say that the subject of the swab had had sexual intercourse within a recent time of the taking of the swab. I can say that such intercourse definitely occurred within forty-eight hours of the taking of the swab, and in all probability, within a very much shorter time. I can illustrate and support my conclusions if necessary.

After examination, I resealed the exhibit in sterile material and placed it in a safe place in the laboratory.

Signed:　Ernest Espinasse　　　Witnessed:　Dennis Bracton D/S

Previous convictions of defendants and witness

CONVICTIONS RECORDED AGAINST: Henry Edward Coke

CONVICTED IN NAME OF: (As above)

C.R.O. No: HEC 3421   D.O.B.: 4/3/66

DATE	COURT	OFFENCE	SENTENCE
16/4/81	Oxbridge Crown	Rape (M/O Induced girl to visit him to listen to records and raped her)	Borstal training (released on 14/10/82)

CONVICTIONS RECORDED AGAINST: Martin Stephen Littleton

CONVICTED IN NAME OF:

C.R.O. No: D.O.B.: 11/2/51

DATE	COURT	OFFENCE	SENTENCE
		NONE RECORDED	

CONVICTIONS RECORDED AGAINST: Margaret Ann Blackstone

CONVICTED IN NAME OF: (As above)

C.R.O. No: D.O.B.: 3/5/67

DATE	COURT	OFFENCE	SENTENCE
28/11/83	Oxbridge Juvenile	Theft (shoplifting)	Conditional discharge 2 years

Notice of alibi

THOMAS, WATSON & CO

Solicitors and
Commissioners for
Oaths

19 College Row
Oxbridge
Oxshire XX5 3BR
Tel: Oxbridge 7541

A. Hughes-Thompson
R. Simms LLB

Our Ref: RS/MSL
Your Ref:

The Prosecuting Solicitor
Oxbridge Constabulary
Police Headquarters
Oxbridge

23 July 1984

Dear Sir,

The Queen v Coke and Littleton

We act in the above matter for the defendant Martin Stephen Littleton, who is charged with indecent assault.

We are instructed by our client to supply you now, at the first practicable opportunity, with details of our client's alibi, which will be his defence at trial.

On 8 July 1984, a Sunday, our client was asleep in bed until about 2 o'clock that afternoon, having retired to bed after a heavy day's work on the Saturday, shortly before midnight. He got up between about 2.30 and 3 p.m., had something to eat, and feeling slightly unwell, went out for a walk at about 4.15 p.m. or a little after. This was the first time our client had left his house at 17 Eldon Villas, Oxbridge, on that day. It was in the course of that walk that he was stopped by police and arrested.

There are no witnesses in support of the alibi. Our client was alone at home at all material times.

Yours faithfully

Thomas, Watson & Co

BRIEF FOR THE DEFENCE

Instructions to Counsel on behalf of the defendant Coke

Counsel is instructed on behalf of the defendant Coke, who is charged with rape, as appears from the indictment and statements of the prosecution witnesses sent herewith. The defendant wishes to plead not guilty to this charge, and Counsel will see from his proof of evidence which follows, that he does not deny having sexual intercourse with Margaret Blackstone on the relevant occasion, but says that such intercourse took place with her consent. Counsel will please consider the implications of this defence, and of the fact that according to Coke, the girl is somewhat promiscuous, in the light of the defendant's previous conviction for rape.

The defendant Littleton is of course separately represented, because of the clear conflict of interest between the two, and it is not known what he may say about Coke. It is believed that he may be putting forward a defence of alibi, which would result in a direct conflict of evidence between the defendants. Littleton is apparently a man of previous good character.

Counsel will see that Coke has some serious challenges to the police evidence, both with regard to the search of his flat and his arrest, and his subsequent treatment at the police station. It may be that these matters will affect the admissibility of Coke's alleged oral and written admissions to the police, which on the face of it are very damaging to his case. There is also concern about the written notes found by the police. Coke is adamant that he did not write these, and Counsel will no doubt wish to consider carefully the evidence of the handwriting expert.

Counsel will please consider these matters and the evidence in general.

Proof of evidence of Coke

HENRY EDWARD COKE of 52 Plowden Drive, Oxbridge, will state as follows:

I have been charged with raping a girl called Margaret Blackstone at my flat on 8 July 1984. To this charge I wish to plead not guilty. I admit that I had sexual intercourse with her, but it was with her consent. What happened was as follows.

I have known Margaret for quite a long time, because we both go to the same youth club at weekends. Margaret is a really good-looking girl, and all my mates fancy her as well. I have never made any secret of the fact that I do. I have tried chatting her up at the club on various occasions, and although she was usually with someone else, she gave me the impression that I would be all right if I played my cards right. I decided to try my luck. By this, I mean that I was going to try to have sexual intercourse with her, but not by force or against her will. I saw Margaret the night before the alleged rape, Saturday the 7th at the club, and I made up my mind to meet her 'accidentally' the next afternoon when she was walking with her sister in the park, as she usually does.

In fact, the next morning, my mate Martin Littleton came round. He is a fair bit older than my crowd, and is married, but he helps out at the pub I use as my local and we get on very well. I told him about what I had in mind while we were having a drink at lunchtime. Martin agreed to talk to the little girl while I made my number with Margaret, if we could persuade them to come back to my place with us. We went round the park, and there they were, so we asked them back to listen to a new album from the Least, which all the kids like at the moment, and they came. Margaret seemed quite happy about it. She came and sat next to me on the divan bed and we drank coffee while we listened to the album. She took her shoes off. We were getting on really well. Martin was laughing and talking to the little girl the other side of the room near the window.

Margaret and I then lay down on the sofa, and she made it clear that she wanted to have sexual intercourse with me. She took off her pants, and we had intercourse. This was entirely with her consent. The story she has told to her mother and the police is quite untrue. I think she has made this up because she is embarrassed about doing it with her sister there, and because obviously she was going to be asked how her younger sister came to be interfered with while Margaret was with her. Also, Margaret was not a virgin at the time. Several of my mates have had it off with her. She will do it with anyone. Apparently she threatened to complain that my mate Kevin had raped her last year, when he hadn't at all. She was convicted of shoplifting last year, and it seems she is rather dishonest.

I want to make it clear that I had nothing to do with Martin interfering with the little girl. All I saw was that he was touching her up, when Margaret and I had finished. Margaret must have seen that as well, because she dragged the little girl off pretty quickly. She didn't even wait to put on her shoes, which she carried, and she left her pants behind. I threw them away later on. I was disgusted with Martin. We had a big row, and I threw him out.

I thought then that the police would be round, but there was nothing I could do. Mr Glanvil and Mr Bracton came round at about 5.30 that afternoon. They did not say anything to me, as they say. They rushed in without a word, and started searching the room. I knew who they were. I did say: 'I was expecting you,' which was true, but this was while they were searching the room. I also asked them if they had a search warrant, and was told to shut up. Glanvil found some pieces of paper with a few bawdy remarks about Margaret on them. I think they had been there for ages. My mates used to come round and we would talk about girls and so on, and I think one of them must have written it for a laugh. I certainly did not. I did give the police specimens of my handwriting later, and I am surprised at the conclusions reached by the expert. I definitely did not write those remarks, and I note that he cannot say for certain that I did.

After they had finished the search, Glanvil just said: 'Right, come on.' They took me to the police station. I was not told I was being arrested, and I was not cautioned. Later that day, the officers came to see me in an office and questioned me. It is true that I signed a statement under caution, but this was only because the officers shouted at me and threatened me that if I did not admit raping Margaret, they would do me for interfering with the little girl as well, and Glanvil said they would 'lock me up and throw away the key' for that. I believed this, because I was really horrified by the idea of touching up children, and I could see that they could make it look bad for me. So I made up the statement and dictated it to them. Some of it was of course true, but not the bit about how the intercourse came about. I did not say before making the statement: 'Yes, I may as well. With form for the same thing, I reckon I'm going down for a while.' I just agreed at the end of a session of threats to make one.

It is true that, unfortunately, I have been convicted of rape before. This was in April 1981. I was sent to Borstal, and was there until October 1982. On this occasion, I was guilty and pleaded guilty. I did intend to persuade the girl to make love but I went too far. However, I learned my lesson from this, and I would not have done this again. I have never been in trouble apart from this, and am now apprentice to a tailor. I started this after a course we had in Borstal, and I want to get on with it and lead a useful life.

Instructions to Counsel on behalf of the defendant Littleton

Counsel is instructed on behalf of the defendant Littleton, a man of good character who has been charged with indecently assaulting a girl of thirteen, as appears from the indictment and statements of the witnesses for the prosecution. Littleton wishes to plead not guilty to this charge, and sets out his defence in the proof of evidence which follows. A proof of evidence from Mrs Littleton is also available, which supports what the defendant has to say in certain important respects.

Counsel will appreciate that in view of the defence of alibi, the issue of identification is crucial to the case. The admissibility and quality of the evidence for the prosecution must be questionable in this respect. Unfortunately, no witness is available to support the alibi itself. It will be particularly important to ensure that the jury hear the whole of the tape of the conversation between the defendant and his wife if it is used in evidence at all, but Counsel will no doubt be anxious to exclude it if this can be done.

Unfortunately, it is believed that the defendant Coke will say that Littleton was at his flat on the day in question and may say that Littleton did in some way assault the girl. In this connection, it is worth observing that Coke has a previous conviction for rape, and it may be that he is protecting the man who was actually there.

Counsel will please consider the matters of evidence which arise in this case.

Proof of evidence of Littleton

MARTIN STEPHEN LITTLETON of 17 Eldon Villas, Oxbridge, will state as follows:

I have been charged with indecently assaulting a girl of thirteen called Angela Blackstone. I wish to plead not guilty. I am a man of thirty-three years of age, married, and I am of good character.

I have a number of part-time occupations, one of which is helping out at a public house called the Turk's Head in Oxbridge. I have come across a youth called Henry Coke there, and I have been to his place in Plowden Drive once or twice. On Sunday, 8 July 1984, the day of the alleged assault, I got up late, about 2.30 or 3 o'clock, as far as I can remember. My wife had been at her sister's over the previous night. I had a bite to eat. Then, because I felt a bit headachy, I went out for a walk in the direction of the park.

I started walking down Plowden Drive in the course of my walk, as this road is on the way from my house to the park. I noticed that there was a car coming towards me rather slowly, but I thought nothing of it until it stopped, and a small girl whom I have never seen before in my life got out with a woman and two men, and came up to me. The girl said something like: 'That's him' and pointed at me. I had no idea what was going on. The police officers then told me what was alleged, and they have correctly recorded my answers, which were to the effect that there had been a mistake over the identity of the attacker. I am sure the girl is genuinely convinced that I assaulted her, but I was not at Coke's flat that day and have no idea what happened. The police did not believe me, and I was arrested and taken to the police station.

Later on, the officers wanted to ask me some more questions, but I refused to answer until I had seen my solicitor, and I was not allowed to see him. Because of this, I was kept in overnight, which really upset me. My wife was due back that afternoon and would have been worried. In fact, the police contacted her, and she arrived at the station to see me later that evening. It now appears that the police recorded what we said to each other during the few minutes we were allowed in my cell. It is true that we had the conversation to which D/I Glanvil refers in his statement, but as should appear from the cassette, my wife's question was asked under the great stress which she felt at what had happened. I very foolishly lost my temper and answered in an ironical vein, intended to convey nothing more than anger that she should even have asked the question. I had in fact told her the truth already, exactly as it appears in this statement, and I hope this is also recorded on the cassette. I was not making any sort of admission that I had committed the offence.

I see that Henry Coke has told the police that I was at his flat and somehow helped him in his plan to rape Margaret Blackstone, and then myself molested her sister. This is quite untrue. I cannot think why he should have said this, as I have never offended him as far as I know, except that he is obviously trying to shield whoever was there, to cover up his own guilt. Coke has been in trouble of this sort before. He has been to Borstal for some offence involving a different girl, although I do not know the details of this.

Proof of evidence of Mrs Littleton

DAVINA MARY LITTLETON of 17 Eldon Villas, Oxbridge, will state as follows:

I am the wife of Martin Stephen Littleton and live with him at the above address.

On Saturday, 7 July 1984, I went for the day to my sister who lives at Winchelham, because it was her little boy's birthday. Martin was working all day on that Saturday, so he remained at home, and I arranged to stay the night and return the next day.

On Sunday, 8 July, I arrived home at about 6 o'clock in the evening to find the house empty. This was rather unusual, as Martin usually stays in if he is not working. By 8 o'clock, I was getting worried. Just about then, I had a telephone call from the Oxbridge police saying that Martin had been arrested. They wouldn't tell me why over the phone. I was frantic. I got to the police station as quickly as I could and I saw Inspector Glanvil, who told me what they said had happened. I told him it was absurd, and said I wanted to see my husband. After some discussion, I was granted permission to do this, and after some delay, I was shown into a cell, where he was.

It appears that our conversation was recorded by the police, and I have done my best to recall it. Unfortunately, I was in such a state that only two things stand out clearly. Firstly, Martin told me that there must have been a mistake because he had been at home when the offence was supposed to have been committed. Then, a bit later, I very foolishly begged him to tell me whether there was any truth in what was said about him. I only did this because of the state I was in. It caused Martin to lose his temper, and he did reply in the words recorded by the police. However, it was quite clear that he was speaking in a bitter, sarcastic tone, and he did not mean that he was really guilty. If he had meant that, I think I would have had complete hysteria on the spot, and it would have shown on the recording. I would have been very angry and distressed.

From my knowledge of Martin, which goes back about nine years, six of them as his wife, the suggestion that he would interfere with children sexually is ludicrous. I have often seen him with children of friends and relatives, and his attitude towards them has always been quite normal. He is very popular with everyone who knows him, and has a good reputation for honesty and helpfulness.

B: *BLACKSTONE V COKE*

BRIEF FOR THE PLAINTIFF

Instructions to Counsel

Counsel is instructed on behalf of the plaintiff in this action, which arises from the rape of the plaintiff by the defendant in July 1984. Counsel will observe that the plaintiff is assisted by the defendant's conviction of this offence in the Crown Court on 10 January 1985. The defendant asserts that he was wrongly convicted, and Counsel will no doubt consider how the matter should be presented, in the light of s. 11 of the Civil Evidence Act 1968. The defendant has never, so far as is known to your instructing solicitors, attempted to deny his paternity of the child until these proceedings, but it is thought that he may try to impute this to one Henneky, who is in the United States at the present time. No notice has been given on behalf of the defendant of an intention to adduce his hearsay evidence, but counsel will find interesting the letter from Henneky's American lawyer.

The plaintiff has available expert evidence from Dr Gray dealing with the plaintiff's psychological sufferings, and from Dr Vesey, who saw her just after the rape and subsequently, dealing with the reasons why the pregnancy was not terminated. Both will be available as witnesses. On instructing solicitors' advice, the plaintiff has declined to submit herself or the child to blood tests. Frankly, we regard the evidence as very strong, and were not prepared to risk exacerbating her suffering. The other side may seek to make some capital out of this.

The defendant's solicitors have issued a subpoena *duces tecum* against the Director of the Oxbridge City Children's Department apparently in the belief that Miss Blackstone made some damaging admission to him about paternity when consulting the Department on the subject of long-term fostering. The Director has refused to answer enquiries from either side, claiming that public policy prevents this, and it seems that the issue may have to be determined by the court. Miss Blackstone states that she said nothing inconsistent with her case. For our part, we have issued a subpoena to a Fr. Wigmore, a Roman Catholic priest consulted by Mr Coke. It is thought that the defendant may well have said something incriminating to Fr. Wigmore, who, subject to counsel's advice, seems to us to be compellable to repeat it to the court. This information was gleaned from a letter which the defendant's solicitors inadvertently enclosed with a letter to instructing solicitors, and a copy of which counsel will find herewith. The original was returned to Mansfield & Co. in accordance with counsel's advice, but it is hoped that the copy may be useful in evidence.

Counsel will please consider the evidence and advise generally, and appear for the plaintiff.

Pleadings

IN THE HIGH COURT OF JUSTICE   1985 B No: 123
QUEEN'S BENCH DIVISION
OXBRIDGE DISTRICT REGISTRY
Writ issued the 20th day of May 1985
BETWEEN:

MARGARET ANN BLACKSTONE   Plaintiff

and

HENRY EDWARD COKE   Defendant

STATEMENT OF CLAIM

1. On or about the 8th day of July 1984 the Defendant lured the Plaintiff to his flat at 52 Plowden Drive in the City and County of Oxbridge under pretence of a social occasion for listening to music and drinking coffee and there assaulted and beat the Plaintiff by having sexual intercourse with her by force and without her consent.

2. Further and alternatively the Defendant falsely and against her will imprisoned the Plaintiff in his said flat by force despite the Plaintiff's repeated requests that she be allowed to leave.

3. Pursuant to the provisions of section 11 of the Civil Evidence Act 1968 the Plaintiff will rely upon the conviction of the Defendant on indictment on the 10th day of January 1985 at the Oxbridge Crown Court before the Honourable Mr Justice Holt and a jury of having raped the Plaintiff on the 8th day of July 1984. Such conviction is relevant in this suit to the Plaintiff's allegations herein that the Defendant had sexual intercourse with the Plaintiff on the said date, that he did so without the Plaintiff's consent and that the Defendant is the father of the Plaintiff's child referred to in the particulars under paragraph 4 hereof.

4. By reason of the Defendant's assault and battery and/or false imprisonment of the Plaintiff as aforesaid the Plaintiff has suffered personal injury, loss and damage.

PARTICULARS OF PERSONAL INJURY

(i)   Severe pain and irritation of the genital region;
(ii) Unwanted pregnancy resulting in the confinement of the Plaintiff and the birth to her on the 22nd day of April 1985 of a male child, Kenneth Arthur Blackstone;
(iii) Post-natal complications and depression;
(iv) Continuing depression, emotional distress, fear of social ostracism, anxiety over normal social contact with others and lack of self-confidence, all requiring psychiatric treatment.

PARTICULARS OF LOSS AND DAMAGE

Expenses of confinement and birth:	£1,000.00
Psychiatrist's fees:	£2,500.00
(and continuing)	
	£3,500.00

5.   Further, pursuant to section 35A of the Supreme Court Act 1981, the Plaintiff is entitled to and claims to recover interest on the amount found to be due to the Plaintiff at such rate and for such period as the court thinks fit.

AND the plaintiff claims:
(i)   The said sum of £3,500.00
(ii)   Damages.
(iii)   The aforesaid interest pursuant to section 35A of the Supreme Court Act 1981, to be assessed.

ALEXANDER NOY

Served this 19th day of May 1985 by Eldon & Co., 12, The Low, Oxbridge, Solicitors for the Plaintiff.

IN THE HIGH COURT OF JUSTICE   1985 B No: 123
QUEEN'S BENCH DIVISION
OXBRIDGE DISTRICT REGISTRY
BETWEEN:

MARGARET ANN BLACKSTONE   Plaintiff

— and —

HENRY EDWARD COKE   Defendant

Defence

1.   With reference to paragraph 1 of the Statement of Claim the Defendant admits only
that on the 8th day of July 1984 at his said flat he had sexual intercourse with the Plaintiff.
The Plaintiff consented to such intercourse. The Defendant denies that he used any force
or assaulted or beat the Plaintiff as alleged or at all. Save as expressly admitted above the
Defendant denies each and every allegation contained in the said paragraph 1.
2.   With reference to paragraph 2 of the Statement of Claim the Defendant denies that he
falsely imprisoned the Plaintiff as alleged or at all. At all material times the Plaintiff was a
willing visitor to the Defendant's flat and was free to leave as she wished.
3.   With reference to paragraph 3 of the Statement of Claim the Defendant admits that
he was in fact convicted of rape as alleged but denies that he was guilty of the said or any
offence. The Defendant will seek to show that he was wrongly convicted and will invite
this Honourable Court so to find.
4.   The Defendant admits that the Plaintiff gave birth to a child on the date alleged but
denies that he is the father of the said child.
5.   The Defendant makes no admissions with regard to the alleged or any personal
injury, loss or damage. If (which is not admitted) the Plaintiff suffered any personal
injury, loss or damage the Defendant denies that such injury, loss or damage was caused
or contributed to by his said sexual intercourse with the Plaintiff or that he is in any
manner responsible therefor.
6.   Further and alternatively such injury, loss or damage as the Plaintiff may prove
flowing from her said pregnancy, confinement or giving birth (which is not admitted) was
caused by or contributed to by the Plaintiff's refusal or failure to undergo an abortion at
the proper time after conception.
7.   In the premises the Defendant denies that the Plaintiff is entitled to the relief claimed
or any relief.

HORACE ATKYN

Served this 13th day of June 1985 by Mansfield & Co, Oldschool Buildings, Oxbridge,
Solicitor for the Defendant.

Correspondence

ELDON & Co

Solicitors
Commissioners for Oaths

12, The Low,
Oxbridge XX5 2BR
Tel: Oxbridge 62847

Geoffrey J. Eldon LL.B
Paul Birch
Stephen M. Paynter B.A.
Mary L. Driver LL.B
Kenneth Stacey
Geraldine C. Eldon M.A.

Messrs. Mansfield & Co.,
Oldschool Bldgs.,
Oxbridge.

Our ref: GJE/MAB
Your ref: SPM/HEC

5 February 1985

Dear Sirs,

    <u>Re</u>:

<u>Miss Margaret Blackstone</u>

We act for Miss Blackstone in matters arising from the rape committed on her by your client Mr Henry Coke on the 8 July, 1984, an offence of which he was convicted by a jury at the Oxbridge Crown Court on the 10 January of this year. As a result of this act, our client is now pregnant with Mr Coke's child, and is expected to give birth in April.

We are advised by Counsel that our client is entitled to substantial damages against Mr Coke in respect of the birth, and her severe psychological injury and distress. Your client may consider himself fortunate that our client wishes no more to do with him and is prepared to maintain the child herself with the help of her family. Unless we hear from you within 14 days of this letter with your proposals for settlement of our client's claim, we shall have no alternative but to instruct Counsel to settle proceedings in the High Court.

        Yours Faithfully,

        <u>Eldon & Co.</u>

MANSFIELD & Co.

	Stanley P. Mansfield
	Philip Garrity LL.B
Solicitors and Commissioners for Oaths	Heather L. Morris
	Peter G. Bullimore

Oldschool Buildings,
Oxbridge
Tel: 0411

Messrs. Eldon & Co.
12, The Low,
Oxbridge.

Our ref: SPM/HEC
Your ref: GJE/MAB

8 February 1985

Dear Sirs,

    <u>Re:</u>

<u>Miss Blackstone and Mr Coke</u>

We are in receipt of your letter of the 5th, inst. and confirm that we act for Mr Coke in this matter. If your client does not require maintenance for the child, we are unable to see what damages your client may be entitled to. Our client instructs us that Miss Blackstone was offered the opportunity of an abortion, but declined it. In those circumstances, her damages are no more than nominal. Mr Coke is prepared to pay her the sum of £500 to avoid this unnecessary litigation, provided that it is understood that this is to end the matter once and for all.

Yours Faithfully,

<u>Mansfield & Co.</u>

ELDON & Co.

Solicitors
Commissioners for Oaths

12, The Low,
Oxbridge XX5 2BR
Tel: Oxbridge 6284

Geoffrey J. Eldon LL.B
Paul Birch
Stephen M. Paynter B.A.
Mary L. Driver LL.B
Kenneth Stacey
Geraldine C. Eldon M.A.

Messrs. Mansfield & Co.,
Oldschool Bldgs.,
Oxbridge.

Our ref: GJE/MAB
Your ref: SPM/HEC

14 February 1985

Dear Sirs,

   <u>Re:</u>

<u>Miss Margaret Blackstone</u>

   We are in receipt of your letter of the 8 February, which both we and our client consider to be outrageous. In our view, an unwelcomed pregnancy induced by forcible sexual intercourse, and the inevitable mental and emotional complications which this must entail in one so young can hardly be written off as 'nominal'. Your client's offer is rejected.

   In view of your client's attitude, we see no purpose in discussing this matter with you any further, and we are sending our papers to Counsel.

Yours Faithfully,

<u>Eldon & Co</u>.

MANSFIELD & Co.

Solicitors and Commissioners for Oaths

Stanley P. Mansfield
Philip Garrity LL.B
Heather L. Morris
Peter G. Bullimore

Oldschool Buildilngs,
Oxbridge
Tel: 0411

Messrs. Eldon & Co.,
12, The Low,
Oxbridge.

Our ref: SPM/HEC
Your ref: GJE/MAB

20 February 1985

Dear Sirs,

Re:

Miss Blackstone and Mr Coke

Thank you for your letter of the 14th inst. We regret that this matter cannot be concluded without resort to the courts. We have instructions to accept service. We shall of course have to apply for Legal Aid on our client's behalf, and you may in due course like to let us know what kind of 'substantial damages' you feel our client, who is an apprentice tailor approaching his 19th birthday, should be in a position to pay.

We wish to advise you that our client continues to maintain his innocence, and will if necessary seek to prove that the verdict of the jury was wrong. He instructs us that both Miss Blackstone and himself know who the father of her child is, and we hope to have evidence available to confirm what he tells us. You may take this letter as notice to your client to submit herself and the child, when it is born, to a suitable blood test.

If in these circumstances, you wish to proceed, so be it.

Yours Faithfully,

Mansfield & Co.

ELDON & Co.

Solicitors

Commissioners for Oaths

12, The Low,

Oxbridge XX5 2BR

Tel: Oxbridge 6284

Geoffrey J. Eldon LL.B

Paul Birch

Stephen M. Paynter B.A.

Mary L. Driver LL.B

Kenneth Stacey

Geraldine C. Eldon M.A.

Messrs. Mansfield & Co.,

Oldschool Bldgs.,

Oxbridge.

Our ref: GJE/MAB

Your ref: SPM/HEC

4 March 1985

Dears Sirs,

Re:

Miss Blackstone and Mr Coke

Thank you for your letter of the 20 February. We too regret that proceedings should be necessary, but your client's attitude leaves us no alternative. It seems to us extraordinary that a man convicted of the offence of rape after a full trial should respond in this way.

We are instructed to reply particularly to your observations as to the paternity of the child with which Miss Blackstone is pregnant. Firstly, while there may be no reason why Miss Blackstone should not have undergone an abortion, we find it incredible that your client should have the temerity, having impregnated ours by force, to dictate to Miss Blackstone what she should or should not do in this regard. If our client had wished to terminate the pregnancy, she was perfectly free to do so, but it was and is for her to decide on these matters and not for your client. Nor is our client prepared to submit herself or her child to any blood test. Our client has indeed no doubt as to the identity of the father, and we have advised her that in view of the available evidence, no further proof is called for.

We take this opportunity of enclosing a letter which, no doubt by inadvertence, you enclosed with your letter to us of the 20 February. On the advice of Counsel, we apprehend that you are entitled to have the original back, but we wish to make it clear that we have copied it for our own use and will in due course tender it as evidence, unless the original is produced or admitted.

Yours Faithfully,

Eldon & Co.

MANSFIELD & Co.

Stanley P. Mansfield
Philip Garrity LL.B
Solicitors and Commissioners for Oaths   Heather L. Morris
Peter G. Bullimore

Oldschool Buildings,
Oxbridge
Tel: 0411

H.E. Coke Esq.,
52, Plowden Drive,
Oxbridge.

STRICTLY PERSONAL AND CONFIDENTIAL

Our ref: SPM/HEC
Your ref: GJE/MAB

20 February, 1985

Dear Henry,

Re:

Yourself and Miss Blackstone

As we discussed yesterday, I have written to the other side in fairly strong terms. As I explained when you telephoned this morning, the court will look at the matter from a strictly legal point of view, although you may see it in other terms too. Certainly, I would not object to your seeking personal advice from Fr. Wigmore about your moral position, but I shall continue, as your solicitor, to uphold your legal rights, subject of course to your instructions.

I have noted what you said about the possibility that Margaret may have given a quite different account of the paternity to the Local Authority Children's Department, and of course I shall look into it.

With my best wishes,

Yours Sincerely,

Stanley P. Mansfield

WARREN B. WITKIN

Attorney at Law   3251 Wontshire Blvd.,
                         Suite 3400,
                         Los Angeles, Ca. 90064
                         Tel: (213) 500 5000

Ms. Margaret A. Blackstone
4, The Hyde,
Oxbridge, England.

8 November 1984

Re: Mr Anthony F. Henneky

Dear Ms. Blackstone:

Mr Anthony F. Henneky has asked me to reply to your recent letter, which hinted obliquely that he might be the father of a child with which you are pregnant at this point in time.

My client tells me that nothing could be further from the truth, and that you are both aware that the father is a Mr Henry E. Coke. Mr Henneky and I hope that this will be the end of the matter, and that you will not repeat such allegations.

If this was not the intent of your letter, please forgive the presumption of this letter.

Very Truly Yours,

Warren B. Witkin

Attorney for Anthony F. Henneky

BRIEF FOR THE DEFENDANT

Instructions to Counsel

Counsel will be familiar with this case, having appeared for Mr Coke at his criminal trial, and having settled the pleadings and advised throughout. There is little to add to what Counsel already knows. The plaintiff's solicitors have not disclosed any expert medical evidence apart from Dr Gray, and have never responded to our request for blood tests.

Mr Henneky refuses to return from the United States to give evidence, and it seems that we shall have to rely on his written statement under the Civil Evidence Act 1968. Unfortunately, the plaintiff's solicitors have issued a subpoena against Fr. Wigmore, of whom they learnt when regrettably, your instructing solicitors sent astray a letter to Mr Coke. It is hoped that Counsel will be able to rely on some privilege for Mr Coke's confidence in Fr. Wigmore, who is minded to refuse to answer any questions on the subject and will no doubt be held in contempt unless some privilege can be found.

The Director of the Children's Department continues to object to revealing any communications passing between his department and the plaintiff, and Counsel is asked to ask the judge to rule on this matter, as it may be of some significance to the defence.

As Counsel requested, a transcript of the evidence given at the criminal trial has been agreed with the other side and will be available at court for the judge's use.

Counsel will please advise as may be necessary and appear for Mr Coke.

Proof of evidence of Anthony Filbert Henneky

1245, Robert E. Lee Boulevard, Gilroy, California USA
5 June 1985.
I am now 32 years of age and reside at the above address. Between 1981 and 1984 I was a student at Oxbridge College of Technology, studying Botany and the technical and economic aspects of market gardening. I came to college rather later in life compared to most of the students, because I worked in market gardening for some years after leaving school. A paper I wrote on the California garlic industry while at college attracted the attention of Mr Jefferson T. Budweiser III, the President of Budweiser Garlic, of Gilroy, California. Mr Budweiser wrote to me and offered me an executive position with his company in Gilroy, which is the major garlic production center in the world. I accepted, and having obtained permission to reside and work in the United States, I moved here in September 1984.

During my stay in Oxbridge, I met a girl called Margaret Blackstone. I think this would be early in 1982. I can only describe Margaret as somewhat promiscuous. She was attracted to me as a rather older person than her other friends. We started to have sexual intercourse on a regular basis. On legal advice, I am not prepared to state when this intercourse began. We had sexual intercourse during 1984, and quite frequently during May and June 1984, when my course was ending and I was preparing to move to the States. I recall specifically the weekend when Margaret states that she was raped by Henry Coke. To my certain recollection, Margaret and I had sexual intercourse on the Friday and Saturday nights in the back of my car after attending the youth club. We might well have seen each other on the Sunday night as well, had it not been for what happened with Coke. After this, we had sexual intercourse once or twice two or three weeks after the Coke incident, and that was the end of our relationship.

After I arrived in the United States, I received a letter from Margaret, to the effect that she was pregnant. She asked me to destroy the letter after reading it which unfortunately I did. I cannot now remember the date on which I received the letter, but it must have been sometime in October 1984. Although the letter did not say so expressly, I formed the impression that Margaret was hinting that the child was mine. This is possible, as we were rather lax over contraception, and often took risks. I took legal advice, and did not reply. I was told by someone I know in England that Henry Coke had been charged with raping Margaret, and it was suggested to me that I might return to give evidence for him. I know nothing of what happened between Coke and Margaret, except that I had the impression that she wasn't interested in him, but I must say that it would not surprise me to hear that she consented to have sex with him, or anyone, for that matter. In any event, I was not then and am not now prepared to return to England to give evidence, as my attorney has advised me not to do so. If this statement is of any use, I am happy for Coke to make use of it, but I am not prepared to leave the United States or to give evidence.

3   The Burden and Standard of Proof

A: THE BURDEN OF PROOF

(Suggested preliminary reading: *A Practical Approach to Evidence,* pp. 74–89.)

Abrath v Northern Eastern Railway Co. (1883) 11 QBD 440 (CA)

The plaintiff, a surgeon, had attended one M for injuries alleged to have been sustained in a collision upon the defendants' railway. M brought an action against the defendants, which was compromised by the defendants paying a large sum for damages and costs. Subsequently the directors of the defendants' company, having received certain information, caused the statements of certain persons to be taken by a solicitor; these statements tended to show that the injuries of which M complained were not caused at the collision, but were produced wilfully by the plaintiff, with the consent of M, for the purpose of defrauding the defendants. These statements were laid before counsel, who advised that there was good ground for prosecuting the plaintiff and M for conspiracy. The defendants accordingly prosecuted the plaintiff, but he was acquitted. In an action for malicious prosecution, an issue arose as to whether the burden of proving absence of reasonable and probable cause as well as the prosecution lay on the plaintiff. The Divisional Court held that it did and ordered a new trial.
   The defendants appealed.

BOWEN LJ: 'Whenever litigation exists, somebody must go on with it; the plaintiff is the first to begin; if he does nothing, he fails; if he makes a *prima facie* case, and nothing is done to answer it, the defendant fails. The test, therefore, as to the burden of proof or onus of proof, whichever term is used, is simply this: to ask oneself which party will be successful if no evidence is given, or if no more evidence is given than has been given at a particular point of the case, for it is obvious that as the controversy involved in the litigation travels on, the parties from moment to moment may reach points at which the onus of proof shifts, and at which the tribunal will have to say that if the case stops there, it must be decided in a particular manner. The test being such as I have stated, it is not a burden that goes on for ever resting on the shoulders of the person upon whom it is first cast. As soon as he brings evidence which, until it is answered, rebuts the evidence against which he is contending, then the balance descends on the other side, and the burden rolls over until again there is evidence which once more turns the scale. That being so, the question of onus of proof is only a rule for deciding on whom the obligation of going further, if he wishes to win, rests. It is not a rule to enable the jury to decide on the value of conflicting evidence. . . .
   Now in an action for malicious prosecution the plaintiff has the burden throughout of establishing that the circumstances of the prosecution were such that a judge can see no reasonable or probable cause for instituting it. In one sense that is the assertion of a negative, and we have been pressed with the proposition that when a negative is to be made out the onus of proof shifts. That is not so. If the assertion of a negative is an essential part of the plaintiff's case, the proof of the assertion still rests upon the plaintiff.

The terms "negative" and "affirmative" are after all relative and not absolute. In dealing with a question of negligence, that term may be considered either as negative or affirmative according to the definition adopted in measuring the duty which is neglected. Wherever a person asserts affirmatively as part of his case that a certain state of facts is present or is absent, or that a particular thing is insufficient for a particular purpose, that is an averment which he is bound to prove positively. It has been said that an exception exists in those cases where the facts lie peculiarly within the knowledge of the opposite party. The counsel for the plaintiff have not gone to the length of contending that in all those cases the onus shifts, and that the person within whose knowledge the truth peculiarly lies is bound to prove or disprove the matter in dispute. I think a proposition of that kind cannot be maintained, and that the exceptions supposed to be found amongst cases relating to the game laws may be explained on special grounds. . . .

Who had to make good their point as to the proposition whether the defendants had taken reasonable and proper care to inform themselves of the true state of the case? The defendants were not bound to make good anything. It was the plaintiff's duty to show the absence of reasonable care.'

Appeal dismissed.

Joseph Constantine Steamship Line v *Imperial Smelting Corporation* [1942] AC 154 (HL)

The charterers of a ship claimed damages from the owners for failure to load. The defendants pleaded that the contract had been frustrated by the destruction of the ship owing to an explosion, the cause of which was unclear. Such frustration would have concluded the case in favour of the defendants in the absence of any fault on their part. Atkinson J held that the onus of proving that the frustration was induced by the defendant's default lay upon the charterers. The Court of Appeal reversed this decision and the defendants appealed to the House of Lords.

VISCOUNT SIMON LC: 'The question here is where the onus of proof lies; i.e., whether, when a supervening event has been proved which would, apart from the defendant's "default" put an end to the contract, and when at the end of the case no inference of "default" exists and the evidence is equally consistent with either view, the defence fails because the defendant has not established affirmatively that the supervening event was not due to his default.

I may observe, in the first place, that, if this were correct, there must be many cases in which, although in truth frustration is complete and unavoidable, the defendant will be held liable because of his inability to prove a negative—in some cases, indeed, a whole series of negatives. Suppose that a vessel while on the high seas disappears completely during a storm. Can it be that the defence of frustration of the adventure depends on the owner's ability to prove that all his servants on board were navigating the ship with adequate skill and that there was no "default" which brought about the catastrophe? Suppose that a vessel in convoy is torpedoed by the enemy and sinks immediately with all hands. Does the application of the doctrine require that the owners should affirmatively prove that those on board were keeping a good look-out, were obscuring lights, were steering as directed, and so forth? There is no reported case which requires us so to hold. The doctrine on which the defence of frustration depends is nowhere so stated as to place this onus of proof on the party relying on it . . .

In this connection it is well to emphasise that when "frustration" in the legal sense occurs, it does not merely provide one party with a defence in an action brought by the other. It kills the contract itself and discharges both parties automatically. The plaintiff sues for breach at a past date and the defendant pleads that at that date no contract existed. In this situation the plaintiff could only succeed if it were shown that the determination of the contract were due to the defendant's "default," and it would be a strange result if the party alleging this were not the party required to prove it.'

VISCOUNT MAUGHAM: 'I think the burden of proof in any particular case depends on the circumstances under which the claim arises. In general the rule which applies is "*Ei qui affirmat non ei qui negat incumbit probatio*". It is an ancient rule founded on considerations of good sense and it should not be departed from without strong reasons. The position as to proof of non-responsibility for the event in such a case as the present is not very different from the position of a plaintiff in an action for negligence where contributory negligence on his part is alleged. In such a case the plaintiff must prove that there was some negligent act or omission on the part of the defendant which caused or materially contributed to the injury, but it is for the defendant to prove affirmatively, if he so contends, that there was contributory negligence on the part of the person injured, though here again the onus may easily be shifted . . .'

LORD WRIGHT: 'The appeal can, I think, be decided according to the generally accepted view that frustration involves as one of its elements absence of fault, by applying the ordinary rules as to onus of proof. If frustration is viewed (as I think it can be) as analogous to an exception, since it is generally relied on as a defence to a claim for failure to perform a contract, the same rule will properly be applied to it as to the ordinary type of exceptions. The defence may be rebutted by proof of fault, but the onus of proving fault will rest on the plaintiff. This is merely to apply the familiar rule which is applied, for instance, where a carrier by sea relies on the exception of perils of the sea. If the goods owner then desires to rebut that *prima facie* defence on the ground of negligence or other fault on the part of the shipowner, it rests on the goods owner to establish the negligence or fault.'

(LORDS RUSSELL of KILLOWEN and PORTER delivered concurring judgments.)
Appeal allowed.

Levison and another v *Patent Steam Carpet Cleaning Co. Ltd* [1978] QB 69 (CA)

The defendants were guilty of the unexplained loss of a Chinese carpet which had been delivered to them for cleaning and which belonged to the plaintiffs. A clause in the contract signed by the plaintiffs would have exempted the defendants from liability for negligence, but not for any fundamental breach. The plaintiffs sued the cleaners for the loss of the carpet. The county court judge gave judgment against the cleaners who appealed.

LORD DENNING MR: 'This brings me to the crux of the case. On whom is the burden of proof? Take the present case. Assuming that clause 2(a) or clause 5, or either of them, limits or exempts the cleaners from liability for negligence: but not for a fundamental breach. On whom is the burden to prove that there was fundamental breach?

Upon principle, I should have thought that the burden was on the cleaners to prove that they were not guilty of a fundamental breach. After all, Mrs Levison does not know what happened to it. The cleaners are the ones who know, or should know, what happened to the carpet, and the burden should be on them to say what it was. It was so held by McNair J in *Woolmer* v *Delmer Price Ltd* [1955] 1 QB 291; and by me in *J Spurling Ltd* v *Bradshaw* [1956] 1 WLR 461, 466, and by the East African Court of Appeal in *United Manufacturers Ltd* v *WAFCO Ltd* [1974] EA 233. A contrary view was expressed by this court in *Hunt & Winterbotham (West of England) Ltd* v *BRS (Parcels) Ltd* [1962] 1 QB 617, 635. And there is a long line of shipping cases in which it has been held that, if a shipowner makes a *prima facie* case that the cause of the loss was one of the excepted perils, the burden is on the shipper to prove that it was not covered by the exceptions: see *The Glendarroch* [1894] P 226 and *Munro, Brice & Co.* v *War Risks Association Ltd* [1918] 2 KB 78. To which there may be added *Joseph Constantine Steamship Line Ltd* v *Imperial Smelting Corporation Ltd* [1942] AC 154 on frustration.

It is, therefore, a moot point for decision. On it I am clearly of the opinion that, in a contract of bailment, when a bailee seeks to escape liability on the ground that he was not negligent or that he was excused by an exception or limitation clause, then he must show what happened to the goods. He must prove all the circumstances known to him in which the loss or damage occurred. If it appears that the goods were lost or damaged without any negligence on his part, then, of course, he is not liable. If it appears that they were lost or damaged by a slight breach—not going to the root of the contract—he may be protected by the exemption or limitation clause. But, if he leaves the cause of loss or damage undiscovered and unexplained—then I think he is liable: because it is then quite likely that the goods were stolen by one of his servants; or delivered by a servant to the wrong address; or damaged by reckless or wilful misconduct; all of which the offending servant will conceal and not make known to his employer. Such conduct would be a fundamental breach against which the exemption or limitation clause will not protect him.

The cleaning company in this case did not show what happened to the carpet. They did not prove how it was lost. They gave all sorts of excuses for non-delivery and eventually said it had been stolen. Then I would ask: By whom was it stolen? Was it by one of their own servants? Or with his connivance? Alternatively, was it delivered by one of their servants to the wrong address? In the absence of any explanation, I would infer that it was one of these causes. In none of them would the cleaning company be protected by the exemption or limitation clause.

(ORR LJ AND SIR DAVIS CAIRNS agreed.)

Appeal dismissed.

Woolmington v *DPP* [1935] AC 462 (HL)

The defendant was charged with the murder of his wife from whom he was separated. He gave evidence to the effect that whilst endeavouring to induce her to return to live with him by threatening to shoot himself, he had shot her and killed her accidentally. The jury were directed that, once it was proved that the defendant shot his wife, it was for him to prove the absence of malice, although malice was an essential element of the charge of murder. The defendant was convicted of murder and appealed unsuccessfully to the Court of Criminal Appeal. He further appealed to the House of Lords.

VISCOUNT SANKEY LC: 'If at any period of a trial it was permissible for the judge to rule that the prosecution had established its case and that the onus was shifted on the prisoner to prove that he was not guilty and that unless he discharged that onus the prosecution was entitled to succeed, it would be enabling the judge in such a case to say that the jury must in law find the prisoner guilty and so make the judge decide the case and not the jury, which is not the common law. It would be an entirely different case from those exceptional instances of special verdicts where a judge asks the jury to find certain facts and directs them that on such facts the prosecution is entitled to succeed. Indeed, a consideration of such special verdicts shows that it is not till the end of the evidence that a verdict can properly be found and that at the end of the evidence it is not for the prisoner to establish his innocence, but for the prosecution to establish his guilt. Just as there is evidence on behalf of the prosecution so there may be evidence on behalf of the prisoner which may cause a doubt as to his guilt. In either case, he is entitled to the benefit of the doubt. But while the prosecution must prove the guilt of the prisoner, there is no such burden laid on the prisoner to prove his innocence and it is sufficient for him to raise a doubt as to his guilt; he is not bound to satisfy the jury of his innocence . . . Throughout the web of the English Criminal Law one golden thread is always to be seen, that it is the duty of the prosecution to prove the prisoner's guilt subject to what I have already said as to the defence of insanity and subject also to any statutory exception. If, at the end of and on the whole of the case, there is a reasonable doubt, created by the evidence given by either the prosecution or the prisoner, as to whether the prisoner killed the deceased with a malicious intention, the prosecution has not made out the case and the prisoner is entitled to an acquittal. No matter what the charge or where the trial, the principle that the prosecution must prove the guilt of the prisoner is part of the common law of England and no attempt to whittle it down can be entertained. When dealing with a murder case the Crown must prove (*a*) death as the result of a voluntary act of the accused and (*b*) malice of the accused. It may prove malice either expressly or by implication. For malice may be implied where death occurs as the result of a voluntary act of the accused which is (i) intentional and (ii) unprovoked. When evidence of death and malice has been given (this is a question for the jury) the accused is entitled to show, by evidence or by examination of the circumstances adduced by the Crown that the act on his part which caused death was either unintentional or provoked. If the jury are either satisfied with his explanation or, upon a review of all the evidence, are left in reasonable doubt whether, even if his explanation be not accepted, the act was unintentional or provoked, the prisoner is entitled to be acquitted. It is not the law of England to say, as was said in the summing-up in the present case: "If the Crown satisfy you that this woman died at the prisoner's hands then he has to show that there are circumstances to be found in the evidence which has been given from the witness-box in this case which alleviate the crime so that it is only manslaughter or which excuse the homicide altogether by showing it was a pure accident."'

(LORDS ATKIN, HEWART, TOMLIN and WRIGHT concurred.)

Appeal allowed.

Homicide Act 1957

2(1)   Where a person kills or is party to the killing of another, he shall not be convicted of murder if he was suffering from such abnormality of mind (whether arising from a condition of arrested or retarded development of mind or any inherent causes or induced by disease or injury) as substantially impaired his mental responsibility for his acts and omissions in doing or being a party to the killing.

(2) On a charge of murder, it shall be for the defence to prove that the person charged is by virtue of this section not liable to be convicted of murder.

Magistrates' Courts Act 1980

101 Where the defendant to an information or complaint relies for his defence on any exception, exemption, proviso, excuse or qualification, whether or not it accompanies the description of the offence or matter of complaint in the enactment creating the offence or on which the complaint is founded, the burden of proving the exception, exemption, proviso, excuse or qualification shall be on him; and this notwithstanding that the information or complaint contains an allegation negativing the exception, exemption, proviso, excuse or qualification.

Daniel M'Naghten's Case (1843) 10 Cl & F 200

The defendant, intending to murder Sir Robert Peel, killed the statesman's secretary by mistake. He was acquitted of murder on the ground of insanity. The verdict was made the subject of debate in the House of Lords and it determined to take the opinion of all the judges on the law governing such cases. The judges attended and five questions were put to them:

TINDAL CJ: 'Your Lordships are pleased to inquire of us, secondly:

What are the proper questions to be submitted to the jury when a person alleged to be afflicted with insane delusion respecting one or more particular subjects or persons is charged with the commission of a crime (murder, for example), and insanity is set up as a defence?

And, thirdly:

In what terms ought the question to be left to the jury as to the prisoner's state of mind at the time when the act was committed?

As these two questions appear to us to be more conveniently answered together we have to submit our opinion to be that the jurors ought to be told in all cases that every man is to be presumed to be sane and to possess a sufficient degree of reason to be responsible for his crimes until the contrary be proved to their satisfaction, and that to establish a defence on the ground of insanity it must be clearly proved that, at the time of committing of the act the party accused was labouring under such a defect of reason, from disease of the mind, as not to know the nature and quality of the act he was doing, or, if he did know it, that he did not know he was doing what was wrong.'

R v Edwards [1975] QB 27 (CA)

The defendant was convicted of selling intoxicating liquor without a justices' licence contrary to section 160(1)(a) of the Licensing Act 1964. He was unrepresented at the trial and did not give evidence, but made an unsworn statement denying the occupation of the premises. He appealed agianst conviction on the ground that, since the prosecution had access to the register of licences under section 34(2) of the Act, the prosecution should have called evidence to prove that there was no justices' licence in force.

LAWTON LJ, reading the judgment of the court: 'Mr Leonard, on behalf of the prosecution, submitted that section 81 [of the Magistrates' Courts Act 1952, the precursor of s. 101 of the Magistrates' Courts Act 1980, see p. 61 *ante*] is a statutory statement of a common law rule applicable in all criminal courts. If it were not, the law would be in an unsatisfactory state, because the burden of proof in summary trials would be different from that in trials on indictment.

Mr Underhill, for the defendant, submitted, however, that at common law the burden of proving an exception, exemption, proviso, excuse or qualification only shifts when the facts constituting it are peculiarly within the accused's own knowledge and that they were not in this case because section 30(1) of the Licensing Act 1964 requires the clerk to the licensing justices for a licensing district to keep a register of licences, containing particulars of all justices' licences granted in the district, the premises for which they were granted, the names of the owners of thos : premises, and the names of the holders of the licences. It follows, submitted Mr Underhill, that the Brixton police had available to them in their own area a public source of knowledge which they could go to at any reasonable time: see section 34(2). If the rule about shifting the onus of proof only applies when the facts initiating the operation of the exception are peculiarly in the accused's own knowledge, there is much to be said for Mr Underhill's submission.

Mr Underhill accepted that there are three exceptions to the fundamental rule of our criminal law that the prosecution must prove every element of the alleged offence. The first relates to insanity and the second to those cases in which a statute expressly imposes a burden of proof upon an accused. The third exception has been under consideration in this appeal and questions have arisen as to its nature and the circumstances in which it applies.

The phrase which Mr Underhill used in making his submission, namely, "facts peculiarly within the accused's own knowledge" has been used many times in textbooks and judgments: for example, *per* Lord Goddard CJ in *John* v *Humphreys* [1955] 1 WLR 325, 327; *Phipson on Evidence*, 11th ed (1970), p.108 and *Cross, Evidence*, 3rd ed (1967), p.81. It has been taken from the judgment of Bayley J in *R* v *Turner* (1816) 5 M & S 206, 211. If the rule only applies when the facts constituting exculpation are peculiarly within the defendant's own knowledge, we would have expected to have found reported cases giving some help as to how the courts were to decide this. If a query arises, should the judge or the jury decide who had what knowledge? Should evidence be called on this issue? If not, why not? In the century and a half since 1816 the defendant is unlikely to have been the first defendant wishing to query the extent of the prosecution's knowledge. Counsel brought no such cases to our attention and we have found none for ourselves. Despite the many times in the cases and textbooks reference has been made to the words used by Bayley J in *R* v *Turner*, we thought it necessary to examine that case carefully in its historical setting. For many decades before *R* v *Turner* there had been much discussion amongst lawyers as to how negative averments were to be pleaded in informations and indictments.

By the end of the 17th century a pleading distinction was drawn between a proviso in a statute and an exception: see *Hale's Pleas of the Crown* (1800 ed), vol. 2, pp.170–171 (which was written about 1650) and *Jones* v *Axen* (1696) 1 Ld Raym 119. Exceptions had to be pleaded and disproved whereas there was no need either to plead or disprove provisos. In *R* v *Jarvis* (1754) 1 East 643 and referred to in *R* v *Stone* (1801) 1 East 639, 646, Lord Mansfield CJ stated the rule as follows:

> For it is a known distinction that what comes by way of proviso in a statute must be insisted on by way of defence by the party accused; but where exceptions are in the enacting part of a law, it must appear in the charge that the defendant does not fall within any of them.

In some cases, however, it was difficult to decide whether provisions in the enacting part of a statute were in the nature of a proviso. This is shown by the cases arising on *certiorari* out of the notorious game laws. These laws, which were statutory, prohibited those without certain qualifications (some 10 in number set out in the statute 22 & 23 Car 2, c. 25) from keeping a gun or being in possession of game. The problem for those drafting informations under these laws and conducting prosecutions was whether the defendant's alleged lack of qualification should be pleaded and proved. By the end of the 18th century it seems to have been accepted that in actions for penalties under the game laws lack of qualifications did not have to be proved: see *R* v *Stone* (1801) 1 East 639, 646, 650, 654. The problem of what had to be proved in a criminal case came before the King's Bench on *certiorari* in *R* v *Stone*. Before the justices the prosecution had not proved the defendant's lack of qualification. The court was equally divided, two of the judges (Lord Kenyon CJ and Grose J) being strongly of the opinion that the prosecution had to prove lack of qualification, whereas the other two (Lawrence and Le Blanc JJ) were of the contrary view. The court being equally divided, the conviction stood.

The approach to the problem by all four judges was substantially the same: to wit, their understanding of the rules of pleading. In the course of argument counsel adverted to the difficulty of proving negative averments and there was some discusson about this. Lord Kenyon CJ thought that some general evidence should be given from which lack of qualification could be inferred, whereas Lawrence J thought that proof of the act forbidden by the statute was enough to place the burden on the accused to show that he was qualified to do it. Lord Kenyon CJ's judgment is the foundation of the submissions which have been made in recent years that even when the prosecution seeks to rely upon the exception to the burden of proof rule which is said to derive from *R* v *Turner*, 5 M & S 206, it can only do so after having given some evidence, albeit slight, from which no lawful excuse can be inferred: see *R* v *Putland and Sorrell* [1946] 1 All ER 85 and *Buchanan* v *Moore* [1963] NI 194; both these cases will be discussed later in this judgment. The opinions of Lawrence and Le Blanc JJ were in accord with what was said in *Hawkins's Pleas of the Crown*, 7th ed (1795), vol. 4, bk. 2, c. 25, s. 113, p. 68:

> It seems agreed, that there is no need to allege in an indictment, that the defendant is not within the benefit of the provisos of a statute whereon it is founded; and this hath been adjudged, even as to those statutes which in their purview expressly take notice of the provisos; as by saying, that none shall do the thing prohibited, otherwise than in such special cases, etc. as are expressed in this act.

He cites a number of authorities starting with *Southwell's Case* (1595) Poph 93, where, in the enacting clause, the wording was "otherwise than in such special cases . . . expressed in this Act." An illustration of how Serjeant Hawkins envisaged this rule would apply appears from a passage in *Pleas of the Crown*, 7th ed., vol. 2, c. 89, s. 17, p. 460, which was noted and approved in *R* v *Oliver* [1944] KB 68, 74. He was commenting on the form of indictment alleging an offence under the statute 9 & 10 Will. 3, c. 41, which enacted that no warlike naval stores should be made by any person

> . . . not being a contractor with or authorised by the principal officers or commissioners of our said Lord the King, of the navy, ordinance, or . . . victualling office, for the use of our said Lord the King, . . .

It was his opinion that the indictment should allege that the prisoner was not an authorised person but he went on to say

> yet it is not incumbent on the prosecutors to prove this negative averment, but that it is incumbent on the defendant to show, if the truth be so, that he is within the exception in the statute.

These passages indicate first that by Serjeant Hawkins's time the old distinction between provisos and exceptions was becoming blurred, secondly that he, like the judges, based his opinion upon rules of pleading and thirdly that he did not associate the rule with the fact that the positive of a negative averment would, or might be, peculiarly within the defendant's own knowledge.

In our judgment *R* v *Turner*, 5 M & S 206 must be considered against this historical background. The point for discussion was the same as in *R* v *Stone*, 1 East 639. The information had alleged that the defendant, a carrier

> "not . . . qualified or authorised by the laws of this realm" had had in his custody and possession pheasants and hares "the same not being sent up or placed in [his] hands . . . by any person or persons qualified to kill game, . . ."

No evidence was called by the prosecution to prove want of qualification. The defendant's case on *certiorari* was argued by Scarlett, probably the most able advocate of his generation. He took two points: the first was technical as to the way the conviction had been drawn up; the second was an echo of what Lord Kenyon CJ had said in *R* v *Stone* about the need for *prima facie* evidence. The leading judgment was delivered by Lord Ellenborough CJ. He commented on the difficulty which would rest upon the prosecution of proving the lack of qualification and the ease with which the defendant could show he was qualified; but towards the end of his judgment he referred to Lord Mansfield CJ's opinion expressed in *Spieres* v *Parker* (1786) 1 Term Rep 141, as to the burden of proof resting on the defendant in actions upon the game laws and gave his own which was that he saw no reason why the same rule should not be applied to informations as well as actions. He ended at p. 211 as follows:

> I am, therefore, of opinion, that this conviction, which specifies negatively in the information the several qualifications mentioned in the statute, is sufficient, without going on to negative, by the evidence, those qualifications.

We read Lord Ellenborough CJ's judgment as being based on common law concepts of pleading, rather than on difficulties of proof, such difficulties being the reason why the rule of pleading had developed as it had. The second judgment was delivered by Bayley J. He started by referring at p. 211 to rules of pleading, namely:

"I have always understood it to be a general rule, that if a negative averment be made by one party, . . ." and added descriptive words qualifying the negative averment, "which is peculiarly within the knowledge of the other, . . ."

As far as we have been able to discover from our researches this was the first time the rules of pleading which had been applied for so long were qualified in this way. The qualification cannot apply to all negative averments. There is not, and never has been, a general rule of law that the mere fact that a matter lies peculiarly within the knowledge of the defendant is sufficient to cast the onus on him. If there was any such rule, anyone charged with doing an unlawful act with a specified intent would find himself having to prove his innocence because if there ever was a matter which could be said to be peculiarly within a person's knowledge it is the state of his own mind. Such rule as there is relating to negative averments in informations and indictments developed from the rules for pleading provisos and exceptions in statutes and is limited in its application. No doubt the reason why the rules developed as they did was the common sense of the matter to which Lord Ellenborough CJ referred. In our judgment what Bayley J was doing was to state the reason for the rule as if it was the rule. The third judge, Holroyd J, at p. 213 used the phrase "peculiarly within the knowledge of the party" but did so in order to demolish the argument that this case was an exception to the general rule of pleading.

It seems likely that practitioners in the decades which followed *R* v *Turner* did not regard Bayley J's words of qualification as a limitation upon an established rule. Thus in *Apothecaries' Co.* v *Bentley* (1824) Rv & M 159, which was an action for penalties under the statute 55 Geo. 3, c. 194, for practising as an apothecary without having obtained a certificate from the Society of Apothecaries of the City of London as required by that Act, no evidence was called by Scarlett, who appeared for the plaintiffs, to prove that they had not issued the defendant with a certificate or that he was exempted from the statute by the fact that he had been in practice before August 1815. Brougham, who was to become Lord Chancellor six years later, is reported at p. 160 as having put his argument as follows:

The distinction he conceived was this, that where an exception was created by a distinct clause, the burden of showing that he was within it lay upon the defendant; but here the exception was introduced to qualify the penal clause in its very body, the negative therefore must be both stated and proved by the plaintiffs.

There was no submission that as a statutory corporation charged with the duty of examining apothecaries and issuing certificates to those qualified to practise, the plaintiffs would have known whether the defendant had obtained a certificate from them or had been in practice before the commencement of the Act so that the necessary qualification, or lack of it, was not peculiarly within his knowledge. *R* v *Turner*, 5 M & S 206 was cited to the court by Scarlett in answer to Brougham's submission. Abbott CJ's ruling was that the onus was on the defendant to prove he had a certificate and was based on concepts of pleading, not on the plaintiffs' opportunities of knowing. In our judgment it is most unlikely that an experienced advocate such as Brougham would have failed to appreciate that *R* v *Turner* only applied when the facts showing exception were peculiarly within the defendant's knowledge. *Starkie's Law of Evidence*, 2nd ed. (1833), vol. I, p. 365, states the rule in these terms:

> And in general, where it has been shown that the case falls within the scope of any general principle or rule of law, or the provision of any statute, whether remedial or even penal, it then lies on the opposite party to show by evidence that the case falls within an exception or proviso.

In 1848, by the Summary Jurisdiction Act 1848 (Jervis's Act), 11 & 12 Vict. c. 43, Parliament consolidated, amended and extended various statutes which had conferred summary jurisdiction on justices. The modern courts of summary jurisdiction came into being. The Act provided a statutory framework for the conduct of proceedings in those courts at all stages. Section 14 of the Act dealt with proceedings at the trial stage. It is clear that what Parliament was trying to do by this section was to adapt proceedings on indictment to the new type of court. The section had a proviso to the effect that if the information or complaint should negative "any exception, proviso or condition" the prosecutor or complainant need not prove such negative, but the defendant might prove the affirmative. In our judgment the object of the proviso to section 14 was to apply the common law relating to exceptions and provisos to the new courts. After 1848 the courts put a restricted meaning on the word "exception" in this proviso: see *Taylor* v *Humphries* (1864) 34 LJMC 1 and *Davis* v *Scrace* (1869) LR 4 CP 172. Parliament stopped this restricting tendency by the terms of section 39(2) of the Summary Jurisdiction Act 1879 as Lord Pearson said in *Nimmo* v *Alexander Cowan & Sons Ltd* [1968] AC 107, 135:

> . . . these show an intention to widen the provision and to direct attention to the substance and effect rather than the form of the enactment to which it is to be applied.

Section 39(2) of the Act of 1879 was repealed by the Magistrates' Courts Act 1952 and replaced by section 81 of that Act. In our judgment section 81 of the Magistrates' Courts Act 1952 sets out the common law rule in statutory form. Paragraph 5(2) of Schedule 1 to the Indictments Act 1915 contained a similar provision relating to the form of an indictment. This is now rule 6(c) of the Indictment Rules 1971, which provides as follows:

> It shall not be necessary [when charging an offence created by or under any enactment] to specify or negative an exception, exemption, proviso, excuse or qualification.

If it is not necessary to specify or negative exceptions and the like in a count, it is difficult to see on principle why it should be necessary to prove an element in the offence charged which has not been set out in the count.

Since 1816 there are a number of cases in the reports illustrating the shifting of the onus of proof on to the defendant to prove either that he held a licence to do an act which was otherwise prohibited by a statute or that he was exempted in some way. Thus in *R* v *Scott* (1921) 86 JP 69 the question arose whether the prosecution should have proved, which they did not, that the defendant, who was charged with an offence under the Dangerous Drugs Act 1920, was not authorised to supply specified drugs. That Act provided that no person should supply any of the specified drugs unless he was licensed by the Secretary of

State to do so. Swift J held that if the defendant was licensed, it was a fact which was peculiarly within his own knowledge and there was no hardship on him in being put to the proof. We can see no difference between that case (which was approved by the Court of Criminal Appeal in *R* v *Oliver* [1944] KB 68 and cited by Lord Pearson with approval in *Nimmo* v *Alexander Cowan & Sons Ltd* [1968] AC 107) and this. There would have been no difficulty whatsoever in calling someone on the Secretary of State's staff to say that the defendant had not been licensed to supply the drugs.

The statutory prohibition of acts otherwise than under licence granted by a government department was a commonplace of life during the war years 1939 to 1945 and for some time afterwards. The problem as to who was to prove lack of a licence was considered fully in *R* v *Oliver* [1944] KB 68, 69–70. The appellant had been convicted on an indictment charging him with supplying sugar otherwise than under the terms of a licence, permit or other authority granted by the Ministry of Food, contrary to regulation 55 of the Defence (General) Regulations 1939 and Article 2 of the Sugar Control Order 1940. The prosecution did not prove that he had not been granted a licence and he appealed on that ground. Mr Slade, for the appellant, submitted that the rule shifting the onus to the defendant to prove he came within an exception did not apply "as the information could easily have been obtained by the prosecution from official sources": see p. 69. The Solicitor-General who appeared for the prosecution, put his case in these terms, at p. 70:

If a statute lays down that an act is prohibited except in the case of persons who are excepted, the onus is on the defendant to prove that he is within the excepted class.

The Court of Criminal Appeal accepted this submission; and in his judgment Viscount Caldecote CJ dealt with two points which Mr Slade had put forward in support of his main submission. Both had been canvassed in the 18th century and had echoed through the courts in the 19th; first, that although there was no need for the prosecution to prove that a proviso in a statute did not apply, this was not so with an exception; and secondly, the prosecution should have given *prima facie* evidence of the non-existence of a licence. As we have sought to show in this judgment, the old distinction between provisos and exceptions had been moribund, if not dead, for well over a century, although some life had been injected into it by Lord Alverstone CJ in *R* v *James* [1902] 1 KB 540, 545. As to this, Viscount Caldecote CJ said in *R* v *Oliver* [1944] KB 68, 73:

With the greatest respect to the judgment of Lord Alverstone in *R* v *James*, it seems to us to be very difficult to make the result depend on the question whether the negative is of a proviso or of an exception. We think it makes no difference at all that the order was drafted as it now appears instead of being in a form which absolutely prohibits the supply of sugar except as thereinafter provided, with a later clause providing that if a person is supplied under a licence he should be excused.

As to the second point Viscount Caldecote CJ said plainly that the prosecution were under no necessity of giving *prima facie* evidence of the non-existence of a licence. As this point had been raised we infer that the court did not consider that the availability of evidence to the prosecution was a relevant factor in shifting the burden of proof.

R v *Oliver* was cited to the House of Lords in *Nimmo* v *Alexander Cowan & Sons Ltd* [1968] AC 107, which was concerned with the onus of pleading and proving in cases under section 29(1) of the Factories Act 1961 that it was not reasonably practicable to make and keep working places safe. Where the onus lay would, of course, be the same in both civil and criminal cases brought under that Act, although the standard of proof would be higher in criminal cases than in civil. None of their Lordships criticised *R* v *Oliver*; Lord Pearson clearly approved it. Not everyone has done so; for an example, see *Glanville Williams, Criminal Law*, 2nd ed [1961], pp. 901–904. In *R* v *Putland and Sorrell* [1946] 1 All ER 85 some judicial doubt was expressed as to how far *R* v *Oliver* went. The appellants were charged with having conspired to acquire, and having acquired, rationed goods, namely, silk stockings, without surrendering the appropriate number of coupons, in contravention of the Consumer Rationing Order 1944. No evidence was called by the prosecution to prove that coupons had not been surrendered. *R* v *Oliver* was cited, but Humphreys J, who delivered the judgment of the court, distinguished that case by stating that there was a very broad distinction between a statutory prohibition against doing an act, in which case it was for the defendant to prove that he might do it lawfully, and a statutory prohibition against doing an act otherwise than in a particular way, as for example by surrendering coupons, in which case it was for the prosecution to give *prima facie* evidence that the specified lawful way had not been followed. We have been unable to appreciate the difference between the two types of case. The court had clearly been impressed, as had Lord Kenyon CJ, 150 years before in *R* v *Stone*, 1 East 639, by the argument that the shifting of the onus of proof could be oppressive; but under the Defence (General) Regulations the only difference between a wholesaler of sugar called upon to justify his trade in that commodity and a man wearing a new shirt (one of the examples given by Humphreys J) called upon to prove that he had acquired it lawfully might be that one could do so more easily than the other. We find this difference not substantial enough to justify distinguishing *R* v *Oliver*.

In *John* v *Humphreys* [1955] 1 WLR 325 the Divisional Court had to consider the problem of the onus of proof in a case of a defendant who had been charged with driving a motor vehicle on a road without being the holder of a licence. He did not appear at the hearing before the justices and no evidence was called other than to prove that he had driven a motor vehicle along a road. The justices were of the opinion that mere proof of driving (that not being in itself an unlawful act) was not enough to support the charge and that before the burden of proving that he was the holder of a licence passed to the defendant the prosecution should have established a *prima facie* case. They dismissed the information. The prosecutor appealed. Before the justices he had argued that the burden of proving the holding of a licence lay on the defendant since it was a fact peculiarly within his knowledge; as indeed it was. It would have been impracticable for the prosecution to have proved that no licensing authority had issued a licence. It follows that this case is of little help on the question whether *R* v *Turner* (1816) 5 M & S 206 applies when the prosecution can prove a defendant's lack of qualification or lawful excuse. The court decided that there was no need for the prosecution to establish a *prima facie* case. Ormerod J expressed some hesitation on this point but concluded that the court was bound by the decision in *R* v *Oliver*. . . .

In our judgment this line of authority establishes that over the centuries the common law, as a result of experience and the need to ensure that justice is done both to the community and to defendants, has evolved an exception to the fundamental rule of our criminal law that the prosecution must prove every element of the offence charged. This exception, like so much else in the common law, was hammered out on the anvil of pleading. It is limited to offences arising under enactments which prohibit the doing of an act save in specified circumstances or by persons of specified classes or with specified qualifications or with the licence or permission of specified authorities. Whenever the prosecution seeks to rely on this exception, the court must construe the enactment under which the charge is laid. If the true construction is that the enactment prohibits the doing of acts, subject to provisos, exemptions and the like, then the prosecution can rely upon the exception.

In our judgment its application does not depend upon either the fact, or the presumption, that the defendant has peculiar knowledge enabling him to prove the positive of any negative averment. As Wigmore pointed out in his great *Treatise on Evidence* [1905], vol. 4 p. 3525, this concept of peculiar knowledge furnishes no working rule. If it did, defendants would have to prove lack of intent. What does provide a working rule is what the common law evolved from a rule of pleading. We have striven to identify it in this judgment. Like nearly all rules it could be applied oppressively; but the courts have ample powers to curb and discourage oppressive prosecutors and do not hesitate to use them.

Two consequences follow from the view we have taken as to the evolution and nature of this exception. First, as it comes into operation upon an enactment being construed in a particular way, there is no need for the prosecution to prove a *prima facie* case of lack of excuse, qualification or the like; and secondly, what shifts is the onus: it is for the defendant to prove that he was entitled to do the prohibited act. What rests on him is the legal or, as it is sometimes called, the persuasive burden of proof. It is not the evidential burden.

When the exception as we have adjudged it to be is applied to this case it was for the defendant to prove that he was the holder of a justices' licence, not the prosecution.'

Appeal dismissed.

• Can this decision be reconciled with the speech of Lord Sankey LC in *Woolmington* v *DPP*, *ante* at p. 60?
• Do you agree with Lawton LJ's statement that the burden of proof had to be placed on the accused 'to ensure that *justice* [emphasis added] is done both to the community and to defendants'?

R v *Hunt* [1987] AC 352

The Misuse of Drugs Regulations 1973, as amended, provide by reg. 4(1) that the Misuse of Drugs Act 1971, ss. 3(1) and 5(1), which prohibit the importation, exportation and possession of controlled drugs, do not have effect in relation to the controlled drugs specified in Sch. 1 to the regulations.

The appellant was convicted of possessing a controlled drug contrary to the 1971 Act, s. 5(2). A quantity of white powder had been found at his house which, when analysed, was found to contain morphine mixed with caffeine and atropine. On appeal it was held that the burden of proving that the preparation of morphine fell within the exceptions contained in the 1973 Regulations rested on the appellant. He appealed to the House of Lords arguing, *inter alia*, that *R* v *Edwards* [1975] QB 27 [ante, p. 61] had been wrongly decided.

LORD GRIFFITHS: 'I propose first to consider the argument based upon *Woolmington* v *Director of Public Prosecutions*. The starting point is the celebrated passage in the speech of Viscount Sankey LC, at pp. 481–482:

> Throughout the web of the English criminal law one golden thread is always to be seen, that it is the duty of the prosecution to prove the prisoner's guilt subject to what I have already said as to the defence of insanity and subject also to any statutory exception. If, at the end of and on the whole of the case, there is a reasonable doubt, created by the evidence given by either the prosecution or the prisoner, as to whether the prisoner killed the deceased with a malicious intention, the prosecution has not made out the case and the prisoner is entitled to an acquittal. No matter what the charge or where the trial, the principle that the prosecution must prove the guilt of the prisoner is part of the common law of England and no attempt to whittle it down can be entertained.

The appellant submits that in using the phrase "any statutory exception" Lord Sankey LC was referring to statutory exceptions in which Parliament had by the use of express words placed the burden of proof on the accused, in the same way as the judges in *M'Naghten's Case* (1843) 10 Cl & Fin 200 had expressly placed the burden of proving insanity upon the accused. There are, of course, many examples of such statutory drafting of which a number are to be found in this Act—see section 5(4): "In any proceedings for an offence under subsection (2) above in which it is proved that the accused had a controlled drug in his possession, it shall be a defence for him to prove—. . ." (see also section 28(2)(3)). Examples in other Acts are to be found conveniently collected in *Phipson on Evidence*, 13th ed (1982), p. 51, note 68.

The appellant also relies upon a passage in the speech of Viscount Simon LC in *Mancini* v *Director of Public Prosecutions* [1942] AC 1 in which he said, at p. 11:

> *Woolmington's* case is concerned with explaining and reinforcing the rule that the prosecution must prove the charge it makes beyond reasonable doubt, and, consequently, that if, on the material before the jury, there is a reasonable doubt, the prisoner should have the benefit of it. The rule is of general application in all charges under the criminal law. The only exceptions arise, as explained in *Woolmington's* case, in the defence of insanity and in offences where onus of proof is specially dealt with by statute.

It is submitted that the use of the word "specially" indicates that Lord Simon LC considered that the reference in *Woolmington* [1935] AC 462 was limited to express statutory burdens of proof.

From this premise, it is argued that as it is well settled that if a defendant raises any of the common law defences such as accident, self-defence, provocation or duress and there is evidence to support such a defence the judge must leave it to the jury with a direction that the burden is on the prosecution to negative that defence, so it must follow that if a defendant raises any statutory defence the same rule must apply, and provided there is evidence to support such a defence the burden lies on the prosecution to negative it, the only exceptions to this rule being those cases in which the statute has by express words placed the burden of proving the defence upon the defendant.

However, in *Woolmington* the House was not concerned to consider the nature of a statutory defence or upon whom the burden of proving it might lie. The House was considering a defence of accident to a charge of murder and were concerned to correct a special rule which appeared to have emerged in charges of murder whereby once it was proved that the defendant had killed the deceased a burden was held to lie upon the defendant to excuse himself by proving that it was the result of an accident or that he had been provoked to do so or had acted in self-defence. This in effect relieved the prosecution of the burden of proving an essential element in the crime of murder, namely the malicious intent and placed the burden upon the accused to disprove it. It was this aberration that was so trenchantly corrected by Lord Sankey LC in the passage already cited [1935] AC 462, 481–482. In *Mancini* the House dealt with the duty of the judge to lay before the jury any line of defence which the facts might reasonably support and they also dealt with the particular nature of the defence of provocation. In neither appeal was the House concerned with a statutory defence and no argument was addressed on the nature or scope of statutory exceptions.

Before the decision in *Woolmington* [1935] AC 462 there had been a number of cases in which in trials on indictment the courts had held that the burden of establishing a statutory defence fell upon the defendant although the statute did not expressly so provide: see for example *R v Turner* (1816) 5 M & S 206, a decision under the Gaming Acts, and *Apothecaries' Co.* v *Bentley* (1824) 1 C & P 538 and *R v Scott* (1921) 86 JP 69, decisions in which it was held that the defendant had the burden of proving that he was licensed to perform an otherwise prohibited act.

I cannot accept that either Viscount Sankey LC or Lord Simon LC intended to cast doubt on these long-standing decisions without having had the benefit of any argument addressed to the House on the question of statutory exceptions. I am, therefore, unwilling to read the reference to "any statutory exception" in *Woolmington*, at p. 481, in the restricted sense in which the appellant invites us to read it. It is also to be observed that Lord Devlin in *Jayesena* v *The Queen* [1970] AC 618, a decision of the Privy Council, commenting upon *Woolmington* said, at p. 623:

> The House laid it down that, save in the case of insanity or of a statutory defence, there was no burden laid on the prisoner to prove his innocence and that it was sufficient for him to raise a doubt as to his guilt.

Lord Devlin does not appear to restrict a statutory defence to one in which the burden of proof is expressly placed upon the defendant.

In *R* v *Edwards* [1975] QB 27, the defendant had been convicted in the Crown Court of selling intoxicating liquor without a justices' licence contrary to section 160(1)(a) of the Licensing Act 1964. Section 160(1)(a) provides:

> Subject to the provisions of this Act, if any person—(a) sells or exposes for sale by retail any intoxicating liquor without holding a justices' licence or canteen licence authorising him to hold an excise licence for the sale of that liquor . . . he shall be guilty of an offence under this section.

The prosecution had called no evidence that the defendant did not have a licence and he appealed on the ground that the burden was on the prosecution to establish the lack of a licence. The Court of Appeal held that the burden was on the defendant to prove that he held a licence and that as he had not done so he was rightly convicted.

After an extensive review of the authorities the Court of Appeal held that the same rule applied to trials on indictment as was applied to summary trial by section 81 of the Magistrates' Court Act 1952 which provided:

Where the defendant to an information or complaint relies for his defence on any exception, exemption, proviso, excuse or qualification, whether or not it accompanies the description of the offence or matter of complaint in the enactment creating the offence or on which the complaint is founded, the burden of proving the exception, exemption, proviso, excuse or qualification shall be on him; and this notwithstanding that the information or complaint contains an allegation negativing the exception, exemption, proviso, excuse or qualification.

(Section 81 of that Act has now been repealed and re-enacted in identical language in section 101 of the Magistrates' Courts Act 1980.)

A study of the old cases and practitioners' books led the court to conclude that when Parliament established a new system of summary jurisdiction by the Summary Jurisdiction Act 1848 (Jervis's Act), (11 & 12 Vict. c. 43) and enacted in section 14, which deals with proceedings on the hearing of complaints and informations, the following proviso:

Provided always, that if the information or complaint in any such case shall negative any exemption, exception, proviso, or condition in the statute on which the same shall be framed, it shall not be necessary for the prosecutor or complainant in that behalf to prove such negative, but the defendant may prove the affirmative thereof in his defence, if he would have advantage of the same

they were there stating the common law rule as to proof that the judges then applied to trials on indictment.

Mr Zucker in a most interesting argument has challenged that conclusion and submitted that the common law rule at that time was that an exception contained in the same clause of the Act which created the offence had to be negatived by the prosecution but if the exception or proviso were in a subsequent clause of a statute or, although in the same section, were not incorporated with the enabling clause by words of reference it was a matter of defence. From this general rule Mr Zucker submits that there were but two exceptions, namely, the burden on a defendant under the gaming laws to show that he was qualified to keep guns, bows, dogs, etc., and, secondly, that where an act was prohibited unless done pursuant to a stipulated licence or authority the defendant had to prove that he possessed the necessary licence or authority.

The authorities certainly show that a rule of pleading had evolved by the beginning of the last century, and probably well before that, in the form of the general rule stated by Mr Zucker. One of the more celebrated statements of the rule is Lord Mansfield CJ's *dictum* in *R v Jarvis* (1754) 1 East 643, 645n:

For it is a known distinction that what comes by way of proviso in a statute must be insisted on by way of defence by the party accused; but where exceptions are in the enacting part of a law, it must appear in the charge that the defendant does not fall within any of them.

However, as Mr Zuckerman demonstrates in his learned article "The Third Exception to the *Woolmington* Rule" (1976) 92 LQR 402 the judges did not always regard the rules of pleading and the rules as to the burden of proof as being the same. In *Spieres* v *Parker* (1786) 1 Durn & E 141 Lord Mansfield CJ said, at p. 144, that the prosecutor must "negative the exceptions in the enacting clause, though he threw the burden of proof upon the other side." And in *Jelfs* v *Ballard* (1799) 1 Bos & Pul 467, 468 Buller J said: "The plaintiff must state in his *scire facias* everything that entitles him to recover; but it is a very different question what is to be proved by one party and what by the other."

Sometimes, however, the judges do appear to have applied the old pleading rules to determine the burden of proof. In *Taylor* v *Humphries* (1864) 17 CBNS 539, a publican was charged with opening his premises on a Sunday before 12.30 in the afternoon otherwise than for the refreshment of travellers. The question for the court was upon whom the burden of proof lay to show that those found drinking in the premises at 11.20 in the morning were "travellers." In the course of giving judgment Erle CJ, referring to the argument on behalf of the publican, said, at p. 549:

He further contended, that, as the exception of refreshment to a traveller is contained in the clause creating the prohibition, the burden of proving that the prohibition has been infringed, and that the case is not within the exception, is cast on the informer . . . In this argument we think the appellant is well founded, and that the statute ought to be construed on the principles that he has contended for.

In *Davis* v *Scrace* (1869) LR 4 CP 172 a publican had been prosecuted under the Metropolitan Police Act 1839 (2 & 3 Vict. c. 47) for selling liquor before one in the afternoon on a Sunday. The Act provided, by section 42: no licensed victualler or other person shall open his house within the metropolitan police district for the sale of wine, spirits [etc.] on Sundays, Christmas Day, and Good Friday before the hour of one in the afternoon, except refreshment for travellers.

The court held that they were bound to follow *Taylor* v *Humphries*, 17 CBNS 539. Brett J said, at pp. 176–177:

It is quite impossible to distinguish this case from *Taylor* v *Humphries* . . . They seem to have held that, though the word 'except' is used in 11 & 12 Vict. c. 49, s. 1, it is not in truth an exception within the meaning of the proviso in section 14 of 11 & 12 Vict. c. 43 [Summary Jurisdiction Act 1848] and that therefore that proviso had no application to the case in hand. I think we must adopt the same construction here.

It seems likely that these cases played their part in leading Parliament to repeal section 14 of the Act of 1848 and to replace it by section 39(2) of the Summary Jurisdiction Act 1879 (42 & 43 Vict. c. 49) which was in substantially the same language as the present section 101 of the Act of 1980. As Lord Pearson pointed out in *Nimmo* v *Alexander Cowan & Sons Ltd* [1968] AC 107, Parliament was here emphasising that it was the substance and effect as well as the form of the enactment that mattered when considering upon whom it was intended that the burden of proof should lie under any particular Act.

It seems to me that the probabilities are that Parliament when it enacted section 14 of the Act of 1848 was intending to apply to summary trial that which they believed to be the rule relating to burden of proof evolved by the judges on trials on indictment. It seems unlikely that Parliament would have wished to introduce confusion by providing for different burdens of proof in summary trials as opposed to trials on indictment. Looking back over so many years, this must, to some extent, be speculation and I bear in mind that whereas the defendant could give evidence on his own behalf in a summary trial it was not until 1898 that he was allowed to do so in a trial on indictment which might be a reason for placing a heavier burden of proof on the prosecution in trials on indictment.

However, my Lords, the common law adapts itself and evolves to meet the changing patterns and needs of society; it is not static. By the time the Act of 1879 was passed there were already many offences that were triable both summarily and on indictment. This list of offences has been growing steadily and the very crime with which we are concerned in this appeal is such an example. It is conceded that in the case of exceptions within the meaning of section 101 of the Act of 1980 the burden of proving the exception has been specifically placed upon the defendant. The law would have developed on absurd lines if in respect of the same offence the burden of proof today differed according to whether the case was heard by the magistrates or on indictment. I observe that there would be no possibility of presenting such a submission in respect of a crime triable in Scotland for the Criminal Procedure (Scotland) Act 1975, by sections 66 and 312(v), applies the same rule as to the burden of proof in respect of exceptions to both trials on indictment and summary trials. Although the language of sections 66 and 312(v) is slightly different from section 101 of the Act of 1980 it is to the like effect.

There have been a number of cases considered by the Court of Appeal since *Woolmington* v *Director of Public Prosecutions* [1935] AC 462 concerning the burden of proof in licensing cases both on indictment and on summary trial. There is no indication in any of these cases that the court considered that there should be any difference of approach to the burden of proof according to whether the case was tried summarily or on indictment: see *R* v *Oliver* [1944] KB 68, *R* v *Putland and Sorrell* [1946] 1 All ER 85, *John* v *Humphreys* [1955] 1 WLR 325, *Robertson* v *Bannister* [1973] RTR 109; see also *R* v *Ewens* [1967] 1 QB 322 in which it was held that the Drugs (Prevention of Misuse) Act 1964 on its true construction placed an onus on the defendant to show that he was in possession of a prohibited drug by virtue of the issue of a prescription by a duly qualified medical practitioner.

Mr Zucker relied upon three recent decisions of the Court of Appeal which he submitted support his submission that a statutory defence only places an evidentiary burden on the defendant to raise the defence and that if this is done the burden remains on the prosecution to negative the defence. They are *R* v *Burke* (1978) 67 Cr App R 220, *R* v *MacPherson* [1973] RTR 157, *R* v *Cousins* [1982] QB 526. In none of these cases was *R* v *Edwards* [1975] QB 27 either cited in argument or referred to in the judgment. In each case the Court of Appeal construed the relevant statutory provision as requiring the burden of proof to be discharged by the prosecution. I do not regard these cases as intending to cast any doubt upon the correctness of the decision in *R* v *Edwards*, or as support for the proposition for which they were cited.

Whatever may have been its genesis I am satisfied that the modern rule was encapsulated by Lord Wilberforce in *Nimmo* v *Alexander Cowan & Sons Ltd* [1968] AC 107, 130, when speaking of the Scottish section which was then the equivalent of the present section 101 of the Magistrates' Courts Act 1980: "I would think, then, that the section merely states the orthodox principle (common to both the criminal and the civil law) that exceptions, etc., are to be set up by those who rely on them."

I would summarise the position thus far by saying that *Woolmington* [1935] AC 462 did not lay down a rule that the burden of proving a statutory defence only lay upon the defendant if the statute specifically so provided: that a statute can, on its true construction, place a burden of proof on the defendant although it does not do so expressly: that if a burden of proof is placed on the defendant it is the same burden whether the case be tried summarily or on indictment, namely, a burden that has to be discharged on the balance of probabilities.

The real difficulty in these cases lies in determining upon whom Parliament intended to place the burden of proof when the statute has not expressly so provided. It presents particularly difficult problems of construction when what might be regarded as a matter of defence appears in a clause creating the offence rather than in some subsequent proviso from which it may more readily be inferred that it was intended to provide for a separate defence which a defendant must set up and prove if he wishes to avail himself of it. This difficulty was acutely demonstrated in *Nimmo* v *Alexander Cowan & Sons Ltd* [1968] AC 107. Section 29(1) of the Factories Act 1961 provides:

> There shall, so far as is reasonably practicable, be provided and maintained safe means of access to every place at which any person has at any time to work, and every such place shall, so far as is reasonably practicable, be made and kept safe for any person working there.

The question before the House was whether the burden of proving that it was not reasonably practicable to make the working place safe lay upon the defendant or the plaintiff in a civil action. However, as the section also created a summary offence the same question would have arisen in a prosecution. In the event, the House divided three to two on the construction of the section, Lord Reid and Lord Wilberforce holding that the section required the plaintiff or prosecution to prove that it was reasonably practicable to make the working place safe, the majority, Lord Guest, Lord Upjohn and Lord Pearson, holding that if the plaintiff or prosecution proved that the working place was not safe it was for the defendant to excuse himself by proving that it was not reasonably practicable to make it safe. However, their Lordships were in agreement that if the linguistic construction of the statute did not clearly indicate upon whom the burden should lie the court should look to other considerations to determine the intention of Parliament such as the mischief at which the Act was aimed and practical considerations affecting the burden of proof and, in particular, the ease or difficulty that the respective parties would encounter in discharging the burden. I regard this last consideration as one of great importance for surely Parliament can never lightly be taken to have intended to impose an onerous duty on a defendant to prove his innocence in a criminal case, and a court should be very slow to draw any such inference from the language of a statute.

When all the cases are analysed, those in which the courts have held that the burden lies on the defendant are cases in which the burden can be easily discharged. This point can be demonstrated by what, at first blush, appear to be two almost indistinguishable cases that arose under wartime regulations. In *R* v *Oliver* [1944] KB 68 the defendant was prosecuted for selling sugar without a licence. The material part of the Sugar (Control) Order 1940 (SR & O 1940 No. 1068) by article 2 provided: Subject to any directions given or except under and in accordance with the terms of a licence permit or other authority granted by or on behalf of the Minister no . . . wholesaler shall by way of trade . . . supply . . . any sugar.

The Court of Criminal Appeal held that this placed the burden upon the defendant to prove that he had the necessary licence to sell sugar. In *R* v *Putland and Sorrell* [1946] 1 All

ER 85, the defendant was charged with acquiring silk stockings without surrendering clothing coupons. The material part of the Consumer Rationing (Consolidation) Order 1944 (SR&O 1944 No. 800) article 4 provided: A person shall not acquire rationed goods . . . without surrendering . . . coupons. The Court of Criminal Appeal there held that the burden was upon the prosecution to prove that the clothing had been bought without the surrender of coupons. The real distinction between these two cases lies in the comparative difficulty which would face a defendant in discharging the burden of proof.

In *Oliver's* case [1944] KB 68 it would have been a simple matter for the defendant to prove that he had a licence if such was the case but in the case of purchase of casual articles of clothing it might, as the court pointed out in *Putland's* case, be a matter of the utmost difficulty for a defendant to establish that he had given the appropriate number of coupons for them. It appears to me that it was this consideration that led the court to construe that particular regulation as imposing the burden of proving that coupons had not been surrendered upon the prosecution.

In *R v Edwards* [1975] QB 27, 39–40 the Court of Appeal expressed their conclusion in the form of an exception to what they said was the fundamental rule of our criminal law that the prosecution must prove every element of the offence charged. They said that the exception: "is limited to offences arising under enactments which prohibit the doing of an act save in specified circumstances or by persons of specified classes or with specified qualifications or with the licence or permission of specified authorities."

I have little doubt that the occasions upon which a statute will be construed as imposing a burden of proof upon a defendant which do not fall within this formulation are likely to be exceedingly rare. But I find it difficult to fit *Nimmo v Alexander Cowan & Sons Ltd* [1968] AC 107 into this formula, and I would prefer to adopt the formula as an excellent guide to construction rather than as an exception to a rule. In the final analysis each case must turn upon the construction of the particular legislation to determine whether the defence is an exception within the meaning of section 101 of the Act of 1980 which the Court of Appeal rightly decided reflects the rule for trials on indictment. With this one qualification I regard *R v Edwards* as rightly decided.

My Lords, I am, of course, well aware of the body of distinguished academic opinion that urges that wherever a burden of proof is placed upon a defendant by statute the burden should be an evidential burden and not a persuasive burden, and that it has the support of the distinguished signatories to the 11th Report of the Criminal Law Revision Committee, Evidence (General) (1972) (Cmnd. 4991). My Lords, such a fundamental change is, in my view, a matter for Parliament and not a decision of your Lordships' House.'

(The House held that on its true construction regulation 4(1) of the 1973 Regulations dealt not with exceptions to what would otherwise be unlawful but with the definition of the essential ingredients of an offence; and that, as it was not an offence to possess morphine in one form but an offence to possess it in another form, it had been for the prosecution to prove that the morphine in the possession of the appellant had been in the prohibited form, which it had not done, and no burden had fallen on the appellant.)

(LORDS KEITH of KINKEL and MACKAY of CLASHFERN agreed with LORD GRIFFITHS. LORDS TEMPLEMAN and ACKNER also delivered a judgment in favour of allowing the appeal.)

Appeal allowed.

What effect does this decision have on the previous law?

R v *Lobell* [1957] 1 QB 547 (CCA)

The appellant was convicted of wounding with intent to do grievous bodily harm. At the trial the sole defence was that in inflicting the wound the appellant was acting in self-defence. The trial judge directed the jury that it was for the defence to establish that plea to the jury's satisfaction.

LORD GODDARD, reading the judgment of the court: 'The onus was clearly put in the summing-up on the defendant. There is no doubt that in so doing the judge had the support of *R* v *Smith* (1837) 8 C & P 160 where Bosanquet J apparently with the approval of Bolland B and Coltman J, charged the jury that before a person can avail himself of this defence he must satisfy the jury that the defence was necessary, that he did all he could to avoid it, and that it was necessary to protect his own life, or to protect himself from such serious bodily harm as would give a reasonable apprehension that his life was in immediate danger. In that case the judge said that the accused would be justified. He no doubt had in mind the provisions of 9 Geo. 4, c. 31, s. 10, now replaced and re-enacted by section 7 of the Offences against the Person Act 1861, which enacts that no punishment or forfeiture shall be incurred by any person who shall kill another by misfortune or in his own defence, or in any other manner without felony. This passage from the summing-up has for many years appeared in *Archbold's Criminal Pleading and Practice* as the proper direction to be given in such cases and certainly puts the onus of establishing a defence of killing *se defendendo* on the accused. It is a defence of justification, or, to put it in terms of pleading, a confession and avoidance. In civil cases this plea is always to be proved by the party setting it up; and it is perhaps not altogether easy to see why it should not be so in a criminal case, more especially as when self-defence is set up the facts must often be known only to the defendant who relies upon it.

But in the opinion of the court the cases of *Woolmington* v *Director of Public Prosecutions* [1935] AC 462 and *Mancini* v *Director of Public Prosecutions* [1942] AC 1 establish that in murder or manslaughter the rule that the onus is on the prosecution permits of no exception except as to proof of insanity. In the recent case of *Chan Kau* v *The Queen* [1955] AC 206 this was stated in terms by Lord Tucker, who referred to *R* v *Smith* and said that the passage from the summing-up quoted in Archbold clearly needed some modification in the light of modern decisions. It must, however, be understood that maintaining the rule that the onus always remains on the prosecution does not mean that the Crown must give evidence-in-chief to rebut a suggestion of self-defence before that issue is raised, or indeed need give any evidence on the subject at all. If an issue relating to self-defence is to be left to the jury there must be some evidence from which a jury would be entitled to find that issue in favour of the accused, and ordinarily no doubt such evidence would be given by the defence. But there is a difference between leading evidence which would enable a jury to find an issue in favour of a defendant and in putting the onus upon him. The truth is that the jury must come to a verdict on the whole of the evidence that has been laid before them. If on a consideration of all the evidence the jury are left in doubt whether the killing or wounding may not have been in self-defence the proper verdict would be not guilty. A convenient way of directing the jury is to tell them that the burden of establishing guilt is on the prosecution, but that they must also consider the evidence for the defence which may have one of three results: it may convince them of the innocence of the accused, or it may cause them to doubt, in which case the defendant is entitled to an acquittal, or it may and sometimes does strengthen the case for the prosecution. It is perhaps a fine distinction to say that before a jury can find a particular issue in favour of an accused person he must give some evidence on which it can be found but none the less the onus remains on the prosecution; what it really amounts to is that if in the result the jury are left in doubt where the truth lies the verdict should be not guilty, and this is as true of an issue as to self-defence as it is to one of provocation, though of course the latter plea goes only to a mitigation of the offence.'

Appeal allowed.

Hill v *Baxter* [1958] 1 QB 277 (DC)

The defendant drove a van across a road junction at a fast speed, ignoring a 'Halt' sign. At his trial for dangerous driving, he gave evidence that he had become unconscious as a result of a sudden illness. No evidence of this was produced. The magistrates acquitted him and the prosecutor appealed to the Divisional Court.

LORD GODDARD CJ: 'The first thing to be remembered is that the Road Traffic Act, 1930, contains an absolute prohibition against driving dangerously or ignoring "Halt" signs. No question of *mens rea* enters into the offence; it is no answer to a charge under those sections to say: "I did not mean to drive dangerously" or "I did not notice the 'Halt' sign." The justices' finding that the respondent was not capable of forming any intention as to the manner of driving is really immaterial. What they evidently mean is that the respondent was in a state of automation. But he was driving and, as the case finds, exercising some skill, and undoubtedly the onus of proving that he was in a state of automation must be on him. This is not only akin to a defence of insanity, but it is a rule of the law of evidence that the onus of proving a fact which must be exclusively within the knowledge of a party lies on him who asserts it. This, no doubt, is subject to the qualification that where an onus is on the defendant in a criminal case the burden is not as high as it is on a prosecutor.'

DEVLIN J: 'I am satisfied that even in a case in which liability depended upon full proof of *mens rea*, it would not be open to the defence to rely upon automatism without providing some evidence of it. If it amounted to insanity in the legal sense, it is well established that the burden of proof would start with and remain throughout upon the defence. But there is also recognized in the criminal law a lighter burden which the accused discharges by producing some evidence, but which does not relieve the prosecution from having to prove in the end all the facts necessary to establish guilt. This principle has manifested itself in different forms; most of them relate to the accused's state of mind and put it upon him to give some evidence about it. Thus the fact that an accused is found in possession of property recently stolen does not of itself prove that he knew of the stealing. Nevertheless, it is not open to the accused at the end of the prosecution's case to submit that he has no case to answer; he must offer some explanation to account for his possession though he does not have to prove that the explanation is true: *R* v *Aves* [1950] 2 All ER 330. In a charge of murder it is for the prosecution to prove that the killing was intentional and unprovoked, and that burden is never shifted: *Woolmington* v *Director of Public Prosecutions* [1935] AC 462. But though the prosecution must in the end prove lack of provocation, the obligation arises only if there is some evidence of provocation fit to go to the jury: *Holmes* v *Director of Public Prosecutions* [1946] AC 588. The same rule applies in the case of self-defence: *R* v *Lobell* [1957] 1 QB 547. In any crime involving *mens rea* the prosecution must prove guilty intent, but if the defence suggests drunkenness as negativing intent, they must offer evidence of it, if, indeed, they do not have to prove it: *Director of Public Prosecutions* v *Beard* [1920] AC 479, 507. It would be quite unreasonable to allow the defence to submit at the end of the prosecution's case that the Crown had not proved affirmatively and beyond a reasonable doubt that the accused was at the time of the crime sober, or not sleepwalking or not in a trance or black out. I am satisfied that such matters ought not to be considered at all until the defence has produced at least *prima facie* evidence. I should wish to reserve for future consideration when necessary the question of where the burden ultimately lies.

As automatism is akin to insanity in law there would be great practical advantage if the burden of proof was the same in both cases. But so far insanity is the only matter of defence in which under the common law the burden of proof has been held to be completely shifted.

In my judgment there is not to be found in the case stated evidence of automatism of a character which would be fit to leave to a jury. It must be remembered that the justices were required to presume that the accused was not suffering from any disease of the mind, since he did not challenge the legal presumption of sanity. Although he was asserting that he did not know the nature and quality of his act and so, inevitably, that he was suffering from a defect of reason or understanding, he was not saying that he was a victim of any disease of the mind. Unless there was evidence which showed that his irrationality was due to some cause other than disease of the mind, the justices were not entitled simply to acquit.'

(PEARSON J agreed with DEVLIN J.)

Appeal allowed.

• How does the approach of Lord Goddard CJ differ from that of Devlin J? Which is to be preferred?

Bratty v *Attorney-General for Northern Ireland* [1963] AC 386 (HL)

The appellant was convicted of the murder by strangulation of an 18-year-old girl. Two of his defences were insanity and automatism. He appealed to the Court of Criminal Appeal in Northern Ireland and the House of Lords against the trial judge's refusal to put the defence of automatism to the jury.

VISCOUNT KILMUIR LC: 'Where the defence succeeds in surmounting the initial hurdle (see *Mancini* v *Director of Public Prosecutions* [1942] AC 1), and satisfies the judge that there is evidence fit for the jury to consider, the question remains whether the proper direction is: (*a*) that the jury will acquit if, and only if, they are satisfied on the balance of probabilities that the accused acted in a state of automatism, or (*b*) that they should acquit if they are left in reasonable doubt on this point. In favour of the former direction it might be argued that, since a defence of automatism is (as Lord Goddard said in *Hill* v *Baxter* [1958] 1 QB 277) very near a defence of insanity, it would be anomalous if there were any distinction between the onus in the one case and in the other. If this argument were to prevail it would follow that the defence would fail unless they established on a balance of probabilities that the prisoner's act was unconscious and involuntary in the same way as, under the M'Naughten Rules, they must establish on a balance of probabilities that the necessary requirements are satisfied.

Nevertheless, one must not lose sight of the overriding principle, laid down by this House in *Woolmington's* case [1935] AC 462, that it is for the prosecution to prove every element of the offence charged. One of these elements is the accused's state of mind; normally the presumption of mental capacity is sufficient to prove that he acted consciously and voluntarily, and the prosecution need go no further. But if, after considering evidence properly left to them by the judge, the jury are left in real doubt whether or not the accused acted in a state of automatism, it seems to me that on principle they should acquit because the necessary *mens rea*—if indeed the *actus reus*—has not been proved beyond reasonable doubt.

I find support for this view in the direction given by Barry J to the jury in *R* v *Charlson* [1955] 1 WLR 317. In that case the prisoner was charged on three counts, namely, causing grievous bodily harm with intent to murder, causing grievous bodily harm with intent to cause grievous bodily harm, and unlawful wounding. The defence raised the issue of automatism and called medical evidence in support of it. The learned judge, on the basis—which has aroused some discussion—that insanity did not come into the case, after directing the jury that on each of the first two charges the prosecution must prove the specific intent, went on to deal with the third charge, that is, unlawful wounding, in these words: "Therefore, in considering this third charge you will have to ask yourselves whether the accused knowingly struck his son, or whether he was acting as an automaton without any knowledge of or control over his acts. . . . If you are left in doubt about the matter, and you think that he may well have been acting as an automaton without any real knowledge of what he was doing, then the proper verdict would be 'not guilty.' . . ."

I am also supported by the words of Sholl J in *R* v *Carter* [1959] VR 105 when he said: "It must be for the defence in the first instance genuinely to raise the issue, but if the defence does raise the issue in a genuine fashion then the Crown, which of course may call rebutting evidence on the matter, is bound in the long run to carry the ultimate onus of proving all the elements of the crime including the conscious perpetration thereof."

My conclusion is, therefore, that once the defence have surmounted the initial hurdle to which I have referred and have satisfied the judge that there is evidence fit for the jury's consideration, the proper direction is that, if that evidence leaves them in a real state of doubt, the jury should acquit.'

LORD DENNING: 'In the present case the defence raised both automatism and insanity. And herein lies the difficulty because of the burden of proof. If the accused says he did not know what he was doing, then, so far as the defence of automatism is concerned, the Crown must prove that the act was a voluntary act, see *Woolmington's* case. But so far as the defence of insanity is concerned, the defence must prove that the act was an involuntary act due to disease of the mind, see *M'Naughten's* case. This apparent incongruity was noticed by Sir Owen Dixon, the Chief Justice of Australia, in an address which is to be found in 31 Australian Law Journal, p. 255, and it needs to be resolved. The defence here say: Even though we have not proved that the act was involuntary, yet the Crown have not proved that it was a voluntary act: and that point at least should have been put to the jury.

My Lords, I think that the difficulty is to be resolved by remembering that, whilst the *ultimate* burden rests on the Crown of proving every element essential in the crime, nevertheless in order to prove that the act was a voluntary act, the Crown is entitled to rely on the *presumption* that every man has sufficient mental capacity to be responsible for his crimes: and that if the defence wish to displace that presumption they must give some evidence from which the contrary may reasonably be inferred. Thus a drunken man is presumed to have the capacity to form the specific intent necessary to constitute the crime, unless evidence is given from which it can reasonably be inferred that he was incapable of forming it, see the valuable judgment of the Court of Justiciary in *Kennedy* v *HM Advocate* (1944) SC(J) 171 which was delivered by Lord Normand. So also it seems to me that a man's act is presumed to be a voluntary act unless there is evidence from which it can reasonably be inferred that it was involuntary. To use the words of Devlin J, the defence of automatism "ought not to be considered at all until the defence has produced at least *prima facie* evidence," see *Hill* v *Baxter* [1958] 1 QB 277, 285; and the words of North J in New Zealand "unless a proper foundation is laid," see *R* v *Cottle* [1958] NZLR 999, 1025. The necessity of laying the proper foundation is on the defence: and if it is not so laid, the defence of automatism need not be left to the jury, any more than the defence of drunkenness (*Kennedy* v *HM Advocate*), provocation (*R* v *Gauthier* (1943) 29 Cr App R 113) or self-defence (*R* v *Lobell* [1957] 1 QB 547) need be.

What, then, is a proper foundation? The presumption of mental capacity of which I have spoken is a provisional presumption only. It does not put the legal burden on the defence in the same way as the presumption of sanity does. It leaves the legal burden on the prosecution, but nevertheless, until it is displaced, it enables the prosecution to discharge the ultimate burden of proving that the act was voluntary. Not because the presumption is evidence itself, but because it takes the place of evidence. In order to displace the presumption of mental capacity, the defence must give sufficient evidence from which it may reasonably be inferred that the act was involuntary. The evidence of the man himself will rarely be sufficient unless it is supported by medical evidence which points to the cause of the mental incapacity. It is not sufficient for a man to say "I had a black-out": for "black-out" as Stable J said in *Cooper* v *McKenna, Ex parte Cooper* "is one of the first refuges of a guilty conscience and a popular excuse." The words of Devlin J in *Hill* v *Baxter* should be remembered: "I do not doubt that there are genuine cases of automatism and the like, but I do not see how the layman can safely attempt without the help of some medical or scientific evidence to distinguish the genuine from the fraudulent." When the only cause that is assigned for an involuntary act is drunkenness, then it is only necessary to leave drunkenness to the jury, with the consequential directions, and not to leave automatism at all. When the only cause that is assigned for it is a disease of the mind, then it is only necessary to leave insanity to the jury, and not automatism. When the cause assigned is concussion or sleep-walking, there should be some evidence from which it can reasonably be inferred before it should be left to the jury. If it is said to be due to concussion, there should be evidence of a severe blow shortly beforehand. If it is said to be sleep-walking, there should be some credible support for it. His mere assertion that he was asleep will not suffice.

Once a proper foundation is thus laid for automatism, the matter becomes at large and must be left to the jury. As the case proceeds, the evidence may weigh first to one side and then to the other: and so the burden may appear to shift to and fro. But at the end of the day the legal burden comes into play and requires that the jury should be satisfied beyond reasonable doubt that the act was a voluntary act.'

LORD MORRIS of BORTH-Y-GEST: 'The "golden" rule of the English criminal law that it is the duty of the prosecution to prove an accused person's guilt (subject to any statutory exception and subject to the special position which arises where it is given in evidence that an accused person is insane), does not involve that the prosecution must speculate as to and specifically anticipate every conceivable explanation that an accused person might offer. The evidence of the commission of certain acts may suffice to prove that they were intentional. In a charge of murder, malice may by implication be proved where death occurs as the result of a voluntary act of the accused which is (i) intentional and (ii) unprovoked. When evidence of death and malice has been given an accused person may, however, either by adducing evidence or by examining the circumstances adduced by the Crown, show that his actions were either unintentional or provoked. In such a situation the continuing and constant obligation of the prosecution to satisfy the jury beyond any reasonable doubt is in no way abated (see *Woolmington* v *Director of Public Prosecutions*). In the conceivably possible case that I have postulated (of a violent act committed by a sleep-walker) it would not necessarily be the duty of the prosecution in leading their evidence as to the commission of the act specifically to direct such evidence to negativing the possibility of the act having been committed while sleep-walking. If, however, during the trial the suggested explanation of the act was advanced and if such explanation was so supported that it had sufficient substance to merit consideration by the jury, then the onus which is upon the prosecution would not be discharged unless the jury, having considered the explanation, were sure that guilt in regard to the particular crime charged was established so that they were left in no reasonable doubt. The position would be analogous to that which arises where a defence of self-defence is raised. Though the onus is upon the prosecution to negative that defence, the obligation to do so only arises effectively when there is a suggestion of such defence (see *R* v *Lobell* [1957] 1 QB 547).

Before an explanation of any conduct is worthy of consideration such explanation must be warranted by the established facts or be supported by some evidence that has been given by some witness. Though questions as to whether evidence should or should not be accepted or as to the weight to be attached to it are for the determination of the jury, it is a province of the judge to rule whether a theory or a submission has the support of evidence so that it can properly be passed to the jury for their consideration. As human behaviour may manifest itself in infinite varieties of circumstances it is perilous to generalise, but it is not every facile mouthing of some easy phrase of excuse that can amount to an explanation. It is for a judge to decide whether there is evidence fit to be left to a jury which could be the basis for some suggested verdict.'

Appeal dismissed.

R v *Johnson* [1961] 1 WLR 1478 (CCA)

The appellant was convicted of robbery with violence. At his trial he denied taking part in the robbery and put forward an alibi, calling witnesses to support it. The trial judge, in summing up, indicated that the appellant had assumed the burden of proof when he put forward his defence of alibi.

ASHWORTH J, delivering the judgment of the court: 'The main ground of appeal is based on an alleged misdirection by the judge in regard to the answer which the appellant put forward in the shape of the alibi. As Mr Skellhorn submits, an alibi is commonly called a defence, but it is to be distinguished from some of the statutory defences, such as the defence of diminished responsibility under the Homicide Act 1957, where Parliament has specifically provided for a defence, and has further indicated that the burden of establishing such a defence rests on the accused. It may be that the true view of an alibi is the same as that of self-defence or provocation. It is the answer which a defendant puts forward, and the burden of proof, in the sense of establishing the guilt of the defendant, rests throughout on the prosecution. If a man puts forward an answer in the shape of an alibi or in the shape of self-defence, he does not in law thereby assume any burden of proving that answer. So much, in the opinion of the court, is plain on the authorities.'

Appeal allowed.

R v *Gill* [1963] 1 WLR 841 (CCA)

At his trial on two counts charging him with conspiracy to steal and larceny pursuant to that conspiracy the defendant gave evidence admitting that he had participated in the conspiracy but said that he had repented of that decision soon afterwards and decided not to carry out the theft; that his fellow conspirators had threatened violence to his wife and himself if he failed to carry out his part of the plan; and that it was for fear of that violence that he was compelled, against his will, to commit the theft. He thus relied on duress as a defence to the larceny. The trial judge directed the jury that it was for the defendant to satisfy the jury that he was acting under duress. The defendant appealed against his conviction.

EDMUND DAVIES J, reading the judgment of the court: 'The issue of duress was left to the jury in the present case, and that may well have been the prudent course. Having been left, did the burden rest upon the Crown conclusively to destroy this defence, in the same way as it is required to destroy such other defences as provocation or self-defence? Or was the accused required to establish it, on the balance of probabilities? For the latter view, reliance was placed on the judgment of Lord Goddard CJ in *R* v *Steane* [1947] KB 997, in the course of which he said: ". . . before any question of duress arises, a jury must be satisfied that the prisoner had the intention which is laid in the indictment. Duress is a matter of defence and the onus of proving it is on the accused. As we have already said, where an intent is charged on the indictment, it is for the prosecution to prove it, so the onus is the other way." On the other hand, in *R* v *Purdy* [1946] 10 J Crim Law 182, where a British prisoner of war was charged with treason, Oliver J, directing the jury on the defence of duress, said: "If you believe, or if you think that it might be true, that he only did that because he had the fear of death upon him, then you will acquit him on that charge, because to act in matters of this sort under threat of death is excusable." Similarly, in *R* v *Shiartos* (unreported, September 29, 1961, CCA), where duress was relied upon by an accused charged with arson, Lawton J directed the jury that: "If, in all the circumstances of this case, you are satisfied that what he did he did at pistol point and in fear of his life, he is entitled to be acquitted. If, although you are not satisfied, you think it might well be that he was forced at pistol point to do what he had to do, then again you should acquit him, because the prosecution would not have made you feel sure that what he did he did maliciously."

In our judgment, the law on this matter is to be found correctly stated in Dr Glanville Williams' *Criminal Law*, 2nd ed (1961), p. 762, in this way: ". . . although it is convenient to call duress a 'defence', this does not mean that the ultimate (persuasive) burden of proving it is on the accused. . . . But the accused must raise the defence by sufficient evidence to go to the jury; in other words, the evidential burden is on him." The Crown are not called upon to anticipate such a defence and destroy it in advance. The defendant, either by the cross-examination of the prosecution witnesses or by evidence called on his behalf, or by a combination of the two, must place before the court such material as makes duress a live issue fit and proper to be left to the jury. But, once he has succeeded in doing this, it is then for the Crown to destroy that defence in such a manner as to leave in the jury's minds no reasonable doubt that the accused cannot be absolved on the grounds of the alleged compulsion. It is true that this approach appears to conflict with the literal reading of the passage from Lord Goddard CJ's judgment in *R* v *Steane*. It is to be observed, however, that that passage was *obiter* in that the real decision there was that it was for the Crown to prove the specific intent laid and that in the particular circumstances of that case an inference could not be drawn that the prisoner intended the natural consequences of his act. We agree with Dr Glanville Williams that the *dictum* must be read as relating only to what the author calls the "evidential" burden cast upon the accused, and not to the ultimate (or "persuasive") burden placed upon the Crown of destroying the defence of duress where it has been substantially raised.'

Appeal dismissed. (The court stating that the passages complained of must be read in the light of the whole summing-up, which was impeccable).

• Is there any rational distinction between those cases where the defendant bears an evidential burden of proving an issue and those where the legal burden of proving some issue is cast upon him?

B: THE STANDARD OF PROOF

(Suggested preliminary reading: *A Practical Approach to Evidence*, pp. 89–98)

Miller v Minister of Pensions [1947] 2 All ER 372

The applicant's husband served in the army from 1915 until his death in 1944. He served in the Middle East from 1940 until 1944, when he became hoarse and found difficulty in eating. He reported sick and he was diagnosed as having cancer of the gullet. He died within a month of reporting sick. The tribunal rejected the applicant's claim for the higher pension granted to widows of soldiers whose death was due to war service. The applicant appealed on the ground that the tribunal had not properly directed itself as to the burden of proof.

DENNING J: '[T]he degree of cogency . . . required in a criminal case before an accused person is found guilty . . . is well settled. It need not reach certainty, but it must carry a high degree of probability. Proof beyond reasonable doubt does not mean proof beyond a shadow of a doubt. The law would fail to protect the community if it admitted fanciful possibilities to deflect the course of justice. If the evidence is so strong against a man as to leave only a remote possibility in his favour which can be dismissed with the sentence "of course it is possible, but not in the least probable," the case is proved beyond reasonable doubt, but nothing short of that will suffice. . . .

[T]he degree of cogency . . . required to discharge a burden in a civil case . . . is well settled. It must carry a reasonable degree of probability but not so high as is required in a criminal case. If the evidence is such that the tribunal can say, "We think it more probable than not," the burden is discharged, but, if the probabilities are equal, it is not.'

R v Hepworth and Fearnley [1955] 2 QB 600 (CCA)

LORD GODDARD CJ: 'The appellants were convicted before the recorder of Bradford of the offence of receiving wool, an offence which is by no means uncommon in Yorkshire. I have no doubt that for the most part, at any rate, juries drawn from the citizens of Bradford know perfectly well what their duty is in trying offences of that description. They have to find and feel sure that the goods have been stolen, that they have got into the possession of the accused persons and that the accused knew that they were stolen.

Having read the evidence in this case one is not surprised that the jury found these men guilty, but complaint is made in the case—and the jury were certainly out a very long time before they arrived at their verdict—that the recorder in summing up did not give the jury any direction with regard to the burden of proof, and did not give them a sufficient direction with regard to the duty of a jury and how they were to regard the evidence and the degree of certainty they were to feel.

First, with regard to the burden of proof, it is always desirable that a jury should be told that the burden of proof is on the prosecution. I have no doubt that, in most cases, they know it, but it is desirable that they should be told that it is for the prosecution to prove the case. It is also most desirable that emphasis should be laid upon that in a receiving case. In such a case it is generally desirable, although there may be circumstances in the particular case which would not render it necessary, to remind the jury first, that the burden of proof remains on the prosecution; secondly, to tell them that if an explanation for possession of the goods is given by the accused, although the jury may not be convinced that it is true, if they think that it may be true it would mean that the prosecution have not proved the case because the jury would remain in some degree of doubt. It is not necessary to use on all occasions the formula which was used in *R v Schama and Abramovitch* (1914) 11 Cr App R 45 because that case, which is constantly cited in these matters relating to receiving, as I have said more than once in giving judgment in appeals, lays down no more than this: if the explanation given by the accused persons which, when they have given it becomes part of the sum of evidence in the case, leaves the jury in doubt whether the accused honestly or dishonestly received the goods, they are entitled to be acquitted because the case has not been proved. A case is never proved if any jury is left in any degree of doubt.

Another thing that is said in the present case is that the recorder only used the word "satisfied". It may be, especially considering the number of cases recently in which this question has arisen, that I misled courts because I said in *R v Summers* (1952) 36 Cr App R 14—and I still adhere to it—that I thought that it was very unfortunate to talk to juries about "reasonable doubt" because the explanations given as to what is and what is not a reasonable doubt are so very often extraordinarily difficult to follow and it is very difficult to tell a jury what is a reasonable doubt. To tell a jury that it must not be a fanciful doubt is something that is without any real guidance. To tell them that a reasonable doubt is such a doubt as to cause them to hesitate in their own affairs never seems to me to convey any particular standard; one member of the jury might say he would hesitate over something and another member might say that that would not cause him to hesitate at all. I therefore suggested that it would be better to use some other expression, by which I meant to convey to the jury that they should only convict if they felt sure of the guilt of the accused. It may be that in some cases the word "satisfied" is enough. Then, it is said that the jury in a civil case has to be satisfied and, therefore, one is only laying down the same standard of proof as in a civil case. I confess that I have had some difficulty in understanding how there is or there can be two standards; therefore, one would be on safe ground if one said in a criminal case to a jury: "You must be satisfied beyond reasonable doubt" and one could also say: "You, the jury, must be completely satisfied," or better still: "You must feel sure of the prisoner's guilt." But I desire to repeat what I said in *R* v *Kritz* [1950] 1 KB 82, 89: "It is not the particular formula that matters: it is the effect of the summing-up. If the jury are made to understand that they have to be satisfied and must not return a verdict against a defendant unless they feel sure, and that the onus is all the time on the prosecution and not on the defence," that is enough. I should be very sorry if it were thought that these cases should depend on the use of a particular formula or particular word or words. The point is that the jury should be directed first, that the onus is always on the prosecution; secondly, that before they convict they must feel sure of the accused's guilt. If that is done, that will be enough.

Comment has been made on the use by the recorder of the word "satisfied" only, and we have come to the conclusion that the summing-up was not satisfactory; but again I emphasise that this is a case of receiving and in such a case it is always important that the onus of proof should be emphasised and explained. The jury should be told that the possession of goods recently stolen calls for an explanation, and if none is given, or one is given which the jury are convinced is untrue, that entitles them to convict. But if the explanation given leaves them in doubt as to whether the accused received the goods honestly or dishonestly the prosecution have not proved the case and they should acquit.

For the reasons I have endeavoured to give—I hope it will not be thought that we are laying down any particular form of words, but we are saying it is desirable that something more should be said than merely "satisfied"—we think that the conviction should be quashed.'

Appeal allowed.

• Which formula is to be preferred: 'beyond reasonable doubt' or 'feeling sure of guilt'? Why?

Walters v *R* [1969] 2 AC 26 (PC)

The petitioner was charged with murder. In the course of his summing up the trial judge sought to explain the phrase 'a reasonable doubt' as follows: 'Sometimes it is put this way, that a reasonable doubt is that quality and mind of doubt which, when you are dealing with matters of importance in your own affairs, you allow to influence you one way or the other.' The Court of Appeal of Jamaica confirmed the conviction and refused the petitioner leave to appeal against his conviction for murder. The petitioner applied to the Privy Council for special leave to appeal.

LORD DIPLOCK delivering the judgment of the court: 'At the trial of the petitioner the judge thought it desirable to explain to the jury what was meant by the time-honoured phrase "a reasonable doubt". In the course of doing so he said: "a reasonable doubt is that quality and kind of doubt which, when you are dealing with matters of importance in your own affairs, you allow to influence you one way or the other."

It has for many years been a common practice of judges in England and other common law jurisdictions when directing the jury on the onus of proof to expand the bare expression "reasonable doubt" by using this or a similar analogy. On behalf of the petitioner, however, it was contended that a direction in terms such as these is erroneous because it invites the jury to apply a "subjective" test instead of an "objective" one. A similar contention had been upheld in *Ramroop* v *The Queen* (1963) 6 WIR 425 by the Court of Appeal of Trinidad and Tobago, where the actual words used at p. 429 were: "It is better . . . merely to look at it as being satisfied, as you have to be in some important matter concerning yourselves."

That court considered that an explanation in these terms would: "suggest no particular standard"—(of proof)—"because whereas one juryman might feel satisfied from certain facts to act in a particular way in some matter of importance to him another on the same facts might feel differently."

Ramroop v *The Queen* was followed by the Court of Appeal of Jamaica in *R* v *Bromfield* (1965) 8 WIR 273 where the phrase used was "such a standard of proof or state of mind as you would act upon in a matter of great consequence in your own affairs", and subsequently in *R* v *Powe* (1985) 8 WIR 395 and *R* v *Plinton* (1965) 9 WIR 44 where almost identical phraseology had been used. In *Lesmond* v *The Queen* (No. 1) (1967) 10 WIR 252, however, the Court of Appeal of the West Indies Associated States approved as part of a "proper and adequate" direction the phrase "such a doubt as would weigh with you in your own important affairs of everyday life". The court distinguished these words from those condemned in *R* v *Bromfield* on the grounds that the latter did whereas the former did not equate "the standard of proof itself with the personal standards of conduct of individual jurors".

In their Lordships' view the correctness or otherwise of a direction to a jury on the onus of proof cannot depend upon such fine semantic distinctions. No jury, whether in the West Indies or England, as it listens to an oral summing-up by the judge is capable of appreciating them. As Lord Goddard CJ said in *R* v *Kritz* [1950] 1 KB 82, at p. 89:

> It is not the particular formula that matters: it is the effect of the summing-up. If the jury are made to understand that they have to be satisfied and must not return a verdict against a defendant unless they feel sure, and that the onus is all the time on the prosecution and not on the defence, then whether the judge uses one form of language or another is neither here nor there.

The expressions "objective test" and "subjective test" are currently in popular use among lawyers, sometimes in contexts in which they are helpful in indicating a meaningful contrast. But in the context of "doubt", which cannot be other than personal to the doubter, it is meaningless to talk of doubt as "objective" and otiose to describe it as "subjective". It is the duty of each individual juror to make up his own mind as to whether the evidence that the defendant committed the offence with which he is charged is so strong as to convince him personally of the defendant's guilt. Inevitably, because of differences of temperament or experience some jurors will take more convincing than others. That is why there is safety in numbers. And shared responsibility and the opportunity for discussion after retiring serves to counteract individual idiosyncrasies.

By the time he sums up the judge at the trial has had an opportunity of observing the jurors. In their Lordships' view it is best left to his discretion to choose the most appropriate set of words in which to make *that* jury understand that they must not return a verdict against a defendant unless they are sure of his guilt; and if the judge feels that any of them, through unfamiliarity with court procedure, are in danger of thinking that they are engaged in some task more esoteric than applying to the evidence adduced at the trial the common sense with which they approach matters of importance to them in their ordinary lives, then the use of such analogies as that used by Small J in the present case, whether in the words in which he expressed it or in those used in any of the other cases to which reference has been made, may be helpful and is in their Lordships' view unexceptionable. Their Lordships would deprecate any attempt to lay down some precise formula or to draw fine distinctions between one set of words and another. It is the effect of the summing-up as a whole that matters.'

Petition dismissed.

R v *Ching* (1976) 63 Cr App R 7 (CA)

The defendant was charged with theft from a supermarket. After retiring, the jury returned to the court and the foreman asked the judge to give further directions about the standard of proof. The judge gave a further direction in these terms: 'It is the duty of the prosecution to prove the charge on the whole of the evidence beyond a reasonable doubt. A reasonable doubt, it has been said, is a doubt to which you can give a reason as opposed to a mere fanciful sort of speculation such as "Well, nothing in this world is certain, nothing in this world can be proved." It is sometimes said the sort of matter which might influence you if you were to consider some business matter. A matter, for example, of a mortgage concerning your house, something of that nature.' The jury convicted the defendant who appealed.

LAWTON LJ, giving the judgment of the court: 'Mr Latham accepted that when this Court comes to consider the effect of the final direction which the judge gave to the jury, it must be looked at against the whole background of the case, and in particular against the whole of the summing-up. That has been said time and time again in this Court. If any authority is required for the proposition it is to be found in *R* v *Hepworth and Fearnley* (1955) 39 Cr App R 152; [1955] 2 QB 600. There Lord Goddard CJ said: "But I desire to repeat what I said in the case of *R* v *Kritz* (1949) 33 Cr App R 169; [1950] 1 KB 82: 'It is not the particular formula of words that matters; it is the effect of the summing up. If the jury are charged whether in one set of words or in another and are made to understand that they have to be satisfied and must not return a verdict against a defendant unless they feel sure, and that the onus is all the time on the prosecution and not on the defence,' that is enough. I should be very sorry if it were thought that cases should depend on the use of a particular formula or particular word or words."

The task therefore for us has been to consider what was the effect of the summing-up as a whole, including the final direction. Mr Latham attacked that final direction on three grounds. He said that it was unsatisfactory for a judge to define a "reasonable doubt" as one for which a reason could be given; he pointed to a criticism of that phrase which was made by Lord Justice Edmund Davies (as he then was) in *R* v *Stafford and Luvaglio* (1968) 53 Cr App R 1. Edmund Davies LJ, sitting with Fenton Atkinson LJ and Waller J said at p. 2: "We do not, however, ourselves agree with the trial judge when, directing the jury upon the standard of proof, he told them to 'Remember that a reasonable doubt is one for which you could give reasons if you were asked,' and we dislike such a description or definition." So do we. It does not help juries. But that is not the problem in this case. The problem is whether its use made this conviction unsafe.

The next ground of complaint was that by using the mortgage of a house analogy, the learned judge was doing something which had been condemned a number of times in this

Court. Counsel called our attention to two recent decisions. One was *R* v *Gray* (1973) 58 Cr App R 177. In that case the phrase which was disapproved of was "doubt which might affect you in the conduct of your everyday affairs." The other, even more recently, is the decision of this Court, on January 13, 1976, in *R* v *Knott*, unreported. In that case the phrase "the sort of doubt that can influence you as prudent men and women in the conduct of your everyday affairs." In the past this Court has criticised trial judges for using that kind of analogy. The use of any analogy is to be avoided whenever possible.

The final criticism was that when giving the direction of which complaint is made, the judge did not emphasise once again that the jury had to be sure. But we have no doubt that by the time the jury retired for the last time, they must have appreciated that they had to be sure before they could return a verdict of guilty.

Nevertheless, in most cases—but not in this one—judges would be well advised not to attempt any gloss upon what is meant by "sure" or what is meant by "reasonable doubt". In the last two decades there have been numerous cases before this Court, some of which have been successful, some of which have not, which have come here because judges have thought it helpful to a jury to comment of what the standard of proof is. Experience in this Court has shown that such comments usually create difficulties. They are more likely to confuse than help. But the exceptional case does sometimes arise. This is the sort of case in which, as I have already pointed out, the jury possibly wanted help as to what was meant by "doubt". The judge thought they wanted help and he tried to give them some. He was right to try and that is all he was doing. He seems to have steered clear of the formulas which have been condemned in this Court such as "such doubt as arises in your everyday affairs or your everyday life"; or using another example which has been before the Court, "the kind of doubts which you may have when trying to make up your minds what kind of motor car to buy."

Mr Latham said that the judge did not stress that the relevant doubts were those which have to be overcome in *important* business affairs. What he did was to pick an example, which for sensible people would be an important matter. We can see nothing wrong in his so doing.

In conclusion we invite attention to what was said in *Walters* v *The Queen* [1969] 2 AC 26, where the Board had to consider the kind of problem which is now before us. In that case the trial judge in Jamaica gave the jury a long explanation as to what was meant by "reasonable doubt". That explanation was criticised upon the same lines as the final direction given by the trial judge in this case was criticised by Mr Latham. The Privy Council considered the criticisms. It objected to certain phrases which had been put forward in the course of argument, and the opinion of Lord Diplock, at p. 30 ended as follows: "By the time he sums-up the judge at the trial has had an opportunity of observing the jurors. In their Lordships' view it is best left to his discretion to choose the most appropriate set of words in which to make *that* jury understand that they must not return a verdict against a defendant unless they are sure of his guilt; and if the judge feels that any of them, through unfamiliarity with court procedure, are in danger of thinking that they are engaged in some task more esoteric than applying to the evidence adduced at the trial the common sense with which they approach matters of importance to them in their ordinary lives, then the use of such analogies as that used by Small J in the present case, whether in the words in which he expressed it or in those used in any of the other cases to which reference has been made, may be helpful and is in their Lordships' view unexceptionable." That opinion is the opinion of this Court.

There is no reason for saying in this case that the verdict was unsafe. As I said earlier, and I repeat, this is one of a large number of cases which have come before this Court in recent years, raising fine points about the terms in which judges have directed the jury as to the standard of proof. We point out and emphasise that if judges stopped trying to define that which is almost impossible to define there would be fewer appeals. We hope there will not be any more for some considerable time.'

Appeal dismissed.

Ferguson v *R* [1979] 1 WLR 94 (PC)

The defendant was charged with murder. The trial judge directed: '. . . it is required to satisfy you beyond reasonable doubt that from the evidence before you . . . the defendant is guilty of murder . . . If you entertain the kind of doubt, which might affect the mind of a person in the conduct of important affairs, then you entertain a reasonable doubt . . .' The defendant was convicted of murder and appealed on the ground, *inter alia*, that the judge misdirected the jury as to the intent necessary to establish the crime of murder.

LORD SCARMAN, delivering the judgment of their Lordships: 'It is submitted that the judge encouraged "too subjective" an approach by telling the jury that the doubt must be such as "might affect the mind of a person in the conduct of important affairs."

Their Lordships were told and accepted that in certain Commonwealth jurisdictions some judges avoid this formulation. It is criticised as being unhelpful and possibly dangerous, in that questions arising in the conduct of important affairs often have little resemblance to the issues in a criminal trial and individual jurors may well decide such questions by applying standards lower than satisfaction beyond reasonable doubt and analogous, if to anything, to the civil standard of the balance of probabilities. In *Walters* v *The Queen* [1969] 2 AC 26 their Lordships had to consider a direction almost identical in part with that in this case. Delivering the judgment in that case (which was not an appeal, but an application for special leave to appeal) Lord Diplock pointed out that a distinction between "objective" and "subjective" tests is not apt in this context. The Board expressed the view in that case that the formula used in summing up does not matter so long as it is made clear to the jury, whatever words are used, that they must not return a verdict against a defendant unless they are sure of his guilt. Their Lordships' Board agree with these comments with one reservation. Though the law requires no particular formula, judges are wise, as a general rule, to adopt one.

The time-honoured formula is that the jury must be satisfied beyond reasonable doubt. As Dixon CJ said in *Dawson* v *The Queen* (1961) 106 CLR 1, 18, attempts to substitute other expressions have never prospered. It is generally sufficient and safe to direct a jury that they must be satisfied beyond reasonable doubt so that they feel sure of the defendant's guilt. Nevertheless, other words will suffice, so long as the message is clear.'

Appeal dismissed.

R v *Carr-Briant* [1943] KB 607 (CCA)

The defendant who was charged with corruption contrary to the Prevention of Corruption Act 1906, was a director of a firm which entered into a contract for work to be done with the War Department. Payments in respect of work done under the contracts were made on the certificate of an engineer named Baldock, an employee of the War

Department, that it had been satisfactorily performed. The appellant gave or lent to Baldock £60 so that Baldock might pay for a car which he had agreed to buy. The trial judge directed the jury that the defendant had not only to discharge the burden of proof and show that he gave the money without a corrupt motive, but had also to do so beyond all reasonable doubt. The defendant was convicted and appealed.

HUMPHREYS J, reading the judgment of the court: 'We agree with and adopt for the purpose of this judgment the language of Lord Hailsham LC, in delivering the judgment of the Privy Council in *Sodeman* v *R* [1936] 2 All ER 1138, [1936] WN 190, 191, where he said: "The suggestion made by the petitioner was that the jury may have been misled by the judge's language into the impression that the burden of proof resting upon the accused to prove the insanity was as heavy as the burden of proof resting upon the prosecution to prove the facts which they had to establish. In fact there was no doubt that the burden of proof for the defence was not so onerous . . .. It was certainly plain that the burden in cases in which an accused had to prove insanity might fairly be stated as not being higher than the burden which rested upon a plaintiff or defendant in civil proceedings. That that was the law was not challenged."

What is the burden resting on a plaintiff or defendant in civil proceedings can, we think, best be stated in the words of the classic pronouncement on the subject by Willes J in *Cooper* v *Slade* 6 HL Cas 746. That learned judge referred to an ancient authority in support of what he termed "the elementary proposition that in civil cases the preponderance of probability may constitute sufficient ground for a verdict." The authority in question was the judgment of Dyer CJ and a majority of the justices of the Common Pleas in *Newis* v *Lark* (1531) Plowd 403, decided in the reign of Queen Elizabeth. The report contains this passage: "Where the matter is so far gone that the parties are at issue . . . so that the jury is to give a verdict one way or other, there, if the matter is doubtful, they may found their verdict upon that which appears the most probable and by the same reason that which is most probable shall be good evidence."

In our judgment, in any case where, either by statute or at common law, some matter is presumed against an accused person "unless the contrary is proved," the jury should be directed that it is for them to decide whether the contrary is proved, that the burden of proof required is less than that required at the hands of the prosecution in proving the case beyond a reasonable doubt, and that the burden may be discharged by evidence satisfying the jury of the probability of that which the accused is called upon to establish.'

Appeal allowed.

Hornal v *Neuberger Products Ltd* [1957] 1 QB 247 (CA)

The plaintiff in an action for damages for breach of warranty or, alternatively, for fraudulent misrepresentation, alleged that the director of the defendant company had in the course of negotiations for the purchase of a used capstan lathe stated that it had been reconditioned by a reputable firm of toolmakers. The defendants denied that the statement had been made. If it had been made, the director must have known it to be untrue.

The county court judge found that the statement had been made, but held on the claim for breach of warranty that it had not been made contractually. On the claim based on fraud he said that he was satisfied on the balance of probability that the statement had been made, and that that was the correct standard to apply; but that he would not have been so satisfied if the criminal standard of proof was to be applied. He gave judgment for the defendants on the ground that the plaintiff had not shown that he had suffered damage by relying on the fraudulent misrepresentation. The plaintiff appealed.

DENNING LJ: 'I must say that, if I was sitting as a judge alone, and I was satisfied that the statement was made, that would be enough for me, whether the claim was put in warranty or on fraud. I think it would bring the law into contempt if a judge were to say that on the issue of warranty he finds the statement was made, and that on the issue of fraud he finds it was not made.'

HODSON LJ: 'Notwithstanding the existence of some cases where the point appears to have been argued and decided in a contrary sense, I think the true view, and that most strongly supported by authority, is that which the judge took, namely that in a civil case the balance of probability standard is correct . . ..

Students are familiar with Professor Kenny's *Outlines of Criminal Law* (16th ed (1952)), where the following passage appears at p. 416: "A larger minimum of proof is necessary to support an accusation of crime than will suffice when the charge is only of a civil nature. For in the latter it is sufficient that there be a *preponderance* of evidence in favour of the successful party, whereas in criminal cases the burden rests upon the prosecution to prove that the accused is guilty 'beyond reasonable doubt.' When therefore the case for the prosecution is closed after sufficient evidence has been adduced to necessitate an answer from the defence, the defence need do no more than show that there is a *reasonable doubt* as to the guilt of the accused. See *R* v *Stoddart* (1909) 25 TLR 612. Even in civil proceedings, e.g., in actions of debt, a mere scintilla of evidence would not warrant the jury in finding a verdict for the plaintiff; for there must (as we have seen) be so much evidence that a reasonable man might accept it as establishing the issue. But in criminal cases the presumption of innocence is still stronger, and accordingly a still higher minimum of evidence is required; and the more heinous the crime the higher will be this minimum of necessary proof. The progressive increase in the difficulty of proof, as the gravity of the accusation to be proved increases, is vividly illustrated in an extract from Lord Brougham's speech in defence of Queen Caroline: 'The evidence before us,' he said, 'is inadequate even to prove a debt—impotent to deprive of a civil right—ridiculous for convicting of the pettiest offence—scandalous if brought forward to support a charge of any grave character—monstrous if to ruin the honour of an English Queen.'" This passage appears in the earlier editions of this work for which the late Professor Kenny was responsible.

Denning LJ referred both to criminal and civil cases when he expressed the same idea in *Bater* v *Bater* [1951] P 35: "The difference of opinion which has been evoked about the standard of proof in recent cases may well turn out to be more a matter of words than anything else. It is of course true that by our law a higher standard of proof is required in criminal cases than in civil cases. But this is subject to the qualification that there is no absolute standard in either case. In criminal cases the charge must be proved beyond reasonable doubt, but there may be degrees of proof within that standard. As Best CJ, and many other great judges have said, 'in proportion as the crime is enormous, so ought the proof to be clear.' So also in civil cases, the case may be proved by a preponderance of probability, but there may be degrees of probability within that standard. The degree depends on the subject-matter. A civil court, when considering a charge of fraud, will naturally require for itself a higher degree of probability than that which it would require when asking if negligence is established. It does not adopt so high a degree as a criminal court, even when it is considering a charge of a criminal nature; but still it does require a degree of probability which is commensurate with the occasion."

This citation comes from a judgment given on appeal in a divorce case. The House of Lords has now held in *Preston-Jones* v *Preston-Jones* [1951] AC 391 that the words of the Divorce Act [the Matrimonial Causes Act, 1950] produce the same result as the rule in criminal cases although divorce cases are civil actions. Nevertheless, on the general question of the standard of proof in criminal and civil cases, I would like to express my complete concurrence with the words used by Denning LJ in the passage I have cited. Just as in civil cases the balance of probability may be more readily tilted in one case than in another, so in criminal cases proof beyond reasonable doubt may more readily be attained in some cases than in others.'

MORRIS LJ: 'In a criminal case a jury must be directed that the onus is all the time upon the prosecution and that before they convict they must feel sure of the accused's guilt. Authoritative guidance in regard to directing juries in criminal cases is to be found in the judgment of Lord Goddard CJ in *R* v *Hepworth and Fearnley* [1955] 2 QB 600, and in other cases. It has, however, been emphasised that what is vital is not the mere using of some particular formula of words but the effect of a summing-up in giving true guidance as to the right approach.

It is, I think, clear from the authorities that a difference of approach in civil cases has been recognised. Many judicial utterances show this. The phrase "balance of probabilities" is often employed as a convenient phrase to express the basis upon which civil issues are decided. It may well be that no clear-cut logical reconciliation can be formulated in regard to the authorities on these topics. But perhaps they illustrate that "the life of the law is not logic but experience". In some criminal cases liberty may be involved; in some it may not. In some civil cases the issues may involve questions of reputation which can transcend in importance even questions of personal liberty. Good name in man or woman is "the immediate jewel of their souls".

But in truth no real mischief results from an acceptance of the fact that there is some difference of approach in civil actions. Particularly is this so if the words which are used to define that approach are the servants but not the masters of meaning. Though no court and no jury would give less careful attention to issues lacking gravity than to those marked by it, the very elements of gravity become a part of the whole range of circumstances which have to be weighed in the scale when deciding as to the balance of probabilities. This view was denoted by Denning LJ when in his judgment in *Bater* v *Bater* he spoke of a "degree of probability which is commensurate with the occasion" and of "a degree of probability which is proportionate to the subject-matter".

In English law the citizen is regarded as being a free man of good repute. Issues may be raised in a civil action which affect character and reputation, and these will not be forgotten by judges and juries when considering the probabilities in regard to whatever misconduct is alleged. There will be reluctance to rob any man of his good name: there will also be reluctance to make any man pay what is not due or to make any man liable who is not or not liable who is. A court will not be deterred from a conclusion because of regret at its consequences: a court must arrive at such conclusion as is directed by the weight and preponderance of the evidence.'

(The court held that, although the judge had applied the correct standard of proof, the plaintiff had suffered damage and was entitled to judgment.)

Appeal allowed.

Re Dellow's Will Trusts [1964] 1 WLR 451 (Ch D)

A husband and wife made mutual wills, the husband leaving all his estate to his wife, provided that she survived him, with other bequests if she did not, and the wife providing in similar terms for the husband with gifts over. On 1 January 1958, both spouses were found dead in their homes from coal gas poisoning. The trustees of the wills issued a summons asking, *inter alia*, whether the husband or the wife had died first or whether, if the evidence was not conclusive, the presumption in section 184 of the Law of Property Act 1925, was applicable and the husband, being the elder, should be presumed to have died first. If the latter proposition was correct, the summons asked for an inquiry as to whether the wife feloniously killed the husband. Thereupon the question arose as to the standard of proof required in civil matters to establish felonious killing . . .

UNGOED-THOMAS J: 'Is it, then, established that the wife killed the husband? It is conceded that, in a case of this kind before me in the Chancery Division dealing with the devolution of property, the standard of proof required is not so severe as that required by the criminal law. The standard of proof was considered in *Hornal* v *Neuberger Products Ltd* [1957] 1 QB 247, where Morris LJ stated: "Though no court and no jury would give less careful attention to issues lacking gravity than to those marked by it, the very elements of gravity become a part of the whole range of circumstances which have to be weighed in the scale when deciding as to the balance of probabilities."

It seems to me that in civil cases it is not so much that a different standard of proof is required in different circumstances varying according to the gravity of the issue, but, as Morris LJ says, the gravity of the issue becomes part of the circumstances which the court has to take into consideration in deciding whether or not the burden of proof has been discharged. The more serious the allegation the more cogent is the evidence required to overcome the unlikelihood of what is alleged and thus to prove it. This is perhaps a somewhat academic distinction and the practical result is stated by Denning LJ [1957] 1 QB 247, 258: "The more serious the allegation the higher the degree of probability that is required: but it need not, in a civil case, reach the very high standard required by the criminal law." In this case the issue is whether or not the wife feloniously killed the husband. There can hardly be a graver issue than that, and its gravity weighs very heavily against establishing that such a killing took place, even for the purposes of deciding a civil issue.'

Order accordingly.

Bastable v **Bastable and Sanders** [1968] 1 WLR 1684 (CA)

The husband petitioned for divorce on the ground of desertion and also adultery with S. The evidence of adultery was purely circumstantial. The judge granted the husband a decree on both grounds. The wife did not dispute the desertion, but she and S appealed against the finding of adultery.

WILLMER LJ: 'I confess that I have found the question raised by this appeal an exceedingly difficult one. It seems to me that much must depend upon what is the appropriate standard of proof to be expected in relation to a charge such as that made here. If I may say so with all possible respect, sitting in this court I do not find it altogether easy to follow the directions contained in various statements made by members of the

House of Lords. There have been two cases in relatively recent years in which various members of the House of Lords expressed views with regard to the standard of proof required in matrimonial cases. One was *Preston-Jones* v *Preston-Jones* [1951] AC 391 and the other was *Blyth* v *Blyth* [1966] AC 643 (HL) in both of which various members of the House made statements which we can treat only with the utmost respect in relation to the standard of proof required. But it is fair to say that in both cases what they said was not strictly necessary for the decision of the matter in hand, but must be regarded as *obiter*. In *Preston-Jones* v *Preston-Jones* the question being debated was whether adultery was to be inferred from an unusual period of gestation, and their lordships were concerned with an argument that in such circumstances nothing short of proof with scientific certainty would satisfy the burden upon a petitioner. The House of Lords rejected that submission. But Lord MacDermott [1951] AC 417, in a passage in his speech which has often been cited, expressed the view that nothing short of proof beyond a reasonable doubt would be sufficient to satisfy the burden of proof on a petitioner. With that expression of view Lord Simonds agreed, and so did Lord Morton of Henryton.

In *Blyth* v *Blyth* the question under consideration was not the standard of proof required in relation to a matrimonial offence, but what was the standard of proof in relation to condonation. Again the members of the House discussed in their speeches what they conceived to be the appropriate standard of proof in support of an allegation of a matrimonial offence. The dissenting minority, consisting of Lord Morris of Borth-y-Gest and Lord Morton of Henryton, adhered to the view which had been expressed in *Preston-Jones*, to which I have already referred. On the other hand, Lord Denning thought that a considerably lower standard of proof could be adopted. He pointed out [1966] AC 667 *et seq*, that what had been said in *Preston-Jones* was *obiter*, and he for his part preferred the view which had been expressed in an Australian case of *Wright* v *Wright* [1948] 77 CLR 191, as against that which had been decided by the Court of Appeal in this country in *Ginesi* v *Ginesi*, Lord Pearce took the same view as Lord Denning had taken. So far, therefore, the House of Lords in *Blyth* v *Blyth* was divided, two against two, on the question what is the appropriate standard of proof to be exacted in support of a charge of a matrimonial offence. The fifth member of the House, Lord Pearson, adopted what I can only describe as an intermediate position. Having quoted at some length from what Lord MacDermott said in *Preston-Jones* v *Preston-Jones*, Lord Pearson commented:

> This language is consistent with the view that the word 'satisfied' does not, as a matter of interpretation, mean 'satisfied beyond reasonable doubt,' and that the requirement of proof beyond reasonable doubt may be limited to the grounds for dissolution and may not extend to the matters referred to in subparagraphs (*b*) and (*c*).

which relate to matters of connivance, condonation, and so forth. In other words, as I read what Lord Pearson was saying, he would have been disposed to apply the standard of "satisfaction beyond reasonable doubt" where proof of a matrimonial offence is being considered, but would not apply that standard in relation to such matters as condonation, which was the subject-matter of the appeal to the House of Lords in that case. It will be seen, therefore, that for us who sit in this court it is not altogether easy to determine exactly what standard of proof should be applied in relation to proof of a matrimonial offence such as adultery.

When *Blyth* v *Blyth and Pugh* [1965] P 411 (CA) was before this court I ventured to say that I agreed with the view expressed by Denning LJ in *Bater* v *Bater* [1951] P 35 and adopted by this court in *Hornal* v *Neuberger Products Ltd* [1957] 1 QB 247. In that oft-quoted passage Denning LJ said [1951] P 37: "The difference of opinion which has been evoked about the standard of proof in recent cases may well turn out to be more a matter of words than anything else. It is, of course, true that by our law a higher standard of proof is required in criminal cases than in civil cases. But this is subject to the qualification that there is no absolute standard in either case. In criminal cases the charge must be proved beyond reasonable doubt, but there may be degrees of proof within that standard. As Best CJ and many other great judges have said: 'in proportion as the crime is enormous, so ought the proof to be clear.' So also in civil cases, the case may be proved by a preponderance of probability, but there may be degrees of probability within that standard. The degree depends on the subject-matter. A civil court, when considering a charge of fraud, will naturally require for itself a higher degree of probability than that which it would require when asking if negligence is established. It does not adopt so high a degree as a criminal court, even when it is considering a charge of a criminal nature; but still it does require a degree of probability which is commensurate with the occasion. Likewise, a divorce court should require a degree of probability which is proportionate to the subject-matter."

Until the matter has been further considered by the House of Lords, and further guidance has been received, I propose to direct myself in accordance with that statement of principle.

In the present case, what is charged is "an offence." True, it is not a criminal offence; it is a matrimonial offence. It is for the husband petitioner to satisfy the court that the offence has been committed. Whatever the popular view may be, it remains true to say that in the eyes of the law the commission of adultery is a serious matrimonial offence. It follows, in my view, that a high standard of proof is required in order to satisfy the court that the offence has been committed.'

EDMUND-DAVIES LJ: 'It has been pointed out by Professor Cross in *Cross on Evidence*, 3rd ed. (1967), p. 94, that when *Ginesi* v *Ginesi* [1948] P 179 decided that the standard of proof of adultery required was that of proof "beyond a reasonable doubt," the earlier decision of the High Court of Australia in *Briginshaw* v *Briginshaw* (1938) 60 CLR 336 was not cited, nor was this court referred to *Mordaunt* v *Moncreiffe* (1874) LR 2 HL Sc Div 374, in which the House of Lords decided that matrimonial proceedings arising from adultery are purely civil in character.

In *Preston-Jones*, Lord MacDermott reiterated that the standard to be applied with regard to all grounds for divorce was that of "proof beyond reasonable doubt," Lord Simonds expressing his concurrence therewith. But in *Blyth* v *Blyth*, to which my Lord has made reference, Lord Denning, disagreeing with that view, said that what Lord MacDermott laid down in *Preston-Jones* was said *obiter* and without argument. Lord Denning drew a distinction between the standards required to be attained in relation to proof of the *grounds* for a decree of dissolution and proof of a *bar* to relief by saying:

> . . . so far as the *grounds* for divorce are concerned, the case, like any civil case, may be proved by a preponderance of probability, but the degree of probability depends on the subject-matter. In proportion as the offence is grave, so ought the proof to be clear. So far as the *bars* to divorce are concerned, like connivance or condonation, the petitioner need only show that on balance of probability he did not connive or condone or as the case may be.

I diffidently entertain doubt as to the capacity of a judge (certainly as to my own capacity) to convey in intelligible terms to the ordinary juryman, were jury trials in civil matters as commonplace as they were years ago, the almost metaphysical difference between such varying standards of proof as those to which Lord Denning there referred. The observations made in the High Court of Australia in *Rejfek* v *McElroy* [1966] ALR 270, on the other hand, are such as I think any average juryman *could* be expected to follow, the judge there saying:

> The difference between the criminal standard of proof and the civil standard of proof is no mere matter of words. It is a matter of critical substance. No matter how grave the fact which is to be found in a civil case, the mind has only to be reasonably satisfied, and has not with respect to any matter in issue in such a proceeding to attain that degree of certainty which is indispensable to the support of a conviction upon a criminal charge.

When one is thus contrasting the standard of proof in criminal charges on the one hand with that applicable to civil cases on the other, the distinction is certainly capable of being expressed in terms which a juryman can be expected to understand. But how he is to be instructed in the proper approach to his duty when he is trying civil cases of a matrimonial character is not very clear to me. "In proportion as the offence is grave, so ought the proof to be clear," observed Lord Denning in *Blyth* v *Blyth*, but with the utmost deference I take leave to doubt that such a distinction could effectively be made by a jury, or indeed by many judges and lawyers. I should have thought, with respect, that an offence is either proved or it is not proved, in accordance with the standard (civil or criminal) appropriate to the case under consideration.

Be that as it may, *Blyth's* case dealt solely with a matter of condonation, and in relation to that it decisively and authoritatively laid down that the petitioner need show, only on a balance of probability, that he did not connive or condone, as the case may be. Lord Denning's observations in relation to the standard of proof appropriate to the establishment of a matrimonial offence, on the other hand, must *ex necessitatis* be regarded as *obiter*. As to this, Professor Cross in *Cross on Evidence* at pp. 96–97, has observed that: "All that can be said with certainty on the present law is that it is only necessary to negative the *bars* to matrimonial relief on a preponderance of probability. So far as the *grounds* for such relief are concerned there is, it is submitted, every reason why the views of Lord Denning in *Blyth* v *Blyth* should be adopted; and, at the level of the House of Lords, no authority precludes their adoption. Whether lower courts will treat *Blyth* v *Blyth* as an authority for the proposition that proof on a preponderance of probability is all that is required throughout every matrimonial cause remains to be seen.'"

(WINN LJ agreed with WILLMER LJ.)

Appeal allowed.

Questions for discussion

R v *Coke; R* v *Littleton*

1   Who bears the burden of proof on the issue of guilt or innocence of Coke and Littleton?

2   Compose directions to the jury which adequately explain both the incidence of the legal burden of proof and the standard of proof required on the issue of guilt or innocence.

3   Are there any issues in the case as to which Coke or Littleton bears any legal burden of proof?

4   Are there any issues in the case as to which Coke or Littleton bears any evidential burden of proof?

5   What must the prosecution do in order to establish a *prima facie* case as to the charges against Coke and Littleton respectively? What effect would this have on the further conduct of the defence by each defendant?

6   The following is an extract from the summing-up of the trial judge in *R* v *Coke*; *R* v *Littleton*:

Now, members of the jury, I have explained to you the meaning in law of these two charges, rape and indecent assault. You now know that each charge consists of a number of elements, and I will now tell you who must prove what elements and to what standard of proof. Let me deal first with the charge of rape against Coke. Once the prosecution prove the fact that sexual intercourse took place between Coke and Miss Blackstone on the relevant date, you are then faced with the problem of consent. The prosecution have had no trouble proving that sexual intercourse took place, because Coke does not dispute it. So there you have no difficulty. The difficulty focuses on consent. Coke says she consented. Miss Blackstone says she did not consent. How do you decide? Well, members of the jury, you may think it would be a matter of some difficulty for the prosecution to prove a negative. If Coke says she did consent, let him prove the affirmative to you. Consider whether he has succeeded in proving that consent to you on the whole of the evidence.

Littleton, members of the jury, has told you that he was not at Coke's flat at the time of the alleged assault on Angela Blackstone. He has raised what is sometimes termed an alibi. Of course, he is therefore doing more than just saying, "I didn't do it"; he is saying "I wasn't there". Now if he had confined himself to denying the assault ("I was there, but I didn't touch her") well, that would be one thing—you would have to ask yourselves, "Have the prosecution proved their case?" But where the defendant asserts a positive defence which goes beyond a mere denial, that is quite another thing, and it is then up to him to prove that fact before you need consider it.

But members of the jury, in both cases, you must bear in mind that these are criminal charges. The law says that you must not convict either man, unless you are fairly sure it is right to do so on the whole of the evidence. You must be satisfied, in other words be pretty certain of their guilt. Otherwise you should acquit.

(a)   Criticise this passage, and suggest grounds of appeal on behalf of Coke and Littleton.

(b)   Would the first paragraph, which refers to Coke, be a correct statement of the law if applied to the civil case of *Blackstone* v *Coke*?

7   How much difference *in practice* would it make if the burden of proof in a criminal case lay on the defendant?

Blackstone v Coke

1   Review the pleadings. On what facts in issue do Margaret Blackstone and Coke respectively bear the legal burden of proof?

2   At the outset of the case, who bears the evidential burden of proof as to the underlying evidential facts? How may this change as the case proceeds?

3   Assume that Coke was never charged with an offence against Margaret Blackstone, but that Margaret has brought the present action in the same form, but omitting paragraph 3 of the statement of claim. What standard of proof would be required of the plaintiff in proving her claim?

4   In the light of the fact that the standard of proof in a civil case is no more than the balance of probabilities, does the burden of proof really matter in a civil case?

Additional questions

1   Angus is charged with the murder of his wife, Bunty, by shooting her. In his defence he states that his shotgun went off accidently as he was cleaning it. He further states that he is subject to blackouts and claims this as an alternative reason for firing the gun.

How would you as the trial judge direct the jury as to the question of the burden and standard of proof in the case?

2   Consider the following passage from the judgment of Windeyer J in the Australian case of *Thomas* v *R* (1960) 102 CLR 584: 'The "golden thread that runs through the web of English criminal law" is broken by the defence of insanity. It is better to recognise this than to rationalise it. For there is really no logical answer to the rhetorical question of Harlan J, asked in the course of delivering the impressive judgment of the Supreme Court of the United States in *Davis* v *United States*, "How, then, upon principle or consistently with humanity can a verdict of guilty be properly returned if the jury entertain a reasonable doubt as to the existence of a fact which is essential to guilt, namely, the capacity in law of the accused to commit that crime?" 160 US 469 at 488 (1895). Nevertheless, it is the firmly established rule of our law that when insanity is put forward as a defence to a criminal charge, it is for the defence to show that the accused was, in the relevant sense, insane.'

Is there an answer to this?

Further reading

Eggleston, *Evidence, Proof and Probability*, 2nd ed. (1983), Chs. 8-10.
Healy, Proof and policy: no golden threads [1987] Crim LR 355.
C.R. Williams, 'Placing the burden of proof' in *Well and Truly Tried* (ed. Campbell & Waller) (1982).
G. Williams, 'Statutory exceptions to liability and the burden of proof' (1976) 126 New LJ 1032.
G. Williams, 'The evidential burden: some common misapprehensions' (1977) 127 New LJ 156.
G. Williams, 'Evidential burdens on the defence' (1977) 127 New LJ 182.
Zuckerman, 'The third exception to the *Woolmington* rule' (1976) 92 LQR 402.

4   Evidence of Character

A: USES OF THE WORD 'CHARACTER'; ADMISSIBILITY OF CHARACTER EVIDENCE IN GENERAL

(Suggested preliminary reading: *A Practical Approach to Evidence*, pp. 100–115)

R v Rowton (1865) Le & Ca 520 (CCR)

The defendant was charged with indecent assault on a boy and called several witnesses to his character. The prosecution called a witness to give evidence in rebuttal, and the witness was asked about the defendant's general character for decency and morality of conduct. He replied: 'I know nothing of the neighbourhood's opinion, because I was only a boy at school when I knew him; but my own opinion, and the opinion of my brothers who were also pupils of his, is that his character is that of a man capable of the grossest indecency and the most flagrant immorality'.

COCKBURN CJ: 'There are two questions to be decided. The first is whether, when evidence of good character has been given in favour of a prisoner, evidence of his general bad character can be called in reply. I am clearly of opinion that it can be. It is true that I do not remember any case in my own experience where such evidence has been given; but that is easily explainable by the fact that evidence of good character is not given when it is known that it can be rebutted; and it frequently happens that the prosecuting counsel, from a spirit of fairness, gives notice to the other side, when he is in a position to contradict such evidence. But, when we come to consider whether the evidence is admissible, it is only possible to come to one conclusion. It is said that evidence of good character raises only a collateral issue; but I think that, if the prisoner thinks proper to raise that issue as one of the elements for the consideration of the jury, nothing could be more unjust than that he should have the advantage of a character which, in point of fact, may be the very reverse of that which he really deserves.

Assuming, then, that evidence was receivable to rebut the evidence of good character, the second question is, was the answer which was given in this case, in reply to a perfectly legitimate question, such an answer as could properly be left to the jury? Now, in determining this point, it is necessary to consider what is the meaning of evidence of character. Does it mean evidence of general reputation or evidence of disposition? I am of opinion that it means evidence of general reputation. What you want to get at is the tendency and disposition of the man's mind towards committing or abstaining from committing the class of crime with which he stands charged; but no one has ever heard the question—what is the tendency and disposition of the prisoner's mind?—put directly. The only way of getting at it is by giving evidence of his general character founded on his general reputation in the neighbourhood in which he lives. That, in my opinion, is the sense in which the word "character" is to be taken, when evidence of character is spoken of. The fact that a man has an unblemished reputation leads to the presumption that he is incapable of committing the crime for which he is being tried. We are not now considering whether it is desirable that the law of England should be altered—whether it is expedient to import the practice of other countries and go into the prisoner's antecedents for the purpose of shewing that he is likely to commit the crime with which he is charged, or, stopping short of that, whether it would be wise to allow the prisoner to go into facts for the purpose of shewing that he is incapable of committing the crime charged against him. It is quite clear that, as the law now stands, the prisoner cannot give evidence of particular facts, although one fact would weigh more than the opinion of all his friends and neighbours. So too, evidence of antecedent bad conduct would form equally good ground for inferring the prisoner's guilt, yet it is quite clear evidence of that kind is inadmissible. The allowing evidence of good character has arisen from the fairness of our laws and is an anomalous exception to the general rule. It is quite true that evidence of character is most cogent, when it is preceded by a statement shewing that the witness has had opportunities of acquiring information upon the subject beyond what the man's neighbours in general would have; and in practice the admission of such statements is often carried beyond the letter of the law in favour of the prisoner. It is, moreover, most essential that a witness who comes forward to give a man a good character should himself have a good opinion of him; for otherwise he would only be deceiving the jury; and so the strict rule is often exceeded. But, when we consider what, in the strict interpretation of the law, is the limit of such evidence, in my judgment it must be restricted to the man's general reputation, and must not extend to the individual opinion of the witness. Some time back, I put this question—suppose a witness is called who says that he knows nothing of the general character of the accused, but that he had had abundant opportunities of forming an individual opinion as to his honesty or the particular moral quality that may be in question in the particular case. Surely, if such evidence were objected to, it would be inadmissible.

If that be the true doctrine as to the admissibility of evidence to character in favour of the prisoner, the next question is, within what limits must the rebutting evidence be confined? I think that that evidence must be of the same character and confined within the same limits—that, as the prisoner can only give evidence of general good character, so the evidence called to rebut it must be evidence of the same general description, shewing that the evidence which has been given in favour of the prisoner is not true, but that the man's general reputation is bad.'

ERLE CJ (dissenting): 'Now, what is the principle on which evidence of character is admitted? It seems to me that such evidence is admissible for the purpose of shewing the disposition of the party accused, and basing thereon a presumption that he did not commit the crime imputed to him. Disposition cannot be ascertained directly; it is only to be ascertained by the opinion formed concerning the man, which must be founded either on personal experience, or on the expression of opinion by others, whose opinion again ought to be founded on their personal experience. The question between us is, whether the Court is at liberty to receive a statement of the disposition of a prisoner, founded on the personal experience of the witness, who attends to give evidence and state that estimate which long personal knowledge of and acquaintance with the prisoner has enabled him to form? I think that each source of evidence is admissible. You may give in evidence the general rumour prevalent in the prisoner's neighbourhood, and, according to my experience, you may have also the personal judgment of those who are capable of forming a more real, substantial, guiding opinion than that which is to be gathered from general rumour. I never saw a witness examined to character without an inquiry being made into his personal means of knowledge of that character. The evidence goes to the jury depending entirely upon the personal experience of the witness who has offered his testimony. Suppose a witness to character were to say, "This man has been in my employ for twenty years. I have had experience of his conduct; but I have never heard a human being express an opinion of him in my life. For my own part, I have always regarded him with the highest esteem and respect, and have had an abundant experience that he is one of the worthiest men in the world." The principle the Lord Chief Justice has laid down would exclude this evidence; and that is the point where I differ from him. To my mind personal experience gives cogency to the evidence; whereas such a statement as, "I have heard some persons speak well of him," or "I have heard general report in favour of the prisoner," has a very slight effect in comparison. Again, to the proposition that general character is alone admissible the answer is that it is impossible to get at it. There is no such thing as general character; it is the general inference supposed to arise from hearing a number of separate and disinterested statements in favour of the prisoner. But I think that the notion that general character is alone admissible is not accurate. It would be wholly inadmissible to ask a witness what individual he has ever heard give his opinion of a particular fact connected with the man. I attach considerable weight to this distinction, because, in my opinion, the best character is that which is the least talked of.'

(WILLES J also dissented. The other learned judges concurred in the judgment delivered by COCKBURN CJ.)

R v Redgrave (1981) 74 Cr App R 10 (CA)

The appellant was charged with persistently importuning for an immoral purpose contrary to section 32 of the Sexual Offences Act 1956. The appellant sought to tender detailed evidence of his heterosexual relationships with girls to rebut inferences from his conduct, as observed by police officers, that he had been making homosexual approaches to them. The judge ruled that evidence inadmissible and the appellant was convicted on a majority verdict. The appellant appealed on the ground, *inter alia*, that the judge's ruling was wrong.

LAWTON LJ, giving the judgment of the court: 'In this court Mr Still put forward four propositions on behalf of his client. The first was that as the *mens rea* of the offence is an intention of a homosexual character, the defendant in a case of this kind is entitled to show that he is not of a homosexual disposition. Secondly, if the prosecution in this class of case, can, in order to rebut such defences as mistaken identity or innocent association, put in evidence showing that the defendant has homosexual tendencies, in the same way a defendant ought to be allowed to put in evidence showing that he has no homosexual tendencies, if his defence is that the prosecution have drawn wrong inferences from the proven facts. Thirdly he submitted that the decision in *R v Rowton* (1865) Le & Ca 520, which is now nearly 120 years old, has been overtaken by developments in the law and is no longer good law. Finally he submitted to the court that as the object of evidence is to obtain a just result, the law ought not to exclude any evidence which common sense says goes to prove that an offence has not been committed.

He developed these points citing well known cases. It is necessary to refer only to three: *R v Ferguson* (1909) 2 Cr App R 250; *R v Samuel* (1956) 40 Cr App R 8 and *R v Bellis* (1965) 50 Cr App R 88; [1966] 1 WLR 234. We do not consider it necessary to refer in detail to *R v Ferguson (supra)* as the matter which was canvassed in that case was considered more fully in *R v Samuel (supra)*, which was heard in 1956 before Lord Goddard CJ, Hilbery and

Stable JJ. The issue in that case was this: the accused had been charged with larceny by finding. He stated in his evidence that on two previous occasions he had restored property found by him. The prosecution took the view that what he was doing was putting in evidence of good character. They sought leave to cross-examine him about his previous convictions. Counsel was allowed to do so. The issue before the Court of Criminal Appeal was whether by saying what he did say about having returned property found by him on two previous occasions, he was giving evidence of his own good character. In the course of discussing that problem Lord Goddard in his judgment referred to the evidence which he had given about having returned goods found by him on two previous occasions as evidence clearly going to show that he was an honest man. The court was not concerned with the question as to whether what the defendant had said about his honest acts on other occasions was properly admissible. We get no help from this case. In *R* v *Bellis* (*supra*) the court was concerned with a direction by the judge about evidence as to character. The court decided that a jury should be directed that the possession of good character by a defendant is primarily a matter which goes to his credibility. But the judgment of the court, delivered by Widgery J (as he then was) said it could also go to probability.

On the basis of these cases Mr Still submitted that the law has altered since the decision in *R* v *Rowton* (*supra*) and if the law has altered, said Mr Still, it follows that any evidence going to show the improbability of the accused having committed the offence with which he was charged is evidence which a jury ought to consider, and even more so when common sense says that such evidence may tend to show that the accused has not committed the offence.

We make at this stage a comment about the so called common sense aspect of the case. It may well be that in many cases, perhaps in most cases, those who have homosexual dispositions and commit homosexual acts, do not have much inclination towards heterosexual activity, but this is not always so. It is a matter of both history and judicial experience that many who commit homosexual acts also indulge in heterosexual activity. Whether they do so because of genetic tendencies, or whether they do so out of what used to be called lust, is not a matter into which we need inquire. Some men and women do commit both kinds of acts.

Mr Smith's argument, on behalf of the Crown, was simple, clear and concise. It came to this: that the law of evidence has grown up over the centuries, largely as a result of the experience of the judges who have decided that certain types of evidence shall be admitted and certain types shall be excluded. The object has been to ensure that there is a fair trial before a jury and that there is a just verdict. Sometimes the rules which have evolved are not all that logical. But those are our rules and it is the duty of the courts to follow them. Parliament from time to time has intervened and has altered the law.

When everything has been taken into consideration, according to Mr Smith, the law is at present as follows. The prosecution can call evidence to prove directly that the accused committed the act. What they cannot do, save in special circumstances, is to call evidence to prove that the defendant had a propensity to commit the kind of crime with which he is charged. The exception either arises at common law, as set out in the well known case of *Makin* v *Attorney-General of New South Wales* [1894] AC 57; 17 Cox CC 704, or under statute, as in the circumstances referred to in the Criminal Evidence Act 1898. That is clear; and Mr Still did not seek to say that that was not the law so far as the prosecution was concerned. What he submitted was that the rules applying to the prosecution ought not to, and do not, apply to the defendant, because he is in a different situation to the prosecution and should not be bound by the same exclusions.

In our judgment the defendant is bound by the same rules as the prosecution. He can call evidence to show that he did not commit the acts which are alleged against him, but he is not allowed, by reference to particular facts, to call evidence that he is of a disposition which makes it unlikely that he would have committed the offence charged.

That this is the common law of England is shown clearly by the decision in *R* v *Rowton* (1865) Le & Ca 520. In the course of his judgment in that case Cockburn CJ said at p. 530: "It is quite clear that, as the law now stands, the prisoner cannot give evidence of particular facts, although one fact would weigh more than the opinion of all his friends and neighbours." That is what the appellant was trying to do in this case. He was trying, by his evidence about his relations with particular women and by the production of these letters and photographs, to show that he had had intimate heterosexual relationships with the writers of the letters and the girls in the photographs, and he was relying on those particular facts to show that he had not got a disposition to behave in the sort of way which the prosecution alleged.

The problem in this case is whether there is any exception in law to the general proposition laid down by Cockburn CJ nearly 120 years ago. The Court of Crown Cases Reserved in *R* v *Rowton* (*supra*), made up of no less than 12 judges, came to the conclusion, with two dissensions, that when a defendant wishes to show he has not got a disposition to commit the kind of offence with which he is charged, he is limited in what he can say. In 1866 he could call evidence to show that his general reputation made it unlikely that he would commit the kind of offence with which he was charged. He could do that by calling people who knew him, but beyond that he could not go.

It follows therefore, so it seems to us, that in this case, although disposition to commit the kind of offence charged was relevant, the law is as decided in *R* v *Rowton* (*supra*), viz that the defendant could do no more than say, or call witnesses to prove, that he was not by general repute the kind of young man who would have behaved in the kind of way that the Crown alleged.

The circumstances of this case show the undesirability of the law going further. Giving evidence and producing documents of this kind would be so easy for somebody who was putting a false defence forward. Clearly it would have been undesirable for this young man to have given evidence that he has had sexual intercourse with a number of named women who were not in court; and it would also not be in the public interest that he should be allowed to subpoena young women to give evidence on oath that they had had sexual intercourse with him. These are the sort of factors which no doubt before 1866 were taken into account by the judges when, during the seventeenth, eighteenth and early part of the nineteenth century, they formulated the rules dealing with evidence.

It seems to us that it is in the public interest generally that evidence of this kind should be limited as laid down in *R* v *Rowton* (*supra*). But it is not for us to consider whether the law is good law or bad law, unjust or fair law. We are here to apply the law.

It was brought to our attention by Mr Smith that nowadays, as a matter of practice in this class of case, defendants are often allowed to say that they are happily married and having a normal sexual relationship with their wives. We are not seeking to stop defending counsel putting that kind of information before a jury. It has long been the practice for judges to allow some relaxation of the law of evidence on behalf of defendants. Had this young man been a married man, or alternatively, had he confined his relationship to one girl, it might not have been all that objectionable for him to have given evidence in general terms that his relationship with his wife or the girl was satisfactory. That would have been an indulgence on the part of the court. It would not have been his right to have it said. Until such time as Parliament amends the law of evidence, it is the duty of this court, and of judges, to keep to the rules, and the rules are clear.'

Appeal dismissed.

- What are the practical implications of the decisions in *Rowton* and in *Redgrave*?

R v *Winfield* [1939] 4 All ER 164 (CCA)

The defendant, who was charged with indecent assault on a woman, called a witness and asked her questions to establish his good character with regard to sexual morality. The witness and/or the defendant (there being a conflict between the two reports of the case, in [1939] 4 All ER 164 and in 27 Cr App R 139) were cross-examined on the defendant's previous convictions of offences involving dishonesty. On appeal against conviction, it was contended that the evidence as to his general character was improperly admitted.

HUMPHREYS J, delivering the judgment of the court: 'The deputy chairman knew, though probably the prisoner did not, that there is no such thing known to our procedure as putting half your character in issue and leaving out the other half. A man is not entitled to say, "Well, I may have a bad character as a dishonest rogue, but at all events nobody has ever said that I have acted indecently towards women." That cannot be done. If a man who is accused chooses to put his character in issue, he must take the consequences. It is quite clear that this man did. He asked questions about his character quite apart from the facts of this case. The result was that he was properly cross-examined as to character.'

(The appeal was, however, allowed and conviction quashed on the ground of want of corroboration.)

- 'If a man is charged with forgery, cross-examination as to his convictions for cruelty can have no purpose but prejudice.' (Nokes, *Introduction to Evidence* (1952), p. 111.)
Is this a sound criticism of the decision in *R* v *Winfield*?

R v *Bryant and Oxley* [1979] QB 108 (CA)

The defendants were jointly charged with robbery. One defendant, who did not testify, applied for leave to appeal against his conviction on the ground that the trial judge had misdirected the jury in stating that evidence given of his good character went to credibility and, in the circumstances, had little relevance to the issue whether he had committed the offence.

WATKINS J, reading the judgment of the court: 'If . . . the judge was intending to convey to the jury the impression that a good character is relevant only when a defendant gives evidence and, therefore, is a matter only to be taken into consideration when the credibility of what he and other witnesses have said is being assessed, he was being too restrictive about its possible uses. The possession of a good character is a matter which does go primarily to the issue of credibility. This has been made clear in a number of recent cases. But juries should be directed that it is capable of bearing a more general significance which is best illustrated by what was said by Williams J in *R* v *Stannard* (1837) 7 C & P 673, 675:

> I have no doubt, if we are put to decide the unwelcome question, that evidence to character must be considered as evidence in the cause. It is evidence, as my brother Patteson has said, to be submitted to the jury, to induce them to say whether they think it likely that a person with such a character would have committed the offence.

The "unwelcome question" related to counsel's right to sum up after defence evidence of character only had been given.

We have no doubt that the omission to direct the jury in this way in the present case could not possibly have had the effect of rendering the jury's verdict unsafe or unsatisfactory.'

Application refused.

B: CROSS-EXAMINATION OF THE DEFENDANT IN CRIMINAL CASES; THE CRIMINAL EVIDENCE ACT 1898 SECTION 1(e) AND (f)

(Suggested preliminary reading: *A Practical Approach to Evidence*, pp. 115–136)

Criminal Evidence Act 1898 s.1(e) and (f)

(e)   A person charged and being a witness in pursuance of this Act may be asked any question in cross-examination notwithstanding that it would tend to criminate him as to the offence charged:

(f)   A person charged and called as a witness in pursuance of this Act shall not be asked, and if asked shall not be required to answer, any question tending to show that he has committed or been convicted of or been charged with any offence other than that wherewith he is then charged, or is of bad character, unless—

(i)   the proof that he has committed or been convicted of such other offence is admissible evidence to show that he is guilty of the offence wherewith he is then charged; or

(ii)   he has personally or by his advocate asked questions of the witnesses for the prosecution with a view to establish his own good character, or has given evidence of his good character, or the nature or conduct of the defence is such as to involve imputations on the character of the prosecutor or the witnesses for the prosecution; or

(iii)   he has given evidence against any other person charged in the same proceedings.

Maxwell v DPP [1935] AC 309 (HL)

The appellant was charged with manslaughter of a woman by performing upon her an illegal operation. He gave evidence of his good character. Thereupon counsel for the prosecution asked him the following questions:

'*Q* This is the second time that sudden death has come to a woman patient of yours, is it not?—*A* Yes.

Q The first time was in 1927?—*A* In 1927, yes . . ..

Q And were you tried for manslaughter?—*A* Something like that; I could not tell you exactly.

Q And you were acquitted by the jury?—*A* Yes.

The appellant was convicted of manslaughter and appealed unsuccessfully to the Court of Criminal Appeal. He further appealed to the House of Lords.

VISCOUNT SANKEY LC: 'The substantive part of proviso (f) is negative in form and as such is universal and is absolute unless the exceptions come into play. Then come the three exceptions: but it does not follow that when the absolute prohibition is superseded by a permission, that the permission is as absolute as the prohibition. When it is sought to justify a question it must not only be brought within the terms of the permission, but also must be capable of justification according to the general rules of evidence and in particular must satisfy the test of relevance. Exception (i) deals with the former of the two main classes of evidence referred to above, that is, evidence falling within the rule that where issues of intention or design are involved in the charge or defence, the prisoner may be asked questions relevant to these matters, even though he has himself raised no question of his good character. Exceptions (ii) and (iii) come into play where the prisoner by himself or his witnesses has put his character in issue, or has attacked the character of others. Dealing with exceptions (i) and (ii), it is clear that the test of relevance is wider in (ii) than in (i); in the latter, proof that the prisoner has committed or been convicted of some other offence, can only be admitted if it goes to show that he was guilty of the offence charged. In the former (exception (ii)), the questions permissible must be relevant to the issue of his own good character and if not so relevant cannot be admissible. But it seems clear that the mere fact of a charge cannot in general be evidence of bad character or be regarded otherwise than as a misfortune. It seemed to be contended on behalf of the respondent that a charge was *per se* such evidence that the man charged, even though acquitted, must thereafter remain under a cloud, however innocent. I find it impossible to accept any such view. The mere fact that a man has been charged with an offence is no proof that he committed the offence. Such a fact is, therefore, irrelevant; it neither goes to show that the prisoner did the acts for which he is actually being tried nor does it go to his credibility as a witness. Such questions must, therefore, be excluded on the principle which is fundamental in the law of evidence as conceived in this country, especially in criminal cases, because, if allowed, they are likely to lead the minds of the jury astray into false issues; not merely do they tend to introduce suspicion as if it were evidence, but they tend to distract the jury from the true issue—namely, whether the prisoner in fact committed the offence on which he is actually standing his trial. It is of the utmost importance for a fair trial that the evidence should be *prima facie* limited to matters relating to the transaction which forms the subject of the indictment and that any departure from these matters should be strictly confined.

It does not result from this conclusion that the word "charged" in proviso (f) is otiose: it is clearly not so as regards the prohibition; and when the exceptions come into play there may still be cases in which a prisoner may be asked about a charge as a step in cross-examination leading to a question whether he was convicted on the charge, or in order to elicit some evidence as to statements made or evidence given by the prisoner in the course of the trial on a charge which failed, which tend to throw doubt on the evidence which he is actually giving, though cases of this last class must be rare and the cross-examination permissible only with great safeguards.

Again, a man charged with an offence against the person may perhaps be asked whether he had uttered threats against the person attacked because he was angry with him for bringing a charge which turned out to be unfounded. Other probabilities may be imagined. Thus, if a prisoner has been acquitted on the plea of *autrefois convict* such an acquittal might be relevant to his credit, though it would seem that what was in truth relevant to his credit was the previous conviction and not the fact that he was erroneously again charged with the same offence; again, it may be, though it is perhaps a remote supposition, that an acquittal of a prisoner charged with rape on the plea of consent may possibly be relevant to a prisoner's credit.

But these instances all involve the crucial test of relevance. And in general no question whether a prisoner has been convicted or charged or acquitted should be asked or, if asked, allowed by the judge, who has a discretion under proviso (f), unless it helps to elucidate the particular issue which the jury is investigating, or goes to credibility, that is, tends to show that he is not to be believed on his oath; indeed the question whether a man has been convicted, charged or acquitted ought not to be admitted, even if it goes to credibility, if there is any risk of the jury being misled into thinking that it goes not to credibility but to the probability of his having committed the offence of which he is charged. I think that it is impossible in the present case to say that the fact that the prisoner had been acquitted on a previous charge of murder or manslaughter, was relevant, or that it tended in the present case to destroy his credibility as a witness.'

(LORDS ATKIN, BLANESBURGH, THANKERTON and WRIGHT agreed.)

Appeal allowed.

Stirland v *DPP* [1944] AC 315 (HL)

The appellant, on trial for forgery, put his character in issue and said in examination-in-chief that he had never been 'charged' with any offence. He was asked in cross-examination questions suggesting that on a previous occasion he had been 'questioned about a suggested forgery' by his former employers. The appellant was convicted and appealed.

VISCOUNT SIMON LC: 'It is necessary . . . to guard against a possible confusion in the use of the word "charged". In para (f) of s. 1 of the Act of 1898 the word appears five times and it is plain that its meaning in the section is "accused before a court" and not merely "suspected or accused without prosecution". When the appellant denied that he had ever been "charged", he may fairly be understood to use the word in the sense it bears in the statute and to mean that he had never previously been brought before a criminal court. Questions whether his former employer had suspected him of forgery were not, therefore, any challenge to the veracity of what he had said. Neither were they relevant as going to disprove good character. The most virtuous may be suspected, and an unproved accusation proves nothing against the accused, but the questions, while irrelevant both to the charge which was being tried and to the issue of good character, were calculated to injure the appellant in the eyes of the jury by suggesting that he had been in trouble before, and were, therefore, not fair to him. They should not have been put, and, if put, should have been disallowed . . .

It is most undesirable that the rules which should govern cross-examination to credit of an accused person in the witness box should be complicated by refined distinctions involving a close study and comparison of decided cases, when, in fact, these rules are few and can be simply stated. The following propositions seem to cover the ground (I am omitting the rule which admits evidence tending to prove other offences where this evidence is relevant to the issue being tried as helping to negative accident or to establish system, intent or the like): (i) The accused in the witness box may not be asked any question "tending to show that he has committed or been convicted of or been charged with any offence other than that wherewith he is then charged, or is of bad character, unless" one or other of the three conditions set out in para (f) of s. 1 of the Act of 1898 is fulfilled. (ii) He may, however, be cross-examined as to any of the evidence he has given in chief, including statements concerning his good record, with a view to testing his veracity or accuracy or to showing that he is not to be believed on his oath. (iii) An accused who "puts his character in issue" must be regarded as putting the whole of his past record in issue. He cannot assert his good conduct in certain respects without exposing himself to inquiry about the rest of his record so far as this tends to disprove a claim for good character. (iv) An accused is not to be regarded as depriving himself of the protection of the section, because the proper conduct of his defence necessitates the making of injurious reflections on the prosecutor or his witnesses: *R* v *Turner* [1944] KB 463. (v) It is no disproof of good character that a man has been suspected or accused of a previous crime. Such questions as "Were you suspected?" or, "Were you accused?" are inadmissible because they are irrelevant to the issue of character, and can only be asked if the accused has sworn expressly to the contrary. (vi) The fact that a question put to the accused is irrelevant is in itself no reason for quashing his conviction, though it should have been disallowed by the judge.'

(LORDS RUSSELL OF KILLOWEN, THANKERTON, WRIGHT and PORTER agreed.)

(The House applied the proviso to s. 4(1) of the Criminal Appeal Act 1907 on the ground that there had been no miscarriage of justice.)

Appeal dismissed.

Jones v *DPP* [1962] AC 635 (HL)

The appellant was charged with the murder of a young girl guide in October 1960. He had previously been convicted of raping another girl guide during September 1960. Although the earlier conviction would have been relevant to the offence charged, in that both involved attacks on girl guides, the prosecution did not lead evidence of it because of a desire to spare the victim of the earlier crime the ordeal of giving evidence again. In statements to the police about the murder charge, the appellant gave an alibi which was false. Subsequently, he admitted that this alibi was false and put forward a second alibi. The second alibi was almost identical to an alibi which the appellant had advanced at his trial on the earlier rape charge. The similarity extended to details of conversations that the appellant alleged he had had with his wife, which were almost 'word for word' the same. At the trial, the appellant sought to explain his giving the first, false alibi by giving evidence that he had been 'in trouble' with the police. He was cross-examined about the suspicious similarity of his second alibi for the murder to his alibi on what was referred to as 'another occasion'—no details of the previous conviction being revealed to the jury. The appellant appealed on the ground that the cross-examination should not have been permitted.

LORD REID: 'It is well established that the 1898 Act has no application to evidence given by any person other than the accused: where it was competent before that Act for a witness to prove or refer to a previous conviction of the accused, that is still competent. What the Act does is to alter the old rules as regards the accused. It might merely have provided that the accused should be a competent witness; then the ordinary rules would have applied to him. But it goes on to afford to him protection which the ordinary rules would not give him: it expressly prohibits certain kinds of question being put to him. That must mean questions which would be competent and relevant under the ordinary rules, because there was no need to prohibit any question which would in any event have been excluded by the ordinary rules. So what must now be considered is what kinds of question, which would have been competent and relevant under the ordinary rules of evidence, does the Act prohibit. . . .

This raises at once the question what is the proper construction of the words in proviso (e), "tend to criminate him, as to the offence charged." Those words could mean "tend to convince or persuade the jury that he is guilty," or they could have the narrower meaning—"tend to connect him with the commission of the offence charged." If they have the former meaning, there is at once an insoluble conflict between provisos (e) and (f). No line of questioning could be relevant unless it (or the answers to it) might tend to persuade the jury of the guilt of the accused. It is only permissible to bring in previous convictions or bad character if they are so relevant, so, unless proviso (f) is to be deprived of all content, it must prohibit some questions which would tend to criminate the accused of the offence charged if those words are used in the wider sense. But if they have the narrower meaning, there is no such conflict. So the structure of the Act shows that they must have the narrower meaning.

So I turn to consider proviso (f). It is an absolute prohibition of certain questions unless one or other of three conditions is satisfied. It says the accused "shall not be asked, and if asked shall not be required to answer," certain questions. It was suggested that this applies to examination-in-chief as well as to cross-examination. I do not think so. The words "shall not be required to answer" are quite inappropriate for examination-in-chief. The proviso is obviously intended to protect the accused. It does not prevent him from volunteering evidence, and does not in my view prevent his counsel from asking questions leading to disclosure of a previous conviction or bad character if such disclosure is thought to assist in his defence.

The questions prohibited are those which "tend to show" certain things. Does this mean tend to prove or tend to suggest? Here I cannot accept the argument of the Attorney-General. What matters is the effect of the questions on the jury. A veiled suggestion of a previous offence may be just as damaging as a definite statement. In my judgment, "tends to show" means tends to suggest to the jury. But the crucial point in the present case is whether the questions are to be considered in isolation or whether they are to be considered in the light of all that had gone before them at the trial. If the questions or line of questioning has to be considered in isolation I think that the questions with which this appeal is concerned would tend to show at least that the accused had previously been charged with an offence. The jury would be likely to jump to that conclusion, if this was the first they had heard of this matter. But I do not think that the questions ought to be considered in isolation. If the test is the effect the questions would be likely to have on the minds of the jury that necessarily implies that one must have regard to what the jury had already heard. If the jury already knew that the accused had been charged with an offence, a question inferring that he had been charged would add nothing and it would be absurd to prohibit it. If the obvious purpose of this proviso is to protect the accused from possible prejudice, as I think it is, then "show" must mean "reveal", because it is only a revelation of something new which could cause such prejudice.

I shall not detain your Lordships by analysing the questions to which objection is taken to see whether they contained any material revelation of anything which the jury were unlikely to infer from the evidence already given by the accused in chief. I need only refer to the speech about to be delivered by my noble and learned friend, Lord Morris of Borthy-Gest, and to the judgment of the Court of Criminal Appeal. For the reasons which they give, I am of opinion that this appeal should be dismissed on the ground that these questions were not prohibited because they did not "tend to show" any of the matters specified in proviso (f).

But, in case it should be thought that some of the views which I have expressed are not in accord with what was said by Lord Simon in *Stirland* v *Director of Public Prosecutions* [1944] AC 315, I must say something about that case. That was a case where the accused had put his character in issue and the questions which it was held ought not to have been put to him in cross-examination dealt with an occasion when a former employer had questioned him about a suspected forgery. But the case did not turn on proviso (f) because the second exception in the proviso was satisfied by the accused having given evidence of his good character and therefore the proviso was excluded.

Lord Simon did, however, state six rules which should govern cross-examination to credit of an accused person. First he set out proviso (f). Then comes the rule which gives rise to the difficulty: "(ii) He may, however, be cross-examined as to any of the evidence he has given in chief, including statements concerning his good record, with a view to testing his veracity or accuracy or to showing that he is not to be believed on his oath." Applied to a case where the accused has put his character in issue I think that is correct, because then proviso (f) does not apply. But I do not think that Lord Simon can have meant it to apply in its general form to a case where proviso (f) does operate, because earlier in his speech he said [at p. 322]: "This House has laid it down in *Maxwell* v *Director of Public Prosecutions* [1935] AC 309 that, while paragraph (f) of this section absolutely prohibits any question of the kind there indicated being put to the accused in the witness box unless one or other of the conditions (i), (ii) or (iii) is satisfied, it does not follow that such questions are in all circumstances justified whenever one or other of the conditions is fulfilled." Thus he recognised the absolute character of the prohibition except where one or other of the conditions is satisfied, so he cannot have intended to say that there is another case, not covered by the conditions, where the proviso also does not apply, namely, where questions are put with a view to testing the veracity of the accused's evidence in chief. But if he did mean that it was certainly *obiter* and I would not agree with it. It would in effect be legislating by adding a fourth condition to proviso (f). The Attorney-General refused to take this point and I think he was perfectly right.

It is said that the views which I have expressed involve overruling two decisions of the Court of Criminal Appeal, *R* v *Chitson* [1909] 2 KB 945 and *R* v *Kennaway* [1917] 1 KB 25, CCA. I do not think so. I think the decisions were right but the reasons given for them were not. In the former case the accused was charged with having had carnal knowledge of a girl aged 14. Giving evidence, she said that the accused told her that he had previously done the same thing to another girl, who, she said, was under 16. No objection was taken to this evidence, I assume rightly. So before the accused gave evidence the jury already knew that he was alleged to have committed another offence. If the views which I have already expressed are right, cross-examining the accused about this matter disclosed nothing new to them and therefore did not offend against the prohibition in proviso (f). But the judgment of the court was not based on that ground: it was said that although the questions tended to prove that the accused was of bad character they also tended to show that he was guilty of the offence with which he was charged. For the reasons which I have given I do not think that that is sufficient to avoid the prohibition in proviso (f).

R v *Kennaway* was a prosecution for forgery. Accomplices giving evidence for the prosecution described the fraudulent scheme of which the forgery was a part and related a conversation with the accused in which he stated to them that some years earlier he had forged another will in pursuance of a similar scheme. Then in cross-examination the accused was asked a number of questions about this other forgery. Those questions were held to have been properly put to him. Here, again, these questions disclosed nothing new to the jury and I can see no valid objection to them. But again that was not the ground of the court's decision. Their ground of decision was similar to that in *Chitson's* case, and I need not repeat what I have said about that case.'

LORD DENNING: 'My Lords, much of the discussion before your Lordships was directed to the effect of section 1(f) of the Criminal Evidence Act 1898: and, if that were the sole paragraph for consideration, I should have thought that counsel for the Crown ought not to have asked the questions he did. My reasons are these:

First: The questions *tended* to show that Jones had previously been charged in a court of law with another offence. True it is that they did not point definitely to that conclusion, but they conveyed that impression, and that is enough. Counsel may not have intended it, but that does not matter. What matters is the impression the questions would have on the jury. The Attorney-General said that, if the questions left the matter evenly balanced, so that there was some other conclusion that could equally well be drawn, as, for instance, that Jones had not been "charged" in a court of law but had only been interrogated in a police station, there was no bar to the questions being asked. I cannot agree. If the questions asked by the Crown are capable of conveying two impressions—one objectionable and the other not—then they "tend to show" each of them: and the questions must be excluded, lest the jury adopt the worse of the two impressions. I do not think that it is open to the prosecution to throw out prejudicial hints and insinuations— from which a jury might infer that the man had been charged before—and then escape censure under the cloak of ambiguity.

Second: I think that the questions tended to *show* that Jones had been charged with an offence, even though he had himself brought out the fact that he had been "in trouble" before. It is one thing to confess to having been in trouble before. It is quite another to have it emphasised against you with devastating detail. Before these questions were asked by the Crown, all that the jury knew was that at some unspecified time in the near or distant past, this man had been in trouble with the police. After the questions were asked, the jury knew, in addition, that he had been very recently in trouble for an offence on a Friday night which was of so sensational a character that it featured in a newspaper on the following Sunday—in these respects closely similar to the present offence—and that he had been charged in a court of law with that very offence. It seems to me that questions which tend to reveal an offence, thus particularised, are directly within the prohibition in section 1(f) and are not rendered admissible by his own vague disclosure of some other offence. I do not believe that the mere fact that he said he had been in trouble before with the police—referring as he did to an entirely different matter many years past—let in this very damaging cross-examination as to recent events.

Third: The questions do not come within the exception (i) to section 1(f). There was no evidence before the court of any "other offence" which would be admissible evidence to show that he had been guilty of this murder. If the prosecution had given evidence of the previous rape with its attendant circumstances, there might have been such similarities as to render the proof of that offence admissible to prove identity, see *R* v *Straffen* [1952] 2 QB 911: but in the absence of such evidence, I do not see how these questions could be justified in cross-examination under exception (i). Before any cross-examination is permissible under exception (i), the prosecution must lay a proper foundation for it by showing some "other offence which is admissible evidence to show that he is guilty." The prosecution should normally do it by giving evidence in the course of their case; though there may be cases in which they might, with the leave of the judge, do it for the first time in cross-examination. No such foundation was laid here.

If the case rested solely on section 1(f), I would therefore have held that these questions were inadmissible. But I do not think it rests on section 1(f). In my judgment, the questions were admissible under section 1(e), which says that a person charged "may be asked any question in cross-examination notwithstanding that it would tend to criminate him as to the offence charged." As to this subsection, Viscount Sankey LC, speaking for all in this House in *Maxwell's* case, said that under section 1(e) "a witness may be cross-examined in respect of the offence charged, and cannot refuse to answer questions directly relevant to the offence on the ground that they tend to incriminate him: thus if he denies the offence, he may be cross-examined to refute the denial." I would add that, if he gives an explanation in an attempt to exculpate himself, he may be cross-examined to refute his explanation. And nonetheless so because it tends incidentally to show that he had previously been charged with another offence.

Let me first say why I think in this case the questions were directly relevant to the offence charged. They were directly relevant because they tended to refute an explanation which the accused man had given. He had given a detailed explanation of his movements on the crucial weekend, and so forth, all in an attempt to exculpate himself. The prosecution sought to show that this explanation was false: and I think it was of direct relevance for them to do so. From the very earliest times, long before an accused man could give evidence on his own behalf, the law has recognised that, in considering whether a man is guilty of the crime charged against him, one of the most relevant matters is this: What explanation did he give when he was asked about it? Was that explanation true or not? If he gives a true explanation, it tells in his favour. If he gives a false explanation, it tells against him. The prosecution have, therefore, always been entitled, as part of their own case, to give evidence of any explanation given by the accused and of its truth or falsity. Thus if a man, who is found in possession of a stolen watch, tells a policeman that he bought it for £5 from a tradesman whom he names, the prosecution can call that tradesman, as part of their case, to say whether that was true or not. If true, it is an end of the case against the accused. If false, it goes a long way to prove his guilt, see *R* v *Crowhurst* (1844) 1 Car & Kir 370 by Alderson B, *R* v *Henry Smith* (1845) 2 Car & Kir 207 by Lord Denman CJ. So also if a man, who is charged with murder at a specified time and place, tells a policeman that he was at the house of his sister-in-law at the time, as Jones did here, the prosecution can call the sister-in-law, as part of their case, to say it was false and that he was not at her house at all. So also if he tries, as Jones did, to get his sister-in-law to say that he was at her house at that time, contrary to the fact, the prosecution can call the sister-in-law to say that he tried to suborn her to give false testimony: for the simple reason that "the recourse to falsehood leads fairly to an inference of guilt," see

Moriarty v *London, Chatham & Dover Railway Co.* (1870) LR 5 QB 314 by Cockburn CJ. In this very case Jones's sister-in-law, Mrs Eldridge, gave such evidence for the prosecution without any objection being taken to it, even though it tended to show that he was guilty of another offence, namely, the offence of attempting to pervert the course of justice.

Now, suppose the man does this further thing which Jones did here. He discards the story that he went to his sister-in-law's house and puts forward a different story. He says that he went up to London and was with a prostitute, but he does not identify her. So the prostitute cannot be called to falsify his story. Nevertheless the prosecution can falsify it by other evidence, if they have it available. They can call such evidence as part of their own case, even though it tends incidentally to show that he was guilty of another offence. For instance, they could prove that his finger-prints were on the window of a house that was broken into at Yateley that night. ". . . the mere fact that the evidence adduced tends to show the commission of other crimes does not render it inadmissible if it be relevant to an issue before the jury," see *Makin* v *Attorney-General of New South Wales* [1894] AC 57. Evidence that he had committed burglary would not be admissible to prove that he had committed murder: but evidence that he was at Yateley would be admissible to prove that he was in the vicinity and had recourse to falsehood to explain his whereabouts. The prosecution would be entitled to call this evidence, even though it tended to show that he was guilty of burglary.

Such is the law as it is, and always has been, as to the evidence which can be called for the prosecution. They can, in the first place, give evidence of any explanation given by the accused of his movements and they can, in the second place, give evidence that his explanation is false, even though it tends incidentally to show the commission by him of some other offence. Now, when Parliament in 1898 enabled an accused man to give evidence on his own behalf, they did not cut down evidence of this kind for the prosecution. And when the prosecution gives such evidence, it must be open to the accused man himself to answer it. He must be able to give evidence about it and to be cross-examined upon it. He can be cross-examined as to any explanation he has given and as to its truth or falsity: and he can be cross-examined upon it nonetheless because incidentally it may tend to show that he has been guilty of some other offence.

No one, surely, can doubt the validity of *R* v *Chitson* [1909] 2 KB 945, and *R* v *Kennaway* [1917] 1 KB 25 at least to this extent, that when the prosecution have legitimately given in evidence any explanation or statement made by the accused relative to the offence charged, he can be cross-examined as to the truth or falsity of it, even though incidentally it may tend to show that he has been guilty of some other offence or is of bad character.

Now, the only difference is that, whereas in those cases the accused man made his explanation or statement *before* the trial, in the present case he made his explanation (about his conversations with his wife, and so forth) for the first time *at* the trial when he went into the witness box to give evidence on his own behalf. But this cannot give him any protection from a cross-examination to which he would otherwise be exposed. His explanation is not made sacrosanct, it is not made incapable of challenge, simply because he gives it at the trial instead of at an earlier stage. The prosecution are entitled to expose its falsity, no matter whether he gives it at the trial or beforehand. And they are not precluded from doing so merely because the exposure of it tends to show that he has been guilty of some other offence or is of bad character. The situation is precisely covered by the second proposition in *Stirland's* case [1944] AC 315 where Viscount Simon LC, in this

House, with the assent of all present, said that, notwithstanding the prohibition in section 1(f), the accused man "may, however, be cross-examined as to any of the evidence he has given in chief, including statements concerning his good record," and including, I would add, any explanation offered by him, "with a view to testing his veracity or accuracy or to showing that he is not to be believed on his oath."

It is noteworthy that everyone at the trial of Jones acted on this view of the law. No one suggested that the questions were absolutely prohibited. All that was suggested was that it was a matter of discretion. And that is, I think, the true position. The judge was entitled in his discretion to exclude them if he thought they were so prejudicial as to outweigh their probative value. It was his discretion, not that of the prosecution. He did not exclude them but permitted them to be asked. They were, therefore, properly put.

In conclusion I would say that I view with concern the suggestion that the reasoning in *R* v *Chitson* and *R* v *Kennaway* was wrong and that what Viscount Simon LC said in *Stirland* v *DPP* is no longer a safe guide. Those cases have governed the practice in our criminal courts for years: and the result has been wholly beneficial. It is not, in my opinion, right to resort now to a literal reading of the Act so as to displace them.'

LORD MORRIS OF BORTH-Y-GEST: 'My Lords, it seems to me that the clearest guidance as to provisos (e) and (f) was given in *Maxwell's* case. In his speech, Viscount Sankey LC said: "In section 1, proviso (e), it has been enacted that a witness may be cross-examined in respect of the offence charged, and cannot refuse to answer questions directly relevant to the offence on the ground that they tend to incriminate him: thus if he denies the offence, he may be cross-examined to refute the denial. These are matters directly relevant to the charge on which he is being tried. Proviso (f), however, is dealing with matters outside, and not directly relevant to, the particular offence charged; such matters, to be admissible at all, must in general fall under two main classes: one is the class of evidence which goes to show not that the prisoner did the acts charged, but that, if he did these acts, he did them as part of a system or intentionally, so as to refute a defence that if he did them he did them innocently or inadvertently, as for instance in *Makin* v *Attorney-General for New South Wales* [1894] AC 57, where the charge was one of murder; another illustration of such cases is *R* v *Bond* [1906] 2 KB 389. This rule applies to cases where guilty knowledge or design or intention is of the essence of the offence.

The other main class is where it is sought to show that the prisoner is not a person to be believed on his oath, which is generally attempted by what is called cross-examination to credit. Closely allied with this latter type of question is the rule that, if the prisoner by himself or his witnesses seeks to give evidence of his own good character, for the purpose of showing that it is unlikely that he committed the offence charged, he raises by way of defence an issue as to his good character, so that he may fairly be cross-examined on that issue, just as any witness called by him to prove his good character may be cross-examined to show the contrary. All these matters are dealt with in proviso (f). . .".

In his speech in *Stirland* v *Director of Public Prosecutions* Viscount Simon LC said that he was disposed to think that in (f), where the word "character" occurs four times, there is a combination of the conceptions of general reputation and of actual moral disposition.

Having regard to what has been laid down in *Maxwell's* case and in *Stirland's* case, I do not find it necessary to embark upon "a close study and comparison" of earlier cases such as *R* v *Chitson* and *R* v *Kennaway*. If the results reached in those cases can be supported it must not be on any line of reasoning that runs counter to what has been laid down in *Maxwell's* case and in *Stirland's* case.'

LORD DEVLIN: 'My Lords, I would dismiss this appeal on the short ground that the questions objected to were relevant to an issue in the case upon which the appellant had testified in chief. It is not disputed that the issue to which the questions related was a relevant one. It concerned the identification of the appellant as being at the material time at the scene of the crime. He testified that at the material time he was with a prostitute in the West End and he supported this alibi by giving evidence of a conversation which he had with his wife about it a day or two later. The purpose of the questions objected to was to obtain from the appellant an admission (which was given) that when he was being questioned about his movements in relation to another incident some weeks earlier he had set up the same alibi and had supported it with an account of a conversation with his wife in almost identical terms; the prosecution suggested that these similarities showed the whole story of the alibi to be an invented one. . ..'

(VISCOUNT SIMONDS delivered a judgment agreeing with LORD REID and LORD MORRIS of BORTH-Y-GEST.)

Appeal dismissed.

Referring to the Criminal Evidence Act 1898 s. 1(e) and (f) Professor J C Smith ([1962] Crim LR 244) said:

Proviso (e) provides that the accused may be asked '*any question* in cross-examination notwithstanding that it would tend to criminate him as to the offence charged'. Proviso (f) provides that he shall not be asked, *inter alia*, any question tending to show that he has committed or been convicted of any other offence. Now it is apparent that a question which shows that the accused has committed or been convicted of some other offence may also tend to criminate him as to the offence charged. Proviso (e) apparently allows such a question, proviso (f) apparently forbids it. One or other must give way.

• How did the House of Lords in *Jones* v *DPP* deal with this problem?

Selvey v DPP [1970] AC 304 (HL)

The appellant was charged with buggery. There was medical evidence that the complainant had been sexually interfered with by someone on the day in question, and also indecent photographs were found in the appellant's room. The defence was that the complainant had told him that he had already "been on the bed" with a man for £1 and that he would do the same for him for £1. The appellant denied knowledge of the photographs and suggested that they had been planted on him by the complainant in annoyance at the rejection of the offer. The trial judge allowed the appellant to be cross-examined on his previous convictions for homosexual offences. The appellant was convicted and appealed on the ground, *inter alia*, that as the nature of his defence necessarily involved the imputation against the complainant, the judge in accordance with 'the general rule' should have exercised his discretion under s. 1(f)(ii) of the Criminal Evidence Act 1898, in his favour by excluding his previous record.

VISCOUNT DILHORNE: 'The cases to which I have referred, some of which it is not possible to reconcile, in my opinion finally establish the following propositions:

(1)   The words of the statute must be given their ordinary natural meaning (*R* v *Hudson* [1912] 2 KB 464; *R* v *Jenkins* (1945) 31 Cr App R 1; *R* v *Cook* [1959] 2 QB 340).

(2)   The section permits cross-examination of the accused as to character both when imputations on the character of the prosecutor and his witness are cast to show their unreliability as witnesses independently of the evidence given by them and also when the casting of such imputations is necessary to enable the accused to establish his defence (*R* v *Hudson*; *R* v *Jenkins*; *R* v *Cook*).

(3)   In rape cases the accused can allege consent without placing himself in peril of such cross-examination (*R* v *Sheean*, 21 Cox CC 561; *R* v *Turner* [1944] KB 463). This may be because such cases are *sui generis* (per Devlin J in *R* v *Cook* [1959] 2 QB 340, 347), or on the ground that the issue is one raised by the prosecution.

(4)   If what is said amounts in reality to no more than a denial of the charge, expressed, it may be, in emphatic language, it should not be regarded as coming within the section (*R* v *Rouse* [1904] 1 KB 184; *R* v *Grout* (1909) 3 Cr App R 64; *R* v *Jones* (1923) 17 Cr App R 117; *R* v *Clark* [1955] 2 QB 469).

Applying these propositions to this case, it is in my opinion clear beyond all doubt that the cross-examination of the accused was permissible under the statute.

I now turn to the question whether a judge has discretion to refuse to permit such cross-examination of the accused even when it is permissible under the section. Mr Caulfield submitted that there was no such discretion and contended that a judge at a criminal trial had no power to exclude evidence which was admissible. He submitted that the position was correctly stated by Bankes J in *R* v *Fletcher* (1913) 9 Cr App R 53, 56, when he said:

> Where the judge entertains a doubt as to the admissibility of evidence, he may suggest to the prosecution that they should not press it, but he cannot exclude evidence which he holds to be admissible.

Since that case it has been said in many cases that a judge has such a discretion. In *R* v *Christie* [1914] AC 545 where the question was as to the admissibility of a statement made in the presence and hearing of the accused, Lord Moulton said, at p. 559:

> Now, in a civil action evidence may always be given of any statement or communication made to the opposite party, provided it is relevant to the issues. The same is true of any act or behaviour of the party. The sole limitation is that the matter thus given in evidence must be relevant. I am of opinion that, as a strict matter of law, there is no difference in this respect between the rules of evidence in our civil and in our criminal procedure. But there is a great difference in the practice. The law is so much on its guard against the accused being prejudiced by evidence which, though admissible, would probably have a prejudicial influence on the minds of the jury which would be out of proportion to its true evidential value, that there has grown up a practice of a very salutary nature, under which the judge intimates to the counsel for the prosecution that he should not press for the admission of evidence which would be open to this objection, and such an intimation from the tribunal trying the case is usually sufficient to prevent the evidence being pressed in all cases where the scruples of the tribunal in this respect are reasonable. Under the influence of this practice, which is based on an anxiety to secure for everyone a fair trial, there has grown up a custom of not admitting

certain kinds of evidence which is so constantly followed that it almost amounts to a rule of procedure.

In *R* v *Watson*, 8 Cr App R 249, 254, the first case when the exercise of discretion in relation to cases coming within the section was mentioned, Pickford J said: "It has been pointed out that to apply the rule" [in *R* v *Hudson* [1912] 2 KB 464] "strictly is to put a hardship on a prisoner with a bad character. That may be so, but it does not follow that a judge necessarily allows the prisoner to be cross-examined to character; he has a discretion not to allow it, and the prisoner has that protection." In *Maxwell* [1935] AC 309 and in *Stirland* [1944] AC 315 it was said in this House that a judge has that discretion. In *R* v *Jenkins*, 31 Cr App R 1, 15, Singleton J said:

If and when such a situation arises [the question whether the accused should be cross-examined as to character] it is open to counsel to apply to the presiding judge that he may be allowed to take the course indicated . . . Such an application will not always be granted, for the judge has a discretion in the matter. He may feel that even though the position is established in law, still the putting of such questions as to the character of the accused person may be fraught with results which immeasurably outweigh the result of questions put by the defence and which make a fair trial of the accused person almost impossible. On the other hand, in the ordinary and normal case he may feel that if the credit of the prosecutor or his witnesses has been attacked, it is only fair that the jury should have before them material on which they can form their judgment whether the accused person is any more worthy to be believed than those he has attacked. It is obviously unfair that the jury should be left in the dark about an accused person's character if the conduct of his defence has attacked the character of the prosecutor or the witnesses for the prosecution within the meaning of the section. The essential thing is a fair trial and that the legislature sought to ensure by section 1, subsection (f).

Similar views were expressed in *Noor Mohamed* v *The King* [1949] AC 182 by Lord du Parcq, in *Harris* v *Director of Public Prosecutions* [1952] AC 594, in *R* v *Cook* [1959] 2 QB 340, in *Jones* v *Director of Public Prosecutions* [1962] AC 635, and in other cases.

In the light of what was said in all these cases by judges of great eminence, one is tempted to say, as Lord Hewart said in *R* v *Dunkley* [1927] 1 KB 323 that it is far too late in the day even to consider the argument that a judge has no such discretion. Let it suffice for me to say that in my opinion the existence of such a discretion is now clearly established.

Mr Caulfield posed the question, on what principles should such a discretion be exercised. In *R* v *Flynn* [1963] 1 QB 729, 737 the court said:

. . . where . . . the very nature of the defence necessarily involves an imputation, against a prosecution witness or witnesses, the discretion should, in the opinion of this Court, be as a general rule exercised in favour of the accused, that is to say, evidence as to his bad character or criminal record should be excluded. If it were otherwise, it comes to this, that the Act of 1898, the very Act which gave the charter, so to speak, to an accused person to give evidence on oath in the witness box, would be a mere trap because he would be unable to put forward any defence, no matter how true, which involved an imputation on the character of the prosecutor or any of his witnesses, without running the risk, if he had the misfortune to have a record, of his previous convictions being brought up in court while being tried on a wholly different matter.

No authority is given for this supposed general rule. In my opinion, the court was wrong in thinking that there was any such rule. If there was any such general rule, it would amount under the guise of the exercise of discretion, to the insertion of a proviso to the statute of the very kind that was said in *R* v *Hudson* [1912] 2 KB 464 not to be legitimate.

I do not think it possible to improve upon the guidance given by Singleton J in the passage quoted above from *R* v *Jenkins*, 31 Cr App R 1, 15, by Lord du Parcq in *Noor Mohamed* [1949] AC 182 or by Devlin J, in *R* v *Cook* [1959] 2 QB 340 as to the matters which should be borne in mind in relation to the exercise of the discretion. It is now so well established that on a charge of rape the allegation that the woman consented, although involving an imputation on her character, should not expose an accused to cross-examination as to character, that it is possible to say, if the refusal to allow it is a matter of discretion, that there is a general rule that the discretion should be so exercised. Apart from this, there is not, I think, any general rule as to the exercise of discretion. It must depend on the circumstances of each case and the overriding duty of the judge to ensure that a trial is fair.

It is desirable that a warning should be given when it becomes apparent that the defence is taking a course which may expose the accused to such cross-examination. That was not given in this case but the failure to give such a warning would not, in my opinion, justify in this case the allowing of the appeal.'

LORD GUEST: 'If I had thought that there was no discretion in English law for a judge to disallow admissible evidence, as counsel for the Crown argued, I should have striven hard and long to give a benevolent construction to section 1(f)(ii), which would exclude such cases as *R* v *Rouse* [1904] 1 KB 184, "liar," *R* v *Rappolt*, 6 Cr App R 156, "horrible liar," *R* v *Jones*, 17 Cr App R 117, "fabricated evidence," *R* v *Turner* [1944] KB 463, rape and other sexual offences, *R* v *Brown* (1960) 44 Cr App R 181, "self defence." I cannot believe that Parliament can have intended that in such cases an accused could only put forward such a defence at peril of having his character put before the jury. This would be to defeat the benevolent purposes of the 1898 Act which was for the first time to allow the accused to give evidence on his own behalf in all criminal cases. This would deprive the accused of the advantage of the Act. But I am not persuaded by the Crown's argument and I am satisfied upon a review of all the authorities that in English law such a discretion does exist. It was exercised for the first time in relation to this section in *R* v *Watson*, 8 Cr App R 249. Discretion as such has the general blessing of Lord Moulton in *R* v *Christie* [1914] AC 545 and thereafter it has been the uniform practice of judges to exercise it in this class of case. Discretion was recognised in this House in *Maxwell* v *Director of Public Prosecutions* [1935] AC 309; *Stirland* [1944] AC 315; *Harris* v *Director of Public Prosecutions* [1952] AC 694; and *Jones* v *Director of Public Prosecutions* [1962] AC 635. And in the Privy Council in *Noor Mohamed* v *The King* [1949] AC 182 and *Kuruma* [1955] AC 197. In face of this long established practice it is, in my opinion, now too late to say that the judge has no discretion. While I leave to others more versed than I am in English criminal law and practice to discuss the origin of this discretion, I would assume that it springs from the inherent power of the judge to control the trial before him and to see that justice is done in fairness to the accused . . .

I find it unnecessary to say much more on the principles upon which discretion should be exercised. The guiding star should be fairness to the accused. This idea is best expressed by Devlin J in *R* v *Cook* [1959] 2 QB 340. In following this star the fact that the imputation was a necessary part of the accused's defence is a consideration which will no doubt be taken into account by the trial judge. If, however, the accused or his counsel goes beyond developing his defence in order to blacken the character of a prosecution witness, this no doubt will be another factor to be taken into account. If it is suggested that the exercise of this discretion may be whimsical and depend on the individual idiosyncrasies of the judge, this is inevitable where it is a question of discretion; but I am satisfied that this is a lesser risk than attempting to shackle the judge's power within a straitjacket.'

LORD PEARCE: 'My Lords, ever since the Criminal Evidence Act, 1898, came into force there has been difficulty and argument about the application of the words in section 1(f)(ii) "the nature or conduct of the defence is such as to involve imputations on the character of the prosecutor or the witnesses for the prosecution."

Two main views have been put forward. One view adopts the literal meaning of the words. The prosecutor is cross-examined to show that he has fabricated the charge for improper reasons. That involves imputations on his character. Therefore, it lets in the previous convictions of the accused. The practical justification for this view is the "tit for tat" argument. If the accused is seeking to cast discredit on the prosecution, then the prosecution should be allowed to do likewise. If the accused is seeking to persuade the jury that the prosecutor behaved like a knave, then the jury should know the character of the man who makes these accusations, so that it may judge fairly between them instead of being in the dark as to one of them.

The other view would limit the literal meaning of the words. For it cannot, it is said, have been intended by Parliament to make a man liable to have his previous convictions revealed whenever the essence of his defence necessitates imputations on the character of the prosecutor. This revelation is always damaging and often fatal to a defence. The high-water mark of this argument is the ordinary case of rape. In this the vital issue (as a rule) is whether the woman consented. Consent (as a rule) involves imputations on her character. Therefore, in the ordinary case of rape, the accused cannot defend himself without letting in his previous convictions. The same argument extends in varying degrees to many cases.

The argument in favour of a construction more liberal to the accused is supported in two ways.

First, it is said that character is used in the sense in which it was used in *R* v *Rowton*, 10 Cox CC 25, where the full court ruled that evidence of good character must be limited solely to general reputation and not to a man's actual disposition; and no imputation on the prosecutor's general reputation is involved by allegations that he acted as a knave in matters relevant to the offence charged. So far as the meaning of "character" is concerned, there is much force in this argument. It would accord with the word "character" as used three times previously in the same subsection. See the judgment delivered by Lord Hewart CJ in *R* v *Dunkley* [1927] 1 KB 323, 329, where the argument was described as formidable but was rejected:

Nevertheless, when one looks at the long line of cases beginning very shortly after the passing of the Criminal Evidence Act, 1898, it does not appear that that argument has ever been so much as formulated. It was formulated yesterday. One can only say that it is now much too late in the day even to consider that argument, because that argument could not now prevail without the revision, and indeed to a great extent the overthrow, of a very long series of decisions.

A similar view was expressed by Lord Denning in *Jones* v *Director of Public Prosecutions* [1962] AC 635, 671 (see also Lord Devlin, at p. 709), a case which dealt with a kindred problem under section 1(f)(i). Viscount Simon, however, in *Stirland* v *Director of Public Prosecutions* [1944] AC 315, 325, after discussing the two conceptions, that is reputation and real disposition, said "I am disposed to think that in para (f) (where the word 'character' occurs four times) both conceptions are combined."

Late as it may be, it might be justifiable to consider whether "character" means in the context solely general reputation, if a reassessment could lead to any clarification of the problem. But in my opinion it leads nowhere. For I cannot accept the proposition that to accuse a person of a particular knavery does not involve imputations on his general reputation. The words "involve" and "imputations" are wide. It would be playing with words to say that the allegation of really discreditable matters does not involve imputations on his general reputation, if only as showing how erroneous that reputation must be. The argument is, however, a valuable reminder that the Act is intending serious and not trivial imputations.

The second part of the argument in favour of a construction more liberal to the accused is concerned with the words "the conduct or nature of the defence." One should, it can be argued, read conduct or nature as something superimposed on the essence of the defence itself. In *O'Hara* v *HM Advocate* 1948 SC (J) 90, 98, the learned Lord Justice-Clerk (Lord Thomson), after a careful review of the English cases, construed "conduct" as meaning the actual handling of the case by the accused or his advocate. He found difficulty with "nature" but said: "But the more general considerations which I have mentioned persuade me to the view that 'nature' is to be read, not as meaning something which is inherent in the defence, but as referable to the mechanism of the defence; nature being the strategy of the defence and conduct the tactics." This argument has obvious force, particularly in a case of rape, where the allegation of consent is in truth no more than a mere traverse of the essential ingredient which the Crown have to prove, namely, want of consent. But the argument does not, and I think cannot, fairly stop short of contending that *all* matters which are relevant to the crime, that is, of which rebutting evidence could be proved, are excluded from the words "conduct or nature of the defence."

To take the present case as an example, the evidence having established physical signs on the victim of the alleged offence, his admission that he had previously committed it with somebody else was relevant. So, too, was his admission that he had been paid £1 for it, since, when the conversation was relevant, it could not be right to bowdlerise it. And, therefore, it is said, the putting of the allegation in cross-examination and the evidence given by the accused was an essentially relevant part of the defence and therefore was not within the words "the nature or conduct of the defence." If Mr Jeremy Hutchison's forceful argument on the proper construction of the subsection is right, the story told by the accused did not let in the convictions.

So large a gloss upon the words is not easy to justify, even if one were convinced that it necessarily produced a fair and proper result which Parliament intended. But there are two sides to the matter. So liberal a shield for an accused is in many cases unfair to a prosecution. Provided it is all linked up to the defence put forward by an accused there would be no limit to the amount of mud which could be thrown against an unshielded prosecutor while the accused could still crouch behind his own shield.'

(LORD HODSON delivered a concurring judgment. LORD WILBERFORCE agreed with LORD PEARCE.)

Appeal dismissed.

- In view of the purpose for which cross-examination is allowed under the second limb of s. 1(f)(ii), does it strike you as odd that in *Selvey* v *DPP* the trial judge should allow the prosecution to cross-examine the accused on his previous convictions for dishonesty?

R v *Bishop* [1975] QB 274 (CA)

On a charge of burglary, the defendant sought to explain his presence in a room where his fingerprints were found by alleging that he had had a homosexual relationship with the occupier, who was a witness for the prosecution. The prosecution were allowed to cross-examine the defendant about his previous convictions for offences of dishonesty and he was convicted.

STEPHENSON LJ, reading the judgment of the court: 'Mr Bate submitted that in these progressive (or permissive) days it was no longer an imputation on a man's character to say of him that he was a homosexual or that he practised homosexuality. Since 1967, when section 1 of the Sexual Offences Act 1967 became law, it was no longer an offence to commit a homosexual act with another man of full age in private. No reasonable person would now think the worse of a man who committed such acts; he might not wish to associate with him but he would not condemn him. We think that this argument goes too far and that the gap between what is declared by Parliament to be illegal and punishable and what the common man or woman still regards as immoral or wrong is not wide enough to support it. Most men would be anxious to keep from a jury in any case the knowledge that they practised such acts and many would be debarred from going to the police to charge another with any offence if they thought that he might defend himself by making such an allegation, whether baseless or not. If this is still true, we are not behind the times in holding that Mr Price's character was clearly impugned by the allegation of homosexual conduct made against him by the defendant.

Then it is contended that even if the allegation reflects upon his character, it does not reflect upon his integrity, his honesty or his reliability so that he is thereby rendered less likely to be a truthful witness, or if in fact it has that effect it was not made with that intention.

Mr Bate says that the defendant's allegation against Mr Price was made not for the purpose of discrediting his testimony but for the purpose of explaining his presence in Mr Price's room.

We do not consider that this argument can succeed against the plain words of section 1(f)(ii) given their natural and ordinary meaning. If we give them that meaning, as we are now required to do by the House of Lords in *Selvey's* case (see for instance what Viscount Dilhorne said [1970] AC 304, 339), they cannot be restricted in the way suggested by the words of the judgment which we have just quoted. Though we agree that the general nature of the Act and the general principle underlying it are as there stated we do not accept the submission that an imputation of homosexual immorality against a witness may not reflect upon his reliability—generally or in the witness box; nor do we accept the submission that a defendant can attack the character of a witness without risk of the jury's learning that his own character is bad by disclaiming any intention to discredit the witness's testimony. Such a construction of the section would enable many guilty men to resort to variations of "the Portsmouth defence" with success by unfairly keeping the jury in ignorance of their true character and would fly in the face of the decision in *Selvey's* case to strip the plain words of section 1(f)(ii) of the gloss put upon them in earlier cases.

'. . . Once it is conceded, as Mr Bate rightly conceded, that an imputation on character covers charges of faults or vices, whether reputed or real, which are not criminal offences it is difficult to restrict the statutory exception of s. 1(f)(ii) in any such way as has been suggested on behalf of the defendant.'

Appeal dismissed.

R v *Britzmann and Hall* [1983] 1 WLR 350 (CA)

A woman telephoned the police after she discovered that her writing bureau had been opened and damaged by one of two men who had entered her house, posing as water board employees. The police stopped and arrested Britzmann and Hall, who fitted the descriptions given by the woman, although at a subsequent identification parade she did not pick them out. Britzmann and Hall were charged with burglary. At their trial, police officers gave evidence of what Britzmann had said during interviews after his arrest, and when shouting to Hall while they were in their cells, from which guilt could be inferred. Britzmann's evidence was that those conversations had not taken place and that the officers must have been mistaken. The judge granted the prosecution leave to cross-examine Britzmann upon his previous convictions under section 1(f)(ii) of the Criminal Evidence Act 1898. Britzmann and Hall were convicted and appealed.

LAWTON LJ, reading the judgment of the court: 'Mr Ingram, who appeared for Britzmann and who is an experienced advocate in criminal cases, appreciated that putting his client's case to these police officers in cross-examination, as he had to do, was like walking through a legal minefield, because of the provisions of section 1(f)(ii) of the Criminal Evidence Act 1898. It is clear from the way Britzmann gave his evidence that he too knew of the dangers, perhaps because his acquaintance with the criminal courts was longer than that of his counsel.

Any denial that the conversations had taken place at all necessarily meant by implication that the police officers had given false evidence which they had made up in order to get the appellants convicted. On the facts of this case there could be no question of mistake, misunderstanding or confusion. If Detective Inspector Whyte and Detective Constable Boal had made up this story, they had conspired together to commit perjury and had committed it. Detective Constable Self must have committed perjury when giving evidence about the alleged conversation on May 29, and Detective Constable Boal must have done the same about the cell conversation. The conversation on June 1 about which two officers gave evidence was long and of a kind which could have appeared in a television film script for a crime series.

A defence to a criminal charge which suggests that prosecution witnesses have deliberately made up false evidence in order to secure a conviction must involve imputations on the characters of those witnesses with the consequence that the trial judge may, in the exercise of his discretion, allow prosecuting counsel to cross-examine the defendant about offences of which he has been convicted. In our judgment this is what Parliament intended should happen in most cases. When allegations of the fabrication of evidence are made against prosecution witnesses, as they often are these days, juries are entitled to know about the characters of those making them.

The duty of the judge in such cases to exercise a discretion whether to allow prosecuting counsel to cross-examine a defendant about previous convictions puts defending counsel in a difficulty because some judges, so Mr Ingram told us and we accept from our own experience when we were at the Bar, will exercise their discretion in favour of the defendant if either he or his counsel avoids making specific allegations of misconduct. This practice has a long history and support for it can be found in *R* v *Clark* [1955] 2 QB 469 and *R* v *Jones (William)* (1923) 17 Cr App R 117. With such judges a suggestion that a witness is mistaken or has misunderstood usually attracts a favourable exercise of discretion.

Britzmann seems to have thought that Mr Recorder Titheridge might be such a judge, because he said in evidence that Detective Inspector Whyte had been mistaken in thinking that he had said what he was alleged to have done on June 1. Mr Ingram in cross-examination contented himself with suggesting to the officers that the alleged conversations had not taken place at all.

Mr Recorder Titheridge would have none of this delicate forensic language. When prosecuting counsel applied for leave to cross-examine Britzmann about his previous convictions he ruled that he could do so. He gave a reasoned ruling, the essence of which is contained in the following passage:

> In my judgment, the delicacy with which cross-examination was conducted on behalf of this defendant cannot hide the basic commonsense position, which is this; there is no room for error or mistake; it must be clear to the jury that the only real issue for their consideration, although, I repeat, it has never been so put to these police officers, that the only real issue for their consideration is whether the statements were made, or in the case of the conversation between the two defendants whether the conversation took place, or whether those officers have made them up: there is simply no other possibility.

Mr Ingram submitted that this ruling was wrong, because the defence amounted in reality to no more than a denial of the charge. In putting his case in that way he adopted what Viscount Dilhorne had said in *Selvey* v *DPP* [1970] AC 304, 339.

In our judgment the nature and conduct of the defence did involve imputations on the characters of the three officers, despite the delicacy of Britzmann's language and the forensic skill of Mr Ingram. The jury had to decide whether these officers had made up what they alleged had been said. If in any case that is the reality of the position and would be seen by a jury to be so, there is no room for drawing a distinction between a defence which is so conducted as to make specific allegations of fabrication and one in which the allegation arises by way of necessary and reasonable implication. Nor can any distinction be validly drawn between an allegation to commit perjury and one of conspiring to commit perjury; but when the allegation is one of perjury, discretion may have to be exercised in favour of the defendant more readily than with a conspiracy allegation, having regard to what was said by Viscount Dilhorne in *Selvey* v *DPP*.

This opinion is in accord with two decisions of this court, namely *R* v *Tanner* (1977) 66 Cr App R 56 and *R* v *McGee and Cassidy* (1980) 70 Cr App R 247. In *R* v *Tanner*, in a reserved judgment, Browne LJ said, at p. 64:

> In some cases the distinction may be a very narrow one, but that it exists in principle is clear. The decision whether a case is on one side of the line or the other must depend on the facts of each particular case. In our judgment, the nature and conduct of the defence in the present case did involve imputations on the character of the police officers. This was not a case of a denial of a single answer, nor was there any suggestion or possibility of mistake or misunderstanding. The appellant was denying not only his admission,

but in the case of each interview a series of subsequent important answers attributed to him by the police. In spite of [defending counsel's] skilful handling of the cross-examination of the police officers, and of the defendant's evidence-in-chief, it necessarily followed, in the circumstances of this case, that the appellant was saying impliedly that the police officers had made up a substantial and vital part of their evidence and that [the two] had conspired together to do so. He also said expressly that one of the police officers said that if he admitted the offence he would get bail. The judge's interventions were, in our judgment, merely bringing into the open what was already necessarily implicit.

That passage applies aptly to this case.

In *R v Nelson (G)* (1979) 68 Cr App R 12, which was decided about 12 months after *R v Tanner*, this court came to a different conclusion. Two grounds for this decision were given, both purporting to be based on the second of the propositions set out in Viscount Dilhorne's speech in *Selvey v DPP* [1970] AC 304, 339. The first was that the attempt to demonstrate a detective constable's unreliability as to a disputed interview was not based on any matter independent of his evidence. That ground will not apply in this case to the interview of June 1, to which Detective Inspector Whyte and Detective Constable Boal spoke, since each gave evidence of what had happened. The second ground was that the appellant's case was that the cross-examination was only directed at supporting his denials of the contents of the disputed interview: it was not directed at casting imputations to establish a defence. Without the challenge he had no defence as he was alleged to have confessed. We prefer the decisions in *R v Tanner* and *R v McGee* to that in *R v Nelson (Gerrard)*. In our judgment the recorder's ruling was right.

In deciding as we have, we have not overlooked the potentiality of unfairness to defendants with previous convictions which a rigid application of section 1(f)(ii) of the Act of 1898 would cause and the difficulties in advising and deciding tactics which defending counsel have. No doubt it was appreciation of the potentiality of unfairness to defendants which led the House of Lords in *Selvey v DPP* [1970] AC 304 to reject the Crown's submission in that case that judges had no discretion to refuse leave to cross-examine about previous convictions.

We hope that it will be helpful for both judges and counsel if we set out some guidelines for the exercise of discretion in favour of defendants. First, it should be used if there is nothing more than a denial, however emphatic or offensively made, of an act or even a short series of acts amounting to one incident or in what was said to have been a short interview. Examples are provided by the kind of evidence given in pickpocket cases and where the defendant is alleged to have said: "Who grassed on me this time?" The position would be different however if there were a denial of evidence of a long period of detailed observation extending over hours and just as in this case and in *R v Tanner*, 66 Cr App R 56 where there were denials of long conversations.

Secondly, cross-examination should only be allowed if the judge is sure that there is no possibility of mistake, misunderstanding or confusion and that the jury will inevitably have to decide whether the prosecution witnesses have fabricated evidence. Defendants sometimes make wild allegations when giving evidence. Allowance should be made for the strain of being in the witness box and the exaggerated use of language which sometimes results from such strain or lack of education or mental instability. Particular care should be used when a defendant is led into making allegations during cross-examination. The defendant who, during cross-examination, is driven to explaining away the evidence by saying it has been made up or planted on him usually convicts himself without having his previous convictions brought out. Finally, there is no need for the prosecution to rely upon section 1(f)(ii) if the evidence against a defendant is overwhelming.'

Appeals dismissed.

• Why should there be any difference between a denial of a brief incriminating statement and a denial of a long and detailed interrogation if in both cases the accused implies perjury by the police?

• Of what practical value are the guidelines laid down by Lawton LJ?

R v *Watts* [1983] 3 All ER 101 (CA)

The appellant, who was of low intelligence and had two previous convictions for sexual offences against children, was interviewed by the police after a young married woman was indecently assaulted near his home by a man whose description fitted the appellant. The appellant made plain admissions to the police both orally and in a statement and he was later charged with the indecent assault. At his trial he advanced an alibi defence and in effect claimed that the police had fabricated the admission evidence. The prosecution then sought, and was granted, leave pursuant to section 1(f)(ii) of the Criminal Evidence Act 1898 to cross-examine him as to his previous convictions. The jury found him guilty of the offence. The appellant appealed, contending that the judge had wrongly exercised his discretion by allowing the cross-examination as to previous convictions.

LORD LANE CJ, delivering the judgment of the court: 'There is no doubt that the law on this particular topic is in an unhappy state. There are numerous decisions of this court and of the House of Lords to the effect that the only relevance of the previous convictions of the defendant admitted by virtue of s. 1 of the Criminal Evidence Act 1898, is as to the credibility of the prisoner, and that the jury must not be asked to infer guilt from such convictions. This in many cases requires the jury to perform difficult feats of intellectual acrobatics. In the view of this court the present case is a good example.

We have been referred to a number of authorities, amongst them *R* v *France* [1979] Crim LR 48 and a further decision of this court, *R* v *Duncalf* [1979] 2 All ER 1116, [1979] 1 WLR 918. We have had the opportunity of seeing a transcript of the judgment in *R* v *France* and it is quite plain that the text is corrupt. There are a number of obvious misprints and mistakes. The transcript was not apparently approved by the judge who delivered the judgment, and we view *R* v *France* therefore with considerable suspicion.

In any event it seems to us that where the exercise of discretion is concerned, which is the problem here, each case is a case on its own and has to be considered on its own particular facts.

The jury in the present case was charged with deciding the guilt or innocence of a man against whom an allegation of indecent assault on a woman was made. They were told that he had previous convictions for indecent assaults of a more serious kind on young girls. They were warned that such evidence was not to be taken as making it more likely that he was guilty of the offence charged, which it seems it plainly did, but only as affecting his credibility, which it almost certainly did not.

The passage in which the judge directed the jury to that effect runs as follows:

And then his previous offences were put to him, members of the jury. And of course you will not use that knowledge in any way as being evidence against him of committing this offence. It is not. The fact that a person has committed an offence on a previous occasion does not make him any more or less likely to be guilty of committing an offence on a subsequent occasion. It is not evidence. It was only allowed to be brought to your knowledge because of the serious allegations of misconduct which are made by the defendant, albeit he is a man of low intelligence, against the police. You are entitled to know that a person has previous offences when such assertions are made, but not as evidence against him.

The direction was, of itself, sound in law but in the circumstances of this case it would have been extremely difficult, if not practically impossible, for the jury to have done what the judge was suggesting. The prejudice which the appellant must have suffered in the eyes of the jury when it was disclosed that he had previous convictions for offences against young children could hardly have been greater. The probative value of the convictions, on the sole issue on which they were admissible, was, at best, slight. The previous offences did not involve dishonesty. Nor were they so similar to the offence which the jury were trying that they could have been admitted as evidence of similar facts on the issue of identity. In short, their prejudicial effect far outweighed their probative value. We would not have allowed this particular man to have been cross-examined about these particular convictions in these particular circumstances. That is not, however, the end of the matter. This court will not simply substitute its own discretion for that of the judge. But in the present case it seems to us that the judge was not given an opportunity to exercise his discretion on a proper basis. In fairness to him neither counsel placed all the relevant considerations before him. It was all done in a hurry and in the presence of the jury. We cannot help feeling that if the matter had been argued before him in the absence of the jury and in the same care as that with which we have examined the case today, he would have exercised his discretion differently.

There is a passage in the opinion of their Lordships in *Maxwell* v *DPP* [1935] AC 309 at 321, [1934] All ER Rep 168 at 174 which seems to us to be appropriate. It is in the speech of Viscount Sankey LC. It relates, *inter alia*, to the exercise of the judge's discretion, and reads as follows: ". . . the question whether a man has been convicted . . . ought not to be admitted . . . if there is any risk of the jury being misled into thinking that it goes not to credibility but to the probability of his having committed the offence of which he is charged." That exactly fits the present circumstances, and, for the reasons which we have endeavoured to indicate, this grave risk was overlooked by the judge.'

Appeal allowed. Conviction quashed.

R v *Powell* (1985) 82 Cr App R 165 (CA)

The appellant owned premises consisting of a shop with residential accommodation above. He was charged with knowingly living wholly or in part on the earnings of prostitution contrary to section 30 of the Sexual Offences Act 1956. The Crown case was that police officers had kept watch on the premises and that they had seen the appellant take money from prostitutes who took their customers to the first floor of the premises; that prostitutes solicited passers-by in the presence of the appellant; and that the appellant was seen to warn them of the presence of police in the area. He was also seen to tell prostitutes where to stand for the purpose of soliciting; to separate prostitutes who were having an argument; and to give a prostitute the key to a side door leading to the first floor room. The defence was that that evidence was a complete fabrication and the appellant put his own character in issue to show that he had no need to take money from prostitutes. At the conclusion of his evidence-in-chief the Crown applied to cross-examine him on his previous convictions since he had both put his own character in issue and attacked the police witnesses by alleging that they had lied on oath.

His previous convictions were for allowing his premises to be used for the purposes of prostitution. The judge ruled that although had the application been made solely on the ground of an attack on the police evidence, he would have refused it, yet since the appellant had gone further and put his own character in issue, then under section 1(f)(ii) of the Criminal Evidence Act 1898, in his discretion, the application would be allowed. The appellant was convicted and appealed on the ground that the judge had wrongly exercised his discretion in allowing the application.

LORD LANE CJ, giving the judgment of the court: 'Much of the difficulty in the present case springs from two decisions of this Court, to each of which I was a party. They are *R* v *Watts* (1983) 77 Cr App R 126; [1983] 3 All ER 101 . . . and *R* v *John and Braithwaite* (unreported), decided on November 24, 1983. Both were *ex tempore* judgments. In neither case were the speeches of their Lordships in *Selvey* v *Director of Public Prosecutions* (1968) 52 Cr App R 443; [1970] AC 304 drawn to the attention of the Court, nor, regrettably, did the Court have them in mind when giving the judgment.

Giving the judgment of the Court in *Watts* (*supra*) I referred to the speech of Viscount Sankey LC, in *Maxwell* v *Director of Public Prosecutions* (1935) 24 Cr App R 152, 173; [1935] AC 309, 321. This is what he said: ". . . in general no question as to whether a prisoner has been convicted or charged or acquitted should be asked or, if asked, allowed by the judge, who has a discretion under proviso (f), unless it helps to elucidate the particular issue which the jury is investigating, or goes to credibility, that is, tends to show that he is not to be believed on his oath; indeed the question whether a man had been convicted, charged or acquitted, even if it goes to credibility, ought not to be admitted, if there is any risk of the jury being misled into thinking that it goes not to credibility but to the probability of his having committed the offence with which he is charged."

In *Watts* (*supra*) the circumstances were somewhat special, and it may be that the decision would have been the same even if we had had the speeches of their Lordships in *Selvey* v *DPP* (*supra*).

The same cannot be said of *John Braithwaite and* (*supra*). The facts in that case were these. The police saw two youths in Oxford Street jostle a woman and steal her purse. They chased and arrested the youths. The defence at trial was that the policemen had fabricated their evidence; they had not seen what they said. The judge gave leave to cross-examine the youths as to their convictions. Each of them had to admit a number of convictions for offences closely resembling that with which they were charged.

In allowing the appeal the judgment of the Court referred to the decision in *Watts* (*supra*) and to Viscount Sankey's observations in *Maxwell* v *DPP* (*supra*), and went on, "It is necessary however to look to see precisely what their convictions were; for the reason that in fact, we are told, the precise nature of those previous convictions was put to them in cross-examination. . . . In the light of those records, it seems to us that a jury might think that these two young men had a specific disposition to snatch bags from the person every bit as much as Mr Watts could be said to have a specific disposition to indecently assault females. In those circumstances, as in the case of *Watts* (*supra*), it would have been extremely difficult, if not practically impossible, for the jury to have done what the judge had suggested, namely use those convictions to judge the respective credibility of the appellants and the police officers, but not as evidence that they had committed the offence charged. However careful the direction, there was, to echo the words of Viscount Sankey LC, a very real risk of the jury being misled into thinking that they went not to credibility but to the probability of them having committed the offence with which they were charged."

When one turns to consider *Selvey* v *Director of Public Prosecutions* (1968) 52 Cr App R 443; [1970] AC 304 decided by their Lordships 33 years after *Maxwell* v *Director of Public Prosecutions (supra)*, the possible misapprehensions in *Watts* and *John Braithwaite and (supra)* begin to emerge.

Selvey was indicted for buggery with a young man M. The prosecution at the trial before Stable J and a jury adduced evidence from M himself, police officers and a doctor who had examined M shortly after the alleged crime and said that M had been buggered within the previous six hours or so. The appellant in evidence stated that M had met him in the street and asked if he could see the appellant's room: when they got there M had asked for the loan of £1, and said that he was "prepared to go on the bed", and that he had already been with a person for £1: that he, the appellant, was not interested and that M had then left.

The judge in the absence of the jury expressed the view that Selvey had alleged in effect that the incident was a blackmail operation which had involved an attack on M's character. Thereupon counsel for the prosecution applied for leave to put to Selvey his previous convictions. Leave was granted.

When the jury returned to court the judge told them that since it had been suggested that M should not be believed as he was a man of bad character, they were entitled to hear Selvey's record. The judge told them that they would not decide the case "purely on matters of character"; that they would deal with the case upon the evidence they had heard; but at least they would not "go into the jury room having heard what was put to M without knowing anything about the previous record of the man by whom those charges are now brought".

Counsel for the Crown then put to Selvey that he had been in 1956 convicted of indecent assaults on two boys aged eight and six; in 1960 of two similar offences against other young boys; that he had been sentenced to two years' imprisonment in 1961 for persistently soliciting for an immoral purpose and in 1964 to six months' imprisonment on a similar offence. Thus the judge was permitting evidence to go before the jury which was at least as prejudicial to the defendant as that which was admitted in *Watts (supra)* and in *John and Braithwaite (supra)*.

Their Lordships in *Selvey* v *DPP (supra)* examined the authorities on this difficult aspect of the law, including *Maxwell* v *Director of Public Prosecutions (supra)* but nowhere expressed disapproval of the course which Stable J had taken at the trial.

The results of their Lordships' opinions in *Selvey* v *DPP (supra)* in so far as they are relevant to the instant case were analysed by another division of the Court in *R* v *Burke* decided on June 21, 1985. We respectfully agree with the judgment in that case delivered by Ackner LJ and cannot improve upon his analysis, which was as follows:

1   The trial judge must weigh the prejudicial effect of the questions against the damage done by the attack on the prosecution's witnesses, and must generally exercise his discretion so as to secure a trial that is fair both to the prosecution and the defence

(thus approving the observations of Devlin J, as he then was, when giving the judgment of the full Court (five judges) of the Court of Criminal Appeal in *R* v *Cook* (1959) 43 Cr App R 138, 143; [1959] 2 QB 340, 345.

2   Cases must occur in which it would be unjust to admit evidence of a character gravely prejudicial to the accused, even though there may be some tenuous grounds for holding it technically admissible (thus approving the observation made by Lord du Parcq, giving the opinion of the Privy Council in *Noor Mohamed* v *R* [1949] AC 182, at 192). Thus, although the position is established in law, still the putting of the questions as to character of the accused person may be fraught with results which immeasurably outweigh the results of questions put by the defence and which make a fair trial of the accused almost impossible (thus approving the observations of Singleton J in *R* v *Jenkins* (1945) 31 Cr App R 1, 15).

3   In the ordinary and normal case the trial judge may feel that if the credit of the prosecutor or his witnesses has been attacked, it is only fair that the jury should have before them material on which they can form their judgment whether the accused person is any more worthy to be believed than those he has attacked. It is obviously unfair that the jury should be left in the dark about an accused person's character if the conduct of his defence has attacked the character of the prosecutor or the witnesses for the prosecution within the meaning of the section (thus approving the observations of Singleton J in *Jenkins* (*supra*) again at p. 15).

4   In order to see if the conviction should be quashed, it is not enough that the Court thinks it would have exercised its discretion differently. The Court will not interfere with the exercise of a discretion by a judge below unless he has erred in principle, or there is no material on which he could properly have arrived at his decision (see Lord Dilhorne at p. 469, quoting Pickford J in *R* v *Watson* (1913) 8 Cr App R 249, at p. 254 and Devlin J in *Cook* (*supra*) at p. 147).

It may be helpful to make particular reference to a passage in the judgment of Devlin J in *R* v *Cook* at p. 146 and pp. 347, 348 respectively as follows: "The cases on this subject-matter . . . indicate the factors to be borne in mind and the sort of question that a judge should ask himself. Is a deliberate attack being made upon the conduct of the police officer calculated to discredit him wholly as a witness? If there is, a judge might well feel that he must withdraw the protection which he would desire to extend as far as possible to an accused who was endeavouring only to develop a line of defence. If there is a real issue about the conduct of an important witness which the jury will inevitably have to settle in order to arrive at their verdict, . . . the jury is entitled to know the credit of the man on whose word the witness's character is being impugned."

In the light of all these considerations, it is clear that in *John and Braithwaite*, (*supra*) and possibly to a lesser extent in *Watts* (*supra*), the Court fell into error. First of all, we interfered too lightly with the exercise of the judge's discretion, thereby overlooking the observations of Viscount Dilhorne already mentioned. Secondly, we overlooked the "tit for tat" principle as enunciated by Devlin J in *Cook* (*supra*) and by Lord Pearce in *Selvey* v *DPP* at p. 485 and p. 353 of the respective reports, at the same time paying too much attention, at least in *Watts* (*supra*), to the question whether the previous offences did or did not involve dishonesty in the ordinary sense of that word. We further suggested that care should be taken to conceal from the jury that the previous convictions of the prisoner were of a similar nature to the offence being charged. We have said enough about the speeches of their Lordships in *Selvey* v *DPP* and the facts of that case to show that those views were wrong.

Moreover, the words used by Viscount Sankey, in *Maxwell* v *Director of Public Prosecutions* (*supra*), which were largely the foundation of the judgment in *Watts* (*supra*), cannot in the light of *Selvey's* case (*supra*) be interpreted as meaning that convictions for the same or kindred offences can never be admitted. A defendant with previous convictions for similar offences may indeed have a very great incentive to make false allegations against prosecution witnesses for fear of greater punishment on conviction. It does however require careful direction from the judge to the effect that the previous convictions should not be taken as indications that the accused has committed the offence.

In short, if there is a deliberate attack being made upon the conduct of a prosecution witness calculated to discredit him wholly; if there is a real issue about the conduct of an important witness which the jury will have to settle in order to reach their verdict, the judge is entitled to let the jury know the previous convictions of the man who is making the attack. The fact that the defendant's convictions are not for offences of dishonesty, the fact that they are for offences bearing a close resemblance to the offences charged, are matters for the judge to take into consideration when exercising his discretion, but they certainly do not oblige the judge to disallow the proposed cross-examination.

Applying these principles to the present appeal, we have no doubt that the learned judge rightly exercised his discretion in permitting cross-examination.'

Appeal dismissed.

R v *Owen* (1986) 83 Cr App R 100 (CA)

The appellant was charged, *inter alia*, with theft of a purse. Police officers who arrested him said they had seen him reach inside his jacket and drop the purse. When interviewed, the appellant said the officers had lied; they had not seen him drop the purse. Evidence of that interview was given at his trial and was not challenged. The prosecution then applied for leave to cross-examine the appellant about his previous convictions, pursuant to s. 1(f)(ii) of the Criminal Evidence Act 1898 and that was granted to the extent that he could be asked if he had been found guilty of or had pleaded guilty to offences of dishonesty on previous occasions, without revealing that those offences were similar to the one charged. The appellant was convicted and appealed against conviction *inter alia*, on the ground that the judge had wrongly exercised his discretion in allowing him to be cross-examined about his previous convictions.

NEILL LJ, reading the judgment of the court: 'In order to consider this aspect of the case it is necessary to bear the following points in mind:

(1) When an application is made on behalf of the Crown for leave to cross-examine the accused as to his previous convictions on the basis that the nature or conduct of the defence has been such as to involve imputations on the character of the prosecutor, or the witnesses for the prosecution, the judge at trial has two tasks to perform:

(a) first he must form a judgment as to "the nature or conduct of the defence" in order to decide whether the condition set out in paragraph (ii) of section 1(f) of the 1898 Act has been satisfied; and

(b)   if he is so satisfied, he must decide whether in the exercise of his discretion he should allow the cross-examination to take place.

(2)   In forming a judgment as to the nature and conduct of the defence the judge will have to consider the facts of the individual case. Where explicit allegations of the fabrication of evidence have been made against prosecution witnesses, his task will be easy. But it is clear that in many cases imputations on the character of the witnesses for the prosecution may be made even though no explicit allegation of fabrication is made and even though counsel for the accused has conducted his cross-examination with delicacy and restraint. A challenge to the evidence of a witness, where there can be no question of mistake or misunderstanding or confusion, may well bear the necessary implication that the evidence has been fabricated. If the reality of the position is that the jury will have to decide whether the evidence of the witness whose testimony has been challenged, has been made up, then, in the words of Lawton LJ in *R* v *Britzmann* (1983) 76 Cr App R 134, 138; [1983] 1 WLR 350, 354 "there is no room for drawing a distinction between a defence which is so conducted as to make specific allegations of fabrication and one in which the allegation arises by way of necessary and reasonable implication." See also *R* v *Tanner* (1977) 66 Cr App R 56, 64.

(3)   Where the condition set out in paragraph (ii) of section 1(f) of the 1898 Act has been satisfied, the trial judge must weigh the prejudicial effect of the questions to be directed to the accused against the damage done by the attack on the prosecution's witness, and must generally exercise his discretion so as to secure a trial that is fair to the prosecution and the defence: see *R* v *Burke* [1985] Crim LR 660 and *R* v *Powell* (1985) 82 Cr App R 165; [1985] 1 WLR 1364 where the guidance to this effect given by the Court of Criminal Appeal in *Cook* (1959) 43 Cr App R 138, 143; (1959) 2 QB 340, 348, was approved.

(4)   Cases must occur in which, although the grounds for putting questions to the accused about his previous convictions have been established, the effect of allowing such questions might be fraught with results which would unreasonably outweigh the result of the questions put by the defence and might make a fair trial of the accused almost impossible: see *Burke* (*supra*) and *Powell* (*supra*), approving the observations of Singleton J in *Jenkins* (1945) 31 Cr App R 1, 15.

(5)   In the normal and ordinary case, however, the trial judge may feel that if the credit of the prosecutor or his witnesses has been attacked, it is only fair that the jury should have before them material on which they can form their judgment whether the accused person is any more worthy to be believed than those he has attacked: see *Burke* (*supra*) and *Powell* (*supra*). If imputations on the character of a prosecution witness have been made and if there is a real issue about the conduct of that witness which the jury will inevitably have to settle in order to arrive at their verdict, then, in the words of Devlin J delivering the judgment of the full Court in *R* v *Cook* (*supra*) at p. 143 and p. 348 of the respective reports, ". . . the jury is entitled to know the credit of the man on whose word the witness's character is being impugned." Devlin J was considering the case of a police officer whose evidence had been attacked, but it seems clear that the same principle is to be applied in the case of any important witness against whom such an imputation has been made and about whose conduct the jury will have to reach a conclusion.

(6)   The fact that the accused's convictions are not for offences of dishonesty, but may be for offences bearing a close resemblance to the offences charged, are matters for

the judge to take into consideration when exercising his discretion, but they certainly do not oblige the judge to disallow the proposed cross-examination: see *Powell* (*supra*).

(7) An appellate court will not interfere with the exercise by the trial judge of his discretion unless he has erred in principle or there was no material on which he could properly arrive at his decision: see *Selvey* v *DPP* (1968) 52 Cr App R 443, 468; [1970] AC 304, 342 and *Powell* (*supra*). The Court will not quash a conviction merely because it would have exercised the discretion differently.

It seems to us that the judge was fully entitled to conclude that there could be no question of honest mistake and that despite the restraint which counsel exercised, there was a necessary implication in the questions which were addressed to the police officers that they had made their evidence up.

Counsel further submitted that even if imputations had been made against prosecution witnesses, the judge was wrong to exercise his discretion in the way that he did, because counsel had done his best to avoid making any imputation. We are unable to accept this submission. The effect and purport of the cross-examination must be judged objectively. We consider that there was ample material on which the judge could decide to allow cross-examination of the appellant on his previous convictions and it is to be noted that the judge restricted the cross-examination so that the prejudicial effect of the details of the previous offences should not be made known to the jury. We can see no basis for interfering with the exercise by the judge of his discretion.'

• In view of the recent cases on s. 1(f)(ii) does the jury still have to perform the 'intellectual acrobatics' referred to by Lord Lane CJ in *R* v *Watts* [1983] 3 All ER 101?

Murdoch v *Taylor* [1965] AC 574 (HL)

Murdoch, who had a criminal record, was jointly tried with Lynch, who was previously of good character. Each was charged with receiving stolen cameras. Lynch gave evidence implicating Murdoch and Murdoch gave evidence alleging that Lynch alone was in control and possession of a box containing the stolen cameras. The judge held that Lynch's counsel was entitled to take advantage of section 1(f)(iii) and cross-examine as to his previous convictions. Murdoch was convicted and appealed.

LORD REID: 'My Lords, two questions of law are before your Lordships in this case. On the question of the discretion of the court I entirely agree with the view expressed by my noble and learned friend, Lord Donovan. But on the other question I find great difficulty in agreeing with what I understand to be the unanimous view of your Lordships. The words which we have to construe are those of section 1(f)(iii) of the Criminal Evidence Act, 1898—"he has given evidence against any other person charged with the same offence." In proviso (e) of the same section there is reference to any question which "would tend to criminate," and I have difficulty in believing that the word "against" in proviso (f)(iii) could have been used if the intention had been that this proviso should apply to all evidence which would tend to criminate the co-accused. If that had been the intention the obvious course would have been to say "tending to criminate" instead of "against." And there are other reasons which tend to strengthen my doubts. If this provision has this wide meaning, an accused person with previous convictions, whose story contradicts in any material respect the story of a co-accused who has not yet been convicted, will find it almost impossible to defend himself, and if he elects not to give evidence his plight will be just as bad. But I have been unable to find any satisfactory solution for the problem set by this proviso and therefore I shall not dissent.'

LORD MORRIS OF BORTH-Y-GEST: 'If an accused person becomes a witness his sworn testimony, if admissible, becomes a part of the evidence in the case. What he says in cross-examination is just as much a part of that evidence as is what he says in examination-in-chief. The word "against" is one that is well understood. It is a clear and robust word. It has more decisiveness than is possessed by such phrases as "tending to show" or "such as to involve." It is a word that needs neither explanation nor translation. It calls for no synonym.

The Act does not call for any investigation as to the motives or wishes which may have prompted the giving of evidence against another person charged with the same offence. It is the nature of the evidence that must be considered. Its character does not change according as to whether it is the product of pained reluctance or of malevolent eagerness. If, while ignoring anything trivial or casual, the positive evidence given by the witness would rationally have to be included in any survey or summary of the evidence in the case which, if accepted, would warrant the conviction of the other person charged with the "same offence," then the witness would have given evidence against such other person. Such other person would then have that additional testimony against him. From his point of view that testimony would be just as damaging whether given with regret or whether given with relish. Such other person might then wish, in order to defend himself, to show that credence ought not to be attached to the evidence which had been given against him. In such circumstances the Act removes one barrier which would otherwise be in his way.

It may be noted that if A and B are jointly charged with the same offence and if A chooses to give evidence which is purely in defence of himself and is not evidence against B he may be asked questions in cross-examination by B notwithstanding that such questions would tend to criminate him (A) as to the offence charged. In similar circumstances B would be likewise placed. But questions of the kind denoted by section 1(f) could not be put. No doubt during any such cross-examination a judge would be alert to protect a witness from being cajoled into saying more than it was ever his plan or wish or intention to say.'

LORD PEARCE (dissenting on the question of discretion): 'It is common ground that, until the case of *R* v *Ellis* [1961] 1 WLR 1064 decided briefly to the contrary, the practice and the general view of Bench and Bar alike was that a judge had a discretion whether to give leave to cross-examine under section 1(f)(iii). Moreover, it has long been established practice and law that the right to cross-examine under section 1(f)(ii) is subject to the judge's discretion (see the cases of *R* v *Jenkins* [1945] 114 LJ KB 425 and *R* v *Cook* [1959] 2 KB 340). Therefore, the right under section 1(f)(iii) would also seem, *prima facie* at least, to be subject to the judge's discretion. For there is nothing in the words of the Act which justifies any discrimination between the two subsections on the point in issue.

Admittedly the situation arising under section 1(f)(ii) differs from that arising under section 1(f)(iii). Under the former, an exercise of discretion could only deprive the prosecution of a right which they would otherwise have had; and the courts have always been ready to do that when fairness seemed to demand it. Under section 1(f)(iii), however, the judge, in using a discretion to refuse the introduction of a defendant's bad record, could only do so at the expense of a co-defendant. And how, it is argued, can he properly do this?

It is certainly not an easy problem. But the difficult burden of holding the scales fairly, not only as between the prosecution and defendants, but also as between the defendants themselves, and of doing his best thereby to secure a fair trial for all concerned, falls inevitably on the trial judge and is generally achieved in practice with considerable success. The use of a judicial discretion under section 1(f)(iii) as between co-defendants would be but an addition to the judge's existing burden.

The exercise of such a discretion would be within fairly narrow limits and the *prima facie* right could only be withheld for good judicial reasons. Two obvious examples occur to one of situations in which the judge ought to use a discretion to refuse a defendant's request to introduce a co-defendant's bad character. The first is where that defendant's counsel has deliberately led a co-defendant into the trap, or has, for the purpose of bringing in his bad record, put questions to him in cross-examination which will compel him, for the sake of his own innocence, to give answers that will clash with the story of the other defendant, or compel him to bring to the forefront implications which would otherwise have been unnoticed or immaterial. The second type of situation is where the clash between the two stories is both inevitable and trivial, and yet the damage by the introduction of a bad record (perhaps many years previous) will in the circumstances be unfairly prejudicial. Any attempt to deal with such a situation by means of the maxim *de minimis* is really to import some sort of discretion in disguise. For if a defendant is entitled to an absolute right, he can claim it on any technical ground that exists, whether it be large or small, fair or unfair: and however unfair or technical the ground may be, the right will be equally valuable to a defendant who can make his escape over the (perhaps innocent) body of a co-defendant.

In such a difficult matter which may not infrequently arise in borderline cases, the judge, who sees the general run of the case as it unfolds before him, can produce a fairer result by the exercise of a judicial discretion than by the strict and fettered application of an arbitrary rule of law. . . .

In my view, there should not be denied to the judges the discretion which in practice they exercised for so many years before the decision in the case of *Ellis* took it out of their capable hands.'

LORD DONOVAN: 'It is now contended on behalf of Murdoch, first, that he had given no evidence against Lynch within the meaning of proviso (f)(iii). That expression in its context connotes, it is said, only evidence given in examination-in-chief and not evidence given in cross-examination. Alternatively, it refers only to evidence given with a hostile intent against a co-accused so that the test to be applied is subjective and not objective. In the further alternative, it is argued that, whatever be the true meaning of the expression, a trial judge has in all cases a discretion whether or not to allow questions to be put pursuant to proviso (f)(iii) just as he has in relation to proviso (f)(ii) of the section.

Prior to the Act of 1898 coming into force an accused person could not (speaking generally) give evidence in his own defence. The Act begins by enacting by section 1 that: "Every person charged with an offence . . . shall be a competent witness for the defence at every stage of the proceedings. . . ." Then follow a number of provisos, the first of which is: (a) "A person so charged shall not be called as a witness in pursuance of this Act except upon his own application." An accused person was thus given a new right of defending himself, if he wished, by his own sworn testimony. There is thus some initial impetus, at least, towards the view that when the legislature contemplated that he might give evidence against a co-accused, it was thinking of evidence produce directly by the testimony which the accused chose to give and not testimony which he might have preferred not to give but which was extracted from him under the pressure of cross-examination. Be that as it may, the words of the proviso are, in my opinion, too clear to admit of any such distinction. The object of proviso (f)(iii) is clearly to confer a benefit upon a co-accused. If evidence is given against him by another accused he may show, if he can, by reference to the latter's previous offences that his testimony is not worthy of belief. It is the effect of the evidence upon the jury which is material and which may be lessened or dissipated by invoking the proviso. The effect upon the jury is the same whether the evidence be given in examination-in-chief or in cross-examination; and the desirability of the co-accused being able to meet it by cross-examination as to credit is of the same importance, however the evidence is given. I feel no difficulty in holding that the first of the appellant's contentions must be rejected.

The like considerations also lead me to reject the argument that proviso (f)(iii) refers only to evidence given by one accused against the other with hostile intent. Again, it is the effect of the evidence upon the minds of the jury which matters, not the state of mind of the person who gives it. Were that the test, there would have to be something of the nature of a trial within a trial in order to determine the state of mind of the accused who gave the evidence, as was pointed out by the Court of Criminal Appeal in the case of *R* v *Stannard* [1965] 2 QB 1. The language of the Act gives no support for the view that this was the intention. In my opinion, the test to be applied in order to determine whether one accused has given evidence against his co-accused is objective and not subjective.

What kind of evidence is contemplated by proviso (f)(iii), that is, what is "evidence against" a co-accused is perhaps the most difficult part of the case. At one end of the scale is evidence which does no more than contradict something which a co-accused has said without further advancing the prosecution's case in any significant degree. I agree with the view expressed by Winn J in giving judgment in *Stannard* that this is not the kind of evidence contemplated by proviso (f)(iii). At the other end of the scale is evidence which, if the jury believes it, would establish the co-accused's guilt, for example, in a case of theft: "I saw him steal the purse" or in a case of assault, "I saw him strike the blow." It is this kind of evidence which alone, so the appellant contends, will satisfy the words "has given evidence against." Again, I regret I cannot share that view. There may well be evidence which regarded in isolation would be quite innocuous from the co-accused's point of view and, so regarded, could not be regarded as evidence "against" him. For example, what would be proved if one co-accused said of his co-accused: "He told me he knew of an easy job and persuaded me to help him"? If such evidence is kept unrelated to anything else it proves nothing criminal. But juries hear the whole of the evidence and they will consider particular parts of it, not in isolation but in conjunction with all the other evidence, and part of that other evidence may establish that "job" meant a housebreaking job. Then the item of evidence I have taken as an example obviously becomes evidence "against" the accused. If, therefore, the effect of the evidence upon the minds of the jury is to be taken as the test, it cannot be right to regard it in isolation in order to decide whether it is evidence against the co-accused. If Parliament had meant by proviso (f)(iii) to refer to evidence which was by itself conclusive against the co-accused it would have been easy to say so.

The test prescribed by the Court of Criminal Appeal in *Stannard* was whether the evidence in question tended to support the prosecution's case in a material respect or to undermine the defence. I have no substantial quarrel with this definition. I would, however, observe that some danger may lurk in the use of the expression "tended to." There will probably be occasions when it could be said that evidence given by one accused "tended to" support the prosecution's case simply because it differed from the evidence of his co-accused; and the addition of the words "in a material respect" might not wholly remove the danger. The difficulty is not really one of conception but of expression. I myself would omit the words "tended to" and simply say that "evidence against" means evidence which supports the prosecution's case in a material respect or which undermines the defence of the co-accused.

The evidence in the present case was clearly against Lynch in that sense. It was evidence which, if the jury accepted it, put Lynch in sole control and possession of property which according to the rest of the evidence had been stolen the day before, and which Lynch had tried to sell for a price which was a fraction of its real value. Murdoch's evidence thus supported the case of the prosecution in a material respect and none the less so because Coles had already given evidence to a somewhat similar effect.

On the question of discretion, I agree with the Court of Criminal Appeal that a trial judge has no discretion whether to allow an accused person to be cross-examined as to his past criminal offences once he has given evidence against his co-accused. Proviso (f)(iii) in terms confers no such discretion and, in my opinion, none can be implied. It is true that in relation to proviso (f)(ii) such a discretion does exist; that is to say, in the cases where the accused has attempted to establish his own good character or where the nature and conduct of the defence is such as to involve imputations on the character of the prosecutor or of a witness for the prosecution.

But in these cases it will normally, if not invariably, be the prosecution which will want to bring out the accused's bad character—not some co-accused; and in such cases it seems to me quite proper that the court should retain some control of the matter. For its duty is to secure a fair trial and the prejudicial value of evidence establishing the accused's bad character may at times wholly outweigh the value of such evidence as tending to show that he was guilty of the crime alleged.

These considerations lead me to the view that if, in any given case (which I think would be rare), the prosecution sought to avail itself of the provisions of proviso (f)(iii) then here, again, the court should keep control of the matter in the like way. Otherwise, if two accused gave evidence one against the other, but neither wished to cross-examine as to character, the prosecution could step in as of right and reveal the criminal records of both, if both possessed them. I cannot think that Parliament in the Act of 1898 ever intended such an unfair procedure. So far as concerns the prosecution, therefore, the matter should be one for the exercise of the judge's discretion, as it is in the case of proviso (f)(ii). But when it is the co-accused who seeks to exercise the right conferred by proviso (f)(iii) different considerations come into play. He seeks to defend himself; to say to the jury that the man who is giving evidence against him is unworthy of belief; and to support that assertion by proof of bad character. The right to do this cannot, in my opinion, be fettered in any way.

Finally, it is said that the decision in *Stannard* [1965] 2 QB 1, if upheld, will make it impossible for a person to defend himself at all effectively if he has a criminal record and is charged jointly with some other person. If he knows that the other person is guilty, and if in the witness box he speaks the truth, then he is liable to have his criminal past disclosed with fatal results.

This would, indeed, be a melancholy result, but I do not think the prospect is so gloomy. To test the matter, let me assume the case of two accused each charged with the same offence—No. 1 in fact being guilty but having no criminal record, No. 2 being in fact innocent but having such a record. No. 1 has nothing to lose by going into the witness box and accusing No. 2 of the crime; No. 2 quite truthfully in his evidence accuses No. 1, whereupon the past criminal record of No. 2 is disclosed to the jury by or on behalf of No. 1. It is said that No. 2 would have practically no hope of avoiding a conviction—hence the argument for an overriding discretion in the judge, although this would not necessarily cure the situation.

But in the case supposed, what would be the position in practice? In the first place, if No. 2 were in fact innocent, it would be in the highest degree unlikely that he would be found relying simply on his own denial. There would almost invariably be some evidence to support his defence. In the second place, his counsel or the judge or both would explain to the jury just how it was that accused No. 1 was able to force the revelation of No. 2's record. The judge would probably go on to exhort the jury not to let that revelation sway their minds and to consider the case against No. 2 primarily on the basis of the other evidence. The assistant recorder in the present case indeed went further and told the jury to ignore Murdoch's past altogether. It would be a very unusual jury which, in these circumstances, did not require cogent proof of guilt before convicting. Indeed, the effect of the disclosure of No. 2's past might have the result of causing the jury to give consideration to the case surpassing in carefulness even their usual high standard.'

(LORD EVERSHED agreed with LORD DONOVAN.)

Appeal dismissed.

R v Hatton (1976) 64 Cr App R 88 (CA)

The appellant and two co-defendants were charged with stealing scrap metal. The first defendant (Hildon) denied that there was a plan to steal the metal, while the other two agreed there was such a plan but denied dishonesty. The trial judge allowed counsel for the first defendant to cross-examine the appellant as to his previous convictions on the ground that the appellant had given evidence against the first defendant, a person charged with the same offence pursuant to section 1(f)(iii) of the Criminal Evidence Act 1898, in that the appellant's evidence undermined the first defendant's story. All three were convicted. The appellant appealed on the ground that evidence which undermined part of a co-defendant's defence was not necessarily evidence 'against' him.

STEPHENSON LJ, giving the judgment of the court: 'It is well known that in *Murdoch* v *Taylor* (1965) 49 Cr App R 119, the House of Lords (1) adopted in substance the interpretation—or gloss—put upon the statutory language in *Stannard* (1962) 48 Cr App R 81; [1965] 2 QB 1 and held that "evidence against" means evidence, not necessarily given with hostile intent, which supports the prosecution's case in a material respect or which undermines the defence of the co-accused; (2) decided (by a majority) that, once the judge has ruled that the witness has given evidence against his co-accused, he has no discretion whether or not to allow him to be cross-examined on his past criminal offences. In *R* v *Bruce* (1975) 61 Cr App R 123; [1975] 1 WLR 1252 (which was decided a few months before this trial) this Court found it necessary to explain that interpretation—or to put a gloss upon that gloss—in "wholly exceptional circumstances" and to hold that evidence which undermined part of a co-accused's defence and damaged his credibility was wrongly considered to be evidence against him, because on balance it was given more in his favour than against him and did more to undermine the prosecution's case than the co-accused's defence.

Before the judge it was submitted, both by counsel for Hildon and by counsel for the Crown, that the question whether the evidence of Hatton had provided a further defence for Hildon was irrelevant; by counsel for Hildon, that the test was whether the defence in fact put forward by him would be undermined; by counsel for the Crown, whether Hildon's credit would be undermined. In this Court the argument took account of what was said in *Bruce* (*supra*) that evidence which damaged a co-accused's credibility by contradicting his evidence, or which provided a co-accused with a different and possibly a better defence, does not thereby make it evidence given against him but only if it makes his acquittal less likely.

In *Bruce* (*supra*) the prosecution's case was that Bruce and seven others, including McGuinness, set out together to rob a Pakistani; they found a Burmese gentleman and robbed him. They were all acquitted of robbing him but convicted of stealing money from him. None of the defendants supported the prosecution's case of an agreement to rob except McGuinness. He admitted that there was such a plan but denied taking any part in it. Bruce gave evidence that there was no such plan and denied taking any money from the victim: he did not give evidence that McGuinness had taken any money from the victim. Yet the judge ruled that Bruce had given evidence against McGuinness because he had contradicted McGuinness's evidence that there was a plan to rob and so undermined his credit.

Hatton's evidence about Hildon is very different from Bruce's evidence about McGuinness. Bruce, as his counsel told the judge, had not said anything which directly involved McGuinness in the robbery or theft. He had merely denied a part of the prosecution's case which McGuinness had admitted. He had not supported the prosecution's case in any material respect. Hatton, on the other hand, had supported a material part of the prosecution's case which Hildon had denied, namely that Hildon had set out for the site with Hatton and Ripley to collect scrap for Hildon's step-brother and he had contradicted Hildon's evidence that he had only joined them later on the site. That evidence of Hatton, if believed, brought Hildon into a plan to collect scrap, albeit honest; and although it provided Hildon with another defence, it not merely undermined his credit but on balance did more to undermine his defence than to undermine the prosecution's case. Indeed it supported the prosecution's case in a material respect, that there was a plan to take scrap from the site, and thereby rendered Hildon's conviction more likely and reduced his chances of acquittal.

There being no discretion to exclude prejudicial evidence of other offences committed by a defendant who gives evidence against a co-accused, it is important that the evidence should be clearly given against the co-accused, as it was not in *Bruce's* case (*supra*) but was in this. Respectfully adopting the language of Lord Morris of Borth-y-Gest, to which we were referred in *Murdoch v Taylor* (*supra*) at pp. 124, 125 and p. 584B of the respective reports, we think that (unlike the evidence of Bruce) the positive evidence of Hatton (and Ripley) associating Hildon with them in their mission to the site "would rationally have to be included in any survey or summary of the evidence in the case, which, if accepted, would warrant the conviction of" Hildon. The words "if accepted" clearly refer to the survey or summary, not to the positive evidence, and Lord Morris is not saying that "the positive evidence" must be accepted *in toto* or that it must by itself warrant the conviction of the other person charged with the same offence.

For these reasons we are of opinion that the judge was right to admit the cross-examination of Hatton as to his previous convictions.'

Appeal dismissed.

R v Varley [1982] 2 All ER 519 (CA)

The appellant and Dibble were jointly charged with robbery. At their trial Dibble admitted that they had both participated in the robbery but stated that he had been forced to do so by threats on his life by the appellant. The appellant denied that he had taken any part in the robbery and asserted that Dibble's evidence was untrue. On the basis that the appellant's evidence was evidence 'against' Dibble for the purposes of section 1(f)(iii) of the Criminal Evidence Act 1898, Dibble's counsel applied for and was granted leave to cross-examine the appellant as to his previous convictions. Dibble and the appellant were both convicted. The appellant appealed, contending that his evidence was not evidence 'against' Dibble and that leave to cross-examine him about his previous convictions should not have been granted.

KILNER BROWN J, reading the judgment of the court: 'The operation of this particular part of the proviso seems to have given rise to no difficulty and no detailed analysis for well over 60 years. No doubt, as Lord Pearce indicated in his speech in *Murdoch* v *Taylor* [1965] 1 All ER 406 at 411, [1965] AC 574 at 586, "the practice and the general view of Bench and Bar alike was that a judge had a discretion whether to give leave to cross-examine under s. 1(f)(iii)" and, in difficult cases where it was not easy to determine whether the evidence could be categorised as "against" or where such questioning could well be unduly prejudicial, a judge would decline to rule that the proposed questions could be put. But this discretionary power was removed from trial judges by the Court of Criminal Appeal in *R* v *Ellis*, *R* v *Ellis* [1961] 2 All ER 928, [1961] 1 WLR 1064, when it was decided that cross-examination of a co-defendant who had given evidence against a person jointly charged with him was a matter of right and not of discretion.

The decision was approved by four of the Lords of Appeal (Lord Pearce dissenting) in *Murdoch's* case [1965] 1 All ER 406, [1965] AC 574. This decision created difficult problems in practice because either to establish or to destroy this right involved, in many cases, an acute analysis of whether or not the evidence which had been given was "against" the other party charged. It sparked off a whole series of cases which have come before this court and at least the one (*Murdoch's* case) in the House of Lords. The instant case is a very good example of the additional burden placed on the trial judge. The application and the resistance to it occupied many hours of judicial time and took up no less than 57 pages of recorded transcript.

Although the judgment of the Court of Criminal Appeal in *R* v *Stannard* [1964] 1 All ER 34, [1965] 2 QB 1 was undoubtedly meant to have been of assistance to trial judges in their consideration of whether evidence was "against" or not, in practice, it has in fact added to their burden and it has caused considerable anxiety to other divisions of this court as it did to Lord Reid and was tacitly ignored by Lord Morris in *Murdoch's* case. What was the nature of the guidance in *R* v *Stannard* [1964] 1 All ER 34, [1965] 2 QB 1? It was this, approved as amended by Lord Donovan in *Murdoch's* case [1965] 1 All ER 406 at 416, [1965] AC 574 at 592: ". . .'evidence against' means evidence which supports the prosecution's case in a material respect or which undermines the defence of the co-accused." There are three reported cases in the Court of Appeal, Criminal Division, in which this interpretation has been considered and to which we were referred. They are *R* v *Davis (Alan Douglas)* [1975] 1 All ER 233, [1975] 1 WLR 345, *R* v *Bruce* [1975] 3 All ER 277, [1975] 1 WLR 1252 and *R* v *Hatton* (1976) 64 Cr App R 88. Now, putting all the reported cases together, are there established principles which might serve as guidance to trial judges when called on to give rulings in this very difficult area of the law? We venture to think that they are these and, if they are borne in mind, it may not be necessary to investigate all the relevant authorities. (1) If it is established that a person jointly charged has given evidence against the co-defendant that defendant has a right to cross-examine the other as to previous convictions and the trial judge has no discretion to refuse an application. (2) Such evidence may be given either in chief or during cross-examination. (3) It has to be objectively decided whether the evidence either supports the prosecution case in a material respect or undermines the defence of the co-accused. A hostile intent is irrelevant. (4) If consideration has to be given to the undermining of the other's defence care must be taken to see that the evidence clearly undermines the defence. Inconvenience to or inconsistency with the other's defence is not of itself sufficient. (5) More denial of participation in a joint venture is not of itself sufficient to rank as evidence against the co-defendant. For the proviso to apply, such denial must lead to the conclusion that if the witness did not participate then it must have been the other who did. (6) Where the one defendant asserts or in due course would assert one view of the joint venture which is directly contradicted by the other such contradiction may be evidence against the co-defendant.

We apply these principles to the facts of this case and particularly the latter two. Here was Dibble going to say, as he did, that he took part in the joint venture because he was forced to do so by Varley. The appellant, Varley, was saying that he was not a participant and had not gone with Dibble and had not forced Dibble to go. His evidence therefore was against Dibble because it amounted to saying that not only was Dibble telling lies but that Dibble would be left as a participant on his own and not acting under duress. In our view, the judge was right to rule that cross-examination as to previous convictions was permissible.'

Appeal dismissed.

R v *Butterwasser* [1948] 1 KB 4 (CCA)

The defendant was convicted of wounding with intent to do grievous bodily harm. At the trial the evidence for the prosecution was given by the prosecutor and his wife. The defendant's counsel in cross-examination attacked the character of the prosecutor and his wife, putting to them a number of previous convictions including convictions of offences of violence, which they admitted, and thereby suggesting that it was really the prosecutor who attacked the defendant. The defendant was not called to give evidence and he neither called witnesses to his character nor cross-examined the witnesses for the prosecution on this subject. Thereupon, with the leave of the court, a police officer was called for the prosecution and read out a record of the defendant's previous convictions.

LORD GODDARD CJ, giving the judgment of the court: 'It is elementary law that ever since it became the practice, as it has been for the last 150 or 200 years, of allowing a prisoner to call evidence of good character, or where he has put questions to witnesses for the Crown and obtained or attempted to obtain admissions from them that he is a man of good character, in other words, where the prisoner himself puts his character in issue, evidence in rebuttal can be given by the prosecution to show that he is in fact a man of bad character. Evidence of character nowadays is very loosely given and received, and it would be as well if all courts paid attention to a well-known case in the Court of Crown Cases Reserved, *R* v *Rowton* 10 Cox CC 25, in which a court of 12 judges laid down the principles which should govern the giving of evidence of character and of evidence in rebuttal of bad character. It was pointed out that the evidence must be evidence of general reputation and not dependent upon particular acts or actions. But however that may be, there is no case to be found in the books—and it is certainly contrary to what all the present members of the court have understood during the whole of the time they have been in the profession—that where the prisoner does not put his own character in issue, but has merely attacked the witnesses for the prosecution, evidence can be called for the prosecution to prove that the prisoner is a man of bad character. It is, of course, permissible, where a prisoner takes advantage of the Act of 1898, which made prisoners competent witnesses on their trial in all cases, and goes into the witness box and attacks the witnesses for the prosecution, to cross-examine him with regard to convictions and matters of character; and no doubt if a conviction is put to him and he denies it, the provisions of Denman's Act would apply and the conviction could be proved against him. But it is admitted that there is no authority, and I do not see on what principle it could be said, that if a man does not go into the box and put his own character in issue, he can have evidence given against him of previous bad character when all that he has done is to attack the witnesses for the prosecution. The reason is that by attacking the witnesses for the prosecution and suggesting they are unreliable, he is not putting his character in issue; he is putting their character in issue. And the reason why, if he gives evidence, he can be cross-examined if he has attacked the witnesses for the prosecution is that the statute says he can. It seems to the court, therefore, that it is impossible to say that because the prisoner in this case attacked the witnesses for the prosecution but did not himself give evidence, evidence of his bad character was admissible. In those circumstances, the learned recorder should have declined to allow the evidence to be given, and therefore inadmissible evidence on a most vital point was admitted in this case.'

Appeal allowed.

Questions for discussion

R v *Coke: R* v *Littleton*

1   May the prosecution make use of Coke's previous conviction for rape, in order to assist in proving his guilt on the charge of raping Margaret Blackstone?

2   May Littleton seek to establish his good character, by way of defence? If so:

   (a)   What matters may be canvassed, by way of 'character evidence' for this purpose?

   (b)   By what means may Littleton establish his good character?

   (c)   If Littleton were not of good character, what steps might the prosecution take to deal with a false or misleading assertion of good character by him?

   (d)   What will be the evidential value of Littleton's good character, if established?

3   What advice would you give to Coke about the voluntary exposure of his character to the jury, if it were contemplated?

4   Assuming that Coke gives evidence in his defence, what would be the effect of the following:

(a) Coke's counsel has cross-examined Margaret, seeking to show that she consented to have sexual intercourse with him on the occasion of the alleged rape?

(b) Coke's counsel has cross-examined Margaret seeking to show that (i) she is promiscuous; and (ii) that last year, she falsely accused Kevin of raping her?

(c) Coke's counsel has suggested to Margaret in cross-examination that she is dishonest, as evidenced by her conviction for shoplifting, and is given to telling lies?

(d) Coke has given evidence in chief that he went to a good school and is honest and hard-working?

5   What would be the effect of the matters raised in question 4(a), (b) and (c) if Coke declined to give evidence?

6   What would be the effect of Coke's giving evidence in chief that Littleton was with him throughout the relevant Sunday, and in particular while Margaret and Angela were at his flat?

7   Littleton wishes to give evidence that he has no sexual attraction to children, that he is happily married and enjoys a normal sexual relationship with his wife. Would this evidence be admissible?

8   Assuming that the prosecution is permitted to cross-examine Coke about his previous conviction for rape:

(a)   Would it be permissible to cross-examine with a view to showing that the *modus operandi* was inducing the girl to visit his home to listen to records?

(b)   How should the judge direct the jury about the previous conviction?

Blackstone v Coke

1   May Margaret Blackstone give evidence at trial that she is a young woman of virtuous character, with a view to showing that it is likely that she did not consent to have sexual intercourse with Coke on the occasion in question?

2   May Coke call witnesses at trial to state that they had previously had sexual relations with Margaret, with a view to showing that it is likely that she did consent on the occasion in question?

3   May Coke introduce evidence that Margaret had sexual intercourse with Anthony Henneky, in order to show that Henneky may be the father of her child?

Additional questions

1   You are acting for Charlie, a man of 40, on two charges of indecent assault committed in May and August 1987 respectively: in both cases, it is alleged that he laid in wait in some bushes on a University campus, seized a girl as she was returning to her hall of residence, and assaulted her before releasing her. Charlie has previous convictions: (i) for several indecent assaults committed during the 1960s; (ii) for a rape, committed on the same campus and in a similar manner to the present charges, for which he was sentenced to seven years' imprisonment in 1978; (iii) several offences of fraud, committed in the 1970s. Prosecuting counsel has notified you that if Charlie gives evidence, he will cross-examine him as to the conviction for rape in 1978, and as to two occasions in the summer of 1987 when he chased other girls on the campus but failed to catch them.

The prosecution also rely on a written confession signed by Charlie: on one occasion he told you that he had made and signed a statement, although he disputed the accuracy of the contents; on another occasion, he told you that the document was a fabrication and that his signature was forged by one of the police officers. You cannot foresee what version he would give in evidence under oath. What factors will you take into account in conducting the defence?

2   Dan and Ed are charged jointly with the murder of Fred. The case for the prosecution is that Dan (who is a man of previous good character) employed Ed (who has a series of convictions for violence) to kill Fred for a sum of £10,000. The prosecution have evidence of a telephone conversation between Dan and Ed arranging the killing, and of a statement by Ed who admits killing Fred but says that he did so in self-defence following an unprovoked attack: the statement contains no reference to Dan. Dan's defence is that he was in no way involved in the matter, and that he never spoke to Ed on the telephone. When giving evidence in his own defence, Ed alleged, for the first time, that he had once had a homosexual relationship with Fred who had been trying to blackmail him ever since, and that Fred had also had a homosexual relationship with Dan who 'wanted to get rid of him'. Can either the prosecution or Dan cross-examine Ed as to his previous convictions? If so, for what purpose may cross-examination be allowed?

Further reading

Cohen, 'Challenging police evidence of interviews and the second limb of section 1(f)(ii)—another view' [1981] Crim LR 523.

Gooderson, 'Is the prisoner's character indivisible?' [1953] 11 CLJ 377.

McNamara, 'Cross-examination of an accused as to collateral crimes relevant to guilt' (1983) 9 Adelaide LR 290.

Munday, 'Reflections on the Criminal Evidence Act 1898' [1985] 44 CLJ 62.

Munday, 'Stepping beyond the bounds of credibility: the application of section 1(f)(ii) of the Criminal Evidence Act 1898' [1986] Crim LR 511.

Munday, 'The wilder permutations of section 1(f) of the Criminal Evidence Act 1898 (1987) 7 LS 137.

Pattenden, 'The purpose of cross-examination under section 1(f) of the Criminal Evidence Act 1898' [1982] Crim LR 707.

Seabrooke, 'Closing the credibility gap: a new approach to section 1(f)(ii) of the Criminal Evidence Act 1898' [1987] Crim LR 231.

Tapper, 'The meaning of section 1(f)(i) of the Criminal Evidence Act 1898' in *Crime, Proof and Punishment* (ed. Tapper) (1981).

Wolchover, 'Cross-examination of the accused on his record when a confession is denied or retracted' [1981] Crim LR 312.

5   *Similar Fact Evidence*

(Suggested preliminary reading: *A Practical Approach to Evidence*, pp. 138-155).

Makin and Makin v *Attorney-General for New South Wales* [1894] AC 57 (PC)

The defendants were charged with the murder of a baby, whose body was found in the back yard of a house occupied by them. The defendants had 'adopted' it from its mother in return for a sum of money, stating that they wished to bring it up because they had lost their own child. The facts were consistent with an allegation that the defendants had killed the child for the maintenance, but equally were consistent with death by natural causes followed by an irregular burial. There was, however, evidence that the bodies of other babies, similarly adopted by the defendants, were found buried in the yards of houses occupied by the defendants. This evidence was held to be admissible, and the defendants were convicted. They appealed to the Supreme Court of New South Wales and from there to the Privy Council.

LORD HERSCHELL LC, delivering the judgment of the court: 'In their Lordships' opinion the principles which just govern the decision of the case are clear, though the application of them is by no means free from difficulty. It is undoubtedly not competent for the prosecution to adduce evidence tending to show that the accused has been guilty of criminal acts other than those covered by the indictment, for the purpose of leading to the conclusion that the accused is a person likely from his criminal conduct or character to have committed the offence for which he is being tried. On the other hand, the mere fact that the evidence adduced tends to show the commission of other crimes does not render it inadmissible if it be relevant to an issue before the jury, and it may be so relevant if it bears upon the question whether the acts alleged to constitute the crime charged in the indictment were designed or accidental, or to rebut a defence which would otherwise be open to the accused. The statement of these general principles is easy, but it is obvious that it may often be very difficult to draw the line and to decide whether a particular piece of evidence is on the one side or the other. . .

The leading authority relied on by the Crown was the case of *R* v *Geering* (1849) 18 LJMC 215, where on the trial of a prisoner for the murder of her husband by administering arsenic evidence was tendered, with the view of showing that two sons of the prisoner who had formed part of the same family, and for whom as well as for her husband the prisoner had cooked their food, had died of poison, the symptoms in all these cases being the same. The evidence was admitted by Pollock CB, who tried the case; he held that it was admissible, inasmuch as its tendency was to prove that the death of the husband was occasioned by arsenic, and was relevant to the question whether such taking was accidental or not. The Chief Baron refused to reserve the point for the consideration of the judges, intimating that Alderson B, and Talfourd J, concurred with him in his opinion.

This authority has been followed in several subsequent cases. And in the case of *R* v *Dossett* 2 C & K 306, which was tried a few years previously, the same view was acted upon by Maule J, on a trial for arson, where it appeared that a rick of wheatstraw was set on fire by the prisoner having fired a gun near to it. Evidence was admitted to show that the rick had been on fire the previous day, and that the prisoner was then close to it with a gun in his hand. Maule J, said: "Although the evidence offered may be proof of another felony, that circumstance does not render it inadmissible, if the evidence be otherwise receivable. In many cases it is an important question whether a thing was done accidentally or wilfully."

'Under these circumstances their Lordships cannot see that it was irrelevant to the issue to be tried by the jury that several other infants had been received from their mothers on like representations, and upon payment of a sum inadequate for the support of the child for more than a very limited period, or that the bodies of infants had been found buried in a similar manner in the gardens of several houses occupied by the prisoners.'

Appeal dismissed.

R v Ball [1911] AC 47 (HL)

A brother and sister were charged with incest between named dates in 1910. There was incontrovertible evidence that they had occupied the same bed in the house in which they were living. The trial judge admitted evidence that they had lived together as husband and wife in 1907 when incest was not a criminal offence. They were convicted and appealed successfully to the Court of Criminal Appeal. The prosecution appealed to the House of Lords.

LORD LOREBURN: 'My Lords, the law on this subject is stated in the judgment of Lord Chancellor Herschell in *Makin* v *Attorney-General for New South Wales* [1894] AC 57 PC; it is well known and I need not repeat it—the question is only of applying it. In accordance with the law laid down in that case, and which is daily applied in the Divorce Court, I consider that this evidence was clearly admissible on the issue that this crime was committed—not to prove the *mens rea*, as Darling J considered, but to establish the guilty relations between the parties and the existence of a sexual passion between them as elements in proving that they had illicit connection in fact on or between the dates charged. Their passion for each other was as much evidence as was their presence together in bed of the fact that when there they had guilty relations with each other.

My Lords, I agree that Courts ought to be very careful to preserve the time-honoured law of England, that you cannot convict a man of one crime by proving that he had committed some other crime; that, and all other safeguards of our criminal law, will be jealously guarded; but here I think the evidence went directly to prove the actual crime for which these parties were indicted.'

(EARL OF HALSBURY and LORDS ASHBOURNE, ALVERSTONE CJ, ATKINSON, GORELL, SHAW OF DUNFERMLINE, MERSEY and ROBSON all concurred.)

Appeal allowed.

• Can the decision in *R v Ball* be reconciled with Lord Herschell's first proposition in *Makin* v *Attorney General for NSW* [1894] AC 57 *ante*, p. 145?

Thompson* v *R [1918] AC 221 (HL)

The appellant was convicted of committing acts of gross indecency with boys on 16 March. At his trial his defence was that he was not the man and he adduced evidence to establish an alibi. It was proved that the man who committed the offence made an appointment to meet the boys on 19 March at the time and place where the offence was committed and that the appellant met the boys at the appointed time and place and gave them money. The prosecution tendered evidence that on this occasion, when he was arrested, the appellant was carrying powder puffs and that he had indecent photographs of boys in his rooms.

LORD FINLAY LC: 'The whole question is as to the identity of the person who came to the spot on 19 March with the person who committed the acts on the 16 March. What was done on the 16 March shows that the person who did it was a person with abnormal propensities of this kind. The possession of the articles tends to show that the person who came on the 19 March, the prisoner, had abnormal propensities of the same kind. The criminal of the 16 March and the prisoner had this feature in common, and it appears to me that the evidence which is objected to afforded some evidence tending to show the probability of the truth of the boys' story as to identity. In my opinion Lawrence J was right in admitting the evidence, and this appeal should be dismissed.'

LORD ATKINSON: 'It would be strange, indeed, if one man should commit with the boys the offence charged on the 16 March, and make an assignation with them to commit it again upon the 19 March, that another man should, with an intent to do the same, take up and fulfil the first man's engagement, personate him as it were, and keep the appointment the first had made. It would appear to me that evidence which goes to prove that the prisoner had in his transactions with these boys on the 19 March an intent or desire to commit an indecent offence with them, if circumstances should permit, becomes evidence to identify him as the person who actually committed on the 16 March the offence for which he was indicted. Apparently the prisoner himself fully appreciated this, for while he stated that the boys did follow him, stared into his face, waited for him while he was in the shop, and watched him through the window, yet he gave them two shillings and told them to go away as the tall man, pointing to a man, was a policeman. The tall man he pointed to was, he said, not Sergeant Blackmore, but one of his own friends, and that he then told them they should wash their dirty faces. The contest then narrows it down to this: Were the sets of acts deposed to in the main by each side as having taken place on the 19 March done with the wicked intent the prosecution alleges, or with the innocent intent the prisoner in his defence alleged? When he is searched powder puffs are found on his person. It is stated that powder puffs are some of the things with which persons who commit abominable and indecent crimes with males furnish themselves for the purpose of carrying out their criminal designs. For what purpose could the prisoner carry upon him on this day the powder puffs? He could not, by them, promote the cause of charity or cleanliness. He could not have carried them for such a purpose—the time had not arrived for their use; but can it be reasonably doubted that they were carried to be used when needed? The possession of them is in my opinion admissible in evidence to show, when taken in connection with the facts proved, that the prisoner harboured on that day an intent to commit an act of indecency with these boys should occasion offer. Well, if these photographs of naked boys, some when apparently approaching adolescence, all I think indecent in their attitude, and some apparently depraved in suggestion, had been found on the person of the accused I do not see how any distinction could well have been drawn between them and the powder puffs. They too are, it is stated, implements for carrying out the same design. I do not know, and it is not stated, whether they are used to stimulate the depraved lusts of those given to such practices, or to corrupt the mind of those whose assistance or sufferance such people seek; but this I think is clear, that they could not be needed for the work of a hygienic enthusiast so devoted to youthful cleanliness that he gave to two boys he had never met before, and who had teased him by staring at him, two shillings to get their dirty faces washed. The fact that they were found in the prisoner's drawer and not on his person may make them less cogent evidence of a criminal intent towards these boys than if they had been found upon his person; but still, in my view, the possession of them is some evidence of the existence of a criminal intent towards these boys on 19 March, and, if so, some evidence of the identity of the person harbouring that intent with the person who had committed the crime charged upon 16 March. I think they belong to the class of evidence mentioned by Lord Herschell in *Makin's Case*, namely, evidence designed and intended to rebut a defence which would be otherwise open to the accused—in this case an alibi for 16 March.'

LORD SUMNER: 'The actual criminal made an appointment to meet the same boys at the same time and place three days later and presumably for the same purpose. This tends to show that his act was not an isolated act, but was an incident in the habitual gratification of a particular propensity. The appellant, as his possession of the photographs tends to show, is a person with the same propensity. Indeed, he went to the place of the appointment with some of the outfit, and he had the rest of it at home. The evidence tends to attach to the accused a peculiarity which, though not purely physical, I think may be recognised as properly bearing that name. Experience tends to show that these offences against nature connote an inversion of normal characteristics which, while demanding punishment as offending against social morality, also partake of the nature of an abnormal physical property. A thief, a cheat, a coiner, or a housebreaker is only a particular specimen of the genus rogue, and, though no doubt each tends to keep to his own line of business, they all alike possess the by no means extraordinary mental characteristic that they propose somehow to get their livings dishonestly. So common a characteristic is not a recognisable mark of the individual. Persons, however, who commit the offences now under consideration seek the habitual gratification of a particular perverted lust, which not only takes them out of the class of ordinary men gone wrong, but stamps them with the hall-mark of a specialised and extraordinary class as much as if they carried on their bodies some physical peculiarity. . .

[T]he photographs, found as they were and after a short interval of time, tend to show that the accused had this recognisable propensity, which it was shown was also the propensity of the criminal of 16 March. It was accordingly admissible evidence of his identity with that criminal. Its weight was for the jury. No doubt it required considerable discretion in introducing it at all and a careful direction from the learned judge, but it is admitted that this was given in unexceptionable terms.

My Lords, if the person who committed the offence had, either by word or conduct, established any connection between what passed on that occasion and the photographs themselves, their admissibility, found as they were so soon afterwards, would present no difficulty. If, on the other hand, there had been nothing to show a propensity in the criminal to the practice of such acts, such as the making of the appointment, I should have thought that the photographs were merely objects going to the accused's bad character and not to his identity with the criminal in the particular case. I certainly do not think it could be held that, as a matter of course, even in the case of crimes of this class, the articles found in a man's possession, not as parts of the transaction which is being inquired into, but at a separate time and place, could, as such, be put in evidence against him merely because they were such as criminals possess or use, and in the absence of any circumstance in the crime tending to show a specific connection between it and the articles in question. If a man could be convicted of a particular burglary, in which it was clear that no tools had been used at all, merely because at another place and time burglar's implements were found on his premises, it is difficult to see what limit could be put to the admissibility of general evidence of bad character, and the fact that evidence of articles found on the premises of accused persons is constantly given without much question, though I doubt not in the vast majority of cases quite rightly, is really only misleading, unless at the same time we ask the question what exactly does this purport to prove and by what probative nexus does it seek to prove it.'

(LORDS DUNEDIN and PARKER OF WADDINGTON concurred. LORD PARMOOR also delivered a judgment dismissing the appeal.)

Appeal dismissed.

• Is the reasoning in the case of *Thompson* v *R* consistent with that in *Makin* v *Attorney General for New South Wales* [1894] AC 57, *ante*, p. 145?

R v *Sims* [1946] KB 531 (CCA)

The defendant was charged with sodomy with three men and gross indecency with a fourth. All the offences were alleged to have taken place on different occasions. At the trial the defendant made an application that the charges be tried separately in respect of each separate man. The application was refused and the defendant was convicted subsequently of sodomy on each of the three charges, but acquitted on the indecency charge.

LORD GODDARD CJ: 'We start with the general principle that evidence is admissible if it is logically probative, that is, if it is logically relevant to the issue whether the prisoner has committed the act charged. To this principle there are exceptions. One of the most important exceptions is this: Evidence that the accused has a bad reputation or has a bad disposition is not admissible unless he himself opens the door to it by giving evidence of good character or otherwise under the Criminal Evidence Act 1898. The reason for excluding evidence of bad character was said by Willes J to be policy and humanity. He thought that evidence of bad character was just as relevant as evidence of good character, but the unfair prejudice created by it was so great that more injustice would be done by admitting it than by excluding it: see *R* v *Rowton* (1865) Le & Ca 520. Lord Sumner, however, thought it was irrelevant: see *Thompson* v R [1918] AC 221. We do not stay to consider which view is correct. The exception is well settled. The question is what are its limits. In our opinion it does not extend further than the interests of justice demand. Evidence is not to be excluded merely because it tends to show the accused to be of a bad disposition, but only if it shows nothing more. There are many cases where evidence of specific acts or circumstances connecting the accused with specific features of the crime has been held admissible, even though it also tends to show him to be of bad disposition. The most familiar example is when there is an issue whether the act of the accused was designed or accidental or done with guilty knowledge, in which case evidence is admissible of a series of similar acts by the accused on other occasions, because a series of acts with the self-same characteristics is unlikely to be produced by accident or inadvertence: see *Makin* v *Attorney-General for New South Wales* [1894] AC 57.

Another example is where there is an issue as to the nature of an act done by the accused with or to another person, in which case evidence is admissible of a series of similar acts between them, because human nature has a propensity to repetition and a series of acts is likely to bear the same characteristics: see *R* v *Ball* [1911] AC 47. So also where there is an issue as to the identity of the accused, we think that evidence is admissible of a series of similar acts done by him to other persons, because, while one witness to one act might be mistaken in identifying him, it is unlikely that a number of witnesses identifying the same person in relation to a series of acts with the self-same characteristics would all be mistaken. In all these cases the evidence of other acts may tend to show the accused to be of bad disposition, but it also shows something more. The other acts have specific features connecting him with the crime charged and are on that account admissible in evidence. A similar distinction exists in respect of articles found in possession of the accused. If they have no connection with the crime except to show that the accused has a bad disposition, the evidence is not admissible; but if there are any circumstances in the crime tending to show a specific connection between it and the articles, the evidence is admissible; see per Lord Sumner in *Thompson* v *R*. Thus, in the case of burglary, evidence is admissible that housebreaking implements such as might have been used in the crime were found in the possession of the accused. In the case of abortion, evidence is admissible that the apparatus of an abortionist such as might have been used in the crime was found in the possession of the accused. The admissibility does not, however, depend on the circumstance that the articles might have been used in the crime. If there is any other specific feature connecting the articles with the crime, it will suffice. Thus, in the case of *Thompson*, there was no suggestion that the photographs were used in the crime charged, but the House of Lords found a connection between the crime and the photographs in that the criminal on the 16 March showed a propensity to unnatural practices by making an appointment for the 19 March and the accused showed a like propensity by the photographs found in his possession. In the cases of *R* v *Twiss* [1918] 2 KB 853 and *R* v *Gillingham* (1939) 27 Cr App R 143 there was also no suggestion that the photographs were used in the crime charged, but the court found a connection between the two in that the crime itself showed a propensity to unnatural practices and the photographs showed a like propensity. The specific feature in such cases lies in the abnormal and perverted propensity which stamps the individual as clearly as if marked by a physical deformity. We think that in all the cases where evidence has been admitted there have been specific features connecting the evidence with the crime charged as distinct from evidence that he is of a bad disposition. This is illustrated by the cases on false pretences where evidence can be given of other transactions when similar false pretences were used, because they have that specific feature in common; but not of different transactions which only show that the accused was of a generally fraudulent disposition.

It has often been said that the admissibility of evidence of this kind depends on the nature of the defence raised by the accused: see, for instance, the observations of Lord Sumner in *Thompson* v *R*, and of this court in *R* v *Cole* (1941) 28 Cr App R 43. We think that that view is the result of a different approach to the subject. If one starts with the assumption that all evidence tending to show a disposition towards a particular crime must be excluded unless justified, then the justification of evidence of this kind is that it tends to rebut a defence otherwise open to the accused; but if one starts with the general proposition that all evidence that is logically probative is admissible unless excluded, then evidence of this kind does not have to seek a justification but is admissible irrespective of the issues raised by the defence, and this we think is the correct view. It is plainly the sensible view. It is only fair to the prosecution, because the depositions have often to be taken and the evidence called before the nature of the defence is known. It is also only fair to the accused, so that he should have notice beforehand of the case he has to meet. In any event, whenever there is a plea of not guilty, everything is in issue and the prosecution have to prove the whole of their case, including the identity of the accused, the nature of the act and the existence of any necessary knowledge or intent. The accused should not be able, by confining himself at the trial to one issue, to exclude evidence that would be admissible and fatal if he ran two defences; for that would make the astuteness of the accused or his advisers prevail over the interests of justice. An attempt was made by the defence in *R* v *Armstrong* [1922] 2 KB 555 to exclude evidence in that way, but it did not succeed.

Applying these principles, we are of opinion that on the trial of one of the counts in this case, the evidence on the others would be admissible. The evidence of each man was that the accused invited him into the house and there committed the acts charged. The acts they describe bear a striking similarity. That is a special feature sufficient in itself to justify the admissibility of the evidence; but we think it should be put on a broader basis. Sodomy is a crime in a special category because, as Lord Sumner said [1918] AC 235, "persons who commit the offences now under consideration seek the habitual gratification of a particular perverted lust, which not only takes them out of the class of ordinary men gone wrong, but stamps them with the hall-mark of a specialised and extraordinary class as much as if they carried on their bodies some physical peculiarity." On this account, in regard to this crime we think that the repetition of the acts is itself a specific feature connecting the accused with the crime and that evidence of this kind is admissible to show the nature of the act done by the accused. The probative force of all the acts together is much greater than one alone; for, whereas the jury might think one man might be telling an untruth, three or four are hardly likely to tell the same untruth unless they were conspiring together. If there is nothing to suggest a conspiracy their evidence would seem to be overwhelming. Whilst it would no doubt be in the interests of the prisoner that each case should be considered separately without the evidence on the others, we think that the interests of justice require that on each case the evidence on the others should be considered, and that, even apart from the defence raised by him, the evidence would be admissible.

In this case the matter can be put in another and very simple way. The visits of the men to the prisoner's house were either for a guilty or an innocent purpose: that they all speak to the commission of the same class of acts upon them tends to show that in each case the visits were for the former and not the latter purpose. The same considerations would apply to a case where a man is charged with a series of indecent offences against children, whether boys or girls: that they all complain of the same sort of conduct shows that the interest the prisoner was taking in them was not of a paternal or friendly nature but for the purpose of satisfying lust.

If we are right in thinking that the evidence was admissible, it is plain that the accused would not be prejudiced or embarrassed by reason of all the counts being tried together, and there was no reason for the judge to direct the jury that, in considering whether a particular charge was proved, they were to shut out other charges from their minds.'

Appeal dismissed.

Noor Mohamed v R [1949] AC 182 (PC)

The appellant, a goldsmith, was convicted of murdering by potassium cyanide poisoning a woman, Ayesha, who was living with him as his wife. At his trial, evidence, led for the purpose of meeting a possible defence of accident or suicide, was admitted that some two years earlier his wife, Gooriah, had died of potassium cyanide poisoning in similar circumstances although her death had not been the subject of any criminal charge.

LORD DU PARCQ, delivering the judgment of the court: 'The first comment to be made on the evidence under review is that it plainly tended to show that the appellant had been guilty of a criminal act which was not the act with which he was charged. In *Makin* v *Attorney-General for New South Wales* [1894] AC 57, 65, Lord Herschell LC, delivering the judgment of the Board, laid down two principles which must be observed in a case of this character. Of these the first was that "it is undoubtedly not competent for the prosecution to adduce evidence tending to show that the accused has been guilty of criminal acts other than those covered by the indictment, for the purpose of leading to the conclusion that the accused is a person likely from his criminal conduct or character to have committed the offence for which he is being tried." In 1934 this principle was said by Lord Sankey LC, with the concurrence of all the noble and learned Lords who sat with him, to be "one of the most deeply rooted and jealously guarded principles of our criminal law" and to be "fundamental in the law of evidence as conceived in this country." (*Maxwell* v *The Director of Public Prosecutions* [1935] AC 309, 317, 320.)

The second principle stated in *Makin's* case was that "the mere fact that the evidence adduced tends to show the commission of other crimes does not render it inadmissible if it be relevant to an issue before the jury, and it may be so relevant if it bears upon the question whether the acts alleged to constitute the crime charged in the indictment were designed or accidental, or to rebut a defence which would otherwise be open to the accused." The statement of this latter principle has given rise to some discussion. A plea of not guilty puts everything in issue which is a necessary ingredient of the offence charged, and if the Crown were permitted, ostensibly in order to strengthen the evidence of a fact which was not denied and, perhaps, could not be the subject of rational dispute, to adduce evidence of a previous crime, it is manifest that the protection afforded by the "jealously guarded" principle first enunciated would be gravely impaired. This aspect of the matter was considered by the House of Lords in *Thompson* v *The King* [1918] AC 221. Their Lordships need not allude to the facts of that case. It is enough to say that the evidence there admitted was held to be relevant as one of the indicia by which the accused man's identity with the person who had committed the crime could be established. (See per Lord Parker of Waddington at p. 231.) In the words of Lord Atkinson, it rebutted the defence of an alibi which otherwise would have been open. Nothing of the kind can be suggested in the present case. The value of the case for the present purpose is that Lord Sumner dealt particularly with the difficulty to which their Lordships have referred, and stated his conclusion as follows: "Before an issue can be said to be raised, which would permit the introduction of such evidence so obviously prejudicial to the accused, it must have been raised in substance if not in so many words, and the issue so raised must be one to which the prejudicial evidence is relevant. The mere theory that a plea of not guilty puts everything material in issue is not enough for this purpose. The prosecution cannot credit the accused with fancy defences in order to rebut them at the outset with some damning piece of prejudice."

Their Lordships respectfully agree with what they conceive to be the spirit and intention of Lord Sumner's words, and wish to say nothing to detract from their value. On principle, however, and with due regard to subsequent authority, their Lordships think that one qualification of the rule laid down by Lord Sumner must be admitted. An accused person need set up no defence other than a general denial of the crime alleged. The plea of not guilty may be equivalent to saying: "Let the prosecution prove its case, if it can," and having said so much the accused may take refuge in silence. In such a case it may appear (for instance) that the facts and circumstances of the particular offence charged are consistent with innocent intention, whereas further evidence, which incidentally shows that the accused has committed one or more other offences, may tend to prove that they are consistent only with a guilty intent. The prosecution could not be said, in their Lordships' opinion, to be "crediting the accused with a fancy defence" if they sought to adduce such evidence. It is right to add, however, that in all such cases the judge ought to consider whether the evidence which it is proposed to adduce is sufficiently substantial, having regard to the purpose to which it is professedly directed, to make it desirable in the interest of justice that it should be admitted. If, so far as that purpose is concerned, it can in the circumstances of the case have only trifling weight, the judge will be right to exclude it. To say this is not to confuse weight with admissibility. The distinction is plain, but cases must occur in which it would be unjust to admit evidence of a character gravely prejudicial to the accused even though there may be some tenuous ground for holding it technically admissible. The decision must then be left to the discretion and the sense of fairness of the judge.

Their Lordships have considered with care the question whether the evidence now in question can be said to be relevant to any issue in the case. They have asked themselves, adopting the language of Lord Sumner in *Thompson's* case [1918] AC 221, 236, "What exactly does this purport to prove?" At the trial the learned counsel for the Crown, when submitting that the evidence should be admitted, referred to the possible defences of accident and suicide. In his address to the jury he said, according to the note, that the evidence was led "to meet the defence of suicide," and pointed out that the circumstances surrounding the deaths of the two women "followed a similar pattern." At their Lordships' bar it was submitted that this similarity of circumstances would lead to the inference that the appellant administered poison to Ayesha with felonious intent.

There can be little doubt that the manner of Ayesha's death, even without the evidence as to the death of Gooriah, would arouse suspicion against the appellant in the mind of a reasonable man. The facts proved as to the death of Gooriah would certainly tend to deepen that suspicion, and might well tilt the balance against the accused in the estimation of a jury. It by no means follows that this evidence ought to be admitted. If an examination of it shows that it is impressive just because it appears to demonstrate, in the words of Lord Herschell in *Makin's* case [1894] AC 57 "that the accused is a person likely from his criminal conduct or character to have committed the offence for which he is being tried," and if it is otherwise of no real substance, then it was certainly wrongly admitted. After fully considering all the facts which, if accepted, it revealed, their Lordships are not satisfied that its admission can be justified on any of the grounds which have been suggested or on any other ground. Assuming that it is consistent with the evidence relating to the death of Ayesha that she took her own life, or that she took poison accidentally (one of which assumptions must be made for the purpose of the Crown's argument at the trial) there is nothing in the circumstances of Gooriah's death to negative these possible views. Even if the appellant deliberately caused Gooriah to take poison (an assumption not lightly to be made, since he was never charged with having murdered her) it does not follow that Ayesha may not have committed suicide. As to the argument from similarity of circumstances, it seems on analysis to amount to no more than this, that if the appellant murdered one woman because he was jealous of her, it is probable that he murdered another for the same reason. If the appellant were proved to have administered poison to Ayesha in circumstances consistent with accident, then proof that he had previously administered poison to Gooriah in similar circumstances might well have been admissible. There was, however, no direct evidence in either case that the appellant had administered the poison. It is true that in the case of Gooriah there was evidence from which it might be inferred that he persuaded her to take the poison by a trick, but this evidence cannot properly be used to found an inference that a similar trick was used to deceive Ayesha, and so to fill a gap in the available evidence. The evidence which was properly adduced as to Ayesha shows her to have been acquainted, as were, it may be supposed, most of the inhabitants of the village in which the appellant lived, with the fact that suspicion rested on him in respect of Gooriah's death, and the theory that Ayesha was deceived into taking poison by a similar ruse to that which is supposed to have succeeded with Gooriah seems to their Lordships to rest on an improbable surmise. The effect of the admission of the impugned evidence may well have been that the jury came to the conclusion that the appellant was guilty of the murder of Gooriah, with which he had never been charged, and having thus, adjudged him a murderer, were satisfied with something short of conclusive proof that he had murdered Ayesha. In these circumstances the verdict cannot stand. . ..

Their Lordships are aware that their statement of the principles to be applied to such a case as this, and of the right way of applying them, may not accord with some, at least, of the *dicta* contained in a recent decision of the Court of Criminal Appeal in England, to which counsel rightly directed their attention. In *R v Sims* [1946] KB 531 the Lord Chief Justice, delivering judgment, expressed the opinion of the court as to the proper method of approaching a question concerning the admissibility of evidence of other offences than that charged in these words: "If one starts with the assumption that all evidence tending to show a disposition towards a particular crime must be excluded unless justified, then the justification of evidence of this kind is that it tends to rebut a defence otherwise open to the accused; but if one starts with the general proposition that all evidence that is logically probative is admissible unless excluded, then evidence of this kind does not have to seek a justification but is admissible irrespective of the issues raised by the defence, and this we think is the correct view. It is plainly the sensible view." With all due deference to the Court of Criminal Appeal, their Lordships feel bound to say that they are not convinced that the method of approach which it thus approved has any advantage over that which it rejects as incorrect. The expression "logically probative" may be understood to include much evidence which English law deems to be irrelevant. Logicians are not bound by the rules of evidence which guide English courts, and theories of probability sometimes cause a clash of philosophic opinion. It would no doubt be wrong to interpret the observations of the Court of Criminal Appeal as meaning that evidence can sometimes be admitted merely for the reason that it shows a propensity in the accused to commit crimes of the nature of that with which he is charged. It cannot be supposed that the court intended to lay down a proposition which would conflict with principles which have been laid down, or approved, by the House of Lords. It may be assumed that it is still true to say, as Lord Sumner said 30 years ago: "No one doubts that it does not tend to prove a man guilty of a particular crime to show that he is the kind of man who would commit a crime, or that he is generally disposed to crime and even to a particular crime." (*Thompson* v *The King* [1918] AC 232.) If all that the court meant to say was that evidence of the kind specified in the first of the principles stated in *Makin's* case may be admitted if it is relevant for other reasons, then the *dictum* has no novelty. It does seem, however, that the passage quoted was intended at least to bear the meaning that evidence ought to be admitted which is in any way relevant to a matter which can be said to be in issue, however technically, between the Crown and the accused, because a little later in the judgment the following passage occurs: "In any event, whenever there is a plea of not guilty, everything is in issue and the prosecution have to prove the whole of their case, including the identity of the accused, the nature of the act and the existence of any necessary knowledge or intent". The Court of Criminal Appeal would thus appear to have rejected altogether the opinion of Lord Sumner which, although, as their Lordships have said, they believe that it must in one respect be somewhat qualified, has hitherto been generally accepted as a governing principle. Recent *dicta* of the Court of Criminal Appeal, though carrying great weight, do not necessarily outweigh earlier *dicta* in the House of Lords or the Court of Crown Cases Reserved, or in the Court of Criminal Appeal itself, and if their Lordships have correctly understood those which they have quoted, they can only regard them as in some degree inconsistent with settled principle. Their Lordships think that a passage from the judgment of Kennedy J in the well-known case of *R* v *Bond* [1906] 2 KB 389 may well be quoted in this connection: "If, as is plain, we have to recognise the existence of certain circumstances in which justice cannot be attained at the trial without a disclosure of prior offences, the utmost vigilance at least should be maintained in restricting the number of such cases, and in seeing that the general rule of the criminal law of England, which (to the credit, in my opinion, of English justice) excludes evidence of prior offences, is not broken or frittered away by the creation of novel and anomalous exceptions.''

Their Lordships respectfully approve this statement, which seems to them to be completely in accord with the later statement of the Lord Chancellor in *Maxwell's* case [1935] AC 309, when he said "It is of the utmost importance for a fair trial that the evidence should be *prima facie* limited to matters relating to the transaction which forms the subject of the indictment and that any departure from these matters should be strictly confined". They would regret the adoption of any doctrine which made the general rule subordinate to its exceptions. They must add, however, that though they have been unwilling to adopt the approach to the problem which the Court of Criminal Appeal has recommended, they of course refrain from expressing any opinion as to the propriety of the actual decision in *Sims's* case. It is unnecessary, and therefore undesirable, that they should do so.'

Appeal allowed.

Harris v DPP [1952] AC 694 (HL)

A series of eight larcenies having common characteristics occurred in May, June and July 1951, in an office in an enclosed and extensive market at times when most of the gates were shut and in periods during part of which the defendant, a police officer, was on solitary duty there. The precise time of only one larceny, the last which occurred in July, was known and then the defendant was found to be in the immediate vicinity of the office. He was charged on indictment with all the larcenies and, having been tried on all eight counts simultaneously, he was acquitted on the first seven and convicted on the eighth, that relating to the larceny in July.

VISCOUNT SIMON LC: 'In my opinion, the principle laid down by Lord Herschell LC in *Makin's* case [1894] AC 57 remains the proper principle to apply and I see no reason for modifying it. *Makin's* case [1894] AC 57 was a decision of the Judicial Committee of the Privy Council, but it was unanimously approved by the House of Lords in *R v Ball* [1911] AC 47, 71, and has been constantly relied on ever since. It is, I think, an error to attempt to draw up a closed list of the sort of cases in which the principle operates: such a list only provides instances of its general application, whereas what really matters is the principle itself and its proper application to the particular circumstances of the charge that is being tried. It is the application that may sometimes be difficult, and the particular case now before the House illustrates that difficulty. . .When Lord Herschell speaks of evidence of other occasions in which the accused was concerned as being admissible to "rebut" a defence which would otherwise be open to the accused, he is not using the vocabulary of civil pleadings and requiring a specific line of defence to be set up before evidence is tendered which would overthrow it. If it were so, instances would arise where magistrates might be urged not to commit for trial, or it might be ruled at the trial, at the end of the prosecution's case, that enough had not been established to displace the presumption of innocence, when all the time evidence properly available to support the prosecution was being withheld. "In criminal cases, and especially in those where the justices have summary jurisdiction, the admissibility of evidence has to be determined in reference to all the issues which have to be established by the prosecution, and frequently without any indication of the particular defence that is going to be set up": *per* Avory J in giving the judgment of the Divisional Court in *Perkins* v *Jeffery* [1915] 2 KB 702, 707.

Lord du Parcq pointed out in *Noor Mohamed* v *The King* [1949] AC 182, 191 in commenting on what Lord Sumner had said in *Thompson* v *The King* [1918] AC 221, 232: "An accused person need set up no defence other than a general denial of the crime alleged. The plea of not guilty may be equivalent to saying 'let the prosecution prove its case, if it can,' and having said so much the accused may take refuge in silence. In such a case it may appear (for instance) that the facts and circumstances of the particular offence charged are consistent with innocent intention, whereas further evidence, which incidentally shows that the accused has committed one or more other offences, may tend to prove that they are consistent only with a guilty intent. The prosecution could not be said, in their Lordships' opinion, to be 'crediting the accused with a fancy defence' if they sought to adduce such evidence."

Lord Herschell's statement that evidence of "similar facts" may sometimes be admissible as bearing on "the question whether the acts alleged to constitute the crime charged in the indictment were designed or accidental" deserves close analysis. Sometimes the purpose properly served by such evidence is to help to show that what happened was not an accident; if it was, the accused had nothing to do with it. Sometimes the purpose is to help to show what was the intention with which the accused did the act which he is proved to have done. In a proper case, and subject to the safeguards which Lord Herschell indicates, either purpose is legitimate. Scrutton J points out the distinction very clearly in *R* v *Ball* [1911] AC 47. Sometimes the two purposes are served by the same evidence.

The substance of the matter appears to me to be that the prosecution may adduce all proper evidence which tends to prove the charge. I do not understand Lord Herschell's words to mean that the prosecution must withhold such evidence until after the accused has set up a specific defence which calls for rebuttal. Where, for instance, *mens rea* is an essential element in guilt, and the facts of the occurrence which is the subject of the charge, standing by themselves, would be consistent with mere accident, there would be nothing wrong in the prosecution seeking to establish the true situation by offering, as part of its case in the first instance, evidence of similar action by the accused at another time which would go to show that he intended to do what he did on the occasion charged and was thus acting criminally. *R* v *Mortimer* (1936) 25 Cr App R 150 is a good example of this. What Lord Sumner meant when he denied the right of the prosecution to "credit the accused with fancy defences" (in *Thompson* v *The King*) was that evidence of similar facts involving the accused ought not to be dragged in to his prejudice without reasonable cause.

There is a second proposition which ought to be added under this head. It is not a rule of law governing the admissibility of evidence, but a rule of judicial practice followed by a judge who is trying a charge of crime when he thinks that the application of the practice is called for. Lord du Parcq referred to it in *Noor Mohamed* v *The King* [1949] AC 182, 192 immediately after the passage above quoted, when he said that "in all such cases the judge ought to consider whether the evidence which it is proposed to adduce is sufficiently substantial, having regard to the purpose to which it is professedly directed, to make it desirable in the interest of justice that it should be admitted. If, so far as that purpose is concerned, it can in the circumstances of the case have only trifling weight, the judge will be right to exclude it. To say this is not to confuse weight with admissibility. The distinction is plain, but cases must occur in which it would be unjust to admit evidence of a character gravely prejudicial to the accused even though there may be some tenuous ground for holding it technically admissible. The decision must then be left to the discretion and the sense of fairness of the judge."

This second proposition flows from the duty of the judge when trying a charge of crime to set the essentials of justice above the technical rule if the strict application of the latter would operate unfairly against the accused. If such a case arose, the judge may intimate to the prosecution that evidence of "similar facts" affecting the accused, though admissible, should not be pressed because its probable effect "would be out of proportion to its true evidential value" (*per* Lord Moulton in *Director of Public Prosecutions* v *Christie* (1914) 24 Cox CC 249, 257). Such an intimation rests entirely within the discretion of the judge.

It is, of course, clear that evidence of "similar facts" cannot in any case be admissible to support an accusation against the accused unless they are connected in some relevant way with the accused and with his participation in the crime. (See Lord Sumner in *Thompson* v *The King* [1918] AC 221, 234.) It is the fact that he was involved in the other occurrences which may negative the inference of accident or establish his *mens rea* by showing "system." Or, again, the other occurrences may sometimes assist to prove his identity, as, for instance, in *Perkins* v *Jeffery* [1915] 2 KB 702. But evidence of other occurrences which merely tend to deepen suspicion does not go to prove guilt. This is the ground, as it seems to me, on which the Judicial Committee of the Privy Council allowed the appeal in *Noor Mohamed* v *The King* [1949] AC 182. The Board there took the view that the evidence as to the previous death of the accused's wife was not relevant to prove the charge against him of murdering another woman, and if it was not relevant it was at the same time highly prejudicial. It is to be noted that the Judicial Committee did not question the decision in *R* v *Sims* [1946] KB 531.

It remains to examine certain reported cases dealing with admissibility of evidence of "similar facts" decided since *Makin's* case, to which the Attorney-General referred us. Rightly understood, these cases do not seem to me to involve any enlargement of the area within which evidence of "similar facts" might be admitted.

In *R* v *Smith* [1915] WN 309 the accused was charged with murdering a woman, immediately after going through a form of marriage with her, by drowning her in a bath in the lodging where they were staying. Evidence was held to be rightly admitted of very similar circumstances which connected the accused with the deaths at a later date of two other women who were drowned in their baths after the accused had gone through a form of marriage with each of them in turn. In all three cases it was shown that the accused benefited by the death. In all three cases the prisoner urged the woman to take a bath and was on the premises when she prepared to do so. The ground on which the evidence of the two later occurrences was admissible was that the occurrences were so alike and the part taken by the accused in arranging what the woman would do was so similar in each case as to get rid of any suggestion of accident. The decision in *R* v *Smith* therefore involved no extension of the principle laid down in *Makin's* case. The challenged evidence was admissible both to show that what happened in the case of the first woman was not an accident and also to show what was the intention with which the accused did what he did.

In *R* v *Armstrong* [1922] 2 KB 555 the accused was indicted for the murder of his wife by administering arsenic to her. The wife was shown to have died from arsenical poisoning, but the defence urged that it was not shown that the husband had administered the poison to her, but that she had committed suicide. The accused had purchased a quantity of arsenic and made it up into a number of small packets, each containing what would constitute a fatal dose, but offered the explanation that he had purchased the poison merely to use it as a weed-killer in his garden. The prosecution called evidence to show that, eight months after the death of his wife, he secretly administered arsenic to another person. The Court of Criminal Appeal held that this evidence was admissible because it went to disprove the suggestion that he had purchased and kept arsenic for an innocent purpose. The decision in *R* v *Armstrong* appears to me to involve no enlargement of the principle in *Makin's* case. Lord Hewart CJ rightly observed at p. 566: "The fact that he was subsequently found not merely in possession of but actually using for a similar deadly purpose the very kind of poison that caused the death of his wife was evidence from which the jury might infer that that poison was not in his possession at the earlier date for an innocent purpose."

In *R* v *Sims* there is a passage in the judgment of Lord Goddard CJ which appears to have raised doubts in some quarters as to whether the principle in *Makin's* case was being extended. The Lord Chief Justice there observed that one method of approaching the relevant problem is to start with the general proposition that all evidence that is "logically probative" is admissible unless excluded by established rules, and that it would follow that evidence for the prosecution "is admissible irrespective of the issues raised by the defence." It is the words "logically probative" which have raised doubts in some minds. Such a phrase may seem to invite philosophic discussion which would be ill-suited to the practical business of applying the criminal law with justice to all concerned. But I do not understand the Lord Chief Justice by the use of such a phrase to be enlarging the ambit of the principle in *Makin's* case at all or to be disregarding the restrictions which Lord Herschell indicated. In one sense, evidence of previous bad conduct or hearsay evidence, might be regarded as having, logically, a probative value, but, of course, the judgment in *Sims'* case is not opening the door to that. I understand the passage quoted to mean no more than what I have already formulated, viz., that the prosecution may advance proper evidence to prove its case without waiting to ascertain what is the line adopted by the defence. Lord du Parcq, in *Noor Mohamed* v *The King*, points out the possibility of misunderstanding the Lord Chief Justice's words and proceeds to put his own construction upon them. In substance, I agree with his interpretation. There is, however, this to be added. The proper working of the criminal law in this connection depends on the due observance of both the propositions which I have endeavoured to expound in this judgment. While the prosecution may adduce all proper evidence which tends to prove the charge, it must do so with due regard to the warnings contained in the judgments of Kennedy J in *R* v *Bond* [1906] 2 KB 389 and Lord Sankey LC in *Maxwell* v *Director of Public Prosecutions* [1935] AC 309. A criminal trial in this country is conducted for the purpose of deciding whether the prosecution has proved that the accused is guilty of the particular crime charged, and evidence of "similar facts" should be excluded unless such evidence has a really material bearing on the issues to be decided. This, in my opinion, is the way in which Lord Sumner's observations in *Thompson* v *The King* should be regarded. It should be noted that in that case Lord Parker was careful to insist that it would be wrong to treat the decision as "laying down any principle capable of general application." With this explanation, I see no reason to differ from the conclusion in *R* v *Sims*.

(His Lordship held that as regards the larceny of July, the evidence of the previous larcenies, which occurred when he was not proved to have been near the office, should have been excluded from the consideration of the jury and, the judge having omitted to direct them to that effect, the conviction should be quashed. LORDS PORTER, TUCKER, and MORTON OF HENRYTON agreed. LORD OAKSEY agreed with the principles stated by the LORD CHANCELLOR as to the admissibility of evidence, but disagreed with the application of those principles to the facts of the case.)

Appeal allowed.

DPP v *Boardman* [1975] AC 421 (HL)

The appellant, the headmaster of a boarding school for boys, was charged, *inter alia*, with buggery with S, a pupil aged 16, and inviting H, a pupil aged 17, to commit buggery with him. The defence was that S and H were lying and that the alleged incidents never took place. The trial judge ruled that the evidence of H was admissible on the count concerning S and *vice versa.* This was because, in each case, the homosexual conduct alleged by both boys against the appellant was of an unusual kind, in that it involved a request by a middle aged man to an adolescent to play the active role in buggery. There were, however, other similarities in the evidence of S and H. Both said that they were woken up by the appellant at about midnight whilst asleep in the dormitory; both said that he used similar words to induce their participation. The jury convicted the appellant, and his appeal against conviction on the ground, *inter alia*, that the judge's ruling had been wrong was dismissed by the Court of Appeal. A further appeal was made to the House of Lords. The point of law of general public importance certified was as follows: 'Whether on a charge involving an allegation of homosexual conduct where there is evidence that the accused person is a man whose homosexual proclivities take a particular form, that evidence is thereby admissible although it tends to show that the accused has been guilty of criminal acts other than those charged.'

LORD WILBERFORCE: 'My Lords, the question for decision in this appeal is whether, on a charge against the appellant of buggery with one boy, evidence was admissible that the appellant had incited another boy to buggery, and *vice versa*. The judge ruled that, in the particular circumstances of this case, the evidence was admissible. We have to decide whether this ruling was correct; for reasons which others of your Lordships have given, we cannot answer the question certified in the terms in which it is stated. Whether in the field of sexual conduct or otherwise, there is no general or automatic answer to be given to the question whether evidence of facts similar to those the subject of a particular charge ought to be admitted. In each case it is necessary to estimate (i) whether, and if so how strongly, the evidence as to other facts tends to support, i.e., to make more credible, the evidence given as to the fact in question, (ii) whether such evidence, if given, is likely to be prejudicial to the accused. Both these elements involve questions of degree.

It falls to the judge, in the first place by way of preliminary ruling, and indeed on an application for separate trials if such is made (see the opinion of my noble and learned friend Lord Cross of Chelsea), to estimate the respective and relative weight of these two factors and only to allow the evidence to be put before the jury if he is satisfied that the answer to the first question is clearly positive, and, on the assumption, which is likely, that the second question must be similarly answered, that on a combination of the two the interests of justice clearly require that the evidence be admitted.

Questions of this kind arise in a number of different contexts and have, correspondingly, to be resolved in different ways. I think that it is desirable to confine ourselves to the present set of facts, and to situations of a similar character. In my understanding we are not here concerned with cases of "system" or "underlying unity" (cf. *Moorov* v *HM Advocate*, 1930 JC 68), words whose vagueness is liable to result in their misapplication, nor with a case involving proof of identity, or an alibi, nor, even, is this a case where evidence is adduced to rebut a particular defence. It is sometimes said that evidence of "similar facts" may be called to rebut a defence of innocent association, a proposition which I regard with suspicion since it seems a specious manner of outflanking the exclusionary rule. But we need not consider the validity or scope of this proposition. The Court of Appeal dealt with the case on the basis, submitted by the appellants's counsel, that no defence of innocent association was set up; in my opinion we should take the same course.

This is simply a case where evidence of facts similar in character to those forming the subject of the charge is sought to be given in support of the evidence on that charge. Though the case was one in which separate charges relating to different complainants were tried jointly, the principle must be the same as would arise if there were only one charge relating to one complainant. If the appellant were being tried on a charge relating to S, could the prosecution call H as a witness to give evidence about facts relating to H? The judge should apply just as strict a rule in the one case as in the other. If, as I believe, the general rule is that such evidence cannot be allowed, it requires exceptional circumstances to justify the admission. This House should not, in my opinion, encourage erosion of the general rule.

We can dispose at once of the suggestion that there is a special rule or principle applicable to sexual, or to homosexual, offences. This suggestion had support at one time—eminent support from Lord Sumner in *Thompson* v *The King* [1918] AC 221— but is now certainly obsolete: see *per* Lord Reid (at p. 751) and the other learned lords in *R* v *Kilbourne* [1973] AC 729. Evidence that an offence of a sexual character was committed by A against B cannot be supported by evidence that an offence of a sexual character was committed by A against C, or against C, D and E.

The question certified suggests that the contrary may be true if the offences take a "particular form". I do not know what this means: all sexual activity has some form or other and the varieties are not unlimited: how particular must it be for a special rule to apply? The general salutary rule of exclusion must not be eroded through so vague an epithet. The danger of it being so is indeed well shown in the present case for the judge excluded the (similar fact) evidence of one boy because it showed "normal" homosexual acts while admitting the (similar fact) evidence of another boy because the homosexual acts assumed a different, and, in his view, "abnormal," pattern. Distinctions such as this, rightly called fine distinctions by the judge, lend an unattractive unreality to the law.

If the evidence was to be received, then, it must be on some general principle not confined to sexual offences. There are obvious difficulties in the way of formulating any such rule in such a manner as, on the one hand, to enable clear guidance to be given to juries, and, on the other hand, to avoid undue rigidity. The prevailing formulation is to be found in the judgment of the Court of Criminal Appeal in *R* v *Sims* [1946] KB 531 where it was said, at pp. 539-540: "The evidence of each man was that the accused invited him into the house and there committed the acts charged. The acts they describe bear a striking similarity. That is a special feature sufficient in itself to justify the admissibility of the evidence;. . .The probative force of all the facts together is much greater than one alone; for, whereas the jury might think that one man might be telling an untruth, three or four are hardly likely to tell the same untruth unless they were conspiring together. If there is nothing to suggest a conspiracy their evidence would seem to be overwhelming."

Sims has not received universal approbation or uniform commentary, but I think that it must be taken that this passage has received at least the general approval of this House in *R v Kilbourne* [1973] AC 529. For my part, since the statement is evidently related to the facts of that particular case, I should deprecate its literal use in other cases. It is certainly neither clear nor comprehensive. A suitable adaptation, and, if necessary, expansion, should be allowed to judges in order to suit the facts involved. The basic principle must be that the admission of similar fact evidence (of the kind now in question) is exceptional and requires a strong degree of probative force. This probative force is derived, if at all, from the circumstance that the facts testified to by the several witnesses bear to each other such a striking similarity that they must, when judged by experience and common sense, either all be true, or have arisen from a cause common to the witnesses or from pure coincidence. The jury may, therefore, properly be asked to judge whether the right conclusion is that all are true, so that each story is supported by the other(s).

I use the words "a cause common to the witnesses" to include not only (as in *R v Sims* [1946] KB 531) the possibility that the witnesses may have invented a story in concert but also the possibility that a similar story may have arisen by a process of infection from media or publicity or simply from fashion. In the sexual field, and in others, this may be a real possibility: something much more than mere similarity and absence of proved conspiracy is needed if this evidence is to be allowed. This is well illustrated by *R v Kilbourne* [1973] AC 529 where the judge excluded "intra group" evidence because of the possibility, *as it appeared to him*, of collaboration between boys who knew each other well. This is, in my respectful opinion, the right course rather than to admit the evidence unless a case of collaboration or concoction is made out.

If this test is to be applied fairly, much depends in the first place upon the experience and common sense of the judge. As was said by Lord Simon of Glaisdale in *R v Kilbourne*, at p 756, in judging whether one fact is probative of another, experience plays as large a place as logic. And in matters of experience it is for the judge to keep close to current mores. What is striking in one age is normal in another: the perversions of yesterday may be the routine or the fashion of tomorrow. The ultimate test has to be applied by the jury using similar qualities of experience and common sense after a fair presentation of the dangers either way of admission or of rejection. Finally, whether the judge has properly used and stated the ingredients of experience and common sense may be reviewed by the Court of Appeal.

The present case is, to my mind, right on the border-line. There were only two relevant witnesses, S and H. The striking similarity as presented to the jury was and was only the active character of the sexual performance to which the accused was said to have invited the complainants. In relation to the incident which was the subject of the second charge, the language used by the boy was not specific: the "similarity" was derived from an earlier incident in connection with which the boy used a verb connoting an active role. I agree with, I think, all your Lordships in thinking that all of this, relating not very specifically to the one striking element, common to two boys only, is, if sufficient, only just sufficient. Perhaps other similarities could have been found in the accused's approaches to the boys (I do not myself find them particularly striking), but the judge did not rest upon them to direct the jury as to their "similarity." I do not think that these ought now to be relied upon. The dilution of the "striking" fact by more prosaic details might have weakened the impact upon the jury rather than strengthened it. The judge dealt properly and fairly with the possibility of a conspiracy between the boys.

These matters lie largely within the field of the judge's discretion, and of the jury's task; the Court of Appeal has reviewed the whole matter in a careful judgment. I do not think that there is anything which justifies the interference of this House. But I confess to some fear that the case, if regarded as an example, may be setting the standard of "striking similarity" too low.'

LORD HAILSHAM OF ST MARYLEBONE: 'My Lords, I will confess that, after this House had disposed of the two appeals in *R* v *Hester* [1973] AC 296 and *R* v *Kilbourne* [1973] AC 729, your Lordships had sufficiently tidied up a notoriously difficult branch of the criminal law to justify the hope that it would be unnecessary to trouble your Lordships with further cases upon it for a considerable period of time.

However, the variety of human circumstances is infinite, and the fertility of ingenuity in counsel considerable, and in the present case we were constrained once more to traverse the pitted battlefield of "similar fact" evidence and corroboration, from *Makin* v *Attorney-General for New South Wales* [1894] AC 57 to the latest decisions of all. Nevertheless, since it springs eternal in the human breast, I, for one, cannot resist expressing once more the hope that this case at least may give a quietus to the series of cases on this topic reaching the highest tribunal. . ..

The position, as I see it, is this. The passage in *R* v *Sims* [1946] KB 531, 537 which appears to say that: ". . .evidence is admissible if it is logically probative, that is, if it is logically relevant to the issue whether the prisoner has committed the act charged," must now be read in the light of Lord du Parcq's criticism of it in *Noor Mohamed* v *The King* [1949] AC 182 where he said, at p. 194: "The expression 'logically probative' may be understood to include much evidence which English law deems to be irrelevant." Lord du Parcq was clearly referring there not merely to the first rule in Lord Herschell LC's famous exposition in *Makin* v *Attorney-General for New South Wales* [1894] AC 57, 65, to which I shall be referring shortly, but matters like the exclusion of hearsay evidence, which can clearly be relevant and logically probative on occasion, evidence consisting in secondary evidence of documents and, of course, the whole complex set of rules contained in the law relating to confessions, and the so-called Judges' Rules. As Lord du Parcq truly said, at p. 194: "Logicians are not bound by the rules of evidence which guide English courts, . . ." Nonetheless, if these technical rules of exclusion in the interests of the accused are for any reason not applicable, to ask whether evidence can be corroboration or is relevant is really to ask the same question in two different ways. The reason for this is clearly seen from the speech in *R* v *Kilbourne* [1973] AC 729 of Lord Simon of Glaisdale when he points out (see especially at p. 756) that: ". . . relevant (i.e., logically probative or disprobative) evidence is evidence which makes the matter which requires proof more or less probable," and, at p. 758: "Corroboration is . . . nothing other than evidence which 'confirms' or 'supports' or 'strengthens' other evidence . . . It is, in short, evidence which renders other evidence more probable."

Another contention put forward by appellant's counsel was that the decision in *R* v *Sims* [1946] KB 531 was wrong, and that any cases founded on *Sims* fell with it. It is true, as I have said, that the passage relating to evidence which is logically probative, at p. 537, must now be read in the light of Lord du Parcq's criticisms in *Noor Mohamed* v *The King* [1949] AC 182, 194. It is also true that in *R* v *Kilbourne* [1973] AC 729 both Lord Reid and I expressed the view that the opinion expressed in *R* v *Sims* [1946] KB 531, 540, which seems to put sodomy as a "crime in a special category" goes a great deal too far, and that Lord Sumner's statement in *Thompson* v *The King* [1918] AC 221, 222 ought not to be read in this sense. Lord Reid said, at p. 751: "Then there are indications of a special rule for homosexual crimes. If there ever was a time for that, that time is past, and on the view which I take of the law, any such special rule is quite unnecessary."

Both Lord Morris of Borth-y-Gest and I said the same by implication. But, subject to these two points, and the specific point decided in *Kilbourne, Sims* has never been successfully challenged and was expressly approved in general terms in *Kilbourne* by myself, Lord Reid and Lord Morris of Borth-y-Gest, and by implication by Viscount Simon in *Harris* v *Director of Public Prosecutions* [1952] AC 694, 708, and followed in *R* v *Campbell* [1956] 2 QB 432.

The truth is that, apart from these qualifications, *Sims* was never in need of support, for in the sense explained in Professor Cross's book on *Evidence*, 3rd ed, p. 319, it was only a particular example of a general principle which stems from *Makin* v *Attorney-General for New South Wales* [1894] AC 57, especially at p. 65, and goes down through a long list of cases, English and Scottish, including *Moorov* v *HM Advocate*, 1930 JC 68 and *Ogg* v *HM Advocate*, 1938 JC 152 to the present time. This rule is contained in the classic statement of Lord Herschell LC in *Makin*, at p. 65, cited above, which I quote here once again solely for convenience:

> It is undoubtedly not competent for the prosecution to adduce evidence tending to show that the accused has been guilty of criminal acts other than those covered by the indictment, for the purpose of leading to the conclusion that the accused is a person likely from his criminal conduct or character to have committed the offence for which he is being tried. On the other hand, the mere fact that the evidence adduced tends to show the commission of other crimes does not render it inadmissible if it be relevant to an issue before the jury, and it may be so relevant if it bears upon the question whether the acts alleged to constitute the crime charged in the indictment were designed or accidental, or to rebut a defence which would otherwise be open to the accused.

This statement may be divided into its component parts. The first sentence lays down a general rule of exclusion. "Similar fact" evidence, or evidence of bad character is not admissible for the purpose of leading to the conclusion that a person, from his criminal conduct or character, is likely to have committed the offence for which he is being held.

Two theories have been advanced as to the basis of this, and both have respectable judicial support. One is that such evidence is simply irrelevant. No number of similar offences can connect a particular person with a particular crime, however much they may lead the police, or anyone else investigating the offence, to concentrate their inquiries upon him as their prime suspect. According to this theory, similar fact evidence excluded under Lord Herschell LC's first sentence has no probative value and is to be rejected on that ground. The second theory is that the prejudice created by the admission of such evidence outweighs any probative value it may have. An example of this view is to be found in the speech of Lord Simon of Glaisdale in *R* v *Kilbourne* [1973] AC 729 where he said, at p 757: "The reason why the type of evidence referred to by Lord Herschell LC in the first sentence of the passage is inadmissible is, not because it is irrelevant, but because its logically probative significance is considered to be grossly outweighed by its prejudice to the accused, so that a fair trial is endangered if it is admitted;. . ."

With respect, both theories are correct. When there is nothing to connect the accused with a particular crime except bad character or similar crimes committed in the past, the probative value of the evidence is nil and the evidence is rejected on that ground. When there is some evidence connecting the accused with the crime, in the eyes of most people, guilt of similar offences in the past might well be considered to have probative value (cf the statutory exceptions to this effect in the old law of receiving and under the Theft Act 1968). Nonetheless, in the absence of a statutory provision to the contrary, the evidence is to be excluded under the first rule in *Makin* [1894] AC 57, 65 because its prejudicial effect may be more powerful than its probative effect, and thus endanger a fair trial because it tends to undermine the integrity of the presumption of innocence and the burden of proof. In other words, it is a rule of English law which has its roots in policy, and by which, in Lord du Parcq's phrase in *Noor Mohamed* v *The King* [1949] AC 182, 194, logicians would not be bound.

But there is a third case, to which the second rule in *Makin* [1894] AC 57, 65 applies. The mere fact that the evidence adduced tends to show the commission of other crimes does not by itself render it inadmissible *if it is relevant to an issue before the jury and it may be so relevant if it bears upon the question whether the acts alleged to constitute the crime charged in the indictment were designed or accidental, or to rebut a defence which would otherwise be open to the accused.*

Contrary to what was suggested in argument for the appellant, this rule is not an exception grafted on to the first. It is an independent proposition introduced by the words: "On the other hand" and the two propositions together cover the entire field. If one applies, the other does not.

Thus in *R* v *Ball* [1911] AC 47, evidence of inclination and affection of a sexual kind was admitted to show inclination in a case of brother and sister incest; in *Thompson* v *The King* [1918] AC 221, evidence of a particular tendency was admitted to show that the accused was present at a particular time and place of meeting as the result of a previous assignation, and was not purely fortuitous as claimed by the accused; in *R* v *Smith* (1915) *The Trial of George Joseph Smith*, edited by Eric R Watson, *Notable British Trials Series* (1922) (the "brides in the bath" case) evidence of similar circumstances was admitted to exclude coincidence where there was no other evidence either of the fact of killing or the intent; similar considerations seem to have prevailed in *R* v *Straffen* [1952] 2 QB 911. The permutations are almost indefinite. In *Moorov* v *HM Advocate*, 1930 JC 68 coincidence of story as distinct from coincidence in the facts was held to be admissible and corroborative, and this, after some fairly agonised appraisals, was what was thought in *R* v *Kilbourne* [1973] AC 729. The fact is that, although the categories are useful classes of example, they are not closed (see *per* Viscount Simon in *Harris* v *Director of Public Prosecutions* [1952] AC 694, 705), and they cannot in fact be closed by categorisation. The rules of logic and common sense are not susceptible of exact codification when applied to the actual facts of life in its infinite variety.

What is important is not to open the door so widely that the second proposition merges in the first: see, for example, what was said in *R* v *Flack* [1969] 1 WLR 937, *R* v *Chandor* [1959] 1 QB 545 and *Ogg* v *HM Advocate* 1938 JC 152. Contrary to what was said in *R* v *Flack* [1969] 1 WLR 937 and *R* v *Chandor* I do not see the logical distinction between innocent association cases and cases of complete denial, since the permutations are too various to admit of universally appropriate labels. The truth is that a mere succession of facts is not normally enough (see *Moorov* v *HM Advocate*, 1930 JC 68 on "a course of criminal conduct"), whether the cases are many or limited to two as in *HM Advocate* v *AE*, 1937 JC 96. There must be something more than mere repetition. What there must be is variously described as "underlying unity" (*Moorov* v *HM Advocate*), "system" (see *per* Lord Reid in *R* v *Kilbourne*), "nexus", "unit of intent, project, campaign or adventure" (*Moorov* v *HM Advocate*), "part of the same criminal conduct," "striking resemblance" (*R* v *Sims* [1946] KB 531). These are all highly analogical not to say metaphorical expressions and should not be applied pedantically. It is true that the doctrine "must be applied with great caution" (see *Ogg* v *HM Advocate*, 1938 JC 152, *per* the Lord Justice-Clerk (Lord Aitchison), at p 158), but: "The test in each case, and in considering each particular charge, is, was the evidence with regard to other charges relevant to that charge?" (*per* Lord Wark, at p 160). The test is (*per* Lord Simon of Glaisdale in *R* v *Kilbourne* [1973] AC 729, 759) whether there is ". . . such an underlying unity between the offences as to make coincidence an affront to common sense" or, to quote Hallett J in *R* v *Robinson* (1953) 37 Cr App R 95, 106-107, in the passage cited by Professor Cross, *Evidence*, 3rd ed, p 316: "If a jury are precluded by some rule of law from taking the view that something is a coincidence which is against all the probabilities if the accused person is innocent, then it would seem to be a doctrine of law which prevents a jury from using what looks like ordinary common sense."

This definition would seem easy enough were it not for the fact that the judge must, as a matter of law, withhold from the jury evidence which is outside the definition. The jury can treat the matter as one of degree and weight, which it is. The judge is constrained to assert a line of principle before he allows it to go to the jury. I do not know that the matter can be better stated that it was by Lord Herschell LC in *Makin* v *Attorney-General for New South Wales* [1894] AC 57, 65, remembering the note of caution sounded in *Ogg* v *HM Advocate*, 1938 JC 152 and perhaps finding useful as guides, but not as shackles, the kind of factor enumerated there, as, for example, the number of instances involved, any interrelation between them, the intervals or similarities of time, circumstances and the details and character of the evidence. Reference may also be made to the passage in Lord du Parcq's judgment in *Noor Mohamed* v *The King* [1949] AC 182, 192 noticed with approval by Viscount Simon in *Harris* v *Director of Public Prosecutions* [1952] AC 694, 707. It is perhaps helpful to remind oneself that what is *not* to be admitted is a chain of reasoning and not necessarily a state of facts. If the inadmissible chain of reasoning is the *only* purpose for which the evidence is adduced as a matter of law, the evidence itself is not admissible. If there is some other relevant, probative purpose than for the forbidden type of reasoning, the evidence is admitted, but should be made subject to a warning from the judge that the jury must eschew the forbidden reasoning. The judge also has a discretion, not as a matter of law but as a matter of good practice, to exclude evidence whose prejudicial effect, though the evidence be technically admissible on the decided cases, may be so great in the particular circumstances as to outweigh its probative value to the extent that a verdict of guilty might be considered unsafe or unsatisfactory if ensuing (cf *per* Lord Simon in *Harris* v *Director of Public Prosecutions* [1952] AC 694, 707). In all these cases it is for the judge to ensure as a matter of law in the first place, and as a matter of discretion where the matter is free, that a properly instructed jury, applying their minds to the facts, can come to the conclusion that they are satisfied so that they are sure that to treat the matter as pure coincidence by reason of the "nexus," "pattern," "system," "striking resemblances" or whatever phrase is used is "an affront to common sense" [*R* v *Kilbourne* [1973] AC 729, *per* Lord Simon of Glaisdale, at p 759]. In this the ordinary rules of logic and common sense prevail, whether the case is one of burglary and the burglar has left some "signature" as the mark of his presence, or false pretences and the pretences alleged have too many common characteristics to have happened coincidentally, or whether the dispute is one of identity and the accused in a series of offences has some notable physical features or behaviourial or psychological characteristics or, as in some cases, is in possession of incriminating articles, like a jemmy, a set of skeleton keys or, in abortion cases, the apparatus of the abortionist. Attempts to codify the rules of common sense are to be resisted. The first rule in *Makin* [1894] AC 57, 65 is designed to exclude a particular kind of inference being drawn which might upset the presumption of innocence by introducing more heat than light. When that is the only purpose for which the evidence is being tendered, it should be excluded altogether, as in *R* v *Horwood* [1970] 1 QB 133. Where the purpose is an inference of another kind, subject to the judge's overriding discretion to exclude, the evidence is admissible, if in fact the evidence be logically probative. Even then it is for the jury to assess its weight, which may be greater or less according as to how far it accords with other evidence, and according as to how far that other evidence may be conclusive.

There are two further points of a general character that I would add. The "striking resemblances" or "unusual features," or whatever phrase is considered appropriate, to ignore which would affront common sense, may either be in the objective facts, as for instance in *R* v *Smith, Notable British Trials Series*, or *R* v *Straffen* [1952] 2 QB 911, or may constitute a striking similarity in the accounts by witnesses of disputed transactions. For instance, whilst it would certainly not be enough to identify the culprit in a series of burglaries that he climbed in through a ground floor window, the fact that he left the same humorous limerick on the walls of the sitting room, or an esoteric symbol written in lipstick on the mirror, might well be enough. In a sex case, to adopt an example given in argument in the Court of Appeal, whilst a repeated homosexual act by itself might be quite insufficient to admit the evidence as confirmatory of identity or design, the fact that it was alleged to have been performed wearing the ceremonial head-dress of a Red-Indian chief or other eccentric garb might well in appropriate circumstances suffice.

The second general observation I wish to make is as to the nature of corroboration as decided in *R* v *Kilbourne* [1973] AC 729. This is correctly described in the opinion of Lord Reid as follows, at p. 750:

> There is nothing technical in the idea of corroboration. When in the ordinary affairs of life one is doubtful whether or not to believe a particular statement one naturally looks to see whether it fits in with other statements or circumstances relating to the particular matter; the better it fits in, the more one is inclined to believe it. The doubted statement is corroborated to a greater or lesser extent by the other statements or circumstances with which it fits in.

I make this point because at one time counsel seemed to be arguing from a remark of mine in *R* v *Kilbourne*, at p. 746, to the effect that, before S's evidence was used to corroborate H, it was necessary for the jury to accept it without doubt and vice versa. With respect, this is quite wrong and, if accepted, would overthrow both *R* v *Kilbourne* and *R* v *Hester* [1973] AC 296 and, indeed, *R* v *Sims* [1946] KB 531, *Moorov* v *HM Advocate* 1930 JC 68 and other cases. When a jury is satisfied beyond doubt that a given witness is telling the truth, they can, after a suitable warning, convict without corroboration. What I said in *R* v *Kilbourne* was not that to give or require corroboration a witness must be believed without doubt. What I said, and what I meant, was that unless a witness's evidence was intrinsically credible he could neither afford corroboration nor be thought to require it. In such cases, the witness's evidence is rejected before the question of corroboration arises. Of course, a conviction in such a case can sometimes result if, notwithstanding the unreliable testimony, the independent evidence is strong enough. But this is because the independent evidence has proved the case independently of the unreliable witness, not because the unreliable witness is corroborated. Unless this is the case there must, as happened in relation to the third count in *R* v *Kilbourne* [1973] AC 729, be an acquittal. To attempt to explain the cases, whether in Scotland or England, in any other sense is to miss the whole point about corroboration as explained by Lord Reid, at p. 750.

I am now in a position to dispose both of the merits of this appeal and of the question of law certified by the Court of Appeal (Criminal Division).

It is fair to the appellant's argument to say that there is undoubted force in the criticism that, by fastening on the purely passive role said to have been adopted by the appellant towards the act of buggery suggested or performed as the sole element of "striking resemblance" between S's testimony and that of H, the trial judge was on dubious ground, partly because it might be said that, as between two witnesses only, the fact, although perhaps unusual, was perhaps not so unusual as to render the evidence admissible, and partly because over the sequence of all the evidence, including that of A, it was not perhaps so unambiguously and consistently displayed as to render it a kind of signature which would make it an "affront to common sense" (*R* v *Kilbourne* [1973] AC 729, 759) in the jury to disregard it as coincidental. But I hope that I have exposed enough of the evidence to indicate that, if the learned judge erred here, he erred by giving too little weight to the case for a conviction. There were other points of resemblance sufficiently striking to have their value as corroboration whether in conjunction with or without the "catamite" feature left to the jury and, in S's case, there was admittedly strong independent corroboration in the testimony of the police officer. If the jury convicted on a presentation of the case which may have been unduly favourable to the appellant, it cannot be doubted that they would have convicted if the matter had been exposed on its real, and stronger, impact.

So far as regards the question certified, I cannot say that the question admits of an absolutely categorical answer which would not be misleading. I therefore propose the following several points:

(1) There is not, as the question rather suggests, a separate category of homosexual cases. The rules of logic and common sense must be the same for all trials where "similar fact" or other analogous evidence is sought to be introduced. This can be inferred from *R* v *Kilbourne* [1973] AC 729.

(2) The mere fact that the homosexual acts take a "particular form" is not by itself enough to make the evidence admissible as a universal rule, as is rather suggested in the word "thereby" as it appears in the question. The rule is as stated by Lord Herschell LC in *Makin* v *Attorney-General for New South Wales* [1894] AC 57, 65 and by Lord du Parcq in *Noor Mohamed* v *The King* [1949] AC 182, 192 in the passage quoted by Lord Simon in *Harris* v *Director of Public Prosecutions* [1952] AC 694, 707, and is subject also to the judge's discretion as defined by Lord Simon, at p. 707.

(3) *R* v *Sims* [1946] KB 531 was rightly decided, but must be read subject to the criticisms of it in *Noor Mohamed* v *The King* and *R* v *Kilbourne* [1973] AC 729 and in paragraph (1) above, and to the rejection of the "circular argument" heresy in *R* v *Manser* (1934) 25 Cr App R 18 as rejected in *R* v *Kilbourne* and *R* v *Hester* [1973] AC 296.

(4) There is no ground for relaxing the "cautious approach" recommended in *Ogg* v *HM Advocate* 1938 JC 152 by the Lord Justice-Clerk (Lord Aitchison), at p. 158, or for reducing the force of the first of Lord Herschell LC's rules in *Makin* v *Attorney-General for New South Wales* [1894] AC 57, 65. If this were done the result would be to admit a number of cases in which the forbidden type of inference would be the real reason for adducing the evidence.

(5) The second of Lord Herschell's rules in *Makin* is not capable of codification into a series of tight propositions or categories of case. Each case must be looked at in the light of all the circumstances and of the sentence containing the rule and of the observations upon it of Lord du Parcq in *Noor Mohamed* v *The King* [1949] AC 182 and Lord Simon in *Harris* v *Director of Public Prosecutions* [1952] AC 694, and of the ordinary rules of logic and common sense.

(6) Despite differences of pedigree and extent of application, there is no relevant difference in this context between the English doctrine of corroboration and the Scottish doctrine as defined in *Moorov* v *HM Advocate*, 1930 JC 68 and *Ogg* v *HM Advocate*, 1938 JC 152 and explained in *R* v *Kilbourne* [1973] AC 729.'

LORD CROSS OF CHELSEA: 'My Lords, on the hearing of a criminal charge the prosecution is not as a general rule allowed to adduce evidence that the accused has done acts other than those with which he is charged in order to show that he is the sort of person who would be likely to have committed the offence in question. As my noble and learned friend, Lord Simon of Glaisdale, pointed out in the recent case of *R* v *Kilbourne* [1973] AC 729, 757, the reason for this general rule is not that the law regards such evidence as inherently irrelevant but that it is believed that if it were generally admitted jurors would in many cases think that it was more relevant than it was, so that, as it is put, its prejudicial effect would outweigh its probative value. Circumstances, however, may arise in which such evidence is so very relevant that to exclude it would be an affront to common sense. Take, for example, *R* v *Straffen* [1952] 2 QB 911. There a young girl was found strangled. It was a most unusual murder for there had been no attempt to assault her sexually or to conceal the body though this might easily have been done. The accused, who had just escaped from Broadmoor and was in the neighbourhood at the time of the crime, had previously committed two murders of young girls, each of which had the same peculiar features. It would, indeed, have been a most extraordinary coincidence if this third murder had been committed by someone else and though an ultra-cautious jury might still have acquitted him it would have been absurd for the law to have prevented the evidence of the other murders being put before them although it was simply evidence to show that Straffen was a man likely to commit a murder of that particular kind. As Viscount Simon said in *Harris* v *Director of Public Prosecutions* [1952] AC 694, 705, it is not possible to compile an exhaustive list of the sort of cases in which "similar fact" evidence—to use a compendious phrase—is admissible. The question must always be whether the similar fact evidence taken together with the other evidence would do no more than raise or strengthen a suspicion that the accused committed the offence with which he is charged or would point so strongly to his guilt that only an ultra-cautious jury, if they accepted it as true, would acquit in face of it. In the end—although the admissibility of such evidence is a question of law, not of discretion—the question as I see it must be one of degree. That, indeed, is how the matter was regarded by the Criminal Law Revision Committee: see sections 3(1) and (2) of their draft Criminal Evidence Bill which was intended to state the existing law.

The setting in which the question arises in this case is familiar enough. When A is charged with an offence against B in what circumstances (if any) can the prosecution strengthen B's evidence by calling C and D to say that A committed similar offences against them? This problem was considered by a full Court of Criminal Appeal in *R* v *Sims* [1946] KB 531. The facts there were that the defendant was charged on different counts with homosexual offences of a similar character involving four different men. Each said that the defendant had invited him to his house and had then had homosexual relations with him. The defendant admitted that each of the men had in fact visited him at his invitation on the occasions in question, but he denied that he had been guilty of any improper conduct with any of them. The court gave three separate reasons for saying that on each count the evidence of the other men as to what the defendant had done to them was admissible to support the evidence of the man with whom the offence to which the count related was alleged to have been committed. The first reason was expressed in the following terms, at pp. 539-540:

> The evidence of each man was that the accused invited him into the house and there committed the acts charged. The acts they describe bear a striking similarity. . . The probative force of all the acts together is much greater than one alone; for, whereas the jury might think one man might be telling an untruth, three or four are hardly likely to tell the same truth unless they are conspiring. If there is nothing to suggest a conspiracy their evidence would seem to be overwhelming.

The second reason was that homosexual offences formed a special class in respect of which "similar fact" evidence was more readily admissible than in other cases. The third reason was that "similar fact" evidence was always admissible to rebut a defence of "innocent association." In *R* v *Kilbourne* [1973] AC 729 several of your Lordships expressed the view that the second reason given in *R* v *Sims* [1946] KB 531 for the admission of the similar fact evidence could not be supported. Those expressions of opinion were only *obiter dicta* since in *R* v *Kilbourne* it was common ground that the similar fact evidence was admissible but I have no hesitation in agreeing with them. The attitude of the ordinary man to homosexuality has changed very much even since *R* v *Sims* was decided and what was said on that subject in 1917 by Lord Sumner in *Thompson* v *The King* [1918] AC 221, 235—from which the view that homosexual offences form a class apart appears to stem—sounds nowadays like a voice from another world. Speaking for myself I have also great difficulty in accepting the third reason. If I am charged with a sexual offence why should it make any difference to the admissibility or non-admissibility of similar fact evidence whether my case is that the meeting at which the offence is said to have been committed never took place or that I committed no offence in the course of it? In each case I am saying that my accuser is lying. Moreover when, as here, the accused is a schoolmaster who was of necessity associating day in and day out with the alleged victim it becomes difficult—as the courts below saw—to say whether his defence to any particular charge can or cannot be fairly described as a defence of "innocent association." In *R* v *Chandor* [1959] 1 QB 545 and *R* v *Flack* [1969] 1 WLR 937, the Court of Appeal approved the distinction between the two types of defence for the purposes of the admission of similar fact evidence. But though the decisions in these two cases may well have been correct, I cannot, as at present advised, agree with that part of the reasoning in them.

If the decision in *R* v *Sims* [1946] KB 531 is to be justified it must, as I see it, be for the first reason. One must, however, bear in mind that such a case as *R* v *Sims* or this case differs materially from such cases as *R* v *Straffen* [1952] 2 QB 911 or *R* v *Smith* (the "brides in the bath" case), 11 Cr App R 229. In those cases there was no direct evidence that the accused had committed the offence with which he was charged but equally there was no question of any witness for the prosecution telling lies. In the first case one started with the undoubted fact that the child had been murdered by someone and in the second case with the undoubted fact that Mrs Smith had been drowned in her bath on her honeymoon. The "similar fact" evidence was equally indisputable—namely, in the first case that Straffen had committed two identical murders and in the second that two other brides of Mr Smith had been drowned in their baths on their honeymoons. If it was admitted this evidence, the truth of which was not open to challenge, provided very strong circumstantial evidence that in each case the accused had committed murder. In such cases as *R* v *Sims* [1946] KB 531 or this case on the other hand there is, it is true, some direct evidence that the offence was committed by the accused but he says that that evidence is false and the similar fact evidence—which he says is also false—is sought to be let in in order to strengthen the case for saying that his denials are untrue. In such circumstances the first question which arises is obviously whether his accusers may not have put their heads together to concoct false evidence and if there is any real chance of this having occurred the similar fact evidence must be excluded. In *R* v *Kilbourne* [1973]

AC 729 it was only allowed to be given by boys of a different group from the boy an alleged offence against whom was being considered. But even if collaboration is out of the way it remains possible that the charge made by the complainant is false and that it is simply a coincidence that others should be making or should have made independently allegations of a similar character against the accused. The likelihood of such a coincidence obviously becomes less and less the more people there are who make the similar allegations and the more striking are the similarities in the various stories. In the end, as I have said, it is a question of degree.

Before I come to the particular facts of this case there is one other matter to which I wish to refer. When in a case of this sort the prosecution wishes to adduce "similar fact" evidence which the defence says is inadmissible, the question whether it is admissible ought, if possible, to be decided in the absence of the jury at the outset of the trial and if it is decided that the evidence is inadmissible and the accused is being charged in the same indictment with offences against the other men the charges relating to the different persons ought to be tried separately. If they are tried together the judge will, of course, have to tell the jury that in considering whether the accused is guilty of the offence alleged against him by A they must put out of mind the fact— which they know—that B and C are making similar allegations against him. But, as the Court of Criminal Appeal said in *R v Sims* [1946] KB 531, 536, it is asking too much of any jury to tell them to perform mental gymnastics of this sort. If the charges are tried together it is inevitable that the jurors will be influenced, consciously or unconsciously, by the fact that the accused is being charged not with a single offence against one person but with three separate offences against three persons. It is said, I know, that to order separate trials in all these cases would be highly inconvenient. If and so far as this is true it is a reason for doubting the wisdom of the general rule excluding similar fact evidence. But so long as there is that general rule the courts ought to strive to give effect to it loyally and not, while paying lip service to it, in effect let in the inadmissible evidence by trying all the charges together.'

LORD SALMON: 'My Lords, evidence against an accused which tends only to show that he is a man of character with a disposition to commit crimes, even the crime with which he is charged, is inadmissible and deemed to be irrelevant in English law. I do not pause to discuss the philosophic basis for this fundamental rule. It is certainly not founded on logic, but on policy. To admit such evidence would be unjust and would offend our concept of a fair trial to which we hold that everyone is entitled. Nevertheless, if there is some other evidence which may show that an accused is guilty of the crime with which he is charged, such evidence is admissible against him, notwithstanding that it may also reveal his bad character and disposition to commit crime.

I have no wish to add to the anthology of guidance concerning the special circumstances in which evidence is relevant and admissible against an accused, notwithstanding that it may disclose that he is a man of bad character with a disposition to commit the kind of crime with which he is charged. The principles upon which such evidence should be admitted or excluded are stated with crystal clarity in the celebrated passage from the judgment delivered by Lord Herschell LC in *Makin v Attorney-General for New South Wales* [1894] AC 57, 65. I doubt whether the learned analyses and explanations of that passage to which it has been subjected so often in the last 80 years add very much to it.

It is plain from what has fallen from your Lordships (with which I respectfully agree) that the principles stated by Lord Herschell are of universal application and that homosexual offences are not exempt from them as at one time seems to have been supposed: see *Thompson* v *The King* [1918] AC 221, *per* Lord Sumner, at p 232, and *R* v *Sims* [1946] KB 531, 537.

My Lords, whether or not evidence is relevant and admissible against an accused is solely a question of law. The test must be: is the evidence capable of tending to persuade a reasonable jury of the accused's guilt on some ground other than his bad character and disposition to commit the sort of crime with which he is charged? In the case of an alleged homosexual offence, just as in the case of an alleged burglary, evidence which proves merely that the accused has committed crimes in the past and is therefore disposed to commit the crime charged is clearly inadmissible. It has, however, never been doubted that if the crime charged is committed in a uniquely or strikingly similar manner to other crimes committed by the accused the manner in which the other crimes were committed may be evidence upon which a jury could reasonably conclude that the accused was guilty of the crime charged. The similarity would have to be so unique or striking that common sense makes it inexplicable on the basis of coincidence. I would stress that the question as to whether the evidence is capable of being so regarded by a reasonable jury is a question of law. There is no easy way out by leaving it to the jury to see how they decide it. If a trial judge wrongly lets in the evidence and the jury convict, then, subject to the proviso [to section 2(1) of the Criminal Appeal Act 1968], the conviction must be quashed. If, for example, A is charged with burglary at the house of B and it is shown that the burglar, whoever he was, entered B's house by a ground floor window, evidence against A that he had commited a long series of burglaries, in every case entering by a ground floor window, would be clearly inadmissible. This would show nothing from which a reasonable jury could infer anything except bad character and a disposition to burgle. The factor of unique or striking similarity would be missing. There must be thousands of professional burglars who habitually enter through ground floor windows and the fact that B's house was entered in this way might well be a coincidence. Certainly it could not reasonably be regarded as evidence that A was the burglar. On the other hand, if, for example, A had a long series of convictions for burglary and in every case he had left a distinctive written mark or device behind him and he was then charged with burglary in circumstances in which an exactly similar mark or device was found at the site of the burglary which he was alleged to have committed, the similarity between the burglary charged and those of which he had previously been convicted would be so uniquely or strikingly similar that evidence of the manner in which he had committed the previous burglaries would, in law, clearly be admissible against him. I postulate these facts merely as an illustration. There is a possibility but only, I think, a theoretical possibility that they might arise. In such a case, A would no doubt say, quite rightly, that, with his record it is inconceivable that he would have left the mark or device behind him had he been the burglar: he might just as well have published a written confession: the mark or device must have been made at the time of or just after the burglary by someone trying to implicate him. This, however, would be a question for the jury to decide.'

(LORD MORRIS OF BORTH-Y-GEST delivered a concurring judgment.)

Appeal dismissed.

• How does the approach of the Law Lords in the case of *DPP* v *Boardman* differ from that of Lord Herschell in *Makin* v *Attorney General for New South Wales, ante* p. 145.

• In view of the decision in *DPP* v *Boardman* would the case of *Thompson* v *R* [1918] AC 221, *ante* p. 147 be decided in the same way today?

R v *Rance; R* v *Herron* (1975) 62 Cr App R 118 (CA)

Rance, the managing director of a building company, was convicted of corruptly procuring a payment of money to Herron, a local councillor (who was convicted of corruptly receiving the money). The payment was made on a certificate signed by Rance describing Herron as a 'subcontractor' which he was not. Rance said that he must have been deceived into signing the certificate. Evidence was received of similar payments to other councillors supported by other false certificates. The defendants applied for leave to appeal against conviction.

LORD WIDGERY CJ, delivering the judgment of the court: 'The question whether evidence of those two other cases should be admitted had to depend on the recent conclusions of the House of Lords in the case of *DPP* v *Boardman* (1974) 60 Cr App R 165; [1975] AC 421. There are two very helpful passages which indicate a crisp, modern test to decide the vexed and oft-argued question of how far evidence of similar criminal transactions can be admitted.

I take first a passage from Lord Cross's speech at pp 185, 457. He says:

As Viscount Simon said in *Harris* v *DPP* (1952) 36 Cr App R 39, 51; [1952] AC 694, 705, it is not possible to compile an exhaustive list of the sort of cases in which "similar fact" evidence—to use a compendious phrase—is admissible. The question must always be whether the similar fact evidence taken together with the other evidence would do no more than raise or strengthen a suspicion that the accused committed the offence with which he is charged or would point so strongly to his guilt that only an ultra-cautious jury, if they accepted it as true, would acquit in face of it. In the end—although the admissibility of such evidence is a question of law, not of discretion—the question as I see it must be one of degree.

Then later Lord Salmon, dealing with the same point, uses these words at pp 188 and 462 of the respective reports. He said:

My Lords, whether or not evidence is relevant and admissible against an accused is solely a question of law. The test must be: is the evidence capable of tending to persuade a reasonable jury of the accused's guilt on some ground other than his bad character and disposition to commit the sort of crime with which he is charged? In the case of an alleged homosexual offence, just as in the case of an alleged burglary, evidence which proves merely that the accused has committed crimes in the past and is therefore disposed to commit the crime charged is clearly inadmissible. It has, however, never been doubted that if the crime charged is committed in a uniquely or strikingly similar manner to other crimes committed by the accused, the manner in which the other crimes were committed may be evidence upon which a jury could reasonably conclude that the accused was guilty of the crime charged.

It seems to us that one must be careful not to attach too much importance to Lord Salmon's vivid phrase "uniquely or strikingly similar". The gist of what is being said both by Lord Cross and by Lord Salmon is that evidence is admissible as similar fact evidence if, but only if, it goes beyond showing a tendency to commit crimes of this kind and is positively probative in regard to the crime now charged. That, we think, is the test which we have to apply on the question of the correctness or otherwise of the admission of the similar fact evidence in this case.

We think quite clearly that the evidence of the other transactions—Bowes and McKenna—did, if accepted by the jury, go beyond merely showing that Rance was a person who was not above passing a bribe. The essence of each of these three cases is that a bribe was paid out to a councillor in respect of a contract in which Rance's company was interested, and in every case (each of the three—the instant one and the other two) there is the bogus document of some kind with Rance's signature on it which is the basis upon which the bribe was to be covered up. We have no doubt in saying that in those circumstances the similar fact evidence of Bowes' case and McKenna's case did go beyond merely showing a tendency on the part of Rance to commit the offence. Therefore it passed the test in *DPP v Boardman* (*supra*) and so far was correctly admitted.

However, Mr Steer has other arguments to raise against the admission of this evidence, even if we are against him, as we are, on the first broad question of whether it is on its face admissible at all. He says in particular that similar fact evidence of other transactions is not to be admitted if there is an issue of the guilt or innocence of the parties in those other transactions. In other words, he says that if, as is submitted here, the guilt of Rance in the Bowes case and the McKenna case was still in any sense doubted, the evidence of those transactions should have been eliminated on that account alone.

In this connection he refers us to page 75 of the summing-up where the judge uses this phrase. Right at the end of the summing-up he says: "Well that covers, not in detail but in outline, the transaction regarding McKenna. So what is the position as regards the three transactions?—and we will call them transactions at this stage. There's the Herron cheque of £600; there are the two Bowes' cheques of £500; there's the £800 to Mr McKenna. Don't take it as read, don't take it as a fact that those payments must have been corrupt. There are very serious issues arising as regards each of them." What the judge was saying, we have no doubt, is that, the evidence being before the jury, they should consider whether they were satisfied that those other transactions were in fact corrupt and, if not, of course to ignore them.

Mr Steer says that the matter goes further than that, and that once the judge recognises that there was a possibility that the jury might not accept the evidence of the Bowes and McKenna transactions at all, he should not have let the evidence in. In other words, he contends for a principle whereby the similar fact evidence is not admitted if there is serious question as to the correctness of the facts spoken to in evidence.

In our opinion that is not so. The question of whether the evidence relating to the similar facts is accepted or not is a question for the jury, and that is made particularly clear in the extracts from *DPP v Boardman* (*supra*) to which we have already referred. If the judge is satisfied that the evidence, if accepted by the jury, goes beyond evidence of mere disposition, he should let the evidence in and then leave it to the jury to make what they think of it, subject, however, to the next point which Mr Steer raises.

That is concerned with the requirement of a warning in these similar fact cases. Mr Steer draws upon a sentence in Lord Hailsham's speech in this connection. It is at pp. 453 and 182 of the respective reports referred to. Speaking of the admission of evidence of similar fact, he says: "If there is some other relevant, probative purpose than for the forbidden type of reasoning, the evidence is admitted, but should be made subject to a warning from the judge that the jury must eschew the forbidden reasoning." Using slightly shorter words, what that means is that the judge should point out to the jury that the evidence is admitted before them only because it goes beyond mere evidence of disposition, and should tell them that if they think it merely contains evidence of disposition they should not take any notice of it.

For our part we think that in this type of case it is a very suitable and proper thing that the judge should consider whether to give a warning of that kind, but we decline to say as a matter of principle that it must always be done and at pains of the conviction being set aside if not. If, as in the present case, the whole approach to the admission of similar facts has been for the purpose of showing something other than disposition, we do not regard it as necessarily fatal that the judge has not in terms spelt out to the jury that they must not allow the evidence to be used for what Lord Hailsham calls "the forbidden purpose." In this case we are satisfied, looking at the summing-up as a whole, that it is not.'

Applications refused.

R v Scarrott [1978] 1 All ER 672 (CA)

The defendant was tried on an indictment, containing 13 counts, charging him with buggery, attempted buggery, assault with intent to commit buggery and indecent assault involving eight young boys over a period of $4\frac{1}{2}$ years. Before arraignment, counsel for the defendant applied to sever the indictment and asked for separate trials in respect of each boy, as a multiple indictment would be prejudicial to the defendant. The application was refused. During the course of the trial the judge ruled that the evidence given by each boy relating to the count or counts concerning him had a striking similarity to the evidence given by the other boys, and was admissible on the other counts. The defendant was convicted on one count of buggery, one count of attempted buggery and eight counts of indecent assault on seven boys.

SCARMAN LJ, giving the judgment of the court: 'To be admissible, the evidence by its striking similarity has to reveal an underlying link between the matters with which it deals and the allegations against the defendant on the count under consideration. Subject to one comment, which really goes only to choice of language, we would respectfully accept the way in which the general principle was put by Lord Salmon in *Boardman's* case ([1974] 3 All ER 887 at 913):

. . .whether or not evidence is relevant and admissible against an accused is solely a question of law. The test must be—is the evidence capable of tending to persuade a reasonable jury of the accused's guilt on some ground other than his bad character and disposition to commit the sort of crime with which he is charged? In the case of an alleged homosexual offence, just as in the case of an alleged burglary, evidence which proves merely that the accused has committed crimes in the past and is therefore disposed to commit the crime charged is clearly inadmissible. It has, however, never been doubted that if the crime charged is committed in a uniquely or strikingly similar manner to other crimes committed by the accused, the manner in which the other crimes were committed may be evidence on which a jury could reasonably conclude that the accused was guilty of the crime charged. The similarity would have to be so unique or striking that common sense makes it inexplicable on the basis of coincidence. I would stress that the question whether the evidence is capable of being so regarded by a reasonable jury is a question of law. There is no easy way out by leaving it to the jury to see how they decide it.

Thus, the admissibility of similar fact evidence, even when it is adduced as it is in this case as corroboration of direct evidence, does not depend on whether it is capable of corroborating the evidence of the victim or accomplice; it depends on its positive probative value. Its corroborative capability is a consequence of its probative value and not *vice versa*, for, if the evidence be admissible, it follows that it is capable of corroborating.

The point was succinctly put by Lord Cross in *Director of Public Prosecutions* v *Kilbourne* [1973] 1 All ER 440 where he said: "Once the 'similar fact' evidence is admitted—and it was common ground that it was properly admitted in this case—then of necessity it "corroborates"—i.e., strengthens or supports—the evidence given by the boy an alleged offence against whom is the subject of the count under consideration."

To succeed, therefore, in quashing these convictions counsel for the appellant has to persuade this court that the judge was wrong to treat the similar fact evidence in this case as strikingly similar. I now come to the one comment which this court would make on the statement of general principle made by Lord Salmon. Hallowed though by now the phrase "strikingly similar" is (it was used by Lord Goddard CJ in *R* v *Sims* [1946] 1 All ER 697 in 1946 and has now received the accolade of use in the House of Lords in *Boardman* v *Director of Public Prosecutions*), it is no more than a label. Like all labels it can mislead; it is a possible passport to error. It is, we repeat, only a label and it is not to be confused with the substance of the law which it labels. We think that Lord Widgery CJ had the danger of a label in mind when, in a very different class of case, he made a comment on the passage from Lord Salmon's speech which we have quoted. In *R* v *Rance, R* v *Herron* (1975) 62 Cr App R 118 at 121, Lord Widgery CJ made this comment, and the court is grateful to counsel for the appellant for drawing our attention to it:

It seems to us that one must be careful not to attach too much importance to Lord Salmon's vivid phrase "uniquely or strikingly similar". The gist of what is being said both by Lord Cross and by Lord Salmon is that evidence is admissible as similar fact evidence if, but only if, it goes beyond showing a tendency to commit crimes of this kind and is positively probative in regard to the crime now charged. That, we think, is the test which we have to apply on the question of the correctness or otherwise of the admission of the similar fact evidence in this case.

Positive probative value is what the law requires, if similar fact evidence is to be admissible. Such probative value is not provided by the mere repetition of similar facts; there has to be some feature or features in the evidence sought to be adduced which provides a link, an underlying link as it has been called in some of the cases. The existence of such a link is not to be inferred from mere similarity of facts which are themselves so commonplace that they can provide no sure ground for saying that they point to the commission by the accused of the offence under consideration. Lord Cross put the matter, as we think, in its correct perspective at the end of the day when, in the course of his speech in *Boardman v Director of Public Prosecutions,* he said: "The likelihood of such a coincidence obviously becomes less and less the more people there are who make the similar allegations and the more striking are the similarities in the various stories. In the end, as I have said, it is a question of degree. . ."

In this part of the case counsel for the appellant has referred us to two recent decisions of the Court of Appeal, one of which would appear to support his submission and the other of which would appear to support the assessment of the evidence made by the trial judge. The first of these cases is *R v Novac, R v Raywood, R v Andrew-Cohen, R v Archer* (1977) 65 Cr App R 107. We do not think it necessary to consider the facts of that case in detail; enough can be gleaned as to the nature of the case from one passage in the judgment of Bridge LJ who gave the judgment of the court:

> Three of the boys called by the Crown to give evidence in connection with the conspiracy and related counts testified that Raywood had offered or attempted to bugger them. In each case he had met them in Playland or some similar amusement arcade and picked them up by offering them money to play the pin tables. In each case he had offered them shelter overnight at the place where he was living at the time and the offer or attempt to commit buggery had occurred when Raywood and the boy were sharing a bed. The boy P, the subject of count 7, had similarly been picked up in an amusement arcade and offered shelter, but it is to be observed that he was first taken back by Raywood to the house of a woman friend and it is not alleged that any offence was committed there. According to P he was subsequently taken to another address where the offence alleged in count 7 was committed when the boy and Raywood were sharing a bed.

The boys, having been picked up at the arcade, were taken to a house and there the offence was alleged to have taken place. Bridge LJ continued:

> The fact that the boys may in each case have been picked up by Raywood in the first instance at amusement arcades may be a feature more clearly approximating to a "unique or striking similarity" within the ambit of Lord Salmon's principle. It is not, however, a similarity in the commission of a crime. It is a similarity in the surrounding circumstances and is not, in our judgment, sufficiently proximate to the commission of the crime itself to lead to the conclusion that the repetition of this feature would make the boys' stories inexplicable on the basis of coincidence.

Counsel for the appellant has based a submission on those words that, to be admissible, the similar fact evidence must reveal features of a striking similarity with the offence itself, not its surrounding circumstances. He submits that is all that the rather strange word that Bridge LJ used, "proximate", means.

In our view, we are here in that area of judgment on particular facts from which the criminal law can never depart. Plainly some matters, some circumstances may be so distant in time or place from the commission of an offence as not to be properly considered when deciding whether the subject-matter of similar fact evidence displays striking similarities with the offence charged. On the other hand, equally plainly, one cannot isolate, as a sort of laboratory specimen, the bare bones of a criminal offence from its surrounding circumstances and say that it is only within the confines of that specimen, microscopically considered, that admissibility is to be determined. Indeed, in one of the most famous cases of all dealing with similar fact evidence, "the brides in the bath case", *R v Smith* (1915) 84 LJKB 2153, the court had regard to the facts that the accused man married the women and that he insured their lives. Some surrounding circumstances have to be considered in order to understand either the offence charged or the nature of the similar fact evidence which it is sought to adduce and in each case it must be a matter of judgment where the line is drawn. One cannot draw an inflexible line as a rule of law. We therefore observe that in *R v Novac* the line was drawn where Bridge LJ expressed it to be drawn. No doubt that was a line drawn after a full investigation and assessment of the particular facts of that case. It would be wrong, in our judgment, to elevate the passage which I have quoted from Bridge LJ's judgment into a statement of law. It is a judgment on the particular facts presented to the court for its consideration and decision and the same observations may be made in regard to *R v Johannsen* (1977) 65 Cr App R 101 the other case which, on a superficial view, might appear to be in conflict with *R v Novac*. *R v Johannsen*, on one view of it, could be said to be against counsel for the appellant; but, properly considered, it is no more against him than *R v Novac* is for him. Lawton LJ gave the judgment of the court in *R v Johannsen* and there is, I hesitate to say a striking similarity, but certainly a remarkable similarity between the salient facts of that case and the salient facts of *R v Novac*. Lawton LJ said: "The prosecution's case was that between May and December 1975 he made a practice of accosting boys in amusement arcades and similar places, offering them money or a meal or treating them to a game, taking them to his accommodation or on to the beach and there committing the offences charged. His particular homosexual propensity was to handle the boys' penises and getting them to do the same with his. . .".

Later Lawton LJ, with confidence, said: We have no hesitation in deciding that there were striking similarities about what happened to each of the boys—the accostings in the same kind of places, the enticements, the visits to his accommodation, his homosexual propensities and his ways of gratifying them. It follows that the evidence of each boy was admissible to corroborate the evidence of the others." We therefore have to reach a judgment on the evidence of this particular case, and to determine whether the evidence adduced, that is the similar fact evidence adduced, possesses such features that it is a proper exercise of judgment to say that the evidence is logically probative, that it has positive probative value in assisting to determine the truth.

We have come to the conclusion that the evidence described by Judge Vowden in the terms which I have quoted does possess that positive, probative value, does possess striking similarities. It is necessary to repeat the features which are strikingly similar: the ages of the boys, the way in which their resistance was worn down, the location of the offences and the offences themselves. Taken together, these similarities are inexplicable on the basis of coincidence. We have come to the conclusion, therefore, that the judge was right to admit this evidence and that he was right to submit it to the jury in the way that he did.

That is not however quite the end of the appeal. I have referred already to the fact that counsel for the appellant did submit both before arraignment and later, at the end of the prosecution's case, that there was a real danger that the evidence of these boys was tainted by conspiracy or ganging up, the "group" point as it is called. The judge had to consider this point first before arraignment, when the only material available to him was that contained in the depositions. He had to form a judgment at that stage whether it was, in all the circumstances, safe in the interests of justice to allow the trial to proceed on a multi-count indictment. Clearly there was a suggestion that some, or perhaps all, of these boys might have been party to a ganging up organised by the older brother of Peter B. He took the view that the matter could be dealt with by him in summing up, that whether or not there was such a ganging up should be considered by the jury. It was of course a matter for his discretion whether to accede to the application to sever the indictment or not and, in our judgment, he cannot be said to have erred in the exercise of his discretion in taking the view that in all the circumstances of this case the matter could properly be left to the jury, always assuming, as in the event occurred, that there was a full and proper direction and warning. There is therefore nothing in this point in our judgment. That really disposes of the points taken by counsel for the appellant.

We think, however, that, in this very difficult class of case where trial judges do face a very complex problem in both the conduct of the trial and in summing up, we should attempt to give some practical guidance to judges at certain stages of the trial. What we now say is not to be considered as any advance or development of the law; it is merely an attempt on the basis of *Director of Public Prosecutions* v *Kilbourne* [1973] 1 All ER 440 and *Boardman* v *Director of Public Prosecutions* [1974] 3 All ER 887 to give some guidance which may be helpful to judges who have this very difficult task to discharge.

The help that we can give deals really with a number of phases of the trial process. The first phase is before arraignment when a defendant submits that the indictment should be severed. Of course the question whether a judge should allow an indictment to contain a number of counts initially has to be dealt with under the discretion given to a judge by the Indictment Rules 1971 SI 1971 No 1253, and in particular rule 9 which only repeats the law as it has been ever since 1915:

> Charges for any offences may be joined in the same indictment if those charges are founded on the same facts, or form or are a part of a series of offences of the same or a similar character.

It is not very difficult for a judge to reach a conclusion under that rule, but, having come to the conclusion, as Judge Vowden plainly did in this case, that the offences were of a similar character and a series, he then has to consider how to deal with the application to sever. It appears to us that when such an application at this stage is made a judge must, as Lawton LJ said in *R* v *Johannsen*, act not on some judicial speculation as to what may happen in the trial but on such factual material as is then available to him, i.e., the depositions or the statements, according to the nature of the committal proceedings. He must ask himself at that stage whether in his judgment it would be open to a jury, properly directed and warned, to treat the evidence available on a study of the depositions or statements as strikingly similar to the evidence to be adduced in respect of the various counts and he must, we think, be able even at that stage to take the matter a little further: he must be able to say that if this evidence is believed, it could be accepted as admissible similar fact evidence or, as in the circumstances of this class of case, as evidence capable of corroborating the direct evidence. Of course he will also at this stage, as at all stages of a criminal trial when a ruling is required of him, consider whether the evidence appears to be, on the information then available, independent or untainted evidence and whether there is a real chance that there is falsity or conspiracy to give false evidence and he must also consider at this stage, as at every stage when a ruling is sought, the balance, on the information then available to him, between the possible prejudicial effect of the evidence and its probative value.

If the judge takes all those well-known matters into account, and reaches his decision on the basis of the factual information which is available to him, it does not seem to us possible to fault the exercise of his discretion whichever way it goes. It is important to appreciate that at this stage, the pre-arraignment stage, the ultimate decision of the judge is an exercise of judicial discretion. So long as he does not err in law, takes into account all relevant matters and excludes consideration of irrelevant matters, his discretion will stand. Of course at this stage the judge is taking no final decision as to the admissibility of evidence. If he decides to allow the multi-count indictment to proceed, it will still be for his ruling whether the evidence, for instance, on counts 1 to 7 will be admitted as similar fact evidence to assist in the proof of the offence charged in count 8 and so on throughout the indictment. It does not follow that because a multi-count indictment has been allowed to proceed that therefore the evidence given will be evidence on all the counts contained in the indictment. Similarly, if he decides at that stage to sever and if the trial proceeds on the basis of only, let us say, one count, it will still be open to the prosecution, at the appropriate moment, to adduce evidence relating to the other (and now put aside) counts as similar fact evidence of that count and it will then be for the judge to rule, in accordance with the laws of evidence, whether the evidence is admissible or not.

The next phase of the trial process, on which we think, in the light of the authorities, we can give some practical guidance, is when the judge's ruling is sought as to the admissibility of the similar fact evidence. His task, though a difficult exercise of judgment, can be stated in simple terms. He first has to reach a view on what he then knows of the facts of the case and of the nature of the evidence to be adduced whether the evidence possesses the features of striking similarity or probative value which have been canvassed earlier in this judgment. If he reaches the view that it does, he then has to consider whether the evidence is such that it ought to be put to the jury. He may be impressed with the very real possibility that the evidence is tainted by conspiracy or ganging up, the group objection, or he may, because of the group objection or for some other reason, take the view that, though strikingly similar and therefore, *prima facie*, admissible, the evidence is so prejudicial that its prejudicial effect outweighs its probative value. If he admits the evidence, he will in his summing-up have to make sure that the jury is left with the task of deciding whether to accept the evidence and whether to treat the evidence as in fact corroboration or not. Here Judge Vowden, as I have already mentioned, very correctly did that, notwithstanding he had already made his ruling as to striking similarities.'

Appeal dismissed.

- How does 'positive probative value' differ, if at all, from 'striking similarity'? Which test, if any, is to be preferred?
- Are the cases of *R* v *Johannsen* (1977) 65 Cr App R 101 and *R* v *Novac* (1977) 65 Cr App R 107 (referred to in the judgment in *R* v *Scarrott*), consistent with each other?

R v *Neale* (1977) 65 Cr App R 304 (CA)

The defendant was charged, together with one Burr, with arson and manslaughter. A fire had occurred at a youth hostel where both lived, which had been started deliberately and had caused loss of life. The defendant said that at the time of the fire he had been asleep in bed at the hostel. Counsel for the defendant sought a ruling from the trial judge which would enable him either by cross-examination from prosecution witnesses or if necessary by adducing evidence in the course of the development of the defence case, to elicit that Burr had admitted on five different occasions he had started fires by himself. The trial judge came to the conclusion that that evidence was not relevant—it was evidence of propensity or disposition only and contained nothing which bore upon the defence which was that the defendant was elsewhere and therefore did not do it. The defendant was subsequently convicted. He applied for leave to appeal.

SCARMAN LJ, giving the judgment of the court: "The question is whether that evidence if extracted or adduced would be admissible evidence in the trial of the applicant Neale. It was a co-accused who was seeking to adduce this evidence, and therefore it is clear upon the authorities that if this evidence were relevant either to the case against him or to his defence, he would be able, as of right, to extract it or adduce it, notwithstanding its prejudicial effect upon Burr. The discretionary control the judge has in a joint trial or indeed in any trial, that is to say the discretion to refuse to allow the Crown to adduce, or elicit, evidence which though probative is so prejudicial that it should not be accepted, does not exist or arise when application is being made by a co-defendant. Mr Hillman, for the applicant, was therefore right in our judgment to make the point that the only issue, and it is a very short issue, is whether or not this evidence was relevant.

The learned judge reached the same analysis of the situation as that which I have just given, and he came to the conclusion that the evidence was not relevant. The view that he took was that this was evidence of propensity or disposition only, and contained nothing which bore upon the defence which was that the applicant was elsewhere and did not therefore do it. We have come to the conclusion that the learned judge was right and that it really is, in the circumstances of this case, a *non sequitur* to deduce from the existence of a propensity in Burr to raise fires that Neale was not there or participating when this fire, which did the damage and caused the death, was raised. Mr Hillman really revealed or exposed the logical fallacy in his argument, when in the course of a succinct and extremely well developed submission he submitted that evidence to Burr's propensity to commit wanton and unaided arson was needed in order to support the defence that the applicant Neale was not there at the time the fire was raised.

In our judgment this is a *non sequitur*. We have been referred helpfully to two authorities, both of which reinforce the approach to this problem which we have developed. The earlier, and indeed the famous, case of *R* v *Miller* (1952) 36 Cr App R 169; [1952] 2 All ER 667, was a decision by Devlin J dealing with a case where the facts were very different from those with which we have been confronted. Devlin J said at p. 171 and p. 668 respectively: "The fundamental principle, equally applicable to any question that is asked by the defence as to any question that is asked by the prosecution, is that it is not normally relevant to inquire into a prisoner's previous character, and, particularly, to ask questions which tend to show that he has previously committed some criminal offence. It is not relevant because the fact that he has committed an offence on one occasion does not in any way show that he is likely to commit an offence on any subsequent occasion. Accordingly, such questions are, in general, inadmissible, not primarily for the reason that they are prejudicial, but because they are irrelevant."

Then he goes on to the difference in application of the principle when it is the prosecution which is seeking to lead the evidence as distinct from the case in which, as here, a co-defendant is seeking to lead the evidence. There is a clear general principle, that, in general, evidence of propensity to commit a crime is not evidence that the man with that propensity committed the crime on the particular occasion, but of course in the present case the logical gap is greater. Here the relevance of the evidence has to be borne in mind by reference to the defence, which was, "I was not there."

Mr Hillman also referred us to a recent decision of this court, again on different facts and really dealing with a different question. The cited case is the decision in *Rance* and *Herron* (1976) 62 Cr App R 118. I quote one sentence from the headnote because it again shows an emphasis on the general principle to which Devlin J was referring in *Miller's* case (*supra*). *Rance* (*supra*) was concerned with the problem of similar fact evidence, and the headnote reads as follows: "Evidence is admissible as 'similar fact' evidence if, but only if, it goes beyond showing a tendency on the part of the defendant to commit crimes of the kind charged and is positively probative in regard to the crime charged." Again a little later there is an emphasis on the necessity for some positive probative link between the evidence sought to be adduced and the issue to which it is said to be relevant.'

Application refused.

R v *Inder* (1978) 67 Cr App R 143 (CA)

The appellant was charged with one offence of buggery and with seven of indecent assault relating to six boys living in the same place where he lodged and three of them in the same house. He had a very bad record for similar offences and during the evidence of one boy, the appellant alleged that the evidence against him had been faked and that the boy had been blackmailing him. The trial judge ruled that the appellant had made an imputation of bad character against the boy and, therefore, under the proviso to section 1(f) of the Criminal Evidence Act 1898, he allowed the appellant's bad record to be let in. During the summing-up the judge did not exercise full caution to ensure that the jury were warned from time to time that the information about the appellant's bad character should be used for purposes of credit only. The Crown's case was that evidence of similar facts satisfied the test laid down in *Boardman* v *DPP* (1974) 60 Cr App R 165, [1975] AC 421, in that the offences were strikingly similar, all committed during a period when the appellant was living in the same house as two of the boys and shared the same bed, and further, that the similarities represented the stock in trade of the seducer of small boys. The jury convicted on the one count of buggery and on four of the indecent assault counts.

LORD WIDGERY, giving the judgment of the court: 'The case of *Boardman* v *DPP* (1974) 60 Cr App R 165, [1975] AC 421, is perhaps the one with which we should start. . .. There one sees the beginning, in modern authority, of the proposition that where other offences bear such striking similarity to those charged, then they have probative value in their own right and can properly be used to support the offences charged. That is as far as *Boardman* v *DPP* (*supra*) goes but since *Boardman* we have had other decisions and it is reasonable now to go straight to one of the most recent which is *Scarrott* (1977) 65 Cr App R 125; [1977] 3 WLR 629. I choose this particularly because it does refer to all the modern cases and it has a very useful and up-to-date summary of the situation with which we are concerned. Again to take the headnote in [1977] 3 WLR 629 first: "The defendant was tried on an indictment containing 13 counts, charging him with buggery, attempted buggery, assault with intent to commit buggery and indecent assault involving eight young boys over a period of $4\frac{1}{2}$ years. Before arraignment, counsel for the defendant applied to sever the indictment and asked for separate trials in respect of each boy, as a multiple indictment would be prejudicial to the defendant. The application was refused. During the course of the trial, the judge ruled that the evidence given by each boy relating to the count or counts concerning him, had a striking similarity to the evidence given by the other boys, and was admissible on the other counts and would be capable of corroboration. He did not apply the test of corroboration to decide whether the evidence was admissible, but, after a direction, left to the jury the question whether there was a possible ganging up between the boys to give false evidence and, if not, whether the similar fact evidence was corroborative evidence. The defendant was convicted on one count of buggery, one count of attempted buggery and eight counts of indecent assault on seven boys." He appealed against conviction and the appeal was dismissed on the ground that ". . . although the prosecution sought to adduce evidence of similar facts in the present case because of its corroborative qualities, the test was not whether the evidence was capable of corroboration but, on the authorities, whether the evidence was 'strikingly similar' to the direct evidence; that before evidence was 'strikingly similar' it had to have positive probative value in that it had some feature or features which provided a link with the evidence of the victim and not merely similarity of facts which were so commonplace that they provided no sure ground for saying that they pointed to the commission by the defendant of the offence under consideration. . .".

The judgment of Scarman LJ bears out that headnote and refers to a number of the more important passages which have come into the reports in the last few years. At p. 633 and (1977) 65 Cr App R 125, 128 we have a reference to *Boardman* v *DPP* (*supra*) which I will read now as I did not read it when I read the headnote to that case. Lord Salmon says this ((1974) 60 Cr App R 165, 188, [1975] AC 421, 462): "Whether or not evidence is relevant and admissible against an accused is solely a question of law. The test must be: is the evidence capable of tending to persuade a reasonable jury of the accused's guilt on some ground other than his bad character and disposition to commit the sort of crime with which he is charged? In the case of an alleged homosexual offence as in the case of an alleged burglary, evidence which proves that the accused has committed crimes in the past and is therefore disposed to commit the crime charged is clearly inadmissible. It has, however, never been doubted that if the crime charged is committed in a uniquely or strikingly similar manner to other crimes committed by the accused the manner in which the other crimes were committed may be evidence upon which a jury could reasonably conclude that the accused was guilty of the crime charged. The similarity would have to be so unique or striking that common sense makes it inexplicable on the basis of coincidence. I would stress that the question as to whether the evidence is capable of being so regarded by a reasonable jury is a question of law."

I draw attention to that passage to indicate the strength of the case which has to be put forward in order to justify the admission of what is now called "similar fact evidence." Lord Salmon is saying that the evidence is admissible where it is so uniquely similar that it would associate the accused with the other offences in a probative sense.

Going on further, there is *DPP* v *Kilbourne* (1973) 57 Cr App R 381, [1973] AC 729 and then, in *Rance and Herron* (1976) 62 Cr App R 118 there is a passage from a judgment of my own, quoted in *Scarrott*, *(supra)* which I will read: (62 Cr App R 118, 122) "It seems to us that one must be careful not to attach too much importance to Lord Salmon's vivid phrase 'uniquely or strikingly similar.' The gist of what is being said both by Lord Cross and by Lord Salmon is that evidence is admissible as similar fact evidence if, but only if, it goes beyond showing a tendency to commit crimes of this kind and is positively probative in regard to the crime now charged. That, we think, is the test which we have to apply on the question of the correctness or otherwise of the admission of the similar fact evidence in this case. . .".

Looking at that list of similarities, it seems to us that these are similarities which represent the stock-in-trade of the seducer of small boys and were not unique but appear in the vast majority of cases that come before the courts.'

R v *Seaman* (1978) 67 Cr App R 234 (CA)

The appellant went into a supermarket carrying a shopping bag in which were empty beer bottles. He then ordered a packet of bacon which the assistant wrapped up and which he placed in a wire basket. He then went to the wines and spirits counter where he exchanged some empty beer bottles for some full ones for which he paid, and placed in a bag, slipping the bacon into the same bag. He then left the supermarket without paying for the bacon at the checkout and was stopped by the store manager. At his trial for the theft of the bacon, to show that what the appellant had done was not by mistake, as he averred but was part of his *modus operandi*, evidence was admitted of two previous occasions the year before on which a store detective in the same supermarket had seen the appellant buying bacon. On both occasions he was seen to place bacon in a wire basket. On the first occasion the basket was later seen to be empty, but as the store detective had lost sight of the appellant for a minute or so, no action was taken against him. On the second occasion the appellant, noticing that he was being watched, took the bacon out of the wire basket and returned it to its place on the provisions cabinet from whence he had taken it. The appellant was convicted and appealed on the ground that the aforesaid evidence was wrongly admitted.

LORD WIDGERY CJ, reading the judgment of the court: 'The case raises a point, often raised and always rather troublesome, of how far it is legitimate in a trial for theft of this kind (or indeed any other offence as well, but theft is the example here) where possible to call evidence before the jury of other similar offences which the accused has committed in the past. One thing is perfectly clear, and that is that you cannot call evidence of other offences merely to show that the appellant has a propensity for committing such offences. You could not call Mr Smith in the case of *Smith* (1915) 11 Cr App R 229—the brides in the bath case—merely to prove that he was a man who tended to drown his wives in the bath. But if you call evidence of other offences which is really probative, and evidence which goes beyond merely showing a propensity to commit this sort of offence, if indeed you can go to the point that the evidence which you are calling helps to supply proof of one of the essential features of the offence charged, then on the authorities it is permissible to give evidence of the earlier offences.

These matters are so well known that I forbear to take up time in looking at them in any great detail, but one perhaps ought to say a word about *R* v *Brown, Smith, Woods and Flanagan* (1963) 47 Cr App R 204. In the case of *Brown* a man had been arrested and charged with burglary, and evidence was tendered of other burglaries having taken place in the vicinity. It was tendered with a view to seeing how far it could be shown that Brown was guilty of theft. The headnote reads as follows: "The four appellants"—one of whom was Brown—"were jointly tried for an offence of shopbreaking and larceny. One of the appellants, S, pleaded guilty to another count in the same indictment charging a similar offence committed at a different place five days before. Both offences were committed during the absence of the shopkeeper for his luncheon break and in both cases entry to the premises was effected by the use of a skeleton key. The judge refused applications for separate trials, and admitted on the trial of the four appellants, evidence of the earlier offence to which S had pleaded guilty, but gave the jury a clear warning that such evidence was admissible only in the case of S and should not be considered by the jury in the case of any of the other defendants." It was held "that the evidence of the earlier offences by S should not have been admitted at all, as there was no nexus between it and the later offence; that the clear warning by the judge could not eradicate the mischief which had been done by the admission of the inadmissible evidence and the prejudice which it may have caused to the cases of the other defendants; and that, accordingly, the conviction of all four appellants must be quashed."

One sees there that, in the absence of a nexus or link between the offences under consideration and the earlier offence, evidence of the earlier offence is not permitted because it could do no more than show the accused was a man who was in the habit of committing burglaries or something like that, and the law does not allow prejudicial earlier offences to be introduced for no better purpose than that. I will just make one further reference to authority because in *Makin* v *Attorney-General for New South Wales* [1894] AC 57 one has the most important, if not the newest, authority of this kind to which reference should be made.

The headnote begins at p. 57, and I will read from p. 65 which contains the oft-quoted paragraph on this subject: "In their Lordships' opinion the principles which must govern the decision of the case are clear, though the application of them is by no means free from difficulty. It is undoubtedly not competent for the prosecution to adduce evidence tending to show that the accused has been guilty of criminal acts other than those covered by the indictment, for the purpose of leading to the conclusion that the accused is a person likely from his criminal conduct or character to have committed the offence for which he is being tried. On the other hand, the mere fact that the evidence adduced tends to show the commission of other crimes does not render it inadmissible if it be relevant to an issue before the jury, and it may be so relevant if it bears upon the question whether the acts alleged to constitute the crime charged in the indictment were designed or accidental, or to rebut a defence which would otherwise be open to the accused. The statement of these general principles is easy, but it is obvious that it may often be very difficult to draw the line and to decide whether a particular piece of evidence is on the one side or the other."

To try and apply that to the facts of the instant case, the prosecution are saying, "We want Mrs Osman's evidence in because it tends to show that the appellant has been guilty of similar conduct on another occasion, and tends thereby to rebut the defence of accident which he is putting up, because his answer was, 'Oh, I forgot to pay, I had an innocent explanation.' The prosecution say that letting in Mrs Osman's evidence of the two previous occasions tended to rebut the evidence of honest mistake or accident put forward by the appellant. It was argued, and it is argued today, by the prosecution that the evidence was properly admitted below in accordance particularly with the *dicta* in *Makin's* case (*supra*) to which I have referred.

On the other side, equally forcibly, it is contended by Mr Trotter that the evidence of Mrs Osman does not go far enough for present purposes. It does not get beyond showing a tendency to commit thefts from supermarkets and there really is nothing here to justify the allegation that this evidence goes beyond proving propensity and tends to rebut a mistake which is relied upon as a defence.

We have not found it an easy case. It is essentially a case which is near the borderline, but on the whole we think the prosecution properly adduced this evidence below. Once that conclusion is reached, of course the effect it may have had is a natural and automatic conclusion.'

Appeal dismissed.

R v Clarke (1978) 67 Cr App R 398

The appellant was charged, *inter alia*, on seven counts in an indictment, counts one and two alleging attempted buggery on his stepson, aged 16, and count three an indecent assault on the same boy. He was also charged on counts five and seven of indecently assaulting his stepdaughter, aged between eight and 10 at the time, and on counts four and six with attempting to have sexual intercourse with her.

An application was made to sever the indictment, so that counts four to seven could be tried separately from counts one to three, on the ground that the offences were charged against children, that the offences in both groups were said to consist of two types of act—something partaking of the nature of attempted masturbation and of attempted penetration, that all of them were said to have taken place in one part or another of the children's home and all were said to have been perpetrated by the stepfather of the children. The trial judge ruled against that submission, the trial proceeded and the jury were directed that if they thought that there had been a course of criminal conduct of a similar pattern they could treat the boy as corroborating the girl and *vice versa*, subject to there being corroboration of the girl's unsworn evidence from outside sources. The appellant had made statements, which could be treated as admissions relating to counts one, three and seven, on which the jury convicted him on majority verdicts, but acquitted him on the other four counts.

ORR LJ, reading the judgment of the court: 'On the application to sever, to which we now turn, the judge adopted the course approved by Lord Wilberforce and Lord Cross in *Boardman* v *DPP* (1974) 60 Cr App R 165, [1975] AC 421, and included, subsequent to the trial in the present case, among the guidelines provided by the judgment of this Court in *Scarrott* (1977) 65 Cr App R 125, [1977] 2 WLR 629. He considered on the application not only the terms of rule 9 of the Indictment Rules 1971, but also whether, on the material then before him, the prosecution evidence on the counts relating to the girl would be admissible in the trial as similar fact evidence in relation to the charges concerning the boy and *vice versa*. He came to the conclusion that it would be so admissible. As is pointed out in the judgment of *Scarrott* (at pp. 135 and 639-640) it would have been open to counsel for the appellant, notwithstanding the judge's earlier ruling on the application to sever, to apply during the trial for a ruling that the similar fact evidence was not admissible, but no such application was made, presumably on the basis that the judge had already considered the question of admissibility when giving his earlier ruling and that nothing had emerged in the evidence which would justify a renewed application.

It is clear that on the application to sever the similarities relied on by the Crown were (1) that the offences charged were all against children; (2) that the offences in both groups were said to have consisted of two types of act—"namely something partaking of the nature of attempted masturbation and something partaking of the nature of attempted penetration"; (3) that all of them were said to have taken place in one part or another of the childrens' home; and (4) that all were alleged to have been perpetrated by the stepfather of the children. It is also clear that as to the first of these matters the prosecution relied on passages from the judgments delivered in the Scottish case of *Moorov* v *HM Advocate* 1930 JC 68 and in particular the following passage from the judgment of Lord Sands at p. 90: "Evidence inferring a course of general immorality would not be admissible or corroborative of an indecent offence against an adult. But indecency against children is a rare and peculiar offence, and, accordingly, evidence inferring a course of conduct is admitted as relevant." This passage was cited by Lord Hailsham of St Marylebone LC in *DPP* v *Kilbourne* (1973) 57 Cr App R 381, [1973] AC 729 and he again referred generally to the *Moorov* case in *DPP* v *Boardman* (*supra*) but in our judgment nothing in his speech in the latter case indicates that he was disagreeing in any way with the "striking similarity" test applied by the other members of the House, or was accepting that some special rule applied in the present context to cases involving sexual offences against children, unhappily much less rare today than they were when the *Moorov* judgments were delivered in 1930.

In our judgment, therefore, the test to be applied in the present case was the "striking similarity" test laid down in *Boardman* (*supra*) though we bear in mind that, as pointed out in *Scarrott*, (*supra*) the phrase "striking similarity" is no more than a label. Applying that test to the factors relied on in the present case we cannot, with great respect to the learned judge, hold that it was satisfied. As to the first similarity relied on— that all the acts alleged were sexual offences against children—we reject, for the reasons already given, the view that offences against children fall, for the present purpose, into any special category as respects the admissibility of similar fact evidence. As to the second feature relied on—that there was a sequence of attempted masturbation followed by attempted penetration—the evidence on the various counts does not appear to establish such a sequence, but even if it did we are unable to accept that such a sequence would give rise to a striking similarity in sexual offences. The third and fourth alleged similarities relied on—that the offences all took place in or beside the childrens' home and that the stepfather was the alleged offender—appear to us to fall far short of being striking similarities, and if they were the case of *Boardman* (*supra*) could have been decided on the basis that the accused was headmaster and the victims pupils at a school, without reference to the similar roles in the acts done or the evidence as to the nocturnal visits of the accused to the dormitories, and *Boardman* (*supra*) would not have been the borderline case which it was held by the House of Lords to be.

Equally, in our judgment, the similarities relied on in the present case fall far short in their totality of those relied on in *Moorov* (*supra*) and *Scarrott* (*supra*). For these reasons, with great respect to the learned judge, we have come to the conclusion that he was wrong in refusing to sever the counts and was also wrong in directing the jury as he did that the evidence on one set of counts could provide corroboration as respects the others.'

(The court applied the proviso to s. 2(1) of the Criminal Appeals Act 1968.)

Appeal dismissed.

R v Barrington [1981] 1 WLR 419 (CA)

The appellant and a co-defendant had induced the three complainants, girls aged 11, 13 and 15, to come to the co-defendant's house on the pretext of being employed as baby sitters and there the appellant committed acts of indecency upon them. He was charged, *inter alia*, with three offences of indecency and an offence of having sexual intercourse with a girl under 16. He denied the offences and in cross-examination it was suggested to one complainant that the girls had concocted their evidence between them. The prosecution was given leave to call three other girls whose evidence did not disclose the commission of similar offences but disclosed circumstances similar to those leading to the commission of the offences against the complainants. The appellant was convicted of indecent assault and an attempt to have sexual intercourse with a girl under 16. He appealed against conviction.

DUNN LJ, reading the judgment of the court: 'Mr Lane for the appellant made no complaint about the direction as to the evidence of the three other girls being capable of corroborating the evidence of the complainants if the evidence of the three other girls was admissible. Indeed in the light of the remarks of Lord Cross of Chelsea in *R v Kilbourne* [1973] AC 729, 760, it would have been impossible for him to have done so. Lord Cross said:

> Once the "similar fact" evidence is admitted—and it was common ground that it was properly admitted in this case—then of necessity it "corroborates"—i.e., strengthens or supports—the evidence given by the boy an alleged offence against whom is the subject of the count under consideration.

But Mr Lane submitted that the evidence of the other girls should not have been admitted at all. None of the other girls gave evidence of an indecent assault, or any other act of indecency upon their person. Indeed their evidence related to events after

Susan and Sally had been in the house. It was accordingly incapable of amounting to "similar fact" evidence. Although other grounds were put forward in the notice of appeal, this was the only ground relied on in this court.

Mr Lane referred us first to *R* v *Doughty* [1965] 1 WLR 331, 334-335, where Lord Parker CJ said:

> It is to be observed in the present case that while it might be said that there was evidence capable of being treated in a sinister respect and held to be indecent assault, the acts to which the small girls had spoken were certainly equally consistent with what one might call a paternal or avuncular interest. It is not without interest that neighbours came, and in particular the mother of Carol said that she knew the defendant, that he was highly respected, that she absolutely trusted her children with him, and that he undoubtedly was very fond of children. That there was evidence of familiarity in the sense of a paternal or avuncular interest is undoubted. The evidence that it was not merely for that but in order to satisfy lust was tenuous to a degree. Further, it is to be observed that even if the acts complained of were capable of being interpreted as indecent it was quite a different form of indecency in regard to physical acts from that spoken to by the two girls who were the subject of the counts.
>
> In the circumstances, this court is satisfied that where the evidence of indecency is tenuous to a degree and where even if held to be indecent it is a different form of indecency, then the court can only exercise its discretion in one way, by excluding that evidence, the reason being that its prejudicial value is quite overwhelming. It is well known that this court is very reluctant ever to interfere with the discretion of a trial judge. They will in the ordinary way only do so if he had erred in principle. The court feels, however, that in the circumstances as I have indicated them, this discretion could properly only be exercised in one way, by excluding the evidence. That being so, and this evidence being clearly directed to both counts—both that dealing with Carol as well as that dealing with Shirley—the only proper course the court can take is to quash both convictions.

Nobody could say that the evidence of the three other girls in this case disclosed no more than a paternal or avuncular interest on the part of the appellant and we do not feel that we are assisted by *R* v *Doughty*.

Mr Lane also referred us to more recent and well known authorities on the admissibility of "similar fact" evidence. They are *R* v *Boardman* [1975] AC 421; *R* v *Johannsen* (1977) 65 Cr App R 101; *R* v *Novac* (1977) 65 Cr App R 107 and *R* v *Scarrott* [1978] QB 1016. He also referred to *Cross on Evidence*, 5th ed (1979), p. 356 and to *R* v *Horry* [1949] NZLR 791, 792. In that case the evidence the admission of which was complained of was, first, that of two women, who, as well as [the] complainant, had each replied to [the] accused's newspaper advertisement and had (separately) met him by appointment; each had had an interview with him broadly similar to that between [the] accused and [the] complainant, except that in the case of these two women there was no suggestion of any attempt to kiss or to assault; and, secondly, the evidence of a detective-sergeant (to whom [the] accused was well known as one who had many convictions), who saw him meet and converse with one of these two women. It was contended that the evidence of the two women served merely to show that they, too, had been deceived, which was not an offence, and was irrelevant; that such evidence merely created in the minds of the jury prejudice against [the] accused; and that the evidence of the detective-sergeant, in so far as it revealed [the] accused was known to him and that the detective-sergeant troubled to keep him under observation, implied previous offences, and so prejudiced [the] accused from obtaining a fair trial. The admissibility of the two young women's evidence was argued in chambers before trial, when it was sought to justify its being led on the grounds (i) that it was indicative of system, and (ii) that it assisted in the establishment of the identity of [the] accused as the person against whom [the complainant's] allegations were directed. The learned judge ruled that the evidence was admissible on the latter ground. On appeal to the Court of Appeal, Gresson J said, at p. 793:

> Dealing first with the question as to whether this evidence was properly admitted: in order to be admissible, it must be relevant. It contributed nothing towards establishing that [the] accused improperly kissed or assaulted [the complainant], which was the offence with which he was charged, and, in so far as it revealed deception practised upon other young women, it was prejudicial. But it had relevance on the question of identity, and this, on the depositions, was in issue no less than whether a kiss was forced on an unwilling recipient.

At p. 798, having cited a large number of authorities, the judge said:

> It was in the light of these authorities that Callan J had to rule. As the matter then stood, the evidence, being relevant to the issue of identity, was admissible, but, from counsel's assurance that identity would not be disputed, it became clear that identity would not in fact be the subject of contention. Evidence that goes to an issue not really in contest, and merely prejudices [the] accused, should be excluded.

The judge then referred to the decision of the Privy Council in *Noor Mohamed* v *The King* [1949] AC 182 and said, at pp. 798-799:

> [That decision] has established beyond all question that there is such a discretionary power. But in this case the question goes deeper, and is whether the evidence is admissible at all, since the issue to which it relates no longer exists. Its sole justification is to establish identity, and that the Crown is no longer called upon to do. . . Our view is, therefore, that the learned judge should have disallowed the evidence, not as a matter of discretion, but because it was inadmissible as irrelevant.

So if the question of identity had remained in issue, the evidence would have been relevant to that issue and would have been admitted notwithstanding that it did not disclose the commission of any offence.

In all the cases so far cited, except *R v Doughty* [1965] 1 WLR 331 and *R v Horry* [1949] NZLR 791, the evidence of similar facts included evidence of the commission of an offence similar to that with which the accused was charged. Counsel could find no case in which it did not, and the evidence was held admissible.

Finally counsel relied on a passage in *Archbold Criminal Pleading Evidence and Practice*, 40th ed (1979), para 1324, under the heading "Proximity," which is in the following terms: "The decisions of the Court of Appeal are not consistent on another point, namely whether the 'striking similarity' must relate to the commission of the offence as opposed to the surrounding circumstances.

In *R v Novac*, 65 Cr App R 107, the facts were very like those in *R v Johannsen*, 65 Cr App R 101, but (at p. 112) the court said: 'If a man is going to commit buggery with a boy he picks up, it must surely be a commonplace of such an encounter that he will take the boy home with him and commit the offence in bed. The fact that the boys may in each case have been picked up by Raymond' (one of the appellants) 'in the first instance at amusement arcades may be a feature more approximating to a "unique or striking similarity.". . . It is not, however, a similarity in the commission of the crime. It is a similarity in the surrounding circumstances and is not, in our judgment, sufficiently proximate to the commission of the crime itself to lead to the conclusion that the repetition of this feature would make the boys' stories inexplicable on the basis of coincidence.' In *R v Scarrott* [1978] QB 1016 the court were faced with the apparent conflict between the approach of the differently constituted courts in *R v Johannsen* and *R v Novac* to barely distinguishable facts. After referring to the use by the court in *R v Novac* of 'the rather strange word. . ."proximate"' the court made it plain that they preferred the approach of the court in *R v Johannsen*. They said that 'it would be wrong . . to elevate the passage' [cited above] '. . . into a statement of law.' They also pointed out that 'in one of the most famous of all cases dealing with similar fact evidence, the brides in the bath case, *R v Smith* (1915) 11 Cr App R 229 the court had regard to the facts that the accused man married the women, and that he insured their lives. Some surrounding circumstances have to be considered in order to understand either the offence charged or the nature of the similar fact evidence which it is sought to adduce and in each case it must be a matter of judgment where the line is drawn.'"

Counsel submitted that evidence to be admissible must be probative of an indecent assault, not merely of an intention to commit an indecent assault. And in as much as none of the three other girls had in fact said that they had been indecently assaulted their evidence was not probative of the charges of indecent assault on the three complainants.

Mr Lane submitted that evidence of similar facts to be admissible must relate to the facts of an offence similar to that with which the appellant was charged, and not to the surrounding circumstances, which he submitted were too remote. He conceded however that if the evidence of the three other girls had included evidence of indecent assault, then their evidence, including the evidence of surrounding circumstances, would have been admissible, even though Susan had not been introduced by photographs, although Sally was photographed in the nude.

Counsel for the Crown sought to support the ruling of the judge that the evidence of the three other girls was admissible on the basis that the principal issue in the case was whether the appellant had lured all six girls to the house for a sexual purpose, or whether, as the defence alleged, the purpose was an innocent one, namely baby sitting, and that the evidence tended to rebut that defence. In our judgment the admission of the evidence can certainly be supported on that ground. But admission of the evidence can be supported on another and wider ground.

It is well established that although evidence of a disposition or propensity to commit the offence with which the accused is charged is not admissible, evidence may in certain circumstances be led of similar facts tending to show that the accused is guilty of the offence charged. Such evidence has it appears hitherto only been admitted where it has disclosed the commission of similar offences although it has also included the surrounding circumstances. In some cases the similarity of the surrounding circumstances has been stressed more than the similarity of the mode of commission of the offences themselves. Surrounding circumstances include the preliminaries leading up to the offence, such as the mode and place of the initial approach and the inducement offered or words used.

The two sets of facts must be looked at as a whole. In *R* v *Scarrott* [1978] QB 1016 the very point with which we are concerned was raised although it was not necessary for the decision because there was evidence of the commission of an offence. Scarman LJ, giving the judgment of the court, said, at p. 1025:

> Mr Fallon has based a submission. . . that, to be admissible, the similar fact evidence must reveal features of a striking similarity with the offence itself, not its surrounding circumstances. He submits that is all that the rather strange word that Bridge LJ used [in *R* v *Novac*, 65 Cr App R 107] "proximate" means. In our view, we are here in that area of judgment upon particular facts from which the criminal law can never depart. Plainly some matters, some circumstances may be so distant in time or place from the commission of an offence as not to be properly considered when deciding whether the subject matter of similar fact evidence displays striking similarities with the offence charged. On the other hand, equally plainly, one cannot isolate, as a sort of laboratory specimen, the bare bones of a criminal offence from its surrounding circumstances and say that it is only within the confines of that specimen, microscopically considered, that admissibility is to be determined. Indeed, in one of the most famous cases of all dealing with similar fact evidence, the brides in the bath case, *R* v *Smith* (1915) 11 Cr App R 229, the court had regard to the facts that the accused man married the women, and that he insured their lives. Some surrounding circumstances have to be considered in order to understand either the offence charged or the nature of the similar fact evidence which it is sought to adduce and in each case it must be a matter of judgment where the line is drawn. One cannot draw an inflexible line as a rule of law.

Then Scarman LJ said, at p. 1026:

> We therefore have to reach a judgment upon the evidence of this particular case, and to determine whether the evidence adduced, that is the similar fact evidence adduced, possesses such features that it is a proper exercise of judgment to say that the evidence is logically probative, that it has positive probative value in assisting to determine the truth.

We accept and follow the reasoning of Scarman LJ in *R* v *Scarrott*. The various facts recited by the judge in this case as constituting "similar facts" were so similar to the facts of the surrounding circumstances in the evidence of the complainants that they can properly be described as "striking." That they did not include evidence of the commission of offences similar to those with which the appellant was charged does not mean that they are not logically probative in determining the guilt of the appellant. Indeed we are of opinion that taken as a whole they are inexplicable on the basis of coincidence and that they are of positive probative value in assisting to determine the truth of the charges against the appellant, in that they tended to show that he was guilty of the offences with which he was charged.'

Appeal dismissed.

R v *Butler* (1987) 84 Cr App R 12 (CA)

The appellant was convicted on counts of rape and indecent assault against each of two complainants. The facts involved in the offences were substantially similar, in both cases the appellant offered a lift to the complainant and in the course of the drive forced her, with one hand pushing her head down, to fellate him; he also raped her. Miss W initially made a misleading statement to the police and was unable to identify the appellant three months after the offence. However seminal stains were found on her and on her clothing, which indicated that her attacker had had a vasectomy (there was evidence to show that the appellant had undergone this operation); and tyre impressions which matched the appellant's car were found at the place where she alleged the offences took place. Further an earring mislaid during the attack was found some months later when the appellant's car was searched. Miss C, the other complainant, was of negroid descent; she had identified the appellant, in particular his voice, the type of car he had used, and the place of the offences. Traces of negroid hair similar to hers, and fibres from her clothes were found in the appellant's car and on his clothing.

At the trial application was made by the prosecution to call a witness, Mrs JU, who a few years previously had had a sexual relationship with the appellant involving acts similar to those involved in the alleged offences, and at similar locations, to which she had been a consenting party. The judge ruled in favour of the application.

SIR RALPH KILNER BROWN, reading the judgment of the court: '*Director of Public Prosecutions* v *Boardman* (1975) 139 JP 52, (1974) Cr App R 165, the leading and most authoritative case on the subject, and other authorities establish principles which are now well known. It should therefore not be necessary to quote extensive passages from those cases. Within the well established principles every case is one to be decided on its own particular circumstances. We venture to summarise the effect of the various authorities and state the principles as follows:

(1)   Evidence of similar facts may be admissible in evidence, whether or not they tend to show the commission of other offences. This evidence may be admitted:

(a)   if it tends to show that the accused has committed the particular crime of which he is charged.

(b)   to support the identification of the accused as the man who committed a particular crime and, in appropriate cases, in order to rebut a defence of alibi, or

(c)   to negative a defence of accident or innocent conduct.

(2)   Admissibility is a question of law for the judge to decide. He must, in the analysis of the proffered evidence, be satisfied that:

(a)   the nature and quality of the similar facts show a striking similarity or what Lord Justice Scarman in *R v Scarrott* (1978) 142 JP 198, (1977) 65 Cr App R 125 describes as being of "positive probative value," and

(b)   the evidence of a similar act goes well beyond a propensity to act in a particular fashion.

(3)   Notwithstanding an established admissibility in law the Judge in the exercise of discretion may refuse to admit the evidence if its prejudicial effect outweighs its probative value.'

Appeal dismissed.

- Do the post-*Boardman* cases satisfy the stringent approach in *Boardman* itself?
- It has been said many times by the courts that even if similar fact evidence is admissible in law, the judge has a discretion to exclude it if its prejudicial effect outweighs its probative value. In the light of the modern law on similar fact evidence could circumstances ever arise in which this discretion would be exercised?

Mood Music Publishing Company Limited v De Wolfe Limited [1976] Ch 119 (CA)

The plaintiffs were the owners of the copyright in a musical work called 'Sogno Nostalgico'. They alleged that the defendants had infringed such copyright by supplying for broadcasting a work entitled 'Girl in the Dark'. It was not disputed that the works were similar, but the defendants argued that the similarity was coincidental, and denied copying even though 'Sogno Nostalgico' was composed prior to 'Girl in the Dark'. The plaintiffs were permitted to adduce evidence to show that on other occasions the defendants had reproduced works subject to copyright. The defendants appealed.

LORD DENNING MR: 'The admissibility of evidence as to "similar facts" has been much considered in the criminal law. Some of them have reached the highest tribunal, the latest of them being *R v Boardman* [1975] AC 421. The criminal courts have been very careful not to admit such evidence unless its probative value is so strong that it should be received in the interests of justice: and its admission will not operate unfairly to the accused. In civil cases the courts have followed a similar line but have not been so chary of admitting it. In civil cases the courts will admit evidence of similar facts if it is logically probative, that is, if it is logically relevant in determining the matter which is in issue: provided that it is not oppressive or unfair to the other side: and also that the other side has fair notice of it and is able to deal with it. Instances are *Brown v Eastern & Midlands Railway Co.* (1889) 22 QBD 391: *Moore v Ransome's Dock Committee* (1898) 14 TLR 539 and *Hales v Kerr* [1908] 2 KB 601.

The matter in issue in the present case is whether the resemblances which "Girl in the Dark" bear to "Sogno Nostalgico" are mere coincidences or are due to copying. Upon that issue it is very relevant to know that there are these other cases of musical works which are undoubtedly the subject of copyright, but that the defendants have nevertheless produced musical works bearing close resemblances to them. Whereas it might be due to mere coincidence in one case, it is very unlikely that they would be coincidences in four cases. It is rather like *R v Sims* [1946] KB 531, 540, where it was said: "The probative force of all the acts together is much greater than one alone." So the probative force of four resemblances together is much better than one alone. . . It seems to me the judge was right.'

(ORR LJ and BROWNE LJ agreed.

Appeal dismissed.

• Should the approach of the courts to similar fact evidence be the same in civil as in criminal cases?

Questions for discussion

R v Coke; R v Littleton

1   Is there some striking similarity in Coke's previous conviction for rape, which would give rise to probative value on the present charge?

2   If so, of what does it consist?

3   Is it of importance for any purpose that Coke's defence is one of consent?

4   Is the judge likely to exercise his discretion to exclude the evidence?

5   At what stage would the prosecution be entitled to lead the evidence, and would it make any difference that Coke would be shown to have a previous conviction?

6   If Margaret Blackstone had previously had sexual intercourse with Coke, but denied this in cross-examination, could Coke adduce evidence of such acts as part of his case?

7   Can Coke prove as part of his case that last year, Margaret threatened to complain falsely that she had been raped by his mate, Kevin?

8   May the prosecution adduce evidence of the writings about Margaret found in Coke's flat (exhibit GG1)?

Blackstone v Coke

1   Would Margaret be entitled to adduce evidence of Coke's previous conviction for rape as part of her case? Does the nature of Coke's defence affect your answer in any way?

2   If the judge allows Margaret to adduce evidence of the previous conviction, what degree of detail should be permitted, and how should Margaret prove the necessary facts?

Additional question

You are acting for Alfred, who has previous convictions for fraud in respect of Girl Guide funds when he was acting as the treasurer of his daughter's company in 1974; for indecent exposure towards the captain of another company in 1977; and for indecent assault upon a Girl Guide in 1980: in the last case the facts were that he offered the girl a lift home after a guide meeting, and then took her to a lay-by where he assaulted her and then left her to walk home.

Alfred is now indicted on three counts, the evidence for the prosecution being as follows:

(i) Indecent assault on Belinda, a girl of 6: he waited outside Belinda's school, offered her a lift home, indecently assaulted her, and then took her to the end of the street where she lived.

(ii) Indecent assault on Catherine, a girl of 13: Catherine is a Girl Guide and he waited outside the company's meeting place; he offered her a lift home, took her into the country, assaulted her in a field and left her.

(iii) Attempted assault on Delia, a young woman hitch-hiker; he gave her a lift and attempted to assault her, but she was able to escape and run away.

The prosecution want to have all three cases tried together: they propose to call Ethel, Belinda's mother, who saw her getting into a car and noted the registration number: Catherine and Delia can both identify Alfred. They also propose to call Freda, a Girl Guide, who will say that Alfred tried to lure her into his car, and Gertrude who will say that Alfred drove his car very slowly alongside the kerb for about 100 yards while she was walking along a country road.

Alfred's defence is a total denial of all charges.

What steps, if any, can you take to minimise the risks of Alfred's conviction?

Further reading

Allan, 'Similar fact evidence and disposition: law, discretion and admissibility' (1985) 48 MLR 253.

Carter, 'Forbidden reasoning permissible: similar fact evidence a decade after *Boardman*' (1985) 48 MLR 29.

Cross, 'Fourth time lucky—similar fact evidence in the House of Lords' [1975] Crim LR 62.

Elliott, 'The young person's guide to similar fact evidence' [1983] Crim LR 284, 352.

Eggleston, '*Evidence, Proof and Probability*', 2nd ed. (1983) Ch. 7.

Hoffman, 'Similar facts after *Boardman*' (1975) 91 LQR 193.

Mirfield, 'Similar facts—*Makin* out' [1987] CLJ 83.

Tapper, 'Proof and prejudice' in *Well and Truly Tried* (ed. Campbell and Waller) (1982).

Weinberg, 'Multiple counts and similar fact evidence' in *Well and Truly Tried* (ed. Campbell & Waller) (1982).

Zuckerman, 'Similar fact evidence—the unobservable rule' (1987) 104 LQR 187.

6   The Rule against Hearsay (1)

A: THE EXCLUSIONARY RULE AND THE DOCTRINE OF RES GESTAE

(Suggested preliminary reading: *A Practical Approach to Evidence*, pp. 156-184).

Subramaniam v Public Prosecutor [1956] 1 WLR 965 (PC)

The appellant was charged with unlawful possession of ammunition. It would have been a defence that the appellant had a lawful excuse for his possession, and he sought to give evidence that he had been captured by terrorists and was acting under duress. The trial judge ruled that he could not state in evidence what the terrorists had said to him. The appellant was convicted and appealed.

MR L M D DE SILVA, delivering the judgment of their Lordships: 'Evidence of a statement made to a witness by a person who is not himself called as a witness may or may not be hearsay. It is hearsay and inadmissible when the object of the evidence is to establish the truth of what is contained in the statement. It is not hearsay and is admissible when it is proposed to establish by the evidence, not the truth of the statement, but the fact that it was made. The fact that the statement was made, quite apart from its truth, is frequently relevant in considering the mental state and conduct thereafter of the witness or of some other person in whose presence the statement was made. In the case before their Lordships statements could have been made to the appellant by the terrorists, which, whether true or not, if they had been believed by the appellant, might reasonably have induced in him an apprehension of instant death if he failed to conform to their wishes.'
    Appeal allowed.

R v Rice and Others [1963] 1 QB 857 (CCA)

Rice, Moore and Hoather were tried with other men on two counts of conspiracy. Part of the prosecution case against Rice was that he had taken a flight to Manchester on or about a certain date, in the company of Hoather. This was denied. The prosecution produced an airline ticket to Manchester in respect of a date at about the relevant time, affording two seats in the names of Rice and Moore. The prosecution suggested that Hoather flew in place of Moore. The ticket was put to Rice in cross-examination, and, he having denied all knowledge of it, it was exhibited and shown to the jury. All the defendants were convicted. On appeal it was argued that the ticket was hearsay and had been wrongly admitted.

WINN J, delivering the judgment of the court: 'The court has no doubt that the ticket and the fact of the presence of that ticket in the file or other place where tickets used by passengers would in the ordinary course be found, were facts which were in logic relevant to the issue whether or not there flew on those flights two men either of whom was a Mr Rice or a Mr Moore.

The relevance of that ticket in logic and its legal admissibility as a piece of real evidence both stem from the same root, *viz.*, the balance of probability recognised by common sense and common knowledge that an air ticket which has been used on a flight and which has a name upon it has more likely than not been used by a man of that name or by one of two men whose names are upon it.

A comparable document would be a passport, which is more likely on the whole to be in the possession of the person to whom it was issued than that of anyone having no right to it.

It is, however, essential, whether for the purposes of logical reasoning or for a consideration of the evidentiary effect in law of any such document, to distinguish clearly between its relevance and its probative significance: the document must not be treated as speaking its contents for what it might say could only be hearsay. Thus a passport cannot say "my bearer is X" nor the air ticket "I was issued to Y."'

Appeal dismissed.

• Do you agree with the reasoning of Winn J?

Myers v DPP [1965] AC 1001 (HL)

The appellant was convicted of offences of dishonesty in relation to motor vehicles. His practice was to buy up wrecked cars with their log-books, to disguise stolen cars so that they corresponded as nearly as possible with the wrecks and their log-books, and to sell the stolen cars as if they were the wrecks, repaired by him. In order to prove their case, the prosecution adduced evidence from a witness in charge of records which were kept on microfilm, containing details of every car made at the works of a certain manufacturer. The microfilm was prepared from records compiled by workmen on cards, which were destroyed after being filmed, and which recorded the cylinder-block number of each car. Since the cylinder-block number was stamped indelibly on the engine of each vehicle, the evidence was of some value to the prosecution in proving the true identity of the cars in question. The trial judge admitted this evidence and the Court of Criminal Appeal upheld this.

LORD REID: 'The reason why this evidence is maintained to have been inadmissible is that its cogency depends on hearsay. The witness could only say that a record made by someone else showed that, if the record was correctly made, a car had left the works bearing three particular numbers. He could not prove that the record was correct or that the numbers which it contained were in fact the numbers on the car when it was made. This is a highly technical point, but the law regarding hearsay evidence is technical, and I would say absurdly technical. . ..

At the trial counsel for the prosecution sought to support the existing practice of admitting such records, if produced by the persons in charge of them, by arguing that they were not adduced to prove the truth of the recorded particulars but only to prove that they were records kept in the normal course of business. Counsel for the accused then asked the very pertinent question — if they were not intended to prove the truth of the entries what were they intended to prove? I ask what the jury would infer from them: obviously that they were probably true records. If they were not capable of supporting an inference that they were probably true records, then

I do not see what probative value they could have, and their admission was bound to mislead the jury. . ..

In argument the Solicitor-General maintained that, although the general rule may be against the admission of private records to prove the truth of entries in them, the trial judge has a discretion to admit a record in a particular case if satisfied that it is trustworthy and that justice requires its admission. That appears to me to be contrary to the whole framework of the existing law. It is true that a judge has a discretion to exclude legally admissible evidence if justice so requires, but it is a very different thing to say that he has a discretion to admit legally inadmissible evidence. The whole development of the exceptions to the hearsay rule is based on the determination of certain classes of evidence as admissible or inadmissible and not on the apparent credibility of particular evidence tendered. No matter how cogent particular evidence may seem to be, unless it comes within a class which is admissible, it is excluded. Half a dozen witnesses may offer to prove that they heard two men of high character who cannot now be found discuss in detail the fact now in issue and agree on a credible account of it, but that evidence would not be admitted although it might be by far the best evidence available.'

(LORDS MORRIS OF BORTH-Y-GEST and HODSON delivered concurring judgments holding that the evidence should not be received. LORDS DONOVAN and PEARCE dissented on the question of admissibility. Their Lordships were unanimous in applying the proviso to s. 4(1) of the Criminal Appeal Act 1907.)

Appeal dismissed.

• Were the usual dangers which are said to prevent the admission of hearsay evidence present in the case of *Myers* v *DPP*?

Patel v Comptroller of Customs [1966] AC 356 (PC)

The appellant imported from Singapore into Fiji a quantity of corriander seed, which was shipped in bags. He correctly engrossed the Customs Import Entry Form A in accordance with the particulars contained in the invoice referable to the purchase of the seed. On investigation at arrival, however, five bags were found each to be contained in an outer bag marked with the appellant's trade name, but the inner bags had written on them: "Alberdan/AD/4152/Corriander Favourite Singapore" and at the base of them the legend "Produce of Morocco". In the import entry form the country of origin was stated to be India. The appellant was charged and convicted with making a false declaration in a customs import entry produced to an officer of customs in that in respect of the five bags instead of declaring the origin of the seed to be Morocco he declared it to be India. He appealed against conviction.

LORD HODSON, delivering the judgment of their Lordships: 'The next question was whether there was any evidence upon which the appellant could be convicted of making a false declaration as charged.

The only entry as to which the allegation of falsity is made is the word "India" in the column headed "country of origin," which is part of the import entry form signed by the appellant. The only evidence purporting to show that this entry was false is the legend "Produce of Morocco" written upon the bags. Their Lordships are asked by the respondent to say that the inference can be drawn that the goods contained in the bags were produced in Morocco. This they are unable to do. From an evidentiary point of view the words are hearsay and cannot assist the prosecution. This matter need not be elaborated in view of the decision of the House of Lords in *Myers* v *Director of Public Prosecutions* [1965] AC 1001, given after the Fiji courts had considered the case. The decision of the House, however, makes clear beyond doubt that the list of exceptions to the hearsay rule cannot be extended judicially to include such things as labels or markings. Nothing is to be gained by comparing the legend in this case with the records considered in *Myers* v *Director of Public Prosecutions.* Nothing here is known of when and by whom the markings on the bags were affixed and no evidence was called to prove any fact which tended to show that the goods in question in fact came from Morocco.

Some reliance was placed by the respondent on *R* v *Rice* [1963] 1 QB 857, where a used airline ticket was admitted as an exhibit in a criminal prosecution. It is sufficient to say that the Court of Criminal Appeal in admitting the document said that it must not be treated as speaking its contents, for what it might say could only be hearsay.'

Appeal allowed.

Jones v Metcalfe [1967] 1 WLR 1286 (DC)

A collision took place between two cars, caused by the action of a lorry. An eye witness reported the registration number of the lorry to the police. The appellant was charged with driving without due care and attention. The eye witness gave evidence that he had reported the number to the police, but was unable to quote the number to the court. The other evidence was that of a police officer who said that as a result of information, he interviewed the appellant, put to him what was alleged to have taken place, stated that his information was that the motor lorry concerned was EWH 820 and that the appellant admitted that he was the driver of a lorry bearing that number at the time and date in question, but denied that any accident occurred due to his driving. The appellant was convicted.

LORD PARKER giving the judgment of the court: 'It was no wonder really that in those circumstances a submission was made that no evidence had been adduced to show that the lorry EWH 820 was the lorry concerned in the incident, or put another way, that the appellant was the driver of the lorry involved in the incident. This court is getting a number of cases of this kind; in most it is true the independent witness, who after a lapse of time has forgotten the number which he took, can produce other matters of identification; for instance Mr Dickinson might or might not have been able to say that the lorry concerned was not merely a lorry but was a brewer's lorry, or he might have been able to identify the driver as a man with red hair or with spectacles, and have in this way produced some identification of the lorry which the appellant admitted to be driving. There is no such additional evidence in the present case. This is simply a case where the evidence was that the independent witness gave a number to a policeman, and that a policeman, not necessarily the same policeman, on information obtained, whether from Mr Dickinson or somebody else we do not know, then proceeded to interview the appellant.

The justices, and I have very much sympathy with them, accepted the common sense approach that they were entitled to come to the conclusion that the police officer acted on the information given by Mr Dickinson and that Mr Dickinson must have identified the lorry as EWH 820. In my judgment, however, they were not entitled to do it. To do so is really to make inroads into the principle under which we still act, that hearsay evidence is inadmissible. I also think that if they had been referred at an earlier stage — because I gather they did not hear the case until after they had convicted the appellant — to *Grew* v *Cubitt* [1951] 2 TLR 305, DC, they would have been forced to come to a different conclusion. There the independent witness had not given a number to the police, but he gave evidence that he had got his wife to write it down. Again as the result of information received the police officer went and interviewed the appellant. In that case it is to be observed that the prosecution case could have been proved in one of two ways: they could have called the wife who wrote the number down; equally they could have asked the independent witness whether he had seen the wife write the number down and, if so, on production of the note he could have refreshed his memory and stated what the number was.

As the court there held, although there was a strong probability that the police officer acted on information obtained from the wife or from the wife's note, there was in fact, under our rules of evidence, no connecting link, and the prosecution had not proved their case.

In my judgment the same really applies here. If Mr Dickinson had been able to say that he gave a number to the police officer, that he saw the police officer write it down in his note book and had then been asked to refresh his memory from the production of that note book then albeit it was not in his own handwriting, it was in effect his note and the prosecution could have proved their case.'

DIPLOCK LJ: 'I reluctantly agree. Like my Lord I have every sympathy with the justices because the inference of fact that the appellant was the driver of the lorry at the time of the accident is irresistible as a matter of common sense. But this is a branch of the law which has little to do with common sense. The inference that the appellant was the driver of the lorry was really an inference of what the independent witness had said to the police when he gave them the number of the lorry, and since what he had said to the police would have been inadmissible as hearsay, to infer what he said to the police is inadmissible also.'

Appeal allowed.

• Do you agree with Diplock LJ's statement that this is a branch of law which has little to do with common sense? If so, how should the law be reformed?

R v *Turner and Others* (1975) 61 Cr App R 67 (CA)

The defendant was charged with robbery. The trial judge refused to admit evidence to the effect that a person not called as a witness had admitted having committed the offence charged. The defendant was convicted and appealed.

MILMO J, giving the judgment of the court: 'Assuming for the present purpose that it was relevant to prove that Saunders had been one of the robbers at Ilford, the defence would have been entitled to call witnesses to prove the fact of their own knowledge, such as people who had actually seen him at the bank. They could have called Saunders himself. No such evidence was called and evidence of what Saunders said to a third party was not probative of anything. It would have been hearsay evidence which did not come within any of the well settled exceptions to the general rule that hearsay evidence is not admissible. That the categories of these exceptions is now closed and cannot be added to without legislation was made clear by Lord Reid in his speech in *Myers* v *Director of Public Prosecutions* [1965] AC 1001, 48 Cr App R 348, a case in which it had been sought to extend the exceptions to the ban on the reception of hearsay in evidence. At p. 1021E and p. 362 Lord Reid said: "The common law must be developed to meet the changing economic conditions and habits of thought, and I would not be deterred by expressions of opinion in this House in old cases. But there are limits to what we can or should do. If we are to extend the law it must be by the development and application of fundamental principles. We cannot introduce arbitrary conditions or limitations: that must be left to legislation."

Mr Wright cited a number of authorities which he contended supported his argument that evidence of what Saunders was alleged to have said to the police was admissible. These included *Greenberg* (1923) 17 Cr App R 107; *Phillips* (1936) 26 Cr App R 17; and *Cooper (Sean)* [1969] 1 QB 267, 53 Cr App R 82.

The case of *Greenberg* (*supra*) was one of rape in which the trial had been conducted on the footing that the complainant who had given evidence for the Crown was a modest woman. On appeal leave was given to cross-examine her on her character and to call two witnesses to give evidence of her companionship with men on the basis of their own observations and of statements made by her that she had brought the charge against the accused in order to get money. The Court held that the new evidence was such that the jury might not have convicted had it been before them.

Phillips' case (*supra*) was one of incest. The defence was that the case was fabricated and that the two girls concerned had been schooled by their mother to give false evidence against their father. It was put to each of the girls in cross-examination that they had admitted to another person that their evidence was false and each of them denied it. The defence then sought to call evidence of the making of these admissions, but the trial judge ruled that such evidence went to credit only and declined to admit it. From the report it seems to this Court that the evidence was clearly admissible under s. 4 of the Criminal Procedure Act 1865 and it is stated that the Crown on the hearing of the appeal conceded that it was admissible. The Court of Criminal Appeal held that the evidence which it was sought to call went beyond the credibility of the girls and went to the very foundation of the prisoner's answer to the charge, namely, that the witnesses called for the Crown were biased and were parties to a plot to frame the accused.

Cooper's case (*supra*) was somewhat curious. In the re-examination of a defence witness, hearsay evidence was given without objection by the Crown, that a third person who had not been called as a witness had admitted that he was the person who had committed the offence with which the accused was charged. The Court of Criminal Appeal allowed the appeal upon the ground that the conviction was unsafe or unsatisfactory. It is significant that throughout the report the word "hearsay" does not appear and it would seem that the point was never taken that the admission in question was hearsay and as such inadmissible.

The Court does not find in any of these cases any authority for the proposition advanced in this case that hearsay evidence is admissible in a criminal case to show that a third party who has not been called as a witness in the case has admitted committing the offence charged. The idea, which may be gaining prevalence in some quarters, that in a criminal trial the defence is entitled to adduce hearsay evidence to establish facts, which if proved would be relevant and would assist the defence, is wholly erroneous.'

Appeal dismissed.

Woodhouse v *Hall* (1981) 72 Cr App R 39 (DC)

The defendant was charged with managing a brothel at certain premises, described as a sauna and massage parlour. In order to prove that the premises were being used as a brothel, the prosecution sought to adduce evidence of conversations between police officers and women employed as masseuses at the premises, in which details of the availability and cost of sexual services were discussed. The magistrates rejected this evidence as hearsay and dismissed the charge. The prosecution appealed.

DONALDSON LJ: 'We have been referred to *Ratten* v *R* (1971) 56 Cr App R 18, [1972] AC 378, a Privy Council decision, but one which reflects English law. For my part I think it is sufficient to refer to a short passage in the opinion of the Board which was delivered by Lord Wilberforce and appears at p. 23 and p. 387 of the respective reports: "The mere fact that evidence of a witness includes evidence as to words spoken by another person who is not called, is no objection to its admissibility. Words spoken are facts just as much as any other action by a human being. If the speaking of the words is a relevant fact, a witness may give evidence that they were spoken. A question of hearsay only arises when the words spoken are relied on 'testimonially,' i.e., as establishing some fact narrated by the words. Authority is hardly needed for this proposition, but their Lordships will restate what was said in the judgment of the Board in *Subramaniam* v *Public Prosecutor* [1956] 1 WLR 965, 970: 'Evidence of a statement made to a witness by a person who is not himself called as a witness may or may not be hearsay. It is hearsay and inadmissible when the object of the evidence is to establish the truth of what is contained in the statement. It is not hearsay and is admissible when it is proposed to establish by the evidence, not the truth of the statement, but the fact that it was made.'".

I suspect that the justices were misled by *Subramaniam's* case (*supra*) and thought that this was a hearsay case, because they may have thought that they had to be satisfied as to the truth of what the ladies said or were alleged to have said in the sense they had to satisfy themselves that the words were not a joke but were meant seriously and something of that sort. But this is not a matter of truth or falsity. It is a matter of what was really said — the quality of the words, the message being transmitted.

That arises in every case where the words themselves are a relevant fact. The quality of the words has to be assessed, but that is quite different from the situation where the words are evidence of some other matter. Then their truth and accuracy has to be assessed and they are hearsay.

There is no question here of the hearsay rule arising at all. The relevant issue was did these ladies make these offers? The offers were oral and the police officers were entitled to give evidence of them. The evidence, in my judgment, was wrongly excluded and should have been admitted. What the result would have been is of course another matter.'

COMYN J: 'There is a famous observation in English literature: "What the soldier said was not evidence." That can be misleading.

The subject of hearsay can be misleading, because it looks so simple in outline. I think a case such as this is of particular importance for emphasising that we are not dealing with an exception to the hearsay rule. What we are here dealing with is a more fundamental question as to whether the evidence proffered by the prosecution, rejected by the justices, was hearsay at all.'

Appeal allowed.

R v *Blastland* [1986] AC 41 (HL)

The appellant was charged on indictment with buggery and murder, the case for the prosecution being that he had forcibly buggered a 12-year-old boy and then strangled him with a scarf. He pleaded not guilty. He gave evidence that he had attempted to bugger the boy but had desisted when the boy had complained of pain. Shortly afterwards, he had seen M nearby and, afraid that he had been seen committing a serious offence, had run off and returned to his home. His case was that it had been M, not he, who had committed the offences with which he was charged. He sought to call a number of witnesses to give evidence that M had said, before the boy's body had been discovered, that a young boy had been murdered. The judge ruled that that evidence was hearsay and inadmissible. He also refused an application to call M and treat him as a hostile witness. The appellant was convicted on both counts, and his appeal against conviction, on the ground that the judge had been wrong to exclude the evidence in question, was dismissed by the Court of Appeal. The appellant further appealed to the House of Lords.

LORD BRIDGE Of HARWICH: 'Hearsay evidence is not excluded because it has no logically probative value. Given that the subject matter of the hearsay is relevant to some issue in the trial, it may clearly be potentially probative. The rationale of excluding it as inadmissible, rooted as it is in the system of trial by jury, is a recognition of the great difficulty, even more acute for a juror than for a trained judicial mind, of assessing what, if any, weight can properly be given to a statement by a person whom the jury have not seen or heard and which has not been subject to any test of reliability by cross-examination. As Lord Normand put it, delivering the judgment of the Privy Council in *Teper* v *The Queen* [1952] AC 480, 486:

> The rule against the admission of hearsay evidence is fundamental. It is not the best evidence and it is not delivered on oath. The truthfulness and accuracy of the person whose words are spoken to by another witness cannot be tested by cross-examination, and the light which his demeanour would throw on his testimony is lost.

The danger against which this fundamental rule provides a safeguard is that untested hearsay evidence will be treated as having a probative force which it does not deserve.

It is, of course, elementary that statements made to a witness by a third party are not excluded by the hearsay rule when they are put in evidence solely to prove the state of mind either of the maker of the statement or of the person to whom it was made. What a person said or heard said may well be the best and most direct evidence of that person's state of mind. This principle can only apply, however, when the state of mind evidenced by the statement is either itself directly in issue at the trial or of direct and immediate relevance to an issue which arises at the trial. It is at this point, as it seems to me, that the argument for the appellant breaks down. The issue at the trial of the appellant was whether it was proved that the appellant had buggered and murdered Karl Fletcher. Mark's knowledge that Karl had been murdered was neither itself in issue, nor was it, *per se*, of any relevance to the issue. What was relevant was not the fact of Mark's knowledge but how he had come by that knowledge. He might have done so in a number of ways, but the two most obvious possibilities were either that he had witnessed the commission of the murder by the appellant or that he had committed it himself. The statements which it was sought to prove that Mark made, indicating his knowledge of the murder, provided no rational basis whatever on which the jury could be invited to draw an inference as to the source of that knowledge. To do so would have been mere speculation. Thus, to allow this evidence of what Mark said to be put before the jury as supporting the conclusion that he, rather than the appellant, may have been the murderer seems to me, in the light of the principles on which the exclusion of hearsay depends, to be open to still graver objection than allowing evidence that he had directly admitted the crime. If the latter is excluded as evidence to which no probative value can safely be attributed, the same objection applies *a fortiori* to the admission of the former.

The basic rule that, when a person's state of mind is directly in issue, it may be proved by what was said by or to that person is well illustrated by two very straightforward cases. In *Thomas* v *Connell* (1838) 4 M & W 266, the plaintiff sought to recover money paid to the defendant by one Cheetham on the ground of fraudulent preference. To make good his case, he needed to prove that at or before the time of the disputed payment, Cheetham both was insolvent in fact and knew that he was insolvent. A statement made by Cheetham indicating knowledge of his insolvency was admitted in evidence. Discharging a rule *nisi* for a new trial on the ground of misreception of evidence, the judgments of Lord Abinger CB, Parke B, and Gurney B, make clear that, provided the fact of Cheetham's insolvency could be, as it was, proved *aliunde*, his knowledge of it could be proved by evidence of his statement. There could be no plainer case where the knowledge of the maker of the statement was the very fact in issue.

The classic illustration of a statement admissible to prove the state of mind, again directly in issue, of the person to whom the statement was made is *Subramaniam* v *Public Prosecutor* [1956] 1 WLR 965. The appellant had been captured in the Federation of Malaya by security forces operating against terrorists. He was tried and convicted of unlawful possession of ammunition, which was at that time a capital offence in the Federation of Malaya. His defence was that he acted under duress. At his trial he sought to give evidence of threats made to him by terrorists, but this was ruled inadmissible as hearsay. His appeal against conviction to the Privy Council was allowed on the ground that, if the threats were made to him and he believed them, the excluded evidence went directly to support his defence of duress. As it was put by Mr L M D de Silva, delivering the judgment of the Board, at p. 970:

> In the case before their Lordships statements could have been made to the appellant by the terrorists, which, whether true or not, if they had been believed by the

appellant, might reasonably have induced in him an apprehension of instant death if he failed to conform to their wishes.

The same principle was applied by the Court of Criminal Appeal in *R* v *Willis* [1960] 1 WLR 55. I do not find it necessary to analyse the somewhat complex facts of that case, but content myself with citing a single sentence from the judgment of Lord Parker CJ, delivering the judgment of the court. He said with reference to *Subramaniam,* at p. 59:

> It is true that the Board were there considering the state of mind and conduct of the defendant at the time of the commission of the offence, but *provided the evidence as to his state of mind and conduct is relevant*, it matters not whether it was in regard to the conduct at the time of the commission of the offence or, as here, at a subsequent time, to explain his answers to the police and his conduct when charged. (Emphasis added.)

The decision of your Lordships' House in *Lloyd* v *Powell Duffryn Steam Coal Co. Ltd* [1914] AC 733 requires examination in a little detail. It concerned a claim for compensation under the Workmen's Compensation Act 1906, by a posthumous illegitimate child as a dependant of its putative father, who was killed by accident arising out of and in the course of his employment with the respondents. At the hearing the mother gave evidence that the deceased was the father of her child and that, shortly before his death, he had told her he intended to marry her in plenty of time before the birth of the child. The deceased man's landlady said that he had told her that he was troubled by what he had heard from the mother, "but that it did not matter because he would marry her soon enough" (p. 734). A room-mate spoke of a conversation in which the deceased said the mother was in trouble and it was a case of getting married. He wanted to provide a home for himself and the mother. The county court judge admitted these statements as declarations by a deceased person against interest. The Court of Appeal, allowing the respondents's appeal, held that this ground of admissibility of the statements was not sustainable. In your Lordships' House the admissibility of the statements was argued and affirmed on entirely different grounds, the House concurring in the view taken by the Court of Appeal of the only point that had been argued before them. Their Lordships discussed the relevance and admissibility of the disputed evidence with reference to the issues of both paternity and dependency. This seems strange since counsel for the respondents is reported as saying, at p. 736: "The respondents do not contest the paternity of the child, but they submit that the evidence of the statement of the deceased that he intended to marry the girl is inadmissible and irrelevant: . . ." Admissibility on the issue of dependency was very clearly disputed. The speeches of their Lordships are, if I may say so with all respect, somewhat diffuse, and I do not find it possible to distil from them any single clear-cut *ratio decidendi*. If I found passages in the speeches which appeared to afford support for Mr Judge's argument, I would certainly refer to them. But I do not. I content myself with citing a single passage from the judgment of Lord Moulton, which seems to me to explain the ground of the decision in a way which is clear, convincing, and entirely consistent with the principles which I have discussed earlier in this opinion, which underlie the other authorities already referred to. After expressing his agreement with the reasoning of the Court of Appeal, Lord Moulton continued, at p. 751:

> . . . the argument before your Lordships was based on a wholly different ground, namely, that the state of mind of the deceased, so far as it bore on his acceptance of his position as the father of the child and his intention to fulfil his duties as such, was *relevant to the issue* of dependency, and that the evidence in question was admissible as being proper to determine his state of mind. I am of opinion, my Lords, that on this ground the evidence was admissible. It can scarcely be contested that the state of mind of the putative father and his intentions with regard to the child are matters *relevant to the issue,* whether there was a reasonable anticipation that he would support the child when born. It may be that an intention on his part so to do might be implied from the fact of his paternity and his recognition of it. But whether this be so or not, the attitude of mind of the putative father is that from which alone one can draw conclusions as to the greater or less probability of his supporting the child when born, and therefore evidence to prove that attitude of mind must be admissible if it be the proper evidence to establish such a fact. Now, it is well established in English jurisprudence, in accordance with the dictates of common sense, that the words and acts of a person are admissible as evidence of his state of mind. (Emphasis added.)

I need only make passing reference to *Mawaz Khan* v *The Queen* [1967] 1 AC 454. This was a case where defendants, jointly charged with murder, against whom the primary evidence was circumstantial, had both made statements to the police setting up the same alibi story. The Crown called direct evidence to demonstrate the falsity of the alibi. The direction to the jury of which the defendants complained on appeal against conviction is set out in the headnote as follows, at p. 455:

> A statement which is made by an accused person in the absence of the other is not evidence against the other; it is evidence against the maker of the statement but against him only . . .. The Crown's case here is not that these statements are true and that what one says ought to be considered as evidence of what actually happened. What the Crown say is that these statements have been shown to be a tissue of lies and that they disclose an attempt to fabricate a joint story . . .. If you come to that conclusion then the fabrication of a joint story would be evidence against both. It would be evidence that they had co-operated after the alleged crime.

The Privy Council dismissed the appeal. All that this case demonstrates, which seems elementary common sense, is that, if two men have put their heads together to concoct a false alibi, this is *prima facie* evidence against both of a guilty state of mind. This is far removed from the issue arising in the present appeal and I derive no assistance from it.

The authority on which Mr Judge places greatest reliance is the decision of the Privy Council in *Ratten* v *The Queen* [1972] AC 378, dismissing an appeal from the Supreme Court of Victoria against the appellant's conviction of murder. The appellant's wife had been killed by a cartridge discharged from a shotgun held in the hands of the appellant. The evidence established the time of the shooting as between 1.12

and 1.20 pm. The appellant's defence was that the shooting occurred accidentally while he was in course of cleaning the gun. The evidence of the appellant was that after the shooting he immediately telephoned for an ambulance and that shortly afterwards the police telephoned him upon which he asked them to come immediately. He denied that any telephone call had been made by his wife, and also denied that he had telephoned for the police. To rebut the appellant's account, the prosecution called the evidence of a telephonist at the telephone exchange of a call from the appellant's number received at about 1.15 pm from a woman saying: "Get me the police please." According to the telephonist, the woman was hysterical and sobbing. The Board, in a judgment delivered by Lord Wilberforce, held this evidence admissible on the grounds both that it was directly relevant to the issue and that it was part of the *res gestae*. We need not consider the second ground, which is not raised in the present appeal. On the first ground the reasoning of the Board appears in the following critical passage from the judgment, at pp. 387-388:

> The evidence relating to the act of telephoning by the deceased was, in their Lordships' view, factual and relevant. It can be analysed into the following elements:
>
> (1) At about 1.15 pm the number Echuca 1494 rang. I plugged into that number.
> (2) I opened the speak key and said 'Number please'.
> (3) A female voice answered.
> (4) The voice was hysterical and sobbed.
> (5) The voice said 'Get me the police please.'
>
> The factual items numbered (1)-(3) were relevant in order to show that, contrary to the evidence of the appellant, a call was made, only some three to five minutes before the fatal shooting, by a woman. It not being suggested that there was anybody in the house other than the appellant, his wife and small children, this woman, the caller, could only have been the deceased. Items (4) and (5) were relevant as possibly showing (if the jury thought fit to draw the inference) that the deceased woman was at this time in a state of emotion or fear (cf. *Aveson* v *Lord Kinnaird* (1805) 6 East 188, 193, *per* Lord Ellenborough CJ). They were relevant and necessary, evidence in order to explain and complete the fact of the call being made. A telephone call is a composite act, made up of manual operations together with the utterance of words (cf. *McGregor* v *Stokes* [1952] VLR 347 and remarks of Salmond J therein quoted). To confine the evidence to the first would be to deprive the act of most of its significance. The act had content when it was known that the call was made in a state of emotion. The knowledge that the caller desired the police to be called helped to indicate the nature of the emotion — anxiety or fear at an existing or impending emergency. It was a matter for the jury to decide what light (if any) this evidence, in the absence of any explanation from the appellant, who was in the house, threw upon what situation was occurring, or developing at the time.

Mr Judge emphasises particularly the concluding sentence in this passage. It establishes, he submits, the proposition that evidence of A's state of mind (the wife's fear in *Ratten's* case — Mark's knowledge in the instant case) should be left to the jury to decide what inference they draw from it with respect to B's action (whether the appellant in *Ratten's* case fired deliberately or accidentally — whether or not, in the instant case, the appellant murdered Karl Fletcher).

Ratten's case is not technically binding on your Lordships' House, but considering the constitution of the Board (Lord Reid, Lord Hodson, Lord Wilberforce, Lord Diplock and Lord Cross of Chelsea) is of the highest persuasive authority and, for my part, I should certainly feel constrained to follow it, if persuaded that it established a principle applicable in the appellant's favour in the circumstances of the present appeal. I am not so persuaded and consider *Ratten's* case clearly distinguishable. First, the telephone call in *Ratten's* case was, although it could be analysed into component elements, nevertheless, as Lord Wilberforce said, "a composite act, made up of manual operations together with the utterance of words." The implication is that its admissibility had to be considered as a whole. The very fact that the call had been made contradicted a critically important part of the appellant's evidence. Secondly, the appellant's denial that the call had been made precluded him from either offering any explanation of it or suggesting that it was made in some other room out of his hearing. This led to a powerful inference that what the wife said on the telephone was said in his presence. Thirdly, in these circumstances, both the making of the call and the wife's state of fear manifested by it were directly relevant to the critical issue in the trial as rebutting the appellant's defence of an accidental shooting. There are no analogous considerations applicable in the present case.

R v *Moghal* (1977) 65 Cr App R 56 was a case presenting exceptional, indeed one may hope unique, features. A man named Rashid had been murdered by stabbing. Only two persons, a woman named Sadiga and her current lover, Moghal, were present when the murder was committed. Rashid had been Sadiga's lover for some years previously. Sadiga and Moghal were jointly indicted for Rashid's murder, which had clearly been committed by one or other or both of them. For reasons which I need not examine, an application by Sadiga for separate trials was successful. Sadiga was tried first and acquitted. When Moghal's trial followed, it was accepted by the Crown, as had indeed been the Crown's case throughout, that it was Sadiga by whose hand Rashid died. The case against Moghal was that he was a willing accomplice in the killing. Moghal's defence was that Sadiga was the dominant character and that he was no more than a cowed and terrified spectator of the murder. Moghal was convicted and appealed. The only relevance of the case for present purposes lies in the discussion in the judgment of the Court of Appeal (Criminal Division) (Scarman and Shaw LJJ and Thompson J), delivered by Scarman LJ, of the possible relevance and admissibility of a tape recording of a family conference some six months before Rashid's murder, in which Sadiga's voice could be heard expressing in virulent terms her hatred of Rashid and her determination to kill him. Deprived of the opportunity to cross-examine Sadiga in a joint trial, counsel for Moghal canvassed with the judge, *inter alia*, the possibility of introducing this tape recording in evidence, though he never made any formal application that it be admitted. In the Court of Appeal, therefore, the issue was discussed, not on the basis of any irregularity in the trial, but in relation to the question whether the verdict of guilty against Moghal was safe and satisfactory. The prosecution, who were clearly much concerned to mitigate, as far as they properly could, the difficulties which the separate trial and acquittal of Sadiga presented for the defence of Moghal, had formally admitted, that, at the family conference, Sadiga had uttered threats against the life of Rashid. Against this background it is difficult to see how the court could have reached any other conclusion than that the verdict of guilty was safe and satisfactory. The passage in the judgment on which Mr Judge particularly relies is in the following terms, at p. 63:

> The tape-recording of the family conference is, however, a very different matter. It records what she said at the family conference of her then state of mind and feeling. Being contemporaneous, these statements are admissible: for we accept — and the Crown by making its formal admission, [that at the family conference Sadiga offered threats against the life of Rashid], has really conceded — that her state of mind at that time was relevant to the appellant's defence.

The opinion here expressed that Sadiga's statements at the family conference were admissible was both *obiter* and plainly influenced by the concession implicit in a formal admission made by the Crown. With all respect, I venture to doubt whether it was correct, precisely because I cannot see how a threat by Sadiga against Rashid's life, made six months before the murder, however virulently the threat was expressed, was of any relevance to the issue whether Moghal was a willing accomplice or an unwilling spectator when the murder was committed. I well understand the Court of Appeal's, and indeed the prosecution's sympathetic approach to the difficulties which the wholly exceptional course of ordering separate trials of a joint indictment created for Moghal's defence following Sadiga's acquittal. But I am certainly not prepared to treat this *obiter dictum* as expressing any principle of general application which assists the appellant in the instant case.

Perhaps a still more remarkable case is the recent decision of the Court of Appeal (Criminal Division) in *R v Roberts (John Marcus)* (1985) 80 Cr App R 89. A man was shot in the head in October 1980. His body was buried and was not discovered until March 1982. Roberts and another man named Evans were in due course tried and both convicted of the murder. Roberts alone appealed against his conviction. The appeal was dismissed. The only ground of the appeal which is of any relevance for present purposes was that the trial judge wrongly refused to allow the appellant to call in his defence two witnesses named Passey and Tong who could have testified that Paul Evans, the brother of the appellant's co-accused, made statements to them, at a time before the discovery of the victim's body, which revealed a detailed knowledge of the circumstances in which the murder had been committed. At risk of excessively lengthening this already lengthy opinion, I think I can only do justice to the judgment of the Court of Appeal (May LJ, Boreham and Nolan JJ), delivered by May LJ, by quoting the whole passage in which the admissibility of the evidence of Passey and Tong is examined. The passage reads as follows, at pp. 94–95:

> After considering the point overnight, the learned judge ruled that such evidence could not be called. He accepted that if it were relevant, such evidence would be admissible. If the only purpose of tendering the evidence was to seek to show the state of Paul's knowledge at the material time, but not the correctness or accuracy of the details of that knowledge, then it could not be assailed as being hearsay. However he disagreed that the evidence, if called, did implicate Paul in the murder as counsel for the appellant contended. As we have said, he accepted that it might indeed show knowledge on the part of Paul of relevant details of the murder, but he pointed out that that knowledge could have been obtained either from his brother, the defendant Richard Evans, despite the fact that the

latter denied discussing the matter with Paul; or Paul could have obtained the information from the present appellant; or he could have done so from some other party who had himself obtained the information from either of the two defendants; or he could have acquired the relevant knowledge from someone who had in his turn obtained the information first, second or third hand, but originating from the two defendants; or Paul Evans could himself have visited the farm on either of the two days following the actual killing whilst the burial of Sands' body was still going on. Further, the learned judge felt that as no one then knew what Paul himself would say were he called to give evidence, if counsel were allowed to call Passey and Tong for this purpose, this would open a series of new issues involving the investigation of all people to whom Paul Evans had given other statements revealing the source of his knowledge. Further, given that the real purpose of calling the evidence was to suggest that Paul had taken part in the murder, it would also become relevant to hear evidence where Paul was at the material times. Finally, even if Paul had been present at the time of the killing, this would not have meant that the appellant could not have been there also. The learned judge therefore ruled that the evidence sought to be called was inadmissible. Although the learned judge did not put his ruling in precisely these terms we think that it is clear that his view was that the evidence was admissible to show Paul's knowledge, if that were relevant; for that limited purpose it could not properly be described as hearsay. But nevertheless, even if it were proved that Paul did have that knowledge, it could only be speculation how he acquired it, and it tended neither to prove nor disprove the Crown's contention that the appellant had been a party to the murder, nor any link in the evidentiary chain which it was said led to that conclusion. In those circumstances the evidence was not relevant to the issues before the jury and was thus inadmissible.

Mr Judge relies in particular on the words "it is clear that his view was that the evidence was admissible to show Paul's knowledge, if that were relevant; for that limited purpose it could not properly be described as hearsay." The implication, he submits, is that the Court of Appeal approved the trial judge's view that the disputed evidence was not hearsay.

However, the more carefully I have sought to analyse the whole passage I have cited from the judgment, the more forcibly am I impelled to the conclusion that the basic reasoning refutes, rather than supports, the submission made for the appellant in the instant case. In summary what the judgment is saying seems to me to be:

(1) If Paul Evans' statements were put in evidence solely to prove his knowledge, they would not be excluded as hearsay;

(2) The statements could not, however, be put in evidence as the basis for an inference as to the source of his knowledge for which there was no rational foundation;

(3) Paul Evans' knowledge, *per se*, was of no relevance to the issue whether or not the appellant was guilty of the murder.

If this is a correct distillation of the essence of the decision that the evidence of Paul Evans' statements was rightly ruled inadmissible, I fully agree with it. Indeed, it seems to me to come very near to the reasoning which commends itself to me as applicable in the instant case. If there is to be extracted from the passage some *obiter dictum* which points in the contrary direction, I cannot agree with it.

At the conclusion of the examination of the relevant authorities I have found nothing to displace the opinion I expressed earlier as a matter of principle that the evidence here in question was rightly excluded. On the contrary, with the exception of a single *obiter dictum* in *R* v *Moghal*, 65 Cr App R 56, the authorities, if they are considered, as they should be, with due regard to the nature of the issues to which the evidence examined in each case was directed, seem to me consistently to support that opinion.'

(LORDS FRASER OF TULLYBELTON, EDMUND-DAVIES, BRIGHTMAN and TEMPLEMAN agreed.)

Appeal dismissed.

• Was any injustice done to the accused by the decision in *R* v *Blastland*?

Wright v Doe d Tatham (1837) 7 A & E 313

This was an action concerning land owned by John Marsden, deceased. The defendant, Wright, claimed as devisee under Marsden's will. The plaintiff, Tatham, claimed as heir at law, alleging that the will was void on the ground that the testator had insufficient mental capacity to make a valid will. He introduced the following evidence without objection: that Marsden was treated as a child by his own servants; that in his youth he was called, in the village where he lived, 'Silly Jack', and 'Silly Marsden'; that a witness had seen boys shouting after him, 'There goes crazy Marsden' and throwing dirt at him, and had persuaded a person passing by to see him home. As evidence of competency, Wright sought to produce letters which had been written to Marsden by persons who knew him well to show that they treated him as sane. The trial judge excluded these letters and the jury found for Tatham. Wright filed a bill of exceptions in the Court of Exchequer Chamber.

BOSANQUET J: 'It is obvious that the contents of letters may be dictated by various motives, according to the dispositions and circumstances of the writers. Language of affection, of respect, of rational or amusing information, may be addressed from the best of motives to persons in a state of considerable imbecility, or labouring under the strangest delusions. The habitual treatment of deranged persons as rational is one mode of promoting their recovery. A tone of insult or derision may be employed in a moment of irritation in writing to a person in full possession of his reason; what judgment can be formed of the intention of the writers, without an endless examination into the circumstances which may have influenced them? And what opinion can be collected of the capacity of the receiver without ascertaining how he acted when he read the language addressed to him? To me it appears that the admission in proof of capacity of letters unaccompanied by other circumstances than such as are stated in this record would establish an entirely new precedent in a Court of Common Law, from which very great inconvenience might result upon trials of sanity, as well of the living as of the dead.'

PARKE B: 'It is admitted, and most properly, that you have no right to use in evidence the fact of writing and sending a letter to a third person containing a statement of competence, on the ground that it affords an inference that such an act would not have been done unless the statement was true, or believed to be true, although such an inference no doubt would be raised in the conduct of the ordinary affairs of life, if the statement were made by a man of veracity. But it cannot be raised in a judicial inquiry; and, if such an argument were admissible, it would lead to the indiscriminate admission of hearsay evidence of all manner of facts.

Further, it is clear that an acting to a much greater extent and degree upon such statements to a third person would not make the statements admissible. For example, if a wager to a large amount had been made as to the matter in issue by two third persons, the payment of that wager, however large the sum, would not be admissible to prove the truth of the matter in issue. You would not have had any right to present it to the jury as raising an inference of the truth of the fact, on the ground that otherwise the bet would not have been paid. It is, after all, nothing but the mere statement of that fact, with strong evidence of the belief of it by the party making it. Could it make any difference that the wager was between the third person and one of the parties to the suit? Certainly not. The payment by other underwriters on the same policy to the plaintiff could not be given in evidence to prove that the subject insured had been lost. Yet there is an act done, a payment strongly attesting the truth of the statement, which it implies, that there had been a loss. To illustrate this point still further, let us suppose a third person had betted a wager with Mr Marsden that he could not solve some mathematical problem, the solution of which required a high degree of capacity; would payment of that wager to Mr Marsden's banker be admissible evidence that he possessed that capacity? The answer is certain; it would not. It would be evidence of the fact of competence given by a third party not upon oath.

Let us suppose the parties who wrote these letters to have stated the matter therein contained, that is, their knowledge of his personal qualities and capacity for business, on oath before a magistrate, or in some judicial proceeding to which the plaintiff and defendant were not parties. No one could contend that such statement would be admissible on this issue; and yet there would have been an act done on the faith of the statement being true, and a very solemn one, which would raise in the ordinary conduct of affairs a strong belief in the truth of the statement, if the writers were faith-worthy. The acting in this case is of much less importance, and certainly is not equal to the sanction of an extra-judicial oath.

Many other instances of a similar nature, by way of illustration, were suggested by the learned counsel for the defendant in error, which, on the most cursory consideration, any one would at once declare to be inadmissible in evidence. Others were supposed on the part of the plaintiff in error, which, at first sight, have the appearance of being mere facts, and therefore admissible, though on further consideration they are open to precisely the same objection. Of the first description are the supposed cases of a letter by a third person to any one demanding a debt, which may be said to be a treatment of him as a debtor, being offered as proof that the debt was really due; a note, congratulating him on his high state of bodily vigour, being proposed as evidence of his being in good health; both of which are manifestly at first sight objectionable. To the latter class belong the supposed conduct of the family or relations of a testator, taking the same precautions in his absence as if he were a lunatic; his election, in his absence, to some high and responsible office; the conduct of a physician who permitted a will to be executed by a sick testator; the conduct of a deceased captain on a question of seaworthiness, who, after examining every part of the vessel, embarked in it with his family; all these, when deliberately considered, are, with reference to the matter in issue in each case, mere instances of hearsay evidence, mere statements, not on oath, but implied in or vouched by the actual conduct of persons by whose acts the litigant parties are not to be bound.'

(TINDALL CJ, GURNEY B, and COLTMAN and PARK JJ delivered concurring judgments.)

Trial verdict confirmed. Subsequently the House of Lords also affirmed the verdict in favour of the plaintiff (see (1838) 4 Bing NC 489).

- Should the rule against hearsay apply to implied assertions?

R v *Andrews* [1987] AC 281 (HL)

Two men entered M's flat and attacked him with knives; property was stolen. Shortly afterwards M, grievously wounded, made his way to the flat below his own to obtain assistance. Two police officers arrived within minutes and M informed them that O and the defendant had been the assailants. Two months later M died as a result of his injuries. The defendant was jointly charged with O with aggravated burglary and the murder of M. At the trial the Crown sought to have the deceased's statement admitted, not as a dying declaration, but as evidence of the truth of the facts that he had asserted, namely, that he had been attacked by O and the defendant, and therefore it was admissible in the circumstances as evidence coming within the *res gestae* exception to the hearsay rule. The judge ruled in favour of its admissibility. The defendant was convicted of aggravated burglary and manslaughter. On appeal by the defendant, the Court of Appeal dismissed the appeal. The defendant further appealed.

LORD ACKNER: 'Mr Worsley sought to have the statement of the deceased admitted as evidence of the truth of the facts that he had asserted, namely that he had been attacked by both O'Neill and the appellant. Since evidence of this statement could only be given by a witness who had merely heard it, such evidence was clearly hearsay evidence. It was not being tendered as evidence limited to the fact that an assertion had been made, without reference to the truth of anything alleged in the assertion. The evidence merely of the fact that such an assertion was made would not have related to any issue in the trial and therefore would not have been admissible. Had, for example, the deceased's state of mind been in issue and had his exclamation been relevant to his state of mind, then evidence of *the fact* that such an assertion was made, would not have been hearsay evidence since it would have been tendered without reference to the truth of anything alleged in the assertion. Such evidence is often classified as "original" evidence.

Mr Worsley based his submission that this hearsay evidence was admissible upon the so-called doctrine of *res gestae*. He could not submit that the statement was a "dying declaration" since there was no evidence to suggest that at the time when the deceased made the statement (two months before his ultimate death), he was aware that he had been mortally injured. Mr Worsley in support of his submission, both before the Common Serjeant, the Court of Appeal and in your Lordships' House relied essentially on a decision of the Privy Council, *Ratten* v *The Queen* [1972] AC 378, an appeal from a conviction for murder by the Supreme Court of the State of

Victoria in which the opinion of the Board was given by Lord Wilberforce. Mr Worsley, for whose researches into this field of law I readily express my gratitude, invited your Lordships' attention to American, Canadian and Australian authorities in order to demonstrate their consistency with that decision and to support his contention, which is the real issue in this appeal *viz.* that your Lordships should accept the analysis, reasoning and advice tended by the Privy Council as being good English law.

I do not think it is necessary to burden this speech by travelling again over all the ground, which, if I may say so respectfully, was so admirably covered by Lord Wilberforce in his judgment. Before turning to the decision in *Ratten's* case, it is convenient at this stage to quote from *Cross on Evidence*, 6th ed (1985), p. 585:

> Before Lord Wilberforce's important review of the authorities in *Ratten v The Queen*, the law concerning the admissibility of statements under this exception to the hearsay rule [the *res gestae* doctrine] was in danger of becoming enmeshed in conceptualism of the worst type. Great stress was placed on the need for contemporaneity of the statement with the event, but, what was far more serious, much attention was devoted to the question whether the words could be said to form part of the transaction or event with all the attendant insoluble problems of when the transaction or event began and ended.

The appellant was charged with the murder of his wife by shooting her with a shotgun. He accepted that he had shot her, but his defence was that the gun had gone off accidentally, whilst he was cleaning it. There was evidence that the deceased was alive and behaving normally at 1.12 pm and less than 10 minutes later she had been shot. To rebut that defence, the prosecution called evidence from a telephone operator as to a telephone call which she had received at 1.15 pm from the deceased's home. She said the call came from a female who sounded hysterical and who said "get me the police, please—," gave her address, but before a connection could be made to the police station, the caller hung up. The appellant objected to that evidence on the ground that it was hearsay and did not come within any of the recognised exceptions to the rule against the admission of such evidence. The Judicial Committee held that the telephone operator's evidence had been rightly received. They concluded that the evidence was not hearsay, but was admissible as evidence of facts relevant to the following issues. First, as rebutting the defendant's statement that his call for the ambulance after he had shot his wife was the only call that went out of the house between 1.12 and 1.20, by which time his wife was dead. Secondly, that the telephonist's evidence that the caller was a woman speaking in a hysterical voice was capable of relating to the state of mind of the deceased and was material from which the jury were entitled to infer that Mrs Ratten was suffering from anxiety or fear of an existing or impending emergency. Lord Wilberforce said, at p. 387:

> The mere fact that evidence of a witness includes evidence as to words spoken by another person who is not called, is no objection to its admissibility. Words spoken are facts just as much as any other action by a human being. If the speaking of the words is a relevant fact, a witness may give evidence that they were spoken. A question of hearsay only arises when the words spoken are relied on 'testimonially', i.e., as establishing some fact narrated by the words. Authority is hardly needed for this proposition, but their Lordships will restate what was

said in the judgment of the Board in *Subramaniam* v *Public Prosecutor* [1956] 1 WLR 965, 970: 'Evidence of a statement made to a witness by a person who is not himself called as a witness may or may not be hearsay. It is hearsay and inadmissible when the object of the evidence is to establish the truth of what is contained in the statement. It is not hearsay and is admissible when it is proposed to establish by the evidence, not the truth of the statement, but the fact that it was made.'

Lord Wilberforce then proceeded to deal with the appellant's submission, on the assumption that the words were hearsay in that they involved an assertion of the truth of some facts stated in them and that they may have been so understood by the jury. He said, at pp. 388–390: "The expression *res gestae*, like many Latin phrases, is often used to cover situations insufficiently analysed in clear English terms. In the context of the law of evidence it may be used in at least three different ways:

(1) When a situation of fact (e.g., a killing) is being considered, the question may arise when does the situation begin and when does it end. It may be arbitrary and artificial to confine the evidence to the firing of the gun or the insertion of the knife, without knowing in a broader sense what was happening. Thus in *O'Leary* v *The King* (1946) 73 CLR 566 evidence was admitted of assaults, prior to a killing, committed by the accused during what was said to be a continuous orgy. As Dixon J said at p. 577: 'Without evidence of what, during that time, was done by those men who took any significant part in the matter and especially evidence of the behaviour of the prisoner, the transaction of which the alleged murder formed an integral part could not be truly understood and, isolated from it, could only be presented as an unreal and not very intelligible event.'

(2) The evidence may be concerned with spoken words as such (apart from the truth of what they convey). The words are then themselves the *res gestae* or part of the *res gestae*, i.e., are the relevant facts or part of them.

(3) A hearsay statement is made either by the victim of an attack or by a bystander — indicating directly or indirectly the identity of the attacker. The admissibility of the statement is then said to depend on whether it was made as part of the *res gestae*. A classical instance of this is the much debated case of *R* v *Bedingfield* (1879) 14 Cox CC 341, and there are other instances of its application in reported cases. These tend to apply different standards, and some of them carry less than conviction. The reason, why this is so, is that concentration tends to be focused upon the opaque or at least imprecise Latin phrase rather than upon the basic reason for excluding the type of evidence which this group of cases is concerned with. There is no doubt what this reason is: it is twofold. The first is that there may be uncertainty as to the exact words used and because of their transmission through the evidence of another person than the speaker. The second is because of the risk of concoction of false evidence by persons who have been victims of assault or accident. The first matter goes to weight. The person testifying to the words used is liable to cross-examination: the accused person (as he could not at the time when earlier reported cases were decided) can give his own account if different. There is no such difference in kind or substance between evidence of what was said and evidence of what was done (for example between evidence of what the victim said as to an attack and evidence that

he (or she) was seen in a terrified state or was heard to shriek) as to require a total rejection of one and admission of the other.

The possibility of concoction, or fabrication, where it exists, is on the other hand an entirely valid reason for exclusion, and is probably the real test which judges in fact apply. In their Lordships' opinion this should be recognised and applied directly as the relevant test: the test should be not the uncertain one whether the making of the statement was in some sense part of the event or transaction. This may often be difficult to establish: such external matters as the time which elapses between the events and the speaking of the words (or *vice versa*), and the differences in location being relevant factors but not, taken by themselves, decisive criteria. As regards statements made after the event it must be for the judge, by preliminary ruling, to satisfy himself that the statement was so clearly made in circumstances of spontaneity or involvement in the event that the possibility of concoction can be disregarded. Conversely, if he considers that the statement was made by way of narrative of a detached prior event so that the speaker was so disengaged from it as to be able to construct or adapt his account, he should exclude it. And the same must in principle be true of statements made before the event. The test should be not the uncertain one, whether the making of the statement should be regarded as part of the event or transaction. This may often be difficult to show. But if the drama, leading up to the climax, has commenced and assumed such intensity and pressure that the utterance can safely be regarded as a true reflection of what was unrolling or actually happening, it ought to be received. The expression *res gestae* may conveniently sum up these criteria, but the reality of them must always be kept in mind: it is this that lies behind the best reasoned of the judges' rulings."

Lord Wilberforce then reviewed a number of cases, in England, in Scotland, in Australia and America and concluded, at p. 391, that those authorities: "show that there is ample support for the principle that hearsay evidence may be admitted if the statement providing it is made in such conditions (always being those of approximate but not exact contemporaneity) of involvement or pressure as to exclude the possibility of concoction or distortion to the advantage of the maker or the disadvantage of the accused." Applying that principle to the facts of the *Ratten* appeal [1972] AC 378, there was in their Lordships' judgment ample evidence of the close and intimate connection between the statement ascribed to the deceased and the shooting which occurred very shortly afterwards. Lord Wilberforce commented, at p. 391: "The way in which the statement came to be made (in a call for the police) and the tone of voice used, showed intrinsically that the statement was being forced from the deceased by an overwhelming pressure of contemporary event. It carried its own stamp of spontaneity and this was endorsed by the proved time sequence and the proved proximity of the deceased to the accused with his gun." Thus, on the assumption that there was an element of hearsay in the words used, the Privy Council concluded that they had been properly admitted.

In *R* v *Blastland* [1986] AC 41, 58, my noble and learned friend Lord Bridge of Harwich, regarded the authority of the *Ratten* case [1972] AC 378 as being of the highest persuasive authority. It was followed and applied in the instant case by the Common Serjeant and by the Court of Appeal (Criminal Division) and accordingly the appellant's appeal against his conviction for manslaughter was dismissed. It had previously been applied in *R* v *Nye* (1978) 66 Cr App R 252, by the Court of Appeal where a victim of a criminal assault, which had occurred within a few yards of a police station, in a statement to police officers made within minutes of the assault, identified the defendant as the man who had hit him in the face. Lawton LJ in giving the judgment of the court put, as he described it, a gloss upon Lord Wilberforce's test by adding as an additional factor to be taken into consideration "was there any real possibility of error?" I will return to this particular point later. In *R v Turnbull* (1985) 80 Cr App R 104 the Court of Appeal again applied the *Ratten* approach, where a man who had been mortally wounded staggered into the bar of a public house and in answer to questions put to him in the bar and in the ambulance on the way to hospital he was understood to say that "Ronnie Tommo" had done it. He died half-an-hour later in hospital. The victim had a Scottish accent and had consumed a great quantity of alcohol and the name "Ronnie Tommo" was said to constitute his attempt to name the appellant. There have been two further decisions of the Court of Appeal this year which have followed *Ratten's* case. *R v Boyle* (unreported) decided on 6 March 1986, involved the theft of a grandfather clock from an old lady to whose home the appellant had obtained access by a false representation. When he took away the clock she came out of the house with a piece of paper in her hand and when asked by a neighbour, "what is happening?" she said "I am coming for his address." This statement was admitted to support the victim's account that the removal of the clock was against her will and to negative the defence that it was being taken away by the defendant with her consent, to have it repaired. I, for myself, would doubt whether this evidence was hearsay evidence. A clear issue in the case was the state of mind of the victim in relation to the removal of her clock. Her statement in the circumstances, as the car drove off, was evidence from which the jury could infer that she was not consenting to the clock being taken away. *R v O'Shea* (unreported) decided on 24 July 1986, is a clearer case. The appellant was charged with burglary and manslaughter. The prosecution case against the appellant was that he went to a second floor flat and while he was battering down the door, the occupier of the flat who was 79 years of age, attempted to escape through the window, slipped and fell some 20 feet and sustained bruising to his heart, which resulted in his death a week later. The statement made by the deceased to two passers-by an hour or so later, when they found him lying where he had fallen, that he had tried to get out of his flat because he was frightened that two robbers who were trying to break down his door would kill him and that he had therefore jumped from the window to escape, was admitted, as was a similar statement which he made to two police officers less than 20 minutes later.

Mr Sedley for the appellant submitted, first that there is no such exception to the rule against the admission of hearsay evidence as that said to be covered by the *res gestae* doctrine. Having regard to the authorities there is no substance in this proposition. Secondly, he submitted that a hearsay statement cannot be admitted under the doctrine if made after the criminal act or acts charged have ceased. He contended that the hearsay statement must form part of the criminal act for which the accused is being tried. He relied strongly upon *R v Bedingfield*, 14 Cox CC 341. In that case the accused was charged with murder. The defence was suicide. The accused was seen to enter a house and a minute or two later the victim rushed out of the house with her throat cut and said to her aunt "See what Harry has done." This exclamation was not admitted by Cockburn CJ at pp. 342–343 because "it was something stated by her after it was all over, whatever it was, and after the act was completed." Mr Sedley submits that the decision in *Ratten's* case involved an extension of the existing hearsay rule and so was in conflict with the ruling of the majority in your Lordships' House in *Myers* v *Director of Public Prosecutions* [1965] AC 1001 that it is now too late to add a further exception to the rule against hearsay otherwise than by legislation. This submission is not assisted by the fact that both Lord Reid and Lord Hodson, who were party to the majority decision in the *Myers* case, were also members of the Board in the *Ratten* case [1972] AC 378.

I do not accept that the principles identified by Lord Wilberforce involved any extension to the exception to the hearsay rule. Lord Wilberforce clarified the basis of the *res gestae* exception and isolated the matters of which the trial judge, by preliminary ruling, must satisfy himself before admitting the statement. I respectfully accept the accuracy and the value of this clarification. Thus it must, of course, follow that *R* v *Bedingfield*, 14 Cox CC 341 would not be so decided today. Indeed, there could, as Lord Wilberforce observed, hardly be a case where the words uttered carried more clearly the mark of spontaneity and intense involvement.

My Lords, may I therefore summarise the position which confronts the trial judge when faced in a criminal case with an application under the *res gestae* doctrine to admit evidence of statements, with a view to establishing the truth of some fact thus narrated, such evidence being truly categorised as "hearsay evidence?"

(1) The primary question which the judge must ask himself is — can the possibility of concoction or distortion be disregarded?

(2) To answer that question the judge must first consider the circumstances in which the particular statement was made, in order to satisfy himself that the event was so unusual or startling or dramatic as to dominate the thoughts of the victim, so that his utterance was an instinctive reaction to that event, thus giving no real opportunity for reasoned reflection. In such a situation the judge would be entitled to conclude that the involvement or the pressure of the event would exclude the possibility of concoction or distortion, providing that the statement was made in conditions of approximate but not exact contemporaneity.

(3) In order for the statement to be sufficiently "spontaneous" it must be so closely associated with the event which has excited the statement, that it can be fairly stated that the mind of the declarant was still dominated by the event. Thus the judge must be satisfied that the event, which provided the trigger mechanism for the statement, was still operative. The fact that the statement was made in answer to a question is but one factor to consider under this heading.

(4) Quite apart from the time factor, there may be special features in the case, which relate to the possibility of concoction or distortion. In the instant appeal the defence relied upon evidence to support the contention that the deceased had a motive of his own to fabricate or concoct, namely, a malice which resided in him against O'Neill and the appellant because, so he believed, O'Neill had attacked and damaged his house and was accompanied by the appellant, who ran away on a previous occasion. The judge must be satisfied that the circumstances were such that having regard to the special feature of malice, there was no possibility of any concoction or distortion to the advantage of the maker or the disadvantage of the accused.

(5) As to the possibility of error in the facts narrated in the statement, if only the ordinary fallibility of human recollection is relied upon, this goes to the weight to be attached to and not to the admissibility of the statement and is therefore a matter for the jury. However, here again there may be special features that may give

rise to the possibility of error. In the instant case there was evidence that the deceased had drunk to excess, well over double the permitted limit for driving a motor car. Another example would be where the identification was made in circumstances of particular difficulty or where the declarant suffered from defective eyesight. In such circumstances the trial judge must consider whether he can exclude the possibility of error.

My Lords, the doctrine of *res gestae* applies to civil as well as criminal proceedings. There is, however, special legislation as to the admissibility of hearsay evidence in civil proceedings. I wholly accept that the doctrine admits the hearsay statements, not only where the declarant is dead or otherwise not available but when he is called as a witness. Whatever may be the position in civil proceedings, I would, however, strongly deprecate any attempt in criminal prosecutions to use the doctrine as a device to avoid calling, when he is available, the maker of the statement. Thus to deprive the defence of the opportunity to cross-examine him, would not be consistent with the fundamental duty of the prosecution to place all the relevant material facts before the court, so as to ensure that justice is done.'

Appeal dismissed.

• Is the test approved by the House of Lords in *R* v *Andrews* to be preferred to the traditional approach? Would *R* v *Bedingfield* (1879) 14 Cox CC 341 be decided in the same way today?

Questions for discussion

R v *Coke; R* v *Littleton*

1   In the depositions and defence proofs of evidence in the cases of Coke and Littleton, identify and distinguish any examples you can find of statements made on prior occasions:
(a)   which are admissible, non-hearsay evidence;
(b)   which are inadmissible hearsay;
2   Consider specifically the admissibility of exhibit GG1 (the suspected handwriting of Coke found at his flat by D/I Glanvil).
3   The prosecution wish to adduce the statements made by Angela to her mother on returning home from Coke' flat as part of the *res gestae*. What arguments may be made for and against the admissibility of this evidence?
4   Coke wishes to adduce evidence that, before the alleged rape, he had been told by friends that Margaret was interested in having sexual relations with him. Would this evidence be admissible? If the judge allowed such evidence to be admitted, how should he direct the jury about it?

Additional questions

1   A patient sues a doctor alleging negligence in administering drug X instead of drug Y. The patient wishes to call a nurse to give evidence that the nurse saw the doctor take a jar marked 'drug X' and give pills from the jar to the patient. Hearsay or non-hearsay?

2   A nephew brings an action to set aside his uncle's will on the ground that the uncle lacked testamentary capacity. The nephew wishes to adduce evidence that the uncle frequently told friends that he was Napoleon. Hearsay or non-hearsay?

3   The issue arises whether the uncle intended to omit the nephew from his will. The aunt is prepared to give evidence that, at about the time he executed his will, the uncle said to her, 'Nephew is the most deserving of all my relatives.' Hearsay or non-hearsay?

4   Smuggler is arrested at the airport. In the baggage-claim area, police find a suitcase filled with an illegal drug, attached to which is a label giving Smuggler's correct name and address. Smuggler denies that the suitcase is his. The prosecution wish to adduce evidence of the contents of the label. Hearsay or non-hearsay?

5   It is a criminal offence to import goods into the United Kingdom from the Republic of Hinterland, a foreign country. An importer is charged with the offence. In the importer's warehouse, the police find a crate of goods, stamped on the outside with the words, 'Republic of Hinterland Customs Service. Cleared for export. Produce of Hinterland.' There is no other evidence of the origin of the goods. The prosecution wish to adduce evidence of the stamp. Hearsay or non-hearsay?

6   An occupier is charged with knowingly permitting certain premises to be used for the purpose of producing a controlled drug. A police officer telephones the premises, speaks to Peter and asks him the price of 'speed'. Peter quotes a price and invites the officer to pick up some 'speed' later that day. The prosecution wish to adduce this evidence to prove that the premises were being used to produce a controlled drug. Hearsay or non-hearsay?

7   Catesby and Fawkes are charged with conspiracy to cause explosions. When Catesby is arrested, the police find a letter in his possession, written to him some time before by Fawkes, in which Fawkes sets out arrangements for planting explosives. The prosecution wish to adduce the letter. Hearsay or non-hearsay?

8   John sues his parachute instructor alleging negligence in failing adequately to supervise John in his first parachute jump. Before making the jump, John signs a form which reads, 'Instructor has explained to me that parachuting is a dangerous sport. Having considered this warning, I wish to make a parachute jump.' The instructor wishes to adduce the form. Hearsay or non-hearsay?

Further reading

Ashworth and Pattenden, 'Reliability, hearsay evidence and the English criminal trial' (1986) 102 LQR 292.

Birch, 'Hearsay-logic and hearsay-fiddles: *Blastland* revisited,' in *Criminal Law: Essays in Honour of J. C. Smith* (ed. P. Smith) (1987).

Carter, 'Hearsay, relevance and admissibility: declarations as to state of mind and declarations against penal interest' (1987) 103 LQR 106.

Cross, 'The scope of the rule against hearsay' (1956) 72 LQR 91.

Cross, 'The periphery of the rule against hearsay' (1969) 7 Melb ULR 1.

Cross, 'What should be done about the rule against hearsay' [1965] Crim LR 68.

Finman, 'Implied assertions as hearsay' (1962) 14 Stanford Law Rev 682.

Gooderson, '*Res gestae* in criminal cases' [1956] CLJ 199; [1957] CLJ 55.

Guest, 'The scope of the hearsay rule' (1985) 101 LQR 385.

Morgan, 'Hearsay dangers and the application of the hearsay concept' (1948) 62 Harv
    LR 177.
Nokes, '*Res gestae* as hearsay' (1954) 70 LQR 370.

7   *The Rule against Hearsay (2)*

A: CONFESSIONS

(Suggested preliminary reading: *A Practical Approach to Evidence*, pp. 198-222.)

Police and Criminal Evidence Act 1984

76(1)   In any proceedings a confession made by an accused person may be given in evidence against him in so far as it is relevant to any matter in issue in the proceedings and is not excluded by the court in pursuance of this section.

(2)   If, in any proceedings where the prosecution proposes to give in evidence a confession made by an accused person, it is represented to the court that the confession was or may have been obtained—

(a)   by oppression of the person who made it; or

(b)   in consequence of anything said or done which was likely, in the circumstances existing at the time, to render unreliable any confession which might be made by him in consequence thereof,

the court shall not allow the confession to be given in evidence against him except in so far as the prosecution proves to the court beyond reasonable doubt that the confession (notwithstanding that it may be true) was not obtained as aforesaid.

(3)   In any proceedings where the prosecution proposes to give in evidence a confession made by an accused person, the court may of its own motion require the prosecution, as a condition of allowing it to do so, to prove that the confession was not obtained as mentioned in subsection (2) above.

(4)   The fact that a confession is wholly or partly excluded in pursuance of this section shall not affect the admissibility in evidence—

(a)   of any facts discovered as a result of the confession; or

(b)   where the confession is relevant as showing that the accused speaks, writes or expresses himself in a particular way, of so much of the confession as is necessary to show that he does so.

(5)   Evidence that a fact to which this subsection applies was discovered as a result of a statement made by an accused person shall not be admissible unless evidence of how it was discovered is given by him or on his behalf.

(6)   Subsection (5) above applies—

(a)   to any fact discovered as a result of a confession which is wholly excluded in pursuance of this section; and

(b)   to any fact discovered as a result of a confession which is partly so excluded, if the fact is discovered as a result of the excluded part of the confession.

(7) Nothing in Part VII of this Act shall prejudice the admissibility of a confession made by an accused person.

(8) In this section 'oppression' includes torture, inhuman or degrading treatment, and the use or threat of violence (whether or not amounting to torture).

77(1) Without prejudice to the general duty of the court at a trial on indictment to direct the jury on any matter on which it appears to the court appropriate to do so, where at such a trial—

(a) the case against the accused depends wholly or substantially on a confession by him; and

(b) the court is satisfied—

(i) that he is mentally handicapped; and

(ii) that the confession was not made in the presence of an independent person,

the court shall warn the jury that there is special need for caution before convicting the accused in reliance on the confession, and shall explain that the need arises because of the circumstances mentioned in paragraphs (a) and (b) above.

(2) In any case where at the summary trial of a person for an offence it appears to the court that a warning under subsection (1) above would be required if the trial were on indictment, the court shall treat the case as one in which there is a special need for caution before convicting the accused on his confession.

(3) In this section—

'independent person' does not include a police officer or a person employed for, or engaged on, police purposes;

'mentally handicapped', in relation to a person, means that he is in a state of arrested or incomplete development of mind which includes significant impairment of intelligence and social functioning; and

'police purposes' has the meaning assigned to it by section 64 of the Police Act 1964.

78(1) In any proceedings the court may refuse to allow evidence on which the prosecution proposes to rely to be given if it appears to the court that, having regard to all the circumstances, including the circumstances in which the evidence was obtained, the admission of the evidence would have such an adverse effect on the fairness of the proceedings that the court ought not to admit it.

(2) Nothing in this section shall prejudice any rule of law requiring a court to exclude evidence.

82(1) In this Part of this Act—

'confession', includes any statement wholly or partly adverse to the person who made it, whether made to a person in authority or not and whether made in words or otherwise;. . .

(3) Nothing in this Part of this Act shall prejudice any power of a court to exclude evidence (whether by preventing questions being put or otherwise) at its discretion.

• Would a confession excluded under s. 76(2)(a) always fall to be excluded under s. 76(2)(b)?

• In s. 76(2)(b) the words 'anything said or done which was likely' have been substituted for 'any threat or inducement of a sort likely' which appeared in clause 2(2)(b) of the draft Bill annexed to the 11th Report of the Criminal Law Revision Committee (Cmnd 4991). What difference does this make?

*   Is there a case for a provision on the lines of s. 77 in the case of juveniles? Does s. 77 have any practical importance?

R v *Fulling* [1987] 2 WLR 923 (CA)

At the appellant's trial the prosecution proposed to give evidence of a confession made by her after persistent questioning in police custody. She submitted that the confession should be ruled inadmissible under section 76(2)(a) of the Police and Criminal Evidence Act 1984 in that the confession was or might have been obtained by oppression of her and the prosecution had not proved beyond reasonable doubt that the confession was not so obtained. The judge ruled that oppression meant something above and beyond what was inherently oppressive in police custody and imported some oppression actively applied in an improper manner by the police and that, even accepting the appellant's version of events as accurate, oppression could not be made out on the evidence. The submission was rejected and the appellant was convicted. She appealed.

LORD LANE CJ, reading the judgment of the court: 'Mr Davey has drawn our attention to a number of authorities on the meaning of "oppression." Sachs LJ in *R* v *Priestley (Note)* (1965) 51 Cr App R 1 said, at pp. 1, 2–3:

> . . .to my mind [oppression] in the context of the principles under consideration imports something which tends to sap, and has sapped, that free will which must exist before a confession is voluntary. . . . the courts are not concerned with ascertaining the precise motive of a particular statement. The question before them is whether the prosecution have shown the statement to be voluntary, whatever the motive may be, and that is always the point to which all arguments must return. To solve it, the court has to look to the questions which I have already mentioned. First, was there in fact something which could properly be styled or might well be oppression? Secondly, did whatever happened in the way of oppression or likely oppression induce the statement in question?

R v *Prager* [1972] 1 WLR 260, was another decision on note (e) to the Judges' Rules 1964, which required that a statement by the defendant before being admitted in evidence must be proved to be "voluntary" in the sense that it has not been obtained by fear of prejudice or hope of advantage or by oppression. Edmund Davies LJ, who delivered the judgment of the court, said, at p. 266:

> As we have already indicated, the criticism directed in the present case against the police is that their interrogation constituted 'oppression.' This word appeared for the first time in the Judges' Rules 1964, and it closely followed the observation of Lord Parker CJ in *Callis* v *Gunn* [1964] 1 QB 495, 501, condemning confessions 'obtained in an oppressive manner'.

Edmund Davies LJ, having cited the relevant passage from *R* v *Priestley (Note)*, 51 Cr App R 1 continued:

> In an address to the Bentham Club in 1968, Lord MacDermott described 'oppressive questioning' as 'questioning which by its nature, duration, or other attendant

circumstances (including the fact of custody) excites hopes (such as the hope of release) or fears, or so affects the mind of the subject that his will crumbles and he speaks when otherwise he would have stayed silent.' We adopt these definitions or descriptions. . .

Director of Public Prosecutions v *Ping Lin* [1976] AC 574, was again a case in which the question was whether a statement by the defendant was shown to be voluntary. It was held that a trial judge faced by the problem should approach the task in a common sense way and should ask himself whether the prosecution had proved that the contested statement was voluntary in the sense that it was not obtained by fear of prejudice or hope of advantage excited or held out by a person in authority. Lord Wilberforce, Lord Morris of Borth-y-Gest and Lord Hailsham of St Marylebone expressed the opinion that:

> . . . it is not necessary, before a statement is held to be inadmissible because not shown to have been voluntary, that it should be thought or held that there was impropriety in the conduct of the person to whom the statement was made; . . .

What has to be considered is whether a statement is shown to have been voluntary rather than one brought about in one of the ways referred to.

Finally Mr Davey referred us to a judgment of this court in *R* v *Rennie* [1982] 1 WLR 64.

Mr Davey submits to us that on the strength of those decisions the basis of the judge's ruling was wrong; in particular when he held that the word "oppression" means something above and beyond that which is inherently oppressive in police custody and must import some impropriety, some oppression actively applied in an improper manner by the police. It is submitted that that flies in the face of the opinions of their Lordships in *Director of Public Prosecutions* v *Ping Lin* [1976] AC 574.

The point is one of statutory construction. The wording of the Act of 1984 does not follow the wording of earlier rules or decisions, nor is it expressed to be a consolidating Act, nor yet to be declaratory of the common law. The preamble runs:

> An Act to make further provision in relation to the powers and duties of the police, persons in police detention, criminal evidence, police discipline and complaints against the police; to provide for arrangements for obtaining the views of the community on policing and for a rank of deputy chief constable; to amend the law relating to the Police Federations and Police Forces and Police Cadets in Scotland; and for connected purposes.

It is a codifying Act, and therefore the principles set out in *Bank of England* v *Vagliano Brothers* [1891] AC 107, 144 apply. Lord Herschell, having pointed out that the Bills of Exchange Act 1882 which was under consideration was intended to be a codifying Act, said, at pp. 144–145:

> I think the proper course is in the first instance to examine the language of the statute and to ask what is its natural meaning, uninfluenced by any considerations derived from the previous state of the law, and not to start with inquiring how the law previously stood, and then, assuming that it was probably intended to leave it unaltered, to see if the words of the enactment will bear an interpretation in conformity with this view. If a statute, intended to embody in a code a particular branch of the law, is to be treated in this fashion, it appears to me that its utility will be almost entirely destroyed, and the very object with which it was enacted will be

frustrated. The purpose of such a statute surely was that on any point specifically dealt with by it, the law should be ascertained by interpreting the language used instead of, as before, by roaming over a vast number of authorities in order to discover what the law was, extracting it by a minute critical examination of the prior decisions, dependent upon a knowledge of the exact effect even of an obsolete proceeding such as a demurrer to evidence.

Similar observations are to be found in *Bristol Tramways & Carriage Co. Ltd* v *Fiat Motors Ltd* [1910] 2 KB 831, 836 *per* Cozens-Hardy MR.

Section 76(2) of the Act of 1984 distinguishes between two different ways in which a confession may be rendered inadmissible: (a) where it has been obtained by oppression; (b) where it has been made in consequence of anything said or done which was likely in the circumstances to render unreliable any confession which might be made by the defendant in consequence thereof. Paragraph (b) is wider than the old formulation, namely that the confession must be shown to be voluntary in the sense that it was not obtained by fear of prejudice or hope of advantage, excited or held out by a person in authority. It is wide enough to cover some of the circumstances which under the earlier rule were embraced by what seems to us to be the artificially wide definition of oppression approved in *R* v *Prager* [1972] 1 WLR 260.

This in turn leads us to believe that "oppression" in section 76(2)(a) should be given its ordinary dictionary meaning. The *Oxford English Dictionary* as its third definition of the word runs as follows: "Exercise of authority or power in a burdensome, harsh, or wrongful manner; unjust or cruel treatment of subjects, inferiors, etc.; the imposition of unreasonable or unjust burdens." One of the quotations given under that paragraph runs as follows. "There is not a word in our language which expresses more detestable wickedness than oppression."

We find it hard to envisage any circumstances in which such oppression would not entail some impropriety on the part of the interrogator. We do not think that the judge was wrong in using that test. What however is abundantly clear is that a confession may be invalidated under section 76(2)(b) where there is no suspicion of impropriety. No reliance was placed on the words of section 76(2)(b) either before the judge at trial or before this court. Even if there had been such reliance, we do not consider that the policeman's remark was likely to make unreliable any confession of the appellant's own criminal activities, and she expressly exonerated — or tried to exonerate — her unfaithful lover.

In those circumstances, in the judgment of this court, the judge was correct to reject the submission made to him under section 76 of the Act of 1984.'

Appeal dismissed.

Note: This is an area of the law which is certain to be the subject of much case law in the next few years. It is likely that many of the old cases on the question of confessions will continue to be relevant to the issues under the 1984 Act. Space precludes the treatment of such cases in this book, but attention is directed in particular to *Ibrahim* v *R* [1914] AC 599 (PC); *Commissioners of Customs & Excise* v *Harz and Power* [1967] 1 AC 760 (HL); *Director of Public Prosecutions* v *Ping Lin* [1976] AC 574 (HL); *R* v *Rennie* [1982] 1 WLR 64 (CA); *R* v *Miller* [1986] 1 WLR 1191 (decided before the 1984 Act came into force). See also, Mirfield, 'Confessions' (1985) *passim*.

Police and Criminal Evidence Act 1984

56(1)   Where a person has been arrested and is being held in custody in a police station or other premises, he shall be entitled, if he so requests, to have one friend or relative or other person who is known to him or who is likely to take an interest in his welfare told, as soon as is practicable except to the extent that delay is permitted by this section, that he has been arrested and is being detained there.

(2)   Delay is only permitted—

(a)   in the case of a person who is in police detention for a serious arrestable offence; and

(b)   if an officer of at least the rank of superintendent authorises it.

(3)   In any case the person in custody must be permitted to exercise the right conferred by subsection (1) above within 36 hours from the relevant time, as defined in section 41(2) above.

(4)   An officer may give an authorisation under subsection (2) above orally or in writing but, if he gives it orally, he shall confirm it in writing as soon as is practicable.

(5)   An officer may only authorise delay where he has reasonable grounds for believing that telling the named person of the arrest—

(a)   will lead to interference with or harm to evidence connected with a serious arrestable offence or interference with or physical injury to other persons; or

(b)   will lead to the alerting of other persons suspected of having committed such an offence but not yet arrested for it; or

(c)   will hinder the recovery of any property obtained as a result of such an offence.

(6)   If a delay is authorised—

(a)   the detained person shall be told the reason for it; and

(b)   the reason shall be noted on his custody record.

(7)   The duties imposed by subsection (6) above shall be performed as soon as is practicable.

(8)   The rights conferred by this section on a person detained at a police station or other premises are exercisable whenever he is transferred from one place to another; and this section applies to each subsequent occasion on which they are exercisable as it applies to the first such occasion.

(9)   There may be no further delay in permitting the exercise of the right conferred by subsection (1) above once the reason for authorising delay ceases to subsist.

(10)   In the foregoing provisions of this section references to a person who has been arrested include references to a person who has been detained under the terrorism provisions and 'arrest' includes detention under those provisions.

(11)   In its application to a person who has been arrested or detained under the terrorism provisions—

(a)   subsection (2)(a) above shall have effect as if for the words 'for a serious arrestable offence' there were substituted the words 'under the terrorism provisions';

(b)   subsection (3) above shall have effect as if for the words from 'within' onwards there were substituted the words 'before the end of the period beyond which he may no longer be detained without the authority of the Secretary of State'; and

(c)   subsection (5) above shall have effect as if at the end there were added 'or

(d)   will lead to interference with the gathering of information about the commission, preparation or instigation of acts of terrorism; or

(e)   by alerting any person, will make it more difficult—

(i)   to prevent an act of terrorism; or

(ii)   to secure the apprehension, prosecution or conviction of any person in connection with the commission, preparation or instigation of an act of terrorism.'

58(1)   A person arrested and held in custody in a police station or other premises shall be entitled, if he so requests, to consult a solicitor privately at any time. . ..

(2)   Subject to subsection (3) below, a request under subsection (1) above and the time at which it was made shall be recorded in the custody record.

(3)   Such a request need not be recorded in the custody record of a person who makes it at a time while he is at a court after being charged with an offence.

(4)   If a person makes such a request, he must be permitted to consult a solicitor as soon as is practicable except to the extent that delay is permitted by this section.

(5)   In any case he must be permitted to consult a solicitor within 36 hours from the relevant time, as defined in section 41(2) above.

(6)   Delay in compliance with a request is only permitted—

(a)   in the case of a person who is in police detention for a serious arrestable offence; and

(b)   if an officer of at least the rank of superintendent authorises it.

(7)   An officer may give an authorisation under subsection (6) above orally or in writing but, if he gives it orally, he shall confirm it in writing as soon as is practicable.

(8)   An officer may only authorise delay where he has reasonable grounds for believing that the exercise of the right conferred by subsection (1) above at the time when the person detained desires to exercise it—

(a)   will lead to interference with or harm to evidence connected with a serious arrestable offence or interference with or physical injury to other persons; or

(b)   will lead to the alerting of other persons suspected of having committed such an offence but not yet arrested for it; or

(c)   will hinder the recovery of any property obtained as a result of such an offence.

(9)   If delay is authorised—

(a)   the detained person shall be told the reason for it; and

(b)   the reason shall be noted on his custody record.

(10)   The duties imposed by subsection (9) above shall be performed as soon as is practicable.

(11)   There may be no further delay in permitting the exercise of the right conferred by subsection (1) above once the reason for authorising delay ceases to subsist.

(12)   The reference in subsection (1) above to a person arrested includes a reference to a person who has been detained under the terrorism provisions.

(13)   In the application of this section to a person who has been arrested or detained under the terrorism provisions—

(a)   subsection (5) above shall have effect as if for the words from 'within' onwards there were substituted the words "before the end of the period beyond which he may no longer be detained without the authority of the Secretary of State";

(b)   subsection (6)(a) above shall have effect as if for the words "for a serious arrestable offence" there were substituted the words "under the terrorism provisions"; and

(c)   subsection (8) above shall have effect as if at the end there were added "or

>   (d)   will lead to interference with the gathering of information about the commission, preparation or instigation of acts of terrorism; or
>
>   (e)   by alerting any person, will make it more difficult—
>
>   (i)   to prevent an act of terrorism; or
>
>   (ii)   to secure the apprehension, prosecution or conviction of any person in connection with the commission, preparation or instigation of an act of terrorism.".

(14)   If an officer of appropriate rank has reasonable grounds for believing that, unless he gives a direction under subsection (15) below, the exercise by a person arrested or detained under the terrorism provisions of the right conferred by subsection (1) above will have any of the consequences specified in subsection (8) above (as it has effect by virtue of subsection (13) above), he may give a direction under that subsection.

(15)   A direction under this subsection is a direction that a person desiring to exercise the right conferred by subsection (1) above may only consult a solicitor in the sight and hearing of a qualified officer of the uniformed branch of the force of which the officer giving the direction is a member.

(16)   An officer is qualified for the purpose of subsection (15) above if—

(a)   he is of at least the rank of inspector; and

(b)   in the opinion of the officer giving the direction he has no connection with the case.

(17)   An officer is of appropriate rank to give a direction under subsection (15) above if he is of at least the rank of Commander or Assistant Chief Constable.

(18)   A direction under subsection (15) above shall cease to have effect once the reason for giving it ceases to subsist.

66   The Secretary of State shall issue codes of practice in connection with—. . .

(b)   the detention, treatment, questioning and identification of persons by police officers;

67(9)   Persons other than police officers who are charged with the duty of investigating offences or charging offenders shall in the discharge of that duty have regard to any relevant provision of such a code. . .

(11)   In all criminal and civil proceedings any such code shall be admissible in evidence; and if any provision of such a code appears to the court or tribunal conducting the proceedings to be relevant to any question arising in the proceedings it shall be taken into account in determining that question.

Code of Practice for the Detention, Treatment and Questioning of Persons by Police Officers.

5   Right not to be held incommunicado

(a)   Action

5.1   Any person to whom paragraphs 2.1 [persons brought to a police station under arrest or arrested at the police station having attended there voluntarily] and 3.9 [persons attending a police station voluntarily] apply may on request have one person known to him or who is likely to take an interest in his welfare informed at public expense as soon as practicable of his whereabouts. If the person cannot be contacted the person who has made the request may choose up to two alternatives. If they too cannot be contacted the custody officer has discretion to allow further attempts until the information has been conveyed.

5.2   The exercise of the above right in respect of each of the persons nominated may be delayed only in accordance with Annex B to this code.

5.3   The above right may be exercised on each occasion that a person is taken to another police station.

5.4   The person may receive visits at the custody officer's discretion.

5.5   Where an enquiry as to the whereabouts of the person is made by a friend, relative or person with an interest in his welfare, this information shall be given, if he agrees and if Annex B does not apply.

5.6   The person shall be supplied on request with writing materials. Any letter or other message shall be sent as soon as practicable unless Annex B applies.

5.7   He may also speak on the telephone for a reasonable time to one person unless Annex B applies.

5.8   Before any letter or message is sent, or telephone call made, the person shall be informed that what he says in any letter, call or message (other than in the case of a communication to a solicitor) may be read or listened to as appropriate and may be given in evidence. A telephone call may be terminated if it is being abused. The costs can be at public expense at the discretion of the custody officer.

(b)   Documentation

5.9   A record must be kept of:

    (a)   any request made under this section and the action taken on it;
    (b)   any letters or messages sent, calls made or visits received; and
    (c)   any refusal on the part of a person to have information about himself or his whereabouts given to an outside enquirer.

6   Right to legal advice

(a)   Action

6.1   Subject to paragraph 6.2, any person may at any time consult and communicate privately, whether in person, in writing or on the telephone with a solicitor.

6.2   The exercise of the above right may be delayed only in accordance with Annex B to this code.

6.3   A person who asks for legal advice may not be interviewed or continue to be interviewed until he has received it unless:

(a)   Annex B applies; or

(b)   an officer of the rank of superintendent or above has reasonable grounds for believing that:

(i)   delay will involve an immediate risk of harm to persons or serious loss of, or damage to, property; or

(ii)   where a solicitor, including a duty solicitor, has been contacted and has agreed to attend, awaiting his arrival would cause unreasonable delay to the processes of investigation; or

(c)   the solicitor nominated by the person, or selected by him from a list:

(i)   cannot be contacted;

(ii)   has previously indicated that he does not wish to be contacted; or

(iii)   having been contacted, has declined to attend;

and the person has been advised of the Duty Solicitor Scheme (where one is in operation) but has declined to ask for the duty solicitor, or the duty solicitor is unavailable; or

(d)   the person has given his agreement in writing or on tape that the interview may be started at once.

6.4   Where sub-paragraph 6.3(b)(i) applies, once sufficient information to avert the risk has been obtained, questioning must cease until the person has received legal advice or sub-paragraphs 6.3(a), (b)(ii), (c) or (d) apply.

6.5   Where a person has been permitted to consult a solicitor and the solicitor is available at the time the interview begins or is in progress, he must be allowed to have his solicitor present while he is interviewed.

6.6   The solicitor may only be required to leave the interview if his conduct is such that the investigating officer is unable properly to put questions to the suspect.

6.7   If the investigating officer considers that a solicitor is acting in such a way, he will stop the interview and consult an officer not below the rank of superintendent, if one is readily available, and otherwise an officer not below the rank of inspector who is not connected with the investigation. After speaking to the solicitor, the officer who has been consulted will decide whether or not the interview should continue in the presence of that solicitor. If he decides that it should not, the suspect will be given the opportunity to consult another solicitor before the interview continues and that solicitor will be given an opportunity to be present at the interview.

6.8   The removal of a solicitor from an interview is a serious step and if it occurs, the officer of superintendent rank or above who took the decision will consider whether the incident should be reported to The Law Society. If the decision to remove the solicitor has been taken by an officer below the rank of superintendent, the facts must be reported to an officer of superintendent rank or above who will similarly consider whether a report to The Law Society would be appropriate.

6.9   In this code 'solicitor' means a solicitor qualified to practise in accordance with the Solicitors Act 1974. If a solicitor wishes to send a clerk or legal executive to provide advice on his behalf, then the clerk or legal executive shall be admitted to the police station for this purpose unless an officer of the rank of inspector or above considers that such a visit will hinder the investigation of crime and directs otherwise. Once admitted to the police station, the provisions of paragraphs 6.3 to 6.7 apply.

6.10   If the inspector refused access to a clerk or legal executive or a decision is taken that such a person should not be permitted to remain at an interview, he must forthwith notify a solicitor on whose behalf the clerk or legal executive was to have acted or was acting, and give him an opportunity of making alternative arrangements.

(b)   Documentation

6.11   Any request for legal advice and the action taken on it shall be recorded.

6.12   If a person has asked for legal advice and an interview is commenced in the absence of a solicitor or his representative (or the solicitor or his representative has been required to leave an interview) a record shall be made in the interview record.

10   Cautions

(a)   When a caution must be given

10.1   A person whom there are grounds to suspect of an offence must be cautioned before any questions about it (or further questions if it is his answers to previous questions that provide grounds for suspicion) are put to him for the purpose of obtaining evidence which may be given to a court in a prosecution. He therefore need not be cautioned if questions are put for other purposes, for example, to establish his identity, his ownership of, or responsibility for, any vehicle or the need to search him in the exercise of powers of stop and search.

10.2   When a person who is not under arrest is initially cautioned before or during an interview at a police station or other premises he must at the same time be told that he is not under arrest, is not obliged to remain with the officer but that if he does, may obtain legal advice if he wishes.

10.3   A person must be cautioned upon arrest for an offence unless:

(a)   it is impracticable to do so by reason of his condition or behaviour at the time; or

(b)   he has already been cautioned immediately prior to arrest in accordance with paragraph 10.1 above.

(b)   Action: general

10.4   The caution shall be in the following terms:

You do not have to say anything unless you wish to do so, but what you say may be given in evidence.

Minor deviations do not constitute a breach of this requirement provided that the sense of the caution is preserved.

10.5   When there is a break in questioning under caution the interviewing officer must ensure that the person being questioned is aware that he remains under caution. If there is any doubt the caution should be given again in full when the interview resumes.

(c) Documentation

10.6   A record shall be made when a caution is given under this section, either in the officer's pocket book or in the interview record as appropriate.

11   Interviews: general

(a)   Action

11.1   No police officer may try to obtain answers to questions or to elicit a statement by the use of oppression, or shall indicate, except in answer to a direct question, what action will be taken on the part of the police if the person being interviewed answers questions, makes a statement or refuses to do either. If the person asks the officer directly what action will be taken in the event of his answering questions, making a statement or refusing to do either, then the officer may inform the person what action the police propose to take in that event provided that that action is itself proper and warranted.

11.2   As soon as a police officer who is making enquiries of any person about an offence believes that a prosecution should be brought against him and that there is sufficient evidence for it to succeed, he shall without delay cease to question him.

(b)   Interview records

11.3   (a)   An accurate record must be made of each interview with a person suspected of an offence, whether or not the interview takes place at a police station.

(b)   if the interview takes place in the police station or other premises:

(i)   the record must state the place of the interview, the time it begins and ends, the time the record is made (if different), any breaks in the interview and the names of all those present; and must be made on the forms provided for this purpose or in the officer's pocket book or in accordance with the code of practice for the tape recording of police interviews with suspects;

(ii)   the record must be made during the course of the interview, unless in the investigating officer's view this would not be practicable or would interfere with the conduct of the interview, and must constitute either a verbatim record of what has been said or, failing this, an account of the interview which adequately and accurately summarises it.

11.4   If an interview record is not made during the course of the interview it must be made as soon as practicable after its completion.

11.5   Written interview records must be timed and signed by the maker.

11.6   If an interview record is not completed in the course of the interview the reason must be recorded in the officer's pocket book.

11.7   Any refusal by a person to sign an interview record when asked to do so in accordance with the provisions of this code must itself be recorded.

13   Persons at risk: juveniles, and those who are mentally ill or mentally handicapped

13.1   A juvenile or a person who is mentally ill or mentally handicapped, whether suspected or not, must not be interviewed or asked to provide or sign a written statement in the absence of the appropriate adult unless Annex C applies. If he is cautioned in accordance with section 10 above in the absence of the appropriate adult, the caution must be repeated in the adult's presence (unless the interview has by then already finished).

13.2   If, having been informed of the right to legal advice under paragraph 3.6 above, the appropriate adult considers that legal advice should be taken, then the provisions of section 6 of this code apply.

13.3   Juveniles may only be interviewed at their places of education in exceptional circumstances and then only where the principal or his nominee agrees and is present.

17   Charging of detained persons

(a)   Action

17.1   When an officer considers that there is sufficient evidence to prosecute a detained person he should without delay bring him before the custody officer who shall then be responsible for considering whether or not he should be charged. Any resulting action should be taken in the presence of the appropriate adult if the person is a juvenile or mentally ill or mentally handicapped.

17.2   When a detained person is charged with or informed that he may be prosecuted for an offence he shall be cautioned in the terms of paragraph 10.4 above.

17.3   At the time a person is charged he shall be given a written notice showing particulars of the offence with which he is charged and including the name of the officer in the case, his police station and the reference number for the case. So far as possible the particulars of the charge shall be stated in simple terms, but they shall also show the precise offence in law with which he is charged. The notice shall begin with the following words:

> You are charged with the offence(s) shown below. You do not have to say anything unless you wish to do so, but what you say may be given in evidence.

If the person is a juvenile or is mentally ill or mentally handicapped the notice shall be given to the appropriate adult.

17.4   If at any time after a person has been charged with or informed he may be prosecuted for an offence a police officer wishes to bring to the notice of that person any written statement made by another person or the content of an interview with another person, he shall hand to that person a true copy of any such written statement or bring to his attention the content of the interview record, but shall say or do nothing to invite any reply or comment save to caution him in the terms of paragraph 10.4 above. If the person cannot read then the officer may read it to him. If the person is a juvenile or mentally ill or mentally handicapped the copy shall also be given to, or the interview record brought to the attention of, the appropriate adult.

17.5   Questions relating to an offence may not be put to a person after he has been charged with the offence, or informed that he may be prosecuted for it, unless they are necessary for the purpose of preventing or minimising harm or loss to some other person or to the public or for clearing up an ambiguity in a previous answer or statement, or where it is in the interests of justice that the person should have put to him and have an opportunity to comment on information concerning the offence which has come to light since he was charged or informed that he might be prosecuted. Before any such questions are put he shall be cautioned in the terms of paragraph 10.4 above.

17.6   Where a juvenile is charged with an offence and the custody officer authorises his continuing detention he must try to make arrangements for the juvenile to be taken into the care of a local authority to be detained pending appearance in court unless he certifies that it is impracticable to do so in accordance with section 38(6) of the Police and Criminal Evidence Act 1984.

(b) Documentation

17.7 A record shall be made of anything a detained person says when charged.

17.8 Any questions put after charge and answers given relating to the offence shall be contemporaneously recorded in full on the forms provided and the record signed by that person or, if he refuses, by the interviewing officer and any third parties present. If the questions are tape recorded the arrangements set out in the relevant code of practice apply.

17.9 If it is not practicable to make arrangements for the transfer of a juvenile into local authority care in accordance with paragraph 17.6 above the custody officer must record the reasons and make out a certificate to be produced before the court together with the juvenile.

Annex B: Delay in notifying arrest or allowing access to legal advice

(A) Persons detained under the Police and Criminal Evidence Act 1984

(a) Action

1 The rights set out in sections 5 or 6 of the code (or both) may be delayed if the person is in police detention in connection with a serious arrestable offence, has not yet been charged with an offence and an officer of the rank of superintendent or above has reasonable grounds for believing that the exercise of each right:

(i) will lead to interference with or harm to evidence connected with a serious arrestable offence or interference with or physical harm to other persons;
(ii) will lead to the alerting of other persons suspected of having committed such an offence but not yet arrested for it; or
(iii) will hinder the recovery of property obtained in consequence of the commission of such an offence.

2 Access to a solicitor may not be delayed on the grounds that he might advise the person not to answer any questions or that the solicitor was initially asked to attend the police station by someone else, provided that the person himself then wishes to see the solicitor.

3 These rights may be delayed only for as long as is necessary and, subject to paragraph 6 below, in no case beyond 36 hours after the relevant time as defined in section 41 of the Police and Criminal Evidence Act 1984. If the above grounds cease to apply within this time, the person must as soon as practicable be asked if he wishes to exercise either right and action must be taken in accordance with the relevant section of the code.

4 A detained person must be permitted to consult a solicitor for a reasonable time before any court hearing.

(b) Documentation

5 The grounds for action under this Annex shall be recorded and the person informed of them as soon as practicable.

(B)   Persons detained under the Prevention of Terrorism (Temporary Provisions) Act 1984

(a)   Action

6   The rights set out in sections 5 or 6 of this code (or both) may be delayed if paragraph 1 above applies or if an officer of the rank of superintendent or above has reasonable grounds for believing that the exercise of either right:

> (a)   will lead to interference with the gathering of information about the commission, preparation or instigation of acts of terrorism; or
> (b)   by alerting any person, will make it more difficult to prevent an act of terrorism or to secure the apprehension, prosecution or conviction of any person in connection with the commission, preparation or instigation of an act of terrorism.

7   These rights may be delayed only for as long as is necessary and in no case beyond 48 hours from the time of arrest. If the above grounds cease to apply within this time, the person must as soon as practicable be asked if he wishes to exercise either right and action must be taken in accordance with the relevant section of this code.

(b)   Documentation

8   Paragraph 5 above applies.
9   Any reply given by a person under paragraph 7 above must be recorded and the person asked to endorse the record in relation to whether he wishes to receive legal advice at this point.

Annex C: Urgent interviews

1   If, and only if, an officer of the rank of superintendent or above considers that delay will involve an immediate risk of harm to persons or serious loss of or serious damage to property:

> (a)   a person heavily under the influence of drink or drugs may be interviewed in that state; or
> (b)   an arrested juvenile or a person who is mentally ill or mentally handicapped may be interviewed in the absence of the appropriate adult; or
> (c)   a person who has difficulty in understanding English or who has a hearing disability may be interviewed in the absence of an interpreter.

2   Questioning in these circumstances may not continue once sufficient information to avert the immediate risk has been obtained.
3   A record shall be made of the grounds for any decision to interview a person under paragraph 1 above.

Annex D: Written statements under caution

(a)   Written by a person under caution

1   A person shall always be invited to write down himself what he wants to say.
2   Where the person wishes to write it himself, he shall be asked to write out and sign before writing what he wants to say, the following:

I make this statement of my own free will. I understand that I need not say anything unless I wish to do so and that what I say may be given in evidence.

3   Any person writing his own statement shall be allowed to do so without any prompting except that a police officer may indicate to him which matters are material or question any ambiguity in the statement.

(b)   Written by a police officer

4   If a person says that he would like someone to write it for him, a police officer shall write the statement, but, before starting, he must ask him to sign, or make his mark, to the following:

I,..........., wish to make a statement. I want someone to write down what I say. I understand that I need not say anything unless I wish to do so and that what I say may be given in evidence.

5   Where a police officer writes the statement, he must take down the exact words spoken by the person making it and he must not edit or paraphrase it. Any questions that are necessary (e.g., to make it more intelligible) and the answers given must be recorded contemporaneously on the statement form.

6   When the writing of a statement by a police officer is finished the person making it shall be asked to read it and to make any corrections, alterations or additions he wishes. When he has finished reading it he shall be asked to write and sign or make his mark on the following certificate at the end of the statement:

I have read the above statement, and I have been able to correct, alter or add anything I wish. This statement is true. I have made it of my own free will.

7   If the person making the statement cannot read, or refuses to read it, or to write the above mentioned certificate at the end of it or to sign it, the senior police officer present shall read it over to him and ask him whether he would like to correct, alter or add anything and to put his signature or make his mark at the end. The police officer shall then certify on the statement itself what has occurred.

R v Donaldson and Others (1976) 64 Cr App R 59 (CA)

The defendant was charged, *inter alia*, with handling stolen goods. He made a statement to the police partly denying, partly admitting the charge against him. At his trial he did not give evidence, and the jury were directed that the statement was only evidence to the extent that it might represent an admission. He was convicted and appealed.

JAMES LJ, giving the judgment of the court: 'The argument was advanced in its most extreme form, attractively and with diffidence, by Mr Palmer on behalf of Watson. It was suggested that in principle statements made by a defendant in the course of police investigations into an offence should be treated in the same way as statements made by a defendant from the dock to the jury at a trial, that such statements, as are statements from the dock, should be left in their entirety to the jury, with a direction that the jury should give to them such weight as they think right bearing in mind that the statements are not on oath and have not been tested by cross-examination. Mr Palmer recognised that this would undermine the need for the exception to the hearsay rule in favour of admitting evidence of admissions and confessions. The argument if right would support a conclusion resulting in a much simplified direction to the jury who must experience some difficulty when faced with regarding the same material as evidence for one purpose but not for another. The main argument of Mr Palmer, however, was in support of that advanced by Mr Salts for Donaldson and is based upon the case of *McGregor* (1967) 51 Cr App R 338. In that case the appellant had been a defendant at an earlier trial at which the jury were not able to agree and he was re-tried. In the earlier trial he had admitted possession of the stolen goods. At the second trial the prosecution called evidence to prove his admissions and defending counsel cross-examined in order to bring out further statements and explanations made by the defendant at the first trial to show that he did not know the goods were stolen. The appellant did not give evidence at the second trial. On the appeal counsel argued, on the authority of the old case of *Jones and Jones* (1827) 2 C & P 629, that if the Crown choose to rely upon an admission or confession made by a defendant the whole and not just a selected part must go before the jury, and that if there be no other evidence in the case or no other evidence incompatible with what the defendant said then the jury must take what he had said as true. This Court rejected that argument and ruled that *Jones and Jones (supra)* was no longer authority. Lord Parker CJ said at p. 341: "It was an old case in 1827, long before 1898, and as stated in Archbold's *Criminal Pleadings*, etc. (36th ed) "the better opinion seems to be that as in the case of all other evidence the whole should be left to the jury to say whether the facts asserted by the prisoner in his favour be true." The Court is satisfied that that passage in Archbold sets out the true position." Further arguments in the case of *McGregor (supra)* were that the trial judge had left to the jury the admissions made by the appellant but directed that they should not consider as evidence of fact the explanations which the appellant had himself given at the earlier trial, and that the jury should have been told to attach equal weight to the admissions and the explanations. At p. 342 Lord Parker CJ said: ". . . it seems to this Court that the position was made clear that the jury were to consider the explanations that the appellant had given at the earlier trial but he reminded them that the appellant not having given evidence himself, that they could not be tested," and later on the same page he said: "This Court cannot conceive why the jury should attach equal weight to both. The appellant not having given evidence, not having gone into the box to deny the truth of his earlier statement that he had put the goods into his wife's shopping bag, and not having gone into the witness-box to verify the explanations he had given on the previous occasion, it was only natural and proper that the jury should attach greater weight to the admission than to the explanation." The reason why the jury should be entitled to consider the explanations as evidence of fact is that the explanations have a bearing upon the evaluation of the part of the statement which is relied on as an admission.

Counsel for these appellants have invited our attention to the later case of *Storey and Anwar* (1968) 52 Cr App R 334 (in the report of which there is no reference to *McGregor (supra)* having been cited) and the case of *Thompson* [1975] Crim LR 34 reported only briefly. The transcript of the judgment in *Thompson* shows that the Court dealt very shortly with the question raised in the appeal and, reading it now, I think what I said was so brief that the *ratio* of the case may be open to misconstruction. In that case the appellant on the occasion of his committal for trial had made a voluntary statement in the presence of his solicitor and a police officer to the effect that his acts, the subject of the charge against him, were acts done in self-defence. The statement was not an admission or confession of the offence. The statement was produced by the Crown at the trial as evidence of what the appellant had said. The appellant who did not give evidence sought to use that statement as evidence of the truth of its content. This Court decided that such a self serving statement could not be relied upon by the appellant as evidence of the truth of the content.

In *Storey and Anwar* (*supra*) the appellant Storey was convicted of possessing a quantity of drugs. Evidence for the Crown included that of police officers who found the drugs on a bed in her flat. Miss Storey was taken to a police station where she made a statement in which she explained the presence of the drugs and which, if true, would have provided a complete answer to the charge. At the close of the case for the Crown the trial judge rejected a submission that there was no case to answer in the light of the explanation in the statement.

The question which the Court had to decide was expressed by Widgery LJ (as he then was) at p. 337: ". . .whether the fact that she gave shortly afterwards an explanation which, if true, would provide a completely innocent explanation is enough to produce a situation in which the learned judge's duty was to say that there was no case to answer." Then a little later in the judgment at pp. 337, 338, he said: "The Court has given careful consideration to this important point. We think it right to recognise that a statement made by the accused to the police, although it always forms evidence in the case against him, is not in itself evidence of the truth of the facts stated. A statement made voluntarily by an accused person to the police is evidence in the trial because of its vital relevance as showing the reaction of the accused when first taxed with the incriminating facts. If, of course, the accused admits the offence, then as a matter of shorthand one says that the admission is proof of guilt, and, indeed, in the end it is. But if the accused makes a statement which does not amount to an admission, the statement is not strictly evidence of the truth of what was said, but is evidence of the reaction of the accused which forms part of the general picture to be considered by the jury at the trial. Accordingly, in our judgment, in this case the fact that the cannabis was on the applicant's bed in her flat was in itself some evidence of possession to go to the jury. Her unsworn explanation, although, if true, it would have been a complete answer to the charge, did not cancel out or nullify the evidence which was provided by the presence of the cannabis. It was ultimately for the jury to decide whether that explanation was or might be true, and it was not for the judge necessarily to accept it at the stage when he was considering the submission." It was suggested in argument that that last sentence is inconsistent with the earlier words "is not in itself evidence of the truth of the facts stated," but that it is in accordance with what was said by Lord Parker CJ in *McGregor* (*supra*). The words "It was ultimately for the jury to decide whether that explanation was or might be true. . ." were not necessary to the decision of the Court nor are they, in our view, inconsistent with the earlier passage. In that sentence Lord Widgery is drawing the distinction between the stage at the end of the Crown case and the subsequent stage when the jury have to make a decision.

In our view there is a clear distinction to be made between statements of admission adduced by the Crown as part of the case against the defendant and statements entirely of a self serving nature made and sought to be relied upon by a defendant. When the Crown adduce a statement relied upon as an admission it is for the jury to consider the whole statement including any passages that contain qualifications or explanations favourable to the defendant, that bear upon the passages relied upon by the prosecution as an admission, and it is for the jury to decide whether the statement viewed as a whole constitutes an admission. To this extent the statement may be said to be evidence of the facts stated therein. If the jury find that it is an admission they may rely upon it as proof of the facts admitted. If the defendant elects not to give evidence then in so far as the statement contains explanations or qualifications favourable to the defendant the jury, in deciding what, if any, weight to give to that part of the statement, should take into account that it was not made on oath and has not been tested by cross-examination.

When the Crown adduce evidence in the form of a statement by the defendant which is not relied on as an admission of the offence charged such a statement is evidence in the trial in that it is evidence that the defendant made the statement and of his reaction which is part of the general picture which the jury have to consider but it is not evidence of the facts stated.'

(The court held that although there had been a misdirection, it had not affected the verdict and no miscarriage of justice had occurred.)

Appeal dismissed.

R v *Pearce* (1979) 69 Cr App R 365 (CA)

The appellant was taxed by his employer's security officer with incriminating facts relating to handling stolen goods and denied knowledge of them. Two days later he was arrested by the police for handling stolen goods and taken to a police station where he made two voluntary statements. He was seen there by two detective constables in the presence of his solicitor. The offences involved the sale of two pairs of lambs carcasses. The appellant's first self-serving statement dealt with only the first pair of lambs — he said he had reason to believe they were stolen and that he had sold them for the same price as he paid. Three hours later the detectives again interviewed the appellant during which he denied that he knew the carcasses were stolen; but he said that he sold a second pair of carcasses at a public house; and when asked if he knew the purchasers said that he did not. The detectives made four pages of notes of that interview. The next day the appellant volunteered another self-serving statement in which he stated that he had no suspicion that the second pair of carcasses were stolen. At his trial, counsel expected that the whole of the interview and both statements would go before the jury. The trial judge excluded the two voluntary statements and part of the interview on the ground that they were self-serving statements and as such not admissible. The appellant was convicted and appealed.

LORD WIDGERY CJ, reading the judgment of the court: 'With regard to the statements, Mr Williams argued that to admit the statements would mean extending what was said in *Storey and Anwar* (1968) 52 Cr App R 334. In that case I said, at pp. 337, 338 in giving the judgment of the Court: "A statement made voluntarily by an accused person to the police is evidence in the trial because of its vital relevance as showing the reaction of the accused when first taxed with the incriminating facts."

Mr Williams argued that the voluntary statements in the present case were not made when first taxed with the incriminating facts. The appellant had been taxed with the incriminating facts in his interview with the chief security officer on March 6. By March 8 when he was first interviewed by the police he had had an opportunity of consulting his solicitors, and indeed his solicitors were present when the first statement was made. Mr Williams submitted that what he called the *Storey* principle should not be extended, because of the difficulty sometimes found in explaining to juries the difference between the voluntary statements being evidence of the truth of the facts stated, and evidence merely of the defendant's reaction.

For reasons which will appear later, we cannot accept Mr Williams' submission. Mr Black for the appellant referred us to all the cases starting with the judgment of Sir James Eyre LCJ in *Hardy* (1794) 24 St Tr 199, 1093. He invited us, in effect, to rewrite a chapter in the law of evidence, and to hold that previous consistent statements are always admissible, subject only to certain exceptions. For our part, we are unwilling to take that step.

In our view the present case can be disposed of within the principles stated in *Storey and Anwar* (*supra*) and *Donaldson* (1976) 64 Cr App R 59. Those decisions will be found to contain all the guidance that is necessary in practice. We would ourselves summarise the principles as follows:

(1)   A statement which contains an admission is always admissible as a declaration against interest and is evidence of the facts admitted. With this exception a statement made by an accused person is never evidence of the facts in the statement.

(2)(a)   A statement that is not an admission is admissible to show the attitude of the accused at the time when he made it. This however is not to be limited to a statement made on the first encounter with the police. The reference in *Storey* to the reaction of the accused "when first taxed" should not be read as circumscribing the limits of admissibility. The longer the time that has elapsed after the first encounter the less the weight which will be attached to the denial. The judge is able to direct the jury about the value of such statements

(b)   A statement that is not in itself an admission is admissible if it is made in the same context as an admission, whether in the course of an interview, or in the form of a voluntary statement. It would be unfair to admit only the statements against interest while excluding part of the same interview or series of interviews. It is the duty of the prosecution to present the case fairly to the jury; to exclude answers which are favourable to the accused while admitting those unfavourable would be misleading.

(c)   The prosecution may wish to draw attention to inconsistent denials. A denial does not become an admission because it is inconsistent with another denial. There must be many cases however where convictions have resulted from such inconsistencies between two denials.

(3)   Although in practice most statements are given in evidence even when they are largely self-serving, there may be a rare occasion when an accused produces a carefully prepared written statement to the police, with a view to it being made part of the prosecution evidence. The trial judge would plainly exclude such a statement as inadmissible.

In the light of the principles which we have ventured to state, there can be no reason for casting doubt on the practice to which we have referred at the start of this judgment, namely, the practice of admitting statements by the accused even when their evidential value is small.

The present case falls within both 2(a) and 2(b) above. As to the first statement it was relevant to show the attitude of the appellant at the beginning of the interview. The voluntary statement set the scene. There was no reason to exclude it. When it was decided to admit part of the interview, the only fair course was to admit the statement so as to put the interview in context. The same principle applies to questions and answers which were exluded in the course of the interview, and to the second voluntary statement made on the following day. Fairness requires that when there is a long series of questions and answers, interspersed with one or more voluntary statements, they should all be admissible in evidence.

For the reasons which we have given, we conclude that the judge was wrong to rule as he did.'

Appeal allowed. Conviction quashed.

R v *Duncan* (1981) 73 Cr App R 359 (CA)

The appellant made statements admitting the killing of a woman with whom he was living. At his trial for murder the appellant elected not to give evidence or call witnesses. The trial judge raised the question of provocation and invited submissions. The judge ruled that, in so far as the appellant's statements were self-serving, they could not be evidence of the facts and therefore provocation would not be left to the jury. The appellant was convicted and appealed on the ground that the ruling was wrong.

LORD LANE CJ, delivering the judgment of the court: 'The basic rules are as follows: (1) What a person says out of court is, generally speaking not admissible to prove the truth of what he says. (2) It may be admissible if — (a) it is an exception to the hearsay rule, in which case it is evidence of the truth of what is stated; (b) it falls outside the hearsay rule, that is to say if it is adduced for a purpose other than proving the truth of the statement — an example of this is to be found in *Subramaniam* v *Public Prosecutor* [1956] 1 WLR 965, where a statement was relevant to the question of whether there had been duress or not. The only relevant exception to the hearsay rule in the present circumstances is that relating to admissions against interest or confessions.

The issue between the parties here is the extent to which confessions are properly to be regarded as evidence of the truth of the facts which they state. Both parties are agreed that if a statement is adduced as an admission against interest, the whole of the statement must be admitted. Any other course would obviously be unfair.

It is contended on behalf of the Crown that this rule does not, however, make the contents of the statement evidence of the facts contained therein except in so far as those statements are admissions against interest. Mr Judge, on the other hand, on behalf of the appellant, contends that the whole statement is evidence of the truth of the facts contained therein. He, however, concedes that the judge is entitled to explain to the jury, if indeed it needs explanation, that the weight to be given to those parts of the statement which contain admissions against interest may be very different from the weight to be given to the parts which are self-exculpatory.

One is bound to observe that if the contentions of the Crown are correct, the judge would be faced with a very difficult task in trying to explain to the jury the difference between those parts of a "mixed" statement (if we may call it such) which were truly confessions and those parts which were self-exculpatory. It is doubtful if the result would be readily intelligible. Suppose a prisoner had said "I killed X. If I had not done so, X would certainly have killed me there and then." If the judge tells the jury that the first sentence is evidence of the truth of what it states but that the second sentence is not; that it is merely something to which they are entitled to have regard as qualifying the first sentence and affecting its weight as an admission, they will either not understand or disregard what he is saying. Judges should not be obliged to give meaningless or unintelligible directions to juries.

We turn to examine the authorities. In *McGregor* (1967) 51 Cr App R 338; [1968] 1 QB 371 Lord Parker CJ, at p. 341 and p. 377, 378 respectively said this: "As we understand it, Mr Dovener says and says rightly that, if the prosecution are minded to put in an admission or a confession, they must put in the whole and not merely part of it." He later cited with approval a pasage from the then current edition of *Archbold* (36th ed), para. 1128: ". . .the better opinion seems to be that as in the case of all other evidence the whole should be left to the jury to say whether the facts asserted by the prisoner in his favour be true." Lord Parker went on to consider and reject out of hand a submission by counsel for the appellant that the jury should have been directed to give equal weight to both parts of the appellant's statement, those containing admissions and those containing excuses or explanations.

This case is clear authority for the proposition that in the case of a "mixed" statement both parts are evidence of the facts they state, though they are obviously not to be regarded as having equal weight.

Sparrow (1973) 57 Cr App R 352: [1973] 1 WLR 488, seems to be inconsistent with the primary ruling in *McGregor* (*supra*), which was not cited to the Court, because Lawton LJ says this at p. 357 and p. 492 of the respective reports: "The trial judge had a difficult task in summing up that part of the case which concerned the appellant. First, he had to try to get the jury to understand that the appellant's exculpatory statement to the police after arrest, which he had not verified in the witness box, was not evidence of the facts in it save in so far as it contained admissions. Many lawyers find difficulty in grasping this principle of the law of evidence. What juries make of it must be a matter of surmise, but the probabilities are they make very little." He then turned to consider the extent to which the judge should comment on the way in which the case has been conducted and upon the failure of the accused man to go into the witness box.

Donaldson and Others (1976) 64 Cr App R 59 was another example of a "mixed" statement. At p. 65 James LJ says this: "In our view there is a clear distinction to be made between statements of admission adduced by the Crown as part of the case against the defendant and statements entirely of a self-serving nature made and sought to be relied by a defendant. When the Crown adduce a statement relied upon as an admission it is for the jury to consider the whole statement including any passages that contain qualifications or explanations favourable to the defendant, that bear upon the passages relied upon by the prosecution as an admission, and it is for the jury to decide whether the statement viewed as a whole constitutes an admission. To this extent the statement may be said to be evidence of the facts stated therein."

Finally in *Pearce* (1979) 69 Cr App R 365, the Court gave directions on how three different factual situations should be approached. We are in this case only concerned with the first: "(1) A statement which contains an admission is always admissible as a declaration against interest and is evidence of the facts admitted. With this exception a statement made by an accused person is never evidence of the facts in the statement." It is not clear from this what standing is to be given to the exculpatory parts of a "mixed" statement, but since the Court expressly based themselves upon the principles in *Donaldson* (*supra*) one can assume that the statement is to be viewed as a whole by the jury.

We should add that we were referred to a number of other decisions: *Storey* (1968) 52 Cr App R 334 in which *McGregor* (*supra*) was not cited and which concerned the question of a purely exculpatory statement and its evidential weight upon a submission of no case; *Thompson* [1975] Crim LR 34; *Barbery Doney and Davis* (1975) 62 Cr App R 248 — which were cases of purely exculpatory statements.

Where a "mixed" statement is under consideration by the jury in a case where the defendant has not given evidence, it seems to us that the simplest, and, therefore, the method most likely to produce a just result, is for the jury to be told that the whole statement, both the incriminating parts and the excuses or explanations, must be considered by them in deciding where the truth lies. It is, to say the least, not helpful to try to explain to the jury that the exculpatory parts of the statement are something less than evidence of the facts they state. Equally, where appropriate, as it usually will be, the judge may, and should, point out that the incriminating parts are likely to be true (otherwise why say them?), whereas the excuses do not have the same weight.'

(The court held on the facts that there was nothing in the appellant's statements which amounted to a claim of provocation.)

Appeal dismissed.

• Does the case of *R* v *Duncan* depart from the earlier authorities?

(Space precludes the insertion of cases on the question of a trial within a trial in relation to confessions: see *Vel* v *Chief Constable of North Wales* (1987) *The Times*, 14 February; *R* v *Liverpool Juvenile Court, ex parte R* [1987] 3 WLR 224; and *R* v *Millard* [1987] Crim LR 196.)

B: STATEMENTS IN THE PRESENCE OF THE DEFENDANT

(Suggested preliminary reading: *A Practical Approach to Evidence,* pp. 222-226).

R v *Norton* [1910] 2 KB 496 (CCA)

The defendant was convicted of having unlawful sexual intercourse with a girl under 13. The child was not called at the trial, but evidence was given of statements made by her in the presence of the defendant and his answers to them. The evidence was to the effect that, on being asked by the defendant who had done it, she said, 'You', and, on being asked by another person, she said, 'Stevie Norton,' and pointed to the defendant; that the defendant said, 'No, Madge, you are mistaken'; that she then said, 'You have done it, Stephen Norton', and pointed to him again. According to one witness he then lifted his arms and said 'If I have done it I hope the Lord will strike me dead,' and according to another witness, 'If you say so I might as well put my clothes on and go home.' There was, therefore, nothing in his answers necessarily amounting to an admission of the girl's statements. The trial judge directed the jury to take into consideration the girl's statement as evidence of the facts contained in it, and to consider whether looking at all the circumstances they accepted it or the defendant's denial. On appeal it was argued that they ought to have been directed that the statements were not evidence of the facts stated and that as they were denied by the defendant the jury should disregard them.

PICKFORD J, reading the judgment of the court: As a general rule, statements as to the facts of a case under investigation are not evidence unless made by witnesses in the ordinary way, but to this rule there are exceptions. One is that statements made in the presence of a prisoner upon an occasion on which he might reasonably be expected to make some observation, explanation, or denial are admissible under certain circumstances. We think it is not strictly accurate, and may be misleading, to say that they are admissible in evidence against the prisoner, as such an expression may seem to imply that they are evidence of the facts stated in them and must be considered upon the footing of other evidence. Such statements are, however, never evidence of the facts stated in them; they are admissible only as introductory to, or explanatory of, the answer given to them by the person in whose presence they are made. Such answer may, of course, be given either by words or by conduct, e.g., by remaining silent on an occasion which demanded an answer.

If the answer given amounts to an admission of the statements or some part of them, they or that part become relevant as showing what facts are admitted; if the answer be not such an admission, the statements are irrelevant to the matter under consideration and should be disregarded. This seems to us to be correctly and shortly stated in *Taylor on Evidence*, s. 814, p. 574: "The statements only become evidence when by such acceptance he makes them his own statements."

No objection was taken in this case to the admission of the statements in evidence, but as the prisoner may be tried again on an indictment on which that question may arise, we think it well to state in what cases such statements can be given in evidence. We think that the contents of such statements should not be given in evidence unless the judge is satisfied that there is evidence fit to be submitted to the jury that the prisoner by his answer to them, whether given by word or conduct, acknowledged the truth of the whole or part of them. If there be no such evidence, then the contents of the statement should be excluded; if there be such evidence, then they should be admitted, and the question whether the prisoner's answer, by words or conduct, did or did not in fact amount to an acknowledgment of them left to the jury.

In trials of prisoners on indictment, in which the most numerous and important of these cases arise, there is, as a rule, no difficulty in deciding whether there be such evidence or not, as the prisoner's answer appears upon the depositions, and the chance that the evidence with regard to it may be different on the trial is so small that it may be disregarded. When, however, the evidence of the prisoner's answer does not appear, there does not seem to be any practical difficulty in applying the rule above stated. The fact of a statement having been made in the prisoner's presence may be given in evidence, but not the contents, and the question asked, what the prisoner said or did on such a statement being made. If his answer, given either by words or conduct, be such as to be evidence from which an acknowledgment may be inferred, then the contents of the statement may be given and the question of admission or not in fact left to the jury; if it be not evidence from which such an acknowledgment may be inferred, then the contents of the statement should be excluded. To allow the contents of such statements to be given before it is ascertained that there is evidence of their being acknowledged to be true must be most prejudicial to the prisoner, as, whatever directions be given to the jury, it is almost impossible for them to dismiss such evidence entirely from their minds. It is perhaps too wide to say that in no case can the statements be given in evidence when they are denied by the prisoner, as it is possible that a denial may be given under such circumstances and in such a manner as to constitute evidence from which an acknowledgment may be inferred, but, as above stated, we think they should be rejected unless there is some evidence of an acknowledgement of the truth. Where they are admitted we think the following is the proper direction to be given to the jury — that if they come to the conclusion that the prisoner had acknowledged the truth of the whole or any part of the facts stated they might take the statement, or so much of it as was acknowledged to be true (but no more), into consideration as evidence in the case generally, not because the statement standing alone afforded any evidence of the matter contained in it, but solely because of the prisoner's acknowledgment of its truth; but unless they found as a fact that there was such an acknowledgment they ought to disregard the statement altogether: See *R* v *Smith* (1897) 18 Cox CC 470.'

Conviction quashed.

R v *Christie* [1914] AC 545 (HL)

The respondent was convicted of an indecent assault upon a little boy. At the trial the boy's mother stated in evidence that, as she and her son came up to the respondent shortly after the act complained of, the little boy said in the respondent's hearing 'That is the man' and described what the respondent did to him, and that the respondent replied 'I am innocent.' The Court of Criminal Appeal quashed the conviction on the ground that evidence of a statement made in the presence of the accused was not admissible against him unless he acknowledged the truth of the statement. The Crown appealed.

LORD ATKINSON: '. . . the rule of law undoubtedly is that a statement made in the presence of an accused person, even upon an occasion which should be expected reasonably to call for some explanation or denial from him, is not evidence against him of the facts stated save so far as he accepts the statement, so as to make it, in effect, his own. If he accepts the statement in part only, then to that extent alone does it become his statement. He may accept the statement by word or conduct, action or demeanour, and it is the function of the jury which tries the case to determine whether his words, action, conduct, or demeanour at the time when a statement was made amounts to an acceptance of it in whole or in part. It by no means follows, I think, that a mere denial by the accused of the facts mentioned in the statement necessarily renders the statement inadmissible, because he may deny the statement in such a manner and under such circumstances as may lead a jury to disbelieve him, and constitute evidence from which an acknowledgment may be inferred by them.

Of course, if at the end of the case the presiding judge should be of opinion that no evidence has been given upon which the jury could reasonably find that the accused had accepted the statement so as to make it in whole or in part his own, the judge can instruct the jury to disregard the statement entirely. It is said that, despite this direction, grave injustice might be done to the accused, in as much as the jury, having once heard the statement, could not, or would not, rid their mind of it. It is therefore, in the application of the rule that the difficulty arises. The question then is this: Is it to be taken as a rule of law that such a statement is not to be admitted in evidence until a foundation has been laid for its admission by proof of facts from which, in the opinion of the presiding judge, a jury might reasonably draw the inference that the accused had so accepted the statement as to make it in whole or in part his own, or is it to be laid down that the prosecutor is entitled to give the statement in evidence in the first instance, leaving it to the presiding judge, in case no such evidence as the above mentioned should be ultimately produced, to tell the jury to disregard the statement altogether?

In my view the former is not a rule of law, but it is, I think, a rule which, in the interest of justice, it might be most prudent and proper to follow as a rule of practice.

The course suggested by Pickford J in *R* v *Norton* [1910] 2 KB 496, where workable, would be quite unobjectionable in itself as a rule of practice, and equally effective for the protection of the accused.'

LORD MOULTON: 'Now, in a civil action evidence may always be given of any statement or communication made to the opposite party, provided it is relevant to the issues. The same is true of any act or behaviour of the party. The sole limitation is that the matter thus given in evidence must be relevant. I am of opinion that, as a strict matter of law, there is no difference in this respect between the rules of evidence in our civil and in our criminal procedure. But there is a great difference in the practice. The law is so much on its guard against the accused being prejudiced by evidence which, though admissible, would probably have a prejudicial influence on the minds of the jury which would be out of proportion to its true evidential value, that there has grown up a practice of a very salutary nature, under which the judge intimates to the counsel for the prosecution that he should not press for the admission of evidence which would be open to this objection, and such an intimation from the tribunal trying the case is usually sufficient to prevent the evidence being pressed in all cases where the scruples of the tribunal in this respect are reasonable. Under the influence of this practice, which is based on an anxiety to secure for every one a fair trial, there has grown up a custom of not admitting certain kinds of evidence which is so constantly followed that it almost amounts to a rule of procedure. It is alleged on the part of the respondent that an instance of this is the case of the accused being charged with the crime and denying it, or not admitting it.

It is common ground that, if on such an occasion he admits it, evidence can be given of the admission and of what passed on the occasion when it was made. It seems quite illogical that it should be admissible to prove that the accused was charged with the crime if his answer thereto was an admission, while it is not admissible to prove it when his answer has been a denial of the crime, and I cannot agree that the admissibility or non-admissibility is decided as a matter of law by any such artificial rule. Going back to first principles as enunciated above, the deciding question is whether the evidence of the whole occurrence is relevant or not. If the prisoner admits the charge the evidence is obviously relevant. If he denies it, it may or may not be relevant. For instance, if he is charged with a violent assault and denies that he committed it, that fact might be distinctly relevant if at the trial his defence was that he did commit the act, but that it was in self-defence. The evidential value of the occurrence depends entirely on the behaviour of the prisoner, for the fact that someone makes a statement to him subsequently to the commission of the crime cannot in itself have any value as evidence for or against him. The only evidence for or against him is his behaviour in response to the charge, but I can see no justification for laying down as a rule of law that any particular form of response, whether of a positive or negative character, is such that it cannot in some circumstances have an evidential value. I am, therefore, of opinion that there is no rule of law that evidence cannot be given of the accused being charged with the offence and of his behaviour on hearing such charge where that behaviour amounts to a denial of his guilt. This is said to have been laid down as a rule of law in *R* v *Norton*, and to have been followed by the Courts since that decision. If this be so, I think that the decision was wrong, but I am by no means convinced that it was intended in that case to lay down any such rule of law.

But while I am of opinion that there is no such rule of law, I am of opinion that the evidential value of the behaviour of the accused where he denies the charge is very small either for or against him, whereas the effect on the minds of the jury of his being publicly or repeatedly charged to his face with the crime might seriously prejudice the fairness of his trial. In my opinion, therefore, a judge would in most cases be acting in accordance with the best traditions of our criminal procedure if he exercised the influence which he rightly possesses over the conduct of a prosecution in order to prevent such evidence being given in cases where it would have very little or no evidential value. Subject to these words of caution, I am of opinion that this appeal should be allowed upon this point, because we have to decide upon the admissibility as a matter of law, and so regarded I have no doubt that the evidence in question was rightly admitted.'

LORD READING: 'A statement made in the presence of one of the parties to a civil action may be given in evidence against him if it is relevant to any of the matters in issue. And equally such a statement made in the presence of the accused may be given in evidence against him at his trial.

The principles of the laws of evidence are the same whether applied at civil or criminal trials, but they are not enforced with the same rigidity against a person accused of a criminal offence as against a party to a civil action. There are exceptions to the law regulating the admissibility of evidence which apply only to criminal trials, and which have acquired their force by the constant and invariable practice of judges when presiding at criminal trials. They are rules of prudence and discretion, and have become so integral a part of the administration of the criminal law as almost to have acquired the full force of law. . . .

Such practice has found its place in the administration of the criminal law because judges are aware from their experience that in order to ensure a fair trial for the accused, and to prevent the operation of indirect but not the less serious prejudice to his interests, it is desirable in certain circumstances to relax the strict application of the law of evidence. Nowadays, it is the constant practice for the judge who presides at the trial to indicate his opinion to counsel for the prosecution that evidence which, although admissible in law, has little value in its direct bearing upon the case, and might indirectly operate seriously to the prejudice of the accused, should not be given against him, and speaking generally counsel accepts the suggestion and does not press for the admission of the evidence unless he has good reason for it.

That there is danger that the accused may be indirectly prejudiced by the admission of such a statement as in this case is manifest, for however carefully the judge may direct the jury, it is often difficult for them to exclude it altogether from their minds as evidence of the facts contained in the statement.

In general, such evidence can have little or no value in its direct bearing on the case unless the accused, upon hearing the statement, by conduct and demeanour, or by the answer made by him, or in certain circumstances by the refraining from an answer, acknowledged the truth of the statement either in whole or in part, or did or said something from which the jury could infer such an acknowledgment, for if he acknowledged its truth, he accepted it as his own statement of the facts. If the accused denied the truth of the statement when it was made, and there was nothing in his conduct and demeanour from which the jury, notwithstanding his denial, could infer that he acknowledged its truth in whole or in part, the practice of the judges has been to exclude it altogether. In *R* v *Norton* Pickford J, in delivering the judgment of the Court of Criminal Appeal, said at p. 500: "If there be no such evidence" (that is of acknowledgment by the accused), "then the contents of the statement should be excluded; if there be such evidence, then they should be admitted." If it was intended to lay down rules of law to be applied whenever such a statement is tendered for admission, I think the judgment goes too far; they are valuable rules for the guidance of those presiding at trials of criminal cases when considering how the discretion of the Court, with regard to the admission of such evidence, should be exercised, but it must not be assumed that the judgment in *R* v *Norton* exhausts all the circumstances which may have to be taken into consideration by the Court when exercising its judicial discretion.

It might well be that the prosecution wished to give evidence of such a statement in order to prove the conduct and demeanour of the accused when hearing the statement as a relevant fact in the particular case, notwithstanding that it did not amount either to an acknowledgment or some evidence of an acknowledgment of any part of the truth of the statement. I think it impossible to lay down any general rule to be applied to all such cases, save the principle of strict law to which I have referred.

Upon the whole, therefore, I come to the conclusion that the rules formulated in *R v Norton*, and followed in this and other cases, must be restricted in their application as above indicated, and cannot be regarded as strict rules of law regulating the admissibility of such evidence.

I think, therefore, that this statement was in law admissible as evidence against Christie.'

(VISCOUNT HALDANE LC agreed with LORDS ATKINSON, MOULTON, and READING. LORD PARKER OF WADDINGTON agreed with LORD ATKINSON.)

The Court of Criminal Appeal's order quashing the conviction was affirmed on the ground of misdirection by the trial judge on the question of corroboration

Hall v *R* [1971] 1 WLR 298 (PC)

The appellant was said to be living with G and T in a two-roomed building. During a search of the premises in his absence, police officers found 'ganja' in a shopping bag. T said that the appellant had brought the bag there. When a police officer told the appellant what T had said, he remained silent. 'Ganja' was also found in a grip and a brief-case in the room occupied by G, who admitted that the grip was hers but denied any knowledge of the drug. When the appellant, G and T were cautioned, they said nothing. They were charged with unlawful possession of 'ganja', and at their trial they neither gave evidence nor called witnesses, but the appellant and T made a statement from the dock denying all knowledge of the matter. They were convicted. The Court of Appeal for Jamaica, in dismissing the appellant's appeal, held that his silence, when told of the accusation made against him, amounted to an acknowledgement by him of the truth of the statement made by T against him. The appellant further appealed.

LORD DIPLOCK, delivering the judgment of their Lordships: 'In dealing with this question, the Court of Appeal cited the following paragraph from Archbold, *Criminal Pleading Evidence and Practice*, 37th ed (1969), para. 1126:

> A statement made in the presence of an accused person, accusing him of a crime, upon an occasion which may be expected reasonably to call for some explanation or denial from him, is not evidence against him of the facts stated, save in so far as he accepts the statement so as to make it in effect his own. If he accepts the statement in part only, then to that extent alone does it become his statement. He may accept the statement by word or conduct, action or demeanour and it is the function of the jury which tries the case to determine whether his words, action, conduct or demeanour at the time when the statement was made amount to an acceptance of it in whole or in part.

This statement in their Lordships' view states the law accurately. It is a citation from the speech of Lord Atkinson in *R v Christie* [1914] AC 545, 554. But their Lordships do not consider that in the instant case the Court of Appeal applied it correctly. It is not suggested in the instant case that the appellant's acceptance of the suggestion of Daphne Thompson which was repeated to him by the police constable was shown by word or by any positive conduct, action or demeanour. All that is relied upon is his mere silence.

It is a clear and widely known principle of the common law in Jamaica, as in England, that a person is entitled to refrain from answering a question put to him for the purpose of discovering whether he has committed a criminal offence. *A fortiori* he is under no obligation to comment when he is informed that someone else has accused him of an offence. It may be that in very exceptional circumstances an inference may be drawn from a failure to give an explanation or a disclaimer, but in their Lordships' view silence alone on being informed by a police officer that someone else has made an accusation against him cannot give rise to an inference that the person to whom this information is communicated accepts the truth of the accusation.

This is well established by many authorities such as *R* v *Whitehead* [1929] 1 KB 99 and *R* v *Keeling* [1942] 1 All ER 507. Counsel has sought to distinguish these cases on the ground that in them the accused had already been cautioned and told in terms that he was not obliged to reply. Reliance was placed on the earlier case of *R* v *Feigenbaum* [1919] 1 KB 431 where the accused's silence when told of the accusation made against him by some children was held to be capable of amounting to corroboration of their evidence. It was submitted that the distinction between *R* v *Feigenbaum* and the later cases was that no caution had been administered at the time at which the accused was informed of the accusation.

The correctness of the decision in *R* v *Feigenbaum* was doubted in *R* v *Keeling*. In their Lordships' view the distinction sought to be made is not a valid one and *R* v *Feigenbaum* ought not to be followed. The caution merely serves to remind the accused of a right which he already possesses at common law. The fact that in a particular case he has not been reminded of it is no ground for inferring that his silence was not in exercise of that right, but was an acknowledgment of the truth of the accusation.'

Appeal allowed. Conviction quashed.

R v *Chandler* [1976] 1 WLR 585 (CA)

The defendant was convicted of conspiracy to defraud. He had been interviewed by the police in the presence of his solicitor. Both before and after being cautioned he answered some questions, but in relation to others either remained silent or refused to answer them. At the trial the judge in summing up said that a person who had been cautioned had a right to remain silent, but it was for the jury to decide whether the defendant remained silent before caution because of this right or because he might have thought, if he had answered, he would have incriminated himself.

LAWTON LJ, reading the judgment of the court: '[Counsel] invited our attention to what Lord Diplock said in *Hall* v *The Queen* [1971] 1 WLR 298, 301:

> In their Lordships' view the distinction sought to be made — that is that no caution had been given — is not a valid one . . . The caution merely serves to remind the accused of a right which he already possesses at common law. The fact that in a particular case he has not been reminded of it is no ground for inferring that his silence was not in exercise of that right, but was an acknowledgment of the truth of the accusation.

Earlier he had said, at p. 301:

> It is a clear and widely known principle of the common law in Jamaica, as in England, that a person is entitled to refrain from answering a question put to him for

the purpose of discovering whether he has committed a criminal offence. . . . It may be that in very exceptional circumstances an inference may be drawn from a failure to give an explanation or a disclaimer, but in their Lordships' view silence alone on being informed by a police officer that someone else has made an accusation against him cannot give rise to an inference that the person to whom this information is communicated accepts the truth of the accusation.

We have reservations about these two statements of law because they seem to conflict with *R* v *Christie* [1914] AC 545 and with earlier cases and authorities. For reasons which will appear later in this judgment, it is not necessary in this case to review the law relating to the so-called right of silence. The law has long accepted that an accused person is not bound to incriminate himself; but it does not follow that a failure to answer an accusation or question when an answer could reasonably be expected may not provide some evidence in support of an accusation. Whether it does will depend upon the circumstances. We could not improve on what Lord Atkinson said in *R* v *Christie*, at p. 554:

> . . .the rule of law undoubtedly is that a statement made in the presence of an accused person, even upon an occasion which should be expected reasonably to call for some explanation or denial from him, is not evidence against him of the facts stated save so far as he accepts the statement, so as to make it, in effect, his own. . . . He may accept the statement by word or conduct, action or demeanour, and it is the function of the jury which tries the case to determine whether his words, action, conduct, or demeanour at the time when a statement was made amounts to an acceptance of it in whole or in part. It by no means follows, I think, that a mere denial by the accused of the facts mentioned in the statement necessarily renders the statement inadmissible, because he may deny the statement in such a manner and under such circumstances as may lead a jury to disbelieve him, and constitute evidence from which an acknowledgment may be inferred by them.

This statement of the law reflected legal opinion in the 19th century. Thus in *Phillips & Arnold on the Law of Evidence*, 10th ed (1852), vol. 1, p. 334, the law is stated as follows:

> In some cases, it is allowable to give evidence of written or verbal statements made, or of acts done, by others, and then to show how the party who heard or read the statements, or saw the acts done, was affected by them, — for the purpose of using his conduct, expressions or demeanour as evidence against him by way of admission. The evidence in such cases is altogether presumptive in its quality and character. . . . This species of evidence is very commonly used in criminal cases, although it appears to be somewhat inconsistent to hold, that the prisoner's silence on hearing an accusation is evidence against him, when his denial of the charge upon such an occasion would not be evidence for him.

This principle was applied in *Bessela* v *Stern* (1877) 2 CPD 265. In that case, which was an action for breach of promise of marriage, evidence from the plaintiff's sister was accepted as corroboration for the purpose of the statute 32 & 33 Vict. c. 68. This evidence was to the effect that the defendant had made no denial when the plaintiff had upbraided him for having promised to marry her and failing to do so. In *R* v *Mitchell* (1892) 17 Cox CC 503, 508, Cave J said:

> Undoubtedly, when persons are speaking on even terms, and a charge is made, and the person charged says nothing, and expresses no indignation, and does nothing to repel the charge, that is some evidence to show that he admits the charge to be true.

As Professor Sir Rupert Cross commented in his book, *Evidence*, 4th ed, p. 189, in reference to *R* v *Mitchell*, this 'is a broad principle of common sense." Indeed it is. It should not be forgotten that the law of evidence developed in the 18th century and the early part of the 19th century as a result of the search by the judges for rules which could be applied during a trial to obtain reliable testimony and to ensure a fair trial for the accused. The search had been made necessary by the disquiet and concern which had arisen after the perjury of Oates, Bedloe, Dugdale, Dangerfield and Turberville in the Popist Plot trials became known. Appeals such as Lord Diplock made in *Hall* v *The Queen* to the common law for support for a proposition in the law of evidence means seeking, at the earliest, an 18th century precedent. Between 1554 and 1640 a criminal trial bore little resemblance to a modern trial; indeed the examination of the accused in court by counsel for the Crown "was the very essence of the trial": see Stephen, *History of the Criminal Law in England* (1883), vol. 1, p. 326. This went on until the beginning of the 18th century: see J H Wigmore, *Evidence in Trials at Common Law*, 2nd ed (1923), vol. 1, p. 604. It would be unfortunate if the law of evidence was allowed to develop in a way which was not in accordance with the common sense of ordinary folk. We are bound by *R* v *Christie*, not by *Hall* v *The Queen*. *R* v *Christie*, in our judgment, does accord with common sense.

When the judge's comments are examined against the principles enunciated in both *R* v *Mitchell* and *R* v *Christie* we are of the opinion that the defendant and the detective sergeant were speaking on equal terms since the former had his solicitor present to give him any advice he might have wanted and to testify, if needed, as to what had been said. We do not accept that a police officer always has an advantage over someone he is questioning. Everything depends upon the circumstances. A young detective questioning a local dignitary in the course of an inquiry into alleged local government corruption may be very much at a disadvantage. This kind of situation is to be contrasted with that of a tearful housewife accused of shoplifting or of a parent being questioned about the suspected wrongdoing of his son. Some comment on the defendant's lack of frankness before he was cautioned was justified provided the jury's attention was directed to the right issue, which was whether in the circumstances the defendant's silence amounted to an acceptance by him of what the detective sergeant had said. If he accepted what had been said, then the next question should have been whether guilt could reasonably be inferred from what he had accepted. To suggest, as the judge did, that the defendant's silence could indicate guilt was to short-circuit the intellectual process which has to be followed. Phillips in *A Treatise on the Law of Evidence* pointed out this very error, at p. 334:

> It very commonly happens, that evidence of the description referred to has the effect of misleading juries, who are frequently influenced by it . . . and are unable, notwithstanding any directions from a judge, to regard it solely as exhibiting demeanour and conduct. In many instances, especially where no observation has been made by the party on hearing it, the evidence is particularly liable to produce erroneous conclusions. An acquiescence in the truth of the statement is frequently inferred, though the inference may, from a variety of causes, be incorrect. Thus the

evidence is not only fallacious with reference to its object, but in its collateral effect is prejudicial to the investigation of truth.

The same kind of error is seen in the comment which the judge made as to whether the defendant had been evasive in order to protect himself. He may have been; but that was not what the jury had to decide. It follows, in our judgment, that the comments made were not justified and could have led the jury to a wrong conclusion.'
   Appeal allowed.

• Was Lawton LJ right in saying that the words of Lord Diplock in *Hall* v *R* conflicted with *R* v *Christie*?
• What are the practical implications of the decision in Chandler?

Parkes v R [1976] 1 WLR 1251 (PC)

The defendant was charged with the murder of a woman who had died from stab wounds. At his trial the deceased's mother gave evidence that she had found her daughter injured and had gone to the defendant and said, 'What she do you — Why you stab her?'; that the defendant had made no answer and had tried to stab her when she threatened to hold him until the police came. The judge directed the jury that the defendant's failure to reply to the mother's accusation coupled with his conduct immediately afterwards was evidence from which the jury could infer that the defendant had accepted the truth of the accusation. The defendant was convicted and appealed.

LORD DIPLOCK, delivering the judgment of their Lordships: 'In support of the argument that the defendant's failure to answer Mrs Graham's accusation that he had stabbed her daughter was not a matter from which the jury were entitled to draw any inference that the defendant accepted the truth of the accusation the defendant relied on the following passage in the judgment of this Board in *Hall* v *The Queen* [1971] 1 WLR 298, 301:

> It is a clear and widely known principle of the common law in Jamaica, as in England, that a person is entitled to refrain from answering a question put to him for the purpose of discovering whether he has committed a criminal offence. *A fortiori* he is under no obligation to comment when he is informed that someone else has accused him of an offence. It may be that in very exceptional circumstances an inference may be drawn from a failure to give an explanation or a disclaimer, but in their Lordships' view silence alone on being informed by a police officer that someone else has made an accusation against him cannot give rise to an inference that the person to whom this information is communicated accepts the truth of the accusation.

As appears from this passage itself, it was concerned with a case where the person by whom the accusation was communicated to the accused was a police constable whom he knew was engaged in investigating a drug offence. There was no evidence of the defendant's demeanour or conduct when the accusation was made other than the mere fact that he failed to reply to the constable. The passage cited had been preceded by a quotation from a speech of Lord Atkinson in *R* v *Christie* [1914] AC 545, 554, in which it was said that when a statement is made in the presence of an accused person:

He may accept the statement by word or conduct, action or demeanour, and it is the function of the jury which tries the case to determine whether his words, action, conduct or demeanour at the time when the statement was made amount to an acceptance of it in whole or in part.

In the instant case, there is no question of an accusation being made by or in the presence of a police officer or any other person in authority or charged with the investigation of the crime. It was a spontaneous charge made by a mother about an injury done to her daughter. In circumstances such as these, their Lordships agree with the Court of Appeal of Jamaica that the direction given by Cave J in *R* v *Mitchell* (1892) 17 Cox CC 503, 508 (to which their Lordships have supplied the emphasis) is applicable:

Now the whole admissibility of statements of this kind rests upon the consideration that if a charge is made against a person in that person's presence it is reasonable to expect that he or she will immediately deny it, and that the absence of such a denial is some evidence of an admission on the part of the person charged, and of the truth of the charge. *Undoubtedly, when persons are speaking on even terms*, and a charge is made, and the person charged says nothing, and expresses no indignation, and does nothing to repel the charge, that is some evidence to show that he admits the charge to be true.

Here Mrs Graham and the defendant were speaking on even terms. Furthermore, as the Chief Justice pointed out to the jury, the defendant's reaction to the twice-repeated accusation was not one of mere silence. He drew a knife and attempted to stab Mrs Graham in order to escape when she threatened to detain him while the police were sent for. In their Lordships' view, the Chief Justice was perfectly entitled to instruct the jury that the defendant's reactions to the accusations including his silence were matters which they could take into account along with other evidence in deciding whether the defendant in fact committed the act with which he was charged.'
    Appeal dismissed.

Questions for discussion

R v Coke; R v Littleton

1 What arguments should be made for and against the admissibility of:

(a) Coke's alleged reply to D/I Glanvil on being arrested at his flat;
(b) Coke's oral answers at the police station; and
(c) Coke's written statement under caution?

2 What factors will affect the weight of these pieces of evidence, if admitted?
3 What steps should be taken at trial to decide the admissibility of these pieces of evidence?
4 How should the judge direct the jury as to how to regard Coke's written statement under caution in considering the guilt or innocence of Littleton?
5 How should the judge direct the jury with regard to Littleton's denials and silence when questioned about the offence charged?
6 Should the judge admit evidence of Angela Blackstone's words 'that's him' when

identifying Littleton, in the light of Littleton's reply and his pre-arrest answers to the officers? Would your opinion change if Littleton had made no reply?

7 Discuss the admissibility and weight of the admission made by Littleton to his wife at the police station.

Additional question

For some time, MI5 suspected that information relating to SAS activities was being leaked to the Russians, and they decided that the informant was Oliver, an SAS sergeant, a very powerful man, who passed messages to Peter, an elderly clergyman, who was the vicar of a country parish near the SAS barracks. One night, three MI5 officers, Roland, Stephen and Thomas, accompanied by four military policemen, shadowed Oliver, and watched him place some papers in a broken tomb in Peter's churchyard. Roland's evidence is then as follows: 'The four policemen pounced on Oliver, pinned him to the ground and bundled him into a truck; I went with them: Oliver was shaking like a jelly; he said: "It's all Peter's fault — he's been blackmailing me for years". We took him to a police station; I cautioned him, and he made a statement and signed it'. The statement was to the effect that five years previously Peter had caught him molesting a girl in the village; Peter promised not to report him provided he supplied information relating to SAS activities, which he had been doing ever since.

Stephen and Thomas remained in the churchyard, and about an hour later Peter came and took the papers from the tomb. Stephen says: 'I accosted him. Peter said: "Caught at last: I've been on the job for fifty years; I'm a founder-member". He invited us into the vicarage; he showed us the piece of paper, which appeared to refer to a wedding, but Peter said 'It's in code: it's a description of a new machine gun'. I cautioned him: he then spent several hours writing out a statement in longhand'. The statement recounted how Peter joined the Communist party at Cambridge in the 1930s, and named several distinguished persons, dead and alive, as Communist spies; he said that he frequently obtained information about the SAS, but the statement contained no reference to Oliver or any other named member of the SAS.

Oliver and Peter are now on trial: both have retracted their statements. Explain the steps which will be taken, and the factors which the judge will take into account, to decide whether the statements are admissible.

At the first trial-within-the-trial, Oliver gave evidence to the effect that he had been rendered unconscious and remembered nothing between leaving his barracks and waking up in the police station: he was interrogated over several days but never made a confession: eventually, Roland wrote out a statement and asked him to sign it; when he refused, Roland forged his signature. In cross-examination, Roland admitted that Oliver was interrogated over several days, but otherwise he denied Oliver's allegations.

At the second trial-within-the-trial, Peter said that as soon as he invited Stephen and Thomas into the vicarage, Stephen said: 'We'll do a Blunt: if you tell us all you know and name names, we won't prosecute you'. Peter then explained that, since his wife died, he lived alone and was addicted to spy stories; his statement was a fabrication from beginning to end, designed as a leg-pull. In cross-examination:

Counsel: You say your story is false?
Peter: Pure fantasy.

Counsel:	Not a word of truth?
Peter:	Well, I was a Communist at Cambridge; we all were.
Counsel:	Why did you collect the paper from the tomb?
Peter:	There's a crank in the village who is always leaving messages about weddings there.

When Stephen was cross-examined, he said that it was Peter who had initiated the conversation about Blunt and suggested making a deal. On this evidence, do you think it is likely that the statements will be admitted? If they are admitted, how is this likely to affect the remainder of the trial? Can the prosecution give evidence as to what was said at the trials-within-the-trial? Are there any points which the judge should particularly mention in the summing-up?

Further reading

Mirfield, *Confessions* (1985), *passim*.

8   *The Rule against Hearsay (3)*

A: HEARSAY ADMISSIBLE BY STATUTE IN CIVIL CASES

(Suggested preliminary reading: *A Practical Approach to Evidence*, pp. 227–252).

Civil Evidence Act 1968

1(1) In any civil proceedings a statement other than one made by a person while giving oral evidence in those proceedings shall be admissible as evidence of any fact stated therein to the extent that it is so admissible by virtue of any provision of this Part of this Act or by virtue of any other statutory provision or by agreement of the parties, but not otherwise.

(2) In this section 'statutory provision' means any provision contained in, or in an instrument made under, this or any other Act, including any Act passed after this Act.

2(1) In any civil proceedings a statement made, whether orally or in a document or otherwise, by any person, whether called as a witness in those proceedings or not, shall, subject to this section and to rules of court, be admissible as evidence of any fact stated therein of which direct oral evidence by him would be admissible.

(2) Where in any civil proceedings a party desiring to give a statement in evidence by virtue of this section has called or intends to call as a witness in the proceedings the person by whom the statement was made, the statement—

(a)   shall not be given in evidence by virtue of this section on behalf of the party without the leave of the court; and

(b)   without prejudice to paragraph (a) above, shall not be given in evidence by virtue of this section on behalf of that party before the conclusion of the examination-in-chief of the person by whom it was made, except—

(i) where before that person is called the court allows evidence of the making of the statement to be given on behalf of that party by some other person; or

(ii) in so far as the court allows the person by whom the statement was made to narrate it in the course of his examination-in-chief on the ground that to prevent him from doing so would adversely affect the intelligibility of his evidence.

(3) Where in any civil proceedings a statement which was made otherwise than in a document is admissible by virtue of this section, no evidence other than direct oral evidence by the person who made the statement or any person who heard or otherwise perceived it being made shall be admissible for the purpose of proving it:

Provided that if the statement in question was made by a person while giving oral evidence in some other legal proceedings (whether civil or criminal), it may be proved in any manner authorized by the court.

3(1) Where in any civil proceedings—

(a)   a previous inconsistent or contradictory statement made by a person called as a
        witness in those proceedings is proved by virtue of section 3, 4 or 5 of the
        Criminal Procedure Act, 1865; or

(b)   a previous statement made by a person called as aforesaid is proved for the
        purpose of rebutting a suggestion that his evidence has been fabricated,

that statement shall by virtue of this subsection be admissible as evidence of any fact
stated therein of which direct oral evidence by him would be admissible.

(2) Nothing in this Act shall affect any of the rules of law relating to the circumstances
in which, where a person called as a witness in any civil proceedings is cross-examined on
a document used by him to refresh his memory, that document may be made evidence in
those proceedings: and where a document or any part of a document is received in
evidence in any such proceedings by virtue of any such rule of law, any statement made in
that document or part by the person using the document to refresh his memory shall by
virtue of this subsection be admissible as evidence of any fact stated therein of which
direct oral evidence by him would be admissible.

4(1) Without prejudice to section 5 of this Act, in any civil proceedings a statement
contained in a document shall, subject to this section and to rules of court, be admissible
as evidence of any fact stated therein of which direct oral evidence would be admissible, if
the document is, or forms part of, a record compiled by a person acting under a duty from
information which was supplied by a person (whether acting under a duty or not) who
had, or may reasonably be supposed to have had, personal knowledge of the matters dealt
with in that information and which, if not supplied by that person to the compiler of the
record directly, was supplied by him to the compiler of the record indirectly through one
or more intermediaries each acting under a duty.

(2) Where in any civil proceedings a party desiring to give a statement in evidence by
virtue of this section has called or intends to call as a witness in the proceedings the person
who originally supplied the information from which the record containing the statement
was compiled, the statement—

(a)   shall not be given in evidence by virtue of this section on behalf of that party
        without the leave of the court; and

(b)   without prejudice to paragraph (a) above, shall not without the leave of the
        court be given in evidence by virtue of this section on behalf of that party before
        the conclusion of the examination in chief of the person who originally supplied
        the said information.

(3) Any reference in this section to a person acting under a duty includes a reference to
a person acting in the course of any trade, business, profession or other occupation in
which he is engaged or employed or for the purposes of any paid or unpaid office held by
him.

5(1) In any civil proceedings a statement contained in a document produced by a
computer shall, subject to rules of court, be admissible as evidence of any fact stated
therein of which direct oral evidence would be admissible, if it is shown that the
conditions mentioned in subsection (2) below are satisfied in relation to the statement and
computer in question.

(2) The said conditions are—

(a) that the document containing the statement was produced by the computer during a period over which the computer was used regularly to store or process information for the purposes of any activities regularly carried on over that period, whether for profit or not, by any body, whether corporate or not, or by any individual;

(b) that over that period there was regularly supplied to the computer in the ordinary course of those activities information of the kind contained in the statement or of the kind from which the information so contained is derived;

(c) that throughout the material part of that period the computer was operating properly or, if not, that any respect in which it was not operating properly or was out of operation during that part of that period was not such as to affect the production of the document or the accuracy of its contents; and

(d) that the information contained in the statement reproduces or is derived from information supplied to the computer in the ordinary course of those activities.

(3) Where over a period the function of storing or processing information for the purposes of any activities regularly carried on over that period as mentioned in subsection (2)(a) above was regularly performed by computers, whether—

(a) by a combination of computers operating over that period; or

(b) by different computers operating in succession over that period; or

(c) by different combinations of computers operating in succession over that period; or

(d) in any other manner involving the successive operation over that period, in whatever order, of one or more computers and one or more combinations of computers,

all the computers used for that purpose during that period shall be treated for the purposes of this Part of this Act as constituting a single computer; and references in this Part of this Act to a computer shall be construed accordingly.

(4) In any civil proceedings where it is desired to give a statement in evidence by virtue of this section, a certificate doing any of the following things, that is to say—

(a) identifying the document containing the statement and describing the manner in which it was produced;

(b) giving such particulars of any device involved in the production of that document as may be appropriate for the purpose of showing that the document was produced by a computer;

(c) dealing with any of the matters to which the conditions mentioned in subsection (2) above relate,

and purporting to be signed by a person occupying a responsible position in relation to the operation of the relevant device or the management of the relevant activities (whichever is appropriate) shall be evidence of any matter stated in the certificate; and for the purposes of this subsection it shall be sufficient for a matter to be stated to the best of the knowledge and belief of the person stating it.

(5) For the purposes of this Part of this Act—

(a) information shall be taken to be supplied to a computer if it is supplied thereto in any appropriate form and whether it is so supplied directly or (with or without human intervention) by means of any appropriate equipment;

(b) where, in the course of activities carried on by any individual or body, information is supplied with a view to its being stored or processed for the purposes of those activities by a computer operated otherwise than in the course of those activities, that information, if duly supplied to that computer, shall be taken to be supplied to it in the course of those activities;

(c) a document shall be taken to have been produced by a computer whether it was produced by it directly or (with or without human intervention) by means of any appropriate equipment.

(6) Subject to subsection (3) above, in this Part of this Act 'computer' means any device for storing and processing information, and any reference to information being derived from other information is a reference to its being derived therefrom by calculation, comparison or any other process.

6(1) Where in any civil proceedings a statement contained in a document is proposed to be given in evidence by virtue of section 2, 4 or 5 of this Act it may, subject to any rules of court, be proved by the production of that document or (whether or not that document is still in existence) by the production of a copy of that document, or of the material part thereof, authenticated in such manner as the court may approve.

(2) For the purpose of deciding whether or not a statement is admissible in evidence by virtue of section 2, 4 or 5 of this Act, the court may draw any reasonable inference from the circumstances in which the statement was made or otherwise came into being or from any other circumstances, including, in the case of a statement contained in a document, the form and contents of that document.

(3) In estimating the weight, if any, to be attached to a statement admissible in evidence by virtue of section 2, 3, 4 or 5 of this Act regard shall be had to all the circumstances from which any inference can reasonably be drawn as to the accuracy or otherwise of the statement and, in particular—

(a) in the case of a statement falling within section 2(1) or 3(1) or (2) of this Act, to the question whether or not the statement was made contemporaneously with the occurrence or existence of the facts stated, and to the question whether or not the maker of the statement had any incentive to conceal or misrepresent the facts;

(b) in the case of a statement falling within section 4(1) of this Act, to the question whether or not the person who originally supplied the information from which the record containing the statement was compiled did so contemporaneously with the occurrence or existence of the facts dealt with in that information, and to the question whether or not that person, or any person concerned with compiling or keeping the record containing the statement, had any incentive to conceal or misrepresent the facts; and

(c) in the case of a statement falling within section 5(1) of this Act, to the question whether or not the information which the information contained in the statement reproduces or is derived from was supplied to the relevant computer, or recorded for the purpose of being supplied thereto, contemporaneously with the occurrence or existence of the facts dealt with in that information, and to the question whether or not any person concerned with the supply of information to that computer or with the operation of that computer or any equipment by means of which the document containing the statement was produced by it, had any incentive to conceal or misrepresent the facts.

(4) For the purpose of any enactment or rule of law or practice requiring evidence to be corroborated or regulating the manner in which uncorroborated evidence is to be treated—

(a) a statement which is admissible in evidence by virtue of section 2 or 3 of this Act shall not be capable of corroborating evidence given by the maker of the statement; and

(b) a statement which is admissible in evidence by virtue of section 4 of this Act shall not be capable of corroborating evidence given by the person who originally supplied the information from which the record containing the statement was compiled.

(5) If any person in a certificate tendered in evidence in civil proceedings by virtue of section 5(4) of this Act wilfully makes a statement material in those proceedings which he knows to be false or does not believe to be true, he shall be liable on conviction on indictment to imprisonment for a term not exceeding two years or a fine or both.

7(1) Subject to rules of court, where in any civil proceedings a statement made by a person who is not called as a witness in those proceedings is given in evidence by virtue of section 2 of this Act—

(a) any evidence which, if that person had been so called would be admissible for the purpose of destroying or supporting his credibility as a witness shall be admissible for that purpose in those proceedings; and

(b) evidence tending to prove that, whether before or after he made that statement, that person made (whether orally or in a document or otherwise) another statement inconsistent therewith shall be admissible for the purpose of showing that that person has contradicted himself.

Provided that nothing in this subsection shall enable evidence to be given of any matter of which, if the person in question had been called as a witness and had denied that matter in cross-examination, evidence could not have been adduced by the cross-examining party.

(2) Subsection (1) above shall apply in relation to a statement given in evidence by virtue of section 4 of this Act as it applies in relation to a statement given in evidence by virtue of section 2 of this Act, except that references to the person who made the statement and to his making the statement shall be construed respectively as references to the person who originally supplied the information from which the record containing the statement was compiled and to his supplying that information.

(3) Section 3(1) of this Act shall apply to any statement proved by virtue of subsection (1)(b) above as it applies to a previous inconsistent or contradictory statement made by a person called as a witness which is proved as mentioned in paragraph (a) of the said section 3(1).

8(1) Provision shall be made by rules of court as to the procedure which, subject to any exceptions provided for in the rules, must be followed and the other conditions which, subject as aforesaid, must be fulfilled before a statement can be given in evidence in civil proceedings by virtue of section 2, 4 or 5 of this Act.

(2) Rules of court made in pursuance of subsection (1) above shall in particular, subject to such exceptions (if any) as may be provided for in the rules—

> (a) require a party to any civil proceedings who desires to give in evidence any such statement as is mentioned in that subsection to give to every other party to the proceeding such notice of his desire to do so and such particulars of or relating to the statement as may be specified in the rules, including particulars of such one or more of the persons connected with the making or recording of the statement or, in the case of a statement falling within section 5(1) of this Act, such one or more of the persons concerned as mentioned in section 6(3)(c) of this Act as the rules may in any case require; and

> (b) enable any party who receives such notice as aforesaid by counter-notice to require any person of whom particulars were given with the notice to be called as a witness in the proceedings unless that person is dead, or beyond the seas, or unfit by reason of his bodily or mental condition to attend as a witness, or cannot with reasonable diligence be identified or found, or cannot reasonably be expected (having regard to the time which has elapsed since he was connected or concerned as aforesaid and to all the circumstances) to have any recollection of matters relevant to the accuracy or otherwise of the statement.

(3) Rules of court made in pursuance of subsection (1) above—

> (a) may confer on the court in any civil proceedings a discretion to allow a statement falling within section 2(1), 4(1) or 5(1) of this Act to be given in evidence notwithstanding that any requirement of the rules affecting the admissibility of that statement has not been complied with, but except in pursuance of paragraph (b) below shall not confer on the court a discretion to exclude such a statement where the requirements of the rules affecting its admissibility have been complied with;

> (b) may confer on the court power, where a party to any civil proceedings has given notice that he desires to give in evidence—

>> (i) a statement falling within section 2(1) of this Act which was made by a person, whether orally or in a document, in the course of giving evidence in some other legal proceedings (whether civil or criminal); or
>> (ii) a statement falling within section 4(1) of this Act which is contained in a record of any direct oral evidence given in some other legal proceedings (whether civil or criminal).

> to give directions on the application of any party to the proceedings as to whether, and if so on what conditions, the party desiring to give the statement in evidence will be permitted to do so and (where applicable) as to the manner in which that statement and any other evidence given in those other proceedings is to be proved; and

(c) may make different provision for different circumstances, and in particular may make different provision with respect to statements falling within section 2(1), 4(1) and 5(1) of this Act respectively;

and any discretion conferred on the court by rules of court made as aforesaid may be either a general discretion or a discretion exercisable only in such circumstances as may be specified in the rules.

(4) Rules of court may make provision for preventing a party to any civil proceedings (subject to any exceptions provided for in the rules) from adducing in relation to a person who is not called as a witness in those proceedings any evidence which could otherwise be adduced by him by virtue of section 7 of this Act unless that party has in pursuance of the rules given in respect of that person such a counter-notice as is mentioned in subsection (2)(b) above.

(5) In deciding for the purpose of any rules of court made in pursuance of this section whether or not a person is fit to attend as a witness, a court may act on a certificate purporting to be a certificate of a fully registered medical practitioner.

9(1) In any civil proceedings a statement which, if this Part of this Act had not been passed, would by virtue of any rule of law mentioned in subsection (2) below have been admissible as evidence of any fact stated therein shall be admissible as evidence of that fact by virtue of this subsection.

(2) The rules of law referred to in subsection (1) above are the following, that is to say any rule of law—

(a) whereby in any civil proceedings an admission adverse to a party to the proceedings, whether made by that party or by another person, may be given in evidence against that party for the purpose of proving any fact stated in the admission;

(b) whereby in any civil proceedings published works dealing with matters of a public nature (for example, histories, scientific works, dictionaries and maps) are admissible as evidence of facts of a public nature stated therein;

(c) whereby in any civil proceedings public documents (for example, public registers, and returns made under public authority with respect to matters of public interest) are admissible as evidence of facts stated therein; or

(d) whereby in any civil proceedings records (for example, the records of certain courts, treaties, Crown grants, pardons and commissions) are admissible as evidence of facts stated therein.

In this subsection 'admission' includes any representation of fact, whether made in words or otherwise.

(3) In any civil proceedings a statement which tends to establish reputation or family tradition with respect to any matter and which, if this Act had not been passed, would have been admissible in evidence by virtue of any rule of law mentioned in subsection (4) below—

(a) shall be admissible in evidence by virtue of this paragraph in so far as it is not capable of being rendered admissible under section 2 or 4 of this Act; and

(b) if given in evidence under this Part of this Act (whether by virtue of paragraph (a) above or otherwise) shall by virtue of this paragraph be admissible as evidence of the matter reputed or handed down;

and, without prejudice to paragraph (b) above, reputation shall for the purposes of this Part of this Act be treated as a fact and not as a statement or multiplicity of statements dealing with the matter reputed.

(4) The rules of law referred to in subsection (3) above are the following, that is to say any rule of law—

    (a)   whereby in any civil proceedings evidence of a person's reputation is admissible for the purpose of establishing his good or bad character;

    (b)   whereby in any civil proceedings involving a question of pedigree or in which the existence of a marriage is in issue evidence of reputation or family tradition is admissible for the purpose of proving or disproving pedigree or the existence of the marriage, as the case may be; or

    (c)   whereby in any civil proceedings evidence of reputation or family tradition is admissible for the purpose of proving or disproving the existence of any public or general right or of identifying any person or thing.

(5) It is hereby declared that in so far as any statement is admissible in any civil proceedings by virtue of subsection (1) or (3)(a) above, it may be given in evidence in those proceedings notwithstanding anything in sections 2 to 7 of this Act or in any rules of court made in pursuance of section 8 of this Act.

(6) The words in which any rule of law mentioned in subsection (2) or (4) above is there described are intended only to identify the rule in question and shall not be construed as altering that rule in any way.

10(1) In this Part of this Act—

'computer' has the meaning assigned by section 5 of this Act;

'document' includes, in addition to a document in writing—

    (a)   any map, plan, graph or drawing;

    (b)   any photograph;

    (c)   any disc, tape, sound track or other device in which sounds or other data (not being visual images) are embodied so as to be capable (with or without the aid of some other equipment) of being reproduced therefrom; and

    (d)   any film, negative, tape or other device in which one or more visual images are embodied so as to be capable (as aforesaid) of being reproduced therefrom;

        'film' includes a microfilm;

        'statement' includes any representation of fact, whether made in words or otherwise.

(2) In this Part of this Act any reference to a copy of a document includes—

    (a)   in the case of a document falling within paragraph (c) but not (d) of the definition of 'document' in the foregoing subsection, a transcript of the sounds or other data embodied therein;

    (b)   in the case of a document falling within paragraph (d) but not (c) of that definition, a reproduction or still reproduction of the image or images embodied therein, whether enlarged or not;

    (c)   in the case of a document falling within both those paragraphs, such a transcript together with such a still reproduction; and

(d) in the case of a document not falling within the said paragraph (d) of which a visual image is embodied in a document falling within that paragraph, a reproduction of that image, whether enlarged or not.

and any reference to a copy of the material part of a document shall be construed accordingly.

- How does the Act deal with implied assertions?
- Do ss. 2 and 4 overlap at all? If so, in what way?

Civil Evidence Act 1972

1(1) Subject to the provisions of this section, Part I (hearsay evidence) of the Civil Evidence Act 1968, except section 5 (statements produced by computers), shall apply in relation to statements of opinion as it applies in relation to statements of fact, subject to the necessary modifications and in particular the modification that any reference to a fact stated in a statement shall be construed as a reference to a matter dealt with therein.

(2) Section 4 (admissibility of certain records) of the Civil Evidence Act 1968, as applied by subsection (1) above, shall not render admissible in any civil proceedings a statement of opinion contained in a record unless that statement would be admissible in those proceedings if made in the course of giving oral evidence by the person who originally supplied the information from which the record was compiled; but where a statement of opinion contained in a record deals with a matter on which the person who originally supplied the information from which the record was compiled is (or would if living be) qualified to give oral expert evidence, the said section 4, as applied by subsection (1) above, shall have effect in relation to that statement as if so much of subsection (1) of that section as requires personal knowledge on the part of that person was omitted.

Knight and others v *David and others* [1971] 1 WLR 1671 (ChD)

A claim by the plaintiffs to certain land depended upon events which occurred in 1886, and for the purpose of establishing that claim, the plaintiffs sought to put in evidence a tithe map and tithe apportionment survey, made under the provisions of the Tithe Act 1836.

GOULDING J: ' . . . the plaintiffs rely on section 4 of the Civil Evidence Act 1968, the material part of which is contained in subsection (1) . . .

Mr Francis argued that the tithe document is not within that subsection on either or both of two grounds: First, he says that the statements therein are statements relating to title, and direct oral evidence of title would not be admissible. I find this perhaps the most difficult point in the question I am considering, but, on the whole, I conclude that Mr Francis's argument must fail if a living person could state in evidence that the machinery of the Act was carried out, and that a certain person was, and another was not, entered as proprietor of certain land. In my judgment, such a statement would be admissible.

Mr Francis's second point was that it was not established that the record compiled by the officers under the Act of 1836 was compiled from information supplied by persons who had, or might be supposed to have had, personal knowledge of the matters dealt with. In my judgment, having regard to the nature of the document and the lapse of time, it is right for the court to infer that this condition is satisfied. Therefore . . . I should also be prepared to admit this evidence under section 4 of the Act of 1968.

H v *Schering Chemicals Ltd* [1983] 1 WLR 143 (QBD)

The plaintiffs claimed damages for personal injuries alleged to have been caused by the effect of a drug marketed and manufactured by the defendant pharmaceutical company. They wished to introduce copies of certain specified documents, which they claimed were records for the purposes of s. 4 of the Civil Evidence Act 1968. The documents included summaries of the results of research, articles and letters published in medical journals concerning the drug.

BINGHAM J: 'The first question in this case is whether these documents are records. Mr Weitzman submits that the tendency which the Act was intended to advance is towards admitting hearsay evidence, subject always to the questions of weight which are left for the determination of the trial court. He further points out that the word 'record' is given a wide meaning, and he is certainly right in submitting that in *R* v *Jones (Benjamin)* [1978] 1 WLR 195, a very wide meaning is given to that expression, significantly wider than was indicated in *R* v *Tirado* (1974) 59 Cr App R 80, 90.

Mr Beldam submits that, be that as it may, these documents, in issue in this case, are simply not records. They are, he says, an analysis of records or a digest of records but not themselves a record. He further says that there is a danger in admitting material, sometimes said in the course of the material itself to be tentative, and that there is too much unknown about the research underlying these documents to make it safe to admit them as evidence.

Having considered the matter as best I can in the light of the arguments and the authorities, I have come to the conclusion that the documents which form part of the large bundle before me are not records within the meaning of section 4 of the Act. The intention of that section was, I believe, to admit in evidence records which a historian would regard as original or primary sources, that is, documents which either give effect to a transaction itself or which contain a contemporaneous register of information supplied by those with direct knowledge of the facts.

Judged by this standard, the commercial documents in *R* v *Jones (Benjamin)* [1978] 1 WLR 195; the tithe map in *Knight* v *David* [1971] 1 WLR 1671; the record in *Edmonds* v *Edmonds* [1947] P67 and the transcript in *Taylor (J)* v *Taylor (IL)* [1970] 1 WLR 1148, would rank as records, as in those cases they were held to be. On the other hand, the documents in *Ioannou* v *Demetriou* [1952] AC 84; the file of letters in *R* v *Tirado*, 59 Cr App R 80, and the summary of cases in *In re Koscot Interplanetary (UK) Ltd* [1972] 3 All ER 829, would fail to be admitted as records, as in the first two cases they did.

Judged by the same standard the documents in the present case, I think, are not records and are not primary or original sources. They are a digest or analysis of records which must exist or have existed, but they are not themselves those records. If the plaintiffs' submission were right it would, I think, mean that anyone who wrote a letter to *The Times*, having done research and summarising the result of that research in his letter, would find his letter admissible as evidence of the facts under section 4. That is not, I think, the intent of the section, and accordingly, whatever counter-notice was served in response to the plaintiffs' notice the effect would not, in my judgment, be to make the evidence admissible under section 4.'

Application dismissed.

Rasool v West Midlands Passenger Transport Executive [1974] 3 All ER 638 (QBD)

The plaintiff commenced an action against the defendants for damages in respect of personal injuries sustained by him as a result of the negligence of a bus driver employed by the defendants. The defendants served notice on the plaintiff under RSC, Ord 38, r.21(1), of their intention to give in evidence at the trial a statement made by C who had been an eye-witness to the plaintiff's accident. C's statement was to the effect that the bus driver was in no way to blame for the accident. The defendant's notice asserted that C could not be called as a witness since 'she has left her former address in Birmingham and cannot at present be found. It is understood that she is now beyond the seas and is probably resident in Jamaica'. On the available evidence, this account appeared to be accurate, although the defendants had made no effort to trace C there. It was contended for the plaintiff that C's statement was inadmissible since, although C was beyond the seas, it was still necessary under s.8(2)(b) of the Civil Evidence Act 1968 for the defendants to prove that despite the exercise of reasonable diligence she could not be found.

FINER J: 'In amending the law regarding the admissibility of hearsay evidence in civil proceedings, the Civil Evidence Act 1968, as appears from ss.1 and 8, left much of the detail to be worked out by rules of court which are now to be found in Part III of RSC, Ord 38. Many of the questions which arise thus entail a reading of the 1968 Act and of the rules in close conjunction with each other. The scheme of things, so fas as material in the present circumstances, may be summarised as follows. Section 2(1) of the 1968 Act provides:

> In any civil proceedings a statement made, whether orally or in a document or otherwise, by any person, whether called as a witness in those proceedings or not, shall, subject to this section and to rules of court, be admissible as evidence of any fact stated therein of which direct oral evidence by him would be admissible. . ..

Section 8 of the 1968 Act enacts further that provision shall be made by rules of court as to the procedure which must be followed and the other conditions which must be fulfilled before a statement can be given in evidence by virtue of s.2. Section 8(2) sets out requirements to which the rules must conform. Subject to such exceptions, if any, which may be provided for in the rules themselves they must, in the first instance, require the party desiring to put in the statement to give to every other party to the proceedings notice of such desire, with such particulars, as may be specified in the rules. Secondly, by s.8(2)(b) the rules must—

> . . . enable any party who receives such notice . . . by counter-notice to require any person of whom particulars were given with the notice to be called as a witness in the proceedings unless that person is dead, or beyond the seas, or unfit by reason of his bodily or mental condition to attend as a witness, or cannot with reasonable diligence be identified or found, or cannot reasonably be expected . . . to have any recollection of matters relevant to the accuracy or otherwise of the statement.

Thirdly, it is provided by s.8(3)(a) that although the rules may confer on the court a discretion to allow a statement to be given in evidence notwithstanding that the requirements of the rules have not been complied with, they cannot, subject to immaterial exceptions, "confer on the court a discretion to exclude such a statement where the requirements of the rules . . . have been complied with".

Turning now to the rules, RSC Ord 38, rr.21 and 22(2) provide for the notice to be given in the case of a statement admissible by virtue of s.2 of the 1968 Act and made in a document. Rule 22(3) provides:

> If the party giving the notice alleges that any person, particulars of whom are contained in the notice, cannot or should not be called as a witness at the trial or hearing for any of the reasons specified in rule 25, the notice must contain a statement to that effect specifying the reason relied on.

The reasons specified in r.25 are the same as those mentioned in s.8(2)(b) to which I have already referred, as disentitling the recipient of a notice to require the witness to be called in the proceedings. Rule 26(2) then provides:

> Where any notice under rule 21 contains a statement that any person particulars of whom are contained in the notice cannot or should not be called as a witness for the reason specified therein, a party shall not be entitled to serve a counter-notice under this rule requiring that person to be called as a witness at the trial or hearing of the cause or matter unless he contends that that person can or, as the case may be, should be called, and in that case he must include in his counter-notice a statement to that effect.

Finally, r.27(1) provides:

> Where . . . a question arises whether any of the reasons specified in rule 25 applies in relation to a person particulars of whom are contained in a notice under rule 21, the Court may, on the application of any party . . . determine that question before the trial or hearing of the cause or matter or give directions for it to be determined before the trial or hearing and for the manner in which it is to be so determined.

Now the short effect of all these complicated provisions seems to be as follows: that the system for adducing a written statement in evidence without calling the maker involves the service by the party wishing to take that course on the other parties of a notice in a prescribed form. A party receiving such a notice who objects to the proposal to put in the statement can, by an appropriate counter-notice, require the witness to be called, failing which the statement (subject to an overriding discretion which the court has to admit it under r.29) will be excluded. This right of objection, however, is modified in the case where the stated reason for desiring to put the statement in evidence without calling the witness is one or other of the five reasons mentioned in s.8(2)(b) of the 1968 Act and r.25. In such a case the objecting party must, despite the assertion in the notice that the witness cannot or should not be called because he is dead, or beyond the seas, or as the case may be, state in his counter-notice that the witness can or should be called. This raises the issue as to the truth or validity of the reason relied on, and that issue will be determined, as it is being now, under the procedure laid down by r.27.

In the instant case, the defendants' notice to the plaintiff asserted that Mrs Collum could not be called as a witness at the hearing because—

she has left her former address number 325 Charles Road, Small Heath, Birmingham and cannot at present be found. It is understood that she is now beyond the seas and is probably resident in Jamaica.

Strictly speaking, this probably invokes only one of the five specified reasons, namely that despite the exercise of reasonable diligence it was not possible to find the witness. By common consent however, the notice at the hearing before myself was treated as invoking both that reason and the further reason that Mrs Collum was beyond the seas . . ..

[As] I read s.8(2)(b) of the 1968 Act and the rules which reflect it, the five reasons that may be relied on for not calling a witness are disjunctive reasons. If the maker of the statement is beyond the seas it does not have to be proved also that he cannot by reasonable diligence be found. His whereabouts abroad may be precisely known, yet if it be established that he is indeed abroad that is in itself a sufficient reason for admitting the statement. It would follow that the application in this case (the terms of which were followed in the order) should not have been based on the ground that Mrs Collum had left her former address and could not be found. The real ground was that she was beyond the seas.

In finding, however, that the absence of the maker beyond the seas is a sufficient reason in itself for admitting the statement, even if no effort is made to trace the precise whereabouts of the proposed witness, or even if those whereabouts are known, I have deliberately elided the question whether the court nevertheless has any discretion to exclude it. At first sight it seems peculiar that there should be no such discretion. Take the case of a witness who has been party to a conversation in which it is common ground that the plaintiff and defendant made a contract, but they dispute the terms they agreed. The witness lives at a known address in Paris, despite which the plaintiff seeks to adduce his evidence in the form of a statement, relying on the fact the witness is beyond the seas. Or in the present case, one may imagine that it was Mrs Collum, a professed eye-witness to a serious accident whose statement may damn the plaintiff, who lived at a known address in Paris. Nevertheless, I find it a clear conclusion from the provisions of the statute and the rules which I have earlier mentioned that if the court is satisfied on any of the five specified reasons the statement becomes admissible, and there is no residuary discretion to exclude it by reference to other circumstances. The relevant provisions leave no room for such a discretion. The scheme of the law is that the counter-notice is ineffectual unless it raises an issue regarding the reason alleged in the notice which is ultimately determined in favour of the giver of the counter-notice. If the counter-notice is ineffectual, the notice takes effect. I consider that this would be the result even apart from s.8(3)(a), but that provision clinches the point by providing in terms that the rules cannot—with the exceptions provided for in s.8(3)(b), which has no application to the present case—confer on the court a discretion to exclude a statement where the requirements of the rules affecting its admissibility have been complied with.

The weight to be attached to the statement admitted in evidence remains a matter for the court. In the circumstances postulated in the examples I gave, where the whereabouts abroad of an important witness in a substantial case are known or can be easily ascertained, but the party relying on his evidence nevertheless adopts a method of adducing it which does not permit of cross-examination, no doubt the court would pay little attention to it. It may be that this is a risk which the defendants run if they make no efforts to find Mrs Collum in Jamaica, so as to permit at least the possibility of evidence being taken on commission. But all that will be a matter for the trial judge.

I should add that in deciding as I have on the matter of discretion I have not overlooked s.18(5) of the 1968 Act which provides that nothing in the Act—

> shall prejudice . . . any power of a court, in any legal proceedings, to exclude evidence (whether by preventing questions from being put or otherwise) at its discretion . . .

The exact meaning of this provision would be an interesting field for enquiry in appropriate circumstances, but it has no relevance that I can detect for the present case.

As I have already explained, the defendants' notice was out of order in that it specified a reason which I doubt whether they made out, and did not specify the good reason on which they have succeeded. This matter has been argued, however, on the footing that the defect is waived. I shall vary the registrar's order by substituting for the words 'because she has left her former address number 325 Charles Road, Small Heath, Birmingham and cannot at present be found', the words 'because she is beyond the seas'. The order will otherwise be affirmed.'

Appeal dismissed.

Ford v *Lewis* [1971] 1 WLR 623 (CA)

The infant plaintiff, who was attempting to cross a road, was struck by a van driven by the defendant. The plaintiff was at the material time in the charge of her parents. By the time of the trial (ten years later) the defendant had become a patient in a mental hospital and it was agreed that he was unfit to be called as a witness. At the trial his counsel sought to put in evidence, under s.2(1) of the Civil Evidence Act 1968, a photostat copy of a written statement, proved by the guardian *ad litem* to be in the defendant's handwriting, giving his version of the accident, and also, under s.4(1) of the Act, hospital records relating to the plaintiff's father which stated that he had been in a state of intoxication when admitted to hospital after the accident. No notice of intention to put those documents in evidence had been served on the plaintiff's advisers as required by RSC, Ord 38, rr.21(1), 22 and 23, and the reason for non-compliance was not disclosed to the judge. Plaintiff's counsel refused an adjournment offered by the judge who thereupon, in the exercise of his discretion under RSC, Ord 38, r.29(1), admitted the documents. He found that the statement attributed to the defendant rang true, acquitted him of negligence and dismissed the claim.

The plaintiff appealed on the ground that the judge had wrongly exercised his discretion in permitting the admission of the defendant's statement and the hospital notes.

EDMUND DAVIES LJ: '[T]he point of substance involved in this appeal relates to the application of the Civil Evidence Act 1968 and RSC, Ord 38, to the circumstances of this case . . ..

Section 8(1) provides for the making of rules of court "as to the procedure which, subject to any exceptions provided for in the rules, must be followed before a statement can be given in evidence in civil proceedings by virtue of section 2 . . . of this Act." . . ..

Rule 21 thereof makes it obligatory on the party desiring to adduce hearsay evidence by virtue of section 2 of the Act to serve notice on the other party of his intention to do so. If he does not, he will, subject to the court's discretion under rule 29, be precluded from giving the statement in evidence. Rule 22 provides that 'the notice must contain particulars of —(a) the time, place and circumstances at or in which the statement was made; (b) the person by whom, and the person to whom, the statement was made; . . .' Furthermore, 'If the statement . . . was made in a document, a copy or transcript of the document, or of the relevant part thereof, must be annexed to the notice'. Finally,

> If the party giving the notice alleges that any person, particulars of whom are contained in the notice, cannot or should not be called as a witness at the trial or hearing for any of the reasons specified . . ., the notice must contain a statement to that effect specifying the reason relied on.

Rule 26 enables the party receiving such a notice to serve a counter-notice, requiring the other side to call as a witness at the trial any person to whom the original notice related. If that counter-notice is served, rule 27 provides the machinery whereby the necessity for the absent maker of the statement being actually called as a witness can be decided before the trial.

It is well known that the statutory provisions which led to the formulation of these rules were the subject matter of considerable controversy. On the one hand, there were the die-hards who would have no further relaxation of the prohibition against hearsay than that already provided by the Evidence Act 1938. On the other hand, there were those who clamoured under modern conditions for a far more relaxed approach to the problem. A compromise was finally reached within the terms of section 8 of the Act of 1968 and its offspring RSC, Ord 38. The object of the latter is expressed with admirable clarity in the notes thereto which appear in the *Supreme Court Practice* (1970), and I cannot do better than to quote them. I am quoting from the thin supplement, para. 38/20/6:

> The machinery of Part III of this Order is designed to achieve two main objectives, namely, (a) that all questions concerning the giving of hearsay evidence at the trial should, so far as practicable, be dealt with and disposed of before the trial, so that the trial itself should proceed smoothly without unnecessary objections relating to such hearsay evidence, and (b) that in relation to any hearsay evidence which any party desires to adduce, there should be no surprises at the trial. In this latter respect, it is to be noted that the machinery of Part III of this Order makes a departure from the general rule of practice that a party is not required to disclose the evidence which he intends to adduce at the trial, for these rules do require such disclosure of the proposed hearsay evidence to be made. The principle is that if a party wishes to obtain the advantage of adducing secondary evidence at the trial, he should pay the price of disclosing such evidence before the trial, and affording the other party the opportunity to resist its admission in that form.

That being the object of Order 38, it is common ground that the defendant never did comply with it. For a substantial period his advisers had been in possession of a statement attributed to him which they had it in mind to place before the court in lieu of calling him as a witness. Despite their non-compliance, Veale J allowed them to adduce it in evidence. It clearly played an effective part in leading him to dismiss the plaintiff's claim, for he made express reference to its contents in his judgment, saying: 'It is not necessary for me to read it; it is only necessary for me to say that I think it rings true'.

In proper circumstances, a trial judge is undoubtedly entitled to admit evidence of an out-of-court statement notwithstanding non-compliance with the initially mandatory requirement. Section 8(3)(a) of the Act of 1968 made express provision for this and was the foundation of rule 29 of Order 38. This provides that: '(1) . . . the court may, if it thinks it just to do so, allow a statement falling within section 2(1), . . . of the Act to be given in evidence . . . notwithstanding—(a) that the statement is one in relation to which rule 21(1) applies and that the party desiring to give the statement in evidence has failed to comply with that rule, . . .' It was by virtue of this provision that Veale J admitted the absentee defendant's out-of-court statement.

I think it is imperative to consider briefly the circumstances in which he was led to do so. He had himself addressed some sharp questions to the defence as to why they had not given the statutory notice, and he received no adequate answer—if, indeed, any real answer at all was forthcoming. But, his offer to adjourn the proceedings until the following assizes having been declined by plaintiff's counsel, the judge admitted the statement.

In these circumstances, it is urged on behalf of the defendant that this exercise of his discretion under rule 29 ought not now to be disturbed. For my part, I cannot accept this. Rule 29(1) empowers the court to admit such a statement as is here in question, notwithstanding failing to comply with the preceding rules, "if it thinks it just to do so." In order that the court may adjudicate upon the justice of relaxing the rules in favour of a defaulting party, it must surely be placed in possession of all the relevant facts. In the present case Veale J was left ignorant of the vital fact that non-compliance by the defendant with the statutory requirement was due to no inability, inadvertence, or slackness on the part of his advisers, but resulted from a deliberate decision not to comply. This emerged from the completely candid statement of leading counsel for the defendant, who, in response to a direct inquiry from the Bench, took sole responsibility for the failure to give any notice of the kind required by rule 22. He was equally candid about his reason for advising this course of action, namely, that he suspected that, were the existence, nature and contents of the defendant's written statement made known to the plaintiff and her parents before the trial, it might have led to their evidence being in some way adjusted in order to meet and destroy it in advance. Put in plain words, this means that the tactics adopted were precisely those which the statutory provisions as to notice and counter-notice were designed to prevent, namely, the taking of a party by surprise by suddenly and without warning producing at the trial an out-of-court statement of someone not proposed to be called as a witness.

In these most unfortunate circumstances, it seems to me impossible that the defendant should be permitted to rely upon the judge's purported exercise of his discretion under rule 29. I hold that there can be no valid exercise of such discretion if there has (for any reason) been a deliberate withholding from the court of the reason for non-compliance. Had Veale J known that this was the result of a deliberate decision based upon the tactical value of surprise, I regard it as inconceivable that he would have ruled in favour of admitting the statement . . ..

[E]ven if he had, such an attitude ought not to be countenanced, by this court. A suitor who deliberately flouts the rules has no right to ask the court to exercise in his favour a discretionary indulgence created by those very same rules. Furthermore, a judge who, to his knowledge, finds himself confronted by such a situation would not, as I think, be acting judicially if he nevertheless exercised his discretion in favour of the recalcitrant suitor. The rules are there to be respected, and those who defy them should not be indulged or excused. Slackness is one thing; deliberate disobedience another. The former may be overlooked; the latter never, even though, as here, it derives from mistaken zeal on the client's behalf. To tolerate it would be dangerous to justice.'

(DAVIES LJ also delivered a judgment. Whilst condemning the course adopted on behalf of the defendant, his lordship was against the granting of a new trial on the ground of the already considerable delay and because it seemed to him that the ultimate result must be the same. KARMINSKI LJ agreed with EDMUND DAVIES LJ.)

Appeal allowed. New trial ordered.

Morris v *Stratford-on-Avon RDC* [1973] 1 WLR 1059(CA).

The plaintiff was struck by a lorry driven by an employee of the defendants. At the trial, which took place five years after the event, the driver gave evidence for the defendants. His evidence was inconsistent and confused, and at the end of his examination in chief counsel for the defendants applied for leave to put in evidence, under s.2 of the Civil Evidence Act 1968, a proof of evidence given by the driver to the defendants' insurers some nine months after the accident. Although prior notice had not been given to the other side as required by RSC, Ord 38, r.21(1) and despite objections made by the plaintiff's counsel, the judge exercised his discretion and admitted the statement. He found on the evidence that the plaintiff had failed to establish that the defendants had been in any way negligent and dismissed the claim. The plaintiff appealed.

MEGAW LJ: 'Counsel for the plaintiff submits that the court, under the Civil Evidence Act 1968 and the Rules of Court made thereunder, has, in a case like this, not one but two discretions to exercise. The first discretion is that which is given to it by section 2 of the Act. That section, which provides for the admissibility of out-of-court statements as evidence of the facts stated, does say, in subsection (2)(a), that the statement "shall not be given in evidence by virtue of this section on behalf of that party without the leave of the court": hence there is discretion coming in at *that* stage. Then in RSC, Ord 38, r.29, it is provided that "without prejudice to", *inter alia*, section 2(2)(a) of the Act, "the court may, if it thinks it just to do so, allow a statement falling within section 2(1) . . . of the Act to be given in evidence at the trial or hearing . . ."—and then (departing from the words of the rule), notwithstanding that the advance notices, which are required by the rules to be given where it is intended to seek to take advantage of the Act, have not been given.

I do not think it matters whether one regards these as being two separate discretions or as being one discretion with the matters which are relevant under Ord 38, r.29 being taken into account when the judge is dealing with the exercise of his discretion under section 2 of the Act or *vice versa*. There is no doubt that the judge has to consider all the relevant matters in exercising his discretion; and if the proper notices for which the Act and the rules provide have not been given, then the judge must consider that matter with care and must given the opposite party every opportunity to make submissions before he can properly decide whether or not the non-compliance with the rules is such that justice requires that the statement should be admitted.

Nothing that I say must be taken in any way as suggesting that non-compliance with the rules as to notices is a matter that can be lightly overlooked. On the other hand, there must be cases in which there is, sensibly and reasonably, no ground for supposing that a statement which is in existence is going to be used by a party. It would perhaps be unfortunate if the matter were to be so interpreted that, in every case, those who are advising a party felt it necessary to advise him that, if there is any possibility, however remote, that, as a result of something which may happen hereafter, an application might be sought to be made, then notice should be given in advance. But, quite clearly, if there is reason to suppose, on proper consideration of the evidence, that such an application may be made, then care must be taken that the proper notices should be given.

As I say, it is important that the notices should be given. We were told by counsel for the defendants, and I have no doubt whatever but that it is correct, that in the present case it had not crossed his mind that this statement would be one which there would be occasion to put in in evidence, and that it was only when the evidence of Mr Pattison came to be taken that it occurred to him that it would be desirable that application should be made. In my judgment, no blame whatever attaches to counsel for making the application at that stage.

Let me say that the present case is, in my judgment, totally different from the case in this court of *Ford* v *Lewis* [1971] 1 WLR 623, ...

It is perfectly apparent that this case bears no conceivable relationship to the matters which motivated the court to take the course that it did in that case. However, it is right that careful consideration should always be given, on an application of this sort, to matters such as those that were stressed before us by counsel for the plaintiff: for example, that the statement was taken as a proof of evidence and that it was not closely contemporary with the time of the accident but was taken some nine months later. Those are matters which of course go to weight; but they can also be relevant on the question of a decision as to the exercise of discretion. Another matter which in my judgment must always be carefully watched, when an application of this sort is made under the Civil Evidence Act 1968 without proper notices having been given, is for the judge to make sure, so far as he can, that no injustice will be done to the other party by reason of the statement being allowed to be put in evidence. If there is ground to suppose that there will be any injustice caused, or that the other party will be materially prejudiced or embarrassed, then the judge should either refuse to allow the document to be admitted or, in his discretion, allow it on terms, such as an adjournment at the cost of the party seeking to put in the statement.

If I thought that in the present case there was any possibility that the plaintiff was prejudiced or that injustice might have been done by reason of the admitting of this statement when it was admitted, I should have had no hesitation in saying that the judge would have been wrong in admitting it. But, having regard to all the circumstances of which we have heard in this case, I am satisfied that there has been no such prejudice and that no injustice resulted. Accordingly, I take the view that Stirling J was not wrong in the manner in which he exercised his discretion.'

(DAVIES LJ and WALTON J agreed.)

Appeal dismissed.

• Why is this case 'totally different' from *Ford* v *Lewis*, ante, p. 272?

B: HEARSAY ADMISSIBLE BY STATUTE IN CRIMINAL CASES

(Suggested preliminary reading: *A Practical Approach to Evidence,* pp. 252–259).

Police and Criminal Evidence Act 1984

68(1) Subject to section 69 below, a statement in a document shall be admissible in any proceedings as evidence of any fact stated therein of which direct oral evidence would be admissible if—

 (a) the document is or forms part of a record compiled by a person acting under a duty from information supplied by a person (whether acting under a duty or not) who had, or may reasonably be supposed to have had, personal knowledge of the matters dealt with in that information; and

 (b) any condition relating to the person who supplied the information which is specified in subsection (2) below is satisfied.

(2) The conditions mentioned in subsection (1)(b) above are—

 (a) that the person who supplied the information—
   (i) is dead or by reason of his bodily or mental condition unfit to attend as a witness;
   (ii) is outside the United Kingdom and it is not reasonably practicable to secure his attendance; or
   (iii) cannot reasonably be expected (having regard to the time which has elapsed since he supplied or acquired the information and to all the circumstances) to have any recollection of the matters dealt with in that information;

 (b) that all reasonable steps have been taken to identify the person who supplied the information but that he cannot be identified; and

 (c) that, the identity of the person who supplied the information being known, all reasonable steps have been taken to find him, but that he cannot be found.

(3) Nothing in this section shall prejudice the admissibility of any evidence that would be admissible apart from this section

69(1) In any proceedings, a statement in a document produced by a computer shall not be admissible as evidence of any fact stated therein unless it is shown—

 (a) that there are no reasonable grounds for believing that the statement is inaccurate because of improper use of the computer;

 (b) that at all material times the computer was operating properly, or if not, that any respect in which it was not operating properly or was out of operation was not such as to affect the production of the document or the accuracy of its contents; and

 (c) that any relevant conditions specified in rules of court under subsection (2) below are satisfied.

(2) Provision may be made by rules of court requiring that in any proceedings where it is desired to give a statement in evidence by virtue of this section such information concerning the statement as may be required by the rules shall be provided in such form and at such time as may be so required.

70(1) Part I of Schedule 3 to this Act shall have effect for the purpose of supplementing section 68 above.

(2) Part II of that Schedule shall have effect for the purpose of supplementing section 69 above.

(3) Part III of that Schedule shall have effect for the purpose of supplementing both sections.

72(1) In this Part of this Act—

'copy' and 'statement' have the same meanings as in Part I of the Civil Evidence Act 1968;

SCHEDULE 3

PROVISIONS SUPPLEMENTARY TO SECTIONS 68 AND 69
PART I: PROVISIONS SUPPLEMENTARY TO SECTION 68

1 Section 68(1) above applies whether the information contained in the document was supplied directly or indirectly but, if it was supplied indirectly, only if each person through whom it was supplied was acting under a duty; and applies also where the person compiling the record is himself the person by whom the information is supplied.

2 Where—

(a) a document setting out the evidence which a person could be expected to give as a witness has been prepared for the purpose of any pending or contemplated proceedings; and

(b) it falls within subsection (1) of section 68 above,

a statement contained in it shall not be given in evidence by virtue of that section without the leave of the court, and the court shall not give leave unless it is of the opinion that the statement ought to be admitted in the interests of justice, having regard—

(i) to the cirumstances in which leave is sought and in particular to the contents of the statement; and

(ii) to any likelihood that the accused will be prejudiced by its admission in the absence of the person who supplied the information on which it is based.

3 Where in any proceedings a statement based on information supplied by any person is given in evidence by virtue of section 68 above—

(a) any evidence which, if that person had been called as a witness, would have been admissible as relevant to his credibility as a witness shall be admissible for that purpose in those proceedings;

(b) evidence may, with the leave of the court, be given of any matter which, if that person had been called as a witness, could have been put to him in cross-examination as relevant to his credibility as a witness but of which evidence could not have been adduced by the cross-examining party; and

(c) evidence tending to prove that that person, whether before or after supplying the information, made a statement (whether oral or not) which is inconsistent with it shall be admissible for the purpose of showing that he has contradicted himself.

4 A statement which is admissible by virtue of section 68 above shall not be capable of corroborating evidence given by the person who supplied the information on which the statement is based.

5 In deciding for the purposes of section 68(2)(a)(i) above whether a person is unfit to attend as a witness the court may act on a certificate purporting to be signed by a registered medical practitioner.

6 Any reference in section 68 above or this Part of this Schedule to a person acting under a duty includes a reference to a person acting in the course of any trade, business, profession or other occupation in which he is engaged or employed or for the purposes of any paid or unpaid office held by him.

7 In estimating the weight, if any, to be attached to a statement admissible in evidence by virtue of section 68 above regard shall be had to all the circumstances from which any inference can reasonably be drawn as to the accuracy or otherwise of the statement and, in particular—

(a) to the question whether or not the person who supplied the information from which the record containing the statement was compiled did so contemporaneously with the occurrence or existence of the facts dealt with in that information; and

(b) to the question whether or not that person, or any other person concerned with compiling or keeping the record containing the statement, had any incentive to conceal or misrepresent the facts.

PART II: PROVISIONS SUPPLEMENTARY TO SECTION 69

8 In any proceedings where it is desired to give a statement in evidence in accordance with section 69 above, a certificate—

(a) identifying the document containing the statement and describing the manner in which it was produced;

(b) giving such particulars of any device involved in the production of that document as may be appropriate for the purpose of showing that the document was produced by a computer;

(c) dealing with any of the matters mentioned in subsection (1) of section 69 above; and

(d) purporting to be signed by a person occupying a responsible position in relation to the operation of the computer, shall be evidence of anything stated in it; and for the purposes of this paragraph it shall be sufficient for a matter to be stated to the best of the knowledge and belief of the person stating it.

9 Notwithstanding paragraph 8 above, a court may require oral evidence to be given of anything of which evidence could be given by a certificate under that paragraph. . . .

11 In estimating the weight, if any, to be attached to a statement regard shall be had to all the circumstances from which any inference can reasonably be drawn as to the accuracy or otherwise of the statement and, in particular—

    (a) to the question whether or not the information which the information contained in the statement reproduces or is derived from was supplied to the relevant computer, or recorded for the purpose of being supplied to it, contemporaneously with the occurrence or existence of the facts dealt with in that information; and

    (b) to the question whether or not any person concerned with the supply of information to that computer, or with the operation of that computer or any equipment by means of which the document containing the statement was produced by it, had any incentive to conceal or misrepresent the facts.

12 For the purposes of paragraph 11 above information shall be taken to be supplied to a computer whether it is supplied directly or (with or without human intervention) by means of any appropriate equipment.

PART III: PROVISIONS SUPPLEMENTARY TO SECTIONS 68 AND 69

13 Where in any proceedings a statement contained in a document is admissible in evidence by virtue of section 68 above or in accordance with section 69 above it may be proved—

    (a) by the production of that document; or

    (b) (whether or not that document is still in existence) by the production of a copy of that document, or of the material part of it,

authenticated in such manner as the court may approve.

14 For the purpose of deciding whether or not a statement is so admissible the court may draw any reasonable inference—

    (a) from the circumstances in which the statement was made or otherwise came into being; or

    (b) from any other circumstances, including the form and contents of the document in which the statement is contained.

15 Provision may be made by rules of court for supplementing the provisions of section 68 or 69 above or this Schedule

R v Tirado (1974) 59 Cr App R 80 (CA)

The appellant who was convicted of obtaining property by deception, ran an employment agency in Oxford. He wrote to Moroccans in Morocco stating that he had work for them and inviting them to post their fees to the agency or to do so through a Moroccan bank. The latter method was used in all the examples before the court. The appellant, in the course of his defence, maintained that his business was wholly honest, although muddled and inefficient. He said that on occasions he had made refunds of the sums which he had received and produced a number of cheque stubs from his office in connection with the alleged repayments as evidence of honest conduct. To rebut this the prosecution produced, from a series of files kept by the appellant, various unanswered letters of complaint addressed by the persons aggrieved to the appellant's firm.

LORD WIDGERY CJ, giving the judgment of the court: 'If the appellant was running his defence in that way, and was putting forward these cheque stubs found on his premises as evidence of the honest conduct of the business, it seems to us that there cannot possibly have been any objection to the prosecution producing the appropriate file, putting it before the appellant in the witness box and saying: "In view of what you now tell us what do you say about the file, and what do you say about those letters of complaint?" If the matter had been handled in that way, there would, we think, have been no possible reason for saying that the document had been improperly let in, regardless of any view which might have been formed of their admissibility under the [Criminal Evidence] Act of 1965. [See now s.68 of the Police and Criminal Evidence Act 1984, ante, p. 277]

The procedure, no doubt, did not precisely follow that which I have described, and one of the reasons may have been the judge's ruling in regard to the effect of the 1965 Act, and even assuming for the moment that the judge was wrong in his view on the 1965 Act and that these documents were not let in in evidence on that account, we can see no possible reason for thinking that the use of the documents in the manner which I have described could give rise to a miscarriage of justice and thus result in a decision in this case going in favour of the appellant. Thus in the end it seems to us that, although the documents were not handled in the conventional manner having regard to their nature, yet the result cannot give rise to a miscarriage of justice which would cause us to think that this appeal should be allowed.

But before leaving this point, of course I must return to this decision on the Act of 1965. We do not find it necessary to give a detailed definition of the words used in the section which I have read and which have not, so far as we know, been the subject of judicial comment before, but although we will leave the matter for final decision on another day, we have at least some hesitation in saying that a file of correspondence, maintained simply as a file of correspondence, and added to from time to time as letters come in, is or can be a record relating to any trade or business and compiled from information supplied within the meaning of section 1 of the Act of 1965. The language of section 1 seems on its face to contemplate the making or compilation of a record. That means the keeping of a book or a file, or a card index, into which information is deliberately put in order that it may be available to others another day. A cash book, a ledger, a stock book: all these may be records because they contain information deliberately entered in order that the information may be preserved. We think it at least widely open to question whether a file of the kind referred to in this case, either as a whole or when its individual documents are looked at, can come within the definition of a record within the meaning of the Act.'

Appeal dismissed.

R v Jones; R v Sullivan [1978] 1 WLR 195 (CA)

The defendants, who ran a transport business, were charged with conspiracy to steal goods from containers. One of the containers broken into had been packed with cartons of cotton goods in Hong Kong and from there shipped to Southampton. To prove the number of cartons originally placed in the container, the prosecution put in evidence under s. 1(1) of the Criminal Evidence Act 1965 (see now s. 68 of the Police and Criminal Evidence Act 1984, ante, p. 277) a bill of lading and a cargo manifest both made out in Hong Kong, being the 'record' of a trade or business made by a person beyond the seas. The defendants were convicted and appealed.

GEOFFREY LANE LJ, giving the judgment of the court: 'It is not in dispute that all the necessary ingredients of [section 1 of the Criminal Evidence Act 1965] are fulfilled in this case, apart from the one matter, namely, can it be said that the documents to which I have referred were a record or form part of a record relating to the trade or business? Mr Harvey has, if we may say so, very ably argued before us that on the plain construction of the words they do not form part of a record and what he says is this. He submits that in order to be a record the documents must have some permanence. It must be something which can be referred to as a record in the future although he concedes he is there using the word which he is seeking to define. He goes on to submit that it must not be a document which is used merely to service an individual transaction; it must be going to be kept beyond the limit of that one single transaction; something to be kept, he says, as a record available beyond the immediate transaction, deliberately done with an eye to its use in the future—something which is merely brought into existence to service the one transaction is not enough. Those were the various ways he put the matter although he was in some difficulty in explaining to us the precise degree of permanence which the document must have before it becomes a record.

He drew our attention to the definition of "record" contained in the *Shorter Oxford English Dictionary*, 3rd ed (1944), vol. II p. 1675. There were two passages to which he referred, the first was:

> The fact or condition of being preserved as knowledge, especially by being put into writing; knowledge or information preserved or handed down in this way.

The second was as follows:

> An account of some fact or event preserved in writing or other permanent form; a document, monument, etc., on which such an account is inscribed; also anything or person serving to indicate or give evidence of, or preserve the memory of, a fact or event; a memorial.

It seems to this court that the documents in the present case fall precisely within those definitions, but Mr Harvey's argument did not stop there. He drew to our attention two decisions of this court; the first was *R v Gwilliam* [1968] 1 WLR 1839. That was a case in which the appellant was charged with driving a vehicle with too much alcohol in his blood. At the trial he took the point that proof was required of the approval on the part of the Secretary of State of the breathalyser device which was used in order to test his breath. The recorder before whom the case was tried admitted as evidence the label on the inside of the breathalyser set which stated that the device was approved by the Secretary of State for the purposes of the Road Safety Act. The appellant was convicted. On appeal it was conceded that the label was not admissible as evidence but the further question was raised, namely, whether the consignment note relating to the delivery of the device to the police force in question, which stated that the goods had been sent from a Home Office supply and transport store, was admissible to prove the approval of the device under section 1(1)(a) of the Criminal Evidence Act 1965 as a commercial record. In the course of the judgment Lord Parker CJ said, at p.1843:

> Mr Barnes [for the Crown] puts it in this way: that evidence of the fact of the Secretary of State's approval could be given by direct oral evidence and accordingly any statement contained in a document of the type there described which tends to establish that approval would be admissible. This court is quite satisfied that that submission fails. It may be (and the court is not deciding this case on that basis) that it is quite impossible to say that the consignment note itself is a record or forms part of a record within the meaning of section 1(1).

If that remark had been part of the *ratio decidendi* of the case we should have been bound by it. It was not. It was expressed to be *obiter* and we do not think, bearing in mind the circumstances of the present case, that it is right that consignment notes can never form part of a record.

The other case is *R v Tirado* (1974) 59 Cr App R 80. That was a very different circumstance. The "record" which it was sought to introduce was a file of letters from various people in Morocco who had been writing to the appellant about the prospect of a course in Oxford which he had advertised. We do not feel that the decision in that case is of any value because a file of various letters from various people does not seem to us to be something which could in any event properly be described as a record.

Although it is not an exhaustive definition of the word, "record" in this context means a history of events in some form which is not evanescent. How long the record is likely to be kept is immaterial: it may be something which will not survive the end of the transaction in question, it may be something which is indeed more lasting than bronze, but the degree of permanence does not seem to us to make or mar the fulfilment of the definition of the word "record". The record in each individual case will last as long as commercial necessity may demand.

The documents in the present case seem to us to fall precisely into that category. They are the written records of the particular transaction. They are documents containing the history of this particular transaction, where the goods started from, the method of transport, the name of the ship, the port of arrival and the container depot destination on the one hand and the final consignee's destination on the other. They are carefully and deliberately compiled for the information of those in this country who are going to be the recipients of the goods. There is no necessity, as we see it, for the contents of these documents to be entered into a book or a ledger as was suggested in one of the cases; indeed these very documents themselves might have been copied into a ledger but how, one asks, could that make them any more or less a record than they are at the moment?

We have come to the conclusion, despite Mr Harvey's argument, quite plainly that these documents were records or part of records within the meaning of the section of the Act which I have read and that particular part of his argument therefore fails.'

Appeal dismissed.

R v Pettigrew (1980) 71 Cr App R 39(CA)

The appellant was found in possession of three new £5 notes shortly after the burglary at a house from which some £650 in £5 notes had been stolen. He was charged on indictment with burglary. At his trial the prosecution tendered in evidence, pursuant to section 1(1)(a) of the Criminal Evidence Act 1965, [see now s.68 of the Police and Criminal Evidence Act 1984, ante p. 277] a print-out from a computer operated by an employee of the Bank of England. The print-out was made by a machine into which the operator fed bundles of bank notes with consecutive serial numbers, and he noted on a card the first serial numbers in the bundle. The machine automatically rejected any notes in the bundle fed into it which were defective in any way; further, it recorded the first and last serial numbers of each bundle of 100 notes, which then had consecutive serial numbers save only those of notes which the machine had rejected. An objection on behalf of the appellant to the admission of the print-out in evidence was overruled by the trial judge, the trial proceeded, the print-out was received in evidence and as a result a bundle of £5,000 was traced from the Bank of England to another bank, from which part went to a third bank and into the possession of the owner of the burgled house. The evidence suggested, but did not prove conclusively, that the three new £5 notes in the appellant's possession could have come from the same series of notes that the owner of the burgled house had possessed. The appellant was convicted and appealed on the ground, *inter alia*, that information recorded on the print-out was not, pursuant to section 1(1)(a) of the Criminal Evidence Act 1965, information supplied by any person who had, or who could reasonably be supposed to have had, personal knowledge of the matters dealt with in the information they supplied.

BRIDGE LJ, giving the judgment of the court: 'Mr McHale's perfectly short and simple submission is that, in those circumstances it cannot be said that anyone—if it were to be anyone, it would have to be the machine operator—had personal knowledge of that which emerges from the machine at the end of the day in a computer print-out recording the serial numbers of every note in each bundle to which the print-out relates.

Mr Williamson, in an attractive argument for the Crown, submits that the operator of the machine can fairly be said to have personal knowledge of the serial numbers of the notes in each bundle which he feeds into the machine. Although he has not mentally recorded them, he has the means of knowledge of the bundle of notes he has fed into the machine, which bear consecutive serial numbers, and he records on a card the first number of each bundle which he feeds into the machine.

This is a most attractive argument, and if the machine did nothing but record the totality of the numbers of notes in each bundle fed into it, it may well be—it is not necessary for present purposes to decide the point finally—that the argument for the Crown should prevail. But what at the end of the day has convinced us that we cannot accept it is the recognition that the machine has the important dual function of separating out the defective notes and rejecting them and recording the numbers of those rejected and recording the serial numbers of the notes at the beginning and end of each bundle.

The numbers of the notes which have been rejected can never be said to be in the personal knowledge of the operator or in the mind of anybody. They are recorded purely by the operation of the machine. The operator could never be said to have personal knowledge of those rejected notes, and knowledge of the numbers of the rejected notes is essential to know the serial numbers of the notes in the bundles to which the computer print-out relates.

Accordingly, although the point is highly technical, and one which may be thought to expose a lacuna in the Criminal Evidence Act 1965, the point is one on which the argument for the appellant Pettigrew is entitled to prevail.'

Appeal allowed.

Questions for discussion

R v Coke; R v Littleton

1 Assume that it is desired to prove the age of Angela Blackstone at the time of the assault on her allegedly committed by Littleton; that both parents are now dead; and that a birth certificate, duly signed and filed, is available. Would the certificate be admissible? What foundation would have to be laid? In what form should it be placed before the court?

2 Assume that Dr Espinasse accomplished his work using a computer, and that the results are available in the form of computer data, a print-out of which can be produced. Would such a print-out be admissible, and if so, admissible evidence of what? What foundation would have to be laid?

Blackstone v Coke

1 Discuss the admissibility of the proof of evidence supplied by Anthony Henneky. What weight is it likely to have? What notice should Coke give of his intention to adduce it? Can Margaret serve an effective counter-notice?

2 Discuss the admissibility of the records of the hospital in which Margaret gave birth to her son. What notice would have to be given? What should Coke's solicitors do in response to such notice?

3 Assume that Mrs Blackstone has suffered a serious stroke and cannot give evidence because her memory has failed her. What use might Margaret make of her statement to the police? Would your answer be different in the criminal case of *R v Coke; R v Littleton*?

Additional questions

1 You are preparing the case for the prosecution against Arthur, who is alleged to have sexually assaulted a young girl, Beatrice in 1981. From a description given by Beatrice, the police believe that her assailant was Arthur, but he disappeared and has only recently been arrested in connection with another sexual offence. Shortly after the alleged offence Beatrice had been taken to a doctor who examined her. The doctor described what he found, and his secretary wrote out a record. The doctor says that after a lapse of six years he has now no recollection of the examination, and the secretary has left his employment and cannot be traced. However, the record still exists. What use, if any, can be made of this evidence?

2 Donald was alighting from a bus when the driver, Edward, closed the door prematurely so that Donald had to let go of the handrail before his feet were on the ground; he lost his balance and fell, and before he could get up, a car, driven by Frank, drove into him and caused injuries from which he died. You are acting for Donald's

widow who is suing Barsetshire Bus Co Ltd, Edward's employers, and Frank. Consider whether the following items of evidence are admissible, and whether any procedure has to be followed before they can be put before the court:

(a)   A passenger overheard Edward say 'Sorry, I've trapped your hand' just as he closed the door.

(b)   The conductor told another passenger shortly after the accident: 'Edward is always doing that: I knew there would be an accident sooner or later.' Subsequently, the conductor made a more detailed statement to the same effect which you have on your file.

(c)   In hospital, shortly before he died, Donald said to his wife: 'It was the bus driver's fault: I shouted to him as he was closing the door, but he took no notice'.

(d)   Gwyneth, who was travelling in Frank's car, handed a hastily scribbled note to a bystander, it read: 'Frank's always creeping up on the near side of buses: I told him not to. I saw the man fall: Frank could easily have stopped in time'. She gave the same address as Frank but she is no longer living there.

Further reading

13th Report of the Law Reform Committee on Hearsay Evidence in Civil Proceedings 1966, Cmnd 2964.

9   Opinion Evidence

(Suggested preliminary reading: *A Practical Approach to Evidence*, pp. 260–279).

Folkes v Chadd and Others (1782) 3 Doug 157 (KB)

In an action for trespass the question was whether an embankment erected by the plaintiff caused silting in the defendant's harbour. Mr Smeaton, a distinguished engineer, testified to his opinion as an expert that the silting was not caused by the embankment. The trial judge rejected the evidence on the ground that it was a matter of opinion and not of facts.

LORD MANSFIELD, delivering the opinion of the court: 'It is objected that Mr Smeaton is going to speak, not as to facts, but as to opinion. That opinion, however, is deduced from facts which are not disputed—the situation of banks, the course of tides and of winds, and the shifting of sands. His opinion, deduced from all these facts, is, that, mathematically speaking, the bank may contribute to the mischief, but not sensibly. Mr Smeaton understands the construction of harbours, the causes of their destruction, and how remedied. In matters of science no other witnesses can be called. An instance frequently occurs in actions for unskilfully navigating ships. The question then depends on the evidence of those who understand such matters; and when such questions come before me, I always send for some of the brethren of the Trinity House. I cannot believe that where the question is, whether a defect arises from a natural or an artificial cause, the opinions of men of science are not to be received. Handwriting is proved every day by opinion; and for false evidence on such questions a man may be indicted for perjury. Many nice questions may arise as to forgery, and as to the impressions of seals; whether the impression was made from seal itself, or from an impression in wax. In such cases I cannot say that the opinion of seal-makers is not to be taken. I have myself received the opinion of Mr Smeaton respecting mills, as a matter of science. The cause of the decay of the harbour is also a matter of science, and still more so, whether the removal of the bank can be beneficial. Of this such men as Mr Smeaton alone can judge. Therefore we are of opinion that his judgment, formed on facts, was very proper evidence.'
    Rule for a new trial made absolute.

R v Silverlock [1894] 2 QB 766 (CCR)

The defendant was charged with obtaining a cheque by false pretences. It became necessary to prove that certain documents were in the defendant's handwriting and the solicitor for the prosecution was called as an expert witness for this purpose. It was objected that the solicitor was not an expert, and could not give evidence as to his opinion. The solicitor said that he had since 1884, quite apart from his professional work, given considerable study and attention to handwriting and had on several occasions professionally compared evidence in handwriting. The objection was overruled, and the evidence was admitted. The jury convicted the defendant, who appealed.

LORD RUSSELL OF KILLOWEN CJ: 'It is true that the witness who is called upon to give evidence founded on a comparison of handwritings must be *peritus*; he must be skilled in doing so; but we cannot say that he must have become *peritus* in the way of his business or in any definite way. The question is, is he *peritus*? Is he skilled? Has he an adequate knowledge? Looking at the matter practically, if a witness is not skilled the judge will tell the jury to disregard his evidence. There is no decision which requires that the evidence of a man who is skilled in comparing handwriting, and who has formed a reliable opinion from past experience, should be excluded because his experience has not been gained in the way of his business. It is, however, really unnecessary to consider this point; for it seems from the statement in the present case that the witness was not only *peritus*, but was *peritus* in the way of his business. When once it is determined that the evidence is admissible, the rest is merely a question of its value or weight, and this is entirely a question for the jury, who will attach more or less weight to it according as they believe the witness to be *peritus*.'

(MATHEW, DAY, VAUGHAN, WILLIAMS and KENNEDY JJ concurred.)

   Conviction affirmed.

R v Lanfear [1968] 2 QB 77 (CA)

The appellant was charged with driving a motor vehicle on a road while unfit to drive through drink. The doctor who had examined him at the police station after the offence gave evidence at his trial. The appellant was convicted and appealed on the ground, *inter alia*, that the deputy recorder misdirected the jury in telling them that the doctor's evidence must be accepted unless the doctor showed by his own conduct that it ought not to be accepted.

DIPLOCK LJ, reading the judgment of the court: 'In his notice of appeal he makes a number of complaints about the summing up by the deputy recorder. As regards all of the complaints but one I need say no more than that there is, in the view of this court, no substance in them. But he did complain, with justification, about the terms in which the deputy recorder instructed the jury about the attitude they should adopt towards the medical evidence. There is considerable excuse for the deputy recorder because he read out to them a passage which appears in the current volume of Archbold's Criminal Pleadings, Evidence and Practice 36th ed (1966) para 2849, under the heading "Medical Witness," which is in the following terms:

> The evidence of any doctor, whether a police surgeon or not, should be accepted as the evidence of a professional man giving independent expert evidence with the sole desire of assisting the court, unless the doctor himself shows that his evidence ought not to be accepted.

The deputy recorder paraphrased that slightly. He said this:

> Let me say immediately about medical evidence in general — this again, members of the jury, is a matter of law. The evidence of any doctor, whether a police surgeon or not, is to be accepted as the evidence of a professional man giving independent evidence with the sole desire of assisting the court unless the doctor by his own conduct shows that his evidence ought not to be accepted.

I think the only difference is that instead of 'himself' he has substituted the words 'by his own conduct.' Then he goes on subsequently to say this:

> . . .his evidence is to be accepted as the evidence of a professional man giving independent expert evidence with the sole desire of helping the court. This, then, puts him into a position in which, in the absence of reasons for rejecting his evidence, his evidence ought to be accepted.

In the view of this court that is an incorrect statement of the law and the passage which is cited in Archbold, which comes from *R* v *Nowell* (1948) 64 TLR 277, 278 is taken out of its context. In that case the argument before the court was based on the fact that a doctor who had examined a defendant had explained to him that it might be in his own interests to allow the doctor to examine him. The defendant eventually agreed to be examined and was examined by the doctor, who certified that owing to his consumption of alcohol, the defendant was unfit to drive a car. The argument was that the doctor should be treated as if he were an arm of the police and that there was an inducement held out to the defendant which made the evidence of the doctor as to the result of his examination inadmissible. That argument was sought to be supported by a decision of the Scots court, *Reid* v *Nixon* and *Dumigan* v *Brown* 1948 SC(J) 68, and the passage now incorporated in Archbold appeared at the end of the judgment in the Court of Criminal Appeal where they were dealing with that. After referring to the two cases, the court said (1948) 64 TLR 277, 278:

> It is not necessary to read the judgment of the court which was given by the Lord Justice-General, who made a number of general observations with regard to the principles on which he suggested police officers and doctors should act in examining persons who are charged with such an offence as this. The Lord Advocate, according to the judgment of the Lord Justice-General, had stated that in all such cases the police surgeon or other doctor summoned by the police to conduct an examination was acting as the hand of the police and not as an independent medical referee. This court can only say that it does not agree that that state of affairs, whether it exists in Scotland or not, exists in this country. Our view is that the evidence of a doctor, whether he be a police surgeon or anyone else, should be accepted, unless the doctor himself shows that it ought not to be, as the evidence of a professional man giving independent expert evidence with the sole desire of assisting the court.

What that passage meant in that context was that the evidence should be treated, as regards admissibility and other matters of that kind, like that of any other independent witness. But taken out of its context, the use of the word 'accepted' may well, we think, give to the jury a false impression of the weight to be given to a doctor's evidence. It is therefore desirable that in subsequent editions of Archbold that passage, which was read by the deputy recorder in this case, should be corrected.

Having said that, however, this, in the view of this court, is the clearest possible case in which to apply the proviso. On the evidence before the jury no jury properly directed could have possibly found the appellant otherwise than guilty of the offence.

Appeal dismissed.

Anderson v *R* [1972] AC 100 (PC)

The appellant was charged with murder. He put forward a defence of alibi but was convicted chiefly on circumstantial evidence and sentenced to death. He appealed against conviction to the Appeal Court of Jamaica on the ground, *inter alia*, that there had been a misdirection by the trial judge. The Court of Appeal held that there had been a misdirection but that no substantial miscarriage of justice had occurred and they applied the proviso to s. 13(1) of the Judicature (Appellate Jurisdiction) Law 1962 and dismissed the appeal. A further appeal was made to the Judicial Committee.

LORD GUEST, delivering the judgment of their Lordships: 'The complaint which formed the basis of the Court of Appeal's judgment related to the trial judge's summing up in regard to the condition of the accused's boots. It should be explained that when the accused was arrested on December 25, his water boots were found and also a piece of cardboard from inside the boots. He admitted wearing the boots on the night of December 23. Mr Garriques a forensic expert examined the water boots and the cardboard on December 28. He found no human blood on the water boots. In his summing up the trial judge referred to the water boots in this way:

> He [Mr Garriques] says there was no blood on the shoes — well, that is merely his opinion, members of the jury, you are not bound to accept it because he happens to be an expert in this particular field. An expert is brought before you merely to guide and assist you in evaluating evidence of a particular nature, he being trained in that particular field therefor. You will weigh well what an expert has said before you discard his evidence because neither you nor I is trained in that particular field in the same way that Mr Garriques would weigh well what I would have to say in the field of law, because he is not trained in that particular field. But you are still judges of the facts and you may accept or reject evidence of the expert.

The Court of Appeal considered that this was a serious misdirection because the judge was inviting the jury to disregard the evidence of the expert to the effect that there was no blood on the boots and form their own opinion as to whether there was blood upon the boots.

So far as the piece of cardboard is concerned this was found by Detective Constable Dwyer on his visit to the accused's home on December 25. It was in the right foot of the water boots which the accused said he was wearing on December 23. It had brown marks resembling blood stains. Mr Garriques said that on his examination on December 28 he found that those marks were human blood stains. The stains must have been about two weeks old but they could have been there before two weeks. In his opinion it was not more recent than two weeks. It might have been older. It was definitely not a fresh stain.

The trial judge in his summing up to the jury when dealing with Mr Garriques' evidence said that the witness found human blood. 'In his opinion they were then about two weeks old.' There is no doubt that in the summing up a confusion might have arisen in the jury's mind as to whether blood on the cardboard could have been of more recent origin than two weeks. Their Lordships are prepared to accept, following the Court of Appeal, that there was misdirections by the trial judge in regard to the boots and in regard to the cardboard.

Their Lordships do not agree with counsel for the respondent that these were subsidiary matters. These were serious misdirections as the Court of Appeal have held. There was no evidence of blood on the boots or the cardboard that could have implicated the accused.' (His Lordship went on to consider the question of the proviso and affirmed the judgment of the Court of Appeal of Jamaica.)

Appeal dismissed.

English Exporters (London) Limited v Eldonwall Limited [1973] Ch 415

By an originating summons the plaintiff tenants applied, pursuant to Part II of the Landlord and Tenant Act 1954, for the grant by the defendant landlords of a new tenancy of certain premises. By a summons the landlords applied under s.24(A) of the Act for the determination of an interim rent while the tenancy continued under the provisions of the Act. During the hearing two valuers gave evidence as expert witnesses.

MEGARRY J: 'As is usual in these cases, a number of comparables was adduced. Eight were put forward by the landlords: the tenants put in none of their own. As is also far from unknown, some of the comparables were less comparable than others, and some turned out to be supported only by hearsay evidence, or by evidence that was in other respects less than cogent. There was no formal process of a ruling being made to exclude those comparables which were supported only by hearsay evidence; but I was discouraging, and in the event Mr Ibbotson, though rueful, did not seriously argue the point, or press it. I nevertheless think that I ought to make more explicit the reasons for my having been discouraging, for in my experience the status of hearsay evidence of comparables in valuation cases is a matter that is often misunderstood, and not only by valuers . . ..

Let me put on one side the cases in which exceptions to the rule excluding hearsay evidence have grown up, whether by case law or by statute (and sometimes almost by a side-wind; see, for example, *In re Koscot Interplanetary (UK) Ltd* [1972] 3 All ER 829); and in particular I exclude cases in which, subject to observing the statutory safeguards, hearsay evidence has been made admissible under the Civil Evidence Act 1968. Let me further ignore cases in which questions in cross-examination may have let in evidence that otherwise would be inadmissible, and confine myself to the admissibility of hearsay in chief and in re-examination in these valuation cases. In such circumstances, two of the heads under which the valuers' evidence may be ranged are opinion evidence and factual evidence. As an expert witness, the valuer is entitled to express his opinion about matters within his field of competence. In building up his opinions about values, he will no doubt have learned much from transactions in which he has himself been engaged, and of which he could give first-hand evidence. But he will also have learned much from many other sources, including much of which he could give no first-hand evidence. Textbooks, journals, reports of auctions and other dealings, and information obtained from his professional brethren and others, some related to particular transactions and some more general and indefinite, will all have contributed their share. Doubtless much, or most, of this will be accurate, though some will not; and even what is accurate so far as it goes may be incomplete, in that nothing may have been said of some special element which effects values. Nevertheless, the opinion that the expert expresses is none the worse because it is in part derived from the matters of which he could give no direct evidence. Even if some of the extraneous information which he acquires in this way is inaccurate or incomplete, the errors and omissions will often tend to cancel each other out; and the valuer, after all, is an expert in this field, so that the less reliable the knowledge that he has about the details of some reported transaction, the more his experience will tell him that he should be ready to make some discount from the weight that he gives it in contributing to his overall sense of values. Some aberrant transactions may stand so far out of line that he will give them little or no weight. No question of giving hearsay evidence arises in such cases; the witness states his opinion from his general experience.

On the other hand, quite apart from merely expressing his opinion, the expert often is able to give factual evidence as well. If he has first-hand knowledge of a transaction, he can speak of that. He may himself have measured the premises and conducted the negotiations which led to a letting of them at £x, which comes to £y per square foot, and he himself may have read the lease and seen that it contains no provisions, other than some particular clause, which would have any material effect on the valuation; and then he may express his opinion on the value. So far as the expert gives factual evidence, he is doing what any other witness of fact may do, namely, speaking of that which he has perceived for himself. No doubt in many valuation cases the requirement of first-hand evidence is not pressed to an extreme: if the witness has not himself measured the premises, but it has been done by his assistant under his supervision, the expert's figures are often accepted without requiring the assistant to be called to give evidence. Again, it may be that it would be possible for a valuer to fill a gap in his first-hand knowledge of a transaction by some method such as stating in his evidence that he has made diligent enquiries of some person who took part in the transaction in question, but despite receiving full answers to his enquiries, he discovered nothing which suggested to him that the transaction had any unusual features which would affect the value as a comparable. But basically, the expert's factual evidence on matters of fact is in the same position as the factual evidence of any other witness. Further, factual evidence that he cannot give himself is sometimes adduced in some other way, as by the testimony of some other witness who was himself concerned in the transaction in question, or by proving some document which carried the transaction through, or recorded it; and to the transaction thus established, like the transactions which the expert himself has proved, the expert may apply his experience and opinions, as tending to support or qualify his views.

That being so, it seems to me quite another matter when it is asserted that a valuer may give factual evidence of transactions of which he has no direct knowledge, whether *per se* or whether in the guise of giving reasons for his opinion as to value. It is one thing to say "From my general experience of recent transactions comparable with this one, I think the proper rent should be £x": it is another thing to say "Because I have been told by someone else that the premises next door have an area of x square feet and were recently let on such-and-such terms for £y a year, I say the rent of these premises should be £z a year." What he has been told about the premises next door may be inaccurate or misleading as to the area, the rent, the terms and much else besides. It makes it no better when the witness expresses his confidence in the reliability of his source of information: a transparently honest and careful witness cannot make information reliable if, instead of speaking of what he has seen and heard for himself, he is merely retailing what others have told him. The other party to the litigation is entitled to have a witness whom he can cross-examine on oath as to the reliability of the facts deposed to, and not merely as to the witness's opinion as to the reliability of information which was given to him not on oath, and possibly in circumstances tending to inaccuracies and slips. Further, it is often difficult enough for the courts to ascertain the true facts from witnesses giving direct evidence, without the added complication of attempts to evaluate a witness's opinion of the reliability, care and thoroughness of some informant who has supplied the witness with the facts that he is seeking to recount.

It therefore seems to me that details of comparable transactions upon which a valuer intends to rely in his evidence must, if they are to be put before the court, be confined to those details which have been, or will be, proved by admissible evidence, given either by the valuer himself or in some other way. I know of no special rule giving expert valuation witnesses the right to give hearsay evidence of facts: and notwithstanding many pleasant days spent in the Lands Tribunal while I was at the Bar, I can see no compelling reasons of policy why they should be able to do this. Of course, the long-established technique in adducing expert evidence of asking hypothetical questions may also be employed for valuers. It would, I think, be perfectly proper to ask a valuer "If in May 1972 No. 3, with an area of 2,000 sq ft, was let for £10,000 a year for seven years on a full repairing lease with no unusual terms, what rent would be appropriate for the premises in dispute?" But I cannot see that it would do much good unless the facts of the hypothesis are established by admissible evidence; and the valuer's statement that someone reputable had told him these facts, or that he had seen them in a reputable periodical, would not in my judgment constitute admissible evidence . . ..

Putting matters shortly, and leaving on one side the matters that I have mentioned, such as the Civil Evidence Act 1968 and anything made admissible by questions in cross-examination, in my judgment a valuer giving expert evidence in chief (or in re-examination): (a) may express the opinions that he has formed as to values even though substantial contributions to the formation of those opinions have been made by matters of which he has no first-hand knowledge; (b) may give evidence as to the details of any transactions within his personal knowledge, in order to establish them as matters of fact; and (c) may express his opinion as to the significance of any transactions which are or will be proved by admissible evidence (whether or not given by him) in relation to the valuation with which he is concerned; but (d) may not give hearsay evidence stating the details of any transactions not within his personal knowledge in order to establish them as matters of fact. To those propositions I would add that for counsel to put in a list of comparables ought to amount to a warranty by him of his intention to tender admissible evidence of all that is shown on the list'.

R v Abadom [1983] 1 WLR 126 (CA)

The appellant was charged with robbery and it was alleged that he was one of four masked men armed with cudgels, who had entered an office, broken an internal window pane and demanded money from the occupants. A principal scientific officer gave evidence at the trial that he had analysed fragments of glass from a pair of shoes belonging to the appellant and glass from the office window and found that all the pieces of glass had the same refractive index. It was the practice of the Home Office Central Research Establishment to collate statistics of the refractive index of broken glass which had been analysed in forensic laboratories and, having consulted those statistics, he found that only four per cent of samples had the same refractive index as the glass he had analysed. He expressed the opinion that it was strong evidence that the fragments of glass on the appellant's shoes had come from the broken window pane. The appellant was convicted and appealed.

KERR LJ, reading the judgment of the court: 'The point taken on this appeal was that the evidence of Mr Cooke, that the identical refractive index of the fragments of glass with that of the control sample occurred in only four per cent of all controlled glass samples analysed and statistically collated in the Home Office Central Research Establishment, was inadmissible because it constituted hearsay evidence. It was said to be hearsay because Mr Cooke had no personal knowledge of the analyses whose results were collated in these statistics, save possibly a few for which he may have been personally responsible. This submission was challenged on behalf of the Crown, but no point was taken, in our view clearly rightly, on the ground that the admissibility of this evidence had not been challenged on behalf of the defence at the trial. In our view, the evidence was not inadmissible as hearsay. It is convenient to deal with this issue first on the basis of general principle and then to consider the authorities.

Mr Cooke was admittedly an expert, and was giving evidence as an expert, on the likelihood or otherwise of the fragments of glass having come from the control sample, the broken window. As an expert in this field he was entitled to express an opinion on this question, subject to laying the foundation for his opinion and subject, of course, to his evidence being tested by cross-examination for evaluation by the jury. In the context of evidence given by experts it is no more than a statement of the obvious that, in reaching their conclusion, they must be entitled to draw upon material produced by others in the field in which their expertise lies. Indeed, it is part of their duty to consider any material which may be available in their field, and not to draw conclusions merely on the basis of their own experience, which is inevitably likely to be more limited than the general body of information which may be available to them. Further, when an expert has to consider the likelihood or unlikelihood of some occurrence or factual association in reaching his conclusion, as must often be necessary, the statistical results of the work of others in the same field must inevitably form an important ingredient in the cogency or probative value of his own conclusion in the particular case. Relative probabilites or improbabilities must frequently be an important factor in the evaluation of any expert opinion and, when any reliable statistical material is available which bears upon this question, it must be part of the function and duty of the expert to take this into account.

However, it is also inherent in the nature of any statistical information that it will result from the work of others in the same field, whether or not the expert in question will himself have contributed to the bank of information available on the particular topic on which he is called upon to express his opinion. Indeed, to exclude reliance upon such information on the ground that it is inadmissible under the hearsay rule, might inevitably lead to the distortion or unreliability of the opinion which the expert presents for evaluation by a judge or jury. Thus, in the present case, the probative value or otherwise of the identity of the refractive index as between the fragments and the control sample could not be assessed without some further information about the frequency of its occurrence. If all glass of the type in question had the same refractive index, this evidence would have virtually no probative value whatever. The extent to which this refractive index is common or uncommon must therefore be something which an expert must be entitled to take into account, and indeed must take into account, before he can properly express an opinion about the likelihood or unlikelihood of the fragments of glass having come from the window in question. The cogency or otherwise of the expert's conclusion on this point, in the light of, *inter alia*, the available statistical material against which this conclusion falls to be tested, must then be a matter for the jury.

We therefore consider that Mr Cooke's reliance on the statistical information collated by the Home Office Central Research Establishment, before arriving at his conclusion about the likely relationship between the fragments of glass and the control sample, was not only permissible in principle, but that it was an essential part of his function as an expert witness to take account of this material.

It was submitted that the present case was indistinguishable from the decision in *Myers v Director of Public Prosecutions* [1965] AC 1001 since Mr Cooke had not been personally responsible for the compilation of the Home Office statistics on which he relied, so that the inferences which he drew from them must be inadmissible because they were based on hearsay. In our view this conclusion does not follow, either as a matter of principle or on the basis of authority. We are here concerned with the cogency or otherwise of an opinion expressed by an expert in giving expert evidence. In that regard it seems to us that the process of taking account of information stemming from the work of others in the same field is an essential ingredient of the nature of expert evidence. So far as the question of principle is concerned, we have already explained our reasons for this conclusion. So far as the authorities are concerned, the position can be summarised as follows.

First, where an expert relies on the existence or non-existence of some fact which is basic to the question on which he is asked to express his opinion, that fact must be proved by admissible evidence: see *English Exporters (London) Ltd* v *Eldonwall Ltd* [1973] Ch 415, 421 *per* Megarry J and *R* v *Turner (Terence)* [1975] QB 834, 840. Thus, it would no doubt have been inadmissible if Mr Cooke had said in the present case that he had been told by somebody else that the refractive index of the fragments of glass and of the control sample was identical, and any opinion expressed by him on this basis would then have been based on hearsay. If he had not himself determined the refractive index, it would have been necessary to call the person who had done so before Mr Cooke could have expressed any opinion based on this determination. In this connection it is to be noted that Mr Smalldon was rightly called to prove the chemical analysis made by him which Mr Cooke was asked to take into account. Secondly, where the existence or non-existence of some fact is in issue, a report made by an expert who is not called as a witness is not admissible as evidence of that fact merely by the production of the report, even though it was made by an expert: see for instance *R* v *Crayden* [1978] 1 WLR 604, 607c.

These, however, are in our judgment the limits of the hearsay rule in relation to evidence of opinion given by experts, both in principle and on the authorities. In other respects their evidence is not subject to the rule against hearsay in the same way as that of witnesses of fact: see *English Exporters* v *Eldonwall* [1973] Ch 415, 420d and *Phipson on Evidence*, 12th ed (1976), para. 1207. Once the primary facts on which their opinion is based have been proved by admissible evidence, they are entitled to draw on the work of others as part of the process of arriving at their conclusion. However, where they have done so, they should refer to this material in their evidence so that the cogency and probative value of their conclusion can be tested and evaluated by reference to it.

Thus, if in the present case the statistical tables of analyses made by the Home Office forensic laboratories had appeared in a textbook or other publication, it could not be doubted that Mr Cooke would have been entitled to rely upon them for the purposes of his evidence. Indeed, this was not challenged. But it does not seem to us, in relation to the reliability of opinion evidence given by experts, that they must necessarily limit themselves to drawing on material which has been published in some form. Part of their experience and expertise may well lie in their knowledge of unpublished material and in their evaluation of it. The only rule in this regard, as it seems to us, is that they should refer to such material in their evidence for the reasons stated above.

We accordingly conclude that Mr Cooke's reliance on the Home Office statistics did not infringe the rule against hearsay . . .'

Appeal dismissed.

H and Another v Schering Chemicals Ltd and Another [1983] 1 WLR 143 (CA)

(For facts, see *ante* p. 268)

BINGHAM J: 'It is, as I have said, common ground that these articles can be referred to by experts as part of the general corpus of medical knowledge falling within the expertise of an expert in this field. That of course means that an expert who says (and I am looking at it from the plaintiffs' point of view for purposes of my example) "I consider that there is a causal connection between the taking of the drug and the resulting deformity", can fortify his opinion by referring to learned articles, publications, letters as reinforcing the view to which he has come. In doing so, he can make reference to papers in which a contrary opinion may be expressed but in which figures are set out which he regards as supporting his contention. In such a situation one asks: Are the figures and statistics set out in such an article strictly proved? and I think the answer is no. I think that they are nonetheless of probative value when referred to and relied on by an expert in the manner in which I have indicated. If an expert refers to the results of research published by a reputable authority in a reputable journal the court would, I think, ordinarily regard those results as supporting inferences fairly to be drawn from them, unless or until a different approach was shown to be proper.

Let me apply that to this case. Mr Beldam submits that there are great dangers in relying on these results contained in this material. For example, he says that certain of them refer to pills having been prescribed but leave it uncertain whether the pills were taken. If the pills were taken the results as published often leave it unclear at what stage of a pregnancy they were taken. Were they, for example, taken at a stage when it was too later for the foetus to be affected by the pills, even if they were capable of having an injurious effect in other circumstances? How were the control cases matched? How were the histories taken? How were the cases identified, and so on? All of these are valid points which will fall to be considered and assessed when they are made and when they are put to and discussed with any expert who relies on the articles. It may be that some of the answers will be found in the papers themselves. It may be that other matters will be left in doubt. It may very well be that grounds will emerge for viewing the results of the research with caution or scepticism. But in my judgment the proper approach of this court is to admit the articles, in the sense of reading them, and to give the factual assertions in those articles such weight as appears to the court, having heard any cross-examination or other evidence, to be proper.

That this is the proper approach I think derives support from the judgment of Cooke J in *Seyfang v Searle (GD) & Co.* [1973] QB 148. That was a case in which there was litigation in the United States on a somewhat similar issue to the present issue, the issue in that case being whether there was a causative link between the taking of the contraceptive pill and thrombo-embolic disorder. One of the parties to the United States litigation sought to subpoena certain British experts who had published the results of their research on this subject, for the purpose of establishing the causative link on which they relied. In the course of giving his judgment, Cooke J said, at p. 151:

Mr Baggott says in his affidavit that taking the testimony of the two doctors is the only way in which he can get the contents of the four articles into evidence in the action. While I accept that as a correct statement of Ohio law, in the absence of evidence to the contrary, I must confess that I find it surprising. The four articles now form part of the corpus of medical expertise on this particular subject. I apprehend that in England a medical expert witness with the proper qualifications would be allowed to refer to the articles as part of that corpus of expertise, even though he was not the author of the articles himself. It does appear to me with the greatest respect that a system which does not permit experts to refer in their expert evidence to the publications of other experts in the same field is a system which puts peculiar difficulties in the way of proof of matters which depend on expert opinion.

That seems to me with respect to be the right approach to the matter, and I say so with the greater diffidence having regard to the fact that I think the judge's observations reflect a submission made to him by counsel for the doctors in that case.

Accordingly the plaintiffs are, in my judgment, entitled by means of expert evidence to incorporate the contents of the articles in their evidence in this case, and it will be given such weight as in the light of any other evidence and of any cross-examination appears to be proper.'

R v Chard (1971) 56 Crim App R 268 (CA)

The applicant was convicted of murder. His defence was provocation. He sought to call a doctor who had reported that there was nothing wrong with his mental state but was of the opinion that in the light of his personality he had no intent or *mens rea* to commit murder. The judge ruled that the evidence was inadmissible. The applicant applied for leave to appeal.

ROSKILL LJ giving the judgment of the court: 'Mr Back has not sought to say that that expression of Dr Mansbridge's opinion could have been admissible on the issue of provocation and plainly he was right to make that concession at the trial and to repeat it before this Court. But he has sought to say that Dr Mansbridge's opinion on the question of the supposed inability of the applicant to form any intent to kill or to do grievous bodily injury, which are, of course, the two relevant alternative constituents of murder, was admissible. He put the matter before us in this way. Whenever, he said, a mental element arises, whether the charge be murder or theft or for that matter grievous bodily harm with intent charged under section 18 of the Offences Against the Person Act 1861, and a question arises in which the decision of the jury is difficult because of their lack of experience, the jury is entitled to expert assistance. Mr Back was unable to cite any authority in support of that proposition, not altogether surprisingly, for with the greatest respect to his argument, it seems to this Court that his submission, if accepted, would involve the Court admitting medical evidence in other cases not where there was an issue, for example, of insanity or diminished responsibility but where the sole issue which the jury had to consider, as happens in scores of different kinds of cases, was the question of intent.

As Geoffrey Lane J said in the course of argument, one purpose of jury trials is to bring into the jury box a body of men and women who are able to judge ordinary day-to-day questions by their own standards, that is, the standards in the eyes of the law of theoretically ordinary reasonable men and women. That is something which they are well able by their ordinary experience to judge for themselves. Where the matters in issue go outside that experience and they are invited to deal with someone supposedly abnormal, for example, supposedly suffering from insanity or diminished responsibility, then plainly in such a case they are entitled to the benefit of expert evidence. But where, as in the present case, they are dealing with someone who by concession was on the medical evidence entirely normal, it seems to this Court abundantly plain, on first principles of the admissibility of expert evidence, that it is not permissible to call a witness, whatever his personal experience, merely to tell the jury how he thinks an accused man's mind— assumedly a normal mind—operated at the time of the alleged crime with reference to the crucial question of what that man's intention was. As I have already said, this applicant was by concession normal in the eyes of the law.

Mr Back suggested that if this evidence were of no value, it could have been demolished by counsel for the Crown or perhaps by the learned trial judge in the summing-up. That submission, with respect, is of no relevance on the question whether or not the evidence was admissible. That consideration, if relevant at all, would go to weight, and questions of weight are in general irrelevant on questions of admissibility.'

Application refused.

Lowery v *The Queen* [1974] AC 85 (PC)

The appellant and K were charged with the murder of a young girl. It was a sadistic killing and the only explanation put forward for it was that they had wanted to see what it was like to "kill a chick". The Crown's case was that they had been acting in concert but both the appellant's and K's defence was that the other had killed the girl. The appellant gave evidence of his good character, stressed the unlikelihood of his behaving in such a manner and said that, because of his fear of K, he had been unable to prevent the murder. K alleged that he had been unable to appreciate what was happening and had been powerless to prevent the appellant killing the girl as he had been under the influence of drugs. Despite the appellant's objection, the defence for K was allowed to call the evidence of a psychologist as to their respective personalities and, on that evidence, the jury were invited to conclude that the appellant was the more likely of the two to have killed the girl. They were both convicted and the appellant unsuccessfully appealed to the full Court of the Supreme Court of Victoria on the ground, *inter alia*, that the psychologist's evidence was inadmissible. He further appealed to the Privy Council.

LORD MORRIS OF BORTH-Y-GEST, delivering the judgment of their Lordships: 'Having referred fully to the nature of the evidence given by Professor Cox the question as to its admissibility may now be considered. There was no doubt that Rosalyn Mary Nolte was killed in the bush area some 10 miles out of Hamilton when Lowery and King were present and when no one else was present. As was pointed out in the Court of Criminal Appeal the very nature of the killing showed that it was "a sadistic and otherwise motiveless killing". Any prospect of the acquittal of either of the two accused could only have been on the basis that one alone was the killer and that the other took no part whatsoever. That was what Lowery alleged when he said that King alone was the killer and that he (Lowery) was powerless to save the girl. In *R* v *Miller* (1952) 36 Cr App R 169, Devlin J referred to the duty of counsel for the defence to adduce any admissible evidence which is strictly relevant to his own case and assists his client whether or not it prejudices anyone else. The case for King was that Lowery had alone been the killer and that King had been heavily under the influence of drugs and had been powerless to stop Lowery. It was furthermore the evidence of each of them, in spite of what they said in their statements, that the idea or suggestion of seeing "what it would be like to kill a chick" emanated from the other. In all these circumstances it was necessary on behalf of King to call all relevant and admissible evidence which would exonerate King and throw responsibility entirely on Lowery. If in imaginary circumstances similar to those of this case it was apparent that one of the accused was a man of great physical strength whereas the other was a weakling it could hardly be doubted that in forming an opinion as to the probabilities it would be relevant to have the disparity between the two in mind. Physical characteristics may often be of considerable relevance: see *R* v *Toohey* [1965] AC 595. The evidence of Professor Cox was not related to crime or criminal tendencies: it was scientific evidence as to the respective personalities of the two accused as, and to the extent, revealed by certain well known tests. Whether it assisted the jury is not a matter that can be known. All that is known is that the jury convicted both the accused. But in so far as it might help in considering the probabilities as to what happened at the spot to which the girl was taken it was not only relevant to and indeed necessary for the case advanced by King but it was made relevant and admissible in view of the case advanced by Lowery and in view of Lowery's assertions against King.

The case being put forward by counsel on behalf of King involved posing to the jury the question "which of these two men is the more likely to have killed this girl?" and inviting the jury to come to the conclusion that it was Lowery. If the crime was one which was committed apparently without any kind of motive unless it was for the sensation experienced in the killing then unless both men acted in concert the deed was that of one of them. It would be unjust to prevent either of them from calling any evidence of probative value which could point to the probability that the perpetrator was the one rather than the other.'

Appeal dismissed.

R v *Turner* [1975] QB 834 (CA)

The defendant, who was charged with murder, admitted that he had killed his girl friend by hitting her with a hammer, but pleaded that he had been provoked by her statement that she had had affairs with other men and that he was not the father of her expected child. The defence sought to call a psychiatrist to give his opinion that the defendant was not suffering from a mental illness, that he was not violent by nature but that his personality was such that he could have been provoked in the circumstances and that he was likely to be telling the truth. The judge ruled the psychiatric evidence inadmissible. The defendant was convicted and appealed.

LAWTON LJ, giving the judgment of the court: 'Before this court Mr Mildon submitted that the psychiatrist's opinion as to the defendant's personality and mental make-up as set out in his report was relevant and admissible for three reasons: first, because it helped to establish lack of intent; secondly, because it helped to establish that the defendant was likely to be easily provoked; and thirdly, because it helped to show that the defendant's account of what had happened was likely to be true. We do not find it necessary to deal specifically with the first of these reasons. Intent was not a live issue in this case. The evidence was tendered on the issues of provocation and credibility. The judge gave his ruling in relation to those issues. In any event the decision which we have come to on Mr Mildon's second and third submissions would also apply to his first.

The first question on both these issues is whether the psychiatrist's opinion was relevant. A man's personality and mental make-up do have a bearing upon his conduct. A quick-tempered man will react more aggressively to an unpleasing situation than a placid one. Anyone having a florid imagination or a tendency to exaggerate is less likely to be a reliable witness than one who is precise and careful. These are matters of ordinary human experience. Opinions from knowledgeable persons about a man's personality and mental make-up play a part in many human judgments. In our judgment the psychiatrist's opinion was relevant. Relevance, however, does not result in evidence being admissible; it is a condition precedent to admissibility. Our law excludes evidence of many matters which in life outside the courts sensible people take into consideration when making decisions. Two broad heads of exclusion are hearsay and opinion. As we have already pointed out, the psychiatrist's report contained a lot of hearsay which was inadmissible. A ruling on this ground, however, would merely have trimmed the psychiatrist's evidence: it would not have excluded it altogether. Was it inadmissible because of the rules relating to opinion evidence?

The foundation of these rules was laid by Lord Mansfield in *Folkes* v *Chadd* (1782) 3 Doug KB 157 and was well laid: the opinion of scientific men upon proven facts may be given by men of science within their own science. An expert's opinion is admissible to furnish the court with scientific information which is likely to be outside the experience and knowledge of a judge or jury. If on the proven facts a judge or jury can form their own conclusions without help, then the opinion of an expert is unnecessary. In such a case if it is given dressed up in scientific jargon it may make judgment more difficult. The fact that an expert witness has impressive scientific qualifications does not by that fact alone make his opinion on matters of human nature and behaviour within the limits of normality any more helpful than that of the jurors themselves; but there is a danger that they may think it does.

What, in plain English, was the psychiatrist in this case intending to say? First, that the defendant was not showing and never had shown any evidence of mental illness, as defined by the Mental Health Act 1959, and did not require any psychiatric treatment; secondly, that he had had a deep emotional relationship with the girl which was likely to have caused an explosive release of blind rage when she confessed her wantonness to him; thirdly, that after he had killed her he behaved like someone suffering from profound grief. The first part of his opinion was within his expert province and outside the experience of the jury but was of no relevance in the circumstances of this case. The second and third points dealt with matters which are well within ordinary human experience. We all know that both men and women who are deeply in love can, and sometimes do, have outbursts of blind rage when discovering unexpected wantonness on the part of their loved ones; the wife taken in adultery is the classical example of the application of the defence of "provocation"; and when death or serious injury results, profound grief usually follows. Jurors do not need psychiatrists to tell them how ordinary folk who are not suffering from any mental illness are likely to react to the stresses and strains of life. It follows that the proposed evidence was not admissible to establish that the defendant was likely to have been provoked. The same reasoning applies to its suggested admissibility on the issue of credibility. The jury had to decide what reliance they could put upon the defendant's evidence. He had to be judged as someone who was not mentally disordered. This is what juries are empanelled to do. The law assumes they can perform their duties properly. The jury in this case did not need, and should not have been offered, the evidence of a psychiatrist to help them decide whether the defendant's evidence was truthful.

Mr Mildon submitted that such help should not have been rejected by the judge because in *Lowery* v *The Queen* [1974] AC 85 the Privy Council had approved of the admission of the evidence of a psychologist on the issue of credibility. We had to consider that case carefully before we could decide whether it had in any way put a new interpretation upon what have long been thought to be the rules relating to the calling of evidence on the issue of credibility, *viz.*, that in general evidence can be called to impugn the credibility of witnesses but not led in chief to bolster it up. In *Lowery* v *The Queen* evidence of a psychologist on behalf of one of two accused was admitted to establish that his version of the facts was more probable than that put forward by the other. In every case what is relevant and admissible depends on the issues raised in that case. In *Lowery* v *The Queen* the issues were unusual; and the accused to whose disadvantage the psychologist's evidence went had in effect said before it was called that he was not the sort of man to have committed the offence. In giving the judgment of the Board, Lord Morris of Borth-y-Gest said, at p.103:

The only question now arising is whether in the special circumstances above referred to it was open to King in defending himself to call Professor Cox to give the evidence that he gave. The evidence was relevant to and necessary for his case which involved negativing what Lowery had said and put forward; in their Lordships' view in agreement with that of the Court of Criminal Appeal the evidence was admissible.

We adjudge *Lowery* v *The Queen* [1974] AC 85 to have been decided on its special facts. We do not consider that it is an authority for the proposition that in all cases psychologists and psychiatrists can be called to prove the probability of the accused's veracity. If any such rule was applied in our courts, trial by psychiatrists would be likely to take the place of trial by jury and magistrates. We do not find that prospect attractive and the law does not at present provide for it.

In coming to the conclusion we have in this case we must not be taken to be discouraging the calling of psychiatric evidence in cases where such evidence can be helpful within the present rules of evidence. These rules may be too restrictive of the admissibility of opinion evidence. The Criminal Law Revision Committee in its eleventh report thought they were and made recommendations for relaxing them: see paragraphs 266–271. The recommendations have not yet been accepted by Parliament and until they are, or other changes in the law of evidence are made, this court must apply the existing rules: see *Myers* v *Director of Public Prosecutions* [1965] AC 1001 *per* Lord Reid at pp. 1021–1022. We have not overlooked what Lord Parker CJ said in *Director of Public Prosecutions* v *A and BC Chewing Gum Ltd* [1968] 1 QB 159, 164 about the advance of science making more and more inroads into the old common law principle applicable to opinion evidence; but we are firmly of the opinion that psychiatry has not yet become a satisfactory substitute for the common sense of juries or magistrates on matters within their experience of life.'

Appeal dismissed.

• Can *Lowery* v *The Queen* and *R* v *Turner* be reconciled with each other?

R v Smith [1979] 1 WLR 1445 (CA)

The applicant occupied rooms in the same house as the victim and his wife. The victim arrived home late one evening, having been drinking heavily, and was told by his wife that she had had an altercation with the applicant. The victim went up to the room where the applicant was asleep. A quarrel and fight took place during which the applicant stabbed the victim to death with a knife. While in custody the applicant was examined by two psychiatrists. At his trial for murder the applicant raised the defence of automatism while asleep. The prosecution, who contended that the applicant had recently thought of that defence, sought and obtained leave to cross-examine him about his interviews with the psychiatrists and to call the psychiatrists to give their views on automatism. The applicant was convicted of murder and applied for leave to appeal against conviction on the ground, *inter alia*, that the judge erred in allowing the psychiatrists to give their opinions as to whether the applicant's evidence was consistent with a defence of automatism.

GEOFFREY LANE LJ, giving the judgment of the court: 'The next point Mr Blom-Cooper made is this: as a matter of discretion these reports should not be admitted. In effect, he says this: that in order to be admissible at all the reports must be relevant; that is to say, relevant to some issue which the jury have to determine. He submits that since there was no question of insanity or diminished responsibility, automatism or not was a matter which could and should be decided by the jury in the light of their own experience and they should not be assisted by medical or expert evidence as to the state of mind of the defendant. That being so, he suggests the doctors' evidence was irrelevant and, on that basis, should not have been admitted. Here, again, he cites a number of authorities. First was the decision of this court in *R v Chard* (1971) 56 Cr App R 268:

> Where no issue of insanity, diminished responsibility or mental illness has arisen, and it is conceded on the medical evidence that the defendant is entirely normal, it is not permissible to call a medical witness to state how, in his opinion, the defendant's mind operated at the time of the alleged crime with regard to the question of intent.

He referred to a passage of Roskill LJ's judgment, at p 270:

> Mr Back was unable to cite any authority in support of the proposition, not altogether surprisingly, for with the greatest respect to his argument, it seems to this court that his submission, if accepted, would involve the court admitting medical evidence in other cases not where there was an issue, for example, of insanity or diminished responsibility but where the sole issue which the jury had to consider, as happens in scores of different kinds of cases, was the question of intent . . . .. One purpose of jury trials is to bring into the jury box a body of men and women who are able to judge ordinary day-to-day questions by their own standards, that is, the standards in the eyes of the law of theoretically ordinary reasonable men and women. That is something which they are well able by their ordinary experience to judge for themselves. Where the matters in issue go outside that experience and they are invited to deal with someone supposedly abnormal, for example, supposedly suffering from insanity or diminished responsibility, then plainly in such a case they are entitled to the benefit of expert evidence.

There is a further decision very much to the same effect which we do not find it necessary to cite in detail. I mention it simply for the purpose of completeness. That is *R* v *Turner (Terence)* [1975] QB 834. So, the question seems to be whether or not the applicant exhibited the type of abnormality in relation to automatism that would render it proper and, indeed, desirable for the jury to have expert help in reaching their conclusion. It seems to us without the benefit of authority that that is clearly the case. This type of automatism—sleepwalking—call it what you like, is not something, we think, which is within the realm of the ordinary juryman's experience. It is something on which, speaking for ourselves as judges, we should like help were we to have to decide it and we see not why a jury should be deprived of that type of help . . .

Accordingly, it seems to us this was a case where the jury were entitled to have the benefit of medical evidence and the judge was right on that basis at any rate to admit the evidence in question as he did.'

(His Lordship decided that there was no reason to exclude the evidence because of possible unfairness to the applicant. The court granted leave to appeal, treating the hearing as the appeal.)

Appeal dismissed.

R v *Davies* [1962] 1 WLR 1111 (CMAC)

At a court-martial in Germany the driver of a car involved in a collision was charged with having driven a vehicle on a road while unfit to drive through drink or drugs. Three witnesses were allowed to give evidence about the facts they had observed and also to give their opinions as to the defendant's ability or fitness to drive. The driver was convicted and appealed.

LORD PARKER CJ, giving the judgment of the court: 'The defence had strongly taken the stand that the witness should be allowed to speak only as to facts he had seen, because it was for the court to say what was the appellant's condition. Apparently the judge advocate advised the court that the witness could state the impression he formed as to the appellant's condition at the time he saw him if he was a witness who knew what was entailed in the driving of a car.

It is to be observed that the witness was allowed to speak about two matters which are quite distinct; one is what his impression was as to whether drink had been taken by the appellant, and the second was his opinion as to whether as the result of that drink he was fit or unfit to drive a car.

The court has come clearly to the conclusion that a witness can quite properly give his general impression as to whether a driver had taken drink. He must describe of course the facts upon which he relies, but it seems to this court that he is perfectly entitled to give his impression as to whether drink had been taken or not. On the other hand, as regards the second matter, it cannot be said, as it seems to this court, that a witness, merely because he is a driver himself, is in the expert witness category so that it is proper to ask him his opinion as to fitness or unfitness to drive. That is the very matter which the court itself has to determine. Accordingly, in so far as this witness and two subsequent witnesses, the lance-corporal and the regimental sergeant-major gave their opinion as to the appellant's ability or fitness to drive, the court was wrong in admitting that evidence. [His Lordship considered the evidence as a whole and continued:] This court has come quite clearly to the conclusion that there was ample evidence here to support the verdict and that so far as the wrongful admission of certain evidence is concerned the court would have been bound to come to the same conclusion even if that evidence had not been admitted.'

Appeal dismissed.

Civil Evidence Act 1972

3(1) Subject to any rules of court . . . where a person is called as a witness in any civil proceedings, his opinion on any relevant matter on which he is qualified to give expert evidence, shall be admissible in evidence . . .

(2) It is hereby declared that where a person is called as a witness in any civil proceedings, a statement of opinion by him on any relevant matter on which he is not qualified to give expert evidence, if made as a way of conveying relevant facts personally perceived by him, is admissible as evidence of what he perceived.

(3) In this section 'relevant matter' includes an issue in the proceedings in question.

Criminal Procedure Act 1865

8   Comparison of a disputed writing with any writing proved to the satisfaction of the judge to be genuine shall be permitted to be made by witnesses; and such writings, and the evidence of witnesses respecting the same, may be submitted to the court and jury as evidence of the genuineness or otherwise of the writing in dispute.

R v *Tilley; R* v *Tilley* [1961] 1 WLR 1309 (CCA)

The appellants, G and L, were both charged with the larceny of a car. Their case was that they had bought it from a person claiming to be the owner and from whom they had obtained a receipt, which they produced. At the trial, in cross-examination, each appellant was asked to write out the words of the receipt. G's handwriting was plainly different, but there were similarities between L's writing and that on the receipt. Counsel for the prosecution did not pursue the matter, as it was the prosecution case that the receipt was a document devised by the appellants in order to explain their possession of the car if questioned, and that it was not of great importance whether they or someone else had written it. The matter was not mentioned again until the summing up, when the deputy chairman commented upon the similarities and invited the jury to decide whether or not the receipt was genuine, giving the jury the receipt and the handwriting exhibits to examine. G and L were convicted and appealed.

ASHWORTH J, giving the judgment of the court: '. . .criticism is now made by Mr Simpson on behalf of the two appellants that it was not right or fair that the defence should suddenly be met with this kind of address to the jury on a topic which had never been ventilated throughout the trial. Moreover, it was said that the topic was one on which the Crown had not relied, and in regard to it, if the defendants had had an opportunity they might have been in a position to call expert evidence. Those criticisms were, we think, of considerable force. But the matter goes even further. The question arises whether in any case it was proper for the deputy chairman to indulge in comments himself about these documents and then hand them to the jury for their consideration and decision without any evidence having been called to assist them on that issue.

The matter has come before the court in more than one previous case. One to which our attention was called was *R* v *Harvey* (1869) 11 Cox CC 546. The matter was also raised in *R* v *Rickard* (1918) 13 Cr App R 140. In that case Salter J, giving the judgment of this court, said this, after referring to section 8 of the Criminal Procedure Act, 1865 (Lord Denman's Act) ibid, 143: "That case [*R* v *Crouch* (1850 4 Cox CC 163] does not decide what degree of preparation is necessary to constitute an expert, but it does decide that a person is not entitled to give such evidence if his only knowledge on the subject is that acquired in the course of the case. That was the position of the police officer, and the position of Busby is less satisfactory. Therefore no expert evidence at all was given in the case. This court does not decide that expert evidence in such cases is necessary, and the observations of Blackburn J in *Harvey* 11 Cox CC 546 do not so decide, but it is clear from the nature of things that to leave a question of handwriting to a jury without assistance is a somewhat dangerous course."

In the present case there was no evidence, not even questions directed to alleged similarities, and the matter only arose in the course of the summing up. This court endorses and reaffirms the statement of principle to be found in Salter J's judgment on behalf of this court in *Rickard's* case. A jury should not be left unassisted to decide questions of disputed handwriting on their own.

It is also to be noted that, although *R* v *Day* [1940] 1 All ER 402 raised in the main an utterly different issue, the question of handwriting did occur, and Croom-Johnson J ruled that the jury could not be asked to compare handwriting, without some assistance by way of expert evidence, and that ruling was once again in conformity with the decision in *Rickard's* case.

In these circumstances, in the view of this court, it is right to say that the course pursued by the deputy chairman was not in accordance with the principles previously laid down, and should not be followed in any other case.'

Appeals allowed.

R v *O'Sullivan* [1969] 1 WLR 497 (CA)

The defendant, an employee of a firm whose custom it was to make overnight deposits in the night safe of their bank in wallets, was charged with the larceny as a servant of a wallet containing £411. The evidence was that a man had asked a bank official for the firm's wallet by number, and had signed for it on a register; that the bank official recognised the man as the defendant, whom she had seen several times, and later picked him out at an identification parade; and that only four people besides the defendant knew the number of the firm's wallet. Photostatic copies of the register on which appeared the signature of the man who had taken the wallet, as well as admittedly genuine signatures of the defendant, were given to the jury. At the outset of the trial the defence did not dispute, but later disputed that the signature of the man who had taken the wallet was that of the defendant, but no expert witness on handwriting gave evidence. The deputy chairman warned the jury of the dangers implicit in making comparisons of handwriting without the help of experts.

The defendant appealed against conviction, on the ground that the jury should not have been left to make the handwriting comparisons on their own.

WINN LJ, giving the judgment of the court: 'It seems to this court that possibly there has been a misunderstanding from a very early date of what was said by Blackburn J in *R* v

Harvey (1867) 11 Cox CC 546. That was a case where there had been an objection taken by the defence to certain evidence found in the house of the prisoner, certain copy books said to contain his handwriting, on the ground that police officers are not competent to give evidence as experts as to handwriting. The judge — and he has been accepted as one of the greatest judges this country has ever had the fortune to possess — said at p. 548:

> But the jury can inspect them and compare them with the forged document . . . they are only copy books . . . the evidence is very weak, and I do not think the jury ought to act upon it without the assistance of an expert. The policeman is certainly not a skilled witness.

and in three lines he gave his ruling: "But here we have no expert, and I do not think it would be right to let the jury compare the handwriting without some such assistance. The evidence is very slight." It seems to this court today that that was a ruling of a very narrow character indeed. The judge was saying "in this particular case (a) we have no expert (b) the evidence is of very poor evidentiary value; therefore I am going to exercise my discretion in not allowing it to go to the jury."

There has been a long sequence of authority and really it does not merit the time that otherwise would be taken that this court should go right through all those cases. The case of *R* v *Tilley* [1961] 1 WLR 1309 is undoubtedly the most important, most prominent, of the decisions and was a case where Ashworth J giving the judgment of the Court of Criminal Appeal, of which it happened that I was myself the junior member, used this expression which this court today, no longer the Court of Criminal Appeal but the Court of Appeal, Criminal Division, thinks has been not only misinterpreted to some extent but has been more widely applied and held to be of stricter restrictive effect than really is justified by the words of the court. This was said, at p. 1312: "In the present case there was no evidence, not even questions directed to alleged similarities, and the matter only arose in the course of the summing up." That point stresses the importance of what Mr Gale said to the court today in his submission, that it may very well be the proper practice where the prosecution does or should anticipate that there will be an issue as to the genuineness of some signature, that the prosecution should tender a witness who is properly expert to give evidence on that matter; in *R* v *Tilley*, as in the instant case, the matter only arose long after the trial had begun, at a time when even if the matter were dealt with by rebuttal, almost certainly there would have to be a second trial rather than such a long adjournment as would be required to obtain the expert advice. There was no evidence in *R* v *Tilley*, said the judge, and the matter only arose in the course of the summing up. He went on, at p. 1312:

> This court endorses and reaffirms the statement of principle to be found in Salter J's judgment on behalf of this court in *Rickard's* case (13 Cr App R 140). A jury should not be left unassisted to decide questions of disputed handwriting on their own.

The question arises whether within the proper understanding of those words in the instant case the jury was 'left unassisted to decide questions of disputed handwriting.' The document had to go before the jury in the instant case since it formed part of the probative material establishing the visit by the man who took away the wallet and the fact that he had entered somebody's name in the register of the bank. The jury was not in the instant case invited to make any comparisons, as the jury had been in *R* v *Tilley*. The chairman in the instant case did not himself purport to make any comments of any kind about similarities or dissimilarities as had been done by the deputy chairman in *R v Tilley*. The jury were warned very, very carefully and stringently not to make these comparisons.

In the circumstances, it does not seem to this court that the jury in the instant case can be said to have been left to decide questions of disputed handwriting on their own. It is true they were not effectively prevented from doing it. What could possibly have been done effectively to prevent them from making the comparison passes the comprehension of this court. It can hardly be right to suppose that the documents already before them for a legitimate, proper and necessary purpose should have been snatched away from them since that could only have aroused dissatisfaction and grave doubt in their minds as to the fairness of the proceedings which were being conducted before them.

There have been subsequent references; it is right that I should say that one of them was a part of a judgment of mine in *R v Stannard*, 48 Cr App R 81, a case which was quite a complicated and heavy appeal and I note on looking back at it — I well remember the burden of the judgment — that the judgment when reported extends over no less than twelve pages. A very subsidiary issue on the appeal was whether or not there had been any impropriety in the manner in which the jury were allowed to look at certain signatures. I attempted then, at p. 95, to give what, on looking at it again, I feel was not a very satisfactory paraphrase of the earlier case of *R v Tilley* [1961] 1 WLR 1309. I referred to the undoubtedly correct statement by Salter J in *R v Rickard* (13 Cr App R 140, 143) that the "court does not decide that expert evidence in such cases is necessary and the observations of Blackburn J in *Harvey* (11 Cox CC 546, 548) do not so decide." I referred to the danger involved. Then I said: "The situation here was quite the obverse of the medal, because what [defending counsel] desired to have from the learned judge was a direction that they *should* make this comparison."

It seems to the court that in the instant case the matter was properly dealt with. The fact remains that there is a very real danger where the jury make such comparisons, but as a matter of practical reality all that can be done is to ask them not to make the comparisons themselves and to have vividly in mind the fact that they are not qualified to make comparisons. It is terribly risky for jurors to attempt comparisons of writing unless they have very special training in this particular science. All possible was done, this court thinks, with great care and very fairly by the court in the instant case. It may well be that, despite it, the jury did try to make comparisons. That is really unavoidable and it should be accepted these days that *R v Tilley* [1961] 1 WLR 1309 cannot always be in its literal meaning exactly applied; nevertheless every possible step and regard should be had to what was said by the court in that case, inasmuch as never should it be deliberately a matter of invitation or exhortation to a jury to look at disputed handwriting. There should be a warning of the dangers; further than that, as a matter of practical reality, it cannot be expected that the court will go.'

Appeal dismissed.

Questions for discussion

R v Coke; R v Littleton

1 What primary facts must be proved as a basis for the expert testimony to be given by: (a) Mr Hale; (b) Dr Vesey; (c) Dr Espinasse? What witnesses should be called to prove these primary facts?

2 Frame a series of questions designed to adduce the evidence in chief of Mr Hale for the prosecution. How would you make use of the chart which he has prepared?

3 Assume that you act for Coke, and that your handwriting expert has advised you that Mr Hale's conclusion can be attacked because a leading work on the scientific examination of documents suggests that he had insufficient known samples of Coke's handwriting to enable a valid comparison to be made. How would you cross-examine Mr Hale, and how would the leading work be treated by the court?

4 The following is an extract from the summing-up of the trial judge in *R* v *Coke; R* v *Littleton*: 'Members of the jury, I must now deal with the subject of the handwritten exhibits GG1 and GG3. As you will recall, the prosecution called no evidence from any handwriting expert in order to prove to you that the defendant Coke is the author of Exhibit GG1. The defence on the other hand called a witness, Mr Mansfield, in order to prove the contrary. Now you may think that the reason why the prosecution did not call such a witness is that the documents speak for themselves. You have already seen them more than once in this court, and when you retire to consider your verdict, you will be at liberty to take them with you into the jury room. There you can examine them at your leisure, bearing in mind that it is the prosecution who have set out to prove that the authorship of these documents is one and the same. If necessary, you will be provided with a magnifyng glass, which may enable you to look at the exhibits more closely. But with regard to Mr Mansfield, let me just say this. He claimed for himself some expertise in the field of handwriting, but his profession is that of solicitor. He has, it is true, purely out of interest, spent much time examining documents over the last fifteen years. You may think that he has inevitably acquired some degree of expertise through that. For that reason I permitted him to give evidence as an expert witness. But you may think that in this case no expert witness can do more than you can. Mr Mansfield stated that he was sure that Coke was not the author of Exhibit GG1. But that is entirely a matter for you. And if you all follow my advice, you will not place too much emphasis on opinion evidence in this kind of case. There is no reason why you should not trust your own observation.'

Criticise this passage.

Blackstone v Coke

1 Would the plaintiff be entitled to call evidence from Mrs Helen Blackstone to the effect that:

(a) following the incident involving Coke, her daughter was extremely depressed, occasionally hysterical and given to fits of weeping?

(b) following the same incident, her daughter was subject to serious psychiatric disturbance as a result of which it would have been inadvisable for her to undergo an abortion?

2 If the answer to either question is 'no', by what evidence should these matters be proved?

Additional questions

1 In a criminal case, a witness is called by the defence as an expert on the operation of a

'guilt-o-meter'. This 'guilt-o-meter' is a flat circular piece of wood, attached to which is a revolving pointer. If the operator spins the pointer while holding the 'guilt-o-meter' the pointer will come to rest pointing either to the letter 'G' or the letters 'NG', which are painted alternately around the circumference. The witness claims that by picking up the 'vibrations' from the courtroom, the 'guilt-o-meter' will deliver a true verdict if the pointer is spun in a random manner. Should the judge permit the witness to testify? Why or why not? [With acknowledgement to Professor Irving Younger].

2 Would an expert astrologer be permitted to testify as to the behaviour of the defendant on a certain day, assuming that the astrologer had prepared an astrological chart in strict compliance with the principles of astrology?

3 You are acting for George who is charged jointly with Harry on a charge of murdering Ivan. The case for the prosecution is that both George and Harry committed a joint and deliberate assault on Ivan. Harry, who has pleaded not guilty, has given evidence to the effect that George was the ringleader and that he, Harry, although present, never touched Ivan. You have in your possession statements from two doctors: Dr James says that George, although physically large, is a timid young man and easily led, and not nearly as strong as he looks; Dr Kay says that Harry is mentally unbalanced, given to fits of violence and a pathological liar. What use, if any, can you make of this evidence in defence of George?

Further reading

Jackson, 'The ultimate issue rule: one rule too many' [1984] Crim LR 75.
Kenny, 'The expert in court' (1983) 99 LQR 197.
Munday, 'Excluding the expert witness' [1981] Crim LR 688.
Pattenden, 'Expert opinion evidence based on hearsay' [1982] Crim LR 85.
Pattenden, 'Conflicting approaches to psychiatric evidence in criminal trials: England, Canada and Australia' [1986] Crim LR 92.

10 Public Policy and Privilege

A: PUBLIC POLICY

(Suggested preliminary reading: *A Practical Approach to Evidence,* pp. 291–317.)

Conway v Rimmer [1968] AC 910 (HL)

The plaintiff, a probationary police constable, was prosecuted for theft by the defendant, a superintendent in the same force. The jury stopped the case. The plaintiff now brought an action for malicious prosecution against the defendant. In the course of discovery, the defendant disclosed a list of documents in his possession, admittedly relevant to the plaintiff's action, which included four reports made by him about the plaintiff during his period of probation, and a report in connection with his prosecution. The Home Secretary objected to production of all five documents on the grounds that each fell within a class of documents the production of which would be injurious to the public interest.

LORD REID: 'The question whether such a statement by a Minister of the Crown should be accepted as conclusively preventing any court from ordering production of any of the documents to which it applies is one of very great importance in the administration of justice. If the commonly accepted interpretation of the decision of this House in *Duncan* v *Cammell, Laird & Co. Ltd* [1942] AC 624 is to remain authoritative the question admits of only one answer—the Minister's statement is final and conclusive. Normally I would be very slow to question the authority of a unanimous decision of this House only 25 years old which was carefully considered and obviously intended to lay down a general rule. But this decision has several abnormal features.

Lord Simon thought that on this matter the law in Scotland was the same as the law in England and he clearly intended to lay down a rule applicable to the whole of the United Kingdom. But in *Glasgow Corporation* v *Central Land Board* 1956 SC (HL) 1 this House held that this was not so, with the result that today on this question the law is different in the two countries. There are many chapters of the law where for historical and other reasons it is quite proper that the law should be different in the two countries. But here we are dealing purely with public policy—with the proper relation between the powers of the executive and the powers of the courts—and I can see no rational justification for the law on this matter being different in the two countries.

Secondly, events have proved that the rule supposed to have been laid down in *Duncan's* case is far from satisfactory. In the large number of cases in England and elsewhere which have been cited in argument much dissatisfaction has been expressed and I have not observed even one expression of whole-hearted approval. Moreover a statement made by the Lord Chancellor in 1956 on behalf of the Government, to which I shall return later, makes it clear that that Government did not regard it as consonant with public policy to maintain the rule to the full extent which existing authorities has held to be justifiable.

I have no doubt that the case of *Duncan* v *Cammell, Laird & Co. Ltd* was rightly decided. The plaintiff sought discovery of documents relating to the submarine Thetis including a contract for the hull and machinery and plans and specifications. The First Lord of the Admiralty had stated that "it would be injurious to the public interest that any of the said documents should be disclosed to any person". Any of these documents might well have given valuable information, or at least clues, to the skilled eye of an agent of a foreign power. But Lord Simon LC took the opportunity to deal with the whole question of the right of the Crown to prevent production of documents in a litigation. Yet a study of his speech leaves me with the strong impression that throughout he had primarily in mind cases where discovery or disclosure would involve a danger of real prejudice to the national interest. I find it difficult to believe that his speech would have been the same if the case had related, as the present case does, to discovery of routine reports on a probationer constable.

Early in his speech Lord Simon quoted with approval the view of Rigby LJ, in *Attorney-General* v *Newcastle-upon-Tyne Corporation* [1897] 2 QB 384 that documents are not to be withheld "unless there be some plain overruling principle of public interest concerned which cannot be disregarded". And, summing up towards the end, he said:

> . . . the rule that the interest of the state must not be in jeopardy by producing documents which would injure it is a principle to be observed in administering justice, quite unconnected with the interests or claims of the particular parties in litigation.

Surely it would be grotesque to speak of the interest of the state being put in jeopardy by disclosure of a routine report on a probationer. Lord Simon did not say very much about objections "based upon the view that the public interest requires a particular class of communications with, or within, a public department to be protected from production on the ground that the candour and completeness of such communications might be prejudiced if they were ever liable to be disclosed in subsequent litigation rather than on the contents of the particular document itself." But at the end he said that a Minister "ought not to take the responsibility of withholding production except in cases where the public interest would otherwise be damnified, for example, where disclosure would be injurious to national defence, or to good diplomatic relations, or where the practice of keeping a class of documents secret is necessary for the proper functioning of the public service". I find it difficult to believe that he would have put these three examples on the same level if he had intended the third to cover such minor matters as a routine report by a relatively junior officer. And my impression is strengthened by the passage at the very end of the speech:

> . . . the public interest is also the interest of every subject of the realm, and while, in these exceptional cases, the private citizen may seem to be denied what is to his immediate advantage, he, like the rest of us, would suffer if the needs of protecting the interests of the country as a whole were not ranked as a prior obligation.

Would he have spoken of "these exceptional cases" or of "the needs of protecting the interests of the country as a whole" if he had intended to include all manner of routine communications? And did he really mean that the protection of such communications is a "prior obligation" in a case where a man's reputation or fortune is at stake and withholding the document makes it impossible for justice to be done?

It is universally recognised that here there are two kinds of public interest which may clash. There is the public interest that harm shall not be done to the nation or the public service by disclosure of certain documents, and there is the public interest that the administration of justice shall not be frustrated by the withholding of documents which must be produced if justice is to be done. There are many cases where the nature of the injury which would or might be done to the nation or the public service is of so grave a character that no other interest, public or private, can be allowed to prevail over it. With regard to such cases it would be proper to say, as Lord Simon did, that to order production of the document in question would put the interest of the state in jeopardy. But there are many other cases where the possible injury to the public service is much less and there one would think that it would be proper to balance the public interests involved. I do not believe that Lord Simon really meant that the smallest probability of injury to the public service must always outweigh the gravest frustration of the administration of justice.

It is to be observed that, in a passage which I have already quoted, Lord Simon referred to the practice of keeping a class of documents secret being "*necessary* [my italics] for the proper functioning of the public interest". But the certificate of the Home Secretary in the present case does not go nearly so far as that. It merely says that the production of a document of the classes to which it refers would be "injurious to the public interest:" it does not say what degree of injury is to be apprehended. It may be advantageous to the functioning of the public service that reports of this kind should be kept secret—that is the view of the Home Secretary—but I would be very surprised if anyone said that that is necessary.

There are now many large public bodies, such as British Railways and the National Coal Board, the proper and efficient functioning of which is very necessary for many reasons including the safety of the public. The Attorney-General made it clear that Crown privilege is not and cannot be invoked to prevent disclosure of similar documents made by them or their servants even if it were said that this is required for the proper and efficient functioning of that public service. I find it difficult to see why it should be *necessary* to withhold whole classes of routine "communications with or within a public department" but quite unnecessary to withhold similar communications with or within a public corporation. There the safety of the public may well depend on the candour and completeness of reports made by subordinates whose duty it is to draw attention to defects. But, so far as I know, no one has ever suggested that public safety has been endangered by the candour or completeness of such reports having been inhibited by the fact that they may have to be produced if the interests of the due administration of justice should ever require production at any time . . ..

In my judgment, in considering what it is "proper" for a court to do we must have regard to the need, shown by 25 years' experience since *Duncan's* case [1942] AC 624, that the courts should balance the public interest in the proper administration of justice against the public interest in withholding any evidence which a Minister considers ought to be withheld.

I would therefore propose that the House ought now to decide that courts have and are entitled to exercise a power and duty to hold a balance between the public interest, as expressed by a Minister, to withhold certain documents or other evidence, and the public interest in ensuring the proper administration of justice. That does not mean that a court would reject a Minister's view: full weight must be given to it in every case, and if the Minister's reasons are of a character which judicial experience is not competent to weigh, then the Minister's view must prevail. But experience has shown that reasons given for withholding whole classes of documents are often not of that character. For example a court is perfectly well able to assess the likelihood that, if the writer of a certain class of document knew that there was a chance that his report might be produced in legal proceedings, he would make a less full and candid report than he would otherwise have done.

I do not doubt that there are certain classes of documents which ought not to be disclosed whatever their content may be. Virtually everyone agrees that Cabinet minutes and the like ought not to be disclosed until such time as they are only of historical interest. But I do not think that many people would give as the reason that premature disclosure would prevent candour in the Cabinet. To my mind the most important reason is that such disclosure would create or fan ill-informed or captious public or political criticism. The business of government is difficult enough as it is, and no government could contemplate with equanimity the inner workings of the government machine being exposed to the gaze of those ready to criticise without adequate knowledge of the background and perhaps with some axe to grind. And that must, in my view, also apply to all documents concerned with policy making within departments including, it may be, minutes and the like by quite junior officials and correspondence with outside bodies. Further it may be that deliberations about a particular case require protection as much as deliberations about policy. I do not think that it is possible to limit such documents by any definition. But there seems to me to be a wide difference between such documents and routine reports. There may be special reasons for withholding some kinds of routine documents, but I think that the proper test to be applied is to ask, in the language of Lord Simon in *Duncan's* case, whether the withholding of a document because it belongs to a particular class is really "necessary for the proper functioning of the public service".

It appears to me that, if the Minister's reasons are such that a judge can properly weigh them, he must, on the other hand, consider what is the probable importance in the case before him of the documents or other evidence sought to be withheld. If he decides that on balance the documents probably ought to be produced, I think that it would generally be best that he should see them before ordering production and if he thinks that the Minister's reasons are not clearly expressed he will have to see the documents before ordering production. I can see nothing wrong in the judge seeing documents without their being shown to the parties. Lord Simon said (in *Duncan's* case) that "where the Crown is a party . . . this would amount to communicating with one party to the exclusion of the other". I do not agree. The parties see the Minister's reasons. Where a document has not been prepared for the information of the judge, it seems to me a misuse of language to say that the judge "communicates with" the holder of the document by reading it. If on reading the document he still thinks that it ought to be produced he will order its production.

But it is important that the Minister should have a right to appeal before the document is produced. This matter was not fully investigated in the argument before your Lordships. But it does appear that in one way or another there can be an appeal if the document is in the custody of a servant of the Crown or of a person who is willing to co-operate with the Minister. There may be difficulty if it is in the hands of a person who wishes to produce it. But that difficulty could occur today if a witness wishes to give some evidence which the Minister unsuccessfully urges the court to prevent from being given. It may be that this is a matter which deserves further investigation by the Crown authorities.

The documents in this case are in the possession of a police force. The position of the police is peculiar. They are not servants of the Crown and they do not take orders from the Government. But they are carrying out an essential function of Government, and various Crown rights, privileges and exemptions have been held to apply to them. Their position was explained in *Coomber v Berkshire Justices* [1883] 9 AC 61 (HL) and cases there cited. It has never been denied that they are entitled to Crown privilege with regard to documents, and it is essential that they should have it.

The police are carrying on an unending war with criminals many of whom are today highly intelligent. So it is essential that there should be no disclosure of anything which might give any useful information to those who organise criminal activities. And it would generally be wrong to require disclosure in a civil case of anything which might be material in a pending prosecution: but after a verdict has been given or it has been decided to take no proceedings there is not the same need for secrecy. With regard to other documents there seems to be no greater need for protection than in the case of departments of Government.

It appears to me to be most improbable that any harm would be done by disclosure of the probationary reports on the appellant or of the report from the police training centre. With regard to the report which the respondent made to his chief constable with a view to the prosecution of the appellant there could be more doubt, although no suggestion was made in argument that disclosure of its contents would be harmful now that the appellant has been acquitted. And, as I have said, these documents may prove to be of vital importance in this litigation.

In my judgment, this appeal should be allowed and these documents ought now to be required to be produced for inspection. If it is then found that disclosure would not, in your Lordships' view be prejudicial to the public interest, or that any possibility of such prejudice is, in the case of each of the documents, insufficient to justify its being withheld, then disclosure should be ordered.'

(LORDS MORRIS OF BORTH-Y-GEST, HODSON, PEARCE and UPJOHN delivered concurring judgments.)

Appeal allowed. Documents ordered to be produced.

- Was *Duncan v Cammell, Laird* correctly decided on its own facts?

Rogers v Home Secretary; Gaming Board for Great Britain v Rogers [1973] AC 388 (HL) (also known as *R v Lewes Justices, ex parte Secretary of State for the Home Department*)

Applications made to the Gaming Board by R for certificates of consent in relation to five bingo clubs were refused. He commenced proceedings for criminal libel in respect of a letter written by the assistant chief constable of the county to the board in reply to their request for certain information about him. The Home Secretary applied for an order of *certiorari* to set aside two witness summonses directed to the chief constable and the secretary of the board to give evidence and produce certain documents, including the letter requesting the information and the reply. The board made a similar application in relation to the summons directed to their secretary. On the Home Secretary's application the Divisional Court ordered that the two witness summonses should be set aside; it made no order on the board's application. R appealed and the board cross-appealed.

LORD REID: 'The ground put forward has been said to be Crown privilege. I think that that expression is wrong and may be misleading. There is no question of any privilege in the ordinary sense of the word. The real question is whether the public interest requires that the letter shall not be produced and whether that public interest is so strong as to override the ordinary right and interest of a litigant that he shall be able to lay before a court of justice all relevant evidence. A Minister of the Crown is always an appropriate and often the most appropriate person to assert this public interest, and the evidence or advice which he gives to the court is always valuable and may sometimes be indispensable. But, in my view, it must always be open to any person interested to raise the question and there may be cases where the trial judge should himself raise the question if no one else has done so. In the present case the question of public interest was raised by both the Attorney-General and the Gaming Board. In my judgment both were entitled to raise the matter. Indeed I think that in the circumstances it was the duty of the board to do as they have done.

The claim in the present case is not based on the nature of the contents of this particular letter. It is based on the fact that the board cannot adequately perform their statutory duty unless they can preserve the confidentiality of all communications to them regarding the character, reputation or antecedents of applicants for their consent.

Claims for "class privilege" were fully considered by this House in *Conway* v *Rimmer* [1968] AC 910. It was made clear that there is a heavy burden of proof on any authority which makes such a claim. But the possibility of establishing such a claim was not ruled out. I venture to quote what I said in that case, at p. 952:

> There may be special reasons for withholding some kinds of routine documents, but I think that the proper test to be applied is to ask, in the language of Lord Simon in *Duncan* v *Cammell Laird & Co. Ltd* [1942] AC 624, 642, whether the withholding of a document because it belongs to a particular class is really "necessary for the proper functioning of the public service".

I do not think that "the public service" should be construed narrowly. Here the question is whether the withholding of this class of documents is really necessary to enable the board adequately to perform its statutory duties. If it is, then we are enabling the will of Parliament to be carried out.

There are very unusual features about this case. The board require the fullest information they can get in order to identify and exclude persons of dubious character and reputation from the privilege of obtaining a licence to conduct a gaming establishment. There is no obligation on anyone to give any information to the board. No doubt many law-abiding citizens would tell what they know even if there was some risk of their identity becoming known, although many perfectly honourable people do not want to be thought to be mixed up in such affairs. But it is obvious that the best source of information about dubious characters must often be persons of dubious character themselves. It has long been recognised that the identity of police informers must in the public interest be kept secret and the same considerations must apply to those who volunteer information to the board. Indeed, it is in evidence that many refuse to speak unless assured of absolute secrecy.

The letter called for in this case came from the police. I feel sure that they would not be deterred from giving full information by any fear of consequences to themselves if there were any disclosure. But much of the information which they can give must come from sources which must be protected and they would rightly take this into account. Even if information were given without naming the source, the very nature of the information might, if it were communicated to the person concerned, at least give him a very shrewd idea from whom it had come.

It is possible that some documents coming to the board could be disclosed without fear of such consequences. But I would think it quite impracticable for the board or the court to be sure of this. So it appears to me that, if there is not to be very serious danger of the board being deprived of information essential for the proper performance of their difficult task, there must be a general rule that they are not bound to produce any document which gives information to them about an applicant.

We must then balance that fact against the public interest that the course of justice should not be impeded by the withholding of evidence. We must, I think, take into account that these documents only came into existence because the applicant is asking for a privilege and is submitting his character and reputation to scrutiny. The documents are not used to deprive him of any legal right. The board have a wide discretion. Not only can they refuse his application on the ground of bad reputation although he may say that he has not deserved that reputation; it is not denied that the board can also take into account any unfavourable impression which he has made during an interview with the board.

Natural justice requires that the board should act in good faith and that they should so far as possible tell him the gist of any grounds on which they propose to refuse his application so that he may show such grounds to be unfounded in fact. But the board must be trusted to do that; we have been referred to their practice in this matter and I see nothing wrong in it.

In the present case the board told the appellant nothing about the contents of this letter because they say that they had sufficient grounds for refusing his application without any need to rely on anything in the letter. Their good faith in this matter is not subject to any substantial challenge. If the appellant had not by someone's wrongful act obtained a copy of the letter there was no reason why he should ever have known anything about it.

In my judgment on balance the public interest clearly requires that documents of this kind should not be disclosed, and that public interest is not affected by the fact that by some wrongful means a copy of such a document has been obtained and published by some person'.

LORD PEARSON: 'It seems to me that the proper procedure is that which has been followed, I think consistently, in recent times. The objection to disclosure of the document or information is taken by the Attorney-General or his representative on behalf of the appropriate Minister, that is to say, the political head of the government department within whose sphere of responsibility the matter arises, and the objection is expressed in or supported by a certificate from the appropriate Minister. This procedure has several advantages: (1) The question whether or not the disclosure of the document or information would be detrimental to the public interest on the administrative or executive side is considered at a high level. (2) The court has the assistance of a carefully considered and authoritative opinion on that question. (3) The Attorney-General is consulted and has opportunities of promoting uniformity both in the decision of such questions and in the formulation of the grounds on which the objections are taken. The court has to balance the detriment to the public interest on the administrative or executive side, which would result from the disclosure of the document or information, against the detriment to the public interest on the judicial side, which would result from non-disclosure of a document or information which is relevant to an issue in legal proceedings. Therefore the court, though naturally giving great weight to the opinion of the appropriate Minister conveyed through the Attorney-General or his representative, must have the final responsibility of deciding whether or not the document or information is to be disclosed.

Although that established procedure is the proper procedure, it is not essential as a matter of law. It is not always practicable. If the appropriate Minister is not available, some other Minister or some highly-placed official must act in his stead. If it becomes evident in the course of a trial or in interlocutory proceedings that perhaps some document or information ought in the public interest to be protected from disclosure, it must be open to the party or witness concerned or the court itself to raise the question. If such a situation arises in the course of a trial, the court can adjourn the trial for the appropriate Minister or the Attorney-General to be consulted, but the court will be reluctant to adjourn the trial unless it is really necessary to do so, and in some cases that will be unnecessary because the court is able to give an immediate answer.

The expression "Crown privilege" is not accurate, though sometimes convenient. The Crown has no privilege in the matter. The appropriate Minister has the function of deciding, with the assistance of the Attorney-General, whether or not the public interest on the administrative or executive side requires that he should object to the disclosure of the document or information, but a negative decision cannot properly be described as a waiver of a privilege'.

LORD SIMON OF GLAISDALE: 'My Lords, "Crown privilege" is a misnomer and apt to be misleading. It refers to the rule that certain evidence is inadmissible on the ground that its adduction would be contrary to the public interest. It is true that the public interest which demands that the evidence be withheld has to be weighed against the public interest in the administration of justice that courts should have the fullest possible access to all relevant material (*R* v *Hardy* (1794) 24 State Tr 199, 808; *Marks* v *Beyfus* (1890) 25 QBD 494; *Conway* v *Rimmer* [1968] AC 910); but once the former public interest is held to outweigh the latter, the evidence cannot in any circumstances be admitted. It is not a privilege which may be waived by the Crown (see *Marks* v *Beyfus* at p. 500) or by anyone else. The Crown has prerogatives, not privilege. The right to procure that admissible evidence be withheld from, or inadmissible evidence adduced to, the courts is not one of the prerogatives of the Crown.'

(LORDS MORRIS OF BORTH-Y-GEST and SALMON delivered concurring judgments.)

Appeal dismissed. Cross-appeal allowed.

Norwich Pharmacal Co. and Others v Commissioners of Customs and Excise [1974] AC 133 (HL)

The appellants were the owners and licensees of a patent for a chemical compound known as furazolidone. It appeared that the patent was being infringed by illicit importations of furazolidone manufactured abroad. In order to obtain the names and addresses of the importers the appellants brought actions against the Commissioners alleging infringement of the patent and seeking orders for the disclosure of the relevant information. The Commissioners made a claim for privilege. The judge ordered discovery of the names and addresses of the importers. The Court of Appeal reversed that decision. The appellants appealed.

LORD REID: ' . . . [W]e have to weigh the requirements of justice to the appellants against the considerations put forward by the respondents as justifying non-disclosure. They are twofold. First it is said that to make such disclosures would or might impair or hamper the efficient conduct of their important statutory duties. And secondly it is said that such disclosure would or might be prejudicial to those whose identity would be disclosed.

There is nothing secret or confidential in the information sought or in the documents which came into the hands of the respondents containing that information. Those documents are ordinary commercial documents which pass through many different hands. But it is said that those who do not wish to have their names disclosed might concoct false documents and thereby hamper the work of the Customs. That would require at least a conspiracy between the foreign consignor and the importer and it seems to me to be in the highest degree improbable. It appears that there are already arrangements in operation by the respondents restricting the disclosure of certain matters if the importers do not wish them to be disclosed. It may be that the knowledge that a court might order discovery in certain cases would cause somewhat greater use to be made of these arrangements. But it was not suggested in argument that that is a matter of any vital importance. The only other point was that such disclosure might cause resentment and impair good relations with other traders; but I find it impossible to believe that honest traders would resent failure to protect wrongdoers.

Protection of traders from having their names disclosed is a more difficult matter. If we could be sure that those whose names are sought are all tortfeasors, they do not deserve any protection. In the present case the possibility that any are not is so remote that I think it can be neglected. The only possible way in which any of these imports could be legitimate and not an infringement would seem to be that someone might have exported some furazolidone from this country and then whoever owned it abroad might have sent it back here. Then there would be no infringement. But again that seems most unlikely.

But there may be other cases where there is much more doubt. The validity of the patent may be doubtful and there could well be other doubts. If the respondents have any doubts in any future case about the propriety of making disclosures they are well entitled to require the matter to be submitted to the court at the expense of the person seeking the disclosure. The court will then only order discovery if satisfied that there is no substantial chance of injustice being done'.

VISCOUNT DILHORNE: 'I do not accept the proposition that all information given to a government department is to be treated as confidential and protected from disclosure, but I agree that information of a personal character obtained in the exercise of statutory powers, information of such a character that the giver of it would not expect it to be used for any purpose other than that for which it is given, or disclosed to any person not concerned with that purpose, is to be regarded as protected from disclosure, even though there is no statutory prohibition of its disclosure. But not all information given to a government department, whether voluntarily or under compulsion is of this confidential character and the question is whether the names of the importers of the furazolidone were given in confidence. I do not think that that is established. The names and addresses of the importers had to be given to the master of the ship and made known to all those taking part in securing the transit of the chemicals. Presumably the parcels of furazolidone had on them the names and addresses of the consignees for all to see, though they may, I do not know, have not disclosed that the contents of the parcels were furazolidone. The documents completed for the transit of the chemicals and for Customs which show the names of the consignees and the contents of the parcels do not seem to me more confidential than consignment notes completed for British Railways and British Road Services . . ..

I must confess that I am not in the least impressed by the "candour" argument. I really cannot conceive it to be realistic to suggest that the vast majority of importers who do not infringe patents or do other wrongs, will be in the least deterred from giving proper information to Customs by the knowledge that pursuant to an order of the court the names of the wrongdoers are disclosed by Customs'.

(LORDS MORRIS OF BORTH-Y-GEST, CROSS OF CHELSEA and KILBRANDON delivered concurring judgments.)

Appeal allowed.

Alfred Crompton Amusement Machines Limited v *Commissioners of Customs and Excise (No. 2)* [1974] AC 405 (HL)

The commissioners had obtained information from customers of the company and others, relevant to assessments of the company's liability for purchase tax, which were the subject of an intended arbitration. The commissioners, in an affidavit sworn by their chairman, Sir Louis Petch, claimed privilege for the documents containing the information.

LORD CROSS OF CHELSEA: '"Confidentiality" is not a separate head of privilege, but it may be a very material consideration to bear in mind when privilege is claimed on the ground of public interest. What the court has to do is to weigh on the one hand the considerations which suggest that it is in the public interest that the documents in question should be disclosed and on the other hand those which suggest that it is in the public interest that they should not be disclosed and to balance one against the other. Plainly there is much to be said in favour of disclosure. The documents in question constitute an important part of the material on which the commissioners based their conclusion that the appellants sell to retailers. That is shown by the reply which the commissioners made to the request for particulars under paragraph 5(h) of the defence. Yet if the claim to privilege made by the commissioners is upheld this information will be withheld from the arbitrator. No doubt it will form part of the brief delivered to counsel for the commissioners and may help him to prove the appellants' evidence in cross-examination; but counsel will not be able to use it as evidence to controvert anything which the appellants' witnesses may say. It is said, of course, that the appellants cannot reasonably complain if the commissioners think it right to tie their own hands in this way. But if the arbitrator should decide against them the appellants may feel—however wrongly—that the arbitrator was unconsciously influenced by the fact that the commissioners stated in their pleadings that they had this further evidence in support of their view which they did not disclose and which the appellants had no opportunity to controvert. Moreover, whoever wins it is desirable that the arbitrator should have all the relevant material before him. On the other hand, there is much to be said against disclosure. The case is not, indeed, as strong as the case against disclosing the name of an informer—for the result of doing that would be that the source of information would dry up whereas here the commissioners will continue to have their powers under Section 24(6) [of the Purchase Tax Act 1963]. Nevertheless, the case against disclosure is, to my mind, far stronger than it was in the *Norwich Pharmacal* case. There it was probable that all the importers whose names were disclosed were wrongdoers and the disclosure of the names of any, if there were any, who were innocent would not be likely to do them any harm at all. Here, on the other hand, one can well see that the third parties who have supplied this information to the commissioners because of the existence of their statutory powers would very much resent its disclosure by the commissioners to the appellants and that it is not at all fanciful for Sir Louis to say that the knowledge that the commissioners cannot keep such information secret may be harmful to the efficient working of the Act. In a case where the considerations for and against disclosure appear to be fairly evenly balanced the courts should I think uphold a claim to privilege on the ground of public interest and trust to the head of the department concerned to do whatever he can to mitigate the ill-effects of non-disclosure. Forbes J was so impressed by those possible ill-effects that he failed to appreciate how reasonable Sir Louis' objections to disclosure were and dismissed them with the remark "We are not living in the early days of the Tudor administration". I do not regard Sir Louis as a modern Cardinal Morton. His objections to disclosure were taken in the interest of the third parties concerned as much as in the interests of the commissioners and if any of them is in fact willing to give evidence, privilege in respect of any documents or information obtained from him will be waived'.

   (VISCOUNT DILHORNE, and LORDS REID, MORRIS of BORTH-Y-GEST and KILBRANDON agreed.)

D v *National Society for the Prevention of Cruelty to Children* [1978] AC 171 (HL)

The National Society for the Prevention of Cruelty to Children received and investigated complaints from members of the public about cases of ill-treatment or neglect of children under an express pledge of confidentiality and was authorised under section 1(1) of the Children and Young Persons Act 1969 to bring care proceedings in respect of children. The society received a complaint from an informant about the treatment of a 14-month-old girl, and an inspector of the society called at the parents' home. The mother subsequently brought an action against the society for damages for personal injuries alleged to have resulted from the society's negligence in failing properly to investigate the complaint and the manner and circumstances of the inspector's call which she said had caused her severe and continuing shock. The society denied negligence and applied for an order that there should be no discovery or inspection ordered under RSC Order 24 rule 2(1), of any documents which revealed or might reveal the identity of the complainant, on the grounds, *inter alia,* that the proper performance by the society of its duties under its charter and the Act of 1969 required that the absolute confidentiality of information given in confidence should be preserved, that if disclosure were ordered in the mother's action its sources of information would dry up and that that would be contrary to the public interest, and it also claimed that disclosure of the informant's identity was not necessary for disposing fairly of the action. Master Jacob ordered that the relevant documents be disclosed. On appeal by the society Croom-Johnson J reversed the master's order. On appeal by the mother the Court of Appeal by a majority restored it. The society appealed to the House of Lords.

LORD DIPLOCK: 'The fact that information has been communicated by one person to another in confidence . . . is not of itself a sufficient ground for protecting from disclosure in a court of law the nature of the information or the identity of the informant if either of these matters would assist the court to ascertain facts which are relevant to an issue upon which it is adjudicating: *Alfred Crompton Amusement Machines Ltd v Customs and Excise Commissioners (No. 2)* [1974] AC 405, 433–434. The private promise of confidentiality must yield to the general public interest that in the administration of justice truth will out, unless by reason of the character of the information or the relationship of the recipient of the information to the informant a more important public interest is served by protecting the information or the identity of the informant from disclosure in a court of law.

The public interest which the NSPCC relies upon as obliging it to withhold from the plaintiff and from the court itself material that could disclose the identity of the society's informant is analogous to the public interest that is protected by the well established rule of law that the identity of police informers may not be disclosed in a civil action, whether by the process of discovery or by oral evidence at the trial: *Marks* v *Beyfus* (1890) 25 QBD 494.

The rationale of the rule as it applies to police informers is plain. If their identity were liable to be disclosed in a court of law, these sources of information would dry up and the police would be hindered in their duty of preventing and detecting crime. So the public interest in preserving the anonymity of police informers had to be weighed against the public interest that information which might assist a judicial tribunal to ascertain facts relevant to an issue upon which it is required to adjudicate should be withheld from that tribunal. By the uniform practice of the judges which by the time of *Marks* v *Beyfus*, 25 QBD 494 had already hardened into a rule of law, the balance has fallen upon the side of non-disclosure except where upon the trial of a defendant for a criminal offence disclosure of the identity of the informer could help to show that the defendant was innocent of the offence. In that case, and in that case only, the balance falls upon the side of disclosure.

My Lords, in *R* v *Lewes Justices, ex parte Secretary of State for the Home Department* [1973] AC 388 this House did not hesitate to extend to persons from whom the Gaming Board received information for the purposes of the exercise of their statutory functions under the Gaming Act 1968 immunity from disclosure of their identity analogous to that which the law had previously accorded to police informers. Your Lordships' sense of values might well be open to reproach if this House were to treat the confidentiality of information given to those who are authorised by statute to institute proceedings for the protection of neglected or ill-treated children as entitled to less favourable treatment in a court of law than information given to the Gaming Board so that gaming may be kept clean. There are three categories of persons authorised to bring care proceedings in respect of neglected or ill-treated children: local authorities, constables and the NSPCC. The anonymity of those who tell the police of their suspicions of neglect or ill-treatment of a child would be preserved without any extension of the existing law. To draw a distinction in this respect between information given to the police and that passed on directly to a local authority or to the NSPCC would seem much too irrational a consequence to have been within the contemplation of Parliament when enacting the Children and Young Persons Act 1969. The local authority is under an express statutory duty to bring care proceedings in cases where this is necessary if neither the police nor the NSPCC have started them, while, as respects the NSPCC, the evidence shows that, presumably because it is not associated in the public mind with officialdom, the public are readier to bring information to it than to the police or the welfare services of the local authority itself.

Upon the summons by the NSPCC for an order withholding discovery of documents to the extent that they were capable of revealing the identity of the society's informant, it was for the judge to weigh the competing public interests involved in disclosure and non-disclosure and to form his opinion as to the side on which the balance fell. In a careful judgment in which he reviewed the relevant authorities Croom-Johnson J ordered that disclosure should not be given. Upon an interlocutory summons relating to discovery this was a matter upon which the judge had a discretion with which an appellate court would not lightly interfere, but the reasoning by which his decision was supported is of wider application. It would also rule out any attempt to ascertain the identity of the NSPCC's informant by questions put to witnesses at the trial and would dispose of the plaintiff's claim to disclosure of the informant's identity as part, and perhaps to her the most important part, of the substantive relief she seeks. The interlocutory judgment thus raises matters of principle fit for the consideration of this House.

For my part I would uphold the decision of Croom-Johnson J and reverse that of the Court of Appeal. I would do so upon what in argument has been referred to as the "narrow" submission made on behalf of the NSPCC. I would extend to those who give information about neglect or ill-treatment of children to a local authority or the NSPCC a similar immunity from disclosure of their identity in legal proceedings to that which the law accords to police informers. The public interests served by preserving the anonymity of both classes of informants are analogous; they are of no less weight in the case of the former than in that of the latter class, and in my judgment are of greater weight than in the case of informers of the Gaming Board to whom immunity from disclosure of their identity has recently been extended by this House.

In the Court of Appeal, as in this House, counsel for the NSPCC advanced, as well as what I have referred to as the narrow submission, a broad submission that wherever a party to legal proceedings claims that there is a public interest to be served by withholding documents or information from disclosure in those proceedings it is the duty of the court to weigh that interest against the countervailing public interest in the administration of justice in the particular case and to refuse disclosure if the balance tilts that way. This broad submission, or something rather like it confined to information imparted in confidence, was adopted in his dissenting judgment by Lord Denning MR, but as I have already indicated there is the authority of this House that confidentiality of itself does not provide a ground of non-disclosure; nor am I able to accept the proposition that the basis of all privilege from disclosure of documents or information in legal proceedings is to prevent the breaking of a confidence. For my part, I think this House would be unwise to base its decision in the instant case upon a proposition so much broader than is necessary to resolve the issue between the parties.

The majority of the Court of Appeal rejected both the broad and narrow submissions. In essence their ground for doing so was that "public interest" as a ground for withholding disclosure of documents or information was but another term for what had before *Conway* v *Rimmer* [1968] AC 910 been called "Crown privilege" and was available only where the public interest involved was the effective functioning of departments or other organs of central government. "Crown privilege" they regarded as having always been so confined; *Conway* v *Rimmer* [1968] AC 910 did not extend the ambit of Crown privilege: all it did was to decide that a claim by a minister of the Crown that documents were of a class which in the public interest ought not to be disclosed was not conclusive but that it was for the court itself to decide whether the public interest which would be protected by non-disclosure outweighed the public interest in making available to the court information that might assist it in doing justice between the litigants in the particular case.

This narrow view as to the scope of public interest as a ground for protecting documents and information from disclosure was supported in argument before this House by copious citations of passages taken from judgments in previous cases in the course of which documents for which a claim to non-disclosure had been described as relating to essential functions of government, to the performance of statutory duties, to the public service or to the interests of the state. From this your Lordships were invited to infer that the document in question would not have been entitled to protection from disclosure unless it fell within the description used in the particular case.

My Lords, the maxim *expressio unius, exclusio alterius* is not a canon of construction that is applicable to judgments. To construe a judgment as if its function were to lay down a code of law is a common error into which the English reliance upon precedent makes it easy to fall. A cautious judge expresses a proposition of law in terms that are wide enough to cover the issue in the case under consideration; the fact that they are not also wide enough to cover an issue that may arise in some subsequent case does not make his judgment an authority against any wider proposition.

I see no reason and I know of no authority for confining public interest as a ground for non-disclosure of documents or information to the effective functioning of departments or organs of central government. In *Conway* v *Rimmer* [1968] AC 910 the public interest to be protected was the effective functioning of a county police force; in *In re D (Infants)* [1970] 1 WLR 599 the interest to be protected was the effective functioning of a local authority in relation to the welfare of boarded-out children. In the instant case the public interest to be protected is the effective functioning of an organisation authorised under an Act of Parliament to bring legal proceedings for the welfare of children. I agree with Croom-Johnson J that this is a public interest which the court is entitled to take into consideration in deciding whether the identity of the NSPCC's informants ought to be disclosed. I also agree that the balance of public interest falls on the side of non-disclosure'.

LORD HAILSHAM OF ST MARYLEBONE: 'The appellant society argued, in effect, for a general extension in range of the nature of the exceptions to the rule in favour of disclosure. This, it was suggested, could be summarised in a number of broad propositions, all in support of the view that, where an identifiable public interest in non-disclosure can be established, either there is a firm rule against disclosure (for example, legal professional privilege or state secrets) or the court has a discretion whether or not to order disclosure, and that this discretion must be exercised against disclosure in all cases where, after balancing the relevant considerations, the court decides that the public interest in non-disclosure outweighs the ordinary public interest in disclosure. The appellants contended that new cases will arise from time to time calling for a protection from disclosure in classes of case to which it was not previously extended, and that the courts had in practice shown great flexibility in adapting these principles to new situations as and when these arise. The appellants contended that some of those entitled to the benefits of protection had, and some had not, been subject to statutory or common law duties or been clothed with government authority or been answerable to Parliament or the executive. This contention was aimed at the majority judgments in the Court of Appeal which in substance disallowed the appellants' claim to immunity on the grounds that they are a private society clothed arguably with authority to fulfil a function but not a duty which they are compelled to perform, and that they are not in any sense either an organ of central government or part of the public service. The appellants noted that the dissenting judgment of Lord Denning MR, which was in their favour, largely relied on the confidentiality which the appellants had pledged to potential informants. Their own contention was that, while the mere fact that a communication was made in confidence did not of itself justify non-disclosure, the fact of confidentiality was relevant to reinforce the view that disclosure would be against the public interest. In this connection the appellants cited *Alfred Crompton Amusement Machines Ltd* v *Customs and Excise Commissioners (No. 2)* [1974] AC 405. Lastly the appellants contended that there was no reported case in which the court, once it had identified a public interest in non-disclosure, had ever regarded itself as debarred from taking it into consideration or from weighing its importance against the damage to be apprehended from excluding relevant evidence.

These contentions have at least the merit of propounding a lucid and coherent system. Nevertheless, I am compelled to say that, in the breadth and generality with which they were put forward, I do not find them acceptable.

They seem to me to give far too little weight to the general importance of the principle that, in all cases before them, the courts should insist on parties and witnesses disclosing the truth, the whole truth, and nothing but the truth, where this would assist the decision of the matters in dispute. In the second place, I consider that the acceptance of these principles would lead both to uncertainty and to inconsistency in the administration of justice. If they were to be accepted, we should remember that we should be laying down a large innovation not merely in the law of discovery but equally in the law of evidence, which has to be administered not merely in the High Court, but in the Crown Courts, the county courts and the magistrates' courts throughout the land. What is the public interest to be identified? On what principles can it be defined? On what principles is the weighing-up process to proceed? To what extent, if at all, can the right to non-disclosure be waived? Can secondary or extraneous evidence of the facts not disclosed be permitted? To what extent should the Crown be notified of the fact that the issue has been raised? These questions are all manageable if the categories of privilege from disclosure and public interest are considered to be limited. Indeed, reported authority, which is voluminous, shows that largely they have been solved. But to yield to the appellants' argument on this part of the case would be to set the whole question once more at large, not merely over the admitted categories and the existing field but over a much wider, indeed over an undefined, field.

Thirdly, and perhaps more important, the invitation of the appellants seems to me to run counter to the general tradition of the development of doctrine preferred by the English courts. This proceeds through evolution by extension or analogy of recognised principles and reported precedents. Bold statements of general principle based on a review of the total field are more appropriate to legislation by Parliament which has at its command techniques of inquiry, sources of information and a width of worldly-wise experience far less restricted than those available to the courts in the course of contested litigation between adversaries.

On the other hand, I find equally unattractive the more restricted and even, occasionally, pedantic view of the authorities advanced on behalf of the respondent. This was based on a rigid distinction, for some purposes valuable, between privilege and public interest, and an insistence on a narrow view of the nature of the interest of the public, reflected in the reasoning of the majority in the Court of Appeal, which would virtually have restricted the public interest cases to the narrower interests of the central organs of the state, or what might be strictly called the public service. The effect of the argument would not merely limit the ambit of possible categories of exception to the general rule. In my view, it would virtually ensure that the categories would now have to be regarded as effectively closed. In her printed case the respondent contended that:

> No party is protected from his obligation to disclose documents on the grounds of public interest unless there is some connection between the claim for protection and the functions of central government or the public service of the state: . . . The expression "Crown privilege" has been criticised but, . . . it accurately reflects the basic requirement that there must be a connection with the Crown or public service of the state.

In support of this contention the respondent referred *inter alia* to *Conway* v *Rimmer* [1968] AC 910, to *R* v *Lewes Justices, ex parte Secretary of State for the Home Department* [1973] AC 388 and to *Alfred Crompton Amusement Machines Ltd* v *Customs and Excise Commissioners (No. 2)* [1974] AC 405. There is, of course, a sense, which will become apparent as I proceed, in which the appellants' claim can be brought squarely within the respondent's principle. But the principle is itself, as I shall show, open to criticism. In particular the argument was based on what was described as a fundamental principle that the exceptions to the general rule requiring disclosure all come within one or the other of two rigidly confined categories, one described as privilege, when secondary evidence could be given or the privilege could be waived, and the other as "public interest" where these possible escapes were excluded. But this, it was contended, was virtually restricted to the category formerly, but inaccurately, referred to as "Crown privilege".

The result of this is that I approach the problem with a caution greater than that contended for the appellants, but with a willingness to extend established principles by analogy and legitimate extrapolation more flexible than was admitted by the respondent.

I am emboldened to do so by the reflection that, quite apart from legislation like the Civil Evidence Act 1968, the law of evidence has steadily developed since my own practice at the Bar began in 1932. This can be seen by a consideration of cases like *McTaggart* v *McTaggart* [1949] P 94, *Mole* v *Mole* [1951] P 21, *Theodoropoulas* v *Theodoropoulas* [1964] P 311, which undoubtedly developed from the long recognised category of "without prejudice" negotiations but which in my opinion has now developed into a new category of a public interest exception based on the public interest in the stability of marriage. I think the case, widely canvassed in argument, of *R* v *Lewes Justices, ex parte Secretary of State for the Home Department* [1973] AC 388 was a clear extension of the previous "Crown privilege" type of case by which, for the first time, communications to the Gaming Board were recognised as a suitable object of such "privilege". Possibly *In re D (Infants)* [1970] 1 WLR 599 is another example, for it decided, I think, for the first time, that local authority records of child care investigations were immune from disclosure in wardship proceedings to which they would otherwise be relevant. I believe that traces of similar evolution, for instance in the field of legal professional privilege, can be found in the 19th century authorities.

I find it also interesting to note that the report (Law Reform Committee Sixteenth Report (Privilege in Civil Proceedings) (1967) (Cmnd. 3472) to which judges of every Division of the High Court were signatories, which was referred to extensively by counsel for both sides, shows a definite development in the law and practice in the precise field now under discussion from what it was generally considered to be when I entered the profession in 1932.

According to paragraph 1 of that report, which is before us, but which represents no more than contemporary textbook authority:

> Privilege in the main is the creation of the common law whose policy, pragmatic as always, has been to limit to a minimum the categories of privileges (*sic*) "which a person has an absolute right to claim, *but to accord to the judge a wide discretion to permit a witness, whether a party to the proceedings or not, to refuse to disclose information where disclosure would be a breach of some ethical or social value and non-disclosure would be unlikely to result in serious injustice in the particular case in which it is claimed* (emphasis mine).

This doctrine was not merely an incidental statement at the beginning of the report. It runs right through it, and forms the basis of some of the most notable conclusions (see, for example, paragraph 3, paragraph 7, paragraphs 36, 37, paragraphs 41, 43, paragraphs 48–52).

Counsel for the respondent, who was himself, as he candidly confessed, signatory to the report, was constrained to argue that the report, the authors of which included Lords Pearson and Diplock, Winn and Buckley LJJ, Orr J and the present Vice-Chancellor (Megarry V-C), was an inaccurate representation of the then existing state of the law, and that the two cases (*Attorney-General* v *Clough* [1963] 1 QB 773 and

Attorney-General v *Mulholland*; *Attorney-General* v *Foster* [1963] 2 QB 477) cited in the report to support the proposition did not in truth do so, were wrong if they did and, being modern, departed from legal principle. Speaking for myself, I am sure that the law has in fact developed in this field during my lifetime, and I find it incredible that paragraph 1 of the report cited, bearing the weight of judicial authority I have described, does not represent the current practice of the courts in 1967, although in fact it goes plainly beyond the current practice of my youth.

For these reasons, I feel convinced that I am entitled to proceed more boldly than counsel for the respondent argued, though more timidly than the robust counsels of the appellants' counsel urged.

The authorities, therefore, seem to me to establish beyond doubt that the courts have developed their doctrine in this field of evidence. An example of this is seen in the privilege extended to editors of newspapers in the 19th century, before the present Order 82, rule 6 was passed, to refuse to answer interrogatories in defamation cases where the issue was malice and the plaintiff desired to discover their sources (cf. *Hope* v *Brash* [1897] 2 QB 188; *Hennessy* v *Wright* (1888) 21 QBD 509; *Plymouth Mutual Co-operative and Industrial Society Ltd* v *Traders' Publishing Association Ltd* [1906] 1 KB 403). This practice, robustly developed by the judges of the Queen's Bench Division (in contrast with the contemporary Chancery Division practice even after 1873), can only have been based on public policy. It has been stressed that these cases relate to discovery and not to questions to witnesses at the trial. This may well be so, at least at present, but certainly they illustrate the use of the court of a discretion, and its sensitiveness to public policy where discretion exists. Until the introduction of the new rules it is within my recollection that interrogatories and discovery on the lines disallowed in the newspaper cases were frequently allowed in other defamation cases where malice was in issue, although it was pointed out in argument that the newspaper principle was, at least once, applied, rather strangely, to MP's in *Adam* v *Fisher* (1914) 30 TLR 288.

In all this argument, however, two facts stand out unmistakably as true beyond dispute. The first is that the welfare of children, particularly of young children at risk of maltreatment by adults, has been, from the earliest days, a concern of the Crown as *parens patriae*, an object of legal charities and in latter years the subject of a whole series of Acts of Parliament, of which the Act of 1969 is only an example, and that not the latest. The second is that the information given by informants to the police or to the Director of Public Prosecutions, and now, since *R* v *Lewes Justices, ex parte Secretary of State for the Home Department* [1973] AC 388, to the Gaming Board, is protected from disclosure in exactly the manner demanded by the appellants. The question, and it is I believe the only question, necessary to be decided in this appeal, is whether an extension of this established principle to information relating to possible child abuse supplied to the appellants is a legitimate extension of a known category of exception or not. For this purpose it is necessary to consider the position of the appellants in relation to the enforcement provisions of the Children and Young Persons Act 1969 . . ..

Of the three classes with *locus standi* to initiate care proceedings, it is common ground that information given to the police is protected to the extent demanded by the society. This is clear from many cases including *Marks* v *Beyfus*, 25 QBD 494 (which applied the principle to the Director of Public Prosecutions), and many of the recent cases in your Lordships' House. The rule relating to the immunity accorded to police informants is in truth much older, so old and so well established, in fact, that it was not and could not be challenged in the instant case before your Lordships. Once, however, it is accepted that information given to the police in the instant case would have been protected, it becomes, in my judgment, manifestly absurd that it should not be accorded equally to the same information if given by the same informant to the local authority (who would have been under a duty to act on it) or to the appellant society, to whom, according to the undisputed evidence, ordinary informants more readily resort.

The last point seems to have been realised, at least to some extent, by Sir John Pennycuick: see, for instance, the passage in his judgment, [1978] AC at p. 203. But I cannot see the sense of allowing the immunity where care proceedings actually result, but not in cases where the society or the local authority, after sifting the information, and assessing the credentials of the informants, decide in the event upon an alternative course. It is not for the informant to predict what course the recipient of the information may take, nor does his (or her) right to anonymity depend upon the outcome. The public interest is that the parties with *locus standi* to bring care proceedings should receive information under a cloak of confidentiality. It may well be that neither the police, nor the local authority, nor the society, can given an absolute guarantee. The informant may in some cases have to give evidence under *subpoena*. In other cases their identity may come to light in other ways. But the police, the local authority and the society stand on the same footing. The public interest is identical in relation to each. The guarantee of confidentiality has the same and not different values in relation to each. It follows that the society is entitled to succeed upon the appeal.

Lord Denning MR, in his dissenting judgment, places his own reasoning on the pledge of confidentiality given by the society, and seeks to found the immunity upon this pledge. I do not think that confidentiality by itself gives any ground for immunity (cf., for example, *per* Lord Cross of Chelsea in *Alfred Crompton Amusement Machines Ltd* v *Customs and Excise Commissioners (No. 2)* [1974] AC 405, 433). Confidentiality is not a separate head of immunity. There are, however, cases when confidentiality is itself a public interest and one of these is where information is given to an authority charged with the enforcement and administration of the law by the initiation of court proceedings. This is one of those cases, whether the recipient of the information be the police, the local authority or the NSPCC. Whether there be other cases, and what these may be, must fall to be decided in the future. The categories of public interest are not closed, and must alter from time to time whether by restriction or extension as social conditions and social legislation develop'.

LORD SIMON OF GLAISDALE: 'There have been three attempts to impose a comprehensive and coherent pattern on this branch of the law: I have great sympathy with the object, though I feel bound to express reservations in the case of each. They are that of Lord Denning MR in the instant case, that of the Law Reform Committee in their Sixteenth Report, and that of counsel for the appellants in his main argument. The solution of Lord Denning MR was to suggest confidentiality of a communication (or in the relationship of the parties) as the criterion for exclusion. The Law Reform Committee found a common factor in (paragraph 1):

> . . . a wide discretion [in the court] to permit a witness, whether a party to the proceedings or not, to refuse to disclose information where disclosure would be

a breach of some ethical or social value and non-disclosure would be unlikely to result in serious injustice in the particular case in which it is claimed.

Counsel for the appellants, while relying on much in the Law Reform Committee's report, put his case with slightly different emphasis. He argued that in each case (save those governed by an existing rule against disclosure) the court will weigh any public interest in the withholding of information against the public interest that all relevant evidence should be adduced to the court, and if the former is preponderant the evidence will be excluded.

I do not think that the confidentiality of the communication provides in itself a satisfactory basis for testing whether relevant evidence should be withheld. First, it does not sufficiently reflect the true basis on which any evidence is excluded—namely, the public interest. Even Wigmore (*Evidence,* 1st ed, vol. IV (1905), s. 2285; 3rd ed (1940), vol. VIII, s. 2285), who stipulates for a principle of confidentiality as a condition of testimonial privilege (and I emphasise that he is dealing only with privilege), states (s. 2286): "In general, then, *the mere fact that a communication was made in express confidence,* or in the implied confidence of a *confidential relation,* does not create a privilege. This [3rd ed: "common law"] rule is not questioned today". (His italics.) In the words of Wigmore, for the privilege to attach, the relationship between the parties to the communication: "must be one which in the opinion of the community ought to be sedulously *fostered*" (s. 2285; his italics). Secondly, a juridical basis of confidentiality does not explain why, in relation to certain classes of excluded evidence, there can be no waiver of the immunity. Thirdly, certain evidence is excluded not because it is confidential (even in the sense of being secret) but because it relates to affairs of state. For example, it was on that ground and not irrelevance that Cobbett was precluded in his trial for seditious libel from asking a witness whether it would not be wise to follow his (Cobbett's) advice as to how to deal with current civil disturbance (*R* v *Cobbett* (1831) 2 State Tr (NS) 789, 877). Fourthly, the law would operate erratically and capriciously according to whether or not a particular communication was made confidentially: Delane, the great 19th century editor of *The Times*, always refused to receive information under the seal of secrecy, because sooner rather than later he would get the same information from a source he could use. Fifthly, it is undesirable that exclusion should be conferred by confidentiality irrespective of the public interest: after all, an attempt to bribe is generally made confidentially (cf. *Lewis* v *James* (1887) 3 TLR 527; *In re Hooley, Rucker's Case* (1898) 79 LT 306; *McGuinness* v *Attorney-General of Victoria* (1940) 63 CLR 73). Sixthly, confidentiality was in fact the original and far-reaching ground of exclusion. A man of honour would not betray a confidence, and the judges as men of honour themselves would not require him to. Thus originally legal professional privilege was that of the legal adviser, not the client. (For the foregoing, see *Wigmore, Evidence,* ss. 2286, 2290.) But, with the decline in the ethos engendering the rule, the law moved decisively away from it. The turning point was the *Duchess of Kingston's Case* (1776) 20 State Tr 355, 386–391, where both the duchess's surgeon and a personal friend, Lord Barrington, were compelled to give evidence in breach of confidence. Seventhly, there is massive authority in addition to *Wigmore, Evidence* and the *Duchess of Kingston's Case* against confidentiality by itself conferring exclusion: Sir George Jessel MR in *Wheeler* v *Le Marchant* (1881) 17 ChD 675, 681; Lord Parker of Waddington CJ in *Attorney-General* v *Clough* [1963] 1 QB 773, 787; Lord Denning MR in *Attorney-General* v *Mulholland;*

Attorney-General v *Foster* [1963] 2 QB 477, 489, Donovan LJ and Danckwerts LJ agreeing; Lord Salmon in *R* v *Lewes Justices, ex parte Secretary of State for the Home Department* [1973] AC 388, 411–412; Lord Cross of Chelsea in *Alfred Crompton Amusement Machines Ltd* v *Customs and Excise Commissioners (No. 2)* [1974] AC 405, 433; *O'Brennan* v *Tully* (1935) 69 Ir LT 115 (cited with approval in *Attorney-General* v *Mulholland; Attorney-General* v *Foster*, at p. 491); *McGuinness* v *Attorney-General of Victoria*, 63 CLR 73, which contains a judgment of characteristic authority by Dixon J dealing with the plea of confidentiality (cited with approval in *Attorney-General* v *Clough*, at pp. 790–791 and in *Attorney-General* v *Mulholland; Attorney-General* v *Foster*, at p. 491): see also *Bray on Discovery* (1885), p. 303. I think the true rule is expressed in *Wigmore, Evidence* and in the passage referred to in the speech of Lord Cross of Chelsea in *Alfred Crompton Amusement Machines Ltd* v *Customs and Excise Commissioners (No. 2)* [1974] AC 405, 433:

> "Confidentiality" is not a separate head of privilege, but it may be a very material consideration to bear in mind when privilege is claimed on the ground of public interest.

(It is only right to say that counsel for the appellants did not rely on confidentiality pur sang as a criterion of exclusion, but rather on the way it was put by Lord Cross.) For the reasons I have given I do not myself think that confidentiality in itself establishes any public interest in the exclusion of relevant evidence, but rather that it may indirectly be significant where a public interest extrinsically established (for example, provision of professional legal advice or effective policing) can only be vindicated if its communications have immunity from forensic investigation.

I naturally feel the same temerity in approaching the report of the powerful Law Reform Committee as I do in approaching the judgment of the learned Master of the Rolls. But since counsel for the appellants relied greatly on the report for his wide general proposition, I feel bound to express my reservations. I would start by pointing out that the committee was concerned only with civil proceedings, and within them only with "privilege" from disclosure. Even though the rules of criminal evidence may differ in some respects from civil, any wide judicial discretion to admit or reject evidence should, I think, at least be tested against what would be acceptable in a criminal trial. Secondly, I do not think that *Attorney-General* v *Clough* [1963] 1 QB 773 or *Attorney-General* v *Mulholland; Attorney-General* v *Foster* [1963] 2 QB 477 really supports the existence of such a wide discretionary power as the committee considered to vest in the court (except for the judgment of Donovan LJ in the latter case, at p. 492). Thirdly, the massive authority I referred to in the preceding paragraph of this speech must at least be weighed in the other scale: see also *Marks* v *Beyfus*, 25 QBD 494, *per* Lord Esher MR, at p. 498, Bowen LJ, at p. 500—not a matter of discretion, but a rule of law. Fourthly, I think that the true position is that the judge may not only rule as a matter of law or practice on the admissibility of evidence, but can also exercise a considerable moral authority on the course of a trial. For example, in the situations envisaged the judge is likely to say to counsel: "You see that the witness feels that he ought not in conscience to answer that question. Do you really press it in the circumstances?" Such moral pressure will vary according to the circumstances—on the one hand, the relevance of the evidence; on the other, the nature of the ethical or professional inhibition. Often indeed such a witness will merely require a little gentle guidance from the judge to overcome his reluctance. I have never myself known this procedure to fail to resolve the situations acceptably. But it is far from the exercise of a formal discretion. And if it comes to the forensic crunch, as it did in many of the cases I have referred to (to which can be added the Parnell Inquiry Commission, 103rd day: see footnote to *Wigmore, Evidence*, s. 2286; also another passage cited in *Attorney-General* v *Mulholland; Attorney-General* v *Foster* [1963] 2 QB 477, 490–491), it must be law, not discretion, which is in command. It may be that the members of the Law Reform Committee considered that a consistent use of moral suasion had resulted in a rule of practice emerging; cf. *Povey* v *Povey* [1972] Fam 40, 48–49 (although I am not convinced myself that it has). Lastly, many of the practical objections voiced by my noble and learned friend, Lord Hailsham of St Marylebone, to the main and wider proposition advanced on behalf of the appellants seem to me to apply equally to the proposition of the Law Reform Committee. But it may be that some of the relationships will need re-examination as matters of practice or law; and it is to be borne in mind that it has been found expedient in some jurisdictions to modify the common law rule of disclosure by giving statutory immunity to, for example, doctors or priests.

My Lords, I have dwelt on this matter because, as I said, counsel for the appellants relied considerably on the report for his wide proposition—a general discretion in the court to weigh conflicting public interests in the adduction or exclusion of evidence. He also, of course, relied on *Conway* v *Rimmer* [1968] AC 910, where conflicting public interests were indeed weighed. But your Lordships' House was really there concerned with the validity of claims by the Crown (based on *Duncan* v *Cammell, Laird and Co. Ltd* [1942] AC 624) that the executive could procure the exclusion of evidence by a conclusive ministerial certificate that the evidence belonged to a class the disclosure of any part of which would be detrimental to the public interest. Your Lordships' House overruled *Duncan* v *Cammell, Laird and Co. Ltd* in this respect and further laid down that if in doubt the court could itself look at a document in the light of any ministerial certificate in order to ascertain whether its forensic publication could really affect the public interest adversely. I do not think that *Conway* v *Rimmer* provides any real foundation for the appellants' wide proposition.

That proposition does, on the other hand, reflect the general principles underlying this branch of the law, as I endeavoured to state them near the outset of this speech. Nevertheless, your Lordships are here concerned with public policy, with all the circumspection which such concern enjoins.

The first question on such a circumspect approach is not so much to canvass general principle as to ascertain whether the law has recognised an existing head of public policy which is relevant to this case. Of that there can be no doubt. The need of continuity in society; the legal application to children of the traditional role of the Crown as *parens patriae*; its exercise in the Court of Chancery in such a way as to make the welfare of a child the first and paramount consideration in matters of custody and guardianship (*In re Thain (An Infant)* [1926] Ch 676); a vast code of legislation starting with the Prevention of Cruelty to Children Act 1889 and culminating in the Children Act 1975; *In re D (Infants)* [1970] 1 WLR 599, decided in this very branch of the law—all this attests beyond question a public interest in the protection of children from neglect or ill-usage.

The *patria potestas* in respect of children in need of help has been largely devolved on local authorities. But the appellants, not only by royal charter but also by statutory recognition, have an important role to play. Apart from the police and the local authority, they are the only persons authorised to take care proceedings in respect of a child or young person (Children and Young Persons Act 1969, section 1; Children and Young Persons Act 1969 (Authorisation for the purposes of Section 1) Order 1970). They have, of course, other important functions for the protection of children from neglect or ill-usage; my noble and learned friends who have preceded me have set them out.

Before passing to the next question I must deal with an argument on behalf of the respondent which arises at this point. Counsel emphasised that the appellants have legal and other powers and functions, but no legal duties in this field. Only the local authority has a duty to take care proceedings and, for example, provide places of safety. The law, it was argued, will only exclude sources of information from disclosure in court if the information is given to someone who has a *duty* to act. No authority was cited in support of this assertion, and, with all respect, I cannot agree with it. First, it is the performance of the *function* of safeguarding children who may be in peril which is the concern of society; enjoining a legal *duty* is merely a way of ensuring that the *function* is performed. Secondly, the police too have only a function (not a duty) as regards care proceedings; but it is accepted that police sources of information about children who may be in peril cannot be investigated in court.

This brings me to the penultimate question. Is protection of their sources of information necessary for the proper performance of their functions by the appellants? As to this there is uncontradicted and entirely plausible evidence. The answer is "yes". This satisfies Wigmore's second test: the element of confidentiality is "essential to the full and satisfactory maintenance of the relation between" the appellants and their informants (s. 2285). And the answers to this and the preceding question together meet Wigmore's third criterion: the relation is "one which in the opinion of the community ought to be sedulously fostered" (s. 2285).

The final question, my Lords, is whether the appellants' sources of information can be withheld from forensic investigation by extending on strict analogy an established rule of law. I have already cited long-standing and approved authority to the effect that sources of police information are not subject to forensic investigation. This is because liability to general disclosure would cause those sources of information to dry up, so that police protection of the community would be impaired. Exactly the same argument applies in the instant case if for "police" you read "NSPCC" and for "community" you read "that part of the community which consists of children who may be in peril". There can be no material distinction between police and/or local authorities on the one hand and the appellants on the other as regards protection of children. It follows that, on the strictest analogical approach and as a matter of legal rule, the appellants are bound to refuse to disclose their sources of information'.

LORD EDMUND-DAVIES: 'In the result, I believe that the law applicable to all civil actions like the present one may be thus stated:

(1) In civil proceedings a judge has no discretion, simply because what is contemplated is the disclosure of information which has passed betwen persons in a confidential relationship (other than that of lawyer and client), to direct a party to that relationship that he need not disclose that information even though its disclosure is (a) relevant to and (b) necessary for the attainment of justice in the particular case. If (a) and

(b) are established, the doctor or the priest must be directed to answer if, despite the strong dissuasion of the judge, the advocate persists in seeking disclosure. This is also true of all other confidential relationships in the absence of a special statutory provision, such as the Civil Evidence Act 1968, regarding communications between patent agents and their clients.

(2) But where (i) a confidential relationship exists (other than that of lawyer and client) *and* (ii) disclosure would be in breach of some ethical or social value involving the public interest, the court has a discretion to uphold a refusal to disclose relevant evidence provided it considers that, on balance, the public interest would be better served by excluding such evidence.

(3) In conducting the necessary balancing operation between competing aspects of public interest, the presence (or absence) of involvement of the central government in the matter of disclosure is *not* conclusive either way, though in practice it may affect the cogency of the argument against disclosure. It is true that in *Blackpool Corporation* v *Locker* [1948] 1 KB 349 the Court of Appeal dismissed a local authority's claim to exclude their interdepartmental communications in the public interest, Scott LJ saying, at p. 380: "No such privilege has yet, so far as I know, been conceded by the courts to any local government officer when his employing authority is in litigation". But it is worthy of note that he went on to observe that, although:

> Public interest is, from the point of view of English justice, a regrettable and sometimes dangerous form of privilege, though at times unavoidable; . . . *no such ground was put forward in the plaintiffs' affidavit.* (The italics are mine.)

We therefore cannot be sure how that case would otherwise have been decided, but we do know from *Conway* v *Rimmer* [1968] AC 910 and *In re D (Infants)* [1970] 1 WLR 599 that an organ of central government does not now necessarily have to be involved before a claim for non-disclosure can succeed. In my judgment, Scarman LJ therefore went too far in asserting in the Court of Appeal in the present case [1976] 3 WLR 124, 139 that ". . . state interest alone can justify the withholding of relevant documents . . ." So to assert is, in the wise words of one commentator, ". . . to place too high a value on the arbitrary factor of the status of the possessor of the information. It also assumes that organisations can be classified into those which have the status of a 'central organ of government' . . . and those which do not. Such a classification is surely impracticable". (Joseph Jacob, "Discovery and Public Interest" [1976] PL 134, 138.)

(4) The sole touchstone is the public interest, and not whether the party from whom disclosure is sought was acting under a "duty"—as opposed to merely exercising "powers". A party who acted under some duty may find it easier to establish that public interest was involved than one merely exercising powers, but that is another matter.

(5) The mere fact that relevant information was communicated in confidence does not necessarily mean that it need not be disclosed. But where the subject matter is clearly of public interest, the *additional* fact (if such it be) that to break the seal of confidentiality would endanger that interest will in most (if not all) cases probably lead to the conclusion that disclosure should be withheld. And it is difficult to conceive of *any* judicial discretion to exclude relevant and necessary evidence save in respect of confidential information communicated in a confidential relationship.

(6) The disclosure of all evidence relevant to the trial of an issue being at all times a matter of considerable public interest, the question to be determined is whether it is clearly demonstrated that in the particular case the public interest would nevertheless be better served by excluding evidence despite its relevance. If, on balance, the matter is left in doubt, disclosure should be ordered.'

(LORD KILBRANDON agreed with LORD HAILSHAM.)

Appeal allowed.

Science Research Council v Nassé; Leyland Cars v Vyas [1979] QB 144 (CA); [1980] AC 1028 (HL)

The two appeals were heard together. The complainants alleged that refusal of promotion by their employers was motivated by unlawful discrimination. They sought discovery of confidential reports by their employers concerning both themselves and the other employees who were considered for promotion at the same time. The employers in each case did not object to disclosure of the reports relating to the applicants, but did object to discovery of those dealing with the rivals. The Employment Appeal Tribunal ordered disclosure in both cases. The employers appealed successfully to the Court of Appeal. The complainants appealed to the House of Lords.

LORD WILBERFORCE: 'On these points my conclusions are as follows:

1 There is no principle of public interest immunity, as that expression was developed from *Conway v Rimmer* [1968] AC 910, protecting such confidential documents as those with which these appeals are concerned. That such an immunity exists, or ought to be declared by this House to exist, was the main contention of Leyland. It was not argued for by the SRC; indeed that body argued against it.

2 There is no principle in English law by which documents are protected from discovery by reason of confidentiality alone. But there is no reason why, in the exercise of its discretion to order discovery, the tribunal should not have regard to the fact that documents are confidential, and that to order disclosure would involve a breach of confidence. In the employment field, the tribunal may have regard to the sensitivity of particular types of confidential information, to the extent to which the interests of third parties (including their employees on whom confidential reports have been made, as well as persons reporting) may be affected by disclosure, to the interest which both employees and employers may have in preserving the confidentiality of personal reports, and to any wider interest which may be seen to exist in preserving the confidentiality of systems of personal assessments.

3 As a corollary to the above, it should be added that relevance alone, though a necessary ingredient, does not provide an automatic sufficient test for ordering discovery. The tribunal always has a discretion. That relevance alone is enough was, in my belief, the position ultimately taken by counsel for Mrs Nassé thus entitling the complainant to discovery subject only to protective measures (sealing up, etc.). This I am unable to accept.

4 The ultimate test in discrimination (as in other) proceedings is whether discovery is necessary for disposing fairly of the proceedings. If it is, then discovery must be ordered notwithstanding confidentiality. But where the court is impressed with the need to preserve confidentiality in a particular case, it will consider carefully whether

the necessary information has been or can be obtained by other means, not involving a breach of confidence.

5 In order to reach a conclusion whether discovery is necessary notwithstanding confidentiality the tribunal should inspect the documents. It will naturally consider whether justice can be done by special measures such as "covering up" substituting anonymous references for specific names, or, in rare cases, hearing in camera.

6 The procedure by which this process is to be carried out is one for tribunals to work out in a manner which will avoid delay and unnecessary applications. I shall not say more on this aspect of the matter than that the decisions of the Employment Appeal Tribunal in *Stone* v *Charrington & Co. Ltd* (unreported), February 15, 1977, *per* Phillips J, *Oxford* v *Department of Health and Social Security* [1977] ICR 884, 887, *per* Phillips J and *British Railways Board* v *Natarajan* [1979] ICR 326 *per* Arnold J well indicate the lines of a satisfactory procedure, which must of course be flexible.

7 The above conclusions are essentially in agreement with those of the Court of Appeal. I venture to think however that the formula suggested, namely [1979] QB 144, 173, 182:

> The industrial tribunals should not order or permit the disclosure of reports or references that have been given and received in confidence except in the very rare cases where, after inspection of a particular document, the chairman decides that it is essential in the interests of justice that the confidence should be overridden: and then only subject to such conditions as to the divulging of it as he shall think fit to impose—both for the protection of the maker of the document and the subject of it.

may be rather too rigid. For myself I prefer to rest such rule as can be stated upon the discretion of the court'.

LORD EDMUND DAVIES: 'Learned counsel for the appellants went so far as to submit that the confidential nature of the documents here in question is totally irrelevant to the matter of discovery, and that the tribunal or court should therefore wholly ignore the protests of third parties against the disclosure of information furnished by them in the belief that neither it nor its sources would ever be revealed. Reliance for that submission was placed on cases ranging from *Hopkinson* v *Lord Burghley* (1867) LR 2 Ch App 447 to *McIvor* v *Southern Health and Social Services Board* [1978] 1 WLR 757; and the Industrial Relations Act 1971, section 158(1), and the Employment Protection Act 1975, section 18, were adverted to as illustrating Parliament's ability to provide express safeguards for the preservation of confidences when it thinks this is desirable. But for myself I am wholly unable to spell out from the absence of corresponding statutory provisions applicable to the present cases the conclusion that confidentiality is an irrelevance. It is true that it cannot of *itself* ensure protection from disclosure (*Alfred Crompton Amusement Machines Ltd* v *Customs and Excise Commissioners* [1974] AC 405; *D* v *National Society for the Prevention of Cruelty to Children* [1978] AC 171), but confidentiality may nevertheless properly play a potent part in the way in which a tribunal or court exercises its discretion in the matter of discovery.

There was ample evidence supporting the view expressed by the Court of Appeal that the disclosure to inspection of confidential reports could well create upsets and unrest which would have a general deleterious effect. And a court, mindful of that risk may understandably—and properly—think it right to scrutinise with particular care a request for their inspection. That is not to say, however, that the fear of possible unrest should deter the court from ordering discovery where the demands of justice clearly require it, but it serves to counsel caution in such cases'.

LORD FRASER OF TULLYBELTON: 'The argument based on the need for candour in reporting echoes the argument which was presented in *Conway* v *Rimmer* [1968] AC 910 and I do not think that it has any greater weight now than it had then. The objections by and on behalf of employees other than the complainers to having their confidential reports disclosed, readily understandable as they are, do not create a public interest against disclosure. They are based on a private interest which must yield, in accordance with well-established principles, to the greater public interest that is deemed to exist in ascertaining the truth in order to do justice between the parties to litigation. I am not satisfied that disclosure of the contents of confidential reports of the kind in question here would have serious consequences upon the efficiency of British industry. In any event, the possibility of industrial unrest is not a sufficient reason for the courts to fail to give full effect to the intentions of Parliament; the courts cannot refuse to apply the law between litigants because of threats by third parties. Much reliance was placed in argument on a passage in the speech of Lord Hailsham of St. Marylebone in *D* v *National Society for the Prevention of Cruelty to Children* [1978] AC 171, 230 as follows:

> The categories of public interest are not closed, and must alter from time to time whether by restriction or extension as social conditions and social legislation develop.

Speaking for myself I fully accept that proposition, but any extension can only be made by adding new categories analogous to those already existing, just as in that case immunity was extended to a new category of informers to the NSPCC by analogy with informers to the police who were already entitled to immunity. There is no analogy between the suggested public interest in the present cases and the kinds of public interest that have so far been held to justify immunity from disclosure. Such public interest as there is in withholding the documents from disclosure is not enough to justify the creation of a new head of immunity for a whole class of documents.

Two other considerations point against immunity. One is that in some cases immunity would make it impossible for an employee to enforce his rights under the Acts. The confidential information is almost always in the possession of the employer, and, in cases where discrimination cannot be inferred from the bare fact that someone other than the complainer has been selected for preferment, it may be of vital importance to the complainer to have access to the reports on the preferred individual. This is particularly true where the complaint is based on discrimination on grounds of race or sex, because in those cases the onus of proof is on the complainer. But even where the complaint is of discrimination for trade union activities, and the onus is on the employer, disclosure may be essential in order to do justice between the parties.

The second consideration is that, if public interest immunity applied, it could not be waived either by the employer alone, or by the employer with the consent of the individual who is the subject of a report and of the person who made it. That would be inconvenient, and, in my opinion, quite unnecessarily restrictive'.

LORD SCARMAN: 'For myself, I regret the passing of the currently rejected term "Crown privilege". It at least emphasised the very restricted area of public interest immunity. As was pointed out by Mr Lester QC who presented most helpful submissions on behalf of the two statutory bodies as well as specifically for the appellant, Mr Vyas, the immunity exists to protect from disclosure only information the secrecy of which is essential to the proper working of the government of the state. Defence, foreign relations, the inner workings of government at the highest levels where ministers and their advisers are formulating national policy, and the prosecution process in its pre-trial stage are the sensitive areas where the Crown must have the immunity if the government of the nation is to be effectually carried on. We are in the realm of public law, not private right. The very special case of *D* v *National Society for the Prevention of Cruelty to Children* [1978] AC 171 is not to be seen as a departure from this well established principle. Immunity from disclosure existed in that case because the House recognised the special position of the NSPCC in the enforcement process of the provisions of the Children Act 1969: a position which the House saw as comparable with that of a prosecuting authority in criminal proceedings. But I would not, with respect, go as far as my noble and learned friend, Lord Hailsham of St Marylebone, when he said in that case, at p. 230: "The categories of public interest are not closed;" nor can I agree with the *dictum* of my noble and learned friend, Lord Edmund-Davies, at p. 245 that, where a confidential relationship exists and disclosure would be in breach of some ethical or social value involving the public interest, the court may uphold a refusal to disclose relevant evidence, if, on balance, the public interest would be better served by excluding it.

I do not find anything in *Conway* v *Rimmer* [1968] AC 910 or the cases therein cited which would extend public interest immunity in this way. On the contrary, the theme of Lord Reid's speech is that the immunity arises only if "disclosure would involve a danger of real prejudice to the national interest" (p. 939). The public interest protected by the immunity is that "harm shall not be done to the nation or the public service by disclosure": Lord Reid at p. 940. Whatever may be true generally of the categories of public interest, the "public interest immunity", which prevents documents from being produced or evidence from being given is restricted, and is not, in my judgment, to be extended either by demanding ministers or by the courts. And, though I agree with my noble and learned friend, Lord Edmund-Davies, in believing that a court may refuse to order production of a confidential document if it takes the view that justice does not require its production, I do not see the process of decision as a balancing act. If the document is necessary for fairly disposing of the case, it must be produced, notwithstanding its confidentiality. Only if the document should be protected by public interest immunity, will there be a balancing act. And then the balance will not be between "ethical or social" values of a confidential relationship involving the public interest and the document's relevance in the litigation, but between the public interest represented by the state and its public service, i.e., the executive government, and the public interest in the administration of justice: see Lord Reid. Thus my emphasis would be different from that of my noble and learned friends. "Public interest immunity" is, in my judgment, restricted to what must be kept secret for the protection of government at the highest levels and in the truly sensitive areas of executive responsibility'.

(LORD SALMON delivered a concurring judgment.)

Appeals dismissed.

Burmah Oil Co. Ltd v Governor and Company of the Bank of England [1980] AC 1090 (HL)

The company sought a declaration against the Bank that a sale by the company to the Bank of certain stock at a price required by the government, pursuant to an agreement made in 1975, was inequitable and unfair, and claimed an order for the transfer back of the stock at the 1975 price. The company had, at the time of the agreement, been in dire financial straits because of an international oil crisis, and the agreement had been designed to 'rescue' the company, under the very close control of the government, working through the Bank. The company sought discovery of all relevant documents. The Crown intervened and objected to the production of some sixty-two documents, which for this purpose were divided into three categories. Categories A and B both related to the formulation of government economic policy, at ministerial level and at a lower level. By a majority, the Court of Appeal upheld the Crown's objection. The company appealed.

LORD SCARMAN: 'It is said—and this view commended itself to the majority of the Court of Appeal—that the bank has given very full discovery of the documents directly relevant to the critical issue in the action, namely, the conduct by the bank of the negotiations with Burmah: that Burmah knows as much about this issue as does the bank: and that it can be fully investigated and decided upon the documents disclosed and the evidence available to Burmah without recourse to documents noting or recording the private discussions between the bank and the government. Upon this view, Burmah's attempt to see these documents is no more than a fishing expedition.

I totally reject this view of the case. First, as a matter of law, the documents for which immunity is claimed relate to the issues in the action and, according to the *Peruvian Guano* formulation, 11 QBD 55, may well assist towards a fair disposal of the case. It is unthinkable that in the absence of a public immunity objection and without a judicial inspection of the documents disclosure would have been refused. Secondly, common sense must be allowed to creep into the picture. Burmah's case is not merely that the bank exerted pressure: it is that the bank acted unreasonably, abusing its power and taking an unconscionable advantage of the weakness of Burmah. Upon these questions the withheld documents may be very revealing. This is not "pure speculation". The government was creating the pressure: the bank was exerting it upon the government's instructions. Is a court to assume that such documents will not assist towards an understanding of the nature of the pressure exerted? The assumption seems to me as unreal as the proverbial folly of attempting to understand Hamlet without reference to his position as the Prince of Denmark. I do not understand how a court could properly reach the judge's conclusion without inspecting the documents: and this he refused to do. The judge in my opinion wrongly exercised his discretion when he refused to inspect unless public policy (of which public interest immunity is a manifestation) required him to refuse.

It becomes necessary, therefore, to analyse closely the public interest immunity objection made by the minister and to determine the correct approach of the court to a situation in which there may be a clash of two interests—that of the public service and that of justice.

In *Conway* v *Rimmer* [1968] AC 910 this House had to consider two questions. They were formulated by Lord Reid in these terms, at p.943:

... first, whether the court is to have any right to question the finality of a minister's certificate and, secondly, if it has such a right, how and in what circumstances that right is to be exercised and made effective.

The House answered the first question, but did not, in my judgment, provide, nor was it required to provide, a complete answer to the second.

As I read the speeches in *Conway* v *Rimmer* the House answered the first question by establishing the principle of judicial review. The minister's certificate is not final. The immunity is a rule of law: its scope is a question of law: and its applicability to the facts of a particular case is for the court, not the minister, to determine. The statement of Lord Kilmuir LC of June 6, 1956 (all that is relevant is quoted in *Conway* v *Rimmer* at p. 922) that: "The minister's certificate on affidavit setting out the ground of the claim must in England be accepted by the court . . ." is no longer a correct statement of the law. Whether *Conway* v *Rimmer* be seen as a development of or a departure from previous English case law is a matter of no importance. What is important is that it aligned English law with the law of Scotland and of the Commonwealth. It is the heir apparent not of *Duncan* v *Cammell, Laird & Co. Ltd* [1942] AC 624 but of *Robinson* v *State of South Australia (No. 2)* [1931] AC 704 and of *Glasgow Corporation* v *Central Land Board*, 1956 SC (HL) 1.

Having established the principle of judicial review, the House had in *Conway* v *Rimmer* [1968] AC 910 a simple case on the facts to decide. The question was whether routine reports, albeit of a confidential character, upon a former probationary police constable should in the interests of justice be disclosed in an action brought by him against his former superintendent in which he claimed damages for alleged malicious prosecution. There was a public interest in the confidentiality of such reports, but the Home Secretary, in his affidavit objecting to production on the ground of injury to the public interest, did not go so far as to say that it was necessary for the proper functioning of the public service to withhold production. On the other hand, the reports might be of critical importance in the litigation. Granted the existence of judicial review, here was a justiciable issue of no great difficulty. The House decided itself to inspect the documents, and, having done so, ordered production.

In reaching its decision the House did indicate what it considered to be the correct approach to the clash of interests which arises whenever there is a question of public interest immunity. The approach is to be found stated in two passages of Lord Reid's speech: pp. 940 and 952. The essence of the matter is a weighing, on balance, of the two public interests, that of the nation or the public service in non-disclosure and that of justice in the production of the documents. A good working, but not logically perfect, distinction is recognised between the contents and the classes of documents. If a minister of the Crown asserts that to disclose the contents of a document would, or might, do the nation or the public service a grave injury, the court will be slow to question his opinion or to allow any interest, even that of justice, to prevail over it. Unless there can be shown to exist some factor suggesting either a lack of good faith (which is not likely) or an error of judgment or an error of law on the minister's part, the court should not (the House held) even go so far as itself to inspect the document. In this sense, the minister's assertion may be said to be conclusive. It is, however, for the judge to determine whether the minister's opinion is to be treated as conclusive. I do not understand the House to have denied that even in "contents" cases the court retains its power to inspect or to balance the injury to the public service against the risk of injustice, before reaching its decision.

In "class" cases the House clearly considered the minister's certificate to be more likely to be open to challenge. Undoubtedly, however, the House thought that there were certain classes of documents, which ought not to be disclosed however harmless the disclosure of their contents might be, and however important their disclosure might be in the interest of justice. Cabinet minutes were cited as an example. But the point did not arise for decision. For the documents in *Conway* v *Rimmer* [1968] AC 910, though confidential, were "routine", in no way concerned with the inner working of the government at a high level; and their production might well be indispensable to the doing of justice in the litigation.

The point does arise in the present case. The documents are "high level". They are concerned with the formulation of policy. They are part of the inner working of the government machine. They contain information which the court knows does relate to matters in issue in the action, and which may, on inspection, prove to be highly material. In such circumstances the minister may well be right in his view that the public service would be injured by disclosure. But is the court bound by his view that it is *necessary* for the proper functioning of the public service that they be withheld from production? And, if non-disclosure is necessary for that purpose, is the court bound to hold that the interest in the proper functioning of the public service is to prevail over the requirements of justice?

If the answer to these two questions is to be in the affirmative as Lord Reid appears to suggest in *Conway* v *Rimmer*, I think the law reverts to the statement of Lord Kilmuir. A properly drawn minister's certificate, which is a *bona fide* expression of his opinion, becomes final. But the advance made in the law by *Conway* v *Rimmer* was that the certificate is not final. I think, therefore, that it would now be inconsistent with principle to hold that the court may not—even in a case like the present—review the certificate and balance the public interest of government to which alone it refers, against the public interest of justice, which is the concern of the court.

I do not therefore accept that there are any classes of document which, however harmless their contents and however strong the requirement of justice, may never be disclosed until they are only of historical interest. In this respect I think there may well be a difference between a "class' objection and a "contents" objection—though the residual power to inspect and to order disclosure must remain in both instances. A Cabinet minute, it is said, must be withheld from production. Documents relating to the formulation of policy at a high level are also to be withheld. But is the secrecy of the "inner workings of the government machine" so vital a public interest that it must prevail over even the most imperative demands of justice? If the contents of a document concern the national safety, affect diplomatic relations or relate to some state secret of high importance, I can understand an affirmative answer. But if they do not (and it is not claimed in this case that they do), what is so important about secret government that it must be protected even at the price of injustice in our courts?

The reasons given for protecting the secrecy of government at the level of policy-making are two. The first is the need for candour in the advice offered to ministers: the second is that disclosure "would create or fan ill-informed or captious public or political criticism". Lord Reid in *Conway* v *Rimmer* [1968] AC 910, 952, thought the second "the most important reason". Indeed, he was inclined to discount the candour argument.

I think both reasons are factors legitimately to be put into the balance which has to be struck between the public interest in the proper functioning of the public service (i.e., the executive arm of government) and the public interest in the administration of justice. Sometimes the public service reasons will be decisive of the issue: but they should never prevent the court from weighing them against the injury which would be suffered in the administration of justice if the document was not to be disclosed. And the likely injury to the cause of justice must also be assessed and weighed. Its weight will vary according to the nature of the proceedings in which disclosure is sought, the relevance of the documents, and the degree of likelihood that the document will be of importance in the litigation. In striking the balance, the court may always, if it thinks it is necessary, itself inspect the documents.

Inspection by the court is, I accept, a power to be exercised only if the court is in doubt, after considering the certificate, the issues in the case and the relevance of the documents whose disclosure is sought. Where documents are relevant (as in this case they are), I would think a pure "class" objection would by itself seldom quieten judicial doubts—particularly if, as here, a substantial case can be made out for saying that disclosure is needed in the interest of justice.

I am fortified in the opinion which I have expressed by the trend towards inspection and disclosure to be found both in the United States and in Commonwealth countries. Of course, the United States have a written constitution and a Bill of Rights. Nevertheless both derive from the common law and British political philosophy. *Mutatis mutandis*, I would adopt the principle accepted by the Supreme Court in *Nixon* v *United States*, 418 US 683 which is summarised in 41 LEd 2d 1039, 1046:

> Neither the doctrine of separation of powers, nor the need for confidentiality of high level communications, without more, can sustain an absolute unqualified presidential privilege of immunity from judicial process under all circumstances; although the President's need for complete candor and objectivity from advisers calls for great deference from the courts, nevertheless when the privilege depends solely on the broad, undifferentiated claim of public interest in the confidentiality of such conversations, a confrontation with other values arises; absent a claim of need to protect military, diplomatic or sensitive national security secrets, it is difficult to accept the argument that even the very important interest in confidentiality of Presidential communications is significantly diminished by production of such material for in camera inspection with all the protection that a United States District Court will be obliged to provide.

In Australia the High Court had to consider the problem in a recent case where the facts were, admittedly, exceptional. In *Sankey* v *Whitlam*, 53 ALJR 11 [(1978) 21 ALR 505] the plaintiff sought declarations that certain papers and documents, to which the magistrate in criminal proceedings instituted by the plaintiff against the defendants had accorded privilege, should be produced. The offences alleged against Mr Whitlam, a former Prime Minister, and others were serious—conspiracies to act unlawfully in the conduct of official business. Gibbs ACJ dealt with the issue of Crown privilege as follows:

For these reasons I consider that although there is a class of documents whose members are entitled to protection from disclosure irrespective of their contents, the protection is not absolute, and it does not endure for ever. The fundamental and governing principle is that documents in the class may be withheld from production only when this is necessary in the public interest. In a particular case the court must balance the general desirability that documents of that kind should not be disclosed against the need to produce them in the interests of justice. The court will of course examine the question with especial care, giving full weight to the reasons for preserving the secrecy of documents of this class, but it will not treat all such documents as entitled to the same measure of protection—the extent of protection required will depend to some extent on the general subject matter with which the documents are concerned. If a strong case has been made out for the production of the documents, and the court concludes that their disclosure would not really be detrimental to the public interest, an order for production will be made. In view of the danger to which the indiscriminate disclosure of documents of this class might give rise, it is desirable that the government concerned, Commonwealth or State, should have an opportunity to intervene and be heard before any order for disclosure is made. Moreover no such order should be enforced until the government concerned has had an opportunity to appeal against it, or test its correctness by some other process, if it wishes to do so (cf. *Conway* v *Rimmer* [1968] AC 910, 953)."

Both *Nixon's* case, 418 US 683 and *Sankey* v *Whitlam*, 53 ALJR 11 are far closer to the Scottish and Commonwealth stream of authority than to the English. In the *Glasgow Corporation* case, 1956 SC (HL) 1, Viscount Simonds said, at p. 11 ; "that there always has been and is now in the law of Scotland an inherent power of the court to override the Crown's objection to produce documents on the ground that it would injure the public interest to do so".

In *Robinson* v *State of South Australia (No. 2)* [1931] AC 704 the Privy Council reminded the Supreme Court of South Australia of the existence of this power. The power must be exercised judicially, and all due weight must be given to the objections of the Crown: that is all.

Something was made in argument about the risk to the nation or the public service of an error at first instance. Injury to the public interest—perhaps even very serious injury—could be done by production of documents which should be immune from disclosure before an appellate court could correct the error. The risk is inherent in the principle of judicial review. The House in *Conway* v *Rimmer* [1968] AC 910 recognised its existence, but, nevertheless, established the principle as part of our law. Gibbs J also mentioned it in *Sankey* v *Whitlam*, 53 ALJR 11. I would respectfully agree with Lord Reid's observations on the point in *Conway* v *Rimmer* [1968] AC 910, 953: " . . . it is important that the minister should have a right to appeal before the document is produced".

In cases where the Crown is not a party—as in the present case—the court should ensure that the Attorney-General has the opportunity to intervene before disclosure is ordered.

For these reasons I was one of a majority of your Lordships who thought it necessary to inspect the 10 documents. Having done so, I have no doubt that they are relevant and, but for the immunity claim, would have to be disclosed, but their significance is not such as to override the public service objections to their production. Burmah will not suffer injustice by their non-disclosure, while their disclosure would be, in the opinion of the responsible minister, injurious to the public service. I would, therefore, dismiss the appeal'.

LORD KEITH OF KINKEL: 'In my opinion, it would be going too far to lay down that no document in any particular one of the categories mentioned should never in any circumstances be ordered to be produced . . . Something must turn upon the nature of the subject matter, the persons who dealt with it, and the manner in which they did so. In so far as a matter of government policy is concerned, it may be relevant to know the extent to which the policy remains unfulfilled, so that its success might be prejudiced by disclosure of the considerations which led to it. In that context the time element enters into the equation. Details of an affair which is stale and no longer of topical significance might be capable of disclosure without risk of damage to the public interest. The ministerial certificate should offer all practicable assistance on these aspects. But the nature of the litigation and the apparent importance to it of the documents in question may in extreme cases demand production even of the most sensitive communications at the highest level. Such a case might fortunately be unlikely to arise in this country, but in circumstances such as those of *Sankey* v *Whitlam*, 53 ALJR 11 or *Nixon* v *United States* (1974) 418 US 683 to which reference is made in the speech of my noble and learned friend Lord Scarman, I do not doubt that the principles there expounded would fall to be applied. There can be discerned in modern times a trend towards more open governmental methods than were prevalent in the past. No doubt it is for Parliament and not for courts of law to say how far that trend should go. The courts are, however, concerned with the consideration that it is in the public interest that justice should be done and should be publicly recognised as having been done. This may demand, though no doubt only in a very limited number of cases, that the inner workings of government should be exposed to public gaze, and there may be some who would regard this as likely to lead, not to captious or ill-informed criticism, but to criticism calculated to improve the nature of that working as affecting the individual citizen. I think that considerations of that nature were present in the mind of Lord Denning MR when delivering his dissenting judgment in the Court of Appeal in this case, and in my opinion they correctly reflect what the trend of the law should be.

There are cases where consideration of the terms of the ministerial certificate and of the nature of the issues in the case before it as revealed by the pleadings, taken with the description of the documents sought to be recovered, will make it clear to the court that the balance of public interest lies against disclosure. In other cases the position will be the reverse. But there may be situations where grave doubt arises, and the court feels that it cannot properly decide upon which side the balance falls without privately inspecting the documents. In my opinion the present is such a case.'

(LORDS SALMON and EDMUND-DAVIES agreed that the documents should be inspected. LORD WILBERFORCE dissented on that issue. After inspecting them the majority found (LORD KEITH *dubitante*) that none was of such evidential value as to justify an order for disclosure for the purpose of disposing fairly of the case.)

Appeal dismissed.

Neilson v *Laugharne* [1981] 1 QB 736 (CA)

While the plaintiff was on holiday in July 1978 police officers searched his house in Lancashire pursuant to a warrant obtained in connection with suspected drug offences. They found no drugs, but noticed that the electricity meter appeared to have been tampered with. When the plaintiff returned home he told the police that his house had been burgled and property stolen. On the following day police officers arrested him and interviewed him about a possible offence of abstracting electricity and about the alleged theft from his house. No charges were brought against the plaintiff, and he withdrew the allegations that his house had been burgled or that anything had been stolen. On 7 August 1978, solicitors acting for the plaintiff wrote a letter before action to the defendant, the Chief Constable of Lancashire, complaining of trespass, damage to the plaintiff's property and belongings, false arrest, wrongful imprisonment and assault by police officers, the assault alleged being the failure to supply the plaintiff promptly when requested to do so with his tablets for a heart condition from which he suffered. The defendant instituted the complaints procedure under section 49 of the Police Act 1964, which resulted in a decision that there were no grounds for disciplinary or criminal proceedings against any of the police officers involved. The plaintiff commenced proceedings in the county court claiming damages from the defendant. Lists of documents were ordered, and the defendant's list disclosed the statements, including one by the plaintiff, taken in pursuance of the inquiry under section 49, which (except for the plaintiff's statement) he objected to produce on the grounds that it would be injurious to the public interest and that they were covered by legal professional privilege. The registrar ordered production of the statements. The defendant appealed to the judge, who upheld his claim that the documents were covered by legal professional privilege. The plaintiff appealed.

LORD DENNING MR: 'There have been many cases lately on public interest privilege. They fall into two distinct categories: (1) The old "Crown privilege" Until the year 1973 we spoke only of "Crown privilege". It was held that a government department could intervene in a suit between two litigants and claim, on the ground of public interest, that documents in the hands of one of the litigants should not be produced. The objection had to be taken by the minister himself or by the head of the department, or some highly placed official in an affidavit giving his reasons. His affidavit was, as a rule, conclusive. It was often said that the privilege could not be waived by the Crown, even though it would be to its advantage to do so. And that the judge might take the objection himself. The leading cases are *Duncan* v *Cammell Laird & Co. Ltd* [1942] AC 624; *In re Grosvenor Hotel, London (No. 2)* [1965] Ch 1210, 1241–1247; *Conway* v *Rimmer* [1968] AC 910; *R* v *Lewes Justices, ex parte Secretary of State for the Home Department* [1973] AC 388, 406, *per* Lord Pearson and *Burmah Oil Co. Ltd* v *Governor and Company of the Bank of England* [1980] AC 1090. I do not think that that kind of "public interest" privilege applies here. There is no affidavit by the Home Secretary as there was in *Conway* v *Rimmer* and *R* v *Lewes Justices*. There is here only an affidavit by the deputy chief constable. I should not regard him as "highly placed" for the purpose.

(2) The modern "public interest" Since 1978 there has been rapidly developed another "public interest" privilege. This is a privilege which is asserted, not by a government department, but by one of the litigants himself. It need not be supported by any affidavit of any minister or highly placed official. And it can be waived. I remember well that in *D* v *National Society for the Prevention of Cruelty to Children*

[1978] AC 171 it was strongly argued by Mr David Hirst that there was no such public interest privilege apart from the traditional "Crown privilege", and his argument was accepted by Scarman LJ: see [1978] AC 171, 195–197. But it did not prevail. We extended it to protect the name of the person who informed the NSPCC. It was in the public interest that it should not be disclosed. The seed of this modern public interest was sown by Lord Cross of Chelsea in *Alfred Crompton Amusement Machines Ltd* v *Customs and Excise Commissioners (No. 2)* [1974] AC 405, when he said on behalf of himself and the other Lords of Appeal, at p. 433:

> "Confidentiality" is not a separate head of privilege, but it may be a very material consideration to bear in mind when privilege is claimed on the ground of public interest. What the court has to do is to weigh on the one hand the considerations which suggest that it is in the public interest that the documents in question should be disclosed and on the other hand those which suggest that it is in the public interest that they should not be disclosed and to balance one against the other.

That seed was sown in the old field of "Crown privilege", but it fell also on the new field with which the Crown was not concerned. It bore fruit in the pair of cases *Science Research Council* v *Nassé; Leyland Cars (BL Cars Ltd)* v *Vyas* in this court [1979] QB 144 and in the House of Lords [1980] AC 1028. The decision was ostensibly based on the rule that the court has a general discretion to order discovery, coupled with the qualification that "discovery shall not be ordered if and in so far as the court is of opinion that it is not necessary either for fairly disposing of the proceedings or for saving costs". In applying that rule, this court—as I believe—and most of the members of the House had regard to the public interests involved. We applied the words of Lord Edmund-Davies in the *NSPCC* case [1978] AC 171, 245: "But where (i) a confidential relationship exists . . . *and* (ii) disclosure would be in breach of some ethical or social value involving the public interest, the court has a discretion to uphold a refusal to disclose relevant evidence provided it considers that, on balance, the public interest would be better served by excluding such evidence."

Very recently we applied this principle in *Gaskin* v *Liverpool City Council* [1980] 1 WLR 1549. We held that a local authority was not bound to disclose the case notes and records relating to a child in care. We drew a parallel between child care privilege and legal professional privilege.

This modern development shows that, on a question of discovery, the court can consider the competing public interests involved. The case is decided by the court holding the balance between the two sides. One of them is asserting that, in the interest of justice, the documents should be disclosed. The other is asserting that in the public interest they should not be disclosed. Confidentiality is often to be considered. So is the need for candour and frankness. So is the desirability of co-operation. Or any other factors which present themselves. On weighing them all the judge decides according to which side the balance comes down. Once it is decided that the public interest is in favour of non-disclosure, the decision is regarded as a precedent for later situations of the same kind. So the body of law is built up. As Lord Hailsham of St Marylebone said in the *NSPCC* case [1978] AC 171, 230: "The categories of public interest are not closed, and must alter from time to time whether by restriction or extension as social conditions and social legislation develop".

On the one hand we have a man who is suing the police for damages. He has got legal aid and demands to see all the statements taken by the police. He—or rather his solicitors—want to see the police statements so as to find out something, if they can, to back him up. On the other hand there are the police who, for aught that appears, apart from this man's complaint, have acted perfectly properly. Statements were taken on the basis that they were to be used for a private investigation—to see if the police had acted improperly in any way: and, if they had acted improperly, to be used in criminal or disciplinary proceedings against the police. No improper conduct by the police was disclosed at all.

Yet now the plaintiff wants to see the statements for another purpose altogether—to help him make out a case for damages. I cannot think it can be right to let him do this. Some of the statements may contain the names of informers which should be kept secret anyway. I cannot think it incumbent on the police—or the court—to go through all these statements—or to consider the contents of them—so as to assert a "contents" privilege. It is in the public interest that the whole "class" should be privileged from disclosure to the plaintiff.

If this man has any case at all, he must make it out on his own showing—supported by witnesses whom he can find himself. He should not be allowed to delve through these statements so as to make out a case—which he would not otherwise have.

It is not necessary for us to inspect the documents ourselves. Nor is it desirable. The man might well feel a grievance if the court decided against him on its own view of the documents—without his seeing them. As Viscount Simon LC said in *Duncan v Cammell Laird & Co. Ltd* [1942] AC 624, 640: "it is a first principle of justice that the judge should have no dealings on the matter in hand with one litigant save in the presence of and to the equal knowledge of the other". And as Megaw LJ said in *Gaskin* v *Liverpool City Council* [1980] 1 WLR 1549, 1555: "[Inspection] should not be undertaken lightly or ill-advisedly. It may put upon the court a burden which it is extremely difficult, perhaps in some circumstances impossible, to discharge fairly and satisfactorily".

I have a feeling that the Burmah shareholders might have felt it unfair that the House of Lords should have looked at the documents themselves and said: "They are relevant but we don't think they help much one way or the other"; see the *Burmah Oil* case [1980] AC 1090, 1121, 1130, 1135. In all "class" cases, I think the court should very rarely inspect the documents themselves. *Ex hypothesi* there may be nothing in their contents to object to. At any rate, in this case, I do not think it would be proper to inspect the documents.

In my opinion the statements taken in pursuance of section 49 are privileged from production in a way analogous to legal professional privilege, and child care privilege. This case bears a striking resemblance to the *Gaskin* case [1980] 1 WLR 1549. It looks like a "fishing expedition". Legal aid is being used by complaining persons to harass innocent folk who have only been doing their duty. The complainants make all sorts of allegations—often quite unjustified—and then use legal machinery to try to manufacture a case. We should come down firmly against such tactics. We should refuse to order production'.

OLIVER LJ: 'The danger was touched on in the course of the argument that the liability of documents of this sort to be disclosed on discovery might encourage those whose brushes with the police might have given them a sense of grievance to launch speculative proceedings in the hope of uncovering evidence which might assist them in making good a civil claim; and the suggestion implicit in this is that the documents ought therefore as a matter of public policy to be protected from discovery. Speaking for myself I am unimpressed by this argument which amounts to no more than saying that because discovery may be abused it must therefore be inhibited altogether. A claim to protect a class of documents on the ground of public policy must, I believe, be based upon a firmer foundation than that merely of deterring a particular type of litigant. A citizen who has had past misunderstandings with the law is no more entitled to litigate than any other citizen; but he is no less entitled and there is no presumption that his grievance is speculative or groundless. The possibility of groundless claims cannot therefore, in my judgment, be the touchstone for determining whether relevant documents shall be produced. That possibility, if a relevant consideration at all, is, I think, relevant only in so far as it bears upon what, in my judgment, is the true test, namely whether the production of these documents is likely to impede the carrying out of the public statutory purpose for which they are brought into existence.

The purpose of the legislature in enacting the section was to ensure that all complaints against police officers are fully and properly investigated and that, if the inquiries raise the possibility that a criminal offence has been committed, the matter shall be referred to the Director of Public Prosecutions. The question therefore, as it seems to me, must be this—will liability to disclosure in civil proceedings of statements taken in the course of such inquiry adversely affect the attainment of the legislature's purpose? It seems to me that it will in a number of ways. Take first the position of police officers who are asked to co-operate on the inquiry. They may themselves be potential defendants and, if they are, would clearly be disinclined to provide statements which might subsequently be used to found civil claims against them. They may be called upon to provide information about the activities of superior officers under whose command they are going to have to continue to serve in future. They may well be willing, in the performance of their duty, to do this and to accept that they may be called upon to give evidence if a prosecution or disciplinary proceedings follow. But the complaints which have to be investigated under the Act are not restricted to those which may lead to prosecution or disciplinary proceedings. They cover things as trivial as minor incivility and as serious as assault. Will officers freely co-operate in assisting in inquiries into the conduct of their superiors if they know that, quite regardless of whether a prosecution or disciplinary proceedings ensue, not only the fact that they have participated in the inquiry but the very statements which they have made are liable to come to the knowledge of the officer whose conduct is under investigation and under whom they may have to continue to serve by disclosure as a result of discovery in civil proceedings.

Statements may have to be taken from relatives or associates or neighbours of the complainant—statements which may well, in the event, be adverse to the claim which he seeks to assert and which may result in a decision that disciplinary proceedings or prosecution shall not be instituted. Are such persons likely to be willing to offer free and truthful co-operation in investigations under the section if they know that any statements which they make are liable to be disclosed to the complainant in any civil proceedings which he may be minded to commence?

Finally, there is the position of the complainant himself. Mr Somerset Jones, in the course of argument, stressed the unfairness of a position in which, in effect, the defendant got a proof of the plaintiff's evidence in advance whilst he was deprived of the opportunity of seeing the defendant's. But this seems to me to be an argument in favour of, rather than against, the protection which is sought. There is no compulsion upon the complainant to co-operate in the inquiry. Having made his complaint, he may refuse to give a statement to the investigating officer and he is, I should have thought, very much more likely to do so if he thinks that any statement which he makes may be quoted against him in any civil proceedings which he has in contemplation. If, however, these statements are protected from disclosure in any proceedings, that consequence will be avoided. If public policy prevents disclosure, it prevents it, in my judgment, in all circumstances except to establish innocence in criminal proceedings. It is not like legal professional privilege which is the personal right of the party entitled to it and can be waived: *R v Lewes Justices, ex parte Secretary of State for the Home Department* [1973] AC 388 *per* Lord Simon of Glaisdale, at p. 407, and *per* Lord Salmon at p. 412. As a consequence, therefore, although no doubt the complainant's statement may be included in counsel's brief and may form the basis of a cross-examination, it cannot be used as evidence to controvert anything which the complainant's witnesses may say: *Alfred Crompton Amusement Machines Ltd v Customs and Excise Commissioners (No. 2)* [1974] AC 405, 434, *per* Lord Cross of Chelsea. Thus, it seems to me that, here again, the protection sought in this case would assist the proper carrying out of the statutory purpose if it were allowed and impede it if it were refused'.

(O'CONNOR LJ also delivered a judgment dismissing the appeal.)

Appeal dismissed.

Hehir v *Commissioner of Police for the Metropolis* [1982] 1 WLR 715 (CA)

Following his acquittal for an offence under the Vagrancy Act 1824, the plaintiff complained about the conduct of the two police officers who had arrested him with the result that the defendant, the Commissioner of Police, ordered an inquiry into the police officers' conduct pursuant to section 49 of the Police Act 1964. For the purposes of the investigation, the plaintiff made a statement. He subsequently brought an action against the defendant seeking damages for false imprisonment and malicious prosecution. The defendant in his list of documents claimed privilege for police reports, statements and documents relating to the investigation but, during the trial, the defendant's counsel sought leave to cross-examine the plaintiff on the statement he had made for the purposes of the police investigation. The judge ruled that the defendant could waive the privilege in the document for the purposes of cross-examining the plaintiff. The plaintiff appealed.

LAWTON LJ: 'After the decision of this court in *Neilson v Laugharne* [1981] QB 736 the solicitor concluded that statements taken in the course of a section 49 investigation should not be disclosed, the reason being that the public interest made them immune from discovery; and if they were so immune, they could not be produced at the trial, nor could secondary evidence be given of their contents.

At the trial this claim for immunity put the defendant's counsel in a difficulty. The plaintiff gave evidence in chief. Counsel for the defendant, in the exercise of his forensic judgment, was of the opinion that the plaintiff had deposed to matters which he had not mentioned during the section 49 investigation and had given evidence which was inconsistent with the statement he had then made. He wanted to cross-examine the plaintiff on his section 49 statement. The plaintiff's counsel objected on the ground that the defendant, having claimed public interest immunity for all the statements, could not properly use the plaintiff's statement for the purposes of cross-examining him upon it. The defendant's counsel then claimed that the defendant was entitled to waive his claim for public interest immunity in respect of this document. The trial judge ruled that the defendant's counsel was entitled to cross-examine the plaintiff on the statement he had made as a complainant in the course of the section 49 investigation. The consequences of this ruling reveal the difficulty with which judges trying civil claims against police officers have to deal as a result of the decision in *Neilson* v *Laugharne* [1981] QB 736. The plaintiff had put himself forward as a truthful man who had been the victim of improper and unlawful conduct on the part of two detective constables. The defendant is of the opinion that he is not what he holds himself out to be and that this may be shown by his being cross-examined on his section 49 statement. Forensic experience goes to show that cross-examination on previous statements may reveal this. But if the plaintiff is cross-examined, what is going to happen if and when the two detective constables give evidence? The defendant's counsel has had the plaintiff's statement in his brief because it is in the possession of the defendant. The plaintiff's counsel has not got, and will not get because of the defendant's claim to public interest immunity, copies of any statements made by the two detective constables. If *Neilson* v *Laugharne* applies to this case and the trial judge's ruling is right, police officers are put into a privileged position in this class of litigation.

In the course of counsel's submissions a number of other consequences of the application of the decision in *Neilson* v *Laugharne* were discussed. Its application may prevent prosecutions for offences under section 5(2) of the Criminal Law Act 1967 of persons who cause any wasteful employment of the police by knowingly making false reports about police officers. Further, in the past, when such reports have been made by persons worth suing for defamation, some of their police officer victims, who may have suffered much worry, have claimed damages for libel. Such claims will now be barred because the defamatory statements cannot be put in evidence. The other side to the same forensic coin is the difficulty in which a victim of police misbehaviour may find himself. Those who have injured him may have lied themselves out of trouble during the course of a section 49 investigation. If this has happened, in subsequent civil proceedings the lying police statements would not be available to support the victim's case.

Counsel for the plaintiff accepted that *Neilson* v *Laugharne* could cause difficulties for both parties in civil litigation of this kind. He went on to submit, however, that this was the price which had to be paid for the greater benefit to the public which arose from covering all statements made in section 49 investigations with the mantle of public interest immunity. Some may doubt whether what results from such immunity is worth the price which has to be paid; but if *Neilson* v *Laugharne* does apply to this case any opinion I may have about its merits as an authority are irrelevant: see *Farrell* v *Alexander* [1977] AC 59.

Since it was not suggested that *Neilson* v *Laugharne* [1981] QB 736 came within the rare exceptions set out in *Young* v *Bristol Aeroplane Co. Ltd* [1944] KB 718, that decision is binding upon us if it applies. The first question is whether it does; and, if it does, the second question is whether the defendant could waive such rights, if any, as he had arising out of public interest immunity . . ..

I find it impossible to distinguish *Neilson* v *Laugharne* [1981] QB 736 from this case on the ground that in the earlier case the court did not have to consider specifically whether public interest immunity attached to the complainant's statement.

There remains the question whether it was competent in this case for the defendant to waive public interest immunity. That bare statement of the issue at once poses another question. If the immunity exists in law for the protection of the public interest what right has the defendant to say whether it should be waived in his own interest?

The issue of waiver was not raised in *Neilson* v *Laugharne*, but Lord Denning MR in the course of his judgment said that public interest immunity could be waived: see p. 747. He did not cite any authority in support of his opinion. He may have overlooked what was said in the speech of Lord Simon of Glaisdale in *R* v *Lewes Justices, ex parte Secretary of State for the Home Department* [1973] AC 388. Lord Simon of Glaisdale said, at p. 407:

> It is true that the public interest which demands that the evidence be withheld has to be weighed against the public interest in the administration of justice that courts should have the fullest possible access to all relevant material (*R* v *Hardy* (1794) 24 State Tr 199, 808; *Marks* v *Beyfus* (1890) 25 QBD 494; *Conway* v *Rimmer* [1968] AC 910); but once the former public interest is held to outweigh the latter, the evidence cannot in any circumstances be admitted. It is not a privilege which may be waived by the Crown (see *Marks* v *Beyfus* at p. 500) or by anyone else.

In *Alfred Crompton Amusement Machines Ltd* v *Customs and Excise Commissioners (No. 2)* [1974] AC 405 Lord Cross of Chelsea made an *obiter* comment which suggests that in some circumstances public interest immunity may be waived. That case concerned an assessment for purchase tax. The commissioners claimed "Crown privilege" for a class of routine documents the disclosure of which the head of the department swore would be injurious in the public interest since they would reveal the commissioners' methods and contained confidential information from third parties supplied both voluntarily and pursuant to the exercise of the commissioners' powers under section 24(6) of the Purchase Tax Act 1963. The House of Lords upheld this claim. In the course of commenting on a critical comment which the judge at first instance had made about the chairman of the commissioners Lord Cross said, at p. 434: "His"— that is the chairman's—"objections to disclosure were taken in the interests of the third parties concerned as much as in the interests of the commissioners and if any of them is in fact willing to give evidence, privilege in respect of any documents or information obtained from him will be waived." I find the statement impossible to reconcile with what Lord Simon of Glaisdale said. If the reason for the immunity is the need to protect the public interest individuals should be unable to waive it for their own purposes. Lord Cross of Chelsea seems to have thought that the chairman could waive immunity in respect of any documents or information obtained from third parties who were interested in maintaining non-disclosure if they were willing to give evidence. As I understand his Lordship, waiver would depend on what the provider of the document or information was willing to do, not upon what the chairman wanted. In this case it was the plaintiff who had given the statement. It was the defendant, not the plaintiff, who wanted waiver of the immunity. If there can be waiver of public interest immunity, then the waiver should be by whoever provides the statement, not by him who receives it. This seems to have been Lord Simon of Glaisdale's opinion in *R* v *Lewes Justices, ex parte Secretary of State for the Home Department* [1973] AC 388, 408.

It was for these reasons that I adjudged that the defendant by his counsel could not cross-examine the plaintiff on the statement which he had made in the course of the section 49 investigation.'

(BRIGHTMAN LJ agreed.)

Appeal allowed.

Campbell v *Tameside Metropolitan Borough Council* [1982] QB 1065 (CA)

The prospective plaintiff, a school teacher employed by the defendant education authority, was violently assaulted by an 11-year-old boy in her classroom and suffered severe injuries. Before commencing proceedings against the defendants, the plaintiff applied for an order for disclosure of all documents in their possession relating to the boy including the reports of teachers and of psychologists and psychiatrists. The defendants contended that they were confidential documents of a class which was protected by public interest immunity. Russell J, after he had inspected the relevant documents ordered the defendants to disclose documents in their possession concerning the educational and psychological welfare of the boy. The defendants appealed.

LORD DENNING MR: 'We have many cases about children in the care of local authorities. One side or the other ask to see the reports which the children's officers have made on the children. They are always confidential. Never, I think, have we ordered them to be disclosed. They are privileged—not because of their actual contents— but because as a class they should be kept confidential. We have always found that justice can be done in the individual case without compelling disclosure of these documents.

The first case was *In re D (Infants)* [1970] 1 WLR 599, which was approved by the House of Lords in *D* v *National Society for the Prevention of Cruelty to Children* [1978] AC 171. Another is *Gaskin* v *Liverpool City Council* [1980] 1 WLR 1549. The latest is *R* v *Birmingham City Council, ex parte O* [1982] 1 WLR 679. In every case our task was to hold the balance between the interests involved. On the one hand the public interest in keeping the reports confidential. On the other hand the public interest in seeing that justice is done.

Mr Clegg for the education authority relied on those cases. But in addition he relied particularly on a recent case in this court of *Neilson* v *Laugharne* [1981] QB 736. *Neilson* v *Laugharne* was considered by the court a few weeks ago in *Hehir* v *Commissioner of Police of the Metropolis* [1982] 1 WLR 715. The court doubted its correctness but felt it was bound by it. ∴ . . . I do not think that *Neilson* v *Laugharne* [1981] QB 736 compelled the result. This court was not referred to the line of cases where a man has made a statement in a confidential document and then afterwards goes into the witness box and gives evidence contrary to what he said in the confidential document. It has always been held that he can be cross-examined on the confidential document, in which case the whole document is to be made available: see *North Australian Territory Co.* v *Goldsborough, Mort and Co.* [1893] 2 Ch 381; *Burnell* v *British Transport Commission* [1956] 1 QB 187 and more fully in [1955] 2 Lloyd's Rep 549 and *Alfred Crompton Amusement Machines Ltd* v *Customs and Excise Commissioners (No. 2)* [1974] AC 405, 434, where Lord Cross of Chelsea said: "No doubt it will form part of the brief delivered to counsel for the commissioners and may help him to probe the appellants' evidence in cross-examination."

The reasoning behind it is that the maker of a confidential document can always waive the privilege which attaches to it, or by his conduct become disentitled to it. When he goes into the box and gives evidence which is contrary to his previous statement—then the public interest in the administration of justice outweighs the public interest in keeping the document confidential. He can be cross-examined to show that his evidence in the box is not trustworthy.

I know that in the days of the old Crown privilege it was often said that it could not be waived. That is still correct when the documents are in the vital category spoken of by Lord Reid in *Conway* v *Rimmer* [1968] AC 910, 940. This category includes all those documents which must be kept top secret because the disclosure of them would be injurious to national defence or to diplomatic relations or the detection of crime (as the names of informers). But not where the documents come within Lord Reid's lower category. This category includes those documents which are kept confidential in order that subordinates should be frank and candid in their reports, or for any other good reason. In those cases the privilege can be waived by the maker and recipients of the confidential document. It was so held by Lord Cross of Chelsea in *Alfred Crompton Amusement Machines Ltd* v *Customs and Excise Commissioners (No. 2)* [1974] AC 405, 434H, when he said: "if any of them is in fact willing to give evidence, privilege in respect of any documents or information obtained from him will be waived."

I am still of opinion, therefore, that *Neilson* v *Laugharne* [1981] QB 736 was correctly decided. It is worth noticing that the House of Lords [1981] 2 WLR 553 refused leave to appeal in it. I would, therefore, stand by the principle, at p. 748:

> This modern development shows that, on a question of discovery, the court can consider the competing public interests involved. The case is decided by the court holding the balance between the two sides. One of them is asserting that, in the interest of justice, the documents should be disclosed. The other is asserting that in the public interest they should not be disclosed. Confidentiality is often to be considered. So is the need for candour and frankness. So is the desirability of co-operation. Or any other factors which present themselves. On weighing them all the judge decides according to which side the balance comes down. Once it is decided that the public interest is in favour of non-disclosure, the decision is regarded as a precedent for later situations of the same kind. So the body of law is built up. As Lord Hailsham of St Marylebone said in *D* v *National Society for the Prevention of Cruelty to Children* [1978] AC 171, 230: "The categories of public interest are not closed, and must alter from time to time whether by restriction or extension as social conditions and social legislation develop."

In holding the balance, I would add an additional factor. It applies especially to the lower category spoken of by Lord Reid in *Conway* v *Rimmer* [1968] AC 910, 940. In these cases the court can and should consider the *significance* of the documents in relation to the decision of the case. If they are of such significance that they may well affect the very decision of the case, then justice may require them to be disclosed. The public interest in justice being done—in the instant case—may well outweigh the public interest in keeping them confidential. But, if they are of little significance, so that they are very unlikely to affect the decision of the case, then the greater public interest may be to keep them confidential. In order to assess their significance, it is open to the court itself to inspect the documents. If disclosure is necessary in the interest of justice in the instant case, the court will order their disclosure. But otherwise not. That is the basic reason why the Burmah Oil Company did not get discovery of the documents of the Bank of England. It was not necessary for fairly disposing of the matter: see *Burmah Oil Co. Ltd* v *Government and Company of the Bank of England* [1980] AC 1090, 1121 and 1122, *per* Lord Salmon; pp. 1129 and 1130, *per* Lord Edmund-Davies; p. 1136, *per* Lord Keith of Kinkel; pp. 1145 and 1147 *per* Lord Scarman.

Like the judge, I have looked at the documents. I think that they may be of considerable significance. They go to show whether or not he was of a violent disposition. They go to show whether he should have been allowed to go into this class or not. And so forth. I see no difference between this case and any other school case where a child is injured in the playground by defective equipment, or by want of supervision by the teacher. Full discovery would be ordered there. There is no difference in principle between a child being injured and a teacher being injured. Nor indeed do I see any difference between this case and the ordinary case against a hospital authority for negligence. The reports of nurses and doctors are, of course, confidential; but they must always be disclosed: subject to the safeguard that they are only for use in connection with the instant case and not for any other purpose: see *Riddick* v *Thames Board Mills Ltd* [1977] QB 881 and *Home Office* v *Harman* [1982] 2 WLR 338.

So here, I am quite clear that these documents must be disclosed for use in this litigation. They must not, of course, be used for any other purpose.'

ACKNER LJ: 'Despite the apparent conflict in the able submissions addressed to us, the basic principles which we must apply in the resolution of this dispute do not seem to me to be much in issue. These are:

1 The exclusion of relevant evidence always calls for clear justification. All relevant documents, whether or not confidential, are subject to disclosure unless upon some recognised ground, including the public interest, their non-disclosure is permissible.

2 Since it has been accepted in this court that the documents for which the respondent seeks discovery are relevant to the contemplated litigation, there is a heavy burden upon the appellants to justify withholding them from disclosure; see in particular *Conway* v *Rimmer* [1968] AC 910 and *R* v *Lewes Justices, ex parte Secretary of State for the Home Department* [1973] AC 388, 400, *per* Lord Reid.

3 The fact that information has been communicated by one person to another in confidence is not, of itself, a sufficient ground for protection from disclosure in a court of law, either the nature of the information or the identity of the informant if either of these matters would assist the court to ascertain facts which are relevant to an issue upon which it is adjudicating: *Alfred Crompton Amusement Machines Ltd* v *Customs and Excise Commissioners (No. 2)* [1974] AC 405, 433–443. The private promise of confidentiality must yield to the general public interest, that in the administration of justice truth will out, unless by reason of the character of the information or the relationship of the recipient of the information to the informant a more important public interest is served by protecting the information or identity of the informant from disclosure in a court of law: *per* Lord Diplock, *D* v *National Society for the Prevention of Cruelty to Children* [1978] AC 171, 218. Immunity from

disclosure was permitted in that case because the House of Lords recognised the special position of the NSPCC in the enforcement process of the provisions of the Children and Young Persons Act 1969, a position which the House saw as comparable with that of a prosecuting authority in criminal proceedings. It applied the rationale of the rule as it applies to police informers, that if their identity was liable to be disclosed in a court of law, this source of information would dry up and the police would be hindered in their duty of detecting and preventing crime.

4 Documents in respect of which a claim is made for immunity from disclosure come under a rough but accepted categorisation known as a "class" claim or a "contents" claim. The distinction between them is that with a "class" claim it is immaterial whether the disclosure of the particular contents of particular documents would be injurious to the public interest—the point being that it is the maintenance of the immunity of the "class" from disclosure in litigation that is important. In the "contents" claim, the protection is claimed for particular "contents" in a particular document. A claim remains a "class" even though something may be known about the documents; it remains a "class" even if part of documents are revealed and part disclosed: *per* Lord Wilberforce in *Burmah Oil Co. Ltd* v *Governor and Company of the Bank of England* [1980] AC 1090, 1111.

5 The proper approach where there is a question of public interest immunity is a weighing, on balance, of the two public interests, that of the nation or the public service in non-disclosure and that of justice in the production of the documents. Both in the "class" objection and the "contents" objection the courts retain the residual power to inspect and to order disclosure: *Burmah Oil* case [1980] AC 1090, 1134, *per* Lord Keith of Kinkel; pp. 1143–1144, *per* Lord Scarman.

6 A judge conducting the balancing exercise needs to know whether the documents in question are of much or little weight in the litigation, whether their absence will result in a complete or partial denial of justice to one or other of the parties or perhaps to both, and what is the importance of the particular litigation to the parties and the public. All these are matters which should be considered if the court is to decide where the public interest lies: *per* Lord Pearce in *Conway* v *Rimmer* [1968] AC 910, 987, quoted by Lord Edmund-Davies in the *Burmah Oil* case [1980] AC 1090, 1129. Lord Edmund-Davies commented that a judge may well feel that he cannot profitably embark on such a balancing exercise without himself seeing the disputed documents and cited in support of that view the observations of Lord Reid and Lord Upjohn in *Conway* v *Rimmer* [1968] AC 910, 953, 995.'

(O'CONNOR LJ also delivered a judgment dismissing the appeal.)

Appeal dismissed.

Air Canada and Others v Secretary of State for Trade and Another (No. 2) [1983] 2 AC 394

A number of airlines sued the Secretary of State, alleging that he had acted *ultra vires* and unlawfully in directing the British Airports Authority to increase landing charges at Heathrow airport in an allegedly discriminatory manner. The government objected to the requested production of communications between ministers, and memoranda prepared for the use of ministers, which related to the formulation of government policy as to the Authority and the limitation of public sector borrowing. The judge made an order for inspection but stayed the order pending an appeal. The

Court of Appeal allowed an appeal by the Secretary of State. The airlines appealed to the House of Lords.

LORD FRASER OF TULLYBELTON: 'In considering the present law of England on what has come to be called public interest immunity, in relation to the production of documents, it is not necessary to go further back than *Conway* v *Rimmer* [1968] AC 910 where this House decided that a certificate by a minister stating that production of documents of a certain class would be contrary to the public interest, was not conclusive. Lord Reid said, at p. 952:

> I would therefore propose that the House ought now to decide that courts have and are entitled to exercise a power and duty to hold a balance between the public interest, as expressed by a Minister, to withhold certain documents or other evidence, and the public interest in ensuring the proper administration of justice.

A little further on Lord Reid went on to say:

> I do not doubt that there are certain classes of documents which ought not to be disclosed whatever their content may be. Virtually everyone agrees that Cabinet minutes and the like ought not to be disclosed until such time as they are only of historical interest.

The latter observation was strictly speaking *obiter* in *Conway* where the documents in question were reports on a probationer police constable by his superiors.

I do not think that even Cabinet minutes are completely immune from disclosure in a case where, for example, the issue in a litigation involves serious misconduct by a Cabinet Minister. Such cases have occurred in Australia (see *Sankey* v *Whitlam* (1978) 21 ALR 505) and in the United States (see *United States* v *Nixon* (1974) 418 US 683) but fortunately not in the United Kingdom: see also the New Zealand case of *Environmental Defence Society Inc* v *South Pacific Aluminium Ltd (No. 2)* [1981] 1 NZLR 153. But while Cabinet documents do not have complete immunity, they are entitled to a high degree of protection against disclosure. In the present case the documents in category A do not enjoy quite the status of Cabinet minutes, but they approach that level in that they may disclose the reasons for Cabinet decisions and the process by which the decisions were reached. The reasons why such documents should not normally be disclosed until they have become of purely historical interest were considered in *Burmah Oil Co. Ltd* v *Governor and Company of the Bank of England* [1980] AC 1090, where Lord Wilberforce said this, at p. 1112:

> One such ground is the need for candour in communication between those concerned with policy making. It seems now rather fashionable to decry this, but if as a ground it may at one time have been exaggerated, it has now, in my opinion, received an excessive dose of cold water. I am certainly not prepared—against the view of the minister—to discount the need, in the formation of such very controversial policy as that with which we are here involved, for frank and uninhibited advice from the bank to the government, from and between civil servants and between ministers . . . .. Another such ground is to protect from inspection by possible critics the inner working of government while forming important governmental policy.

I do not believe that scepticism has invaded this, or that it is for the courts to assume the role of advocates for open government. If, as I believe, this is a valid ground for protection, it must continue to operate beyond the time span of a particular episode. Concretely, to reveal what advice was *then* sought and given and the mechanism for seeking and considering such advice, might well make the process of government more difficult *now*. On this point too I am certainly not prepared to be wiser than the minister.

Although Lord Wilberforce dissented from the majority as to the result in that case, I do not think that his statement of the reasons for supporting public interest immunity were in any way in conflict with the views of the majority . . ..

A great variety of expressions has been used in the reported cases to explain the considerations that ought to influence judges in deciding whether to order inspection. In *Conway* v *Rimmer* [1968] AC 910, 953, Lord Reid said if the judge "decides that on balance the documents probably ought to be produced, I think that it would generally be best that he should see them before ordering production and if he thinks that the minister's reasons are not clearly expressed he will have to see the documents before ordering production." (The latter point does not arise in this appeal, because the reasons why the documents ought not to be produced are clearly and fully expressed in Sir Kenneth Clucas's certificate.) In the same case Lord Morris of Borth-y-Gest, at p. 964, said that there was no reason why there should not be a private examination of a document by a court "if such an examination becomes really necessary" and later, at p. 971, he said that the power to examine documents privately was one which should be "sparingly exercised." In *Burmah Oil Co. Ltd* v *Governor and Company of the Bank of England* [1980] AC 1090, 1117, Lord Wilberforce said that it was not desirable for the court to assume the task of inspection "except in rare instances where a strong positive case is made out, certainly not upon a bare unsupported assertion by the party seeking production that something to help him may be found, or upon some unsupported—viz., speculative—hunch of its own."

Of all the formulations I have seen, that is, I think, the one least favourable to inspection. Lord Edmund-Davies in the *Burmah Oil* case, at p. 1129, quoted with approval the passage I have just quoted from Lord Reid's speech in *Conway* v *Rimmer* [1968] AC 910, 953. A little lower down p. 1129 Lord Edmund-Davies, as I understand him, expressed the view that a judge should not hesitate to call for production of documents for his private inspection if they are "'likely' to contain material substantially useful to the party seeking discovery". At p. 1135 Lord Keith of Kinkel referred to "situations where grave doubt arises, and the court feels that it cannot properly decide upon which side the balance falls without privately inspecting the documents." And Lord Scarman said, at p. 1145: "Inspection by the court is, I accept, a power to be exercised only if the court is in doubt, after considering the certificate, the issues in the case and the relevance of the documents whose disclosure is sought."

My Lords, I do not think it would be possible to state a test in a form which could be applied in all cases. Circumstances vary greatly. The weight of the public interest against disclosure will vary according to the nature of the particular documents in question; for example, it will in general be stronger where the documents in question; for example, it willin general be stronger where the documents are Cabinet papers than when they are at a lower level. The weight of the public interest in favour of disclosure will vary even more widely, because it depends upon the probable evidential value to the party seeking disclosure of the particular documents, in almost infinitely variable circumstances of individual cases. The most that can usefully be said is that, in order to persuade the court even to inspect documents for which public interest immunity is claimed, the party seeking disclosure ought at least to satisfy the court that the documents are very likely to contain material which would give substantial support to his contention on an issue which arises in the case, and that without them he might be "deprived of the means of . . . proper presentation" of his case: see *Glasgow Corporation* v *Central Land Board*, 1956 SC (HL) 1, 18, *per* Lord Radcliffe. It will be plain that that formulation has been mainly derived from the speech of my noble and learned friend, Lord Edmund-Davies, in the *Burmah Oil* case [1980] AC 1090, 1129, and from the opinion of McNeill J in *Williams* v *Home Office* [1981] 1 All ER 1151, 1154A. It assumes, of course, that the party seeking disclosure has already shown in his pleadings that he has a cause of action, and that he has some material to support it. Otherwise he would merely be "fishing".

The test is intended to be fairly strict. It ought to be so in any case where a valid claim for public interest immunity has been made. Public interest immunity is not a privilege which may be waived by the Crown or by any party. In *R* v *Lewes Justices, ex parte Secretary of State for the Home Department* [1973] AC 388, 400, Lord Reid said: "There is no question of any privilege in the ordinary sense of the word. The real question is whether the public interest requires that the letter shall not be produced and whether that public interest is so strong as to override the ordinary right and interest of a litigant that he shall be able to lay before a court of justice all relevant evidence." When the claim is a "class" claim judges will often not be well qualified to estimate its strength, because they may not be fully aware of the importance of the class of documents to the public administration as a whole. Moreover, whether the claim is a "class" claim or a "contents" claim, the court will have to make its decision on whether to order production, after having inspected the documents privately, without having the assistance of argument from counsel. It should therefore, in my opinion, not be encouraged to "take a peep" just on the off chance of finding something useful. It should inspect documents only where it has definite grounds for expecting to find material of real importance to the party seeking disclosure.'

LORD SCARMAN: 'The appeal illustrates, if illustration be needed, that the House's decision in *Conway* v *Rimmer* [1968] AC 910 was the beginning, but not the end, of a chapter in the law's development in this branch of the law.

The issue is specific and within a small compass. The Crown having made its objection to production in proper form, in what circumstances should the court inspect privately the documents before determining whether they, or any of them, should be produced?

The court, of course, has a discretion: but the discretion must be exercised in accordance with principle. The principle governing the production of disclosed documents is embodied in RSC, Order 24, rule 13. No order for the production of any documents for inspection or to the court shall be made unless the court is of the opinion that the order is necessary either for disposing fairly of the cause or matter or for saving costs: rule 13(1). And the court may inspect the document for the purpose of deciding whether the objection to production is valid: rule 13(2). The rule provides a measure of protection for a party's documents irrespective of their class or contents and independently of any privilege or immunity. While the existence of all documents in a party's possession or control relating to matters in question in the action must be "discovered", that is to say disclosed, to the other party (or parties), he is not obliged to produce them unless the court is of the opinion that production is necessary.

It may well be that, where there is no claim of confidentiality or public interest immunity or any objection on the ground of privilege, the courts follow a relaxed practice, allowing production on the basis of relevance. This is sensible, bearing in mind the extended meaning given to relevance in *Compagnie Financière et Commerciale du Pacifique* v *Peruvian Guano Co.* (1882) 11 QBD 55. But very different considerations arise if a reasoned objection to production is put forward. In *Science Research Council* v *Nassé* [1980] AC 1028 your Lordships' House ruled that, even where there is no question of public interest immunity but the documents are confidential in character, the court should not order production unless it thought it necessary. An objection based on public interest immunity, if properly formulated, must carry at least as much weight as an objection on the ground of confidentiality.

Faced with a properly formulated certificate claiming public interest immunity, the court must first examine the grounds put forward. If it is a "class" objection and the documents (as in *Conway* v *Rimmer* [1968] AC 910) are routine in character, the court may inspect so as to ascertain the strength of the public interest in immunity and the needs of justice before deciding whether to order production. If it is a "contents" claim, e.g., a specific national security matter, the court will ordinarily accept the judgment of the minister. But if it is a class claim in which the objection on the face of the certificate is a strong one—as in this case where the documents are minutes and memoranda passing at a high level between ministers and their advisers and concerned with the formulation of policy—the court will pay great regard to the minister's view (or that of the senior official who has signed the certificate). It will not inspect unless there is a likelihood that the documents will be necessary for disposing fairly of the case or saving costs. Certainly, if, like Bingham J in this case, the court should think that the documents might be "determinative" of the issues in the action to which they relate, the court should inspect: for in such a case there may be grave doubt as to which way the balance of public interest falls: *Burmah Oil Co. Ltd* v *Governor and Company of the Bank of England* [1980] AC 1090, 1134–35, 1145. But, unless the court is satisfied on the material presented to it that the documents are likely to be necessary for fairly disposing of the case, it will not inspect for the simple reason that unless the likelihood exists there is nothing to set against the public interest in immunity from production.

The learned judge, Bingham J, correctly appreciated the principle of the matter. He decided to inspect because he believed that the documents in question were very likely to be "necessary for the just determination of the second and third issues in the plaintiffs' . . . case." Here I consider he fell into error. For the reasons given in the speech of my noble and learned friend, Lord Templeman, I do not think that the appellants have been able to show that the documents whose production they are seeking are likely to be necessary for fairly disposing of the issues in their "constitutional" case. Indeed, my noble and learned friend has demonstrated that they are unnecessary. Accordingly, for this reason, but for no other, I would hold that the judge was wrong to decide to inspect the documents.

On all other questions I find myself in agreement with the judge. In particular, I am persuaded by his reasoning that the public interest in the administration of justice, which the court has to put into the balance against the public interest immunity, is as he put it:

> In my judgment, documents are necessary for fairly disposing of a cause or for the due administration of justice if they give substantial assistance to the court in determining the facts upon which the decision in the cause will depend.

The learned judge rejected, in my view rightly, the view which has commended itself to the Court of Appeal and to some of your Lordships that the criterion for determining whether to inspect or not is whether the party seeking production can establish the likelihood that the documents will assist his case or damage that of his opponent. No doubt that is what he is seeking; no doubt also, it is a very relevant consideration for the court. But it would be dangerous to elevate it into a principle of the law of discovery. Discovery is one of the few exceptions to the adversarial character of our legal process. It assists parties and the court to discover the truth. By so doing, it not only helps towards a just determination: it also saves costs. A party who discovers timeously a document fatal to his case is assisted as effectively, although less to his liking, as one who discovers the winning card; for he can save himself and others the heavy costs of litigation. There is another important aspect of the matter. The Crown, when it puts forward a public interest immunity objection, is not claiming a privilege but discharging a duty. The duty arises whether the document assists or damages the Crown's case or if, as in a case to which the Crown is not a party, it neither helps nor injures the Crown. It is not for the Crown but for the court to determine whether the document should be produced. Usually, but not always, the critical factor will be whether the party seeking production has shown the document will help him. But it may be necessary for a fair determination or for saving costs, even if it does not. Therefore, although it is likely to make little difference in practice, I would think it better in principle to retain the formulation of the interests to be balanced which Lord Reid gave us in *Conway* v *Rimmer* [1968] AC 910, 940:

> It is universally recognised that here there are two kinds of public interest which may clash. There is the public interest that harm shall not be done to the nation or the public service by disclosure of certain documents, and there is the public interest that the administration of justice shall not be frustrated by the withholding of documents which must be produced if justice is to be done.

And I do so for the reasons given by Lord Pearce in the same case. Describing the two conflicting interests, he said of the administration of justice, at p. 987, that the judge "can consider whether the documents in question are of much or little weight in the litigation, whether their absence will result in a complete or partial denial of justice to one or other of the parties or perhaps to both, and what is the importance of the particular litigation to the parties and the public." Basically, the reason for selecting the criterion of justice, irrespective of whether it assists the party seeking production, is that the Crown may not have regard to party advantage in deciding whether or not to object to production on the ground of public interest immunity. It is its duty to bring the objection, if it believes it to be sound, to the attention of the court. It is for the court, not the Crown, to balance the two public interests, that of the functioning and security of the public service, which is the sphere within which the executive has the duty to make an assessment, and that of justice, upon which the executive is not competent to pass judgment.'

(LORD EDMUND-DAVIES agreed with LORD FRASER. LORDS WILBERFORCE and TEMPLEMAN also delivered concurring judgments.)
Appeal dismissed.

- In the light of the modern case law, by what criteria should an assertion by a minister that documents should be withheld on grounds of public policy be judged?
- Should the courts' approach vary as between 'class claims' and 'contents claims'?
- Should the court ever inspect the document privately?
- Is confidentiality by itself ever sufficient to create public interest immunity?
- May public policy immunity ever be waived?

R v Rankine [1986] 2 WLR 1075 (CA)

Two police officers, who were using an image intensifier to watch a shop from a vantage point about 65 yards away, radioed a description of what they saw to another officer. As a result the appellant was arrested and he was charged with unlawfully supplying a controlled drug. The prosecutor's case was that on ten occasions in the course of an hour the appellant had been seen selling the drug outside the shop. In the absence of the jury the prosecution applied for a ruling that the police officers should not be asked to identify the location of the observation post. The judge ruled that he would not compel any questions to be answered to which an officer objected on the ground that it would embarrass his sources of co-operation. The appellant was convicted and appealed.

MANN J, reading the judgment of the court: 'Mr Offenbach for the appellant raises before this court a single ground of appeal. It is that the judge was wrong in law in permitting the prosecution not to disclose the observation point from where the identification was made.

The single ground raises a point of general importance. We were told that surveillance is a vital form of criminal intelligence and that much of it is carried out from static positions in business premises or private houses. Such positions cannot be occupied without the co-operation of members of the public. We can readily understand that members of the public would be unwilling to co-operate if the identity of their premises was disclosable in court.

For many years it has been well recognised that the detection of crime is assisted by the use of information given to the police by members of the public. Those members may be either professional informers, who give information regularly in the expectation of financial or other reward, or public spirited citizens who wish to see the guilty punished for their offending.

It is in the public interest that nothing should be done which is likely to discourage persons of either class from coming forward. One thing which above all others would be likely to prevent them from coming forward with information would be the knowledge that their identity may be disclosed in court. Accordingly for many years it has been the rule that police and other investigating officers cannot be asked to disclose the sources of their information.

In *Attorney-General* v *Briant* (1846) 15 M & W 169, Pollock CB then regarded the rule as having been extant for 50 years. He said, at p. 184:

It has been, however, contended for the defendant, that, admitting that a witness cannot be asked who was the informer, the informer being a third person, yet he may be asked whether he was himself the informer, and gave the information. On the part of the Crown it was replied, that such a question, addressed to each witness in turn, might be the means of discovering the informer; and that, if the principle and object of the rule was to prevent the informer from being discovered, the question cannot any more be put directly to the witness, whether he himself was the informer, than whether a third person was. It was alleged, and, as far as we can learn or have had any experience, it was correctly alleged, that the practice of this court has been in accordance with this rule. There is no direct authority either way; but the rule clearly established and acted on is this, that, in a public prosecution, a witness cannot be asked such questions as will disclose the informer, if he be a third person. This has been a settled rule for fifty years, and although it may seem hard in a particular case, private mischief must give way to public convenience. This is the ground on which the decision took place in *Hardy's*, (1794) 24 St Tr 816 and in *Watson's* case, (1817) 32 St Tr 98 and we think the principle of the rule applies to the case where a witness is asked if he himself is the informer, and therefore that the question could not be asked.

In *Marks* v *Beyfus* (1890) 25 QBD 494, Lord Esher MR said, at p. 498: "What, then, is the rule as to the disclosure of the names of informants, and the information given by them in the case of a public prosecution? In the case of *Attorney-General* v *Briant*, 15 M & W 169, Pollock CB, discussing the case of *R* v *Hardy*, 24 St Tr 199, says that on all hands it was agreed in the case that the informer, in the case of a public prosecution, should not be disclosed; and later on in his judgment, Pollock CB, says: . . ." and Lord Esher MR quoted the passage to which we have referred. The Master of the Rolls continued:

Now, this rule as to public prosecutions was founded on grounds of public policy, and if this prosecution was a public prosecution the rule attaches; I think it was a public prosecution, and that the rule applies. I do not say it is a rule which can never be departed from; if upon the trial of a prisoner the judge should be of opinion that the disclosure of the name of the informant is necessary or right in order to show the prisoner's innocence, then one public policy is in conflict with another public policy, and that which says that an innocent man is not to be condemned when his innocence can be proved is the policy that must prevail. But except in that case, this rule of public policy is not a matter of discretion; it is a rule of law, and as such should be applied by the judge at the trial, who should not treat it as a matter of discretion whether he should tell the witness to answer or not.

Bowen LJ said, at p. 499:

The only question which remains for our decision is, whether the Director of Public Prosecutions was right in objecting to answer the questions put to him, and whether the judge was right in saying that on grounds of public policy he ought not to be asked to disclose the name of his informant. That depends upon whether this was a public prosecution; if so, then neither upon the criminal trial nor upon any subsequent civil proceedings arising out of it, ought the Director of Public Prosecutions, upon grounds of general policy, to be asked to disclose the name of his informant. The only exception to such a rule would be upon a criminal trial, when the judge if he saw that the strict enforcement of the rule would be likely to cause a miscarriage of justice, might relax it in *favorem innocentiae;* if he did not do so, there would be a risk of innocent people being convicted.

The most recent formulation of the rule is in the judgment of Lawton LJ who delivered the judgment of this court in *R v Hennessey (Timothy)* (1979) 68 Cr App R 419. The Lord Justice said, at p. 426:

The courts appreciate the need to protect the identity of informers, not only for their own safety but to ensure that the supply of information about criminal activities does not dry up: see *Marks v Beyfus* (1890) 25 QBD 494. In general this should be the approach of the courts; but cases may occur when for good reason the need to protect the liberty of the subject should prevail over the need to protect informers. It will be for the accused to show that there is good reason.

It is to be observed that the rule is a rule of exclusion subject to a duty to admit in order to avoid a miscarriage of justice. Lord Esher MR emphasised that the rule is a rule of exclusion by an addendum to his judgment in *Marks v Beyfus*, where he said, at p. 500: "I desire to say, so that there shall be no possibility of mistake as to my opinion, that even if the Director of Public Prosecutions had been willing to answer the questions put to him the judge ought not to have allowed him to do so." Thus even if the prosecution do not invoke the rule, the judge is nonetheless obliged to apply it.

The question is whether the rule protects the identity of the person who has allowed his premises to be used for surveillance and the identity of the premises themselves. The only decision upon the question to which our attention has been drawn is the decision of a Divisional Court in *Webb v Catchlove* (1886) 3 TLR 159. That is not a satisfactory case. Denman J said, at p. 160, that in refusing to allow a police officer to be asked from where he had made his observation, "That magistrates had totally misapprehended the law applicable to the case . . ." It does not appear that the court either paused to consider the basis of that conclusion or examined *Attorney-General v Briant*, 15 M & W 169. The court did not have help from the prosecutor, in that he was not represented. We cannot derive assistance from the case.

In our judgment the reasons which give rise to the rule that an informer is not identified apply with equal force to the identification of the owner or occupier of premises used for surveillance and to the identification of the premises themselves. The cases are indistinguishable, and the same rule must apply to each. That being so the only question could be as to whether the judge in the instant case was correct in not exercising the duty exceptionally to admit in order to avoid a miscarriage of justice. Mr Offenbach for the appellant accepted that if the rule in regard to informers applied, the performance of the duty could not be criticised. We agree.'

Appeal dismissed.

B: PRIVILEGE

(Suggested preliminary reading: *A Practical Approach to Evidence*, pp. 317–332).

Blunt v Park Lane Hotel Ltd and Briscoe [1942] 2 KB 253 (CA)

This was an action for slander based on an allegation that the plaintiff had committed adultery. The plaintiff objected to answering interrogatories which the defendants wished to administer in support of their plea of justification. The defendants were given leave to administer the interrogatories. The plaintiff appealed on the ground, *inter alia*, that an affirmative answer to the interrogatories would expose her to the risk of ecclesiastical penalties.

GODDARD LJ: '[T]he rule is that no one is bound to answer any question if the answer thereto would, in the opinion of the judge, have a tendency to expose the deponent to any criminal charge, penalty, or forfeiture which the judge regards as reasonably likely to be preferred or sued for. This rule was laid down by the Queen's Bench in *R v Boyes* 1 B&S 311, and the words in which I have stated it are those of Stephen J in *Lamb v Munster* (1882) 10 QBD 110. A party can also claim privilege against discovery of documents on the like ground: see *Hunnings v Williamson* (1883) 10 QBD 459. Is there, then, except in a case of a clerk in holy orders, any reasonable likelihood that such interrogatories would expose a person to ecclesiastical penalties? It is purely fantastic to suppose anything of the sort. When Lord Hardwicke decided *Finch v Finch* 2 Ves Sen 493 and *Chetwynd v Lindon* 2 Ves Sen 450, there was, no doubt, a real risk of such proceedings. In those days the courts of the Church exercised a very active jurisdiction over the laity in criminal causes. Heresy, simony, defamation, brawling in church or churchyard, and all forms of immorality and not merely adultery were within their cognisance, *pro reformatione morum et pro salute animae* . . . Such jurisdiction has long been obsolete, so far as the laity are concerned, when it has not been expressly taken away by legislation.

. . . One other argument that was adduced was that an admission of adultery might result in the refusal of the sacrament to the offender. There is a complete air of unreality about such an argument in a case of this sort, and I will only say that, assuming that acts of adultery (of which the offender may have repented) as distinct from living in adultery would furnish "lawful cause" within the Statute 1 Edward 6, C 1, for a minister's refusal to administer the sacrament, that is not a penalty within the rule to which I referred at the beginning of this judgment.'

(LORD CLAWSON delivered a judgment to the same effect.)

Appeal dismissed.

Civil Evidence Act 1968

14(1) The right of a person in any legal proceedings other than criminal proceedings to refuse to answer any question or produce any document or thing if to do so would tend to expose that person to proceedings for an offence or for the recover of a penalty—

    (a)   shall apply only as regards criminal offences under the law of any part of the United Kingdom and penalties provided for by such law; and

    (b)   shall include a like right to refuse to answer any question or produce any document or thing if to do so would tend to expose the husband or wife of that person to proceedings for any such criminal offence or for the recovery of any such penalty.

(2) In so far as any existing enactment conferring (in whatever words) powers of inspection or investigation confers on a person (in whatever words) any right otherwise than in criminal proceedings to refuse to answer any question or give any evidence tending to incriminate that person, subsection (1) above shall apply to that right as it applies to the right described in that subsection; and every such existing enactment shall be construed accordingly.

(3) In so far as any existing enactment provides (in whatever words) that in any proceedings other than criminal proceedings a person shall not be excused from answering any question or giving any evidence on the ground that to do so may incriminate that person, that enactment shall be construed as providing also that in such proceedings a person shall not be excused from answering any question or giving any evidence on the ground that to do so may incriminate the husband or wife of that person.

(4) Where any existing enactment (however worded) that—

(a)   confers powers of inspection or investigation; or
(b)   provides as mentioned in subsection (3) above,

further provides (in whatever words) that any answer or evidence given by a person shall not be admissible in evidence against that person in any proceedings or class of proceedings (however described, and whether criminal or not), that enactment shall be construed as providing also that any answer or evidence given by that person shall not be admissible in evidence against the husband or wife of that person in the proceedings or class of proceedings in question.

(5) In this section "existing enactment" means any enactment passed before this Act; and the references to giving evidence are references to giving evidence in any manner, whether by furnishing information, making discovery, producing documents or otherwise.

Minter v Priest [1930] AC 558 (HL)

The respondent refused to act as a solicitor in a transaction relating to land, and was alleged to have defamed the plaintiff in the course of giving his reasons for so refusing. The respondent pleaded that the slander was uttered on a privileged occasion and under such circumstances as to make it a privileged communication. The jury found for the appellant, but the Court of Appeal upheld the claim of privilege and set aside the judgment.

LORD BUCKMASTER: 'I am not prepared to assent to a rigid definition of what must be the subject of discussion between a solicitor and his client in order to secure the protection of professional privilege. That merely to lend money, apart from the existence or contemplation of professional help, is outside the ordinary scope of a solicitor's business is shown by the case of *Hagart and Burn-Murdoch v Inland Revenue Commissioners* [1929] AC 386. But it does not follow that, where a personal loan is asked for, discussions concerning it may not be of a privileged nature. . . .

The relationship of solicitor and client being once established, it is not a necessary conclusion that whatever conversation ensued was protected from disclosure. The conversation to secure this privilege must be such as, within a very wide and generous ambit of interpretation, must be fairly referable to the relationship, but outside that boundary the mere fact that a person speaking is a solicitor, and the person to whom he speaks is his client affords no protection.'

LORD ATKIN: 'It is I think apparent that if the communication passes for the purpose of getting legal advice it must be deemed confidential. The protection of course attaches to the communications made by the solicitor as well as by the client. If therefore the phrase is expanded to professional communications passing for the purpose of getting or giving professional advice, and it is understood that the profession is the legal profession, the nature of the protection is I think correctly defined. One exception to this protection is established. If communications which otherwise would be protected pass for the purpose of enabling either party to commit a crime or a fraud the protection will be withheld. It is further desirable to point out, not by way of exception but as a result of the rule, that communications between solicitor and client which do not pass for the purpose of giving or receiving professional advice are not protected. It follows that client and solicitor may meet for the purpose of legal advice and exchange protected communications, and may yet in the course of the same interview make statements to each other not for the purpose of giving or receiving professional advice but for some other purpose. Such statements are not within the rule: see per Lord Wrenbury in *O'Rourke* v *Darbishire* [1920] AC 581, 629.'

(VISCOUNT DUNEDIN, and LORDS THANKERTON and WARRINGTON of CLIFFE agreed.)

Appeal allowed.

R v *King* [1983] 1 WLR 411 (CA)

The defendant was charged with an offence of conspiracy to defraud. The prosecution had in their possession a number of documents which, at the request of the defendant's solicitors, they sent to a handwriting expert. With a view to eliciting evidence about other documents which had been sent by the defendant's solicitors to the handwriting expert as "control" documents, the prosecution served *subpoenas ad testificandum* and *duces tecum* on the handwriting expert. At the trial the defence objected to the expert being called to produce any documents in his possession emanating from the defence, claiming that such documents constituted a communication for the purpose of the defendant's solicitors to advise or act in the proceedings, and were therefore privileged. The trial judge ruled that the documents were not privileged. The defendant was convicted and appealed.

DUNN LJ, reading the judgment of the court: 'Mr Smith, on behalf of the appellant, submitted in this court that any communication passing between a solicitor and a third party for the purpose of taking advice was privileged. He relied on a passage in *Cross on Evidence*, 5th ed (1979), p. 286: "The rationale of the head of legal professional privilege under consideration was succinctly stated by the Law Reform Committee to be 'to facilitate the obtaining and preparation of evidence by a party to an action in support of his case'. The privilege is essential to the adversary system of procedure which would be unworkable if parties were obliged to disclose communications with prospective witnesses." While accepting that there is no property in a witness, Mr Smith submitted that at common law an expert who has been consulted by solicitors for one party should not be called as a witness by the other party to give evidence as to any communication sent to him by the solicitors. Mr Smith submitted that exhibit 257 formed part of the communication from the appellant's solicitors to the expert.

Alternatively, Mr Smith submitted that if that was not the general rule, there is a difference between civil actions and criminal trials, and that in criminal trials privilege extends not only to communications requesting advice, but also to the article which the client submits as the subject matter upon which the advice is to be given. He relied in support of that proposition on *dicta* of Swanwick J in *Frank Truman Export Ltd* v *Metropolitan Police Commissioner* [1977] QB 952, 961 and 963.

Dealing first with the general position, the rule is that in the case of expert witnesses legal professional privilege attaches to confidential communications between the solicitor and the expert, but it does not attach to the chattels or documents upon which the expert based his opinion, nor to the independent opinion of the expert himself: see *Harmony Shipping Co. SA* v *Saudi Europe Line Ltd* [1979] 1 WLR 1380, 1385, *per* Lord Denning MR. The reasons for that are that there is no property in an expert witness any more than in any other witness and the court is entitled, in order to ascertain the truth, to have the actual facts which the expert has observed adduced before it in considering his opinion.

In general, then, no privilege will attach to exhibit 257. It was one of the documents examined by Mr Radley, upon which he based his opinion, and the court was entitled to have it adduced in evidence. Is there any difference because the document was examined in criminal proceedings rather than in civil proceedings? On principle we can see no reason why that should be so. It would be strange if a forger could hide behind a claim of legal professional privilege by the simple device of sending all the incriminating documents in his possession to his solicitors to be examined by an expert. The only hint of authority to the contrary is the dicta of Swanwick J in *Frank Truman Export Ltd* v *Metropolitan Police Commissioner* [1977] QB 952. That case was cited, though not referred to in the judgments in *R* v *Peterborough Justice, ex parte Hicks* [1977] 1 WLR 1371. In that case a search warrant was ordered under section 16 of the Forgery Act 1913, empowering police officers to search a solicitor's premises and seize a forged document. On an application for *certiorari* to quash the order for the warrant the Divisional Court held that any privilege which the solicitors may have had in respect of the document was the privilege of the client, and since the client had no lawful excuse for possessing the document, the application was dismissed. Eveleigh J said, at p. 1374:

> The claim of privilege, it is true, applies to documents in the hands of solicitors in a great variety of circumstances; but it is the privilege of the client. When one looks at section 16 there is nothing to indicate that an exception shall be made in the case of documents in the hands of solicitors, which could have been done had Parliament so intended. Right in the forefront of one's consideration of this point is that the solicitor holds the document in the right of his client and can assert in respect of its seizure no greater authority than the client himself or herself possesses. The client in this case would have possessed no lawful authority or excuse

that would prevent the document's seizure. In my view the solicitor himself can be in no better position. The solicitor's authority or excuse in a case like this is the authority or excuse of the client.

In this case it is conceded that if exhibit 257 had been in the possession of the appellant, no privilege would have attached, and, accordingly, no greater privilege can attach to the document because it has passed through the hands of his solicitor. The Divisional Court in *R* v *Peterborough Justice, ex parte Hicks* [1977] 1 WLR 1371 did not consider that any special rule applied because the privilege was claimed in criminal proceedings.

We do not regard *Truman's* case as authority for the proposition that any such rule does exist. The observations of Swanwick J to that effect were not necessary for his decision, which related to the validity of searches and seizures under warrant rather than to questions of privilege. We agree with the observations on that case which appear in *Cross on Evidence* at p. 287:

> In civil cases documents which have come into existence before advice was sought or litigation contemplated have to be disclosed on discovery, but the judgment of Swanwick J in *Frank Truman (Export) Ltd* v *Metropolitan Police Commissioner* [1977] QB 952 suggest that documents and other property left by a client with his solicitor in good faith in order that he may be advised thereon are privileged in criminal proceedings. The fact that there is no pre-trial discovery in a criminal case and the prosecution's inability to oblige the accused to produce documents at the trial render the conception of legal professional privilege somewhat out of place in this context. In the *Truman* case documents were taken from the office of the accused's solicitor by the police pursuant to a search warrant. It was held that the police were entitled to retain a number of them because, although they were privileged, some were covered by the terms of the warrant and others were relevant to a charge of conspiracy pending against the accused. The same result might have been reached on the basis that the documents could, in the circumstances, have been retained if they had been procured by a search of the accused's premises. The problem before the court related to the validity of searches and seizures rather than privilege.

For those reasons the judge was right to allow Mr Radley to be called and to produce exhibit 257.'

Appeal dismissed.

Wheeler v **Le Marchant** (1881) 17 Ch D 675 (CA)

In an action for specific performance of a building contract to take on lease building land from the defendants, the defendants sought to protect from production letters which had passed between their solicitors and their surveyors. The judge held that the letters were privileged. The plaintiff appealed.

JESSEL MR: 'What they contended for was that documents communicated to the solicitors of the defendants by third parties, though not communicated by such third parties as agents of the clients seeking advice, should be protected, because those documents contained information required or asked for by the solicitors, for the purpose of enabling them the better to advise the clients. The cases, no doubt, establish that such documents are protected where they have come into existence after litigation commenced or in contemplation, and when they have been made with a view to such litigation, either for the purpose of obtaining advice as to such litigation, or of obtaining evidence to be used in such litigation, or of obtaining information which might lead to the obtaining of such evidence, but it has never hitherto been decided that documents are protected merely because they are produced by a third person in answer to an inquiry made by the solicitor. It does not appear to me to be necessary, either as a result of the principle which regulates this privilege or for the convenience of mankind, so to extend the rule. In the first place, the principle protecting confidential communications is of a very limited character. It does not protect all confidential communications which a man must necessarily make in order to obtain advice, even when needed for the protection of his life, or of his honour, or of his fortune. There are many communications which, though absolutely necessary because without them the ordinary business of life cannot be carried on, still are not privileged. The communications made to a medical man whose advice is sought by a patient with respect to the probable origin of the disease as to which he is consulted, and which must necessarily be made in order to enable the medical man to advise or to prescribe for the patient, are not protected. Communications made to a priest in the confessional on matters perhaps considered by the penitent to be more important even than his life or his fortune, are not protected. Communications made to a friend with respect to matters of the most delicate nature, on which advice is sought with respect to a man's honour or reputation, are not protected. Therefore it must not be supposed that there is any principle which says that every confidential communication which it is necessary to make in order to carry on the ordinary business of life is protected. The protection is of a very limited character, and in this country is restricted to the obtaining the assistance of lawyers, as regards the conduct of litigation or the rights to property. It has never gone beyond the obtaining legal advice and assistance, and all things reasonably necessary in the shape of communication to the legal advisers are protected from production or discovery in order that that legal advice may be obtained safely and sufficiently.

Now, keeping that in view, what has been done is this: The actual communication to the solicitor by the client is of course protected, and it is equally protected whether it is made by the client in person or is made by an agent on behalf of the client, and whether it is made to the solicitor in person or to a clerk or subordinate of the solicitor who acts in his place and under his direction. Again, the evidence obtained by the solicitor, or by his direction, or at his instance, even if obtained by the client, is protected if obtained after litigation has been commenced or threatened, or with a view to the defence or prosecution of such litigation. So, again, a communication with a solicitor for the purpose of obtaining legal advice is protected though it relates to a dealing which is not the subject of litigation, provided it be a communication made to the solicitor in that character and for that purpose. But what we are asked to protect here is this. The solicitor, being consulted in a matter as to which no dispute has arisen, thinks he would like to know some further facts before giving his advice, and applies to a surveyor to tell him what the state of a given property is, and it is said that the information given ought to be protected because it is desired or required by the solicitor in order to enable him the better to give legal advice. It appears to me that to give such protection would not only extend the rule beyond what has been previously laid down, but beyond what necessity warrants . . .. It is a rule established and maintained solely for the purpose of enabling a man to obtain legal advice with safety.'

(BRETT and COTTON LJJ delivered concurring judgments.)

Appeal allowed.

Waugh v *British Railways Board* [1980] AC 521 (HL)

The plaintiff's husband, an employee of the British Railways Board, was killed in an accident while working on the railways. In accordance with the board's usual practice a report on the accident, called an internal enquiry report, was prepared by two of the board's officers two days after the accident. The report was headed "For the information of the Board's solicitor". However, it appeared from an affidavit produced on behalf of the board that the report was prepared for two purposes: to establish the cause of the accident so that appropriate safety measures could be taken and to enable the board's solicitor to advise in the litigation that was almost certain to ensue. Although the first purpose was more immediate than the second, they were described in the affidavit as being of equal importance. The report contained statements by witnesses and was probably the best evidence available as to the cause of the accident. The plaintiff commenced an action against the board under the Fatal Accidents Act 1846 to 1959 and applied for discovery of the report to assist in preparing and conducting her case. The board resisted discovery on the ground that the report was protected by legal professional privilege. The master ordered disclosure but on appeal the judge reversed the order. The plaintiff appealed to the Court of Appeal which held that a report which came into existence or was obtained for the purpose of anticipated litigation was privileged from production even though it might serve some other even more important purpose, and dismissed her appeal. The plaintiff appealed to the House of Lords.

LORD WILBERFORCE: 'My Lords, before I consider the authorities, I think it desirable to attempt to discern the reason why what is (inaccurately) called legal professional privilege exists. It is sometimes ascribed to the exigencies of the adversary system of litigation under which a litigant is entitled within limits to refuse to disclose the nature of his case until the trial. Thus one side may not ask to see the proofs of the other side's witnesses or the opponent's brief or even know what witnesses will be called: he must wait until the card is played and cannot try to see it in the hand. This argument cannot be denied some validity even where the defendant is a public corporation whose duty it is, so it might be thought, while taking all proper steps to protect its revenues, to place all the facts before the public and to pay proper compensation to those it has injured. A more powerful argument to my mind is that everything should be done in order to encourage anyone who knows the facts to state them fully and candidly—as Sir George Jessel MR said, to bare his breast to his lawyer: *Anderson* v *Bank of British Columbia* (1876) 2 ChD 644, 699. This he may not do unless he knows that his communication is privileged.

But the preparation of a case for litigation is not the only interest which calls for candour. In accident cases " . . . the safety of the public may well depend on the candour and completeness of reports made by subordinates whose duty it is to draw attention to defects": *Conway* v *Rimmer* [1968] AC 910, *per* Lord Reid, at p. 941. This however does not by itself justify a claim to privilege since, as Lord Reid continues: " . . . no one has ever suggested that public safety has been endangered by the candour or completeness of such reports having been inhibited by the fact that they may have to be produced if the interests of the due administration of justice should ever require production at any time."

So one may deduce from this the principle that while privilege may be required in order to induce candour in statements made for the purposes of litigation it is not required in relation to statements whose purpose is different—for example to enable a railway to operate safely.

It is clear that the due administration of justice strongly requires disclosure and production of this report: it was contemporary; it contained statements by witnesses on the spot; it would be not merely relevant evidence, but almost certainly the best evidence as to the cause of the accident. If one accepts that this important public interest can be over-ridden in order that the defendant may properly prepare his case, how close must the connection be between the preparation of the document and the anticipation of litigation? On principle I would think that the purpose of preparing for litigation ought to be either the sole purpose or at least the dominant purpose of it: to carry the protection further into cases where that purpose was secondary or equal with another purpose would seem to be excessive, and unnecessary in the interest of encouraging truthful revelation. At the lowest such desirability of protection as might exist in such cases is not strong enough to outweigh the need for all relevant documents to be made available.

There are numerous cases in which this kind of privilege has been considered. A very useful review of them is to be found in the judgment of Havers J in *Seabrook* v *British Transport Commission* [1959] 1 WLR 509 which I shall not repeat. It is not easy to extract a coherent principle from them. The two dominant authorities at the present time are *Birmingham and Midland Motor Omnibus Co. Ltd* v *London and North Western Railway Co.* [1913] 3 KB 850 and *Ogden* v *London Electric Railway Co.* (1933) 49 TLR 542, both decisions of the Court of Appeal. These cases were taken by the majority of the Court of Appeal in the present case to require the granting of privilege in cases where one purpose of preparing the document(s) in question was to enable the defendants' case to be prepared whether or not they were to be used for another substantial purpose. Whether in fact they compel such a conclusion may be doubtful— in particular I do not understand the *Birmingham* case to be one of dual purposes at all: but it is enough that they have been taken so to require. What is clear is that, though loyally followed, they do not now enjoy rational acceptance: in *Longthorn* v *British Transport Commission* [1959] 1 WLR 530 the manner in which Diplock J managed to escape from them, and the tenor of his judgment, shows him to have been unenthusiastic as to their merits. And in *Alfred Crompton Amusement Machines Ltd* v *Customs and Excise Commissioners (No. 2)* [1974] AC 405 Lord Cross of Chelsea, at p. 432, pointedly left their correctness open, while Lord Kilbrandon stated, at p. 435, that he found the judgment of Scrutton LJ in *Ogden* v *London Electric Railway Co.,* 49 TLR 542, 543–544, "hard to accept". Only Viscount Dilhorne (dissenting) felt able to follow them in holding it to be enough if one purpose was the use by solicitors when litigation was anticipated.

The whole question came to be considered by the High Court of Australia in 1976: *Grant* v *Downs*, 135 CLR 674. This case involved reports which had "as one of the material purposes for their preparation" submission to legal advisers in the event of litigation. It was held that privilege could not be claimed. In the joint judgment of Stephen, Mason and Murphy JJ, in which the English cases I have mentioned were discussed and analysed, it was held that "legal professional privilege" must be confined to documents brought into existence for the sole purpose of submission to legal advisers for advice or use in legal proceedings. Jacobs J put the test in the form of a question, at p. 692: " . . . does the purpose"—in the sense of intention, the intended use—"of supplying the material to the legal adviser account for the existence of the material?" Barwick CJ stated it in terms of "dominant" purpose. This is closely in line with the opinion of Lord Denning MR in the present case that the privilege extends only to material prepared "wholly or mainly for the purpose of preparing [the defendant's] case". The High Court of Australia and Lord Denning MR agree in refusing to follow *Birmingham and Midland Motor Omnibus Co. Ltd* v *London and North Western Railway Co.* [1913] 3 KB 850 and *Ogden* v *London Electric Railway Co.*, 49 TLR 542, as generally understood.

My Lords, for the reasons I have given, when discussing the case in principle, I too would refuse to follow those cases. It appears to me that unless the purpose of submission to the legal adviser in view of litigation is at least the dominant purpose for which the relevant document was prepared, the reasons which require privilege to be extended to it cannot apply. On the other hand to hold that the purpose, as above, must be the sole purpose would, apart from difficulties of proof, in my opinion, be too strict a requirement, and would confine the privilege too narrowly: as to this I agree with Barwick CJ in *Grant* v *Downs*, 135 CLR 674, and in substance with Lord Denning MR.'

LORD EDMUND-DAVIES: 'It is for the party refusing disclosure to establish his right to refuse. It may well be that in some cases where that right has in the past been upheld the courts have failed to keep clear the distinction between (a) communications between client and legal adviser, and (b) communications between the client and third parties, made (as the Law Reform Committee put it) ". . . for the purpose of obtaining information to be submitted to the client's professional legal advisers for the purpose of obtaining advice upon pending or contemplated litigation." (Sixteenth Report, para. 17(c).) In cases falling within (a), privilege from disclosure attaches to communications for the purpose of obtaining legal advice and it is immaterial whether or not the possibility of litigation were even contemplated, Kindersley V-C saying in *Lawrence* v *Campbell* (1859) 4 Drew 485, 490: ". . . it is not now necessary as it formerly was for the purpose of obtaining production that the communications should be made either during or relating to an actual or even to an expected litigation. It is sufficient if they pass as professional communications in a professional capacity." But in cases falling within (b) the position is quite otherwise. Litigation, apprehended or actual, is its hallmark. Referring to "the rule which protects confidential communications from discovery as regards the other side," Sir George Jessel MR said in *Anderson* v *Bank of British Columbia*, 2 Ch D 644, 649:

> The object and meaning of the rule is this: that as, by reason of the complexity and difficulty of our law, litigation can only be properly conducted by professional men, it is absolutely necessary that a man, in order to prosecute his rights or to defend himself from an improper claim, should have recourse to the assistance

of professional lawyers, and it being so absolutely necessary, it is equally necessary, to use a vulgar phrase, that he should be able to make a clean breast of it to the gentleman whom he consults with a view to the prosecution of his claim, or the substantiating his defence against the claim of others; that he should be able to place unrestricted and unbounded confidence in the professional agent, and that the communications he so makes to him should be kept secret, unless with his consent (for it is his privilege, and not the privilege of the confidential agent) that he should be enabled properly to conduct his litigation. This is the meaning of the rule.

And in the Court of Appeal James LJ summed up the position at p. 656, by speaking succinctly of ". . . an intelligible principle, that as you have no right to see your adversary's brief, you have no right to see that which comes into existence merely as the materials for the brief."

Preparation with a view to litigation—pending or anticipated—being thus the essential purpose which protects a communication from disclosure in such cases as the present, what in the last resort is the touchstone of the privilege? Is it sufficient that the prospect of litigation be merely one of the several purposes leading to the communication coming into being? And is that sufficient (as Eveleigh LJ in the present case held) despite the fact that there is also "another . . . and even more important purpose"? Is it enough that the prospect of litigation is a *substantial* purpose, though there may be others equally substantial? Is an *appreciable* purpose sufficient? Or does it have to be *the main* purpose? Or *one* of its *main* purposes (as in *Ogden* v *London Electric Railway Co.*, 49 TLR 542)? Ought your Lordships to declare that privilege attaches only to material which (in the words of Lord Denning MR) "comes within the words, 'wholly or mainly' for the purpose of litigation"? Or should this House adopt the majority decision of the High Court of Australia in *Grant* v *Downs*, 135 CLR 674, that legal professional privilege must be confined to documents brought into existence for the *sole* purpose of submission to legal advisers for advice or for use in legal proceedings?

An affirmative answer to each of the foregoing questions can be supported by one or more of the many reported decisions. And so can a negative answer. But no decision is binding upon this House, and your Lordships are accordingly in the fortunate position of being free to choose and declare what is the proper test. And in my judgment we should start from the basis that the public interest is, on balance, best served by rigidly confining within narrow limits the cases where material relevant to litigation may be lawfully withheld. Justice is better served by candour than by suppression. For, as it was put in the *Grant* v *Downs* majority judgment, at p. 686: ". . . the privilege . . . detracts from the fairness of the trial by denying a party access to relevant documents or at least subjecting him to surprise."

Adopting that approach, I would certainly deny a claim to privilege when litigation was merely one of several purposes of equal or similar importance intended to be served by the material sought to be withheld from disclosure, and *a fortiori* where it was merely a minor purpose. On the other hand, I consider that it would be going too far to adopt the "*sole* purpose" test applied by the majority in *Grant* v *Downs*, which has been adopted in no United Kingdom decision nor, as far as we are aware, elsewhere in the Commonwealth. Its adoption would deny privilege even to material whose outstanding purpose is to serve litigation, simply because another and very minor purpose was also being served. But, inasmuch as the *only* basis of the claim to privilege in such cases as the present one is that the material in question was brought into existence for use in legal proceedings, it is surely right to insist that, before the claim is conceded or upheld, such a purpose must be shown to have played a paramount part. Which phrase or epithet should be selected to designate this is a matter of individual judgment. Lord Denning MR, as we have seen, favoured adoption of the phrase employed in the Law Reform Committee's Sixteenth Report, viz., "material which came into existence . . . *wholly or mainly*" for the purpose of litigation (para. 17). "Wholly" I personally would reject for the same reason as I dislike "solely," but "mainly" is nearer what I regard as the preferable test. Even so, it lacks the element of clear paramountcy which should, as I think, be the touchstone. After considerable deliberation, I have finally come down in favour of the test propounded by Barwick CJ in *Grant* v *Downs*, 135 CLR 674, in the following words, at p. 677:

> Having considered the decisions, the writings and the various aspects of the public interest which claim attention, I have come to the conclusion that the court should state the relevant principle as follows: a document which was produced or brought into existence either with the *dominant* purpose of its author, or of the person or authority under whose direction, whether particular or general, it was produced or brought into existence, of using it or its contents in order to obtain legal advice or to conduct or aid in the conduct of litigation, at the time of its production in reasonable prospect, should be privileged and excluded from inspection." (Italics added.)

Dominant purpose, then, in my judgment, should now be declared by this House to be the touchstone. It is less stringent a test than "sole" purpose, for, as Barwick CJ added, 135 CLR 674, 677: ". . . the fact that the person . . . had in mind other uses of the document will not preclude that document being accorded privilege, if it were produced with the requisite dominant purpose".

Applying such test to the facts of the present case, we have already seen that privilege was claimed in Mr Hasting's affidavit on several grounds. Thus, the report of 6 May 1976, was produced in accordance with the long-standing practice of the board regarding "accidents occurring on or about any railway . . . in order to assist in establishing the causes of such accidents", and this whether or not (so your Lordships were informed) any personal injuries were sustained and even where there was no prospect of litigation ensuing. This particular report was called for in accordance with such practice and:

> *One of the principal purposes* for so doing was so that they could be passed to the board's chief solicitor to enable him to advise the board on its legal liability and if necessary conduct its defence to these proceedings. (Italics added.)

Were the "sole purpose" test adopted and applied, on the board's own showing their claim to privilege must fail. Then what of the "dominant purpose" test which I favour? Dominance again is not claimed by the board, but merely that use in litigation was "one of the principal purposes." Such moderation is only to be expected in the face of a claim arising out of a fatal accident. Indeed, the claims of humanity must surely make the dominant purpose of any report upon an accident (particularly where personal injuries have been sustained) that of discovering what happened and why it happened, so that measures to prevent its recurrence could be discussed and, if possible, devised.

And, although Barwick CJ in *Grant* v *Downs*, 135 CLR 674, observed, at p. 677, that ". . .the circumstance that the document is a 'routine document' will not be definitive. The dominant purpose of its production may none the less qualify it for professional privilege." the test of dominance will, as I think be difficult to satisfy when inquiries are instituted and reports produced automatically whenever any mishap occurs, whatever its nature, its gravity, or even its triviality.

My Lords, if, as I hold, "*dominant* purpose" be the right test of privilege from disclosure, it follows that the board's claim to privilege must be disallowed, and the same applies if the "*sole* purpose" test be applied.

(LORDS SIMON OF GLAISDALE, RUSSELL OF KILLOWEN and KEITH OF KINKEL delivered concurring judgments.)

Appeal allowed.

R v Cox and Railton (1884) 14 QBD 153 (CCR)

The defendants were convicted of a conspiracy to defraud. At the trial a solicitor was called by the prosecution to prove that the defendants had consulted him with reference to drawing up a bill of sale that was alleged to be fraudulent. The reception of this evidence was objected to on the ground that it was privileged.

STEPHEN J, delivering the judgment of the court: 'The question, therefore is, whether, if a client applies to a legal adviser for advice intended to facilitate or to guide the client in the commission of a crime or fraud, the legal adviser being ignorant of the purpose for which his advice is wanted, the communication between the two is privileged? We expressed our opinion at the end of the argument that no such privilege existed. If it did, the result would be that a man intending to commit treason or murder might safely take legal advice for the purpose of enabling himself to do so with impunity, and that the solicitor to whom the application was made would not be at liberty to give information against his client for the purpose of frustrating his criminal purpose. Consequences so monstrous reduce to an absurdity any principle or rule in which they are involved. Upon the fullest examination of the authorities we believe that they are not warranted by any principle or rule of the law of England, but it must be admitted that the law upon the subject has never been so distinctly and fully stated as to shew clearly that these consequences do not follow from principles which do form part of the law, and which it is of the highest importance to maintain in their integrity . . . The case which has always been regarded as the great leading authority on the question of the privilege of legal advisers is *Greenough* v *Gaskell* 1 My & K 98 decided by Lord Brougham in 1833 . . .. In this case the rule as to professional communications was laid down in the following words:— "If, touching matters that come within the ordinary scope of professional employment, they" (legal advisers) "receive a communication in their professional capacity, either from a client or on his account, and for his benefit in the transaction of his business, or, which amounts to the same thing, if they commit to paper in the course of their employment on his behalf, matters which they know only through their professional relation to the client, they are not only justified in withholding such matters, but bound to withhold them, and will not be compelled to disclose the information or produce the papers in any court of law or equity, either as party or as witness."

. . . This rule has been accepted and acted upon ever since, and we fully recognise its authority, but we think that the present case does not fall either under the reason on which it rests, or within the terms in which it is expressed. The reason on which the rule is said to rest cannot include the case of communications, criminal in themselves, or intended to further any criminal purpose, for the protection of such communications cannot possibly be otherwise than injurious to the interests of justice, and to those of the administration of justice. Nor do such communications fall within the terms of the rule. A communication in furtherance of a criminal purpose does not "come into the ordinary scope of professional employment". A single illustration will make this plain. It is part of the business of a solicitor to draw wills. Suppose a person, personating someone else, instructs a solicitor to draw a will in the name of the supposed testator, executes it in the name of the supposed testator, gives the solicitor his fee, and takes away the will. It would be monstrous to say that the solicitor was employed in the "ordinary scope of professional employment". He in such case is made an unconscious instrument in the commission of a crime.'

Conviction affirmed.

R v *Barton* [1973] 1 WLR 115 (Lincoln Crown Court)

The defendant was charged with fraudulent conversion, theft and falsification of accounts alleged to have been committed in the course of his employment as a legal executive with a firm of solicitors. The defence served on a solicitor, a partner in the firm, a subpoena to give evidence at the trial and produce certain documents which had come into existence while the solicitor was acting as the solicitor to the executors or administrators of the estates of deceased persons. The solicitor took the point that the documents were protected by legal professional privilege.

CAULFIELD J: 'I think the correct principle is this, and I think that it must be restricted to these particular facts in a criminal trial, and the principle I am going to enunciate is not supported by any authority that has been cited to me, and I am just working on what I conceive to be the rules of natural justice. If there are documents in the possession or control of a solicitor which, on production, help to further the defence of an accused man, then in my judgment no privilege attaches. I cannot conceive that our law would permit a solicitor or other person to screen from a jury information which, if disclosed to the jury, would perhaps enable a man either to establish his innocence or to resist an allegation made by the Crown. I think that is the principle that should be followed.'

Ruling accordingly.

Goddard v *Nationwide Building Society* [1986] 3 WLR 734 (CA)

The plaintiffs purchased a house with the aid of a mortgage from the defendant. The solicitor acting for the plaintiffs in connection with the purchase of the house was simultaneously acting for the defendant in respect of the grant of the mortgage. The plaintiffs, claiming that a defect in the house, of which they had known before they had purchased it, was more serious than they had been led to believe, brought an action for damages for negligence against the defendant. Having been informed of the proceedings, the solicitor sent the defendant a copy of an attendance note in which were recorded, *inter alia*, conversations which the solicitor had had with the first plaintiff, and the defendant thereupon pleaded the substance of the contents of the note in its defence. The plaintiffs applied to have struck out the passages in the defence which were based on the contents of the note, on the basis that they were confidential and privileged and that the pleading would embarrass the plaintiffs in the fair trial of the action and was an abuse of the process of the court, and sought an injunction restraining the defendant from using or relying on the copy note and requiring it to deliver up the document and any further copies which it might have made of it. The judge held that once the copy of the note had come into the defendant's possession it was entitled to use it in any way it wished, regardless of any legal professional privilege to which the plaintiffs might have been entitled, and dismissed the plaintiffs' applications. The plaintiffs appealed.

MAY LJ: 'In essence the opposing arguments in this case deployed both before the judge and before us were these. For the plaintiffs it was argued that the content of any communication, with immaterial exceptions, between a solicitor and his client is confidential and only the client can waive that confidentiality; at least where it is the solicitor who breaches his fiduciary duty to his client in respect of such a communication, any person who comes into possession of that communication, or a document or a copy of a document setting it out, can be restrained from making any use of the communication or the original or copy documents and can be ordered to return them to the client: see *Lord Ashburton* v *Pape* [1913] 2 Ch 469.

For the defendant it was contended that even though communications between solicitor and client are confidential, nevertheless if a document, original or copy containing or evidencing them, comes into the hands of a third party, even by dishonesty—which of course is not alleged in the instant case—then that third party is entitled to use that original or copy document as evidence in litigation between himself and the erstwhile client: see *Calcraft* v *Guest* [1898] 1 QB 759.

In *Lord Ashburton* v *Pape* [1913] 2 Ch 469 the latter was a bankrupt, whose discharge was opposed by, amongst others, the plaintiff. One Nocton had been Lord Ashburton's solicitor and he employed a clerk by the name of Brooks. By a trick Pape got possession from Brooks of a number of letters which Lord Ashburton had written to Nocton at a time when the relationship of client and solicitor had subsisted between them. Pape's solicitors took copies of these letters and then handed the originals back to Pape. Lord Ashburton then brought an action against Pape, Nocton and others for an injunction restraining them from disclosing or parting with any letters or other documents received by or communicated to Nocton as his solicitor, or the effect of, or copies of, or extracts from, them.

On a motion by Lord Ashburton in the action Neville J made orders that Pape should hand over to Nocton all the original letters which he had in his possession or control and restraining Pape, amongst others, until judgment or further order, from publishing or making any use of the copies of the letters or any information contained in them "except for the purpose of pending proceedings in the defendant . . . Pape's bankruptcy and subject to the direction of the Bankruptcy Court". Lord Ashburton appealed asking that the order of Neville J might be varied by striking out this exception. The Court of Appeal allowed his appeal.

There has been a considerable amount of discussion about the decision in *Lord Ashburton* v *Pape* since it was decided and it is unfortunate that in one important sentence the other reports of the case differ from that in the Law Reports (cf. [1913] 2 Ch 469, 473, with 109 LT 381, 382 and 82 LJ Ch 527, 529, and see C Tapper, "Privilege and Confidence" (1972) 35 MLR 83, 85–86 and J D Heydon, "Legal Professional Privilege and Third Parties" (1974) 37 MLR 601, 604.) However, for my part I think that the ratio of the decision in *Lord Ashburton* v *Pape* was founded upon the confidential nature of the content of the letters written by Lord Ashburton to Nocton. The Court of Appeal was concerned to protect that confidence, in the same way, for instance, as the courts protect the trade secrets of an employer against the unauthorised use of them by an employee, both while he remains such as well as after he has left the employment.

In his judgment Cozens-Hardy MR [1913] 2 Ch 469, 472 quoted with approval the following passage from the judgment of Kay LJ in *Lamb* v *Evans* [1893] 1 Ch 218, 235, 236, which itself referred to an earlier judgment in *Morison* v *Moat* (1851) 9 Hare 241:

> Then the judgment goes on to give several instances, and many of them are of cases where a man, being in the employment of another, has discovered the secrets of the manufacture of that other person, or has surreptitiously copied something which came under his hands while he was in the possession of that trust and confidence, and he has been restrained from communicating that secret to anybody else, and anybody who has obtained that secret from him has also been restrained from using it.

The Master of the Rolls then applied that principle to the case then before him in saying [1913] 2 Ch 469, 472–473: "Apart, therefore, from these pending or threatened proceedings in bankruptcy, it seems to me to be perfectly clear that the plaintiff can obtain the unqualified injunction which he asks for." He then went on to deal with *Calcraft* v *Guest* [1898] 1 QB 759 in a way to which I shall refer shortly.

On the first point Kennedy LJ agreed with Cozens-Hardy MR [1913] 2 Ch 469, 473–474: "The principle which has been stated by the Master of the Rolls upon which a person would be restrained from dealing with documents or using information in documents which he has obtained wrongly . . . is clear."

In his turn Swinfen Eady LJ stated the underlying principle in this way, at p. 475:

> The principle upon which the Court of Chancery has acted for many years has been to restrain the publication of confidential information improperly or surreptitiously obtained or of information imparted in confidence which ought not to be divulged. Injunctions have been granted to give effectual relief, that is not only to restrain the disclosure of confidential information, but to prevent copies being made of any record of that information, and, if copies have already been made . . . to restrain persons into whose possession that confidential information has come from themselves in turn divulging or propagating it.

However, in *Lord Ashburton* v *Pape* the defendant relied on *Calcraft* v *Guest* [1898] 1 QB 759 to support the exception in Neville J's order. Before referring to the way in which the Court of Appeal distinguished the latter it is convenient if I first deal directly with *Calcraft* v *Guest*. The facts of that case were that in 1787 certain documents came into existence in respect of which the owner of a fishery on the River Frome

in Dorset was entitled to legal professional privilege. In 1898 the successor in title
to that fishery, Calcraft, brought an action for trespass to it, the substantial question
being as to the upper boundary of the fishery. He succeeded at first instance. One
of the defendants appealed. Between trial at first instance and the hearing of the appeal
the relevant documents came to light. They had been stored in the coach house of
the grandson of the solicitor who had acted for the 1787 owner of the fishery in
the 1787 litigation. That solicitor had been succeeded by his son and when he died
his business was wound up and his nephew, the owner of the coach house, acted
for his executors. Soon after these documents came to light the solicitors for the appellant
inspected and took copies of them, but thereafter they were handed over to the plaintiff
in the 1898 litigation. Upon the appeal, however, the appellant defendant sought to
put in the copies and in the result two questions arose. First, were the original documents
privileged from production; second, even if they were could the appellant give secondary
evidence of them?

In so far as the first question was concerned, the Court of Appeal, following the
earlier decision in *Minet* v *Morgan* (1873) LR 8 Ch App 361, held in effect that once
privileged, always privileged and that the then owner of the fishery was entitled to
refuse to produce the originals. On the second question, however, the court held that
secondary evidence of the documents was admissible. In his judgment with which
the other members of the court agreed, Lindley MR [1898] 1 QB 759, 764 approved
this dictum of Parke B in *Lloyd* v *Mostyn* (1842) 10 M & W 478, 481–482:

> Where an attorney entrusted confidentially with a document communicates the
> contents of it, or suffers another to take a copy, surely the secondary evidence
> so obtained may be produced. Suppose the instrument were even stolen, and a
> correct copy taken, would it not be reasonable to admit it?

Lindley MR then continued [1898] 1 QB 759, 764:

> The matter dropped there; but the other members of the court . . . all concurred
> in that, which I take it is a distinct authority that secondary evidence in a case
> of this kind may be received.

Subject to the distinction that may be drawn between letters written to a solicitor
for the purpose of obtaining legal advice on the one hand, and a deed entrusted to
one's solicitor to hold in confidence on the other, the decision in *Calcraft* v *Guest*
[1898] 1 QB 759 might have been thought to have been good authority for the admission
in Pape's bankruptcy proceedings of secondary evidence of Lord Ashburton's letters
to Nocton, his solicitor. However, the court distinguished the earlier authority on
the basis that whereas in it the question of the admission of secondary evidence arose
incidentally, in *Lord Ashburton* v *Pape* [1913] 2 Ch 469 this issue of admissibility was
the principal, indeed the sole, issue in the case. In his judgment Cozens-Hardy MR
said, at p. 473.

> The rule of evidence as explained in *Calcraft* v *Guest* merely amounts to this, that
> if a litigant wants to prove a particular document which by reason of privilege
> or some circumstance he cannot furnish by the production of the original, he may
> produce a copy as secondary evidence although that copy has been obtained by

improper means, and even, it may be, by criminal means. The court in such an action is not really trying the circumstances under which the document was produced. That is not an issue in the case and the court simply says "Here is a copy of a document which cannot be produced; it may have been stolen, it may have been picked up in the street, it may have improperly got into the possession of the person who proposes to produce it, but that is not a matter which the court in the trial of the action can go into." But that does not seem to me to have any bearing upon a case where the whole subject-matter of the action is the right to retain the originals or copies of certain documents which are privileged.

In my opinion Kennedy LJ followed the same path when he said, at p. 474:

> I agree that the better view seems to me to be that although it is true that the principle which is laid down in *Calcraft* v *Guest* must be followed, yet, at the same time, if, before the occasion of the trial when a copy may be used, although a copy improperly obtained, the owner of the original can successfully promote proceedings against the person who has improperly obtained the copy to stop his using it, the owner is none the less entitled to protection, because, if the question had arisen in the course of a trial before such proceedings, the holder of the copy would not have been prevented from using it on account of the illegitimacy of its origin. If that is so, it decides this case.

Swinfen Eady LJ put the matter even more clearly in this passage from his judgment, at pp. 476–477:

> There are many similar cases to the like effect, where the use of information improperly obtained has been restrained and the parties into whose possession it has come have been restrained from using or divulging it. Down to that point there can be no dispute as to the law. Then objection was raised in the present case by reason of the fact that it is said that Pape, who now has copies of the letters, might wish to give them in evidence in certain bankruptcy proceedings, and although the original letters are privileged from production he has possession of the copies and could give them as secondary evidence of the contents of the letters, and, therefore, ought not to be ordered either to give them up or to be restrained from divulging their contents. There is here a confusion between the right to restrain a person from divulging confidential information and the right to give secondary evidence of documents where the originals are privileged from production, if the party has such secondary evidence in his possession. The cases are entirely separate and distinct. If a person were to steal a deed, nevertheless in any dispute to which it was relevant the original deed might be given in evidence by him at the trial. It would be no objection to the admissibility of the deed in evidence to say you ought not to have possession of it. His unlawful possession would not affect the admissibility of the deed in evidence if otherwise admissible. So again with regard to any copy he had. If he was unable to obtain or compel production of the original because it was privileged, if he had a copy in his possession it would be admissible as secondary evidence. The fact, however, that a document, whether original or copy, is admissible in evidence is no answer to the demand of the lawful owner for the delivery up of the document, and no answer to an

application by the lawful owner of confidential information to restrain it from being published or copied.

I confess that I do not find the decision in *Lord Ashburton v Pape* logically satisfactory, depending as it does upon the order in which applications are made in litigation. Nevertheless I think that it and *Calcraft v Guest* [1898] 1 QB 759 are good authority for the following proposition. If a litigant has in his possession copies of documents to which legal professional privilege attaches he may nevertheless use such copies as secondary evidence in his litigation: however, if he has not yet used the documents in that way, the mere fact that he intends to do so is no answer to a claim against him by the person in whom the privilege is vested for delivery up of the copies or to restrain him from disclosing or making any use of any information contained in them.

We were referred to a number of other authorities and are grateful for an interesting argument upon what has become known as the "third party exception to legal professional privilege": see the articles in 35 MLR 83 and 37 MLR 601 to which I have already referred, and *Cross on Evidence*, 6th ed (1985), pp. 400–402. Having regard to the view I take of the effect of the decision in *Lord Ashburton v Pape* [1913] 2 Ch 469, however, I do not consider it necessary to refer to the other authorities or the general argument in any detail. In *Butler v Board of Trade* [1971] Ch 680, Goff J took the same view of *Lord Ashburton v Pape* [1913] 2 Ch 469 and would have granted an injunction similar to that sought in the instant case but for the fact that the defendants there were the Crown who intended to use the copy letter in a public prosecution brought by them. However, one may just note that there is a difference between the view taken in England about the admissibility of privileged communications in criminal proceedings—see *R v Tompkins* (1977) 67 Cr App R 181—and that taken in New Zealand—see *R v Uljee* [1982] 1 NZLR 561.

Nevertheless, having regard to the decision in *Lord Ashburton v Pape* [1913] 2 Ch 469, I respectfully think that the judge below was wrong to reject the plaintiffs' claim to relief. I would allow this appeal and make the orders sought.'

NOURSE LJ: 'The question has confronted us, in a simple and straightforward manner, with the task of reconciling the decisions of this court in *Calcraft v Guest* [1898] 1 QB 759 and *Lord Ashburton v Pape* [1913] 2 Ch 469. I agree that those decisions are authority for the proposition which May LJ has stated. However unsatisfactory its results may be thought to be, that proposition must hold sway unless and until it is revised by higher authority.

The apparent conflict between the rule of evidence established by *Calcraft v Guest* [1898] 1 QB 759 and the equitable jurisdiction reaffirmed in *Lord Ashburton v Pape* [1913] 2 Ch 469 was probably not fully recognised until the later case was considered by Goff J in *Butler v Board of Trade* [1971] Ch 680, a decision which itself made a further distinction between most criminal and all civil proceedings. Although, for the reasons given by May LJ, I am in no doubt that our decision must be governed by *Lord Ashburton v Pape* [1913] 2 Ch 469, the confusion which the existing authorities have caused in this case and are liable to cause in others has prompted me to deal with the matter at somewhat greater length than would otherwise have been necessary. The following observations are not made in any order of logic or importance. They are in general confined to a case, such as the present, where the communication is both confidential and privileged and the privilege has not been waived.

First, it is desirable to emphasise that the proceedings in which the rule of evidence denies protection to the confidential communication are not proceedings whose purpose is to seek that protection. The question is an incidental one which arises when the party who desires the protection asserts a right to it as if he were the plaintiff in an action seeking to invoke the equitable jurisdiction. When *Lord Ashburton v Pape* was decided, the practice and procedures of our courts were no doubt such that it was first necessary to issue fresh proceedings. Nowadays I think that we would at the most require an undertaking to issue a pro forma writ, perhaps not even that, a consideration which no doubt explains the agreement not to require fresh proceedings in the present case. The crucial point is that the party who desires the protection must seek it before the other party has adduced the confidential communication in evidence or otherwise relied on it at trial.

Second, although the equitable jurisdiction is of much wider application, I have little doubt that it can prevail over the rule of evidence only in cases where privilege can be claimed. The equitable jurisdiction is well able to extend, for example, to the grant of an injunction to restrain an unauthorised disclosure of confidential communications between priest and penitent or doctor and patient. But those communications are not privileged in legal proceedings and I do not believe that equity would restrain a litigant who already had a record of such a communication in his possession from using it for the purposes of his litigation. It cannot be the function of equity to accord a de facto privilege to communications in respect of which no privilege can be claimed. Equity follows the law.

Third, the right of the party who desires the protection to invoke the equitable jurisdiction does not in any way depend on the conduct of the third party into whose possession the record of the confidential communication has come. Thus, several eminent judges have been of the opinion that an injunction can be granted against a stranger who has come innocently into the possession of confidential information to which he is not entitled: see *Rex Co.* v *Muirhead* (1926) 136 LT 568, 573, *per* Clauson J; *Printers & Finishers Ltd* v *Holloway* [1965] 1 WLR 1, 7, *per* Cross J; and *Butler* v *Board of Trade* [1971] Ch 680, 690, *per* Goff J. This view seems to give effect to the general rule that equity gives relief against all the world, including the innocent, save only a bona fide purchaser for value without notice. It is directly in point in the present case and our decision necessarily affirms it.

Fourth, once it is established that a case is governed by *Lord Ashburton* v *Pape* [1913] 2 Ch 469 there is no discretion in the court to refuse to exercise the equitable jurisdiction according to its view of the materiality of the communication, the justice of admitting or excluding it or the like. The injunction is granted in aid of the privilege which, unless and until it is waived, is absolute. In saying this, I do not intend to suggest that there may not be cases where an injunction can properly be refused on general principles affecting the grant of a discretionary remedy, for example on the ground of inordinate delay.

Fifth, in a case to which *Lord Ashburton* v *Pape* can no longer apply, public policy may nevertheless preclude a party who has acted improperly in the proceedings from invoking the rule of evidence: see *ITC Film Distributors Ltd* v *Video Exchange Ltd* [1982] Ch 436, where the defendant had at an earlier hearing obtained some of the plaintiff's privileged documents by a trick. Warner J, having expressed the view that there were by that stage in the case difficulties in the way of his granting the plaintiff relief on the basis of *Lord Ashburton* v *Pape*, held, at p. 441, that the greater public interest that litigants should be able to bring their documents into court without fear that they may be filched by their opponents, whether by stealth or by a trick, and then used in evidence required an exception to the rule in *Calcraft* v *Guest* [1898] 1 QB 759, save in regard to documents at which he (the judge) had already looked. I emphasise that that decision proceeded not on an exercise of the court's discretion but on grounds of public policy.

Sixth, the distinction between civil proceedings and public prosecutions made in *Butler* v *Board of Trade* [1971] Ch 680 was again one which was made on grounds of public policy. The distinction has since been adopted and applied by the Criminal Division of this court in *R* v *Tompkins*, 67 Cr App R 181. It can now be disregarded only by the House of Lords.

Finally, it is to be noted that the Court of Appeal in New Zealand, after an extensive consideration of the authorities, including *Calcraft* v *Guest, Butler* v *Board of Trade* and *R* v *Tompkins*, recently declined to apply the rule of evidence in a criminal case and held that the evidence of a police constable who had happened to overhear a privileged conversation between the accused and his solicitor (i.e., one which was not itself part of a criminal or unlawful proceeding: see *R* v *Cox and Railton* (1884) 14 QBD 153) was not admissible: see *R* v *Uljee* [1982] 1 NZLR 561. The practical result of the decision would seem to be to leave the spirit of *Lord Ashburton* v *Pape* [1913] 2 Ch 469 supreme in both civil and criminal proceedings in that jurisdiction, a supremacy for which in my respectful opinion there is much to be said in this.'

Appeal allowed.

Contempt of Court Act 1981

10   No court may require a person to disclose, nor is any person guilty of contempt of court for refusing to disclose, the source of information contained in a publication for which he is responsible, unless it be established to the satisfaction of the court that disclosure is necessary in the interest of justice or national security or for the prevention of disorder or crime.

[For the application of s. 10, see *Secretary of State for Defence* v *Guardian Newspaper Ltd* [1984] 3 WLR 986 (HL).]

Questions for discussion

R v *Coke; R* v *Littleton*

1   Assuming that Coke's solicitors, on his instructions, send samples of his handwriting to a handwriting expert for comparison with Exhibit GG1, and that the prosecution wish to make these samples available for trial. May Coke make any claim of privilege?

2   Would the position differ if these samples were seized by the police, acting under a search warrant, from the offices of Coke's solicitors?

3   If Coke and Littleton testify in their defence at trial, may they assert the privilege against self-incrimination in cross-examination with respect to the offences charged against them?

Blackstone v Coke

1 May Coke assert any privilege to prevent Fr Wigmore from being compelled to testify about any confession Coke may have made to him?

2 May the local authority successfully object to Coke's application for production of their files, made with a view to showing that Margaret may have given the authority a different account of how she became pregnant?

3 May Margaret make use of a copy of the letter of 20 February 1985, the original of which was inadvertently sent to her solicitors? Had Margaret's solicitors refused to return the original, what should Coke's solicitors have done?

Additional questions

1 Is there a case for extending the English rules of privilege to other relationships, for example doctor or psychotherapist and patient, or priest and penitent?

2 You are acting for Sharpshooters Ltd, which manufactures small arms for the Ministry of Defence and for customers overseas. During the Falklands War in 1982, the Ministry sent a letter to Sharpshooters Ltd, requesting them to speed up production and a few days later Arnold, a machine operator, was injured whilst working on a sub-machine gun. An enquiry was set up to ascertain how the accident occurred, and a report was produced marked 'Confidential: for the Government's and company's legal advisers' but copies were circulated to the company's managerial staff and shop stewards and to other factories which manufacture similar weapons. Arnold claims that the accident occurred while he was working on a consignment of weapons destined for Auralia, a country situated in the Middle-East, and his solicitors have asked to see correspondence passing between the company and Auralia, together with photographs of the machine and a list of accidents in the workshop during 1981 and 1982, as well as all other relevant material.

Advise Sharpshooters Ltd as to what material should be disclosed to Arnold and what course may be taken to resolve a dispute between the parties.

Further reading

Allen, 'Legal privilege and the principle of fairness in the criminal trial' [1987] Crim LR 449.

Heydon, 'Legal professional privilege and third parties' (1974) 37 MLR 601.

Tapper, 'Privilege and confidence' (Note) (1972) 35 MLR 83.

Zuckerman, 'Privilege and public interest' in *Crime, Proof and Punishment* (ed. Tapper) (1981).

11 Witnesses: Competence and Compellability

A: THE DEFENDANT IN A CRIMINAL CASE

(Suggested preliminary reading: *A Practical Approach to Evidence,* pp. 334–340).

Criminal Evidence Act 1898 (as amended by the Police and Criminal Evidence Act 1984)

1 Every person charged with an offence shall be a competent witness for the defence at every stage of the proceedings, whether the person so charged is charged solely or jointly with any other person. Provided as follows:

(a) A person so charged shall no: be called as a witness in pursuance of this Act except upon his own application;

(b) The failure of any person charged with an offence to give evidence shall not be made the subject of any comment by the prosecution . . .

R v Mutch [1973] 1 All ER 178 (CA)

The accused was arrested and charged with robbery in a grocer's shop. The accused denied the charge claiming that he was not in the shop at the time of the incident. He was released on bail. No formal identification parade was held by the police as it was alleged by the prosecution that, whilst on bail and for the purpose of confusing anyone attending an identification parade of which he was the suspect member, the accused tried to alter his appearance by tinting his hair and moustache and by reshaping the latter. At his trial, a girl assistant in the shop at the time of the incident identified the accused but he elected not to give evidence. He did however call two witnesses to prove that he had not altered his appearance as alleged. The trial judge, in summing up, told the jury, *inter alia*, that they were entitled to draw inferences unfavourable to the accused where he was not called to establish an innocent explanation of facts proved by the prosecution which, without such an explanation, told for his guilt. The accused was convicted and he appealed.

LAWTON LJ, reading the judgment of the court: 'It was submitted that the judge was wrong to tell the jury that they were entitled to draw inferences unfavourable to the appellant because of his absence from the witness box and that he had made his error worse by repeating what he had said. There is nothing in the complaint about repetition. In repeating what he had said the judge was doing nothing more than helping the jury to understand what he thought, and rightly thought, was a somewhat complicated and involved legal formula. The legal concept underlying the formula is one which is founded on authorities over 60 years old. The problem is whether it was applicable in a case such as this where the sole issue was whether an identification was correct. If it is applicable, accused persons faced with evidence of identity, however weak it may be, will be doing themselves no good but positive harm by not giving evidence because the unfavourable inferences to be drawn from their silence may be regarded as strengthening the prosecution's weak evidence to such an extent as to warrant a conviction.

The reference to reading in the passage complained of shows what the judge had done; he had read to the jury the last sentence in para. 1308 of the current edition of *Archbold's Criminal Pleading, Evidence and Practice* [which said: "But the jury are entitled to draw inferences unfavourable to the prisoner where he is not called to establish an innocent explanation of facts proved by the prosecution, which, without such explanation, tell for his guilt."]. In the current edition the editors quote two cases to support the proposition set out, namely, *R* v *Corrie, R* v *Watson* (1904) 20 TLR 365, a decision of the Court of Crown Cases Reserved, and *R* v *Bernard* (1908) 1 Cr App R 218.

In *R* v *Corrie* the question to be decided was whether there was any evidence to go to the jury of the offences charged which were keeping a common gaming house and under statutes relating to gambling. The police had gone to some premises used as a club and had found the accused seated at a table with a racing card in front of them. There was a tape machine recording the names of runners and prices on one side and a telephone on the other. The accused did not give evidence and as far as can be judged from the report the facts testified to by the police witnesses were not in issue. The deputy recorder had taken a special verdict from the jury and on getting their answers to his questions he had directed them to find a verdict of guilty. On its facts this case seems to be a long way from the present one but it has no doubt been quoted as an authority by the editors of Archbold because of the following passage in the judgment of Lord Alverstone CJ:

> No inference should be drawn in support of a weak case from the fact that the defendants were not called; but when transactions were capable of an innocent explanation, then, if the defendants could have given it, it was not improper, once a *prima facie* case had been established, for the jury to draw a conclusion from their not being called.

In our judgment on the facts of *Corrie's case* Lord Alverstone CJ's reference to the accused not being called was but one way of stating that an inference can be drawn from uncontested or clearly established facts which point so strongly to guilt as to call for an explanation; if no explanation is given when the circumstances are such that an innocent man would be expected either to give an explanation or deny the basic facts, this is a factor which can be taken into consideration: see *Bessela* v *Stern* (1877) 2 CPD 265. As Professor Cross has pointed out in his book on evidence whether guilt should be inferred from silence in this kind of case must depend on the facts. The facts of this case were very different from those in *R* v *Corrie*. Nothing here was admitted or had been at any stage of the police investigation.

R v *Bernard* provided another illustration of the principle applied in *R* v *Corrie*. The accused, who had been convicted with another man of conspiracy to defraud, had signed letters containing untrue statements and had been a party to a fraudulent conveyance. The defence put forward at the trial had been that this accused had been nothing more than a paid servant and that there was no evidence that he knew of any fraudulent design. The trial judge, who was Lord Alverstone CJ, when summing up, had referred to the absence of the accused from the witness box and had told the jury they must draw their own conclusions from the absence of his explanation.

Darling J, giving the judgment of the court in *R* v *Bernard*, said:

It is right that the jury should know, and if necessary, be told to draw their own conclusions from the absence of explanation by the prisoner. Here he failed to give any explanation of the circumstances in which he signed letters containing false statements . . . There was abundant evidence of his guilt, and the jury were satisfied, in the absence of explanation by him, in convicting him.

Since the first decade of this century, there have been many cases in which this court and its predecessor have had to rule whether comments about an accused's absence from the witness box or a failure to disclose a defence when questioned by the police were permissible, and as Salmon LJ pointed out in *R v Sullivan* (1966) 51 Cr App R 102: "The line dividing what may be said and what may not be said is a very fine one, and it is perhaps doubtful whether in a case like the present it would be even perceptible to the members of any ordinary jury." Nevertheless, as long as the law recognises the so called right to silence, judges must keep their comments on the correct side of the line even though the differences between what is permissible and what is not may have little significance for many jurors. In the circumstances of this case there would be no point in reviewing the cases, some of which are not easy to reconcile, as we are firmly of the opinion that the trial judge used a form of words which was inappropriate to the case and the evidence which he was summing up. The words he used might have been permissible if the evidence had established a situation calling for "confession and avoidance"; they were not proper for one of flat denial as this case was. The court is of the opinion that the trial judge was led into error by the passage in Archbold to which we have already referred. The concept there set out has a limited application and it would be helpful to both judges and practitioners if this was made clear.

Judges who are minded to comment on an accused's absence from the witness box should remember, first, Lord Oaksey's comment in *Waugh v R* [1950] AC 203:

> It is true that it is a matter for the judge's discretion whether he shall comment on the fact that a prisoner has not given evidence; but the very fact that the prosecution are not permitted to comment on that fact shows how careful a judge should be in making such comment;

and, secondly, that in nearly all cases in which a comment is thought necessary (the *R v Corrie* and *R v Bernard* type of cases being rare exceptions) the form of comment should be that which Lord Parker CJ described in *R v Bathurst* [1968] 2 QB 99, as the accepted form, namely, that:

> . . . the accused is not bound to give evidence, that he can sit back and see if the prosecution have proved their case, and that, while the jury have been deprived of the opportunity of hearing his story tested in cross-examination, the one thing that they must not do is to assume that he is guilty because he has not gone into the witness box.

The trial judge in this case went very near to encouraging this assumption.'
Appeal allowed. Conviction quashed.

R v Sparrow [1973] 1 WLR 488 (CA)

A policeman was shot in the course of a car theft by the appellant and his co-accused. At his trial for murder, the defendant did not give evidence to support his plea that the gun used was only intended to frighten anyone attempting to apprehend them. In his summing up the judge, commenting on the appellant's failure to give evidence, said that if he never contemplated that any shooting would take place it was essential that he should give evidence which could be tested in cross-examination. The appellant was convicted of murder.

LAWTON LJ, reading the judgment of the court: 'Mr Brown, on behalf of the appellant, submitted with his usual incisiveness that that comment could have and would have been understood by the jury as a direction that they should assume that there was nothing in the appellant's defence and that he was guilty because he had not given evidence. In our judgment that is how the trial judge's comment would have been understood, but we think that that is how the jury would have assessed the situation if the judge's comment had not been made. In our experience of trials, juries seldom acquit persons who do not give evidence when there is a clear case for them to answer and they do not answer it. Lord Goddard CJ recognised that, as one would have expected him to do, in his judgment in *R v Jackson* [1953] 1 WLR 591, 595:

> . . . whatever may have been the position immediately after the Criminal Evidence Act 1898 came into operation, everybody knows that absence from the witness box requires a very great deal of explanation . . .

The reason lies in common sense. An innocent man who is charged with a crime, or with any conduct reflecting upon his reputation, can be expected to refute the allegation as soon as he can by giving his own version of what happened. Juries know this, and they must often be perplexed as to why they should be told by judges, as they often have been since the passing of the Criminal Evidence Act 1898, that when considering their verdict they should not take into account the fact that the accused has said not a word in his own defence even though the case against him is a strong one. The law, however, has set limits upon what judges may say about an accused's election not to give evidence. Our task is to adjudge whether the trial judge went too far in this case.

The limits have been set by the judges, and the experience of this court is that in recent years many judges at first instance have come to think that their right to comment on the absence of the defendant from the witness box has been restricted by the report of the Judicial Committee of the Privy Council in *Waugh v The King* [1950] AC 203 and the judgment of this court in *R v Bathurst* [1968] 2 QB 99. Sometimes judges stress the right of the defendant not to give evidence, as Devlin J did in *R v Adams* (unreported), April 9, 1957, and what he said in that case, taken out of context, is often used by defending counsel as an excuse for not calling the defendant.

Two propositions founded on *Waugh v The King* [1950] AC 203 and *R v Bathurst* [1968] 2 QB 99 are argued from time to time: first, that if a judge does decide to comment he should do so once only and that if he makes any more comments he is acting unfairly, and, secondly, that any substantial variation from the form of comment suggested by Lord Parker CJ in *R v Bathurst* [1968] 2 QB 99, 107 is unfair. Present day doubts about what a judge can and cannot say by way of comment have led us to examine what principles, if any, apply.

Before the passing of the Criminal Evidence Act 1898 there was no problem of this kind because the defendant had no right to give evidence. As soon as that Act came into operation, the question arose as to whether a judge had any right to comment on the election of the defendant not to give evidence on his own behalf. It was answered in *R* v *Rhodes* [1899] 1 QB 77 by Lord Russell CJ in these words, at p. 83:

> There is nothing in the Act that takes away or even purports to take away the right of the court to comment on the evidence in the case, and the manner in which the case has been conducted. The nature and degree of such comment must rest entirely in the discretion of the judge who tries the case; and it is impossible to lay down any rule as to the cases in which he ought or ought not to comment on the failure of the prisoner to give evidence, or as to what those comments should be. There are some cases in which it would be unwise to make any such comment at all; there are others in which it would be absolutely necessary in the interests of justice that such comments should be made. That is a question entirely for the discretion of the judge; and it is only necessary now to say that that discretion is in no way affected by the provisions of the Criminal Evidence Act 1898.

That clear statement of the law has never been questioned; it is the law. From 1899 until *Waugh* v *The King* [1950] AC 203 it was the practice of judges when justice required them to do so to comment in robust terms upon a defendant's absence from the witness box. An example of such comments which has been remembered at the Bar is provided by *R* v *Nodder* (unreported), 12 April, 1937. The defendant had been indicted for the murder of a small girl. Swift J began his summing up by reminding the jury that they had heard evidence from several witnesses as to where the murdered girl had been up to a certain time when the defendant had been with her but none from the defendant himself, although he alone could have given evidence of where she had been afterwards. The justice of that case called for that comment, and at the time when it was made informed opinion at the Bar did not question the propriety of it. It would, however, be questioned today. Why?

Many would say that the change in judicial practice resulted from *Waugh* v *The King* [1950] AC 203. There the appellant had been convicted of murder. The case against him was weak, so weak, indeed, that the police authorities, after they had completed their investigations, accepted his explanation as to what had happened and decided not to prosecute him. A coroner, however, ordered his prosecution. The only evidence of any strength against him was provided by a statement which the deceased had made shortly before his death. At the trial the appellant did not give evidence. In his summing up the trial judge commented nine times on the fact and on two of those occasions he made comments in much the same terms as Swift J had done in *R* v *Nodder* (unreported). The Judicial Committee of the Privy Council disapproved of those comments. Lord Oaksey delivered the reasons for the Board's report. He said, at p. 211:

> Whilst much of the summing up is unexceptionable, there are certain parts of it which, in their Lordships' view, do constitute a grave departure from the rules that justice requires, and they are therefore of opinion that the conviction must be quashed. It is true that it is a matter for the judge's discretion whether he shall comment on the fact that a prisoner has not given evidence; but the very fact that the prosecution are not

permitted to comment on that fact shows how careful a judge should be in making such comment.

He went on to point out how weak the prosecution's case had been and continued, at p. 212:

> *In such a state of the evidence*—the italics are ours—the judge's repeated comments on the appellant's failure to give evidence may well have led the jury to think that no innocent man could have taken such a course . . . in the present case their Lordships think that the prisoner's counsel was fully justified in not calling the prisoner, and that the judge, if he made any comment on the matter at all, ought at least have pointed out to the jury that the prisoner was not bound to give evidence and that it was for the prosecution to make out the case beyond reasonable doubt.

Lord Oaksey went on to find that the dying declaration had been wrongly admitted and inaccurately commented upon.

In our judgment *Waugh* v *The King* [1950] AC 203 establishes nothing more than this: it is a wrongful exercise of judicial discretion for a judge to bolster up a weak prosecution case by making comments about a defendant's failure to give evidence, and implicit in the report is the concept that failure to give evidence has no evidential value. We can find nothing in it which qualifies the statement of principle in *R* v *Rhodes* [1899] 1 QB 77. Our view of *Waugh* seems to have been that of Lord Goddard CJ in *R* v *Jackson* [1953] 1 WLR 591 when he said, at p. 594:

> . . . I do not want in the least to appear to be whittling down what their Lordships in the Judicial Committee said on these matters, but each case on such a point as this must depend on its own facts . . . It has to be remembered, among other things, that the charge against the appellant was one of receiving stolen property . . . if ever there was a case in which one would expect him to give evidence to explain his possession of the property that is the case.

In the present case, the charge was murder, and the evidence went to establish that when the police officer was shot by the co-defendant the appellant was standing close by and that after the shooting the pair of them drove off together and that one of them within a short time in the presence of the other reloaded the pistol; there has to be added to that the submission of the appellant's counsel that the prosecution's evidence was consistent with the possibility that the joint enterprise between the co-defendant and the appellant was merely to frighten the police officer with a pistol (which the appellant knew was loaded) and that the co-defendant departed from it by pressing the trigger a number of times.

In the judgment of this court, if the trial judge had not commented in strong terms upon the appellant's absence from the witness box he would have been failing in his duty. The object of a summing up is to help the jury and in our experience a jury is not helped by a colourless reading out of the evidence as recorded by the judge in his notebook. The judge is more than a mere referee who takes no part in the trial save to intervene when a rule of procedure or evidence is broken. He and the jury try the case together and it is his duty to give them the benefit of his knowledge of the law and to advise them in the light of his experience as to the significance of the evidence, and when an accused person elects not to give evidence, in most cases but not all the judge should explain to the jury what the consequences of his absence from the witness box are, and if, in his discretion, he thinks that he should do so more than once he may, but he must keep in mind always his duty to be fair. As A T Lawrence J pointed out in *R v Voisin* [1918] 1 KB 531, 536:

> Comments on the evidence which are not misdirections do not by being added together constitute a misdirection.

How should this be done? In *R v Bathurst* [1968] 2 QB 99 Lord Parker CJ gave judges some guidance, but what he said was, as he appreciated, *obiter*. It was in these terms, at p. 107:

> . . . as is well known, the accepted form of comment is to inform the jury that, of course, he—the defendant—is not bound to give evidence, that he can sit back and see if the prosecution have proved their case, and that while the jury have been deprived of the opportunity of hearing his story tested in cross-examination, the one thing they must not do is to assume that he is guilty because he has not gone into the witness box.

In many cases, a direction in some such terms as these will be all that is required; but we are sure that Lord Parker CJ never intended his words of guidance to be regarded as a judicial directive to be recited to juries in every case in which a defendant elects not to give evidence. What is said must depend upon the facts of each case and in some cases the interests of justice call for a stronger comment. The trial judge, who has the feel of the case, is the person who must exercise his discretion in this matter to ensure that a trial is fair. A discretion is not to be fettered by laying down rules and regulations for its exercise: see *R v Selvey* [1970] AC 304, *per* Lord Hodson, at p. 364. What, however, is of the greatest importance in Lord Parker CJ's advice to judges is his reference to the need to avoid telling juries that absence from the witness box is to be equated with guilt. As we have already said, this was implicit in *Waugh v The King* [1950] AC 203 and Lord Parker CJ's *dictum* on this point has been accepted by this court as the law in *R v Pratt* [1971] Crim LR 234 and *R v Mutch* [1973] Crim LR 111.

How should these principles be applied in this case? In our judgment there is nothing in the complaint about the cumulative effects of the comments, particularly as the trial judge at the beginning of his summing up explained accurately and clearly that the appellant had a right to remain silent and to rest his defence on the presumption that he was innocent until proved guilty. The interests of justice required that the trial judge should get the jury to understand that an exculpatory statement, unverified on oath, such as the appellant had made after arrest, was not evidence save in so far as it contained admissions, and his task was not made easier by the present state of the law which required the Attorney-General to say nothing about the appellant's silence but allowed the co-defendant's counsel to say what he liked and, were he so minded, to put into words what it is almost certain the majority of the jurors were asking themselves, viz., having regard to the strength of the evidence, if the appellant was innocent why had he not gone into the witness box to say so? Our law, however, does not require a defendant to give evidence and a judge must not either by express words or impliedly give jurors to understand that a defence cannot succeed unless the defendant gives evidence. Unfortunately, probably by a slip of the tongue, that is what the trial judge did when he said to the jury:

Is it not essential that he should go into the witness box and tell you that himself and be subject to cross-examination about it? Well, he did not do so and there it is.

He did overstep the limits of justifiable comment; he should not have said what he did.

How far did these few words in a long summing up affect the jury's verdict? This must always be a matter of speculation, but we are confident on the facts of this case that the jury would have come to the same verdict if the trial judge had not said what he did. There has been no miscarriage of justice.'

Appeal dismissed.

- How does the case of *R* v *Sparrow* differ, if at all, from *R* v *Mutch*?

R v Rudd (1948) 32 Cr App R 138 (CCA)

The applicant was convicted of receiving stolen property. It is unnecessary to set out the facts of the case beyond stating that a co-defendant of the applicant named Powell gave evidence implicating the applicant. The applicant applied for leave to appeal.

HUMPHREYS J, delivering the judgment of the court: 'Ever since this Court was established it has been the invariable rule to state the law in the same way—that, while a statement made in the absence of the accused person by one of his co-defendants cannot be evidence against him, if a co-defendant goes into the witness box and gives evidence in the course of a joint trial, then what he says becomes evidence for all the purposes of the case including the purpose of being evidence against his co-defendant. That is the law as we have always understood it, and there is ample authority to that effect, and most assuredly *R v Meredith and Others* (1943) 29 Cr App R 40 said nothing to the contrary. In *Meredith and Others (supra)* there were several prisoners, and the Court was dealing with the question whether the summing-up of the learned Recorder of London correctly directed the jury. The learned Recorder said, no doubt accurately, at the end of his summing-up, " These men all made statements, and it is impossible for you to listen to all those statements and not to realise that they are statements which may implicate some persons other than the men making them. You will do your best, members of the jury, to remember that those statements are only evidence against the persons who make them. I will go further than that. When the individual making a statement of that sort comes into the witness box and gives evidence on oath, it is a different situation. What he says then does become evidence against the other person". He went on to say this: "but I endeavour in this class of case where there are a number of prisoners in the dock always to warn juries that so far as possible they should not use any evidence given by a person who is accused, when he is in the witness box, against any one of his co-defendants". That obviously does not mean: "I am in the habit of directing juries that what a co-defendant has said is not admissible in evidence against another co-defendant", because the learned Recorder has just said to the jury: "what he has said does become evidence against the co-defendant". In our view, it is plain that what the learned Recorder was, in effect, saying to the jury was: "I always take care to warn juries of the danger of convicting solely upon the evidence of a co-defendant". That is good sense and, as the Lord Chief Justice (Lord Caldecote) observed in the judgment of the Court, a proper direction. The Lord Chief Justice, therefore, in that case, in giving the judgment of the Court dealing with the question of law, was clearly of the same opinion as all the other Judges in this Court have always been. When it is said that there was in that case, either by the learned Recorder in the first instance or by the Court of Criminal Appeal, a statement in law that a jury would be wrongly directed if they were told that they may take into consideration in considering the case of one defendant what has been said by a co-defendant, that is nonsense. We are satisfied that that was not the meaning of the learned Recorder or of the Lord Chief Justice when he used the expression (at p. 44): "that was a proper direction, and one that was fair to each of the appellants". I repeat that, in reading the judgment in *Meredith and Others (supra)* it must be remembered that what the Court was dealing with there was not a statement of law of universal application that evidence by a co-defendant in the witness box is always admissible against another co-defendant. They were merely approving of the practice stated by the learned Recorder in that case as being perfectly fair to the then defendants, and for that reason the Court held that the direction was a perfectly proper one and that the appeal should be dismissed. That is the whole of that case, and it would be quite wrong to say that it is an authority for the proposition contended for by Mr Smallwood; if it were, it would mean that the Court was intending to overrule or to differ from a whole series of cases, only one of which need be mentioned. Attached to the report of *Meredith and Others (supra)*, there appears (at p. 46) a note of the decision of this Court in *R v Garland* (November 4, 1941). In giving the judgment of the Court, consisting of the Lord Chief Justice (Lord Caldecote), Lewis J and myself, I said: "The co-defendant of the appellant had given evidence before the jury on her own behalf, and what she said on that occasion was evidence for all purposes in the case and in that sense evidence against the appellant . . . It is said that the learned Recorder [of London] omitted to remind the jury that in the position which she occupied in the case she ought to be treated as an accomplice, because her statement admitted to a great extent the case against her, and went on to state that she did what she did at the instance of the appellant. There is no doubt of the correctness of that proposition of law, and this Court will do nothing to weaken the force of those judgments in which it has been repeatedly said by this Court that it is most desirable that a judge dealing with such a case, where it involves the evidence of an accomplice, should remind the jury of the danger of convicting upon the evidence of an accomplice unless corroborated". We then went on to consider the facts of that case, and inasmuch as there was ample evidence of corroboration in that case, we dismissed the appeal. That disposes of the second of the objections.

R v Turner (1975) 61 Cr App R 67 (CA)

The nineteen appellants were charged with several robberies. One of the defendants, named Smalls, was offered immunity from prosecution by the Director of Public Prosecutions, in return for giving Queen's evidence against the appellants who included many accomplices. Smalls' evidence was the foundation of the prosecution's case against all the appellants. The appellants were convicted and appealed.

LAWTON LJ, giving the judgment of the court: 'Mr Hutchinson did not suggest that Smalls was not a competent witness. He could not have done so because the courts have ruled time and time again since the seventeenth century that accomplices are competent witnesses (see *Wigmore on Evidence*, 2nd ed, para. 2056). He submitted that for some time past there had been a practice for judges not to admit the evidence of accomplices who could still be influenced by continuing inducements and that this Court in *R v Pipe* (1966) 51 Cr App R 17 had adjudged that this practice had become a rule of law. If this is so, *Pipe (supra)* marks an important change in the law relating to giving Queen's evidence.

Despite Mr Hutchinson's admission that Smalls was a competent witness, Barrett's counsel, Mr Wright, in another appeal, submitted that he was not. It is convenient to deal with that submission now. We inferred that Mr Hutchinson used the word "competent" in relation to witnesses in the usual way in which it is used in the law of evidence, viz. the capacity which categories of persons have to give evidence. Smalls came into the category of accomplices and, as we have said already, this category can give evidence. If Mr Wright was using the word "competent" in this sense, his submission was misconceived. He may, however, have used it in a more narrow sense, applying it to a particular witness who for a particular reason should not be allowed to give evidence. If this be so, his submission was really the same as Mr Hutchinson's.

There can be no doubt that at common law an accomplice who gave evidence for the Crown in the expectation of getting a pardon for doing so was a competent witness. The two most persuasive authorities in English law say just that. In *Rudd* (1775) 1 Cowp 331 the Court of King's Bench had to consider an application for bail made by a woman who had given King's evidence and who claimed that in consequence she was entitled to be released on bail pending the grant of the pardon which she submitted she was entitled to as of right. Lord Mansfield CJ adjudged (at p. 334) that hers was not one of the three types of case in which pardons could be claimed as of right (that is, pardons promised by proclamation or given under statute or earned by the ancient procedure of approvement). He continued as follows (at p. 344): "There is besides a practice, which indeed does not give a legal right; and that is where accomplices having made a full and fair confession of the whole truth, are in consequence thereof admitted evidence for the Crown and that evidence is afterwards made use of to convict the other offenders. If in that case they act fairly and openly, and discover the whole truth, though they are not entitled as of right to a pardon, yet the usage, lenity and the practice of the Courts is to stop the prosecution against them and they have an equitable title to a recommendation for the King's mercy."

Blackstone wrote to the same effect; see *Commentaries*, 23rd ed (1854), Vol. 4 at p. 440. It is manifest that in the eighteenth century the courts did not consider an accomplice to be incompetent to give evidence because any inducement held out to him to do so was still operating on his mind when he was in the witness box. Blackstone considered that an accomplice could not expect to receive his pardon unless he gave his evidence "without prevarication or fraud." The nineteenth century brought about no change in the competence of accomplices to give evidence even though the prospect of immunity from prosecution was before them: see all the editions of S M Phillips' *Treatise on the Law of Evidence* which appeared between 1814 and 1952—there were ten. The contribution of the nineteenth century to this topic was the rule of practice that judges should warn juries of the dangers of convicting on the uncorroborated evidence of accomplices. In this century that practice became a rule of law.

It is against that background that the case of *Pipe (supra)* should be considered. There is nothing in either the arguments or the judgment itself to indicate that the Court thought it was changing a rule of law as to the competency of accomplices to give evidence which had been followed ever since the seventeenth century. The facts of that case must be closely examined. Pipe was being tried on an indictment charging him with housebreaking and larceny. He was alleged to have stolen a safe and its contents. A man named Swan was called to prove that he had helped Pipe to break open the safe. Swan, however, before Pipe's trial had begun had himself been charged with complicity in Pipe's crime in relation to the safe. The form of the charge is not stated in the report. He was not indicted with Pipe. It was intended to try him later. The Court adjudged that Swan should not have been called in these circumstances. "In the judgment of this Court," said Lord Parker CJ at p. 21, " . . . it is one thing to call for the prosecution an accomplice, a witness whose evidence is suspect, and about whom the jury must be warned in the recognised way. It is quite another to call a witness who is not only an accomplice but is an accomplice against whom proceedings have been brought which have not been concluded." The Court expressly approved the practice which was then set out in paragraph 1297 of *Archbold,* 36th ed (now para. 401 of the 38th ed).

In our judgment *Pipe (supra)* is limited to the circumstances set out in *Archbold.* Its *ratio decidendi* is confined to a case in which an accomplice, who has been charged, but not tried, is required to give evidence of his own offence in order to secure the conviction of another accused. *Pipe (supra)* on its facts was clearly a right decision. The same result could have been achieved by adjudging that the trial judge should have exercised his discretion to exclude Swan's evidence on the ground that there was an obvious and powerful inducement for him to ingratiate himself with the prosecution and the Court and that the existence of this inducement made it desirable in the interests of justice to exclude it. See *Noor Mohamed* v *The King* [1949] AC 182 *per* Lord du Parcq at p. 192 and followed in *Harris* v *Director of Public Prosecutions* [1952] AC 694 and 36 Cr App R 39 *per* Viscount Simon at p. 707 and p. 57. To have reached the decision on this basis would, we think, have been more in line with the earlier authorities. Lord Parker CJ in *Pipe (supra)* seems, however, to have viewed the admission of Swan's evidence in the circumstances of that case as more than a wrong exercise of discretion. He described what happened as being "wholly irregular". It does not follow, in our judgment, that in all cases calling a witness who can benefit from giving evidence is "wholly irregular". To hold so would be absurd. Examples are provided by the prosecution witness who hopes to get a reward which has been offered "for information leading to a conviction", or even an order for compensation or whose claim for damages may be helped by a conviction.

If the inducement is very powerful, the judge may decide to exercise his discretion; but when doing so he must take into consideration all factors, including those affecting the public. It is in the interests of the public that criminals should be brought to justice; and the more serious the crimes the greater is the need for justice to be done. Employing Queen's evidence to accomplish this end is distasteful and has been distasteful for at least 300 years to judges, lawyers and members of the public. Hale CJ writing about 1650, used strong language of condemnation of the plea of approvement which was the precursor of the modern practice of granting immunity from prosecution, or further prosecution, to accomplices willing to give evidence for the Crown. See Hale, *Pleas of the Crown*, Vol. 2, p. 226. His comments should be remembered by the Director of Public Prosecutions. "The truth is", he wrote, "that more mischief hath come to good men, by these kinds of approvements by false accusations, of desperate villains than benefit to the public by the discovery and convicting of real offenders". The practice has been condemned on ethical grounds. See Professor Sir Leon Radzinowicz, *History of the English Criminal Law* (1956), Vol. 2, p. 53. It is, however, no part of our function to add to the weight of ethical condemnation or to dissipate it. We are concerned to decide what the law is and whether the judge should, as a matter of discretion, have excluded Smalls' evidence, and whether, having admitted it, he gave the jury an adequate warning about acting on it.

When Smalls decided to give the police information about his partners in crime, the prospect of getting himself immunity from further prosecution was a most powerful inducement. It is necessary, however, to consider Smalls' position when he gave evidence. All the charges which had been preferred against him had already been terminated in his favour. By means of the absurd conspiracy charge, the prosecution had tried to give him immunity from prosecution for any offences he had disclosed in his statements. If, after verdicts of "not guilty" had been entered in his favour, he had refused to give evidence, and the prosecution had tried by relying on the differences between a charge of conspiracy to rob and one of robbing to prosecute him for any substantive offences which he had disclosed, his statements would have been inadmissible because they had been obtained from him by inducements. His statements could not, of course, have been used in any prosecution brought against his wife. When Smalls went into the witness box both before the magistrates and at this trial, there was no real likelihood of his being prosecuted if he refused to give evidence. The only risk he ran was that the police might have withdrawn the protection which he had had and have refused to conduct him in secrecy to where he wanted to go. These facts distinguished this case from *Pipe (supra)* and would have justified the judge in refusing to exercise his discretion to exclude Smalls' evidence had he been asked to do so which he was not.'

R v Richardson and Others (1967) 51 Cr App R 381

H, M and others were originally jointly indicted, but at the beginning of the trial a separate trial had been ordered in the case of M. At a later stage in the trial of H and others, H applied for and obtained a witness summons against M, whom he desired to call as a witness in his defence. The question then arose whether M was in law a compellable witness.

LAWTON J: 'Mr Platts-Mills has invited my attention to the decision of the Court for Crown Cases Reserved in *Payne* (1872) LR 1 CCR 349. A number of men had been indicted for entering on other people's land, while armed, for the purpose of taking and destroying game. One of the defendants wanted to call another defendant on his behalf. Could he do so? The problem came before a court consisting of Cockburn CJ, Martin and Channell BB, and Keating and Lush JJ. They thought the problem of such importance that they reserved it for consideration by the full Bench. The arguments of counsel before the full Bench have been reported at length together with comments made by the judges in the course of the argument. The judgment itself is very short. The injustice of a situation in not being able to call a man jointly charged as a witness was duly pointed out to the Court, whereupon Cockburn CJ said (at p. 354) "The remedy for that is to apply to have the prisoners tried separately". The Chief Justice seems to have thought that, if there were separate trials, the problem of calling one defendant in support of another could be overcome; but that is not this problem. Here the problem is not whether Mottram can be called as a witness for Hall (and it is conceded by counsel that he is a competent witness), but whether he is a compellable one.

In 1883 a similar kind of problem arose at the trial of *R v Bradlaugh* 15 Cox CC 217. At his trial Charles Bradlaugh was indicted with two other men and his defence was that he had not published certain allegedly blasphemous libels. He wanted to call his co-defendants to testify that he had not had any part in the publication. The court was disposed to order a separate trial of Bradlaugh in order to enable him to call his co-defendants. The court, however, heard Mr Avory (later to become Avory J) on behalf of one of the co-defendants whom Bradlaugh wanted to call. Mr Avory's argument is reported as follows (at p. 223): "Mr Avory, on behalf of Ramsay, objected that this could not be done unless a verdict of acquittal was taken against Ramsay. He cited the observations of Cockburn CJ in *R* v *Winsor* and *Harris* (1866) LR 1 QB 289, in which Harris was examined as a witness against Winsor, without being first acquitted, that . . . it was much to be lamented. In all cases where two persons are joined in the same indictment, and it is desired to try them separately, and that the evidence of one should be received against the other, it is better that a verdict of not guilty should be taken against the one called". Lord Coleridge CJ pointed out that in *Winsor* and *Harris (supra)* the fellow prisoner had been called for the Crown. Mr Avory continued his argument in this way: "He urged that this did not matter, as if the co-defendant were called for the defence he would be liable to be cross-examined, and could hardly avoid incriminating himself". It seems clear that Mr Avory was objecting to his client being called as a witness. Lord Coleridge CJ dealt with the matter at p. 224. He said he should endeavour to avoid that [that is cross-examination which might be incriminating] by not allowing questions to be asked or answered which might have that effect. As to the dictum cited, he observed that Cockburn CJ did not go to the length of saying that the course taken was not legal even when the fellow-prisoner had been called for the prosecution to make out a case against the prisoner being tried. Here, however, the co-defendant was to be called for the defendant under trial. He could not prevent this, nor compel the prosecution to take a verdict of acquittal as to the co-defendant to be called. The co-defendant was to be called simply to disprove publication by the defendant Bradlaugh, and any questions to show publication by anybody else would either not be admissible, or, if they tended to criminate the witness, he would not be compellable to answer".

That case is authority for the proposition that, if there are separate trials of two men charged in the same indictment, on the trial of one the other can be called as a witness and compelled to answer.

Mr Gardner sought to show that the authority of that case is no longer good law, because of the provisions of the Criminal Evidence Act 1898. He invited my attention to the opening words of section 1, which are as follows. "Every person charged with an offence, and the wife or husband, as the case may be, of the person so charged, shall be a competent witness for the defence at every stage of the proceedings, whether the person so charged is charged solely or jointly with any other person. Provided as follows—(a) A person so charged shall not be called as a witness in pursuance of this Act except upon his own application". In my judgment, the construction of section 1 of the Criminal Evidence Act 1898 is that the word "proceedings" means a trial which is going on. That seems to be clear, not only from the opening words of the section, but also from the language and the proviso. Accordingly, I am of the opinion that there is nothing in the Act of 1898 which derogates from the decisions in *Payne (supra)* and *Bradlaugh (supra)*. Accordingly, I rule and adjudge that Mottram is a compellable witness at this trial.'

Order accordingly.

B: THE SPOUSE OF THE DEFENDANT

(Suggested preliminary reading: *A Practical Approach to Evidence,* pp. 340–348).

Police and Criminal Evidence Act 1984

80(1) In any proceedings the wife or husband of the accused shall be competent to give evidence—

    (a)   subject to subsection (4) below, for the prosecution; and

    (b)   on behalf of the accused or any person jointly charged with the accused.

    (2) In any proceedings the wife or husband of the accused shall, subject to subsection (4) below, be compellable to give evidence on behalf of the accused.

    (3) In any proceedings the wife or husband of the accused shall, subject to subsection (4) below, be compellable to give evidence for the prosecution or on behalf of any person jointly charged with the accused if and only if—

    (a)   the offence charged involves an assault on, or injury or a threat of injury to, the wife or husband of the accused or a person who was at the material time under the age of sixteen; or

    (b)   the offence charged is a sexual offence alleged to have been committed in respect of a person who was at the material time under that age; or

    (c)   the offence charged consists of attempting or conspiring to commit, or of aiding, abetting, counselling, procuring or inciting the commission of, an offence falling within paragraph (a) or (b) above.

    (4) Where a husband and wife are jointly charged with an offence neither spouse shall at the trial be competent or compellable by virtue of subsection (1)(a), (2) or (3) above to give evidence in respect of that offence unless that spouse is not, or is no longer, liable to be convicted of that offence at the trial as a result of pleading guilty or for any other reason.

    (5) In any proceedings a person who has been but is no longer married to the accused shall be competent and compellable to give evidence as if that person and the accused had never been married.

    (6) Where in any proceedings the age of any person at any time is material for the purposes of subsection (3) above, his age at the material time shall for the purposes of that provision be deemed to be or to have been that which appears to the court to be or to have been his age at that time.

    (7) In subsection (3)(b) above "sexual offence" means an offence under the Sexual Offences Act 1956, the Indecency with Children Act 1960, the Sexual Offences Act 1967, section 54 of the Criminal Law Act 1977 or the Protection of Children Act 1978.

    (8) The failure of the wife or husband of the accused to give evidence shall not be made the subject of any comment by the prosecution.

R v *Pitt* [1983] QB 25 (CA)

The appellant was charged with two offences of assault occasioning actual bodily harm to his eight-month-old baby. His wife made a witness statement which was prejudicial to him. She was called as a prosecution witness at his trial, but during her evidence in-chief she gave answers inconsistent with her statement. The judge granted a prosecution application to treat her as hostile, and she was cross-examined on her witness statement. The appellant was convicted.

PETER PAIN J, reading the judgment of the court: 'Up to the point where she goes into the witness box, the wife has a choice: she may refuse to give evidence or waive her right of refusal. The waiver is effective only if made with full knowledge of her right to refuse. If she waives her right of refusal, she becomes an ordinary witness. She is by analogy in the same position as a witness who waives privilege, which would entitle him to refuse to answer questions on a certain topic.

In our view, in these circumstances, once the wife has started upon her evidence, she must complete it. It is not open to her to retreat behind the barrier of non-compellability if she is asked questions that she does not wish to answer. Justice should not allow her to give evidence which might assist, or injure, her husband and then to escape from normal investigation.

It follows that if the nature of her evidence justifies it, an application may be made to treat her as a hostile witness. There is, in our view, no objection in law which will preclude a judge from giving leave to treat as hostile a wife who chooses to give evidence for the prosecution of her husband. We have not been able to find any direct authority upon this point. This makes it particularly important that the wife should understand when she takes the oath that she is waiving her right to refuse to give evidence. It points to the wisdom of the words of Darling J in *R* v *Acaster* (1912) 7 Cr App R 187 when he said, at p. 189:

> The only suggestion made for the appellant is founded on a passage which occurred in the argument in *Leach's* case [(1912) 7 Cr App R 187] in the House of Lords, where the Solicitor-General asked whether it was suggested that the prosecution, when a wife came to give evidence, should raise the question whether she knew she could refuse to give evidence, and Lord Atkinson said it was for the witness to take the point and the Lord Chancellor added "Or for the judge". Speaking for myself, and I think for the other members of the court, in consequence of these observations I shall, when the wife—in any case where she is not a compellable witness—comes to give evidence against her husband, ask her: 'Do you know you may object to give evidence?' and I shall also do so if she is called on behalf of her husband. That I imagine, is what other judges will do for the present, though there is no decision which binds us to do it, and the point is open to argument on an appeal to this court. So far none of us here remember to have ever done it, nor did it occur to us before that it was necessary.

That decision is now 70 years old and we cannot say that Darling J's counsel of prudence has become a rule of law. Nor do we seek to lay down any rule of practice for the future. This is an unusual case and we are reluctant to make it the basis for any general rule. Nonetheless, this case does illustrate very powerfully why it is necessary for the trial judge to make certain that the wife understands her position before she takes the oath. Had that been done here, there would have been no difficulty.

It seems to us to be desirable that where a wife is called as a witness for the prosecution of her husband, the judge should explain to her in the absence of the jury, that before she takes the oath she has the right to refuse to give evidence, but that if she chooses to give evidence she may be treated like any other witness.'

Appeal allowed.

Conviction quashed. (Note that this case was decided before the Police and Criminal Evidence Act 1984 came into operation.)

R v *Naudeer* (1985) 80 Cr App R 9 (CA)

The appellant was charged with theft. He was a man of previous good character and gave evidence at his trial, but his wife was not called on his behalf. The prosecution commented on that fact in contravention of section 1(b) of the Criminal Evidence Act 1898. The appellant was convicted and appealed on the ground that counsel for the prosecution's adverse comments on the failure of his wife to give evidence suggested that the jury had been deprived of what would probably have been material evidence, and that the trial judge had failed in his summing-up to give any direction or warning which would repair the breach of section 1(b) of the 1898 Act.

PURCHAS LJ, reading the judgment of the court: 'Mrs Drew submitted that the appeal should be dismissed for two reasons: first, that since the passing of the 1898 Act the social background in relation to marriage, and in particular to the privilege to be accorded between a husband and wife, had so changed that the provisions of this section should no longer be grounds for a successful appeal, even in the presence of a blatant breach of those provisions. If we understood Mrs Drew's submissions correctly, she compared the sanctity and stability of marriage in the contemporary social context unfavourably with the state of marriage as it existed at the time of, and immediately prior to, the passing of the 1898 Act; that a relationship which had in earlier times demanded respect and protection no longer merited the privilege accorded to it by section 1 of the 1898 Act.

With every respect to Mrs Drew, we found that this submission was so unimpressive as to require no further consideration in this judgment.

Mrs Drew's second submission was that the jury had the benefit not only of her comments but also of the comments of Mr Finucane, and that, although the learned judge had not made further comment in his summing-up, the case was within a very short compass and that no harm had been done by her comment upon the failure to call the appellant's wife. We are unable to accept this submission.

There have been cases, to which we were referred, where an appropriate summing-up was held adequately to have corrected a breach of section 1(b) of the Criminal Evidence Act 1898. In particular, we were referred to the case of *Dickman* (1910) 5 Cr App R 135, 147. It should, however, be remembered that in that case the impact of the breach of section 1(b) of the Criminal Evidence Act 1898 was peripheral to the other matters raised on the appeal, and the Court was able to say that it was not significant so far as the overall justice of the case was concerned. In this case, however, the breach is clearly central. This is particularly so where the accused is a man of good character, which he has put before the jury, and the question of his *bona fides* is central to the offence itself. Moreover, of course, for reasons which he has given and with which we sympathise, the learned assistant recorder took the course, albeit in our view wrongly, of not taking any steps to correct the error in his summing-up to the jury. With respect to his reasoning, he overlooks the reality of the position of leaving the jury, faced with two conflicting submissions about the failure to call the appellant's wife, made in an adversarial manner by opposing counsel, to choose between the two without any assistance from the judge. Particularly in situations of this kind the jury look to assistance from the judge and normally pay very great attention to it.

In this respect the authorities provide that if a judge in the exercise of his discretion decides to comment upon the failure of the accused to call his spouse or to give evidence himself he must, except in exceptional circumstances, do this with a great deal of circumspection. We were referred to a judgment of this Court in the case of *Mitchell* (unreported July 1, 1983) which, although not directly in point with the issue in this case, did review the exercise of the judge's discretion to comment. It is not necessary to refer in detail to that judgment or to the references to *Sparrow* (1973) 57 Cr App R 352, and *Mutch*

(1973) 57 Cr App R 196, which form the basis of the approach to the classic direction taken from the judgment of Lord Parker CJ in *Bathurst* (1968) 52 Cr App R 251; [1968] 2 QB 99. It is undesirable that we should lay down any general principles as to when the trial judge in the exercise of his discretion should make stronger comment than that indicated in *Bathurst (supra)*, but each case must depend upon its own circumstances. In the case of *Mitchell (supra)* a violent attack was made upon the investigating police officers, without the success of which the appellant had no defence at all. In those circumstances the Court held that the judge could not have been criticised for commenting in strong terms about the subsequent failure of the accused to give evidence himself in support of his allegations. The mere statement of these facts shows how very different the facts of *Mitchell* are from the instant case. We are very far from agreeing that this is a case which would call for anything other than the normal comment approved in the classic dictum in *Bathurst (supra)*. The fact remains that the learned assistant recorder gave no directions at all and the jury were left without any assistance in the presence of a confusing and difficult dichotomy originated by a breach of the statutory provisions of the Criminal Evidence Act 1898 on the part of the prosecuting counsel, and followed by an attempt to rescue the situation by defending counsel in speech. This gave rise to a position which was wholly unsatisfactory.'

Appeal allowed.

Conviction quashed. (Note that this case was decided before the Police and Criminal Evidence Act 1984 came into operation.)

C: CHILDREN OF TENDER YEARS AND PERSONS OF DEFECTIVE INTELLECT

(Suggested preliminary reading: *A Practical Approach to Evidence,* pp. 348–351).

Children and Young Persons Act 1933

38(1) Where, in any proceedings against any person for any offence, any child of tender years called as a witness does not in the opinion of the court understand the nature of an oath, his evidence may be received, though not given upon oath, if, in the opinion of the court, he is possessed of sufficient intelligence to justify the reception of the evidence, and understands the duty of speaking the truth . . .

(As to the requirement for corroboration of evidence admitted under this section, see p. 455 post.)

R v *Hayes* [1977] 1 WLR 234 (CA)

The defendant was charged with inciting three young boys to commit acts of gross indecency, and with committing an act of gross indecency with one of the boys. He denied that he was the man involved. At the time of the trial the boys were aged 12, 11 and 9. The youngest boy was permitted to give unsworn evidence. The judge, after questioning the older boys, allowed the oath to be administered to them although the eldest had said that he was ignorant of the existence of God but he did understand the importance of telling the truth, particularly on that occasion. The defendant was convicted. He applied for leave to appeal on the ground that, in the light of the boys' answers to his questions, the judge had exercised his discretion wrongly in permitting them to be sworn.

BRIDGE LJ, giving the judgment of the court: 'It is unrealistic not to recognise that, in the present state of society, amongst the adult population the divine sanction of an oath is probably not generally recognised. The important consideration, we think, when a judge has to decide whether a child should properly be sworn, is whether the child has a sufficient appreciation of the solemnity of the occasion and the added responsibility to tell the truth, which is involved in taking an oath, over and above the duty to tell the truth which is an ordinary duty of normal social conduct.

Against the background of those general considerations of principle, we think it right also to approach the matter on the footing that this is very much a matter within the discretion of the trial judge and we think that this court, although having jurisdiction to interfere if clearly satisfied that the trial judge's discretion was wrongly exercised, should hesitate long before doing so. The judge sees and hears the boy or girl, which means very much more than the bare written word, and it may easily be that the judge comes to the conclusion that the way in which he has initially been phrasing his questions has been such that the child to whom the questions are directed has not sufficiently understood them, and he may then attempt to phrase his questions in a different way.'

Application refused.

• Is there any difference between the test of competence laid down in this case and that under s. 38(1) of the Children and Young Persons Act 1933?

R v Khan (1981) 73 Cr App R 190 (CA)

The appellant was charged with living wholly or in part on the earnings of prostitution of a girl, aged 11. At his trial the girl was called to give evidence for the prosecution. Without previous inquiry by the trial judge the girl, then aged 12, was sworn and gave evidence. The judge warned the jury of the danger of convicting the appellant on the uncorroborated evidence of the girl, but they returned a verdict of guilty. The appellant appealed.

KILNER BROWN J, giving the judgment of the court: 'This was a sexual case. If the evidence given by this young girl was unsworn evidence then it required corroboration and there was none and there could have been no conviction. Some argument has been developed as to the meaning of the words "tender years". The Court is informed, and has no reason to disagree, that there is no direct authority upon that question. This is understandable because it seems to this Court that what is meant by "tender years" may very well differ according to the type of child who is about to give evidence but, as a general working rule, it is the experience of all three members of this Court that for a proffered witness who is under the age of 14 the precaution which has been well established becomes necessary. The matter is made crystal clear, as one may most respectfully say is only to be expected by Lord Goddard CJ in *Reynolds* (1950) 34 Cr App R 60; [1950] 1 KB 606. Although that particular case turned on a slightly different point, the Lord Chief Justice was making it quite plain that where there is a child of tender years there is an obligation upon the judge in the first place to make inquiries of that child as to its understanding of the nature of an oath, and, secondly, that inquiry has to be done—

and other authorities make it quite plain—in the presence of and in the hearing of the jury.

The most recent authority to which reference was made was that of *Hayes* (1977) 64 Cr App R 194; [1977] 2 All ER 288. There the Court of Appeal Criminal Division had to deal with the manner in which the trial judge dealt with the question which he correctly, as the Court of Appeal said, had to put to the proffered witness in the hearing of the jury. If it is authority for anything, it is authority for two propositions. One is that there the Court upheld the necessity for investigation in the case of a child of 12 and, secondly, that it does not necessarily follow that ignorance of the Deity or the existence of the Deity is necessarily fatal to the ability of that child to understand the nature of an oath. It is unnecessary to apportion blame in this instant case. It is one of those most unfortunate cases where everybody seems to have overlooked the fact that it was necessary for this judge to put questions to this witness when she came to the witness box as to the understanding by her of the nature of an oath; nothing was done. We could wish that clerks to the court would follow the old established practice that the officer in the court reminds the judge of the witness's age.'

Appeal allowed. Conviction quashed.

R v Bellamy (1986) 82 Cr App R 222 (CA)

The complainant in a rape trial being mentally handicapped, the trial judge investigated her competence as a witness. He heard evidence from the complainant's social worker and questioned the complainant both about her belief in and knowledge of God and about her understanding of the importance of telling the truth. He decided that she was a competent witness but lacked a sufficient belief in the existence of God to take a binding oath. Accordingly, he required her to affirm. The appellant was convicted of rape and appealed on the ground that the complainant ought to have been required to take the oath.

SIMON BROWN J, giving the judgment of the court: 'The basis of the appeal is that the learned judge was not entitled and had no power in those circumstances to cause the complainant to affirm. And it is said that the fact that the main evidence in the trial (that from the complainant) was given in this unauthorised way goes to the heart of the trial and vitiates the conviction.

As it seems to this Court, the learned judge, although clearly right to investigate whether or not the complainant was a competent witness in so far as having a sufficient understanding of the nature of the proceedings was concerned, ought not to have embarked upon a detailed examination of her theological appreciation.

Applying section 5 of the Oaths Act 1978, given that the judge concluded as he did that the complainant was a competent witness and given that she did not object to being sworn, it is our opinion that he should simply have allowed her to be sworn. Even however, if one took a different view as to that and concluded that the learned judge was entitled also to examine the complainant upon the extent of her belief in God, recent authorities regarding the proper application of section 38(1) of the Children and Young Persons Act 1933 indicate clearly that it is no longer necessary that a witness should have awareness of the divine sanction of the oath in order that that witness may properly be sworn.

This is made abundantly clear by consideration of two decisions of this Court: *Hayes* (1977) 64 Cr App R 194; [1977] 2 All ER 288 and *Campbell* [1983] Crim LR 174. I cite just a short paragraph from each case.

The position in *Hayes* was that two children, respectively aged 12 and 11, had been sworn in a case of gross indecency. They had been examined and had in fact denied having heard of God. The judgment of the Court was given by Bridge LJ (as he then was) in these terms at p. 196 and p. 290 of the respective reports. "If the series of questions and answers started with the question 'Do you think there is a God?' and the answer 'Yes' there would really be no substance in Mr Charlesworth's complaints, but the fact that the earlier questions and answers, on their face, reveal the boy declaring that he is wholly ignorant of the existence of God does lend some force to the submission that if the essence of the sanction of the oath is a divine sanction, and if it is an awareness of that divine sanction which the Court is looking for in a child of tender years, then here was a case where, on the face of it, that awareness was absent. The Court is not convinced that that is really the essence of the Court's duty in the difficult situation where the Court has to determine whether a young person can or cannot properly be permitted to take an oath before giving evidence. It is unrealistic not to recognise that, in the present state of society, amongst the adult population the divine sanction of an oath is probably not generally recognised. The important consideration, we think, when a judge has to decide whether a child should properly be sworn, is whether the child has a sufficient appreciation of the solemnity of the occasion, and the added responsibility to tell the truth, which is involved in taking an oath, over and above the duty to tell the truth which is an ordinary duty of normal social conduct."

Applying that passage in *Campbell*, May LJ, giving the judgment of the Court, said this: "The two principles to be followed when considering whether a child should properly be sworn set out in *Hayes (supra)* were: that the child had a sufficient appreciation of the seriousness of the occasion and a realisation that taking the oath involved something more than the duty to tell the truth in ordinary day to day life".

That this complainant had such a realisation is evident and was clearly found by the learned judge, he having noted her evidence that she realised that if she told a lie in the particular circumstances in which she was to give her evidence, then she could "be put away".

Those cases of course were concerned with the statute governing the position of children of tender years. *A fortiori* they would apply where, in regard to adult persons such as this complainant, there is no ruling statutory provision.'

Appeal dismissed.

Questions for discussion

R v Coke; R v Littleton

1 In what circumstances might Coke and Littleton be competent witnesses (a) for the prosecution; (b) in their own defence; (c) for each other? Would they be compellable in any such case?

2 In what circumstances may Mrs Littleton be a competent witness (a) for the prosecution; (b) for her husband; (c) for Coke? Will she be compellable in any such case?

3 How should the competence of Angela Blackstone as a witness be determined? What options are open to the court with regard to her evidence, and what are their advantages or disadvantages to the prosecution and defence respectively?

4 Should a spouse be (a) a competent and (b) a compellable prosecution witness against the other spouse? Does your answer vary with the nature of the case? What questions of policy are involved?

5 Suppose that at the trial Coke elects not to give evidence in his defence and is subsequently convicted. Coke now complains to the Court of Appeal of the following passage in the summing-up of the trial judge to the jury: 'Members of the jury, so far as the defendant Coke is concerned, it cannot have escaped you that he was conspicuously absent from the witness box. You may have thought, in view of the matters put to the complainant Margaret Blackstone on Coke's behalf in cross-examination, that he would have been anxious to provide you with some evidence of his side of the case. But there has been none. What you make of that is entirely a matter for you. But you may think it not without significance, as prosecuting counsel observed to you in his closing speech, that Coke has chosen to avoid the risk of cross-examination on the detail of his story.'

Has the trial judge misdirected the jury?

Additional question

Anthony and David are charged with indecent assault on Belinda, a girl of seven; the prosecution wish to call Belinda herself, and a witness, Celia, a woman in her 20's, who is thought to be mentally retarded. Anthony has throughout denied having any part in the offence, but David has made a confession which implicates Anthony. Discuss what steps can be taken by the prosecution to call these witnesses, and what factors the judge will take into account in deciding whether to admit their evidence.

Further reading

Gooderson, 'The evidence of co-prisoners' [1953] 1! CLJ 279.

12   Examination-in-Chief

A: REFRESHING THE MEMORY

(Suggested preliminary reading: *A Practical Approach to Evidence*, pp. 357–364.)

R v Richardson [1971] 2 QB 484 (CA)

Before the trial of the defendant on two charges of burglary and attempted burglary relating to offences which had taken place about 18 months earlier, four prosecution witnesses were shown the statements which they had made to the police a few weeks after the offences. Two of those witnesses had positively identified the defendant, and identification was the sole issue at the trial. The defence submitted that the evidence of all four witnesses was, in the circumstances, inadmissible. The trial judge rejected those submissions. The defendant was convicted and appealed.

SACHS LJ, giving the judgment of the court: '. . . it is, . . . necessary to consider what should be the general approach of the court to there being shown in this way to witnesses their statements—which were not "contemporaneous" within the meaning of that word as normally applied to documents used to refresh memory.

First, it is to be observed that it is the practice of the courts not to allow a witness to refresh his memory in the witness box by reference to written statements unless made contemporaneously. Secondly, it has been recognised in a circular issued in April 1969 with the approval of the Lord Chief Justice and the judges of the Queen's Bench Division (the repositories of the common law) that witnesses for the prosecution in criminal cases are normally (though not in all circumstances) entitled, if they so request, to copies of any statements taken from them by police officers. Thirdly, it is to be noted that witnesses for the defence are normally, as is known to be the practice, allowed to have copies of their statements and to refresh their memories from them at any time up to the moment when they go into the witness box—indeed, Mr Sedgemore was careful not to submit that there was anything wrong about that. Fourthly, no one has ever suggested that in civil proceedings witnesses may not see their statements up to the time when they go into the witness box. One has only to think for a moment of witnesses going into the box to deal with accidents which took place five or six years previously to conclude that it would be highly unreasonable if they were not allowed to see them.

Is there, then, anything wrong in the witnesses in this case having been offered an opportunity to see that which they were entitled to ask for and to be shown on request? In a case such as the present, is justice more likely to be done if a witness may not see a statement made by him at a time very much closer to that of the incident?

Curiously enough, these questions are very bare of authority. Indeed, the only case which has a direct bearing on this issue is one which was decided not in this country but on appeal in the Supreme Court of Hong Kong in 1966: *Lau Pak Ngam* v *The Queen* [1966] Crim LR 443. In the view of each member of this court this case contains some sage observations, two of which are apt to be quoted. One of them is:

Testimony in the witness box becomes more a test of memory than of truthfulness if witnesses are deprived of the opportunity of checking their recollection beforehand by reference to statements or notes made at a time closer to the events in question.

The other is:

Refusal of access to statements would tend to create difficulties for honest witnesses but be likely to do little to hamper dishonest witnesses.

With those views this court agrees. It is true that by the practice of the courts of this country a line is drawn at the moment when a witness enters the witness box; when giving evidence there in chief he cannot refresh his memory except by a document which, to quote the words of *Phipson on Evidence*, 11th ed (1970), p. 634, para 1528: "must have been written either at the time of the transaction or so shortly afterwards that the facts were fresh in his memory." (Incidentally, this definition does provide a measure of elasticity and should not be taken to confine witnesses to an over-short period.) This is, moreover, a practice which the courts can enforce: when a witness is in the box the court can see that he complies with it.

The courts, however, must take care not to deprive themselves by new, artificial rules of practice of the best chances of learning the truth. The courts are under no compulsion unnecessarily to follow on a matter of practice the lure of the rules of logic in order to produce unreasonable results which would hinder the course of justice. Obviously it would be wrong if several witnesses were handed statements in circumstances which enabled one to compare with another what each had said. But there can be no general rule (which, incidentally, would be unenforceable, unlike the rule as to what can be done in the witness box) that witnesses may not before trial see the statements which they made at some period reasonably close to the time of the event which is the subject of the trial. Indeed, one can imagine many cases, particularly those of a complex nature, where such a rule would militate very greatly against the interests of justice.

On the basis of this general approach, this court now returns to the facts of the present case. There had been great delay in the matter coming before the court and it appears to this court that nothing unreasonable was done in the particular circumstances.'

Appeal dismissed.

R v Westwell [1976] 2 All ER 812 (CA)

The appellant was charged with assault occasioning actual bodily harm. Before the trial, which took place 11 months after the fight which was the subject of the charge, certain prosecution witnesses asked if they could see their written statements and they were allowed to do so. The prosecution did not inform the defence that this had been done, but the fact that it had become known to the defence, who submitted that in consequence the jury ought to be directed to acquit. The judge refused and the appellant was convicted. He appealed.

BRIDGE LJ, delivering the judgment of the court: 'There is no general rule that prospective witnesses may not, before giving evidence at a trial, see the statements which they made at or near the time of the events of which they are to testify. They may see them whether they make a request to do so or merely accept an offer to allow them to do so. On the other hand, there is no rule that witnesses must be allowed to see their statements before giving evidence. There may be cases where there is reason to suppose that the witness has some sinister or improper purpose in wanting to see his statement and it is in the interests of justice that he should be denied the opportunity. Examples are suggested in the Home Office circular and in the judgment of this court in *R v Richardson* [1971] 2 QB 484. However, in most cases and particularly where, as often happens, there is a long interval between the alleged offence and the trial, the interests of justice are likely to be best served and witnesses will be more fairly treated if, before giving evidence, they are allowed to refresh their recollection by reference to their own statements made near the time of the events in question. As was said by the Supreme Court of Hong Kong in 1966 [in *Lau Pak Ngam* v *The Queen* [1966] Crim LR 443] in passages quoted with approval by this court in *R v Richardson*, if a witness is deprived of this opportunity his testimony in the witness box becomes more a test of memory than truthfulness; and refusal of access to statements would tend to create difficulties for honest witnesses but would be likely to do little to hamper dishonest witnesses. We have all, from time to time, seen the plight of an apparently honest witness, subjected to captious questioning about minor differences between his evidence in the witness box and the statement he made long ago and has never seen since, although his tormentor has it in his hand and has studied it in detail. Although such cross-examination frequently generates in the jury obvious sympathy with the witness and obvious irritation with the cross-examiner, it must leave a witness who has come to court to do his honest best with a smarting sense of having been treated unfairly.

Neither in the approved statement in the Home Office circular, nor in the judgment of the court in *R v Richardson*, is it laid down that the Crown must inform the defence that a prosecution witness has been allowed to look at his written statement before giving evidence. In *R v Richardson* the defence first discovered the fact for themselves in the course of cross-examination of a prosecution witness. The court made no criticism of the Crown on that account, nor was it invited to do so. Moreover, the decision of the trial judge, refusing to allow previous witnesses to be recalled for cross-examination about their statements, was upheld because in the particular facts of that case no prejudice was thereby caused to the defence.

Since hearing the argument in this appeal, our attention has been called to the decision of the Divisional Court in *Worley v Bentley* [1976] 2 All ER 449 in which the same point arose. The court held that it was desirable but not essential that the defence should be informed that witnesses have seen their statements. We agree. In some cases the fact that a witness has read his statement before going into the witness box may be relevant to the weight which can properly be attached to his evidence and injustice might be caused to the defendant if the jury were left in ignorance of that fact.

Accordingly, if the prosecution is aware that statements have been seen by witnesses it will be appropriate to inform the defence. But if, for any reason, this is not done, the omission cannot of itself be a ground for acquittal. If the prosecution tell the defence that the witness has been allowed to see his statement the defence can make such use of the information as it thinks prudent, but in any event the defence, where such a fact may be material, can ask the witness directly when giving evidence whether the witness has recently seen his statement. Where such information is material it does not ultimately matter whether it is volunteered by the prosecution or elicited by the defence. If the mere fact that the prosecution had not volunteered the information were a bar to conviction, this would be an artificial and arbitrary rule more appropriate to a game or a sporting contest than to a judicial process. The question for the court is whether, in the event, the trial can be continued without prejudice or risk of injustice to the defendant.

In the present case the defence knew, before the prosecution case was concluded, that the witnesses had seen their statements. The defence could have applied to recall the witnesses if they thought cross-examination about the statements worthwhile. They could have made whatever points they wished to make with the jury about the weight to be attached to the prosecution evidence.'

Appeal dismissed.

Burrough v *Martin* (1809) 2 Camp 111 (KB)

In an action on a charter-party, a witness was called to give an account of the voyage, and the logbook was laid before him for the purpose of refreshing his memory. Being asked whether he had written it himself, he said that he had not, but that from time to time he examined the entries in it while the events recorded were fresh in his recollection, and that he always found the entries accurate.

The Attorney-General contended that the witness could make no use of the logbook during his examination, notwithstanding his former inspection of it; and that the only case where a witness could refer to a written paper for the purpose of giving evidence, was where he had actually written it himself and had thus the surest means of knowing the truth of its contents.

LORD ELLENBOROUGH: 'If the witness looked at the logbook from time to time, while the occurrences mentioned in it were recent and fresh in his recollection, it is as good as if he had written the whole with his own hand. This collation gave him an ample opportunity to ascertain the correctness of the entries; and he may therefore refer to these on the same principles that witnesses are allowed to refresh their memory by reading letters and other documents which they themselves have written.'

R v *Langton* (1876) 2 QBD 296 (CCR)

The defendant was a timekeeper, and C a pay clerk in the employment of a colliery company. It was the duty of the defendant every fortnight to give a list of the days worked by the workmen to a clerk who entered the days and the wages due in respect of them in a time book. At pay time it was the duty of the defendant to read out from the time book the number of days worked by each workman to C, who paid the wages accordingly. C saw the entries in the time book while the defendant was reading them out. The defendant was convicted of obtaining money by false pretences from the company. The question was whether C should have been permitted to refresh his memory from the time book.

LORD COCKBURN CJ: 'With regard to the first point, the propriety of allowing the witness to refresh his memory by means of the time book, I think he was rightly allowed to do so. If the witness had only seen the entries in the absence of the prisoner, the case might be different. There would then be obvious dangers in admitting such a use of the book, which do not exist in the present case. Here the entries were read aloud by the prisoner himself, and seen by the witness at the time of reading, and he made payments in accordance with them.'

(LORD COLERIDGE CJ, CLEASBY B, POLLOCK B, and FIELD J concurred.)
Conviction affirmed.

R v *Cheng* (1976) 63 Cr App R 20 (CA)

Police officers kept observation on a number of men, including the defendant, who were suspected of peddling heroin. The defendant was later charged with unlawfully supplying a preparation of a dangerous drug, and at his trial one of the officers who had kept observation was called as a prosecution witness. He no longer had the relevant notebook and sought to refresh his memory from a statement he had prepared from his notebook and used at the committal proceedings. The defence objected to the use of the statement because it did not contain the notes about the other men who had been under surveillance and was thus a partial not an exact copy of the notebook. The trial judge ruled that the officer could refer to his statement and the defendant was convicted. He appealed.

LAWTON LJ, giving the judgment of the court: 'The sole question in this case has been whether the judge acted properly and in accordance with law in allowing Constable Moore to refresh his memory from the statement.

Mr Wright, on behalf of the Crown, has reminded the Court that in *Richardson* (1971) 55 Cr App R 244; [1971] 2 QB 484 Sachs LJ, giving the judgment of the Court said this at pp. 251 and 490: "The Courts, however, must take care not to deprive themselves by new, artificial rules of practice of the best chances of learning the truth. The Courts are under no compulsion unnecessarily to follow the lure of the rules of logic in order to produce results on a matter of practice which are unreasonable and would hinder the course of justice."

It is because of that approach by this Court as recently as 1971, that we have felt it necessary to find out how the rules about refreshing memory developed. As far as the researches of counsel go (and their researches seem to be supported by textbooks), the first reported case in which the problem of what documents a witness could use to refresh his memory was discussed was *Doe d Church and Phillips v Perkins* (1790) 3 Term Rep 749. It is clear from the facts of that case that up to that time there had been no certain rule about what witnesses could look at when giving evidence for the purpose of making a deposition. The witness whose evidence was under consideration in that case had been allowed to refer to a document which had been substantially prepared by her solicitor. Lord Kenyon CJ ruled that this was irregular.

In the 60 years which followed, the problem of what witnesses could look at to refresh their memories came before the Courts in a number of cases. It is manifest that as the years went by the Courts came to the conclusion that too strict a rule was not in the interests of justice. It is not necessary for us to deal with each of the cases which were considered in the 60 odd years after the decision in *Doe d Church and Phillips v Perkins (supra)*. It suffices to refer to two.

In *Burton v Plummer* (1834) 2 A & E 341, the question before the Court was whether a witness could look at a copy of an original note which he had made. The Court adjudged that he could; but he had to be able to say that the copy was an accurate copy of the original note.

It was almost inevitable after that case that some lawyer would raise the question as to what was an accurate copy. That very problem was considered by the House of Lords in *Horne v MacKenzie* (1839) 6 Cl & Fin 628. The point arose in this way: I read from the headnote: "A, a surveyor, made a survey or report, which he furnished to his employers:

being afterwards called as a witness, he produced a printed copy of this report, on the margin of which he had, two days before, to assist him in giving his explanations as a witness, made a few jottings. The report had been made up from his original notes, of which it was in substance, though not in words, a transcript . . ." In other words, as appears clear when one looks at the details of the case what he was looking at in the witness box was not strictly a copy at all of his original note. He was allowed to refresh his memory from it and the House of Lords seems to have taken the view, albeit *obiter*, that there was nothing wrong in his doing so.

The judgment of the House was delivered by Lord Cottenham: he said at p. 645: "If your Lordships think that there should be a new trial on this ground, it will be unnecessary to give any decision on the question of evidence. But I may say that in my opinion the witness was, under the circumstances of this case, entitled to refer to the paper to refresh his memory."

In our judgment that opinion of the Lord Chancellor resolves this case. What the police constable was doing in this case was what the surveyor had done in that case. He had transcribed that part of his note which he thought was relevant. We can see nothing wrong in that. Indeed if we had felt bound to say that it was wrong for him to refresh his memory from his statement, we would have brought about an absurdity, because it is now established by *Richardson (supra)* to which I have already referred that a witness can see his original statement outside court. If he could read it right up to the court door and learn it off by heart, but was forbidden in the witness box to look at it at all, this would be a triumph of legalism over common sense.

What seems to us to be the position is this. If the statement in this case, or any other transcription of notes in other cases, is substantially what is in the notes and there is evidence to that effect, then the judge should allow the witness to refresh his memory from the statement or transcription as the case may be. But if, after investigation, it turns out that the statement or transcription bears little relation to the original note, then a different situation arises. The judge in the exercise of his discretion would be entitled to refuse to allow a witness to refresh his memory from such an imperfect source of information.'

Appeal dismissed.

Attorney-General's Reference (No. 3 of 1979) (1979) 69 Cr App R 411 (CA)

(For facts, see below)

LORD WIDGERY CJ, giving the judgment of the court: 'The reference is in these terms. The point of law is in three parts: "(a) Whether a police officer who has taken brief jottings in the course of interviewing an accused person, and within a short time thereafter made a full note in his notebook incorporating not only those brief jottings, but expanding thereon from his then recollection should be permitted to refresh his memory from that notebook at the accused person's subsequent trial.

(b) Whether in the aforementioned circumstances the police officer is bound to retain the original jottings and disclose their existence to the court of trial.

(c) Whether in the above circumstances it is the duty of the prosecution in such circumstances to make available to the court of trial and the defence copies of the police officer's original brief jottings."

The reference then goes on to deal with the facts upon which the matter was determined. "The accused were charged together with another man on two counts of criminal deception by representing to the complainant that work of a particular value either would be or had been effectively done to the plumbing and loft of his home. In the event, the complainant proved to be a senile witness and the Crown relied upon answers given by the defendants to the police. The first police officer to give evidence to the court disclosed that he had kept brief jottings of questions and/or answers during the course of the interviews with the defendants and that within a period of about two hours had compiled his notebook with the assistance of the brief jottings, his own and his fellow interviewing officer's recollections. The notebook was in question and answer form and included the brief jottings originally taken, but were expanded by reason of the recollections then present in the minds of the police officers."

Evidently what happened was, the police officer took brief notes while interrogating the witness, with a view no doubt to getting over the interrogation more quickly than if he were taking full notes at the time. The interview with the witness was concluded. He made up what counsel submitted and properly described as "the note", that being a full note of the questions and answers covered by the interrogation drawn from the jottings and drawn from the note of the other police officer, whose note was made up in the same way.

The trial came up six months later. We need not turn to deal with the trial at all. All we need say about the trial is that at the appropriate time the trial judge was asked to rule on the right of the police officers to refresh their memories from the full note contained in the way I have described. In the trial within a trial the judge was looking at the notebooks having their contents shown to him, and was deciding whether the police officers could refresh their memories from these books. He took the view in the case of the officer who had not made jottings at all, that he could produce his notebook in the ordinary way. But the officer who made the jottings had the ruling against him that only the jottings should be put in evidence and anything he wished to make up additionally was not produced to the jury. The result was bizarre in the extreme, because the officer who merely made an ordinary note had his note taken and the officer who had the two-stage note, as it were, jottings first and then the note, was excluded from everything but the jottings. It was of course meaningless and resulted in insufficient evidence to support a conviction.

Why the learned judge took this attitude, we confess we do not know. Looking at paragraph 515 of *Archbold* (40th ed), a book available to all the judges, one finds this: "The rule may be stated as follows: a witness may refresh his memory by reference to any writing made or verified by himself concerning and contemporaneously with, the facts to which he testifies. 'Contemporaneously' is a somewhat misleading word in the context of the memory refreshing rule. It is sufficient, for the purposes of the rule, if the writing was made or verified at a time when the facts were still fresh in the witness' memory." That, in our view, is the correct rule.

The learned judge unfortunately did not take that course. He made a ruling after long argument and his ruling is in these terms:

The test it seems is one of whether or not the record is contemporaneous. There is no authority that Mr Elfer can produce to me, save the principle of that requirement in *Archbold* and implicitly in *Cheng* (1976) 63 Cr App R 20 to which I will refer in a moment, to suggest that the note to which the officer should refer, or anybody else come to that, should be the first note that he has made, which is the principle which I have adopted throughout my practice. If someone has a note of something which happened, which he made at the time, that is the note to which he should refer. If he later copies it exactly other questions may arise. They do not arise in this case. If another document is produced which includes the whole of that note as it was recorded at the first time, again it might be that he could refer to the second transcript, but that does not arise in this case. What this case is about and what I have to decide is whether he can refer to an enlarged note made as the evidence at this moment, using the first jottings in this book, exhibit 46 . . .

I do not find it necessary to go any further than that. We find it a matter of regret that an experienced judge, equipped, one assumes, with the text book *Archbold Criminal Pleading Evidence and Practice* does not look up the paragraph in which the problem is explained. It seems to us very difficult to know how the judge could find it possible to rely on some rule of thumb, such as the first statement produced, when the right rule, as *Archbold* says, is any statement which is made at the time when the witness's memory is clear. That is the rule and that is the end of this reference.

As a side issue one might bear in mind that the judge says it has always been the practice to make the normal note, if I may so describe it, available to the defence on cross-examination. So one must make a two-stage note. Counsel for the defence is entitled to examine the police officer's notebook to see whether his entries are consistent with his evidence or not. That is exactly the same thing as saying whether the note has been made in two stages rather than one. That is only a subsidiary point.'

R v Kelsey (1982) 74 Cr App R 213 (CA)

The appellant was convicted of offences of burglary and appealed against his conviction on the ground that a witness called for the Crown was wrongly permitted to refresh his memory about a car's registration number by reference to a note made at his, the witnesses, dictation by a police officer and verified orally but not visually as accurate at the time by the witness. The officer in question had given evidence to prove that the note he produced was the one the witness saw him making and heard him read back.

TAYLOR J, reading the judgment of the court: 'The one ground of appeal against conviction is that Hill should not have been allowed to refer to the officer's note. Mr Purnell argues that a witness can only refresh his memory from a note he has made himself or (and here he uses the words of Winn J in *Mills and Rose* (1962) 46 Cr App R 336, 342; [1962] 1 WLR 1152, 1156): "from a note made by some other person which he has contemporaneously, in the sense of within a short time, himself seen, read and adopted as accurate." Mr Purnell asserts it is essential the witness should read the note himself; it is not enough that it should be made in his presence and read over to him.

In *Mills and Rose (supra)* a constable had heard and tape-recorded a conversation between the defendants in the cells. He was allowed to refresh his memory of what they said by reference to a note he made from the tape recording shortly after the event. That procedure was approved on appeal. The Court did not have to decide when A may be allowed to refresh his memory from a note made by B. The *ratio* was simply that A may refresh his memory from a tape recording or from a note he has made from a tape recording. The passage from the judgment of Winn J cited above was therefore *obiter*.

Shortly after that passage, Winn J said (at p. 342 and p. 1156 respectively):

In this case the constable set a machine to perform the functions which otherwise would have been performed by a pen or pencil in his own hand, and used the record produced by that piece of mechanism, which he was employing as his tool, in order to refresh his memory when he was giving evidence. If that be not precisely the right way to look at the matter, though the court thinks it is, an alternative approach is this: that the machine, albeit inanimate, was set by the constable to perform the function of making a record and very soon after the conversations had taken place the constable adopted as accurate the record which that machine had made, and thereupon it became his own record.

So, despite the earlier words of Winn J, upon which Mr Purnell relies, in that very case the officer was verifying the "note" or record on the tape recording by hearing it played back rather than by having "seen, read and adopted it". If the officer in that case had simply played the tape back to satisfy himself, when his recollection was fresh, that it had accurately and wholly recorded what occurred and had not gone on to make a written note therefrom, there can surely be no doubt that he could at the trial have been allowed to refresh his memory by playing the tape again. If that be so, the situation was very similar to the present case. Here Hill dictated the number, not to a machine, but to an officer who recorded it. That officer then "played back", not mechanically but orally, what he had recorded. Hill heard it and satisfied himself the officer had got it right. Providing the officer testified at the trial, as he did, that this was the note which was dictated by Hill and read back to him, the Crown argue that Hill could refresh his memory from it.

We were referred to two more cases. In *Jones* v *Metcalfe* [1967] 3 All ER 205, an eye-witness to an accident mentally noted a lorry's registration number and reported it to the police. On the strength of this information the police interviewed the defendant, who admitted driving a lorry bearing that number. The eye-witness could not at the trial recall the number. There was no document made either by him or the police. It was held, on appeal, that there had been no evidence to prove the identity of the lorry at the scene. Lord Parker CJ referred in his judgment to *Grew* v *Cubitt* (1951) 49 LGR 650, in which an eye witness had got his wife to write down a vehicle number and a police interview with the defendant followed. Lord Parker said, at p. 207F: "In that case it is to be observed that the prosecution case could have been proved in one of two ways; they could have called the wife who wrote the number down; equally they could have asked the independent witness whether he had seen his wife write the number down and if so, on production of the note, he could have refreshed his memory and stated what the number was."

Diplock LJ, at p. 208C, said of the *Jones'* case *(supra)*: "If when the independent witness gave the number of the lorry to the policeman, the policeman had written it down in his presence, the policeman's note could have been shown to the independent witness and he could have used it, not to tell the magistrates what he told the policeman, but to refresh his memory."

In *McLean* (1968) 52 Cr App R 80, the victim of a robbery dictated something shortly afterwards to C, including a car number which C wrote down. The victim did not see the note; nor, it would appear, was it read over for him to check. There was no evidence as to the car number from the victim; C's evidence of the car number from the note was held on appeal to be hearsay and inadmissible and the conviction was quashed.

Commenting on *McLean's* case, the learned editor of *Phipson on Evidence* (12th ed), at para. 1570, note 11, says: "All that this case decided, however, was that where A called out the number of a motor car to B, who recorded it, B cannot give evidence of the number, A having forgotten it. *Non constat* but that if A had seen B's note and checked its accuracy he could have been allowed to say: 'although I have no recollection of the number, I am confident that that is the number'. In any event it is not easy to see why *McLean (supra)* was decided in the way that it was. If A says 'the number I dictated to B is correct' and B says 'I correctly recorded the number', it is difficult to see how this differs in principle from when A has made the note himself".

The learned author of *Cross on Evidence* (5th ed), at p. 468 said of *McLean (supra)*: "This may with some justice appear to be nothing but pedantry run wild". It is important to stress, however, that in *McLean* the Court was dealing with an attempt to prove a car number, not by allowing the witness who took it to refresh his memory from a note he had dictated, but by the evidence of the scribe who wrote it down. Although logically defensible, this mode of proof might, if permitted, open the doors to allowing a witness' whole account of an incident, which he had dictated to an officer at the time and since forgotten, to be given at the trial by the officer.

That problem has been expressly envisaged by Professor Cross (*op cit* at p. 468) and Professor Smith ([1978] Crim LR 58). However, it does not arise if the note is used simply to enable the original witness to refresh his memory on a point of precision. A witness may refresh his memory as to such a fact or figure which easily escapes or eludes human memory. Thus, for example, a date or time or an address, the exact words of a remark, a car or telephone number, are properly matters upon which a witness is entitled to refresh his memory. They are the precise details which sharpen and point his general evidence, and are to be distinguished from the narrative of events itself which the witness gives from his recollection.

The most recent statement of the rule as to when a witness may refresh his memory from a document is contained in *Attorney-General's Reference (No. 3 of 1979)* (1979) 69 Cr App R 411, where this Court at p. 414 approved a passage in *Archbold* (40th ed), at para. 515, as follows: ". . . a witness may refresh his memory by reference to any writing made or verified by himself concerning and contemporaneously with, the facts to which he testifies. 'Contemporaneously' is a somewhat misleading word in the context of the memory refreshing rule. It is sufficient, for the purpose of the rule, if the writing was made or verified at a time when the facts were still fresh in the witness' memory".

The question we have to decide is, therefore, whether witness A can verify a note he dictates to B only by reading it himself, or whether it is sufficient if the note is read back by B to A at the time for confirmation. In most cases we would expect the note to be read by A if it is made in his presence. But what of the instant case, or cases involving the blind or the illiterate? In our view there is no magic in verifying by seeing as opposed to verifying by hearing. *Mills and Rose (supra)*, the tape recording case, illustrates this, and shows that Winn J's words were somewhat too restrictive. What must be shown is that witness A has verified in the sense of satisfying himself whilst the matters are fresh in his mind, (1) that a record has been made, and (2) that it is accurate. If A makes a "contemporaneous" note himself, or if A reads and adopts at the time a "contemporaneous" note made by B, A may refresh his memory from it without need of another witness. In a case such as the present a second witness will be required. Hill dictated the number, heard it read back and confirmed its accuracy. But although he saw the note being made, he did not read it, so it was necessary for the officer also to be called to prove that the note he produced was the one Hill saw him making and heard him read back. Once that was done, we are of the opinion that Hill could refresh his memory from it. To adopt Professor Smith's phrase [(1978) Crim LR 58) the document was made "under the supervision of" Hill.

We consider the learned judge was right to allow him to refresh his memory as he did.'

Appeal dismissed.

- Does the verification of the note by the witness in *R* v *Kelsey* depend on hearsay?

R v *Bass* [1953] 1 QB 680 (CCA)

The appellant was convicted of shopbreaking and larceny. The only evidence against him was contained in statements amounting to a confession of guilt which he was alleged to have made, before he was charged, during an interrogation by two police officers at a police station. At the trial the officers gave evidence and read their accounts of the interview from their notebooks. As these accounts appeared to be identical, and the officers denied that they had been prepared in collaboration, the defendant asked that the jury should be allowed to inspect the notebooks, but the application was refused.

BYRNE J, delivering the judgment of the court: 'With regard to the second ground of appeal, the matter stood in this way. The officers' notes were almost identical. They were not made at the time of the interview. One officer made his notes after the appellant had been charged, and the other officer made his an hour later. Mr Crowder suggested to the officers in cross-examination that they had collaborated. They denied that suggestion. This court has observed that police officers nearly always deny that they have collaborated in the making of notes, and we cannot help wondering why they are the only class of society who do not collaborate in such a matter. It seems to us that nothing could be more natural or proper when two persons have been present at an interview with a third person than that they should afterwards make sure that they have a correct version of what was said. Collaboration would appear to be a better explanation of almost identical notes than the possession of a superhuman memory . . .

The deputy chairman's desire to preserve the confidential nature of the notebooks could probably quite easily have been achieved with the assistance of a pin or a piece of sticking plaster so that only the relevant pages could have been read. Be that as it may, however, the jury should have been permitted to see the notebooks. The credibility and accuracy of the two police officers was a vital mattter, for it was upon their evidence, and their evidence alone, that the whole of the case against the appellant rested, and as they had denied collaboration in the making of their notes, the jury should have been given the opportunity of examining them.'

Appeal allowed.

Owen v *Edwards* (1983) 77 Cr App R 191 (DC)

The defendant was charged with an offence against section 5 of the Public Order Act 1936. A policeman, who was a prosecution witness, made notes about the incident and refreshed his memory from his notebook outside court but did not refer to the notebook while giving evidence at the defendant's trial. Counsel for the defence then asked to see the notebook to check whether there were any discrepancies between the notes contained therein and the oral evidence which had been given. The police witness informed the court that he had only looked at part of his notes, but did not formally object to the proposed inspection. The justices ruled that the defence could inspect the notebook but could not cross-examine on matters contained in it which had not been referred to by the witness. Counsel for the defence then closed her cross-examination without inspecting the notebook and, no adjournment being sought, the justices proceeded to hear the whole of the evidence including that of a civilian witness and the police witness as to identity and that of the defendant himself.

The defendant was convicted and appealed on the ground that on the basis of the ruling on admissibility the case ought not to be remitted to the justices but the only proper course was to quash the conviction.

McNEIL J: 'Curiously, the point whether or not an accused's representative may ask to see the notebook of a police officer, or indeed the statement of a witness, from which the witness has refreshed his memory not in the witness box but outside the door of the court, has not been decided in England. There is a passage in *Archbold* (41st ed 1982) para. 4–324, which reads as follows: "If the witness has not referred to any book in his evidence for the purpose of refreshing his memory, and has merely admitted in cross-examination that he did not make a note, it has been held in Scotland that he cannot be compelled to produce the book: *Hinshelwood* v *Auld* (1926) SC (J) 4 (police officer's notebook)". The learned editors continue: "It is unlikely that this decision would be applied in England or Wales. If, for example, the witness admitted that he had been refreshing his memory from the notebook outside the court door, it would be odd indeed if he could not be required to produce the document after entering the witness box."

We have been referred to cases on the general proposition as to the production of documents. It is of course clear and hardly needs authority but we were referred to *Senat* v *Senat* [1965] 2 All ER 505 and the words in particular of Sir Jocelyn Simon P on p. 512 that where a document has been used to refresh memory in court then clearly the defendant is entitled to see it. Equally, the right to cross-examine on previous inconsistent statements is well recognised: see, for example, the judgment of this Court in *Worley* v *Bentley* (1976) 62 Cr App R 239: [1976] 2 All ER 449, where Kilner Brown J giving the judgment of this Court, seemed to accept it as axiomatic that a statement would have been shown to the defence if inconsistent with the testimony, and the opinion of the Privy Council in *Baksh* v *R* [1958] AC 167, where Lord Tucker makes observations to the same effect. Those observations are to my mind also in line with the guidelines that were issued by the Attorney-General, to be found in (1982) 74 Cr App R 302 as to the making available to the defence of what is called "unused material". Those guidelines, of course, as I read them, apply only to proceedings on committal and have not been applied so far as the Court has been informed to proceedings in the magistrates' court.

The whole tenor of authority appears to indicate that the defence is entitled to see such documents, including notebooks and statements, from which memory has been refreshed subject, of course, only to the well-established rules that a witness can be cross-examined having refreshed his memory upon the material in his notebook from which he has refreshed his memory without the notebook being made evidence in the case, whereas if he is cross-examined beyond those limits into other matters, the cross-examiner takes the risk of the material being evidence and the document being exhibited and therefore available for use by the fact finding tribunal.

As I say, the justices came to the conclusion that counsel was entitled to inspect the notebook but not entitled to cross-examine the witness on matters contained in it and which had not been referred to by the witness. It seems to me that on that aspect of the case I am in total agreement with the learned editors of *Archbold* in saying that the rules which apply to refreshing memory in the witness box should be the same as those which apply if memory has been refreshed outside the door of the court or, in the words of the learned editor. "It would be odd if it were otherwise". It is not for this Court on these facts to determine how much earlier than giving evidence the line is to be drawn. That will be for the fact-finding tribunal or some other court to consider, if necessary. On the point of law as posed by the justices, my answer would be that they were wrong in law.'

(NOLAN J agreed.)

Appeal dismissed.

R v *Virgo* (1978) 67 Cr App R 323 (CA)

The defendant, the head of the Obscene Publications Squad, was convicted of conspiracy and corruptly accepting bribes. At his trial the judge granted the prosecution permission to allow a leading prosecution witness—a self-confessed dealer in pornography and a very unsavoury character—to use his diaries to refresh his memory while giving evidence, and copies of the diaries were before the jury. The object of the diaries was to assist the witness to give accurate dates. In summing up, the judge directed the jury that the diaries were the most important documents in the case against the defendant, that the entries were powerful evidence, pointing to a corrupt relationship between him and the witness, and that although they did not amount to corroboration in law, they were very important in relation to the witness' evidence.

GEOFFREY LANE LJ said: 'There is always a danger in circumstances such as these when attention has been focussed on a particular document for a long period of time, and when the document has been subjected to a minute and line by line analysis, as these diaries were that the document will achieve an importance which it does not warrant. It was most important in this case that the status of these diaries should be clearly understood throughout the trial and particularly at the end of the trial when the learned judge came to sum up the matter to the jury.

Those diaries were never more, at best, than a means whereby Humphreys might be able to give accurate dates and accurate chapter and verse for the incidents in respect of which he was giving evidence. They were never more than documents prepared by Humphreys and Humphreys was a self-confessed dealer in pornography. He was an accomplice and he was, on any view, a highly unsavoury character in many other ways. His evidence, *par excellence*, required corroboration.

The learned judge made perfectly plain to the jury, in impeccable language at the outset of his direction, the general law relating to corroboration. No one complained about that for a moment, nor could they complain. So far as Humphreys' diaries were concerned, not only did his evidence in general require corroboration, but by the same token, the answers which he gave about his diaries required corroboration. At the very highest, if the jury were convinced that the diaries were genuine, they showed a degree of consistency in Humphreys which otherwise might have been lacking, just as a complaint by the victim of a sexual assault, if made at the first reasonable opportunity thereafter, may show consistency in his or her evidence, though that analogy, one concedes, is not altogether apt. What the diaries could not under any circumstances do, was to support the oral evidence of Humphreys other than in a very limited way which we have already endeavoured to describe. In no way were they evidence of the truth of their contents.

Taking the two steps as set out in the decision in *Turner* (1975) 61 Cr App R 67, to which we have been referred, the diaries might assist the jury to say, in the first instance, that the witness in question was not wholly devoid of credit but what they could in no circumstances do was to contribute to the second stage of *Turner (supra)*, namely the search for corroboration.'

Appeal allowed.

Civil Evidence Act 1968, s. 3(2)

Nothing in this Act shall affect any of the rules of law relating to the circumstances in which, where a person called as a witness in any civil proceedings is cross-examined on a document used by him to refresh his memory, that document may be made evidence in those proceedings; and where a document or any part of a document is received in evidence in any such proceedings by virtue of any such rule of law, any statement made in that document or part by the person using the document to refresh his memory shall by virtue of this subsection be admissible as evidence of any fact stated therein of which direct oral evidence by him would be admissible.

R v Britton [1987] 1 WLR 539 (CA)

The appellant, soon after release from arrest, typed out a note of the circumstances of his arrest and later events. In examination-in-chief he referred to the note to refresh his memory about the circumstances of his arrest. Cross-examination on the note was not confined to the matters on which he had refreshed his memory. He applied for the note to be put in evidence and made an exhibit for the jury's inspection. His application was refused and he was convicted. He appealed against conviction.

LORD LANE CJ, giving the judgment of the court: 'There appears to be a long-standing rule of the common law regulating the admissibility of the *aide-mémoire* in these circumstances.

That rule is as follows: cross-examining counsel is entitled to inspect the note in order to check its contents. He can do so without making the document evidence. Indeed he may go further and cross-examine upon it. If he does so and succeeds in confining his cross-examination to those parts of it which have already been used by the witness to refresh his memory, he does not make it evidence. If on the other hand he strays beyond that part of the note which has been so used, the party calling him—in this case the appellant represented by Mr Buchan—may insist on it being treated as evidence in the case, which will thereupon become an exhibit.

The cases upon which that common law rule is based, and to which we have been referred, are these: *Gregory v Tavernor* (1833) 6 C & P 280, 281 where Gurney B observed:

The memorandum itself is not evidence; and particular entries only are used by the witness to refresh his memory. The defendant's counsel may cross-examine on those entries, without making them his evidence. The defendant's counsel cannot go into evidence of the contents of other parts of the book without making it his evidence; but he may cross-examine on the entries already referred to, and the jury may also see those entries if they wish to do so.

More recently Sir Jocelyn Simon P in *Senat* v *Senat* [1965] P 172, 177 observed:

[Counsel] says that where a document is inspected by opposing counsel in the conduct of the suit, it becomes evidence which that counsel must put in. He cited to me a decision of Wrangham J in *Stroud* v *Stroud (No. 1)* [1963] 1 WLR 1080, where he himself was counsel. In my view the mere inspection of a document does not render it evidence which counsel inspecting it is bound to put in. I think that the true rules are as follows: Where a document is used to refresh a witness's memory, cross-examining counsel may inspect that document in order to check it, without making it evidence. Moreover he may cross-examine upon it without making it evidence provided that his cross-examination does not go further than the parts which are used for refreshing the memory of the witness: *Gregory* v *Tavernor* (1833) 6 C & P 280. But if a party calls for and inspects a document held by the other party, he is bound to put it in evidence if he is required to do so: . . .

In view of some of the arguments adduced before the judge in the court below, it should perhaps be noted that there is a distinction to be drawn between looking at notes used by a witness to refresh his memory and calling for and looking at other documents. Once again in an elderly case that is made clear, the case being *Palmer* v *Maclear* (1858) 1 Sw & Tr 149. Sir Creswell Creswell said to counsel, at p. 151: "You may look at the notes made by the witness to refresh his memory; but you cannot look at the letters without putting them in evidence, if required by the plaintiff". The witness there was in fact holding the letters in his hands.

In the present case it is conceded that Mr Aylett did in his cross-examination go outside those parts of the *aide-mémoire* which had been used by the witness in chief to refresh his memory. Consequently, if those authorities are accurate, the document became evidence and should, on the application of counsel for the defence, have been admitted in evidence.

What the effect of exhibiting such a document might be is another matter. The decision of this court in *R* v *Virgo* (1978) 67 Cr App R 323, shows that their effect is solely to show consistency in the witness producing them, and they are not to be used as evidence of the truth of the facts stated in the *aide-mémoire*. Mr Buchan readily accepts that fact and, indeed, expressly accepted it before the court below. He prefaced his submissions with that concession.

As we say, the argument in the court below seems to have gone off on the wrong tack, largely on the question of the applicability of Lord Denman's Act [section 4 of the Common Law Procedure Act 1854 (17 & 18 Vict. c. 125)] which was irrelevant.

Mr Aylett has submitted to us boldly, to use a word which he himself employed, that the rule that we have endeavoured to express no longer obtains, at least so far as criminal trials are concerned. He submits that the *aide-mémoire* can only be put before the jury, to use his own words, if there is a clear allegation of forgery, or if the document is put in to rebut a suggestion of recent fabrication.

It is to be observed that in *Cross on Evidence*, 6th ed (1985) pp. 254–255 the following passage appears: "There is an old general rule, inadequately explored in the modern authorities, that, if a party calls for and inspects a document held by the other party, he is bound to put it in evidence if required to do so. But . . ."—and then he cites the passage from *Senat* v *Senat* [1965] P 172, 177 which we have already quoted, and goes on—"If, therefore, a witness refreshes his memory concerning a date or an address by referring to a diary, he may be cross-examined about the terms or form of the entries used to refresh his memory without there being any question of the right of the party calling him to insist that the diary should become evidence in the case. On the other hand, if the witness is cross-examined about other parts of the diary, the party calling him may insist on its being treated as evidence in the case".

We respectfully adopt that passage. It is, in the view of this court, still good law and accordingly we reject the submission of Mr Aylett that somewhere along the line that old common law rule has now disappeared.

Mr Aylett founds his submission in part upon the judgment of this court in *R* v *Sekhon*, *The Times* 2 January 1987, the judgment of another division of this court presided over by Woolf LJ. There Woolf LJ sets out in tabular form a number of circumstances in which the sort of evidence which the judge here declined to admit should be admitted. But is is to be noted that Woolf LJ, so far from in any way casting a doubt upon the older decisions to which we have referred, said (see the transcript, at p. 8): "Where a document is used to refresh a witness's memory, cross-examining counsel may inspect that document in order to check it, without making it evidence. Moreover he may cross-examine upon it without making it evidence provided that his cross-examination does not go further than the parts which are used for refreshing the memory of the witness . . ." He cites *Gregory* v *Tavernor*, 6 C & P 280. So he too is approving the existence of the common law rule.

It may be a dangerous application for the defendant to make, because it may very well be that the effect of the jury seeing the document will be, to say the least, counterproductive. As indicated by this court in *R* v *Virgo*, 67 Cr App R 323 in any particular case where the judge takes the view that the interests of justice so require, he will have a discretion to refuse to allow the document to go before the jury, if this could give rise to prejudice to the defendant. Here, in contradistinction from the usual case, the application was being made by the defendant and not being made by the prosecution.

Consequently we have come to the view that there was a material irregularity in this case.'

Appeal allowed. Conviction quashed.

B: *PREVIOUS CONSISTENT OR SELF-SERVING STATEMENTS*

(Suggested preliminary reading: *A Practical Approach to Evidence,* pp. 364–377.)

R v *Roberts* [1942] 1 All ER 187 (CCA)

The defendant was convicted of murdering a girl by shooting her. His defence was that the gun went off accidentally while he was trying to make up a quarrel with the girl. Two days after the event he told his father that the defence would be accident. The trial judge would not allow his conversation to be proved.

HUMPHREYS J, delivering the judgment of the court: 'In our view the judge was perfectly right in refusing to admit that evidence, because it was in law inadmissible. It might have been, and, perhaps, by some judges would have been, allowed to be given on the ground that it was the evidence which the defence desired to have given, was harmless, and there was no strenuous opposition on the part of the prosecution. Such evidence might have been allowed to be given, but the judge was perfectly entitled to take the view which he did, that in law that evidence was inadmissible. The law upon the matter is well-settled. The rule relating to this is sometimes put in this way, that a party is not permitted to make evidence for himself. That law applies to civil cases as well as to criminal cases. For instance, if A and B enter into an oral contract, and some time afterwards there is a difference of opinion as to what were the actual terms agreed upon and there is litigation about it, one of those persons would not be permitted to call his partner to say: "My partner a day or two after told me what his view of the contract was and that he had agreed to do" so and so. So, in a criminal case, an accused person is not permitted to call evidence to show that, after he was charged with a criminal offence, he told a number of persons what his defence was going to be, and the reason for the rule appears to us to be that such testimony has no evidential value. It is because it does not assist in the elucidation of the matters in dispute that the evidence is said to be inadmissible on the ground that it is irrelevant. It would not help the jury in this case in the least to be told that the appellant said to a number of persons, whom he saw while he was waiting his trial, or on bail if he was on bail; that his defence was this, that or the other. The evidence asked to be admitted was that the father had been told by his son that it was an accident. We think the evidence was properly refused. Of course, if the statement had been made to the father just at the time of the shooting, that would have been a totally different matter, because it has always been regarded as admissible that a person should be allowed to give in evidence any statement accompanying an act so that it may explain the act. It was put by counsel for the appellant that the statement might be admissible on the ground that the accused had been asked in cross-examination, and it had been suggested to him in cross-examination that this story of accident was one which he had recently concocted. If any such question had been put, undeniably the evidence would have been admissible as showing it was not recently concocted, because the accused had said so on the very day the incident occurred. The answer is that no such question had been put, and no suggestion made, to the accused.'

(The defendant's appeal was allowed on other grounds.)

R v Christie [1914] AC 545 (HL)

(For facts, see p. 248 *ante*).

VISCOUNT HALDANE LC: 'The only point on which I desire to guard myself is the admissibility of the statement in question as evidence of identification. For the boy gave evidence at the trial, and if his evidence was required for the identification of the prisoner that evidence ought, in my ópinion, to have been his direct evidence in the witness box and not evidence of what he said elsewhere. Had the boy, after he had identified the accused in the dock, been asked if he had identified the accused in the field as the man who assaulted him, and answered affirmatively, then that fact might also have been proved by the policeman and the mother who saw the identification. Its relevancy is to shew that the boy was able to identify at the time and to exclude the idea that the identification of the prisoner in the dock was an afterthought or a mistake. But beyond the mere fact of such identification the examination ought not to have proceeded.'

LORD ATKINSON: '. . . it cannot, I think, be open to doubt that if the boy had said nothing more, as he touched the sleeve of the coat of the accused, than "That is the man", the statement was so closely connected with the act which it accompanied, expressing, indeed, as it did, in words little if anything more than would have been implied by the gesture simpliciter, that it should have been admitted as part of the very act of identification itself. It is on the admissibility of the further statement made in answer to the question of the constable that the controversy arises. On the whole, I am of opinion, though not without some doubt, that this statement only amplifies what is implied by the words "That is the man", plus the act of touching him.

A charge had been made against the accused of the offence committed on the boy. The words "That is the man" must mean "That is the man who has done to me the thing of which he is accused." To give the details of the charge is merely to expand, and express in words what is implied under the circumstances in the act of identification. I think, therefore, that the entire statement was admissible on these grounds, even although the boy was not asked at the trial anything about the former identification. The boy had in his evidence at the trial distinctly identified the accused. If on another occasion he had in the presence of others identified him, then the evidence of these eye-witnesses is quite as truly primary evidence of what acts took place in their presence as would be the boy's evidence of what he did, and what expressions accompanied his act. It would, I think, have been more regular and proper to have examined the boy himself as to what he did on the first occasion, but the omission to do so, while the bystanders were examined on the point, does not, I think, violate the rule that the best evidence must be given. His evidence of what he did was no better in that sense than was their evidence as to what they saw him do.'

LORD MOULTON: 'Speaking for myself, I have great difficulty in seeing how this evidence is admissible on the ground that it is part of the evidence of identification. To prove identification of the prisoner by a person, who is, I shall assume, an adult, it is necessary to call that person as a witness. Identification is an act of the mind, and the primary evidence of what was passing in the mind of a man is his own testimony, where it can be obtained. It would be very dangerous to allow evidence to be given of a man's words and actions, in order to shew by this extrinsic evidence that he identified the prisoner, if he was capable of being called as a witness and was not called to prove by direct evidence that he had thus identified him. Such a mode of proving identification would, in my opinion, be to use secondary evidence where primary evidence was obtainable, and this is contrary to the spirit of the English rules of evidence.'

LORD READING: 'No objection was raised by Mr Dickens, for the respondent, to the admission of the first part of the statement, namely, "That is the man." It implied that Christie was the man designated by the boy as the person who had committed the offence, and meant little, if anything, more than the act of touching the sleeve of Christie or pointing to him. The importance is as to the admission of the additional words, describing the various acts done by Christie. These were not necessary to complete the identification or to explain it. There was no dispute that in the presence of his mother and the police constable the boy designated Christie as the man who had committed the offence. According to the constable's evidence the additional statement was made in answer to his question to the boy, "What did he do to you?" (Question 138). At the trial, and before the statement was admitted, the boy identified Christie in Court, and was not cross-examined. The additional statement was not required by the prosecution for the purpose of proving the act of identification by the boy. The statement cannot, in my judgment, be admitted as evidence of the state of the boy's mind when in the act of identifying Christie, as that would amount to allowing another person to give in evidence the boy's state of mind, when he was not asked, and had not said anything about it in his statement to the Court.

If the prosecution required the evidence as part of the act of identification it should have been given by the boy before the prosecution closed their case. In my judgment it would be a dangerous extension of the law regulating the admissibility of evidence if your Lordships were to allow proof of statements made, narrating or describing the events constituting the offence, on the ground that they form part of or explain the act of identification, more particularly when such evidence is not necessary to prove the act, and is not given by the person who made the statement. I have found no case in which any such statement has been admitted.'

(LORD PARKER concurred with LORD ATKINSON.)

R v *Osbourne; R* v *Virtue* [1973] QB 678 (CA)

The defendants were convicted of robbery. Both defendants had been picked out at an identification parade, Osbourne by Mrs B and Virtue by Mrs H. At the trial, some seven months after the parade, Mrs B said that she could not remember having picked out anyone at a parade; and Mrs H first said that she thought one of the defendants to be a man she had picked out at a parade, and then said that she did not think that that man was in court. The police inspector in charge of the parade was then called and gave evidence that the women had identified the defendants.

LAWTON LJ, giving the judgment of the court: 'Now I turn to the point which was taken on behalf of the defendant Osbourne about the admissibility of Chief Inspector Stevenson's evidence. It is right that I should stress that the point was that such evidence was inadmissible. Its weight was another matter altogether and, as I have pointed out already, the trial judge advised the jury to attach little, if any, weight to Mrs Head's evidence of identification. He reminded the jury of Mrs Brookes' lapse of memory. It was strenuously argued before the trial judge and equally strenuously argued before us, that such evidence was not admissible at all and that its wrongful admission made the conviction unsafe. An analogy was drawn between the situation which arose in this case with those two ladies and the situation which can arise in the witness box when a witness for the prosecution gives evidence which the Crown does not like. Our attention was drawn to the Criminal Law Procedure Act 1865. The situation envisaged by section 3 of the Act of 1865 did not arise in this case at all because nobody suggested that those two ladies were acting in the way envisaged by that Act, namely, adversely, or, to use the modern term, hostilely, but it was said that the trial judge allowed the prosecution to call evidence to contradict them, which is not admissible.

We do not agree that Chief Inspector Stevenson's evidence contradicted their evidence. All that Mrs Brookes had said was that she did not remember, and, as I have already indicated, that is very understandable after a delay of seven and a half months. She had, however, done something. Within four days of the robbery she had attended an identification parade. She had been told in the presence and hearing of the defendant Osbourne, as is the usual practice, what she was to do, namely, point out anybody whom she had seen at the time of the raid. She did point somebody out and it was the defendant Osbourne. One asks oneself as a matter of commonsense why, when a witness has forgotten what she did, evidence should not be given by another witness with a better memory to establish what, in fact, she did when the events were fresh in her mind. Much the same situation arises with regard to Mrs Head. She said in the witness box that she had picked somebody out. She did not think that the man she had picked out was in court, but that again is understandable because appearances can change after seven and a half months, and if the experience of this court is anything to go by, accused persons often look much smarter in the dock than they do when they are first arrested. This court can see no reason at all in principle why evidence of that kind should not be admitted.

It was submitted that the admission of that evidence was contrary to a decision of the House of Lords in *R* v *Christie* [1914] AC 545. That case has long been regarded as a difficult one to understand because the speeches of their Lordships were not directed to the same points, but this can be got from the speeches: that evidence of identification other than identification in the witness box is admissible. All that the prosecution were seeking to do was to establish the fact of identification at the identification parades held on November 20. This court can see no reason why that evidence should not have been admitted. The court is fortified in that view by a passage in the judgment of Sachs LJ which appears in *R* v *Richardson* [1971] 2 QB 484, which was a very different case from the present case, but the principle enunciated by Sachs LJ is applicable. Sachs LJ said, at p. 490:

> The courts, however, must take care not to deprive themselves by new, artificial rules of practice of the best chances of learning the truth. The courts are under no compulsion unnecessarily to follow on a matter of practice the lure of the rules of logic in order to produce unreasonable results which would hinder the course of justice.

It is pertinent to point out that in 1914 when the House of Lords came to consider *R* v *Christie* [1914] AC 545 the modern practice of identity parades did not exist. The whole object of identification parades is for the protection of the suspect, and what happens at those parades is highly relevant to the establishment of the truth. It would be wrong, in the judgment of this court, to set up artificial rules of evidence, which hinder the administration of justice. The evidence was admissible.'

Appeal dismissed.

• In *Sparks* v *R* [1964] AC 964, Lord Morris of Borth-y-Gest said, 'There is no rule which permits the giving of hearsay evidence merely because it relates to identity'. Is the decision in *R* v *Osbourne and Virtue* consistent with this?

R v *Lillyman* [1896] 2 QB 167 (CCR)

The defendant was charged with attempted unlawful intercourse with a girl between the ages of thirteen and sixteen; with assault upon her with intent to ravish; and with an indecent assault upon her. The girl gave evidence that the acts complained of had been done without her consent. The prosecution also tendered evidence in chief of a complaint made by her to her mistress, in the absence of the defendant, shortly after the commission of the acts, and proposed to ask the details of the complaint as made by the girl. The defence objected to the admission of the evidence, but the trial judge admitted it. The mistress then deposed to all that the girl had said respecting the defendant's conduct towards her. The defendant was convicted.

HAWKINS J, delivering the judgment of the court: 'It is necessary, in the first place, to have a clear understanding as to the principles upon which evidence of such a complaint, not on oath, nor made in the presence of the prisoner, nor forming part of the *res gestae*, can be admitted. It clearly is not admissible as evidence of the facts complained of: those facts must therefore be established, if at all, upon oath by the prosecutrix or other credible witness, and, strictly speaking, evidence of them ought to be given before evidence of the complaint is admitted. The complaint can only be used as evidence of the consistency of the conduct of the prosecutrix with the story told by her in the witness box, and as being inconsistent with her consent to that of which she complains.

In every one of the old textbooks proof of complaint is treated as a most material element in the establishment of a charge of rape or other kindred charge . . ..

It is too late, therefore, now to make serious objection to the admissibility of evidence of the fact that a complaint was made, provided it was made as speedily after the acts complained of as could reasonably be expected.

We proceed to consider the second objection, which is, that the evidence of complaint should be limited to the fact that *a complaint* was made without giving any of the particulars of it. No authority binding upon us was cited during the argument, either in support of or against this objection. We must therefore determine the matter upon principle. That the *general usage* has been substantially to limit the evidence of the complaint to proof that the woman made a complaint of something done to her, and that she mentioned in connection with it the name of a particular person, cannot be denied; but it is equally true that judges of great experience have dissented from this limitation, and of those who have adopted the usage none have ever carefully discussed or satisfactorily expressed the grounds upon which their views have been based . . ..

After very careful consideration we have arrived at the conclusion that we are bound by no authority to support the existing usage of limiting evidence of the complaint to the bare fact that a complaint was made, and that reason and good sense are against our doing so. The evidence is admissible only upon the ground that it was a complaint of that which is charged against the prisoner, and can be legitimately used only for the purpose of enabling the jury to judge for themselves whether the conduct of the woman was consistent with her testimony on oath given in the witness box negativing her consent, and affirming that the acts complained of were against her will, and in accordance with the conduct they would expect in a truthful woman under the circumstances detailed by her. The jury, and they only, are the persons to be satisfied whether the woman's conduct was so consistent or not. Without proof of her condition, demeanour, and verbal expressions, all of which are of vital importance in the consideration of that question, how is it possible for them satisfactorily to determine it? Is it to be left to the witness to whom the statement is made to determine and report to the jury whether what the woman said amounted to a real complaint? And are the jury bound to accept the witness's interpretation of her words as binding upon them without having the whole statement before them, and without having the power to require it to be disclosed to them, even though they may feel it essential to enable them to form a reliable opinion? For it must be borne in mind that if such evidence is inadmissible when offered by the prosecution, the jury cannot alter the rule of evidence and make it admissible by asking for it themselves.

In reality, affirmative answers to such stereotyped questions as these, "Did the prosecutrix make a complaint" (a very leading question, by the way) "of something done to herself?" "Did she mention a name?" amount to nothing to which any weight ought to be attached; they tend rather to embarrass than assist a thoughtful jury, for they are consistent either with there having been a complaint or no complaint of the prisoner's conduct. To limit the evidence of the complaint to such questions and answers is to ask the jury to draw important inferences from imperfect materials, perfect materials being at hand and in the cognizance of the witness in the box. In our opinion, nothing ought unnecessarily to be left to speculation or surmise.

It has been sometimes urged that to allow the particulars of the complaint would be calculated to prejudice the interests of the accused, and that the jury would be apt to treat the complaint as evidence of the facts complained of. Of course, if it were so left to the jury they would naturally so treat it. But it never could be legally so left; and we think it is the duty of the judge to impress upon the jury in every case that they are not entitled to make use of the complaint as any evidence whatever of those facts, or for any other purpose than that we have stated. With such a direction, we think the interests of an innocent accused would be more protected than they are under the present usage. For when the whole statement is laid before the jury they are less likely to draw wrong and adverse inferences, and may sometimes come to the conclusion that what the woman said amounted to no real complaint of any offence committed by the accused. Moreover, the present usage and consequent uncertainty in practice (for the usage is not universal) provokes many objections to the evidence on the part of the prisoner's counsel, and these are generally looked upon with disfavour by the jury, and the very object of confining the evidence of the complaint to the few stereotyped questions we have referred to is often defeated by a device, not to be encouraged, by which the name of the accused, though carefully concealed as an inadmissible particular of the complaint, is studiously revealed to the jury by some such question and answer as the following: "*Q*   In consequence of that complaint did you do anything? *A*   Yes, I went to the house of the prisoner's mother, where he lives, and accused him." This seems to us to be an objectionable mode of introducing evidence indirectly, which if tendered directly would be inadmissible.'

Conviction affirmed.

• Should the victim of a sexual offence be entitled to relate not only the fact of a recent complaint, but also the substance of what she said? Is the rule regarding recent complaints an anachronism today?

R v *Osborne* [1905] 1 KB 551 (CCR)

The defendant was convicted of an indecent assault on a girl under the age of thirteen years, whose consent to the act was therefore immaterial. At the trial evidence was admitted of the answer given by the girl to a question put by another child, in the absence of the defendant, as to why the girl had not waited for the other child at the defendant's house. The girl's reply was a complaint of the defendant's conduct to her.

RIDLEY J, reading the judgment of the court: 'It was contended for the prisoner that the evidence was inadmissible—first, because the answer made by the girl was not a complaint, but a statement or conversation, having been made in answer to a question; and, secondly, because, as Keziah Parkes was under the age of thirteen, her consent was not material to the charge. As to the first point, the case of *R* v *Merry* 19 Cox CC 442 was quoted. In that case a question had been put to a girl of nine years old by her mother in a case of indecent assault, and the learned judge ruled that, as the proposed evidence was a statement made in answer to a question, it was a conversation and not a complaint, and he declined to allow it to be given in evidence. It does not appear, however, from the report what the question was that was put to the girl. It appears to us that the mere fact that the statement is made in answer to a question in such cases is not of itself sufficient to make it inadmissible as a complaint. Questions of a suggestive or leading character will, indeed, have that effect, and will render it inadmissible; but a question such as this, put by the mother or other person, "What is the matter?" or "Why are you crying?" will not do so. These are natural questions which a person in charge will be likely to put; on the other hand, if she were asked, "Did So-and-so" (naming the prisoner) "assault you?" "Did he do this and that to you?" then the result would be different, and the statement ought to be rejected. In each case the decision on the character of the question put, as well as other circumstances, such as the relationship of the questioner to the complainant, must be left to the discretion of the presiding judge. If the circumstances indicate that but for the questioning there probably would have been no voluntary complaint, the answer is inadmissible. If the question merely anticipates a statement which the complainant was about to make, it is not rendered inadmissible by the fact that the questioner happens to speak first. In this particular case, we think that the chairman of quarter sessions acted rightly, and that the putting of this particular question did not render the statement inadmissible.

Upon the second point it was contended that, although under the decision of *R* v *Lillyman* [1896] 2 QB 167 the particulars of a complaint made may, in some circumstances, be given in evidence on a charge of rape, that ruling does not extend to a charge of criminal knowledge or indecent assault, where, as in the present case, consent is not legally material . . ..

By the judgment in *R* v *Lillyman* it was decided that the complaint was admissible, not as evidence of the facts complained of, nor as being a part of the *res gestae* (which it was not), but as evidence of the consistency of the conduct of the prosecutrix with the story told by her in the witness box, and as being inconsistent with her consent to that of which she complains. Mr Marchant argued upon this that the reasons so given were one only, and that the consistency of the complaint with the story given by the prosecutrix was material only so far as the latter alleged non-consent. If, however, that argument were sound, the words in question might have been omitted from the sentence, and it would have been sufficient to say that the complaint was admissible only and solely because it negatived consent. We think, however, if it were a question of the meaning of words, that the better construction of the judgment is that while the Court dealt with the charge in question as involving in fact, though not in law, the question of consent on the part of the prosecutrix, yet the reasons given for admitting the complaint were two—first, that it was consistent with her story in the witness box; and, secondly, that it was inconsistent with consent. The reasoning proceeded thus: On the second and third counts consent was material in law; on the first it was material in fact; there is, for this purpose, no difference between the two. It is not, therefore, because the charge itself involves proof of the absence of consent that the evidence is admissible; on the contrary, the prosecutrix herself can make it evidence by deposing that she did not consent when that is no part of the charge. In other words, whether non-consent be legally a necessary part of the issue, or whether, on the other hand, it is what may be called a collateral issue of fact, the complaint becomes admissible. But how does non-consent become a collateral issue of fact? The answer must be, in consequence of the story told by the prosecutrix in the witness box. And the judgment treats the two cases on the same footing. If non-consent be a part of the story told by the prosecutrix, or if it be legally a part of the charge, in each case alike the complaint is admissible. But, if that is so, does not the reasoning apply equally to other parts of the story, and not merely to the part in which the prosecutrix has denied consent? If not, it seems illogical to allow, as the Court did allow, that the whole of the story may be given in evidence. The true result is, we think, that, while the decision in *R v Lillyman* is not strictly on all-fours with the present case, yet the reasoning which it contains answers the question now raised for decision. But, however that may be, it appears to us that, in accordance with principle, such complaints are admissible, not merely as negativing consent, but because they are consistent with the story of the prosecutrix. In all ordinary cases, indeed, the principle must be observed which rejects statements made by any one in the prisoner's absence. Charges of this kind form an exceptional class, and in them such statements ought, under proper safeguards, to be admitted. Their consistency with the story told is, from the very nature of such cases, of special importance. Did the woman make a complaint at once? If so, that is consistent with her story. Did she not do so? That is inconsistent. And in either case the matter is important for the jury . . ..

We are, at the same time, not insensible of the great importance of carefully observing the proper limits within which such evidence should be given. It is only to cases of this kind that the authorities on which our judgment rests apply; and our judgment also is to them restricted. It applies only where there is a complaint not elicited by questions of a leading and inducing or intimidating character, and only when it is made at the first opportunity after the offence which reasonably offers itself. Within such bounds, we think the evidence should be put before the jury, the judge being careful to inform the jury that the statement is not evidence of the facts complained of, and must not be regarded by them, if believed, as other than corroborative of the complainant's credibility, and, when consent is in issue, of the absence of consent. For these reasons we think the conviction should be affirmed.'

Conviction affirmed.

R v Wallwork (1958) 42 Cr App R 153 (CCA)

The defendant was convicted of incest with his daughter, aged five. At the trial the child was put in the witness box by the prosecution, but was unable to give any evidence. However, evidence by her grandmother of a complaint made by the child to her, in which she named the defendant as her assailant, was admitted.

LORD GODDARD CJ, giving the judgment of the court, said: '. . . [I]n our opinion, in this particular case that evidence was not admissible. In cases of rape or indecent assault it has always been held that evidence of a complaint and the terms of the complaint may be given, but they may be given only for a particular purpose, not as evidence of the fact complained of, because the fact that the woman says not on oath: "So-and-so assaulted me" cannot be evidence against the prisoner that the assault did take place. The evidence may be and is tendered for the purpose of showing consistency in her conduct and consistency with the evidence she has given in the box. It is material, for instance, where a question of identity is concerned, that she made an immediate complaint or a complaint as soon as she had a reasonable opportunity of making it and made the complaint against the particular man. It is also material, and most material, very often on the point whether the girl or woman was a consenting party. None of these matters arise in this case. The child had given no evidence because when the poor little thing was put into the witness box, she said nothing and could not remember anything. The learned judge had expressly told the jury to disregard her evidence altogether. Therefore, there was no evidence given by her with regard to which it was necessary to say what she had said to her grandmother was consistent; nor could there be any question of the identity of the prisoner or any question of consent. The learned judge, having once admitted that evidence ought—and he omitted to do this—to have told the jury that it was not evidence of the facts complained of by the child.'

(The court dismissed the appeal on the ground that no substantial miscarriage of justice was caused by the irregularities).

R v *Oyesiku* (1971) 56 Cr App R 240 (CA)

The defendant was convicted of assault occasioning actual bodily harm and assaulting a police officer. At the trial the defendant's wife gave evidence that the police officer was the aggressor. During cross-examination it was put to her that her evidence was a late invention and concocted with a view to helping the defendant. The trial judge refused to admit in evidence an earlier statement made by the wife to a solicitor before she had seen her husband after his arrest. This statement was to the same effect as the evidence she gave in court.

KARMINSKI LJ, giving the judgment of the court: 'It was argued with great force before us by Mr Hazan that this decision to exclude the evidence was wrong in law . . . In *Coll* (1889) 24 LR Ir 522 at p. 541, Holmes J said: "It is I think clear that the evidence of a witness cannot be corroborated by proving statements to the same effect previously made by him; nor will the fact that his testimony is impeached in cross-examination render such evidence admissible. Even if the impeachment takes the form of showing a contradiction or inconsistency between the evidence given at the trial and something said by the witness on a former occasion it does not follow that the way is open for proof of other statements made by him for the purpose of sustaining his credit. There must be something either in the nature of the inconsistent statement, or in the use made of it by the cross-examiner, to enable such evidence to be given." We regard that statement of the law as correct, and applicable to the present case.

Our attention has also been drawn to a recent decision in the High Court of Australia, *Nominal Defendant* v *Clement* (1961) 104 CLR 476. I desire to read only one passage from the full judgment of Dixon CJ. He said this (at p. 479): "The rule of evidence under which it was let in is well recognised and of long standing. If the credit of a witness is impugned as to some material fact to which he deposes upon the ground that his account is a late invention or has been lately devised or reconstructed, even though not with conscious dishonesty, that makes admissible a statement to the same effect as the account he gave as a witness, if it was made by the witness contemporaneously with the event or at a time sufficiently early to be inconsistent with the suggestion that his account is a late invention or reconstruction. But, inasmuch as the rule forms a definite exception to the general principle excluding statements made out of court and admits a possibly self-serving statement made by the witness, great care is called for in applying it. The judge at the trial must determine for himself upon the conduct of the trial before him whether a case for applying the rule of evidence has arisen and, from the nature of the matter, if there be an appeal, great weight should be given to his opinion by the appellate court. It is evidence however that the judge at the trial must exercise care in assuring himself not only that the account given by the witness in his testimony is attacked on the ground of recent invention or reconstruction or that a foundation for such an attack has been laid by the party, but also that the contents of the statement are in fact to the like effect as his account given in his evidence and that having regard to the time and circumstances in which it was made it rationally tends to answer the attack. It is obvious that it may not be easy sometimes to be sure that counsel is laying a foundation for impugning the witness's account of a material incident or fact as a recently invented, devised or reconstructed story. Counsel himself may proceed with a subtlety which is the outcome of caution in pursuing what may prove a dangerous course. That is one reason why the trial judge's opinion has an importance."

Dealing with the last paragraph of that quotation from Dixon CJ, there is no doubt at all that in this case counsel was making an attack, because it was clear from what he said at the trial and indeed what he said to us today. That judgment of the Chief Justice of Australia, although technically not binding upon us, is a decision of the greatest persuasive power, and one which this Court gratefully accepts as a correct statement of the law applicable to the present appeal.

That is the position in law, and in our view the learned trial judge was wrong to refuse to allow that evidence to be given. The value of it, of course, was a matter for the jury to assess.'

Conviction quashed.

Civil Evidence Act 1968

3(1) Where in any civil proceedings—. . .

(b) a previous statement made by a person called [as a witness in those proceedings] is proved for the purpose of rebutting a suggestion that his evidence has been fabricated, that statement shall by virtue of this subsection be admissible as evidence of any fact stated therein of which direct oral evidence by him would be admissible.'

C: UNFAVOURABLE AND HOSTILE WITNESSES

(Suggested preliminary reading: *A Practical Approach to Evidence,* pp. 377–381.)

Ewer v Ambrose (1825) 3 B & C 746 (KB)

In an action of assumpsit for money had and received, the defence being that the defendant was jointly liable with a partner against whom judgment had been recovered, B was called as a witness by the defendant to prove the partnership, but he proved the contrary.

HOLROYD J: 'I take the rule of law to be that, if a witness proves a case against the party calling him, the latter may show the truth by other witnesses. But it is undoubtedly true that, if a party calls a witness to prove a fact, he cannot, when he finds the witness proves the contrary, give general evidence to show that that witness is not to be believed on his oath, but he may show by other evidence that he is mistaken as to the fact which he is called to prove.

LITTLEDALE J: 'Where a witness is called by a party to prove his case, and he disproves that case, I think the party is still at liberty to prove his case by other witnesses. It would be a great hardship if the rule were otherwise, for if a party had four witnesses upon whom he relied to prove his case, it would be very hard, that by calling first the one who happened to disprove it, he should be deprived of the testimony of the other three. If he had called the three before the other who had disproved the case, it would have been a question for the jury upon the evidence whether they would give credit to the three or to the one. The order in which the witnesses happen to be called ought not therefore to make any difference.'

Greenough v *Eccles* (1859) 5 CB (NS) 786 (CP)

In an action on a bill of exchange, a witness called by the defendants supported the evidence of the plaintiff. The witness was then asked by the defendant's counsel about a previous statement inconsistent with his present testimony. The defence also proposed to put in evidence the statement. The judge ruled that the witness was not hostile and that therefore he had no power under s. 22 of the Common Law Procedure Act 1854 to admit such evidence.

WILLIAMS J: 'The section [s 22 of the Common Law Procedure Act 1854] lays down three rules as to the power of a party to discredit his own witness, first, he shall not be allowed to impeach his credit by general evidence of his bad character,—secondly, he may contradict him by other evidence,—thirdly, he may prove that he has made at other times a statement inconsistent with his present testimony.

These three rules appear to include the principal questions that have ever arisen on the subject: as may be seen by referring to the chapter in *Phillips on Evidence* which treats "of the right of a party to disprove or impeach the evidence of his own witness." And it will there be further seen that the law relating to the first two of these rules was settled before the passing of the act, while, as to the third, the authorities were conflicting: that is to say, the law was clear that you could not discredit your own witness by general evidence of bad character, but you might nevertheless contradict him by other evidence relevant to the issue. Whether you could discredit him by proving that he had made inconsistent statements, was to some extent an unsettled point.

In favour of construing the word "adverse" to mean merely "unfavourable", the main arguments are, that, taking the words of the section in their natural and ordinary sense, its object appears to be to declare the whole law on the subject by negativing the right as to the first, and affirming it both on the second and third points; but that it proceeds to fetter the right as to both the latter; for, the right is declared to exist in the former as well as the latter of these two instances, "in case the witness shall, in the opinion of the judge, prove adverse,"—with the additional qualification, as to the latter, that the leave of the judge must be obtained. The right, it is argued, according to this enactment, is not to exist in either instance, if the judge is not of that opinion. The fetter thus imposed, it is further said, would be harmless in its operation, if "adverse" be construed "unfavourable", but most oppressive if it means "hostile"; because the party producing the witness would be fixed with his evidence, when it proved pernicious, in case the judge did not think the witness "hostile," which might often happen; whereas, he could not in such a case fail to think him "unfavourable" . . ..

But there are two considerations which have influenced my mind to disregard these arguments. The one is, that it is impossible to suppose the legislature could have really intended to impose any fetter whatever on the right of a party to contradict his own witness by other evidence relevant to the issue,—a right not only fully established by authority, but founded on the plainest good sense. The other is, that the section requires the judge to form an opinion that the witness is adverse, before the right to contradict, or prove that he has made inconsistent statements, is to be allowed to operate. This is reasonable, and indeed necessary, if the word "adverse" means "hostile", but wholly unreasonable and unnecessary if it means "unfavourable".

On these grounds, I think the preferable construction is, that, in case the witness shall, in the opinion of the judge, prove "hostile", the party producing him may not only contradict him by other witnesses, as he might heretofore have done, and may still do, if the witness is unfavourable, but may also, by leave of the judge, prove that he has made inconsistent statements . . ..

Whatever is the meaning of the word "adverse", the mere fact of the witness being in that predicament is not to confer the right of discrediting him in this way. The section obviously contemplates that there may be cases where the judge may properly refuse leave to exercise the right, though in his opinion the witness proves "adverse." And, as the judge's discretion must be principally, if not wholly, guided by the witness's behaviour and language in the witness box (for, the judge can know nothing, judicially, of his earlier conduct), it is not improbable that the legislature had in view the ordinary case of a judge giving leave to a party producing a witness who proves hostile, to treat him as if he had been produced by the opposite party, so far as to put to him leading and pressing questions; and that the purpose of the section is, to go a step further in this direction, by giving the judge power to allow such a witness to be discredited, by proving his former inconsistent statements, as if he were a witness on the other side.'

COCKBURN CJ: 'The solution by my learned brothers is a solution of a difficulty, otherwise incapable of solution, but I am not satisfied therewith, and without actually dissenting from their judgment, I do not altogether assent to it.'

(WILLES J agreed with WILLIAMS J.)

(Note: s. 22 of the Common Law Procedure Act 1854 has been repealed, but it is re-enacted by s. 3 Criminal Procedure Act 1865 which applies to both criminal and civil cases.)

Criminal Procedure Act 1865

3   A party producing a witness shall not be allowed to impeach his credit by general evidence of bad character; but he may, in case the witness shall prove adverse, contradict him by other evidence, or, by leave of the judge prove that he has made at other times a statement inconsistent with his present testimony; but before such last-mentioned proof can be given, the circumstances of the supposed statement sufficient to designate the particular occasion, must be mentioned to the witness, and he must be asked whether or not he has made such statement.

R v Thompson (1976) 64 Cr App R 96 (CA)

The appellant was charged, *inter alia*, with incest with one of his daughters, A. She was called for the prosecution, and after she had been sworn and answered certain preliminary questions, she refused to give evidence. The trial judge said she had to unless she wished to spend some time in prison. He then allowed her to be treated as hostile and be cross-examined about a statement made by her to the police, and the appellant was convicted.

LORD WIDGERY CJ, delivering the judgment of the court: 'Thus, one comes from there to Mr Mylne's main point today, his best point as he described it, which is that the girl Anne ought never to have been treated as hostile. He concedes that she was a hostile witness and that the provisions of section 3 of the Criminal Procedure Act 1865 applied to her, but he says, for a reason which I will endeavour to explain in a moment, that that section did not apply to this case . . .

It is to be observed in the text of that section that the party producing a witness is permitted in certain circumstances to contradict, and that he may produce a statement inconsistent with present testimony. The argument of Mr Mylne is that in order to get the benefit of section 3 it is not enough to show, as in this case, that the girl was hostile and stood mute of malice. It is essential, so the argument goes, that there should be a contradiction of a previous statement and an inconsistent current statement, and since in this case there was no such contradiction, the previous statement standing alone and the girl refusing to produce a second statement either consistent or otherwise, it is contended that the section has no application.

We do not find it necessary to express any view upon the section as applied to cases where there is an inconsistent statement. We think this matter must be dealt with by the provisions of the common law in regard to recalcitrant witnesses. Quite apart from what is said in section 3, the common law did recognise that pressure could be brought to bear upon witnesses who refused to co-operate and perform their duties. We have had the advantage of looking at one or two of the earlier cases prior to the Act to which I have already referred and their treatment of this matter.

The first is *Clarke v Saffery* (1824) Ry & M 126, and the issue before the Vice-Chancellor does not require to be considered in any detail. But it is to be observed that in the course of the trial the plaintiff's counsel called the defendant, who was also one of the assignees, as a witness, and objection was taken by the defendant's counsel to the mode of examining the defendant. There does not seem to be a second statement contradicting the earlier one there, yet Best CJ said, at p. 126: "there is no fixed rule which binds the counsel calling a witness to a particular mode of examining him. If a witness, by his conduct in the box, shows himself decidedly adverse, it is always in the discretion of the judge to allow a cross-examination . . ."

I pause there because the rest of Best CJ's judgment is subject to comment in the later cases, but that part which I have read seems to me to stand uncontradicted. That is what we are dealing with here. We are dealing here with a witness who shows himself decidedly adverse, and whereupon, as Best CJ says, it is always in the discretion of the judge to allow cross-examination. After all, we are only talking about the asking of leading questions. If the hostile witness declines to say anything at all that was inconsistent with his or her duty as making a second and inconsistent statement about the facts, Best CJ is recognising as a feature of the common law the right in the discretion of the judge always to allow cross-examination in those circumstances.

Then in the case of *Bastin* v *Carew* (1824) Ry & M 127 Lord Abbott CJ said, at p 127: "I mean to decide this, and no further. But in each particular case there must be some discretion in the presiding judge as to the mode in which the examination should be conducted, in order best to answer the purposes of justice."

The statement, which is consistently supported in later authorities, again seems to us to cover this case admirably. The short question after all is: was the judge right in allowing counsel to cross-examine in the sense of asking leading questions? On the authority of *Clarke* v *Saffrey* and *Bastin* v *Carew* it seems to us that he was right and there is no reason to suppose that the subsequent statutory intervention into this subject has in any way destroyed or removed the basic common law right of the judge in his discretion to allow cross-examination when a witness proves to be hostile.'

Appeal dismissed.

R v *Golder, Jones and Porritt* [1960] 1 WLR 1169 (CCA)

The defendants were charged with burglary and larceny. A witness, whose evidence on deposition at the committal proceedings incriminated the defendants, repudiated her statement at the trial and, although treated as hostile by the prosecution, refused to admit that her deposition was true. The trial judge, in effect, directed that it was open to the jury to act upon the evidence contained in the deposition and the jury convicted.

LORD PARKER CJ giving the judgment of the court: 'A long line of authority has laid down the principle that while previous statements may be put to an adverse witness to destroy his credit and thus to render his evidence given at the trial negligible, they are not admissible evidence of the truth of the facts stated therein. It is unnecessary to refer to the cases in detail; the following extract from the judgment of this court in *R* v *Harris* (1927) 20 Cr App R 144, 147 is a sufficient statement of the principle: "It was permissible to cross-examine this girl upon the assertions she had previously made, not for the purpose of substituting those unsworn assertions for her sworn testimony, but for the purpose of showing that her sworn testimony, in the light of those unsworn assertions, could not be regarded as being of importance. It is upon that matter that confusion has sometimes arisen. It has undoubtedly sometimes been thought that where a witness is cross-examined upon a previous unsworn statement and admits that the statement was made, but says that the statement was untrue, that unsworn statement may sometimes be treated as if it could be accepted by the jury in preference to the sworn statement in the witness box . . . That of course is all wrong, as has been pointed out on various occasions by this court, and not least in the case of *White* (1922) 17 Cr App R 60".

In both *Harris* and *White* the previous statement was unsworn and not made in the presence of the accused. It could not, therefore, on any view be evidence against him. The principle, however, is equally applicable to earlier statements made on oath as it is to unsworn statements: cf *R* v *Birch* (1924) 18 Cr App R 26). . . ..

In the judgment of this court, when a witness is shown to have made previous statements inconsistent with the evidence given by that witness at the trial, the jury should not merely be directed that the evidence given at the trial should be regarded as unreliable; they should also be directed that the previous statements, whether sworn or unsworn, do not constitute evidence upon which they can act.'

Appeals allowed.

Civil Evidence Act 1968

3(1) Where in any civil proceedings—
(a) a previous inconsistent or contradictory statement made by a person called as a witness in those proceedings is proved by virtue of section 3 of the Criminal Procedure Act 1865 . . . that statement shall by virtue of this subsection be admissible as evidence of any fact stated therein of which direct oral evidence by him would be admissible.

Questions for discussion

R v *Coke*; *R* v *Littleton*

1 Devise a series of questions to take Margaret and Angela Blackstone through their evidence in chief, without leading them.

2 If D/I Glanvil and D/S Bracton apply to refresh their memories from their notebooks, what must the judge take into account before permitting this?

3 Under what circumstances may the officers' notebooks be put in evidence? What evidential value would they have?

4 May Angela Blackstone, her mother or the officers give evidence of the identification of Littleton in the street?

5 May evidence be given of the accounts given to their mother by Margaret and Angela of what had happened at Coke's flat? If so, what evidence may be given, and to what effect?

6 Assume that the trial judge in *R* v *Coke*; *R* v *Littleton* has admitted the statements made by Margaret and Angela to their mother as recent complaints. Construct a passage for inclusion in the judge's summing-up which deals fully and accurately with the evidence of these recent complaints.

7 If at the committal proceedings, Margaret refuses to give evidence, or asserts that she consented to the act of intercourse, what should counsel for the prosecution do?

Blackstone v *Coke*

1 Consider questions 3, 4 and 5 above in the context of *Blackstone* v *Coke*.

(Note: Additional questions relating to the subject-matter of this chapter are to be found at the end of chapter 13.)

Further reading

Gooderson, 'Previous consistent statements' [1968] CLJ 64.
Howard, 'Refreshment of memory out of court' [1972] Crim LR 351.
Libling, 'Evidence of past identification' [1977] Crim LR 276.
Newark and Samuels, 'Refreshing memory' [1978] Crim LR 408.
Newark, 'The hostile witness and the adversary system' [1986] Crim LR 441.

13   *Cross-examination*

A: NATURE AND CONDUCT OF CROSS-EXAMINATION

(Suggested preliminary reading: *A Practical Approach to Evidence*, pp. 383–388).

R v *Thomson* [1912] 3 KB 19 (CCA)

At the trial of the appellant upon a charge of having used an instrument upon a woman in order to procure a miscarriage, his defence was that he had done nothing to her, but that she had performed such an operation upon herself. His counsel, in cross-examination, sought to ask questions of a witness for the prosecution as to statements made by the woman (who was dead) sometime before her miscarriage that she intended to operate upon herself, and shortly after her miscarriage that she had operated upon herself; but the judge refused to permit these questions.

LORD ALVERSTONE CJ, delivering the judgment of the court: 'This point is one of importance and at first appeared to be difficult. Counsel for the appellant was not allowed in cross-examination to put questions to a witness for the prosecution as to what the deceased woman had told her some time before the miscarriage as to her intentions and also a few days before her death as to what she had done. If put in a popular way, the argument for the appellant, that what the woman had said she had done to herself ought to be admissible evidence for the defence, might be attractive; but upon consideration it is seen to be a dangerous argument, and, in the opinion of the Court, the rejection of evidence of that kind is much more in favour of the accused than of the prosecution. If such evidence is admissible for one side it must also be admissible for the other.

   In our opinion there is no principle upon which this evidence is admissible any more than any other hearsay evidence. If it were admissible, then all those decisions in which it was considered whether statements were admissible in evidence as dying declarations, or as part of the *res gestae*, or as admissions against pecuniary or proprietary interest, would have been unnecessary. The only ground upon which it has been suggested in argument that such evidence ought to be admitted is that since the Criminal Evidence Act 1898, and the Criminal Appeal Act 1907, a new rule of evidence has been introduced under which anything must be admitted in evidence which will help the accused to prove his defence. There is a decision of a great authority, Charles J, against that contention. In *R* v *Gloster* 16 Cox CC 471 the prisoner was charged with having caused the death of a woman by an illegal operation, and it was sought to give in evidence statements made by the woman a few days after the operation as to who had caused the injuries from which she died. Charles J refused to admit the evidence and said: "Mr Poland proposes to ask the witness what the deceased said as to her bodily condition and what had been done to her. My judgment is this: that the statements must be confined to contemporaneous symptoms and nothing in the nature of a narrative is admissible as to who caused them or how they were caused". In this case it cannot be argued that the statements were admissible as part of the *res gestae*; the statements sought to be proved were not made at the time when anything was being done to the woman.'

Appeal dismissed.

R v Fenlon, Neal and Neal (1980) 71 Cr App R 307 (CA)

The appellant F and the applicants N were convicted of rape. The victim they were said to have raped had been picked up by them at a public house after which they and four other men had gone with her to the flat of the parents of one of the men. F appealed on the ground, *inter alia*, that the judge wrongly ruled, after F had finished his examination-in-chief, that it was the duty of counsel for the co-defendants to cross-examine him by putting to him their client's case whenever it might differ from F's evidence and thus perform Crown counsel's task.

LORD LANE CJ, giving the judgment of the court: ' We are told (and there is no reason to doubt it) that there seems to have been in the past a difference of approach between judges to this particular matter. We have been referred to a decision of the House of Lords, albeit in a civil case, *Browne v Dunn* (1894) 6 R 67, the material parts of the headnote in which read: "If in the course of a case it is intended to suggest that a witness is not speaking the truth upon a particular point, his attention must be directed to the fact by cross-examination showing that that imputation is intended to be made, so that he may have an opportunity of making any explanation which is open to him, unless it is otherwise perfectly clear that he has had full notice beforehand that there is an intention to impeach the credibility of his story or (*per* Lord Morris) the story is of an incredible and romancing character". The passage in the speeches to which we were referred is at p. 70, the speech of Lord Herschell LC, and reads: "These witnesses all of them depose to having suffered from such annoyances; they further depose to having consulted the defendant on the subject, and to have given him instructions which resulted in their signing this document; and when they were called there was no suggestion made to them in cross-examination that that was not the case. Their evidence was taken; to some of them it was said, 'I have no questions to ask'; in the case of others their cross-examination was on a point quite beside the evidence to which I have just called attention. Now, my Lords, I cannot help saying that it seems to me to be absolutely essential to the proper conduct of a case, where it is intended to suggest that a witness is not speaking the truth on a particular point, to direct his attention to the fact by some questions put in cross-examination showing that that imputation is intended to be made, and not to take his evidence and pass it by as a matter altogether unchallenged, and then, when it is impossible for him to explain, as perhaps he might have been able to do if such questions had been put to him, the circumstances which it is suggested indicate that the story he tells ought not to be believed, to argue that he is a witness unworthy of credit".

Mr Goldberg submits that that is a rule which applies to counsel prosecuting on behalf of the Crown. It is his clear duty, he concedes, to put to witnesses the version of events for which he contends, so that they can answer it. But he further submits that it is not the duty of one defendant to put to another defendant his version of events where it differs from the version given by that other defendant.

We can see no distinction in principle between the one situation and the other. The basis of the rule, as Lord Herschell pointed out, is to give a witness of whom it is going to be said or suggested that he was not telling the truth an opportunity of explaining and if necessary of advancing further facts in confirmation of the evidence which he has given. There seems to be no reason why there should be any different rule relating to defendants between themselves from that applying to the prosecution *vis-à-vis* the defendant or the defence *vis-à-vis* the prosecution. It is the duty of counsel who intends to suggest that a witness is not telling the truth to make it clear to the witness in cross-examination that he challenges his veracity and to give the witness an opportunity of replying. It need not be done in minute detail, but it is the duty of counsel to make it plain to the witness, albeit he may be a co-defendant, that his evidence is not accepted and in what respects it is not accepted.'

Appeal dismissed.

Sexual Offences (Amendment) Act 1976

2(1) If at a trial any person is for the time being charged with a rape offence to which he pleads not guilty, then, except with the leave of the judge, no evidence and no question in cross-examination shall be adduced or asked at the trial, by or on behalf of any defendant at the trial, about any sexual experience of a complainant with a person other than that defendant.

(2) The judge shall not give leave in pursuance of the preceding subsection for any evidence or question except on an application made to him in the absence of the jury by or on behalf of a defendant; and on such an application the judge shall give leave if and only if he is satisfied that it would be unfair to that defendant to refuse to allow the evidence to be adduced or the question to be asked.

R v *Mills* (1978) 68 Cr App R 327 (CA)

The defendant was charged with rape. At the trial an application was made to cross-examine the complainant as to her previous sexual experience with other men. The application was refused and the defendant was subsequently convicted. He applied for leave to appeal.

ROSKILL LJ, giving the judgment of the court: 'Application was made during cross-examination of this complainant by Mr Hunt that he should be allowed to cross-examine her as to her antecedent sexual experience. On the face of it such cross-examination would be contrary to section 2(1). Accordingly the learned judge was only empowered by subsection (2) to give leave "if and only if he is satisfied that it would be unfair to that defendant to refuse to allow the evidence to be adduced or the question to be asked". That was therefore the question to which the learned judge had to direct his attention.

This section has not yet, as far as this Court is aware, been considered by this Court. It was however considered by May J a few months before the present trial, in *Lawrence and Another* [1977] Crim LR 492, which that learned judge heard at Nottingham Crown Court on May 10, 1977. There is a brief report of the learned judge's ruling at pp. 492 and 493, which reads thus:

The important part of the statute which I think needs construction are the words "if and only if he [the judge] is satisfied that it would be unfair to that defendant to refuse to allow the evidence to be adduced or the question to be asked". And, in my judgment, before a judge is satisfied or may be said to be satisfied that to refuse to allow a particular question or a series of questions in cross-examination would be unfair to a defendant he must take the view that it is more likely than not that the particular question or line of cross-examination, if allowed, might reasonably lead the jury, properly directed in the summing up, to take a different view of the complainant's evidence from that which they might take if the question or series of questions was or were not allowed".

This comment follows: "On the facts of the case the learned judge ruled that cross-examination designed to form a basis for the unspoken comment, 'Well, there you are, members of the jury, that is the sort of girl she is,' was not permissible; distinguishing between cross-examination designed to blacken the complainant's sexual character so as to leave such a comment and cross-examination as to the trustworthiness of her evidence, the learned judge ruled that only the latter going to credit properly so called was permissible".

This is, as we pointed out to Mr Hunt in the course of argument, essentially a matter for the exercise of discretion by the trial judge within the framework of the Act, bearing in mind that that statutory provision is designed to secure protection for complainants. The learned judge here exercised his discretion after having had that decision of May J quoted to him.

Mr Hunt found himself unable to say that this was not a matter for the exercise of the learned judge's discretion, but argued that this Court should substitute its own discretion for that of the learned judge.

With respect, it would be entirely wrong for us to do so. In our view the approach adopted by May J in *Lawrence and Another (supra)* was entirely right and Boreham J, following that ruling of May J, exercised his discretion properly. It would be impossible, and it would be quite wrong, for this Court in any way to seek to disturb that exercise of discretion which seems to us to be wholly in accordance with section 2(1) and (2) of the statute. Consequently the application for leave to appeal against conviction fails and must be refused.'

Application refused.

R v Viola [1982] 1 WLR 1138 (CA)

At the appellant's trial on a charge of rape, the issue was whether or not the complainant, who had given evidence in-chief, had consented to the sexual intercourse. The appellant sought leave under s. 2 of the Sexual Offences (Amendment) Act 1976 to cross-examine her about her sexual experiences with other men, the proposed questions being based on statements made by eye witnesses concerning incidents with different men some hours before and some hours after the alleged rape. The judge refused leave and the appellant was convicted. He appealed.

LORD LANE CJ, giving the judgment of the court: 'It is, we think apparent from those words [s.2 of the Sexual Offences (Amendment) Act 1976], without more, that the first question which the judge must ask himself is this: are the questions proposed to be put relevant according to the ordinary common law rules of evidence and relevant to the case as it is being put? If they are not so relevant, that is the end of the matter . . ..

The second matter which the judge must consider is this. If the questions are relevant, then whether they should be allowed or not will of course depend upon the terms of section 2, which limits the admissibility of relevant evidence. That section has been the subject of judicial consideration first of all by May J in *R* v *Lawrence* [1977] Crim LR 492; a passage, which is taken verbatim from the transcript of the ruling, reads, at p. 493:

> The important part of the statute which I think needs construction are the words 'if and only if [the judge] is satisfied that it would be unfair to that defendant to refuse to allow the evidence to be adduced or the question to be asked.' And, in my judgment, before a judge is satisfied or may be said to be satisfied that to refuse to allow a particular question or a series of questions in cross-examination would be unfair to a defendant he must take the view that it is more likely than not that the particular question or line of cross-examination, if allowed, might reasonably lead the jury, properly directed in the summing up, to take a different view of the complainant's evidence from that which they might take if the question or series of questions was or were not allowed.

That statement was approved by this court in *R* v *Mills (Leroy)* (1978) 68 Cr App R 327. Roskill LJ, giving the judgment of the court said, at p. 329:

> The second ground of appeal is different in character. It was alleged that the complainant had had a good deal of earlier sexual experience. As is well known, in former times cross-examination in rape cases was permitted with a view to attacking the character of the complainant on the ground that she had had such previous sexual experience. That practice was the subject of widespread public condemnation and ultimately the Sexual Offences (Amendment) Act 1976 was passed.

Then Roskill LJ reads the contents of section 2 and continues:

> Application was made during cross-examination of this complainant by Mr Hunt that he should be allowed to cross-examine her as to her antecedent sexual experience. On the face of it such cross-examination would be contrary to section 2(1). Accordingly the learned judge was only empowered by subsection (2) to give leave "if and only if he is satisfied that it would be unfair to that defendant to refuse to allow the evidence to be adduced or the question to be asked". That was therefore the question to which the learned judge had to direct his attention.
>
> This section has not yet, as far as this court is aware, been considered by this court. It was however considered by May J a few months before the present trial in *R* v *Lawrence* [1977] Crim LR 492, which that learned judge heard at Nottingham Crown Court . . .

Then Roskill LJ reads out the part of the judgment of May J which we have already read, and continues, on p. 330: "This is, as we pointed out to Mr Hunt in the course of argument, essentially a matter for the exercise of discretion by the trial judge within the framework of the Act, bearing in mind that that statutory provision is designed to secure protection for complainants. The learned judge here exercised his discretion after having had that decision of May J quoted to him. Mr Hunt found himself unable to say that this was not a matter for the exercise of the learned judge's discretion, but argued that this court should substitute its own discretion for that of the learned judge. With respect, it would be entirely wrong for us to do so . . .". Then Roskill LJ said that the court over which he presided felt that the ruling of May J, which they approved, was entirely right, and said, "It would be impossible, and it would be quite wrong, for this court in any way to seek to disturb that exercise of discretion which seems to us to be wholly in accordance with section 2(1) and (2) of the statute". The application was refused.

That approval by this court of the decision in *R v Lawrence* [1977] Crim LR 492 means that we are bound by the words of May J to which we have referred. In the end the judge will have to ask himself the question whether he is satisfied in the terms expounded by May J. It will be a problem for him to apply that *dictum* to the particular facts of the case. In those circumstances it seems to us it would be both improper and, perhaps more important, very unwise for us to try to say in advance what may or may not be unfair in any particular case.

We would further like to say this about the judgment in *R v Mills (Leroy)*, 68 Cr App R 327, and say it with the greatest possible deference to that court. It has been agreed on all hands, not only by the appellant and by the Crown but also by Mr Green who has assisted us as *amicus curiae*, that it is wrong to speak of a judge's "discretion" in this context. The judge has to make a judgment as to whether he is satisfied or not in the terms of section 2. But once having reached his judgment on the particular facts, he has no discretion. If he comes to the conclusion that he is satisfied it would be unfair to exclude the evidence, then the evidence has to be admitted and the questions have to be allowed.

Having said that, when one considers the purposes which lay behind the passing of this Act as expounded by Roskill LJ it is clear that it was aimed primarily at protecting complainants from cross-examination as to credit, from questions which went merely to credit and no more. The result is that generally speaking—I use these words advisedly, of course there will always be exceptions—if the proposed questions merely seek to establish that the complainant has had sexual experience with other men to whom she was not married, so as to suggest that for that reason she ought not to be believed under oath, the judge will exclude the evidence. In the present climate of opinion a jury is unlikely to be influenced by such considerations, nor should it be influenced. In other words questions of this sort going simply to credit will seldom be allowed. That is borne out by the cases to which we have been referred: not only those which I have cited, but other unreported cases which have been before this court, to which perhaps it is not necessary to make reference.

On the other hand if the questions are relevant to an issue in the trial in the light of the way the case is being run, for instance relevant to the issue of consent, as opposed merely to credit, they are likely to be admitted, because to exclude a relevant question on an issue in the trial as the trial is being run will usually mean that the jury are being prevented from hearing something which, if they did hear it, might cause them to change their minds about the evidence given by the complainant. But, I repeat, we are very far from laying down any hard and fast rule.

Inevitably in this situation, as in so many similar situations in the law, there is a grey area which exists between the two types of relevance, namely, relevance to credit and relevance to an issue in the case. On one hand evidence of sexual promiscuity may be so strong or so closely contemporaneous in time to the event in issue as to come near to, or indeed to reach the border between mere credit and an issue in the case. Conversely, the relevance of the evidence to an issue in the case may be so slight as to lead the judge to the conclusion that he is far from satisfied that the exclusion of the evidence or the question from the consideration of the jury would be unfair to the defendant.

We have had drawn to our attention some of the difficulties which face a judge. It is perfectly true to say that normally he has to make this decision at an early stage of the trial. It will be, generally speaking, when the complainant's evidence in chief is concluded that counsel in the absence of the jury will make the necessary application under section 2. At this stage it may not be easy for the judge to reach a conclusion, but this is a problem which is continually being faced by judges, sometimes in even more trying circumstances, for example, when he is asked to determine whether a count should be tried separately or whether defendants should be tried separately and so on, before the trial has got under way at all. He has to reach the best conclusion that he can.

The second matter is: is this court entitled to differ from the conclusions of the judge? As already pointed out, this is the exercise of judgment by the judge not an exercise of his discretion. This court is in many respects in as good a position as the judge to reach a conclusion. The judge has certainly heard the complainant give evidence, but only in chief. So far as the proposed questions are concerned, the statements upon which the questions were to be asked or the way in which the matter was going to be put to the jury are presented in exactly the same way to this court as they were to the judge at first instance. We have been told what it was that counsel sought in the course of his submission to the judge and indeed we have been given the statements which were to be the basis of the questions which he was going to ask. So what we have to decide is whether the judge was right or wrong in the conclusion which he reached, applying the test of May J in *R* v *Lawrence* [1977] Crim LR 492, 493. Like so many decisions in the grey area, it is not an easy decision to make'.

Appeal allowed.

Conviction quashed.

• If the law should both protect the interest of the accused in securing a fair trial and also the interest of the complainant in not having marginally relevant aspects of her private life put before the court, does section 2 of the Sexual Offences (Amendment) Act 1976 as interpreted in the case-law strike the correct balance?

• Is it possible to make a clear distinction between relevance to issue and relevance to credibility?

B: PREVIOUS INCONSISTENT STATEMENTS

(Suggested preliminary reading: *A Practical Approach to Evidence,* pp. 388–391).

Criminal Procedure Act 1865

4 If a witness upon cross-examination as to a former statement made by him relative to the subject-matter of the indictment or proceeding, and inconsistent with his present testimony, does not distinctly admit that he has made such statement, proof may be given that he did in fact make it; but before such proof can be given the circumstances of the supposed statement, sufficient to designate the particular occasion, must be mentioned to the witness, and he must be asked whether or not he has made such statement.

5 A witness may be cross-examined as to previous statements made by him in writing, or reduced into writing, relative to the subject-matter of the indictment or proceeding, without such writing being shown to him; but if it is intended to contradict such witness by the writing, his attention must, before such contradictory proof can be given, be called to those parts of the writing which are to be used for the purpose of so contradicting him: Provided always, that it shall be competent for the judge, at any time during the trial, to require the production of the writing for his inspection, and he may thereupon make such use of it for the purposes of the trial as he may think fit.

Civil Evidence Act 1968

3(1) Where in any civil proceedings—

(a) a previous inconsistent or contradictory statement made by a person called as a witness in those proceedings is proved by virtue of section 3, 4 or 5 of the Criminal Procedure Act, 1865 . . . that statement shall by virtue of this subsection be admissible as evidence of any fact stated therein of which direct oral evidence by him would be admissible.

C: FINALITY OF ANSWERS ON COLLATERAL ISSUES

(Suggested preliminary reading: *A Practical Approach to Evidence,* pp. 391–397).

Attorney-General v *Hitchcock* (1847) 1 Exch 91

The defendant, a maltster, was charged with using a cistern in breach of certain statutory requirements. A prosecution witness was asked in cross-examination whether he had not previously said that he had been offered £20 by officers of the Crown, if he would state in evidence that the cistern had been so used. The witness denied the allegation, whereupon the defence proposed to call a witness of their own to state that the prosecution witness had said this. The judge held that the question tended to raise a collateral issue and ruled that it could not be put. The defence obtained a rule for a new trial on the ground that this evidence was improperly rejected.

POLLOCK CB: ' . . . the test, whether the matter is collateral or not, is this: if the answer of a witness is a matter which you would be allowed on your part to prove in evidence—if it have such a connection with the issue, that you would be allowed to give it in evidence—then it is a matter on which you may contradict him. Or it may be as well put, or perhaps better, in the language of my Brother Alderson this morning, that, if you ask a witness whether he has not said so and so, and the matter he is supposed to have said would, if he had said it, contradict any other part of his testimony, then you may call another witness to prove that he had said so, in order that the jury may believe the account of the transaction which he gave to that other witness to be the truth, and that the statement he makes on oath in the witness box is not true'.

ALDERSON B: 'The reason why a party is obliged to take the answer of a witness is, that if he were permitted to go into it, it is only justice to allow the witness to call other evidence in support of the testimony he has given, and as those witnesses might be cross-examined as to their conduct, such a course would be productive of endless collateral issues. Suppose, for instance, witness A is accused of having committed some offence; witness B is called to prove it, when, on witness B's cross-examination, he is asked whether he has not made some statement, to prove which witness C is called, so that it would be necessary to try all those issues, before one step could be obtained towards the adjudication of the particular case before the Court. On the contrary, if the answer be taken as given, if the witness speaks falsely he may be indicted for perjury. That is the proper remedy. Then in the next place, in my opinion, when the question is not relevant, strictly speaking, to the issue, but tending to contradict the witness, his answer must be taken, although it tends to shew that he, in that particular instance, speaks falsely, and although it is not altogether immaterial to the matter in issue, for the sake of the general public convenience; for great inconvenience would follow from a continual course of those sorts of cross-examinations which would be let in in the case of a witness being called for the purposes of contradiction. I think those are the rules by which these cases have always been governed, and the application of which is easy and short. In this case the party is asked, A have you not said B offered you £20 to make a certain statement, which I agree is material in the cause. He says, no, I have not said any such thing. Is that material to the issue, or does it qualify or contradict anything that he had said before? What he had said before was, that the cistern was used; the offer of a bribe to make a statement to the contrary, if he had not accepted it, would not have had a different tendency. If he had said, that he had been offered a bribe, if he had answered in the affirmative, it would not in the slightest degree have disproved the matter. If it would not, it does not qualify or contradict that which he had before stated; and I think that it is not allowable to call a witness to contradict him in that, which, if answered by him in the affirmative, would not have qualified or contradicted his statement'.

ROLFE B: 'If we lived for a thousand years instead of about sixty or seventy, and every case were of sufficient importance, it might be possible, and perhaps proper, to throw a light on matters in which every possible question might be suggested, for the purpose of seeing by such means whether the whole was unfounded, or what portion of it was not, and to raise every possible inquiry as to the truth of the statements made. But I do not see how that could be; in fact, mankind find it to be impossible'.

Rule discharged.

Criminal Procedure Act 1865

6 A witness may be questioned as to whether he has been convicted of any misdemeanour, and upon being so questioned, if he either denies or does not admit the fact, or refuses to answer, it shall be lawful for the cross-examining party to prove such conviction . . ..

R v Mendy (1976) 64 Cr App R 4 (CA)

The appellant was charged with assault. At her trial all the witnesses were kept out of court in accordance with normal practice. While a detective was giving evidence about the assault, a constable in court noticed a man in the public gallery taking notes. This man was then seen to leave court and the same constable and a court officer saw him discussing the case with the appellant's husband, apparently describing the detective's evidence to him. The husband then gave evidence and in cross-examination denied that the incident with the man had occurred and the prosecution was given leave to call evidence by the constable and the court officer in rebuttal. The appellant was convicted and appealed on the ground that this evidence in rebuttal had been wrongly admitted, as the husband's answers in cross-examination were answers as to credit and the prosecution was not entitled to call evidence to contradict them.

GEOFFREY LANE LJ, reading the judgment of the court: 'Was the evidence admissible? A party may not, in general, impeach the credit of his opponent's witnesses by calling witnesses to contradict him on collateral matters, and his answers thereon will be conclusive—see *Harris* v *Tippett* (1811) 2 Camp 637, and *Phipson on Evidence*, 11th ed, paragraph 1553. The rule is of great practical use. It serves to prevent the indefinite prolongation of trials which would result from a minute examination of the character and credit of witnesses. It seems to have caused very little trouble in operation, judging by the paucity of authority on the subject. Difficulties may sometimes arise in determining what matters are merely collateral, see *Phillips* (1936) 26 Cr App R 17, but no one seriously suggests that the issue in the present case was other than collateral. On the other hand, it seems strange, if it be the case, that the Court and jury have to be kept in ignorance of behaviour by a witness such as that in the present case. The suggestion which lay behind the evidence in question was that Mr Mendy was prepared to lend himself to a scheme designed to defeat the purpose of keeping prospective witnesses out of Court; that he allowed the messenger to give him details of what Detective Constable Price had been saying in the witness box about the assault which the appellant was alleged to have committed. If the evidence of the Court officer and Constable Thatcher was to be believed, the jury could be in little doubt that the witness's object in receiving such instruction must have been to enable him the more convincingly to describe how he and not the appellant had caused the injuries to the policeman.

The truth of the matter is, as one would expect, that the rule is not all-embracing. It has always been permissible to call evidence to contradict a witness's denial of bias or partiality towards one of the parties and to show that he is prejudiced so far as the case being tried is concerned.

Pollock CB in *Attorney-General* v *Hitchcock* (1847) 1 Ex 91 puts the matter thus at p. 101: "It is no disparagement to a man that a bribe is offered to him; it may be a disparagement to the man who makes the offer. If therefore the witness is asked about the fact and denies it or if he is asked whether he said so and so and he denies it he cannot be contradicted as to what he has said. *Lord Stafford's Case* [(1680) 7 How St Tr 1400] was totally different. There the witness himself had been implicated in offering a bribe to some other person. That immediately affected him as proving that he had acted the part of a suborner for the purpose of preventing the truth. In that case the evidence was to show that the witness was offered a bribe in a particular case, and the object was to show that he was so far affected towards the party accused as to be willing to adopt any corrupt course in order to carry out his purposes". In *Lord Stafford's Case, (supra)* the evidence was admitted.

Those words apply almost precisely to the facts in the present case. The witness was prepared to cheat in order to deceive the jury and help the defendant. The jury were entitled to be apprised of that fact'.

Appeal dismissed.

R v Busby (1981) 75 Cr App R 79 (CA)

The appellant was charged with offences of burglary and handling stolen goods. He was alleged to have made certain remarks to the police when interviewed about the alleged offences which were not specific admissions but were very damaging. At his trial he did not give evidence, and on his behalf two police officers were cross-examined to establish, *inter alia*, that the appellant had made the remarks aforesaid and also that one officer, in the presence of the other, had threatened a potential witness for the defence to stop him giving evidence. Both officers denied that they had threatened that witness. The witness was then called. Thereupon the Crown objected to his giving evidence about the officers' visit to him. The trial judge upheld the objection on the ground that that evidence was merely an attack upon credit and did not go to the facts in issue. The trial proceeded and the appellant was convicted. He appealed.

EVELEIGH LJ, giving the judgment of the court: 'It is not always easy to determine when a question relates to facts which are collateral only, and therefore to be treated as final, and when it is relevant to the issue which has to be tried. In *Attorney-General v Hitchcock* (1847) 1 Exch 91, a witness was asked in cross-examination whether he had not told one Cook that excise officers had offered him a bribe to give his evidence. He denied saying this to Cook and it was held that Cook was not to be called on the matter. The fact that he had been offered a bribe would cast no light on his attitude to giving evidence in the case. If it had been suggested that he had actually received a bribe the position would have been different.

We are of the opinion that the learned judge was wrong to refuse to admit the evidence. If true, it would have shown that the police were prepared to go to improper lengths in order to secure the accused's conviction. It was the accused's case that the statement attributed to him had been fabricated, a suggestion which could not be accepted by the jury unless they thought that the officers concerned were prepared to go to improper lengths to secure a conviction.

In *Phillips* (1936) 26 Cr App R 17, the Court of Criminal Appeal held that the accused should have been allowed to call evidence to rebut his daughters' denial that they had been schooled by their mother to give evidence against him. Again, in *Mendy* (1976) 64 Cr App R 4, it was held that evidence in rebuttal could be called after a denial by the witness that he had been spoken to by someone who left the court after hearing evidence. As Professor Sir Rupert Cross summarised the matter in *Cross on Evidence* (5th ed) p. 267: "It was held that evidence in rebuttal might be called because the episode indicated that the husband was a prejudiced witness, prepared to cheat in furtherance of his wife's case". In the present case, the evidence, if true, would have indicated that the officers were prepared to cheat in furtherance of the prosecution.'

Appeal allowed. Convictions quashed.

Toohey v *Commissioner of Police of the Metropolis* [1965] AC 595 (HL)

The appellant was tried, with two other men, on an indictment which included a count of assault with intent to rob M a boy aged 16. The jury having disagreed, a second trial took place. At both trials the prosecution's case was substantially the same, being based mainly on the evidence of M as to the alleged assault and also the evidence of two police officers who stated that they had come upon the accused and M in an alleyway, M being in a dishevelled and hysterical state and asking for police help, while the defendants were denying the assault. The defendants stated that they had come on M in a bad state and apparently the worse for drink and had decided to help him home, that he had become hysterical and that the charge was ridiculous.

The case for the defence at both trials was also substantially the same, being a denial of the assault, save that, at the first trial, evidence for the defence was given by a police surgeon, who had examined M shortly after he had been taken to the police station and who stated that M had been in a state of hysteria at the time. In his evidence in chief he had been asked his opinion as to the part played by alcohol in the condition described as hysteria, and replied that it was hard to say, but that alcohol would exacerbate it. In re-examination he was asked what, from his examination of M, he would consider his normal behaviour to be, and gave his opinion that he might well be more prone to hysteria than the normal person. At the first trial neither the judge nor the prosecution objected to this opinion being elicited, but at the second trial, before the doctor was called, the judge intimated that he would not allow questions designed to elicit the opinions given by the doctor at the first trial, on the ground that they were evidence of the kind held to be inadmissible in *R* v *Gunewardene* [1951] 2 KB 600; namely evidence by a doctor that a witness was suffering from such a mental disease that the doctor would regard his testimony as unreliable.

At the second trial all the accused were convicted on the count of assault with intent to rob. The appellant appealed against conviction on the ground that *R* v *Gunewardene* was distinguishable.

LORD PEARCE: 'It is common knowledge that hysteria can be produced by fear. The hysteria of the victim of an alleged assault may, if he is a person of normal stability, confirm a jury in the belief that he has been assaulted. When, however, the victim is unstable and hysterical by nature, the hysteria can raise a doubt whether in truth an assault ever occurred or whether it was the figment of an hysterical imagination. Here the real question to be determined was whether, as the prosecution alleged, the episode created the hysteria, or whether, on the other hand, as the defence alleged, the hysteria created the episode. To that issue medical evidence as to the hysterical and unstable nature of the alleged victim was relevant. It might be that, on a careful examination of the medical evidence, the predisposition to hysteria and instability was not enough to create an episode of this kind without some assault to provoke it. But, equally, that evidence might have created a real doubt whether there was any assault at all and might have inclined the jury to believe the account given by the accused. On that ground the defence was entitled to have the evidence considered by the jury.

The second question, whether it was permissible to impeach the credibility of Madden, *qua* witness, by medical evidence of his hysterical and unstable nature, raises a wider and more important problem which applies to evidence in criminal and civil cases alike.

The Court of Criminal Appeal held that such evidence was not admissible since they were bound by the case of *Gunewardene*. Undoubtedly they were right in thinking that on this point the present case is not distinguishable from it. In *Gunewardene's* case the appellant (to quote the words of Lord Goddard CJ) "wished to call [Doctor Leigh] to say that he . . . had examined the witness and had come to the conclusion that the man was suffering from a disease of the mind and that therefore he regarded his testimony as unreliable. In our opinion that is exactly what the cases show cannot be done". It was there held that the most that the doctor could have been asked on oath was: "From your knowledge of the witness, would you believe him on his oath?" And although it was open to the other side in cross-examination to probe the particular reasons for the belief, the doctor could not give them in examination-in-chief. Thus, the only evidence which a doctor could give in chief would seem mysterious or meaningless to the jury; and if it was not amplified by questions in cross-examination (from which opposing counsel might well refrain) it would be liable to be robbed of its proper effect. Moreover, the principle in *Gunewardene's* case would exclude altogether the evidence of a doctor who cannot go so far as to say that he would not believe the witness on oath. It would not allow a doctor to testify (as is desired in the present case) to the abnormality and unreliability of the witness, or (as may happen in some other case), to the fact that the witness, by reason of some delusion, would on some matters not be credible, whereas on others he might be quite reliable.

Throughout *Gunewardene's* case the court dealt with the problem created by the mental disease and mental abnormality of the witness as if it were identical with the problem of moral discredit and unveracity. They referred to many cases dealing with bad character and reputation, but to none which dealt with mental disturbance.

From olden times it has been the practice to allow evidence of bad reputation to discredit a witness's testimony. It is perhaps not very logical and not very useful to allow such evidence founded on hearsay. None of your Lordships and none of the counsel before you could remember being concerned in a case where such evidence was called. But the rule has been sanctified through the centuries in legal examinations and textbooks and in some rare cases, and it does not create injustice. Its scope is conveniently summarised by Professor Cross (*Evidence*, 2nd ed (1963), p. 225): "In *Mawson* v *Hartsink* (1802) 4 Esp 102; it was held that the witness must be asked whether he is aware of the impugned witness's reputation for veracity and whether, from such knowledge, he would believe the impugned witness on oath. In *R* v *Watson* (1817) 2 Stark 116, however, it was held that the witness might simply state whether he would believe the oath of the person about whom he was asked, and although *R* v *Rowton* (1865) Le & Ca 520 decides that, when asked about a prisoner's character, the witness must speak to the accused's general reputation and not give his personal opinion of the accused's disposition, *R* v *Brown and Hedley* (1867) 10 Cox CC 453 sanctions the form of question approved in *R* v *Watson*".

Where a witness's general reputation, so far as concerns veracity, has been thus demolished, it seems that it may be reinstated by other witnesses who give evidence that he is worthy of credit or who discredit the discrediting witness (*Taylor on Evidence*, 12th ed, Vol. II, para. 1473; *Stephen on Evidence*, 12th ed, art. 146). Thus far, and no further, it appears, may the process of recrimination go (Taylor, para. 1473, citing *R v Lord Stafford* (1680) 7 How St Tr 1400). How far the evidence is confined to veracity alone or may extend to moral turpitude generally seems a matter of some doubt (see Taylor, para. 1471).

There seems little point, however, for present purposes in exploring these archaic niceties. The old cases are concerned with lying as an aspect of bad character and are of little help in establishing any principle that will deal with modern scientific knowledge of mental disease and its effect on the reliability of a witness. I accept all of the judgment in *Gunewardene's* case in so far as it deals with the older cases and the topic with which they were concerned. But, in my opinion, the court erred in using it as a guide to the admissibility of medical evidence concerning illness or abnormality affecting the mind of a witness and reducing his capacity to give reliable evidence. This unreliability may have two aspects either separate from one another or acting jointly to create confusion. The witness may, through his mental trouble, derive a fanciful or untrue picture from events while they are actually occurring, or he may have a fanciful or untrue recollection of them which distorts his evidence at the time when he is giving it.

The only general principles which can be derived from the older cases are these. On the one hand, the courts have sought to prevent juries from being beguiled by the evidence of witnesses who could be shown to be, through defect of character, wholly unworthy of belief. On the other hand, however, they have sought to prevent the trial of a case becoming clogged with a number of side issues, such as might arise if there could be an investigation of matters which had no relevance to the issue save in so far as they tended to show the veracity or falsity of the witness who was giving evidence which *was* relevant to the issue. Many controversies which might thus obliquely throw some light on the issues must in practice be discarded because there is not an infinity of time, money and mental comprehension available to make use of them.

There is one older case (*R v Hill* (1851) 20 LJMC 222) in which the Court for Crown Cases Reserved considered how it should deal with the evidence of a lunatic who was rational on some points. Evidence was given by doctors as to his credibility. Alderson B in argument made the sensible observation: "It seems to me almost approaching to an absurdity to say that a jury may, by hearing the statement of doctors, be able to say whether a man was insane when he made his will, and yet that they should not be competent to say whether a man be in a state of mind to enable him to give credible evidence when they see him before them". Lord Campbell CJ in giving judgment said: "The true rule seems to me to be that it was for the judge to see whether the witness understands the nature of an oath and, if he does, to admit his testimony. No doubt, before he is sworn, the lunatic may be cross-examined, and evidence may be called to show that he labours under such a diseased mind as to be inadmissible; but, in the absence of such evidence he is *prima facie* admissible, and the jury may give such credit as they please to his testimony". The point was not quite the same as that which is before your Lordships, since the question was whether the lunatic should be allowed to give evidence at all. But there is inherent,

I think, in the judgments an intention that the jury should have the best opportunity of arriving at the truth and that the medical evidence with regard to the witness's credibility should be before them.

Human evidence shares the frailties of those who give it. It is subject to many cross-currents such as partiality, prejudice, self-interest and, above all, imagination and inaccuracy. Those are matters with which the jury, helped by cross-examination and common sense, must do their best. But when a witness through physical (in which I include mental) disease or abnormality is not capable of giving a true or reliable account to the jury, it must surely be allowable for medical science to reveal this vital hidden fact to them. If a witness purported to give evidence of something which he believed that he had seen at a distance of 50 yards, it must surely be possible to call the evidence of an oculist to the effect that the witness could not possibly see anything at a greater distance than 20 yards, or the evidence of a surgeon who had removed a cataract from which the witness was suffering at the material time and which would have prevented him from seeing what he thought he saw. So, too, must it be allowable to call medical evidence of mental illness which makes a witness incapable of giving reliable evidence, whether through the existence of delusions or otherwise.

It is obviously in the interest of justice that such evidence should be available. The only argument that I can see against its admission is that there might be a conflict between the doctors and that there would then be a trial within a trial. But such cases would be rare and, if they arose, they would not create any insuperable difficulty, since there are many cases in practice where a trial within a trial is achieved without difficulty. And in such a case (unlike the issues relating to confessions) there would not be the inconvenience of having to exclude the jury since the dispute would be for their use and their instruction.

Mr Buzzard very fairly expressed himself as unable to support the judgment in the case of *Gunewardene* since, in the Crown's view, the important thing was that the jury should be enabled to arrive at the truth and do justice.

In *R* v *Pedrini*, *The Times* 28 July, 1967 before the Court of Criminal Appeal no reliance was placed on *Gunewardene's* case. Without opposition from the Crown, since justice seemed to demand it, the court considered the evidence of three doctors as to the mental condition at the relevant time of a witness who had subsequently become insane. Lord Parker CJ said of that evidence: "That it is fresh evidence this court is prepared to accept: that it is relevant evidence there is no doubt; that it is credible evidence in the sense that it is capable of belief and of carrying some weight is also clear". In my view, the court was right in not excluding the medical evidence in that case.

Gunewardene's case was, in my opinion, wrongly decided. Medical evidence is admissible to show that a witness suffers from some disease or defect or abnormality of mind that affects the reliability of his evidence. Such evidence is not confined to a general opinion of the unreliability of the witness but may give all the matters necessary to show, not only the foundation of and reasons for the diagnosis, but also the extent to which the credibility of the witness is affected.'

(LORDS REID, MORRIS of BORTH-Y-GEST, HODSON and DONOVAN concurred.)

Appeal allowed.

R v *Richardson*; R v *Longman* [1969] 1 QB 299 (CA)

The defendants were tried on indictment with conspiring together to pervert the course of justice by trying to influence a jury and by suborning witnesses at a trial at which the brother of one of the defendants was among those tried. At the trial the chief prosecution witness gave evidence, and in order to discredit her the defence called a witness (a doctor) who was asked whether he would believe the prosecution witness on her oath and he replied that in certain particulars she could be believed on oath. The judge refused to allow the witness to be asked the further question whether from his personal knowledge of her he would believe the prosecution witness on her oath nor was the witness permitted to qualify his previous answer. The defendants were convicted and appealed.

EDMUND DAVIES LJ, giving the judgment of the court: 'The legal position may be thus summarised:

1 A witness may be asked whether he has knowledge of the impugned witness's general reputation for veracity and whether (from such knowledge) he would believe the impugned witness's sworn testimony.

2 The witness called to impeach the credibility of a previous witness may also express his individual opinion (based upon his personal knowledge) as to whether the latter is to be believed upon his oath and is *not* confined to giving evidence merely of general reputation.

3 But whether his opinion as to the impugned witness's credibility be based simply upon the latter's general reputation for veracity or upon his personal knowledge, the witness cannot be permitted to indicate during his examination-in-chief the particular facts, circumstances or incidents which formed the basis of his opinion, although he may be cross-examined as to them . . . [I]t is said that, while Mr Lassman was permitted to ask Dr Hitchens whether, in the light of Mrs Clemence's general reputation for veracity, he would be prepared to believe her on her oath, the question was never allowed to be answered in its entirety. It is submitted that the form of such answer as Dr Hitchens gave showed that he desired to qualify it in some way and was prevented by the judge from uttering more than the single qualifying word, "But——".

It is clear from the transcript that Mr Lassman also desired to ask another question of Dr Hitchens, and we were told (and we accept) that it would have been in this form: "From your personal knowledge of Mrs Clemence would you believe her on her oath?" That question, in our judgment, he should have been permitted to put, but we have some sympathy with the trial judge suddenly confronted as he was with a situation which so rarely arises that not one of the learned Lords who decided *Toohey's* case [1965] AC 595 had throughout their extensive careers ever experienced it. Nevertheless, we are obliged to hold that the trial judge was technically wrong in ruling out that further question. As to whether he was also wrong in cutting short Dr Hitchens's attempt to qualify his earlier answer is far less clear: for it looks very much as though the witness was proceeding to adduce his reasons for qualifying it, and we know of no authority which permits that to be done'.

(The court applied the proviso to s.4(1) of the Criminal Appeal Act 1907.)

Appeal dismissed.

Questions for discussion

R v *Coke*; *R* v *Littleton*

1 May counsel for Coke cross-examine Margaret Blackstone as to:

(a) The fact that she consented to have sexual intercourse with Coke on 8 July 1979?

(b) The fact that she had led him to believe on other occasions that she was prepared to have sexual intercourse with him?

(c) The fact that Margaret is promiscuous?

(d) The fact that Margaret has had sexual intercourse with Coke's mate, Kevin?

(e) The fact that Margaret threatened to accuse Kevin of raping her?

(f) The fact that Margaret has previous convictions for theft?

2 In relation to any of these matters on which cross-examination is possible, would the defence be entitled to call evidence in rebuttal if Margaret denies them in cross-examination?

3 If Margaret's evidence in chief varies materially from the contents of her statement to the police, what steps may Coke's counsel take? What results will any such course have, and what must counsel bear in mind before embarking on it?

4 If Margaret has a known history of lying, what evidence might be called on behalf of Coke to deal with this?

Blackstone v Coke

1 Consider question 3 above in the context of *Blackstone* v *Coke*.

2 If Coke is permitted to adduce the hearsay statement of Anthony Henneky, what steps might Margaret take to discredit it?

Additional questions

1 Most American jurisdictions limit cross-examination to matters which have been canvassed in examination-in-chief, plus matters affecting credit. A party who wishes to elicit further evidence from the witness must do so by calling the witness as part of his case and conducting his own examination-in-chief. What are the advantages and disadvantages of this system compared with the English practice?

2 You are acting for Albert, a plaintiff who is claiming damages for injuries sustained in a road accident. The evidence in your possession is as follows: Albert was riding a bicycle along a country road near Barton; he knew nothing of the accident and was unconscious for several days afterwards. Bernard, accompanied by his wife, Celia, was driving his car on the same road: after overtaking Albert, he saw in his mirror a blue car driving rapidly behind him; it knocked Albert off his bicycle; the blue car overtook Bernard. Bernard stopped his car, told Celia to take the number of the blue car, and went to look after Albert. Sergeant Douglas accompanied by Edward, a police cadet, arrived about ten minutes later: Celia, in the presence of Bernard, told the police that the blue car's number was ABC 123V, and Douglas wrote this in his notebook. Douglas and Edward ascertained that the car was owned by a partnership, Fred and George, and they visited the premises later that day: Fred was in the office: he said that he had been in the office all day, but that George had

been to visit a client in Barton: later George arrived, and said that he had been out, but in the firm's other car, XYZ 789W, and had not been to Barton: he also said that there was another car in the neighbourhood, ACB 122W, which was sometimes mistaken for theirs; the officers examined ABC 123V which was old and battered. Douglas took a note of the interview: after returning to the police station, Edward copied out Douglas' note. Douglas later decided that there was insufficient evidence to prosecute George and destroyed his note.

Albert is suing George, whose insurers maintain that he was not driving near Barton that day, and that the accident was probably caused by Bernard. You are aware that Bernard was convicted on a charge of fraud some years ago, but do not know if the insurers are aware of this. Albert's medical consultant says that Albert's condition is unusually complex, and that he would have difficulty in explaining this to the court without reference to medical textbooks and statistical tables. Discuss.

3 You are acting for Harry, a young man of previous good character, who is charged with raping Irene on the night of the 1/2 August.

The prosecution are proposing to call the following witnesses:

(a) Irene, who will say that she spent the evening of 1 August drinking with Harry and Jack in the Jolly Sailor; Harry was pestering her all evening and after Jack left at about 10 p.m. Harry enticed her outside and raped her.

(b) Jack, who will say that he and Irene and Harry were drinking together and that Harry was chatting Irene up; he was anxious about leaving Irene and Harry together, but he had to leave at 10 p.m. because his mother got worried if he was late.

(c) Mrs Knowles, Irene's mother, who will say that Irene arrived home at 2 a.m. on the 2 August in a state of distress and said that Harry had raped her.

(d) Dr Lambert, who will say that he examined Irene on the 2 August and found evidence of recent intercourse.

(e) Detective Constable Michael who will say that he interviewed Harry briefly on the 2 August, and that Harry made a statement admitting having intercourse with Irene, but saying that it was with her consent.

Harry has told you that he had been having intercourse with Irene on a regular basis and always with her consent; he says that she has been with all the lads in town. He admits making a statement to DC Michael, but says that the interview lasted an hour and that DC Michael was scribbling in his notebook the whole time. You have taken a statement from Jack, who has told you that while they were in the Jolly Sailor, Irene was egging Harry on; he left at 10 p.m. because he thought they wanted to be left alone together; when asked why he had given the police a different story, he told you that his father was in trouble, and he didn't want to make things worse. You also have on file a statement from Norman whom you previously represented on a charge of unlawful intercourse with Olive, a 15-year-old friend of Irene: Norman pleaded guilty but he told you that he had regularly been having intercourse with Irene, and had only had intercourse with Olive because Irene had told him 'It was time Olive learnt how to do it'. Your clerk has seen Mrs Knowles and, although he cannot be sure, he thinks he has recognised her as a woman who previously lived with a scrap-metal dealer called Peters under the name of Mrs Peters and had a series of convictions for handling stolen metal.

How will you conduct Harry's defence?

(Questions 2 and 3 examine materials in both chapters 12 and 13).

Further reading

Adler, 'Rape—the intention of parliament and the practice of the courts' (1982) 45 MLR 664.

Elliott, 'Rape complainants' sexual experience with third parties' [1984] Crim LR 4.

Temkin, 'Evidence in sexual assault cases' (1984) 47 MLR 625.

Temkin, 'Regulating sexual evidence history: the limits of discretionary legislation' (1984) 33 ICLQ 942.

14 Corroboration

A: WHEN CORROBORATION IS REQUIRED

(Suggested preliminary reading: *A Practical Approach to Evidence*, pp. 414–425).

Affiliation Proceedings Act 1957, as amended

4(1) On the hearing of a complaint under section 1 of this Act the court may adjudge the defendant to be the putative father of the child but shall not do so, in a case where evidence is given by the mother, unless her evidence is corroborated in some material particular by other evidence to the court's satisfaction.

Road Traffic Regulation Act 1984

89(1) A person who drives a motor vehicle on a road at a speed exceeding a limit imposed by or under any enactment to which this section applies shall be guilty of an offence.

(2) A person prosecuted for such an offence shall not be liable to be convicted solely on the evidence of one witness to the effect that, in the opinion of the witness, the person prosecuted was driving the vehicle at a speed exceeding a specified limit.

Children and Young Persons Act 1933

38(1) Where, in any proceedings against any person or for any offence, any child of tender years called as a witness does not in the opinion of the court understand the nature of an oath, his evidence may be received, though not given upon oath, if, in the opinion of the court, he is possessed of sufficient intelligence to justify the reception of the evidence, and understands the duty of speaking the truth; . . .

Provided that where evidence admitted by virtue of this section is given on behalf of the prosecution the accused shall not be liable to be convicted of the offence unless that evidence is corroborated by some other material evidence in support thereof implicating him.

DPP v *Hester* [1973] AC 296 (HL)

The respondent was charged with indecent assault on the complainant, a girl of 12. The complainant gave evidence on oath. Her nine-year-old sister gave unsworn evidence for the prosecution under section 38 of the Children and Young Persons Act 1933. The trial judge directed the jury that the evidence of an unsworn child could, in law, amount to corroboration of evidence given on oath by another child who had been sworn. The respondent was convicted. The Court of Appeal held that the trial judge's direction had been wrong and quashed the conviction. The Crown appealed to the House of Lords.

LORD MORRIS OF BORTH-Y-GEST: 'The accumulated experience of courts of law, reflecting accepted general knowledge of the ways of the world, has shown that there are many circumstances and situations in which it is unwise to found settled conclusions on the testimony of one person alone. The reasons for this are diverse. There are some suggestions which can readily be made but which are only with more difficulty rebutted. There may in some cases be motives of self-interest, or of self-exculpation, or of vindictiveness. In some situations the straight line of truth is diverted by the influences of emotion or of hysteria or of alarm or of remorse. Sometimes it may be that owing to immaturity or perhaps to lively imaginative gifts there is no true appreciation of the gulf that separates truth from falsehood. It must, therefore, be sound policy to have rules of law or of practice which are designed to avert the peril that findings of guilt may be insecurely based. So it has come about that certain statutory enactments impose the necessity in some instances of having more than one witness before there can be a conviction. So also has it come about that in other instances the courts have given guidance in terms which have become rules. Included in such cases are those in which charges of sexual offences are made. It has long been recognised that juries should in such cases be told that there are dangers in convicting on the uncorroborated testimony of a complainant though they may convict if they are satisfied that the testimony is true. As this is no mere idle process it follows that there are no set words which must be adopted to express the warning. Rather must the good sense of the matter be expounded with clarity and in the setting of a particular case. Also included in the types of cases above referred to are those in which children are witnesses. The common sense and the common experience of men and women on a jury will guide them when they have to decide what measure of credence and dependence they should accord to evidence which they have heard.

All the rules which have been evolved are in accord with the central principle of our criminal law that a person should only be convicted of a crime if those in whose hands decision rests are sure that guilt has been established. In England it has not been laid down that such certainty ought never to be reached in dependence upon the testimony of but one witness. It has, however, been recognised that the risk or danger of a wrong decision being reached is greater in certain circumstances than in others. It is where those circumstances exist that rules based upon experience, wisdom and common sense have been introduced . . ..

On the construction of the proviso to section 38(1) the further question arises whether the unsworn evidence of a child could be corroborated by the unsworn evidence of another child. The evidence of the first child would be "evidence admitted by virtue of" the section. Would the evidence of the second child (being evidence supporting that of the first and implicating the accused) be "some other material evidence" within the meaning of the proviso? It would be "other" evidence in the sense that the evidence of the second child would be other than the evidence of the first child. If the language permits of ambiguity it would seem to be more in accord with the intention of the proviso that the words "some other material evidence" should be regarded as denoting evidence other than "evidence admitted by virtue of this section". This would conform with the view which has been generally entertained. The decision in *R* v *Coyle* [1926] NI 208 was to this effect.

Although it has been necessary to refer to the reports (many of them almost too brief to record statements of principle) of many decided cases, it is to those in the cases of *R* v *Manser* (1934) 25 Cr App R 18 and *R* v *Campbell* [1956] 2 QB 432 that attention must chiefly be directed . . ..

In *Manser's* case, 25 Cr App R 18 there was a conviction of carnal knowledge of a girl (Barbara) who was under 13 years of age. A sister of Barbara, Doris, aged nine years, gave evidence without being sworn; her evidence was substantially the only corroboration of the evidence of Barbara. One of the grounds of appeal was that there was no real corroboration of Barbara's story. It does not clearly appear from the report whether Barbara gave evidence on oath but my reading of the report leaves me with the impression that she did. On that basis the important part of the decision of the court lies in the following passage in the judgment, at pp. 20–21:

> There is one further matter which is the most important of all and may indeed be regarded as conclusive. The story of the little child Doris, who was nine years of age and had given evidence without taking the oath, was treated as corroborative of the evidence of the girl Barbara. Now by statute the evidence of the little child who had not been sworn was not to be accepted as evidence at all, unless it was corroborated. The argument for the prosecution is therefore an argument in a circle. Let it be granted that the evidence of Barbara has to be corroborated: it is corroborated by the evidence of Doris. She, however, also needs to be corroborated. The answer is that she is corroborated by the evidence of Barbara, and that is called "mutual corroboration." In truth and in fact the evidence of the girl Doris ought to have been obliterated altogether from the case, in as much as it was not corroborated. It clearly was not corroborated by the evidence of the girl Barbara.

It is the correctness or otherwise of the reasoning there set out that is central to the determination of the main issue in this appeal. The conviction was quashed in *Manser's* case not merely because the summing-up failed sufficiently to direct the jury as to corroboration but also because (on the basis of the reasoning of the above passage) the "intrinsic evidence adduced on the part of the prosecution was deficient" (p. 21). It is to be noted that the headnote of the report was as follows:

> Where the evidence of a young child requires corroboration as a matter of law or practice, the unsworn testimony of another child, which itself requires to be corroborated, cannot be treated as supplying the requisite corroboration."

In *R v Campbell* [1956] 2 QB 432 there was a conviction on each one of seven counts in an indictment each one of which alleged an indecent assault on one of seven different boys under the age of 16. The seven boys, who were about 10 years of age, gave evidence. In some cases one boy gave evidence in corroboration of the evidence of another. As to four counts there was corroborative evidence given by three other children (two boys and one girl) who had not themselves been assaulted and who were not therefore involved in any of the charges. All the children gave evidence on oath. One of the chief points raised on appeal was whether the evidence of complaining children could be corroborated by the evidence of other children (being children not alleged to have been assaulted). The summing up had stressed the importance of having corroboration of the evidence of young boys and the danger of convicting in its absence though the jury had been told that if they fully appreciated the danger they could convict if they were absolutely certain that they were right in doing so.

In giving the judgment of the court dismissing the appeal, Lord Goddard CJ referred to *R v Manser*, 25 Cr App R 18 as authority for the proposition that unsworn evidence cannot be corroborated by other unsworn evidence. As I have indicated, I prefer to regard *Manser* as a case in which the evidence of Barbara was given on oath though that of Doris was not. Lord Goddard CJ proceeded, at p. 436.

> Whether a child is of tender years is a matter for the good sense of the court, and though it may be difficult to decide whether a child understands the obligation of an oath, a court probably would have no difficulty in deciding whether he or she was of tender years. Where, then, such a child gives unsworn evidence, it must be corroborated by some other evidence, and we can see no reason why the corroboration should not be the evidence of another child who in the opinion of the court is capable of being sworn.

Lord Goddard CJ does not in this passage in terms deal with the question whether, accepting that the unsworn evidence of child A can be corroborated by the sworn evidence of child B, the corroboration of that sworn evidence of B may be found in the evidence of A.

Lord Goddard CJ did, however, consider the situation which arises where evidence is given by two people in circumstances where there is a danger in convicting unless the evidence is corroborated. He instanced the case of an indecent assault upon a mother in the presence of her son. He dealt with the matter thus, at p. 436:

> It is true that for very many years the courts have always warned juries that it is dangerous to convict on the uncorroborated evidence of a child, whether of tender years or not, but so also is a similar warning given in all sexual cases. In a case where the complaining party is a grown woman the jury would be advised to look for corroboration and if the evidence is that of a child, that is, of one under the age of 14, but who in the opinion of the court can be sworn, we can find no reason for saying that such evidence could not be accepted by the jury as corroboration. To hold otherwise would mean that if a mother was indecently assaulted in the presence of her son, aged, say, 12 or 13, his evidence could not be accepted as corroboration if the jury believed him. Whether evidence that is legally admissible does corroborate is for a jury to determine. The court points out to them what can be corroboration, and then it is for the jury to decide whether it does corroborate and it is open to them to accept it or to reject it, it may be because they do not think it safe to act upon the evidence of one so young.

In my view, this passage, the principle of which I regard as acceptable, shows that the sworn evidence of A may corroborate the sworn evidence of B which may itself corroborate the sworn evidence of A. But if evidence which needs (following judicial utterances) to be corroborated can be corroborated by evidence which itself (for comparable reasons) needs to be corroborated so that each one of two witnesses may corroborate the other the question may be asked why the legally admitted but unsworn evidence of child A should not corroborate the legally admitted but unsworn evidence of child B and vice versa. The answer to that question must be found by considering the wording of the proviso to section 38(1)—a matter to which I have referred above. In the case of an accomplice who gives sworn evidence it must be accepted that there are special reasons which have guided the laying down of certain rules such as those in *Davies* v

Director of Public Prosecutions [1954] AC 378. I do not find it necessary to discuss those rules.

Though in *Campbell's* case [1956] 2 QB 432 the court was dealing with a case where only sworn evidence was given, it was expressly stated that the court was endeavouring to deal comprehensively with the evidence of children. At the end of the judgment, at p. 438, Lord Goddard CJ summed up the conclusions of the court. They may be stated as follows: (a) The unsworn evidence of a child must be corroborated by sworn evidence; if, then, the only evidence implicating the accused is that of unsworn children the judge must stop the case. (b) It makes no difference whether the child's evidence relates to an assault on himself or herself or to any other charge, for example, where an unsworn child says that he saw the accused person steal an article. (c) The sworn evidence of a child need not as a matter of law be corroborated, but a jury should be warned, not that they must find corroboration, but that there is a risk in acting on the uncorroborated evidence of young boys or girls though they may do so if convinced that the witness is telling the truth. (d) Such warning should also be given where a young boy or girl is called to corroborate the evidence either of another child whether sworn or unsworn or of an adult. (e) As the statute which permits a child of tender years to give unsworn evidence expressly provides for such evidence being given in any proceeding against any person for any offence, the unsworn evidence of a child can be given to corroborate the evidence of another person given on oath but in such case a particularly careful warning should be given.

Subject to my comment as to the last of these I consider that they correctly summarise the law. It is no part of our present province to express any opinion as to whether the law could be improved or should be altered. Nor does any question arise for discussion as to the nature of corroboration or its definition. By the wording of the proviso the unsworn evidence of a child of tender years must (before the accused is liable to be convicted) be "corroborated by some other material evidence in support thereof implicating" the accused. If the jury in the present case were prepared to accept the evidence of June that she saw the accused assault Valerie it could not be doubted that such evidence corroborated that of Valerie that she was assaulted by the accused: nor *per contra* could it be doubted that the evidence of Valerie corroborated that of June. The wording of the proviso to section 38(1) was, therefore, satisfied in as much as the evidence of June which was admitted by virtue of the section was corroborated by the evidence of Valerie which was not admitted by virtue of the section and was evidence in support of the evidence of June and was evidence which implicated the accused.

In my view, the discussion in *Campbell's* case [1956] 2 QB 432 does not fully cover the point under consideration. I accept, as set out under (e) above, that unsworn evidence may be given to corroborate sworn evidence but, as the problem did not arise in *Campbell's* case, the court did not go on to consider the necessity for and the nature of the corroboration of the unsworn evidence itself. There was in *Campbell's* case no analysis or testing of the reasoning in *Manser's* case, 25 Cr App R 18. It is to that that I now turn. I have quoted above the relevant words in the judgment of the court. On the basis that in that case the girl Barbara gave evidence on oath then the wording of the judgment if it were applied to the present case would be as follows: "Now by statute the evidence of the little girl who had not been sworn was not to be accepted as evidence at all, unless it was corroborated. The argument for the prosecution is therefore an argument in a circle. Let it be granted that the evidence of Valerie has to be corroborated: it is corroborated by the evidence of June. She, however, also needs to be corroborated. The answer is that she is corroborated by the evidence of Valerie, and that is called 'mutual corroboration'. In truth and in fact the evidence of the girl June ought to have been obliterated altogether from the case, in as much as it was not corroborated. It clearly was not corroborated by the evidence of the girl Valerie". But why, I ask, is this an argument in a circle? If child A gives evidence and says "I was assaulted by X" and if child B gives evidence and says "I saw X assault A" I would have thought that each corroborates the other. Each gives evidence implicating X. The evidence of each one is parallel with the evidence of the other. The evidence of A of having been assaulted by X is confirmed by the evidence of B of having seen X assault A. The evidence of B of having seen X assault A is confirmed by the evidence of A of having been assaulted by X. One of the elements supplied by corroborative evidence is that there are two witnesses rather than one. The weight of the evidence is for the jury—in cases where there is a trial by jury. It is for the jury to decide whether witnesses are creditworthy. If a witness is not, then the testimony of the witness must be rejected. The essence of corroborative evidence is that one creditworthy witness confirms what another creditworthy witness has said. Any risk of the conviction of an innocent person is lessened if conviction is based upon the testimony of more than one acceptable witness. Corroborative evidence in the sense of some other material evidence in support implicating the accused furnishes a safeguard which makes a conclusion more sure than it would be without such evidence. But to rule it out on the basis that there is some mutuality between that which confirms and that which is confirmed would be to rule it out because of its essential nature and indeed because of its virtue. The purpose of corroboration is not to give validity or credence to evidence which is deficient or suspect or incredible but only to confirm and support that which as evidence is sufficient and satisfactory and credible: and corroborative evidence will only fill its role if it itself is completely credible evidence. All of this emphasises the importance of directing a jury that the evidence of children must be examined with special care. The need for such special care is manifest where vital issues fall to be determined only on the evidence of children.

If, then, the court, being satisfied that the requirements of section 38(1) are met, allows child A to give evidence not on oath and if child A gives evidence of having been assaulted by X there could be no conviction of X unless the evidence of A is corroborated by some other material evidence in support of it implicating X. If child B gives sworn testimony of having seen X assault A then I see no reason why there could not be a conviction. The weight to be given to the evidence of A and of B would be for the jury and undoubtedly a judge would have to warn a jury that they should consider the evidence of A and of B (both being children) with great care. If, however, the jury was satisfied that both A and B were telling the truth then there could be a conviction. This view was presumably adopted as long ago as 1932 in *R* v *Gregg* (1932) 24 Cr App R 13. The accused was charged with indecently assaulting a girl aged seven whose evidence was admitted without her being sworn. A girl aged nine gave evidence on oath of having witnessed the indecent assault. At the trial the recorder omitted to tell the jury that by law the unsworn evidence of the child aged seven required corroboration. The accused was convicted. His appeal was dismissed on the ground that there was corroboration of the unsworn evidence and that though the summing up was defective no injustice had been done.

If child A gave sworn evidence of having been assaulted by X then only if the jury, after having applied their minds to a proper warning, were absolutely sure could there be a conviction in the absence of the support of corroborative evidence. If child B was allowed to give evidence, not on oath, of having seen X assault A there could, in my view, be a conviction if the jury, regarding the evidence of A and of B with great care, were satisfied that each was telling the truth. It was argued that this conclusion would lead to the result that A would be corroborating himself. The argument is, in my view, fallacious. If A and B were independent of each other then clearly what B said would be separate from and independent of what was said by A. If A and B were not independent of each other either for the reason that they had agreed together to concoct a story or for some other reason such as that they had (though with no wrong motive) closely collaborated then their evidence would be either discredited or of little value. Any warning to a jury of the need to examine the evidence of children with care would no doubt in a suitable case include mention of any circumstances affecting the independence of their testimony. But as to this no general rule could be laid down. According to the infinite variety of differing sets of circumstances a judge would exercise his judgment as to the style and language of the guidance that it would be helpful and wise for him to give.

For the reasons which I have given I consider that the point of law as formulated should be answered by saying that the evidence of an unsworn child (admitted pursuant to section 38(1)) can amount to corroboration of evidence given on oath by another child (a complainant) provided that the unsworn evidence is corroborated as required by the proviso. In terms of the present case the evidence of June could corroborate the evidence of Valerie and that of Valerie could corroborate that of June provided that the jury after suitable adequate guidance and warning were satisfied that each child was a truthful and satisfactory witness.'

LORD DIPLOCK: '[I]t [section 38(1) of the Children and Young Persons Act 1933] differs from the common law rule in two respects. Whereas at common law the jury if given adequate warning were entitled to convict upon the uncorroborated evidence of witnesses in the suspect categories, the section imposes an absolute prohibition upon conviction on the uncorroborated evidence of an unsworn child. Secondly, it expressly excludes as a permissible source of such corroboration the evidence of any other unsworn child.

In this latter respect it presents an analogy with the common law rule as to accomplices who are *participes criminis* in the actual offence charged. The practice of giving the warning as to the desirability of confirmation from another source when more than one accomplice gave evidence implicating the accused seems to have originated in the opinion expressed by Littledale J in his summing up in *R v Noakes* (1832) 5 C & P 326. It appears to have been based upon reason—though Littledale J himself gave none—rather than upon precedent which at that date had been confined to the evidence of a single accomplice. There is a continuing logical basis for the practice, for the reason which makes an accomplice a suspect witness, viz., the natural temptation to exculpate himself or to minimise the part which he played in a common crime, applies also to any other accomplice in the same crime, and there is every reason for them to concert together to tell the same false story. But there was in 1832 a possible further justification which no longer subsists. The accused himself was not a competent witness and so was debarred from giving evidence to contradict that of any accomplices as to matters which might well be known only to him and them. Furthermore, had they too been charged in the same indictment, as, being accomplices, they might have been, they too would have been incompetent to give evidence. Common fairness, with which the judges sought to mitigate the rigour of the law which debarred the accused from giving evidence in his own defence, may well have influenced Littledale J and those who subsequently adopted the same practice to limit the advantage which the prosecution could obtain by choosing not to arraign accomplices in the same indictment as the accused.

This practice, as well as that relating to a single accomplice, was accepted as "virtually equivalent to a rule of law," in *R* v *Baskerville* [1916] 2 KB 658, 663. I would not wish to question it today, for although the possible historical justification for it has vanished the logical reason for it still remains. But the same reason does not apply where the reason for regarding each of the witnesses as suspect is different or, although the same, is not one which makes it likely that they will concert together to tell the same false story. There is no case in the books to support the practice of treating the evidence of one suspect witness as incapable in law of corroborating the evidence of another, except where both suspect witnesses are accomplices in the strict sense of being *participes criminis* with the accused in the crime with which he is charged. *R* v *Campbell* [1956] 2 QB 432 is direct authority to the contrary.

I conclude, therefore, that there is not now, and *a fortiori* was not in 1885, any common law rule of *general application* that evidence of a witness which is itself suspect for a reason which calls for a warning of the danger of convicting on it unless it is corroborated is incapable in law of amounting to corroboration of the evidence of another witness whose evidence is also suspect for the same or any other reason which calls for a similar warning. It is, in my view, impossible to infer that Parliament, which expressly provided that the evidence of one unsworn child must be corroborated by some evidence other than that of another unsworn child before the jury could convict upon it, intended by an implication so clear that it goes without saying—for there are no words in the proviso which suggest it—to impose a further but unexpressed limitation upon the power of the jury to rely upon the evidence of an unsworn child in support of a conviction.

For these reasons I would hold: (a) that the sworn evidence of Valerie was capable under the statute of amounting to corroboration of the unsworn evidence of June, notwithstanding that Valerie's evidence, both because she herself was a young child and because she was alleging that she was the victim of a sexual offence, was itself of such a nature as to call for a warning as to the danger of convicting upon it unless it was corroborated; (b) that the unsworn evidence of June was capable at common law of amounting to corroboration of the sworn evidence of Valerie within the meaning of the required warning.

But so to hold, though it decides all points of law, does not dispose of this appeal, for your Lordships are now bound to consider whether under all the circumstances the verdict of the jury was nevertheless so unsatisfactory that it ought to be set aside. The Court of Appeal, who took a contrary view to that of your Lordships on the point of law, held that the summing up contained an erroneous statement of the law on corroboration and allowed the appeal on that ground alone. They did not find it necessary to deal with the more general ground that the verdict was in any event unsatisfactory.

Counsel for the Director of Public Prosecutions has not thought it right to resist the dismissal of the appeal upon this latter ground. It was the ruling of the Court of Appeal upon the law as to mutual corroboration of the evidence of child witnesses which he desired to challenge, because of the many cases of the same type as the instant appeal in which this question arises.

I would be content to say that there were a number of features of the case which in combination make it unsafe to allow the conviction to stand. There is one, however, which I would single out for comment, viz., the nature of summing up on the question of corroboration, for this I believe to be a frequent source of bewilderment to juries in cases of this kind.

To say this is no reproach to the learned [trial judge]. There is scarcely a phrase in his statement to the jury of the law upon this topic which has not at some time or other received the blessing of the Court of Criminal Appeal or the Court of Appeal. As is so often the practice even of very experienced judges in these cases, he followed the course of treating the jury to a general exposition of the law as to the corroboration of the evidence of children using for that purpose a succession of verbal formulae culled from decisions of appellate courts and hallowed by usage.

My Lords, to incorporate in the summing-up a general disquisition upon the law of corroboration in the sort of language used by lawyers may make the summing-up immune to appeal upon a point of law, but it is calculated to confuse a jury of laymen and, if it does not pass so far over their heads that when they reach the jury room they simply rely upon their native common sense, may, I believe, as respects the weight to be attached to evidence requiring corroboration, have the contrary effect to a sensible warning couched in ordinary language directed to the facts of the particular case.

Only too often the sort of direction given to the jury is to tell them at the outset that they must not convict unless they are satisfied beyond reasonable doubt by the evidence put before them that the accused is guilty of the offence with which he is charged. Then, as respects the unsworn evidence of a young child tendered by the prosecution, they are instructed that they are prohibited by statute from paying any regard to that evidence unless it is corroborated by some other evidence, and one of the *Baskerville* formulae— for there are several in that judgment [*R* v *Baskerville* [1916] 2 KB 658]—is used to explain what "corroboration" means. Next they are told that it is for the judge to say whether there is other evidence *capable* of amounting to corroboration of the child's evidence and their attention is drawn to the evidence which falls within this category, but they are then told that it is for the jury, not the judge, to decide whether that evidence *does* amount to corroboration and that only if they do so decide are they entitled to pay any regard to the unsworn child's evidence in deciding to convict.

These complicated formulae about the concept of corroboration and the respective functions of judge and jury are, I believe, unintelligible to the ordinary laymen, even where only one witness whose evidence calls for corroboration is involved. But where the sworn evidence of a young child is tendered by the prosecution in the same case as that of an unsworn child the jury are told that the law as respects the sworn evidence is different. The judge, they are informed, is required by law to give them a solemn warning that it is dangerous to convict upon the sworn child's evidence unless it is corroborated, but that if, bearing in mind that warning, they are nevertheless convinced that the child is telling the truth they *are* entitled to convict upon that evidence alone.

It is common practice to sum up upon these lines and one cannot blame the [trial judge] for following that practice in the instant appeal. It contains no statement of the law that is incorrect but it is seldom of any assistance to the jury in any case, and in a case such as your Lordships are now reviewing where the only evidence inculpating the accused is that of two young children, one sworn and one unsworn, both of whom tell substantially identical stories either of which, if accepted, proves that the accused was guilty of the offence charged, a summing up on these conventional lines must positively bemuse the jury.

My Lords, if a summing up is to perform its proper function in a criminal trial by jury it should not contain a general disquisition on the law of corroboration couched in lawyer's language but should be tailored to the particular circumstances of the case.

It would be highly dangerous to suppose that there is any such thing as a model summing up appropriate to all cases of this kind. No doubt if there is unsupported evidence on oath of a child complainant fit to be left to the jury the judge should tell them that it is open to them to convict upon her evidence alone, though he should remind them forcibly of the danger of doing so. But there is no need for him to tell them of what kind of evidence *could* amount to corroboration of her story if in fact there is none at all.'

(VISCOUNT DILHORNE and LORDS PEARSON and CROSS OF CHELSEA delivered concurring judgments.)

Appeal dismissed.

- Are there any other possible ways of interpreting s. 38 of the Children and Young Persons Act 1933 other than the interpretation given in *DPP* v *Hester*?
- Would they have been preferable?
- It was once supposed that there could be no mutual corroboration. What effect does *DPP* v *Hester* have on this?
- What are the practical implications of the decision in *DPP* v *Hester*?

R v *Morgan* [1978] 1 WLR 735 (CA)

The defendant was tried on a charge of indecent assault on a boy aged 11. Evidence on oath about the incident was given by the victim, his brother aged 12 and a boy aged 16 at the time of the incident, which had occurred some 12 months before the trial. Neither the brother nor the boy aged 16 was a victim. The defendant did not give evidence. In relation to the victim the jury were warned of the risks in convicting on his evidence unless it was corroborated; no such warning was given in relation to the brother or the boy aged 16. The defendant was convicted. He appealed.

ROSKILL LJ, giving the judgment of the court: 'There have been in the last four or five years a number of cases which touch upon the problem which we have to consider. There are three decisions of the House of Lords, *R* v *Hester* [1973] AC 296; *R* v *Kilbourne* [1973] AC 729 and *R* v *Boardman* [1975] AC 421, and we have had a number in this court, the most recent of which is *R* v *Scarrott* [1977] 3 WLR 629, the court consisting of Scarman LJ who gave the judgment of the court, and Wien J and myself. I do not propose in this judgment to go through the ground so fully covered in those three House of Lords decisions and in the recent cases in this court culminating in *R* v *Scarrott*.

One or two observations may usefully be made. First, this is not in the strict sense of the phrase a "similar fact" case such as *R* v *Hester, R* v *Kilbourne, R* v *Boardman* and *R* v *Scarrott*. This case is not one where the prosecution have sought to bring before the court, in support of a charge that child A has been the victim of a sexual assault, evidence from children B, C and D that they have been the victims of similar sexual assaults at the hands of the same accused person. Therefore, many of the problems that the House and this court have had to consider recently do not arise. The problem is different. It arises because the alleged victim was a young boy and one of the witnesses, his brother, whose evidence was relied upon as corroborating the evidence of the victim, was also a young boy and the third witness was also a boy though substantially older in years. The evidence was of a victim alleging assault and of two others, one a boy of about the same age and the other an older boy, giving evidence corroborating, though not in every detail, those incidents of which the victim complained but in relation to which the two other boys were not victims. Therein lies an important difference.

The problem that has to be considered first is whether the judge was wrong in not directing the jury that, when they were considering the weight that they should give to, or whether they would accept, the evidence of the brother, they ought to look and see what corroboration there was in relation to his evidence.

The relevant law was stated by Lord Goddard CJ in *R v Campbell* [1956] 2 QB 432, a decision affirmed in this respect by the House of Lords in *R v Hester* [1973] AC 296. I need only read one passage from the speech of Lord Morris of Borth-y-Gest in *R v Hester*— although other parts of the decision in *R v Campbell* were later criticised in *R v Kilbourne* [1973] AC 729, this part was expressly approved in *R v Hester* [1973] AC 296, 314:

> Though in *Campbell's* case [1956] 2 QB 432 the court was dealing with a case where only sworn evidence was given, it was expressly stated that the court was endeavouring to deal comprehensively with the evidence of children. At the end of the judgment, at p. 438, Lord Goddard CJ summed-up the conclusions of the court. They may be stated as follows: (a) The unsworn evidence of a child must be corroborated by sworn evidence; if, then, the only evidence implicating the accused is that of unsworn children the judge must stop the case.—[That is not relevant here]—(b) It makes no difference whether the child's evidence relates to an assault on himself or herself or to any other charge, for example, where an unsworn child says that he saw the accused person steal an article.—[That is irrelevant]—(c) The sworn evidence of a child need not as a matter of law be corroborated, but a jury should be warned, not that they must find corroboration, but that there is a risk in acting on the uncorroborated evidence of young boys or girls though they may do so if convinced that the witness is telling the truth. (d) Such warning should also be given where a young boy or girl is called to corroborate the evidence either of another child whether sworn or unsworn or of an adult. . ..

We think, with great respect to the judge, whose attention may well not have been drawn to this passage, that he was guilty of an omission in not extending what he said to the jury as to the need for corroboration in the case of the victim to the brother, who was only a little older than the victim. We think that he should have given a similar warning that the jury ought to have in mind that this boy was only 12 years of age at the time of the incident and 13 at the time of the trial and that, therefore, exactly the same considerations applied to testing his evidence and to the need to support from other sources as applied in the case of the victim himself.

So far as the older boy is concerned, reliance was placed on a decision of the Court of Criminal Appeal in *R v Gammon* (1959) 43 Cr App R 155. I have already said, the elder boy was 17 years of age at the time of the trial and 16 at the time of the incidents. He was, therefore, substantially older, and it has been suggested that the omission which I have mentioned in relation to the brother is applicable also to the case of the older boy.

We do not think it possible to state as a general proposition what the age is above which it becomes unnecessary for a judge to give a warning such as I have already mentioned. This is an example of a situation where the trial judge is much better placed to consider the matter than any appellate court can be. The judge will, in those circumstances, obviously apply his mind to the problem and ask himself the question whether, having seen this boy in the witness box, he was of an age which made it desirable to give this warning. He might say to the jury: "If you think that this boy is of an age where the sort of risks exist against which the rule regarding corroboration is a safeguard, then you should look and see what corroboration exists." This is the type of problem which falls within the general discretion of the judge of which this court spoke in *R* v *Scarrott* [1977] 3 WLR 629; I would refer in particular to pp. 639 and 640 of the report of the judgment of the court, which Scarman LJ gave.

There was, therefore, this omission in the summing up regarding at least the brother.'

(The court applied the proviso to s. 2(1) of the Criminal Appeal Act 1968.)

Appeal dismissed.

Davies v *DPP* [1954] AC 378 (HL)

The defendant, together with other youths, attacked with their fists another group, one of whom subsequently died from stab wounds inflicted by a knife. Six youths, including the defendant and one Lawson, were charged with murder but finally the defendant alone was convicted. Lawson having been among four against whom no evidence was offered and who were found not guilty of murder but convicted of common assault. At the defendant's trial Lawson gave evidence for the prosecution as to an admission by the defendant of the use of a knife by him but the judge did not warn the jury of the danger of accepting his evidence without corroboration. The defendant's conviction was affirmed by the Court of Criminal Appeal, and he appealed to the House of Lords.

LORD SIMONDS LC: 'The true rule has been, in my view, accurately formulated by the appellant's counsel in his first three propositions, more particularly in the third. These propositions as amended read as follows:

(1) In a criminal trial where a person who is an accomplice gives evidence on behalf of the prosecution, it is the duty of the judge to warn the jury that, although they may convict upon his evidence, it is dangerous to do so unless it is corroborated.

(2) This rule, although a rule of practice, now has the force of a rule of law.

(3) Where the judge fails to warn the jury in accordance with this rule, the conviction will be quashed, even if in fact there be ample corroboration of the evidence of the accomplice, unless the appellate court can apply the proviso to section 4(1) of the Criminal Appeal Act 1907.

The rule, it will be observed, applies only to witnesses for the prosecution. The remaining questions, therefore, on the main issue are [w]hat is an "accomplice" within the rule? And has the rule, on the proper construction of the word "accomplice" contained in it, any application to Lawson in the present case?

There is in the authorities no formal definition of the term "accomplice": and your Lordships are forced to deduce a meaning for the word from the cases in which X, Y and Z have been held to be, or held liable to be treated as, accomplices. On the cases it would appear that the following persons, if called as witnesses for the prosecution, have been treated as falling within the category:—

(1) On any view, persons who are *participes criminis* in respect of the actual crime charged, whether as principals or accessories before or after the fact (in felonies) or

persons committing, procuring or aiding and abetting (in the case of misdemeanors). This is surely the natural and primary meaning of the term "accomplice". But in two cases, persons falling strictly outside the ambit of this category have, in particular decisions, been held to be accomplices for the purpose of the rule: viz.:

(2) Receivers have been held to be accomplices of the thieves from whom they receive goods on a trial of the latter for larceny (*R* v *Jennings* (1912) 7 Cr App R 242: *R* v *Dixon* (1925) 19 Cr App R 36):

(3) When X has been charged with a specific offence on a particular occasion, and evidence is admissible, and has been admitted, of his having committed crimes of this identical type on other occasions, as proving system and intent and negativing accident; in such cases the court has held that in relation to such other similar offences, if evidence of them were given by parties to them, the evidence of such other parties should not be left to the jury without a warning that it is dangerous to accept it without corroboration. (*R* v *Farid* (1945) 30 Cr App R 168).

In both of these cases (2) and (3) a person not a party or not necessarily a party to the substantive crime charged was treated as an accomplice for the purpose of the requirement of warning. (I say "not necessarily" to cover the case of receivers. A receiver may on the facts of a particular case have procured the theft, or aided and abetted it, or may have helped to shield the thief from justice. But he can be a receiver without doing any of these things.) The primary meaning of the term "accomplice", then, has been extended to embrace these two anomalous cases. In each case there are special circumstances to justify or at least excuse the extension. A receiver is not only committing a crime intimately allied in character with that of theft: he could not commit the crime of receiving at all without the crime of theft having preceded it. The two crimes are in a relationship of "one-side dependence". In the case of "system", the requirement of warning within the special field of similar crimes committed is a logical application within that collateral field of the general principle, though it involves a warning as to the evidence of persons not accomplices to the substantive crime charged.

My Lords, these extensions of the term are imbedded in our case law and it would be inconvenient for any authority other than the legislature to disturb them. Neither of them affects this case. Lawson was not a receiver, nor was there any question of "system"; Lawson, if he was to be an accomplice at all had to be an accomplice to the crime of murder. I can see no reason for any further extension of the term "accomplice". In particular, I can see no reason why, if half a dozen boys fight another crowd, and one of them produces a knife and stabs one of the opponents to death, all the rest of his group should be treated as accomplices in the use of a knife and the infliction of mortal injury by that means, unless there is evidence that the rest intended or concerted or at least contemplated an attack with a knife by one of their number, as opposed to a common assault. If all that was designed or envisaged was in fact a common assault, and there was no evidence that Lawson, a party to that common assault, knew that any of his companions had a knife, then Lawson was not an accomplice in the crime consisting in its felonious use. It should be borne in mind in this connexion that all suggestion of a concerted *felonious* onslaught had, by consent at the instance of counsel for the defence himself, been expunged from the Crown's case and from the issues put to the jury. Your Lordships would, I feel, be slow to permit counsel for the defence, having got that suggestion buried, to disinter it for the purpose of suggesting that Lawson was constructively an accomplice to the crime of murder and for that reason attracted the rule as to warning.

My Lords, I have tried to define the term "accomplice". The branch of the definition relevant to this case is that which covers *participes criminis* in respect of the actual crime charged, "whether as principals or accessories before or after the fact". But, it may reasonably be asked, who is to decide, or how is it to be decided, whether a particular witness was a *particeps criminis* in the case in hand? In many or most cases this question answers itself, or, to be more exact, is answered by the witness in question himself, by confessing to participation, by pleading guilty to it, or by being convicted of it. But it is indisputable that there are witnesses outside these straightforward categories, in respect of whom the answer has to be sought elsewhere. The witnesses concerned may never have confessed, or may never have been arraigned or put on trial, in respect of the crime involved. Such cases fall into two classes. In the first, the judge can properly rule that there is no evidence that the witness was, what I will, for short, call a participant. The present case, in my view, happens to fall within this class, and can be decided on the narrow ground. But there are other cases within this field in which there is evidence on which a reasonable jury could find that a witness was a "participant". In such a case the issue of *accomplice vel non* is for the jury's decision; and a judge should direct them that if they consider on the evidence that the witness was an accomplice, it is dangerous for them to act on his evidence unless corroborated: though it is competent for them to do so if, after that warning, they still think fit to do so.'

(LORDS PORTER, OAKSEY, TUCKER and ASQUITH OF BISHOPSTONE concurred.)

Appeal dismissed.

- What is the justification for treating the evidence of an accomplice with caution? Is the definition of 'accomplice' in *Davies* v *DPP* too narrow?

Sneddon v *Stevenson* [1967] 1 WLR 1051 (DC)

At 11.30 pm one evening a police officer saw the appellant loitering in the street. He drove past and saw her talking to a man. He turned his car round, saw her emerge from an entry with a man, and stopped near to her. He purposely drove in a manner which from his experience he knew would be likely to attact her attention. She went to the car, opened the door and asked if he wanted business. She got into the car and he drove to where his colleague was standing, despite her efforts to get out. She was then cautioned and arrested. She was convicted of loitering and soliciting in the street for the purpose of prostitution contrary to section 1 of the Street Offences Act 1959. She appealed on the grounds that the police officer had incited or encouraged the offence of soliciting and was therefore an accomplice whose evidence required corroboration, and that, since he had been party to the offences, it was improper in the circumstances that she should be convicted.

LORD PARKER CJ: 'In my opinion this never got near a case of aiding and abetting, inciting or encouraging or anything of the sort. All that the officer did was to place himself and the car in such a position that if the appellant desired to solicit there was full opportunity to do so. In my judgment that does not mean that the officer commits any offence at all. I would go further myself and hold that even if it could be said that the officer was, as it were, a party to the offence, partook in the offence, that he was certainly not an accomplice for the purpose of the doctrine of corroboration.

We have been referred to *R* v *Mullins* (1848) 3 Cox CC 526, *R* v *Bickley* (1909) 2 Cr App R 53 and *R* v *Heuser* (1910) 6 Cr App R 76. It seems to me that on a true reading of those cases it can be stated that though a police officer acting as a spy may be said in a general sense to be an accomplice in the offence, yet if he is merely partaking in the offence for the purpose of getting evidence, he is not an accomplice who requires to be corroborated.'

WALLER J: 'I agree. I would only add on the first point, namely, the question of whether corroboration is required, that it seems to me that where a police officer is engaged in obtaining evidence and is thereby, perhaps, participating in the offence, the circumstances are entirely different from that of the true accomplice, being somebody who was intending to carry out an important part in the offence. The reason why the latter ought to be corroborated is that he may have a number of mixed motives when he comes to give evidence, for example, that he will be treated more leniently or something of that sort, and it is for that kind of reason that the court has always thought it necessary to give a warning that corroboration should be looked for. In the case of the police officer, those considerations do not apply at all, and it seems to me that, even if he may be participating, that is why no warning about corroboration is required in the case of his evidence.'

(SWANWICK J agreed.)

Appeal dismissed.

R v *Royce-Bentley* [1974] 1 WLR 535 (CA)

The defendant was charged with theft. A prosecution witness, who on his own evidence could have been an accomplice in the theft, gave evidence which was mainly favourable to the defence but in some respects supported the prosecution's case. Before summing up to the jury, the judge consulted with both counsel as to whether the witness ought to be put before the jury as a potential accomplice. Defence counsel stated that he would prefer that no direction was given on the issue whether the witness was an accomplice. The judge agreed and gave no direction to the jury on the matter. The defendant was convicted. He appealed against conviction on the grounds that the judge failed to leave to the jury the issue whether the witness was an accomplice and that he misdirected the jury by failing to warn them, if they found that the witness was an accomplice, of the danger of convicting the defendant on his uncorroborated evidence.

LORD WIDGERY CJ, delivering the judgment of the court: 'To turn to the principle to be applied, a relevant decision is in this court in *R* v *Peach* (unreported), January 14, 1974. This again was an unusual case because here again the prosecution had called a witness who was intended to give evidence adverse to the defence, and who would on any view have been an accomplice in the sense of his implication in the offence if the case against the defendant was a sound case at all. But in the event the so-called accomplice in *Peach's* case, when he gave his evidence for the Crown, not only failed to come up to proof but failed to give any evidence which was adverse to the defence. In this court it was held that in those circumstances there was no obligation on the judge to give an accomplice warning, because the supposed accomplice having said nothing injurious to the defendant, there was no danger of the jury convicting on the evidence of that accomplice whether it was corroborated or not. In giving the judgment of the court, I said:

But of course the real point here, and one only has to think about the case for a few minutes, is that if Griffin—[that is the accomplice]—was not giving evidence adverse to the accused, the ordinary reason for giving a direction on accomplices and corroboration did not arise. The whole purpose of the well known requirement for directing juries in this sense in a criminal case is that one is normally concerned with an accomplice who has given adverse evidence. If there was no such evidence, then no such direction was necessary because the law does not require a direction on corroboration unless the evidence is adverse.

We start today with that proposition, that if the so-called accomplice does not in fact give evidence adverse to the defendant, no warning is required for the reason there given. Today we have to move on to the slightly different situation in which the alleged accomplice has given some evidence which is favourable to the defence and some evidence which is potentially favourable to the prosecution as well. It seems we have to face up, perhaps for the first time, to laying down a principle as to the conduct of the trial judge in that situation.

We approach it on the footing that in this case there was in the extract from the transcript which I have read some evidence given by the boy which could be treated as adverse to the defendant, and also some evidence given by the boy which might entitle the jury to hold him to be an accomplice, but there was also, as I have said, a good deal of other evidence given by the boy which was favourable to the defence.

Cases will obviously arise in which a witness who gives evidence of these two different characters may wish to be upheld by the defence because, on the whole, he is more favourable to them, and cases will therefore arise where the defence do not want the credibility of the witness attacked by an accomplice direction because they attach too much importance to that evidence themselves.

In our judgment, where a trial judge is faced with the situation which arises here, he should of course consult counsel in the absence of the jury before taking any final decision, but having done that, he ought to consider whether on the whole, more harm to the defence would be done by giving the accomplice direction than by not giving it, and if he comes to the conclusion that on the whole more harm would be done in that way, then it is no irregularity on his part in the conduct of the trial if he decides not to give the accomplice direction.'

Appeal dismissed.

R v Knowlden and Knowlden (1983) 77 Cr App R 94 (CA)

The appellants, members of the same family, were convicted of murder. They gave evidence which was damaging to each other.

WATKINS LJ, reading the judgment of the court: ' . . . [I]t is submitted that the recorder did not direct the jury properly upon the manner in which they should approach the evidence of co-defendants. There is no doubt that each one of them in this case had made damaging accusations about one or more of the others. It was incumbent, therefore, so it is submitted, upon the recorder to give a warning about that evidence to the jury in the form of what is known as a *Prater* direction (see (1959) 44 Cr App R 83; [1960] 2 QB 464) which included the requirement of corroboration. It is, of course, customary and necessary for a warning to be given to the jury, in respect of a witness for the prosecution who may be regarded as an accomplice, to beware of relying upon the evidence of that witness unless, in relevant respects, it is corroborated. Furthermore, it is desirable that a warning should be given that a witness who has come from the dock may be someone with a purpose of his own to serve in giving evidence.

Both of these propositions are plainly stated in *Prater* (1959) 44 Cr App R 83, 85, 86; [1960] 2 QB 464, 466. Edmund Davies J, as he then was, in giving the judgment of the Court said at p. 86 and p. 466 of the respective reports: "This Court in the circumstances of the present appeal is content to express the view that it is desirable that in cases where a person may be regarded as having some purpose of his own to serve, a warning against uncorroborated evidence should be given but every case must be looked at in the light of its own facts. In *Garland* (1941) 29 Cr App R 46n Humphreys J, delivering the judgment of the Court, used words which this Court finds completely apposite to the circumstances of the present case, namely, that if there be clear and convincing evidence to such an extent that this Court is satisfied that no miscarriage of justice has arisen from an omission of a direction to the jury this Court will not interfere."

No rule of law was thereby being laid down, and we do not feel called upon to refer to other authorities used in argument on this subject to state that what was being referred to in *Prater (supra)*, if the case itself did not give rise to it, was a rule of practice, the form of adoption of which, where, as here, the witness is a co-defendant, is always a matter for the discretion of the trial judge.

In exercising his discretion, he is at the least to be expected to give the customary clear warning to a jury where defendants have given damaging evidence against one another to examine the evidence of each with care because each has or may have an interest of his own to serve. Whether he should also advise the jury to look for corroboration of the evidence of a co-defendant and specify what evidence may or may not be corroboration will be decided by him, having regard to the nature and severity of the attack made by one co-defendant on another. The need for this advice should rarely arise in our experience since the simple customary warning will suffice to ensure that the jury regards the evidence in question with proper and adequate caution. The content of whatever kind of warning or advice is given is best formulated by the trial judge and, although invited to, we decline to introduce through this judgment a formula which trial judges should use no matter what circumstances confront them.

In the present case, so far as Harold is concerned there was no corroboration of anything said about him in the witness box by either one of his two sons. And there was none of anything said by him against them nor of what one son said about the other.'

Appeals dismissed.

• If an accomplice is thought to be so unreliable when giving evidence for the prosecution, what is different when he is giving evidence in his own defence?

R v Beck [1982] 1 WLR 461 (CA)

The appellant, who effectively controlled a business, was tried on a charge of conspiracy to defraud a company financing the business. A co-defendant, who pleaded guilty, gave evidence for the prosecution, and prosecution evidence was given also by three witnesses of the finance company in respect of whom there was no suggestion that they were the appellant's accomplices, but they had an alleged purpose of their own to serve in covering up false representations made, or acceded to, by them in an insurance claim unconnected with the charge against the appellant. The judge directed the jury about the need for corroboration of the evidence of the co-defendant as an accomplice, and the appellant was convicted. He appealed on the grounds that the judge should have directed the jury, in relation to the evidence of the three witnesses, as though each were an accomplice since he had a substantial interest of his own to serve in giving evidence, and evidence was capable of amounting to corroboration only if and in so far as it directly corroborated a piece of evidence given by an accomplice.

ACKNER LJ, reading the judgment of the court: 'Mr Lloyd-Eley bases his contention that such a warning should have been given essentially upon *R* v *Prater* [1960] 2 QB 464. In that case a co-prisoner, who could have been considered an accomplice, gave evidence. The Common Serjeant did not give warning in regard to his testimony and the danger of acting upon it unless corroborated. Edmund Davies J, in the course of the judgment of the court, said, at p. 466:

> For the purposes of this present appeal, this court is content to accept that whether the label to be attached to Welham in this case was strictly that of an accomplice or not, in practice it is desirable that a warning should be given that the witness, whether he comes from the dock, as in this case, or whether he be a Crown witness, may be a witness with some purpose of his own to serve . . .. In the circumstances of the present appeal it is sufficient for this court to express the view that it is desirable that, in cases where a person may be regarded as having some purpose of his own to serve, the warning against uncorroborated evidence should be given. But every case must be looked at in the light of its own facts . . .

The court also considered the position of a witness called for the prosecution in regard to whom questions were put in cross-examination suggesting that he was an accomplice. Edmund Davies J said, at p. 466:

> This court has looked in vain at the transcript of the summing-up, and has listened in vain, with respect to Mr Fitch, for any satisfactory indication that there was material upon which the Common Serjeant would have been justified in presenting Truman to the jury as being an accomplice. As my brother Hilbery said, it is easy to make suggestions to a witness. That is one thing. But more than that is required to clothe a witness for the Crown or any other witness with the garment of an accomplice. This court is unable, on the material before it, to hold that it is shown that any warning was in strict law or in prudence called for, for it is by no means satisfied that there was any material upon which Truman could properly be described as an accomplice . . .

In the course of his judgment, Edmund Davies J had referred to the *locus classicus* on accomplices and the requirement of corroboration, namely *Davies* v *Director of Public Prosecutions* [1954] AC 378. Lord Simonds LC, giving the decision of the House, said, at p. 401.

> My Lords, I have tried to define the term "accomplice". The branch of the definition relevant to this case is that which covers *participes criminis* in respect of the actual crime charged, "whether as principals or accessories before or after the fact". But, it may reasonably be asked, who is to decide, or how is it to be decided, whether a

particular witness was a *particeps criminis* in the case in hand? In many or most cases this question answers itself, or, to be more exact, is answered by the witness in question himself, by confessing to participation, by pleading guilty to it or by being convicted of it. But it is indisputable that there are witnesses outside these straightforward categories, in respect of whom the answer has to be sought elsewhere. The witnesses concerned may never have confessed, or may never have been arraigned or put on trial, in respect of the crime involved. Such cases fall into two classes. In the first, the judge can properly rule that there is no evidence that the witness was, what I will, for short, call a participant. The present case, in my view, happens to fall within this class, and can be decided on that narrow ground. But there are other cases within this field in which there is evidence on which a reasonable jury could find that a witness was a "participant". In such a case the issue of "accomplice *vel non*" is for the jury's decision: and a judge should direct them that if they consider on the evidence that the witness was an accomplice, it is dangerous for them to act on his evidence unless corroborated: though it is competent for them to do so if, after that warning, they still think fit to do so.

Prater's case [1960] 2 QB 464 has been the subject of strong comment in the Court of Criminal Appeal in *R* v *Stannard* [1965] 2 QB 1, where Winn J said, at p. 14:

> The rule, if it be a rule, enunciated in *R* v *Prater* [1960] 2 QB 464 is no more than a rule of practice. I say deliberately "if it be a rule" because, reading the passage of the judgment as I have just read it, it really seems to amount to no more than an expression of what is desirable and what, it is to be hoped, will more usually than not be adopted, at any rate, where it seems to be appropriate to the judge. It certainly is not a rule of law . . .

It was looked upon as "a qualified decision" in *R* v *Whitaker* (1976) 63 Cr App R 193.

Mr Lloyd-Eley accepts that an accomplice direction cannot be required whenever a witness may be regarded as having some purpose of his own to serve. Merely because there is some material to justify the suggestion that a witness is giving unfavourable evidence, for example, out of spite, ill-will, to level some old score, to obtain some financial advantage, cannot Mr Lloyd-Eley concedes, in every case necessitate the accomplice warning, if there is no material to suggest that the witness may be an accomplice. But, submits Mr Lloyd-Eley, even though there is no material to suggest any involvement by the witness in the crime, if he has a "substantial interest" of his own for giving false evidence, then the accomplice direction must be given. Where one draws the line, he submits is a question of degree, but once the boundary is crossed the obligation to give the accomplice warning is not a matter of discretion. We cannot accept this contention. In many trials today, the burden upon the trial judge of the summing-up is a heavy one. It would be a totally unjustifiable addition to require him, not only fairly to put before the jury the defence's contention that a witness was suspect, because he had an axe to grind, but also to evaluate the weight of that axe and oblige him, where the weight is "substantial", to give an accomplice warning with the appropriate direction as to the meaning of corroboration together with the identification of the potential corroborative material.

We take the view that if and in so far as *R* v *Prater* [1960] 2 QB 464 was not a decision on its particular facts, it in no way extended the law as laid down in *Davies's* case [1954] AC

378. There was material upon which a reasonable jury could have concluded that Welham was an accomplice. Equally, there was no such material in regard to Truman. In short, the phrase in *R* v *Prater* [1960] 2 QB 464, 466; "it is desirable that, in cases where a person may be regarded as having some purpose of his own to serve, the warning against uncorroborated evidence should be given," is related to cases where witnesses may be participants or involved in the crime charged.

This view is borne out by *R* v *Daniels* (unreported), 13 April 1967. In that case the appellant was convicted of receiving just over 9 cwt. of copper wire knowing it to have been stolen. Copper wire was discovered in a lorry and in the driving cab was the appellant, a man called Fisher, and the owner of the lorry. The owner gave evidence to the effect that he had lent the lorry to the appellant as he wanted to collect some scrap. It was an odd story, since no time was specified for the loan and nothing was paid for the hire of the lorry. The appellant's defence was that he was given £3 to collect a fully-loaded lorry and had driven it away unsuspectingly. The court concluded that theoretically there were three possibilities; one was that the owner of the lorry was telling the truth, the second was that the appellant was wholly innocent and that the owner of the lorry had received the copper wire knowing it to have been stolen and had hired the innocent appellant to drive the lorry away. The third possibility was that both the appellant and the owner of the lorry were liars and in the crime together. Clearly in that situation the owner who was cross-examined to show that he was a liar, had a purpose of his own, if he was lying, which was to hide his own involvement in the offence charged. He was potentially a participant in the crime. Salmon LJ, giving the judgment of the court, referred to *R* v *Prater* [1960] 2 QB 464 and to that part which we have quoted. He was clearly treating that case as being an accomplice or potential accomplice case. He said, in regard to the judge's summing up:

He should then have reviewed the evidence to see what corroboration there was and he should have told them that bearing in mind the lorry owner's strong motives for putting the blame on the appellant and the danger of convicting him on his uncorroborated evidence alone, if nevertheless they felt quite certain that what the lorry owner was saying was true they were still entitled to convict without corroboration.

Mr Lloyd-Eley drew our attention to *Archbold, Criminal Pleading Evidence & Practice*, 40th ed (1979), para. 1425a which reads:

. . . a general rule seems to be developing that when a witness in a criminal case, whether he be a fellow accused or called for the Crown, may reasonably be regarded as having some purpose of his own to serve which may lead him to give false evidence against an accused, the judge should warn the jury of the danger of convicting that accused on that witness's evidence unless it is corroborated: . . .

And then a reference is made to *Prater* and to *R* v *Kilbourne* [1973] AC 729, *per* Lord Hailsham of St Marylebone LC. Significantly in the instant case, where potential corroborative material was discussed in relation to Mayze, who was a self-confessed accomplice, neither counsel for the prosecution, then Mr Farquharson QC, nor Mr Lloyd-Eley suggested in relation to the three directors of Coach House that any special direction was required, let alone the accomplice warning.

While we in no way wish to detract from the obligation upon a judge to advise a jury to proceed with caution where there is material to suggest that a witness's evidence may be tainted by an improper motive, and the strength of that advice must vary according to the facts of the case, we cannot accept that there is any obligation to give the accomplice warning with all that that entails, when it is common ground that there is no basis for suggesting that the witness is a participant or in any way involved in the crime the subject matter of the trial.

Mr Lloyd-Eley accepts that if the single judge who gave leave to appeal did so having regard to the decision of the Court of Appeal (Criminal Division) a few months earlier, it was not a proper foundation for the grant of leave in this case. That case was *R* v *Riley* (1980) 70 Cr App R 1 in which a witness was called for the prosecution in regard to whom there was material to suggest that he might be an accomplice of the defendant.

It is alleged in the notice of appeal:

> . . . on the evidence of Jorg (the chief auditor of the American company which owned First Fortune), the witnesses Noble, Knight and Hochenberg had all lied to him in the period June to September 1975 when they told him that they had no knowledge of the use of personal loan documents by Coach House Finance prior to Jorg raising the question with them. This statement by the three witnesses was vital to an insurance claim of approximately £600,000 which relied in part upon Mayze having introduced and used the personal loan documents over a period from June 1974 to June 1975 without the knowledge or approval of Noble, Knight or Hochenberg.

Thus, it is made palpably clear that the alleged purpose of Noble, Knight and Hochenberg in giving evidence was, we quote again: "to cover up false representations made or acceded to by them in the insurance claim." It was accepted that this insurance claim was not connected with the offence charged against the appellant. It provided no material in support of the proposition nor indeed was it ever suggested that Noble, Knight and Hochenberg were possible accomplices of the appellant. Mr Lloyd-Eley made it clear that he was not seeking to make that contention before us.

We have set out the general ground of our decision in order to assist trial judges by dispelling belief in the "general rule" to which the editors of *Archbold* were referring in paragraph 1425a. We accept of course that there is a far narrower ground which could justify the rejection of the appellant's first contention, namely, the authority of *Whitaker's* case (1976) 63 Cr App R 193, where Lord Widgery CJ, having referred to *Prater's* case said, at p. 197:

> Furthermore, since any question of referring to corroborative evidence in this context is a matter primarily for the trial judge, it is no ground of criticism in this case that the trial judge did not deal with the matter. Indeed, as I have already said, it was not raised in argument for his specific consideration in the case. It seems to us therefore that as a matter of law Mr Temple cannot sustain his argument that there was here a failure to warn of the kind referred to in *Prater's* case.

We prefer, however, to base our decision on the general principles to which we have referred above.'

Appeal dismissed.

R v Spencer and Others; R v Smails and Others [1986] 2 All ER 928 (HL)

The appellants, who were nursing staff at a special hospital, were charged with ill-treating patients, contrary to s 126 of the Mental Health Act 1959. In two separate trials before the same judge, the prosecution relied wholly on the uncorroborated evidence of patients who had criminal convictions or were suffering from mental disorders.

At both trials Judge Hopkin directed the jury to approach the evidence of the patients with great caution but did not warn them that it would be dangerous to convict on the patients' uncorroborated evidence. The appellants were all convicted. They appealed to the Court of Appeal which dismissed the appeals, holding that the evidence of patients at a secure hospital did not fall into the category of evidence of witnesses where a full warning of the danger of conviction on their uncorroborated evidence was necessary. The appellants appealed to the House of Lords.

LORD ACKNER: 'On 11 May 1982 Bagshaw, Holmes and Starkey were found guilty in the Crown Court at Nottingham of ill-treating patients contrary to s 126 of the 1959 Act and were sentenced by Judge Hopkin. They applied to the Court of Appeal, Criminal Division ([1984] 1 All ER 971, [1984] 1 WLR 477) for leave to appeal against these convictions on the grounds that they were unsafe by reason of the inadequacy of the evidence, asserting that it was uncorroborated and unsupported in any material particular and that the patients who gave the evidence were inherently unreliable. We were told that in the application for leave to appeal it was stated in terms that "No criticism is or could be made of the summing-up". The Court of Appeal apparently thought otherwise, and during the hearing gave leave to the appellants to amend their grounds so as to question the adequacy of the judge's direction to the jury as to the treatment of the evidence of the complainants. A short adjournment was granted for this new approach to be considered, and after hearing further submissions the Court of Appeal reserved its judgment.

The warning given by Judge Hopkin in *R v Bagshaw* was in similar, though perhaps stronger, terms. O'Connor LJ, in giving the judgment of the court, said at an early stage in the judgment ([1984] 1 All ER 971 at 973, [1984] 1 WLR 477 at 479):

> We should like to say at once that the judge's summing up is a masterpiece of lucidity and fairness. He gave an impeccable direction to the jury that they should treat the evidence of the complainants with the greatest caution. The question is whether these witnesses were such that a full warning was required, namely that it was dangerous to convict on their unsupported evidence.

The "full warning" to which O'Connor LJ was referring is the warning as to the danger of convicting on uncorroborated evidence, which by rule of practice has to be given if the prosecution is relying on the evidence of an accomplice or the victim of a sexual offence or the sworn evidence of a child.

Having considered the well-known cases of *DPP v Kilbourne* [1973] 1 All ER 440, [1973] AC 729 and *DPP v Hester* [1972] 3 All ER 1056, [1973] AC 296, the judgment continued ([1984] 1 All ER 971 at 977, [1984] 1 WLR 447 at 484):

> Patients in hospital under the [Mental Health Act 1959] are not a category like accomplices or complainants in sexual cases, nor would we wish to make them into an

additional category. Patients detained in a special hospital after conviction for an offence or offences, even if they are not a category, may well fulfil to a very high degree the criteria which justify the requirement of the full warning in respect of witnesses within accepted categories. It seems to us that in such cases nothing short of the full warning that it is dangerous to convict on the uncorroborated evidence of the witness will suffice.

Thus, because Judge Hopkin had not used the words "it is dangerous to convict" the Court of Appeal concluded that the convictions were unsafe and they were therefore quashed. The court, however, in the final paragraph of the judgment commented in relation to the original grounds of appeal that if they had stood alone they might or might not have sufficed adding ([1984] 1 All ER 971 at 977, [1984] 1 WLR 477 at 484):

We say that because we are conscious that in practice it would mean that the protection afforded to patients by s 126 of the 1959 Act would be cut down to a large extent. It would be tantamount to saying that a conviction based on the uncorroborated evidence of such a complainant could not be safe. That would be to step outside the common law and usurp the function of Parliament.

When the appeals with which your Lordships are concerned came to be heard by the Court of Appeal, differently constituted, the first submission made on behalf of the appellants was that the court was bound by the decision in *R* v *Bagshaw* and, since that case could not be distinguished on its facts, the appeals should be allowed. On behalf of the Crown, counsel submitted to the Court of Appeal that the court's decision in *R* v *Bagshaw* was reached *per incuriam*. In *R* v *Bagshaw* counsel had not come prepared to deal with the amendment, which was made only at the suggestion of the court. Although following the short adjournment he sought to deal with the new ground as adequately as he could in his reply, he did not deal with the point as fully as he would otherwise have done, and in particular the court's attention was not drawn to an earlier decision of the Court of Appeal, namely *R* v *Beck* [1982] 1 All ER 807, [1982] 1 WLR 461. In that case the main ground of appeal was that the judge wrongly failed to direct the jury that it would be dangerous to act on the uncorroborated evidence of three witnesses, none of whom could be considered as participants or involved in the crime charged, but who "had a purpose of their own to serve in giving evidence, namely to cover up false representations made or acceded to by them in the insurance claim". In *R* v *Beck* the appellants' counsel based his contention that such a warning should have been given essentially on *R* v *Prater* [1960] 1 All ER 298, [1960] 2 QB 464. In that case a co-prisoner, who could have been considered an accomplice, gave evidence. The Common Serjeant did not give a warning in regard to his testimony and the danger of acting on it unless corroborated. Edmund Davies J in the course of the judgment of the Court of Criminal Appeal said ([1960] 1 All ER 298 at 299–300, [1960] 2 QB 464 at 466):

For the purposes of this present appeal, this court is content to accept that, whether the label to be attached to Welham in this case was strictly that of an accomplice or not, in practice it is desirable that a warning should be given that the witness, whether he comes from the dock, as in this case, or whether he be a Crown witness, may be a witness with some purpose of his own to serve . . . This court, in the circumstances of the present appeal, is content to found itself on the view which it expresses that it is desirable that, in cases where a person may be regarded as having some purpose of his own to serve, the warning against uncorroborated evidence should be given. But every case must be looked at in the light of its own facts . . .

The Court of Appeal in *R* v *Beck* [1982] 1 All ER 807 at 812–813, [1982] 1 WLR 461 at 468, having considered subsequent decisions in which *R* v *Prater* was criticised, concluded that the phrase in *R* v *Prater* [1960] 1 All ER 298 at 300, [1960] 2 QB 464 at 466 "it is desirable that, in cases where a person may be regarded as having some purpose of his own to serve, the warning against uncorroborated evidence should be given" is confined to cases where witnesses may be participants or involved in the crime charged. The Court of Appeal further observed ([1982] 1 All ER 807 at 813, [1982] 1 WLR 461 at 469):

> While we in no way wish to detract from the obligation on a judge to advise a jury to proceed with caution where there is material to suggest that a witness's evidence may be tainted by an improper motive, and the strength of that advice must vary according to the facts of the case, we cannot accept that there is any obligation to give the accomplice warning with all that entails, when it is common ground that there is no basis for suggesting that the witness is a participant or in any way involved in the crime the subject matter of the trial.

The phrase "with all that entails" requires perhaps further explanation. Where there is no corroboration, the rule of practice merely requires that the jury should be warned of the danger of relying on the sole evidence of an accomplice or of the complainant in the sexual case or on the evidence of a child. The warning to be sufficient must explain why it is dangerous so to act, since otherwise the warning will lack significance. The jury are, of course, told that, while as a general rule it is dangerous so to act, they are at liberty to do so if they feel sure that the uncorroborated witness is telling the truth. Where, however, there is evidence before the jury which they can properly consider to be corroborative evidence the position becomes less simple. The trial judge has the added obligation of identifying such material, and explaining to the jury that it is for them to decide whether to treat such evidence as corroboration. He should further warn them against treating as potential corroborative evidence that which may appear to them to be such, but which is not so in law, e.g., evidence of a recent complaint in a sexual offence. Moreover where the prosecution are relying, as potential corroborative material, on lies alleged to have been told by the accused, a particularly careful direction is needed. A special direction is also often needed where evidence of the complainant's distress is relied on by the prosecution in sexual cases as potentially corroborative material. The trial judge has further the additional obligation of directing the jury that accomplices, who are parties to the same charge, cannot corroborate each other.

The Court of Appeal was, in my judgment, fully entitled to conclude that had the court in *R* v *Bagshaw* had the benefit of the full argument which it had had in these two appeals, and, in particular, had its attention drawn to *R* v *Beck*, a different conclusion might have been reached. It accordingly concluded that it was not bound by the decision in *R* v *Bagshaw*. I consider that it was entitled so to decide.

In the submissions before your Lordships' House, there has been little, if any dispute, as to the relevant law. Counsel for the appellants has fully accepted the decision of the Court of Appeal both in *R* v *Bagshaw* and in these two appeals, that patients in hospital under the Mental Health Acts are not in a category like accomplices or complainants in sexual cases or young children. To create from them such a new category would clearly involve considerable problems of definition. What sort of patients, and patients with what sort of criminal records are to be included? The submission of the appellants, in essence, is that without use of the word "danger", in any case analogous to those of the three established categories, and where the evidence of the only or principal witness relied on by the prosecution is inherently unreliable, such a warning must be inadequate. I cannot agree. It has been said, both in the Court of Appeal and in your Lordships' House, that the obligation to warn a jury does not involve some legalistic ritual to be automatically recited by the judge, or that some particular form of words or incantation has to be used and, if not used, the summing up is faulty and the conviction must be quashed (see *R* v *Russell* (1968) 52 Cr App R 147 at 150 per Diplock LJ). There is no magic formula which has to be used with regard to any warning which is given to juries (*R* v *Price* [1968] 2 All ER 282 at 285, [1969] 1 QB 541 at 546 per Sachs LJ). As this is no mere idle process it follows that there are no set words which must be adopted to express the warning. Rather must the good sense of the matter be expounded with clarity and in the setting of a particular case (see *DPP* v *Hester* [1972] 3 All ER 1056 at 1060, [1973] AC 296 at 309 per Lord Morris). The summing-up should be tailored to suit the circumstances of the particular case (see *DPP* v *Kilbourne* [1973] 1 All ER 440 at 447, [1973] AC 729 at 741 per Lord Hailsham LC).

To my mind the question raised by these appeals is both simple to define and simple to answer. Given that it is common ground that a warning was required as to the way in which the jury should treat the evidence of the complainants, the question is: was that warning sufficient? Did it in clear terms bring home to the jury the danger of basing a conviction on the unconfirmed evidence of the complainants?

In the three established categories where the "full warning" is obligatory, the inherent unreliability of the witness may well not be apparent to the jury. Hence the phrase often used in a summing-up: it is the experience of the courts accumulated over many years etc, etc. Complainants of sexual assaults do on occasions give false evidence for a variety of reasons, some of which may not have occurred to a jury. Accomplices may have hidden reasons for lying, and this possibility may again not be apparent to a jury. Children who, although old enough to understand the nature of an oath and thus competent to give sworn evidence, may yet be so young that their comprehension of events and of questions put to them, or their own powers of expression, may be imperfect. All this needs properly to be spelt out to the jury. Hence the well-established rule of practice.

In other cases the potential unreliability of the sole or principal witness for the prosecution is obvious for all to see. These were such cases. The complainants were men of bad character. They had been sent to Rampton rather than to an ordinary prison, because they were mentally unbalanced. That they were anti-authoritarian, prone to lie or exaggerate and could well have old scores which they were seeking to pay off was not disputed. Notwithstanding that the possibility of their evidence being unreliable was patent, that it was clearly dangerous to prefer their evidence to that of the defendants, all men of good character on whose behalf witnesses had spoken in glowing terms, the judge nevertheless told the jury in the clearest possible terms, and repeated himself, that they must approach the evidence of the complainants with great caution. It is common ground that, having given that warning, he then identified the very dangers which justified the exercise of great caution. He gave three reasons: firstly, they were all persons of bad character; secondly, they were all persons suffering from some form of mental disorder; and, thirdly, they may have all conspired together to make false allegations. Thus the judge warned the jury of the dangers of relying on the complainants' testimony because, for the reasons which he gave, such testimony could well be unreliable. The judge, however, did not leave the matter there. As previously stated he pointed out, when dealing with each count, the details of the background of the complainant, his past criminal record, the nature of his mental disturbance and his history in the hospital and, perhaps most important of all, the hospital psychiatrist's view of the personality defects from which the patient suffered and of which I have already given a typical example. I agree with the Court of Appeal that he gave the emphatic warning which was required to meet the justice of the case. Indeed had this been one of the category of cases which required the "full warning" then the judge's direction would have been fully adequate.

The certified point of law is in these terms:

> In a case where the evidence for the Crown is solely that of a witness who is not in one of the accepted categories of suspect witnesses, but who, by reason of his particular mental condition and criminal connection, fulfilled the same criteria, must the judge warn the jury that it is dangerous to convict on his uncorroborated evidence.

I would amend the question by substituting for the words "the same criteria" "analogous criteria": I would then answer the question in the affirmative, adding, for the sake of clarity, that, while it may often be convenient to use the words "danger" or "dangerous", the use of such words is not essential to an adequate warning, so long as the jury are made fully aware of the dangers of convicting on such evidence. Again, for the sake of clarity I would further add that *R* v *Beck* [1982] 1 All ER 807, [1982] 1 WLR 461 was rightly decided and that in a case which does not fall into the three established categories and where there exists potential corroborative material the extent to which the trial judge should make reference to that material depends on the facts of each case. The overriding rule is that he must put the defence fairly and adequately.'

LORD HAILSHAM LC: ' . . . [T]he modern cases, quite correctly in my view, are reluctant to insist on any magic formula or incantation, and stress instead the need that each summing up should be tailor-made to suit the requirements of the individual case; cf *DPP* v *Hester* [1972] 3 All ER 1056 at 1060, 1069, 1073, 1076, [1973] AC 296 at 309, 321, 325, 328 per Lord Morris, Lord Pearson and Lord Diplock. In particular, when, as here, it is agreed that no corroboration exists, a disquisition on what can or could amount to such if corroboration were needed is emphatically not required and greatly to be discouraged (see [1972] 3 All ER 1056 at 1076, [1973] AC 296 at 328 per Lord Diplock). Speaking for myself, I even dislike the expression "categories" as applied to the cases. They are simply classes of cases where the experience of the courts has gradually hardened into rules of practice, owing, as my noble and learned friend points out, partly to the inherent dangers involved, and partly to the fact that the danger is not necessarily obvious to a lay mind. The less juries are confused by superfluous learning and the more their minds are directed to the particular issues relevant to the case before them, the more likely they are, in my view, to arrive at a just verdict.'

(LORDS BRIDGE OF HARWICH, BRANDON OF OAKBROOK and MACKAY OF CLASHFERN agreed.)

• Would it be preferable for the question of whether to give a corroboration warning and what form it should take to be discretionary in all cases?

R v Stewart (1986) 83 Cr App R 327 (CA)

The appellant was charged on indictment with eight counts of contravening section 30 of the Sexual Offences Act 1956. The prosecution case was that he had for a substantial period been letting flats in the West End of London at high rents to persons who he knew to be prostitutes. A, the principal prosecution witness, was one such prostitute. She averred that she became engaged in prostitution in the 1970s when she formed a friendship with the appellant. He had arranged a mortgage for her on a house in the country and loaned her money. She said that she had repaid the loan but that the appellant had refused to transfer the house to her. A also said that she had collected rents for the appellant from prostitutes at the other flats. Other women gave evidence that they had carried on prostitution at two of the flats named in the indictment. The appellant's defence was that he did not encourage the use of his premises for prostitution, he had endeavoured to sell the flats to someone else. He had not charged the exorbitant rents the prostitutes had spoken about, nor had he received rents from prostitutes. A, he said, had given false evidence because she was bitter about the house. He was convicted on counts 4 and 7, acquitted on counts 1, 5 and 8, and the jury failed to reach a verdict on counts 2, 3 and 6. The appellant was re-tried before a different judge and jury on these three counts, renumbered 1, 2 and 3. On counts 1 and 2 he was convicted mainly on the veracity of A's evidence, and on count 3 on evidence, other than that of A, as being capable of founding a conviction. The appellant appealed on the ground, *inter alia*, in the second trial the judge had failed properly to direct the jury on the danger of convicting the appellant on the evidence of the prostitute A alone (he had warned the jury to treat A as an accomplice) that it was necessary to look at her evidence with considerable care, they should look for corroboration but that there was no evidence before them, the jury, that came within that category.

MUSTILL LJ, reading the judgment of the court: 'The appellant maintains that this direction did not go far enough to warn the jury of the dangers involved in convicting on the evidence of Anita alone. We feel constrained to agree with this submission. Whilst the language in which the "full" warning on corroboration as expressed in the judgments has tended to follow a pattern, there is ample authority that no set formula is required, and indeed that the words "danger" and "dangerous" need not themselves be employed. At the same time, however, the courts have emphasised that (as Salmon LJ said in *Henry and Manning* (1968) 53 Cr App R 150) there must be clear and simple language that will without any doubt convey to the jury that it is really dangerous to convict on the evidence of the impugned witness alone: and the danger is, of course, the serious risk that the jury will end by convicting an innocent man (*Holland* [1983] Crim LR 545).

There are undoubtedly indications in the reported cases that the law has already gone at least as far as it need go to protect the accused by making an accomplice direction on corroboration an invariable rule. We have had this very much in mind, as well as the need not to limit the freedom of the trial judge to adapt his direction to the circumstances of the individual case. Even so, and even without the benefit of authority, we would conclude that a reminder of the reasons which an accomplice may have for giving false evidence, and an accurate statement of the reasons which Anita had for such conduct, coupled with an injunction to look at her evidence "with considerable care" did fall short of a decisive warning (however expressed) that if they convicted on the basis of her evidence they were in danger of convicting an innocent man.

Whatever hesitations we have felt in arriving at this conclusion are dispelled by decisions of this Court which show that exhortations to use "great" or "particular" or "the utmost" care are not enough; see *Holland (supra)*; *Price* (1968) 52 Cr App R 295; [1968] 2 All ER 282; *Riley* (1980) 70 Cr App R 1. Moreover, in *Bagshaw, Holmes and Starkey* (1984) 78 Cr App R 163; [1984] 1 WLR 477 and *R v Spencer* [1985] 1 All ER 673 (CA), there were the most elaborate discussions of whether, in relation to a category of witnesses with which we are not here concerned, it was mandatory to give the "full" warning, or whether something similar to the direction given in the present case would suffice. The whole of the debate would have been unnecessary if the latter formula had been understood as conveying the same warning as the "full" direction, albeit in different language.

Thus, so far as concerned the evidence of Anita, we hold that there was a material misdirection, and the convictions at the second trial must be quashed unless there are grounds for applying the proviso to section 2(1) of the Criminal Appeal Act, 1968. That the proviso can be applied where there has been a failure to give an adequate direction on corroboration is undeniable: see *Davies v DPP* (1954) 38 Cr App R 11; [1954] AC 378; *Henry and Manning (supra)*; *Jenkins* (1981) 72 Cr App R 354; and the use of the proviso in this context may not be as exceptional as had at one time been thought: contrast *Trigg* (1963) 47 Cr App R 94, with *Jenkins (supra)*. A useful working guide is to look at the totality of the evidence, and then consider whether, after subtracting the evidence of the impugned witness there would be sufficient left to make the jury sure that the defendant was guilty.'

Appeal allowed.

R v *Midwinter* (1971) 55 Cr App R 523 (CA)

The appellant was convicted of indecent assault on a girl. There had been no visual identification by the girl of the appellant as her assailant either at an identification parade or in court, but she had given a description of her assailant to the police. The summing-up contained no reference to corroboration.

CAIRNS LJ, reading the judgment of the court: 'The rule has been laid down as a rule to which there are few, if any, exceptions that in a case of a sexual nature such as this it is essential that there should be a direction to the jury on corroboration. The case which may be regarded as final in deciding that proposition beyond doubt is *Trigg* (1963) 47 Cr App R 94; [1963] 1 WLR 305. It is true that it was said in the later case of *O'Reilly* (1967) 51 Cr App R 345: [1967] 2 QB 722, that the word "corroboration" need not be used so long as there is given a solemn warning to the same effect, but there may be cases where a direction on corroboration is unnecessary, as in the earlier case of *Rolfe* (1952) 36 Cr App R 4, where the accused had actually gone into the witness box and had admitted in the witness box that he committed the indecent assault. Indeed, in reading the report in the case of *Rolfe (supra)* it is impossible to say, and Mr Clapham was not able to enlighten us, what possible defence or ground of appeal there could have been in that case.

However, Mr Clapham says this was not a case for corroboration because the girl herself had not identified the man at all, it turned upon the alleged confession of the appellant. The Court does not accept that view of the matter. It is true that the girl had not identified the man either at an identification parade or in court, and it may well be that counsel for the prosecution exercised a proper discretion in not inviting the girl to identify the man in court which, as we all know, has its dangers. But when one looks at the summing-up one finds this passage: "And so the sole vital issue which you must determine is: Was the youth who committed that indecent assault and whose description I have read to you as given by Christine, was it this defendant?" The position, therefore, was that the girl had given a description of her assailant and no doubt one question to which the jury would direct their minds was: Does the accused man fit that description? It is on that point that it seems to this Court that it is vital that there should have been added the warning that corroboration of the girl's evidence of the description that she had given was required.

If indeed it were the fact that nothing that the girl had said could be regarded as evidence of identification, then no doubt the warning would have to be in a different form and the word "corroboration" would not be appropriate. That would be in complete accordance with the position in *O'Reilly (supra)*, but in this case it seems to us that the word "corroboration" would have been appropriate and that, whether that actual word was used or not, it was essential that the jury should be directed that the girl's evidence must be supported or confirmed, whatever word one likes to choose, by evidence which the jury accepted. On that ground this Court is of the opinion that the direction here was not a sufficient one.'

Conviction quashed.

B: NATURE AND USE OF CORROBORATIVE EVIDENCE

(Suggested preliminary reading: *A Practical Approach to Evidence,* pp. 406–414, 426–429).

R v Baskerville [1916] 2 KB 658 (CCA)

The defendant was convicted of having committed acts of gross indecency with two boys. The only direct evidence of the commission of the acts charged was that of the boys themselves, who on their own statement were accomplices in the offences. However, a letter was proved to have been sent to one of the boys by the defendant in his handwriting signed by him with his initial B, enclosing a 10s note for both boys, and making an appointment for them to meet the defendant 'as arranged'. The judge told the jury that the letter afforded evidence which they would be entitled to find was sufficient corroboration of the boys' evidence.

LORD READING LC, delivering the judgment of the Court: 'The rule of practice as to corroborative evidence has arisen in consequence of the danger of convicting a person upon the unconfirmed testimony of one who is admittedly a criminal. What is required is some additional evidence rendering it probable that the story of the accomplice is true and that it is reasonably safe to act upon it. If the only independent evidence relates to an incident in the commission of the crime which does not connect the accused with it, or if the only independent evidence relates to the identity of the accused without connecting him with the crime, is it corroborative evidence?. . .

[W]e have come to the conclusion that the better opinion of the law upon this point is that stated in *R v Stubbs* (1855) Dears 555 by Parke B, namely, that the evidence of an accomplice must be confirmed not only as to the circumstances of the crime, but also as to the identity of the prisoner. The learned Baron does not mean that there must be confirmation of all the circumstances of the crime; as we have already stated, that is unnecessary. It is sufficient if there is confirmation as to a material circumstance of the crime and of the identity of the accused in relation to the crime. . . .

We hold that evidence in corroboration must be independent testimony which affects the accused by connecting or tending to connect him with the crime. In other words, it must be evidence which implicates him, that is, which confirms in some material particular not only the evidence that the crime has been committed, but also that the prisoner committed it. The test applicable to determine the nature and extent of the corroboration is thus the same whether the case falls within the rule of practice at common law or within that class of offences for which corroboration is required by statute. The language of the statute, "implicates the accused", compendiously incorporates the test applicable at common law in the rule of practice. The nature of the corroboration will necessarily vary according to the particular circumstances of the offence charged. It would be in high degree dangerous to attempt to formulate the kind of evidence which would be regarded as corroboration, except to say that corroborative evidence is evidence which shows or tends to show that the story of the accomplice that the accused committed the crime is true, not merely that the crime has been committed, but that it was committed by the accused.

The corroboration need not be direct evidence that the accused committed the crime; it is sufficient if it is merely circumstantial evidence of his connection with the crime. A good instance of this indirect evidence is to be found in *R* v *Birkett* (1839) 8 C & P 732. Were the law otherwise, many crimes which are usually committed between accomplices in secret, such as incest, offences with females, or the present case, could never be brought to justice.'

Appeal dismissed.

- Is Lord Reading CJ's statement in *R* v *Baskerville* that evidence in corroboration must be independent *testimony* correct?

R v *Whitehead* [1929] 1 KB 99 (CCA)

On the trial of the appellant for having had unlawful sexual intercourse with a girl under sixteen, the judge directed the jury that although what the girl said to her mother several months after the offence was committed was not evidence, yet the jury could infer what the girl said, namely, that the appellant was responsible for her condition, from what the mother did, because the appellant was at once accused, and that that amounted to corroboration of the girl's story. The appellant was convicted.

LORD HEWART, delivering the judgment of the court, said: 'This is not a case like *R* v *Lillyman* [1896] 2 QB 167 or *R* v *Osborne* [1905] 1 KB 551, because in those cases the complaint was made at the first opportunity which reasonably offered itself after the offence was committed, whereas in the present case the complaint was not made until after the lapse of several months. [His Lordship referred to a passage from the summing-up and continued:] It is said that the opening portion of that passage was likely to convey to the minds of the jury that although the girl's statement to her mother was in the circumstances not admissible in evidence, nevertheless the jury could draw the inference, from what the mother did, that the girl had said that the appellant was responsible for her condition, and that that amounted to corroboration of the girl's story. That direction would be wrong. Any such inference as to what the girl had told her mother could not amount to corroboration of the girl's story, because it proceeded from the girl herself; it was merely the girl's story at second hand. In order that evidence may amount to corroboration it must be extraneous to the witness who is to be corroborated. A girl cannot corroborate herself, otherwise it is only necessary for her to repeat her story some twenty-five times in order to get twenty-five corroborations of it.'

Appeal allowed.

R v Chauhan (1981) 73 Cr App R 232 (CA)

The appellant accompanied his sister to premises where she had applied for employment, and while she was being interviewed he waited in another room where a female employee was working alone. They entered into conversation, whereupon it was alleged by the victim that the appellant touched her breast and tried to kiss her. She extricated herself and ran upstairs to the ladies' lavatory crying. A fellow employee heard her cries and followed her. The victim explained to her fellow employee what had happened. The police later interviewed the appellant who admitted being alone with the victim but denied any incident took place in which he had touched her. He maintained that when she left the room she had been behaving normally. The appellant was charged with indecent assault. At the end of the prosecution case counsel for the appellant submitted that there was insufficient corroboration for the issue to be left to the jury. The recorder ruled that the jury were entitled to regard the victim's distressed condition described by the fellow employee as corroboration if they thought it right to do so. The appellant was convicted. He appealed on the ground, *inter alia*, that the evidence of distress could not amount to corroboration.

LORD LANE CJ, giving the judgment of the court: 'We have been referred to a number of authorities on the matter. It is right that at least brief reference should be made to them. The first one in point of time is the case of *Redpath* (1962) 46 Cr App R 319. The headnote encapsulates adequately the effect of that case. It reads as follows: "In a sexual offence the distressed condition of the complainant is capable of amounting to corroboration of the complainant's evidence, but the weight of such evidence as corroboration will vary according to the circumstances of the case".

At p. 321, Lord Parker CJ said this: "So far as any question of indecent assault is concerned, the learned judge told the jury that her distressed condition observed by Mr Hall and spoken to by Mr Hall was capable of being corroboration. The point in this appeal is whether that is so. Mr Harper has argued that the distressed condition of the complainant is no more corroborative than the complaint, if any, that the complainant makes, and that while the latter merely shows that the story is consistent and is not corroborative, so the distressed condition is not corroborative. This Court is quite unable to accept that argument. It seems to this Court that the distressed condition of a complainant is quite clearly capable of amounting to corroboration. Of course, the circumstances will vary enormously, and in some circumstances quite clearly no weight, or little weight, could be attached to such evidence as corroboration. Thus, if a girl goes in a distressed condition to her mother and makes a complaint, while the mother's evidence as to the girl's condition may in law be capable of amounting to corroboration, quite clearly the jury should be told that they should attach little, if any, weight to that evidence, because it is all part and parcel of the complaint. The girl making the complaint might well put on an act and simulate distress. But in the present case the circumstances are entirely different."

In respect of that, the circumstances there were that the distressed condition of the little girl who had been the subject of the assault was observed by someone whom the little girl did not know to be there.

The next case to which we were referred was *Okoye* [1964] Crim LR 416. That was a judgment of the Court of Criminal Appeal. It is a very brief, sparse report. The second half of the holding reads as follows: "2 The judge did not emphasise sufficiently that a distressed condition at the time of making a complaint can only amount at the most to the very slightest evidence of corroboration . . ."

That was a case, as was the next one, *Luisi* [1964] Crim LR 605, where the only issue was consent and where undoubtedly there had been some form of sexual activity between the parties. It seems to this Court that in those circumstances what was said in that type of case is of very little value in considering this type of case, where, on the appellant's evidence, no form of contact, or sexual contact, or indecent sexual contact took place at all. But I read a very short passage from the judgment in *Luisi (supra)*, as reported, in skeleton form, in the same volume of the *Criminal Law Review*. It reads as follows: "The significance of the girl's distress was over-emphasised. There may be cases (e.g., *Redpath* (1962) 46 Cr App R 319) where there can be no suggestion that the distress was feigned. In normal cases, however, the weight to be given to distress varies infinitely, and juries should be warned that, although it may amount to corroboration they must be fully satisfied that there is no question of it having been feigned".

For purposes of completeness, there are two other cases. The first is *Knight* (1966) 50 Cr App R 122; [1966] 1 WLR 230. I read a passage from p. 125 and p. 233 respectively, from the judgment of the Court given by Lord Parker CJ: "Despite what was said in that judgment", (he is referring there to *Redpath (supra)*, "there has been a tendency since then for judges to leave to the jury almost every case where a complainant is seen to be in a distressed condition, and in several cases since *Redpath (supra)*, and in particular two cases to which we have been referred, *Okoye (supra)*, and *Luisi (supra)*, I endeavoured to stress that the distress shown by a complainant must not be over-emphasised in the sense that juries should be warned that except in special circumstances little weight ought to be given to that evidence."

Finally, the case of *Wilson* (1974) 58 Cr App R 304. I read a passage from the judgment of Edmund-Davies LJ at the foot of page 309: "In granting leave to appeal, the Court drew attention with understandable brevity to the fact that, while the appearance and emotional state of a complainant may in very special circumstances be regarded as capable of constituting corroboration, it is an approach which has to be very guarded, and whether the matter was sufficiently elaborated by the learned judge in the present instance was something which the court thought called for further examination".

One other short passage, at p. 312: "We regard it" (said Edmund-Davies LJ) "as of considerable importance that the type of warning adverted to by Lord Parker CJ in *Knight (supra)* is constantly borne in mind when such cases as the present are before the courts and that a trial judge cannot be too zealous in heeding that warning. For these reasons we allow the appeal . . ."

It seems to us that in this case the circumstances, as we have already indicated, were very different from those in many of the cases which appear in the reports. Here there were only two people in the room. Here there was a total denial by the appellant that anything of an indecent nature, or anything to which exception could be taken ever took place in the room at all. In those circumstances, it seems to us that it was essential for the jury to have before them the evidence of what happened when this lady left the room; evidence coming from Mrs Hindle. If they had not had that evidence before them, they could have legitimately complained that they were being deprived of a valuable aid to them in deciding the case properly according to the directions given to them by the recorder.'

Appeal dismissed.

• Was the evidence of the distress of the complainant in the case of *R* v *Chauhan* truly independent in terms of the *Baskerville* test?

Cracknell v *Smith* [1960] 1 WLR 1239 (DC)

The complainant in affiliation proceedings gave evidence that she had had intercourse with the defendant at about the likely time of conception (March 1958). Her mother testified that the defendant had visited her home to see the complainant in January and February 1958, and had met the complainant at the corner of the street on various occasions. The justices were of opinion that the evidence of the mother was sufficient corroboration of the complainant's evidence, and accordingly adjudged the defendant the putative father of the child. The defendant appealed.

LORD PARKER CJ, giving the judgment of the court: 'For my part, I am perfectly satisfied that the evidence of the mother was not sufficient corroboration or, perhaps more accurately, any corroboration, because the weight to be attached to the evidence is a matter for the justices. Quite apart from the fact that she was only speaking in regard to January and February, 1958, and not in regard to March, it is quite clear that her evidence was as to mere opportunity. Mere evidence of opportunity and nothing more can be no corroboration. There are, of course, cases, of which *Moore* v *Hewitt* [1947] KB 831 is an example, and also *Harvey* v *Anning* (1902) 87 LT 687, in both of which there was something more than mere opportunity. In both cases, unlike the present case, there was evidence that the complainant was not being intimate with or associating with anybody else. Secondly, in *Harvey* v *Anning* there was, as an additional factor, the great difference in the social position of the parties, and in both cases there was real evidence of courtship and association together, and not the very vague association spoken to by the mother in the present case.'

Appeal allowed.

James v *R* (1970) 55 Cr App R 299 (PC)

The appellant was convicted of rape. The complainant alleged that a man whom she subsequently identified as the appellant had raped her at knife point. There was medical evidence showing that the complainant had had sexual intercourse at about a time consistent with her allegation. The trial judge directed that this evidence might corroborate that of the complainant.

VISCOUNT DILHORNE, delivering the judgment of the Board: 'Where the charge is of rape, the corroborative evidence must confirm in some material particular that intercourse has taken place and that it has taken place without the woman's consent, and also that the accused was the man who committed the crime. In sexual cases, in view of the possibility of error in identification by the complainant, corroborative evidence confirming in a material particular her evidence that the accused was the guilty man is just as important as such evidence confirming that intercourse took place without her consent . . .

True it is that the medical evidence and the evidence of what was found on Miss Hall's clothing and on the articles taken from her bed confirmed her testimony that intercourse with her had taken place on her bed, but there was no medical evidence that the intercourse had taken place without her consent; and the judge directed the jury that, if they accepted that evidence, it could amount to corroboration in the sense in which he had already explained to them that the word was to be understood.

In their Lordship's view, this direction was entirely wrong. Independent evidence that intercourse had taken place is not evidence confirming in some material particular either that the crime of rape had been committed or, if it had been, that it had been committed by the accused. It does not show that the intercourse took place without consent or that the accused was a party to it. There was in this case no evidence capable of amounting to corroboration of Miss Hall's evidence that she had been raped, and raped by the accused. The judge should have told the jury that. His failure to do so was a serious misdirection, so serious as to make it inevitable that the conviction should be quashed.'

R v *Jackson* (1953) 37 Cr App R 43 (CCA)

The appellant was convicted of being accessory before the fact to the larceny of a quantity of motor tyres and of receiving the tyres knowing them to have been stolen. The evidence against the defendant on the counts on which he was convicted consisted mainly of that of the thieves. The appellant did not go into the witness box.

LORD GODDARD CJ, giving the judgment of the court: 'The difficulty that arises in this case is on the direction that the learned judge gave. Having pointed out and emphasised the danger of acting on the evidence of accomplices and having indicated who might be regarded as accomplices, in commenting on the fact that the appellant had not gone into the box to give evidence, he said: "You, members of the jury, will attach just what weight you think right to that and if you say: 'Well, that, in our view, forms ample corroboration that those thieves were telling the truth, that he has refrained from going into the witness box because he does not dare; he thinks he will only make matters worse if he does'—if you come to that conclusion—the weight you attach to his silence is entirely a matter for you." That came just at the end of the learned judge's summing-up, and could only, in our view, have been understood by the jury as meaning that the fact that the appellant had not gone into the witness box might amount to corroboration, if they thought fit to treat it as such. In the opinion of the court, that is not correct. One cannot say that the fact that a prisoner had not gone into the witness box to give evidence is of itself corroboration of accomplices' evidence. It is a matter which the jury very properly could, and very probably would, take into account but it should be clearly understood that that direction is wrong in law.'

(The court applied the proviso to s. 4(1) of the Criminal Appeal Act 1907.)
Appeal dismissed.

R v *Lucas* [1981] QB 720 (CA)

The appellant was tried on a count charging her with being knowingly concerned in the fraudulent evasion of the prohibition on importation of a controlled drug. Evidence implicating her was given by an accomplice. The appellant gave evidence which was challenged as being partly lies. The jury were warned of the dangers of convicting on the accomplice's uncorroborated evidence and were directed in terms which suggested that lies told by the appellant in court could be considered as corroborative of the accomplice's evidence. The appellant was convicted and appealed.

LORD LANE CJ, delivering the judgment of the court: 'The fact that the jury may feel sure that the accomplice's evidence is to be preferred to that of the defendant and that the defendant accordingly must have been lying in the witness box is not of itself something which can be treated by the jury as corroboration of the accomplice's evidence. It is only if the accomplice's evidence is believed that there is any necessity to look for corroboration of it. If the belief that the accomplice is truthful means that the defendant was untruthful and if that untruthfulness can be used as corroboration, the practical effect would be to dispense with the need of corroboration altogether.

The matter was put in this way by Lord MacDermott in *Tumahole Bereng* v *The King* [1949] AC 253, 270:

> Nor does an accused corroborate an accomplice merely by giving evidence which is not accepted and must therefore be regarded as false. Corroboration may well be found in the evidence of an accused person; but that is a different matter, for there confirmation comes, if at all, from what is said, and not from the falsity of what is said.

There is, without doubt, some confusion in the authorities as to the extent to which lies may in some circumstances provide corroboration and it was this confusion which probably and understandably led the judge astray in the present case. In our judgment the position is as follows. Statements made out of court, for example, statements to the police, which are proved or admitted to be false may in certain circumstances amount to corroboration. There is no shortage of authority for this proposition: see, for example, *R* v *Knight* [1966] 1 WLR 230, *Credland* v *Knowler* (1951) 35 Cr App R 48. It accords with good sense that a lie told by a defendant about a material issue may show that the liar knew if he told the truth he would be sealing his fate. In the words of Lord Dunedin in *Dawson* v *M'Kenzie*, 1908 SC 648, 649, cited with approval by Lord Goddard CJ in *Credland* v *Knowler*, 35 Cr App R 48, 55:

> . . . the opportunity may have a complexion put upon it by statements made by the defender which are proved to be false. It is not that a false statement made by the defender proves that the pursuer's statements are true, but it may give to a proved opportunity a different complexion from what it would have borne had no such false statement been made.

To be capable of amounting to corroboration the lie told out of court must first of all be deliberate. Secondly it must relate to a material issue. Thirdly the motive for the lie must be a realisation of guilt and a fear of the truth. The jury should in appropriate cases be reminded that people sometimes lie, for example, in an attempt to bolster up a just cause, or out of shame or out of a wish to conceal disgraceful behaviour from their family. Fourthly the statement must be clearly shown to be a lie by evidence other than that of the accomplice who is to be corroborated, that is to say by admission or by evidence from an independent witness.

As a matter of good sense it is difficult to see why, subject to the same safeguards, lies proved to have been told in court by a defendant should not equally be capable of providing corroboration. In other common law jurisdictions they are so treated; see the cases collated by Professor J D Heydon in "Can Lies Corroborate?" (1973) 89 LQR 552, 561, and cited with apparent approval in *Cross on Evidence*, 5th ed (1979), p. 210 (footnote).

It has been suggested that there are dicta in *R* v *Chapman* [1973] QB 774, to the effect that lies so told in court can never be capable of providing corroboration of other evidence given against a defendant. We agree with the comment upon this case in *Cross on Evidence*, 5th ed pp. 210–211, that the court there may only have been intending to go no further than to apply the passage from the speech of Lord MacDermott in *Tumahole Bereng* v *The King* [1949] AC 253, 270 which we have already cited.

In our view the decision in *R* v *Chapman* [1973] QB 774 on the point there in issue was correct. The decision should not, however, be regarded as going any further than we have already stated. Properly understood, it is not authority for the proposition that in no circumstances can lies told by a defendant in court provide material corroboration of an accomplice. We find ourselves in agreement with the comment upon this decision made by this court in *R* v *Boardman* [1975] AC 421, 428–429. That point was not subsequently discussed when that case was before the House of Lords.

The main evidence against Chapman and Baldwin was a man called Thatcher, who was undoubtedly an accomplice in the alleged theft and dishonest handling of large quantities of clothing. The defence was that Thatcher was lying when he implicated the defendants and that he must himself have stolen the goods. The judge gave the jury the necessary warning about accomplice evidence and the requirement of corroboration, and then went on to say, at p. 779:

> If you think that Chapman's story about the disappearance of the van and its contents is so obviously untrue that you do not attach any weight to it at all—in other words, you think Chapman is lying to you—then I direct you that that is capable of corroborating Thatcher, because, members of the jury, if Chapman is lying about the van, can there be any explanation except that Thatcher is telling the truth about how it came to disappear? . . . My direction is that it is capable in law of corroborating Thatcher. Similarly in the case of Baldwin, if you think that Baldwin's story about going up to London and buying these . . . is untrue—in other words he has told you lies about that—then . . . that I direct you, so far as he is concerned, is capable of amounting to corroboration of Thatcher.

That being the direction which this court was then considering, the decision is plainly correct, because the jury were being invited to prefer the evidence of the accomplice to that of the defendant and then without more to use their disbelief of the defendant as corroboration of the accomplice.

Providing that the lies told in court fulfil the four criteria which we have set out above, we are unable to see why they should not be available for the jury to consider in just the same way as lies told out of court. So far as the instant case is concerned, the judge, we feel, fell into the same error as the judge did in *R* v *Chapman* [1973] QB 774. The lie told by the appellant was clearly not shown to be a lie by evidence other than that of the accomplice who was to be corroborated and consequently the apparent direction that a lie was capable of providing corroboration was erroneous.'

Appeal allowed.

DPP v *Kilbourne* [1973] AC 729 (HL)

The respondent was convicted of one offence of buggery, one of attempted buggery, and five offences of indecent assault on two groups of boys. Counts one to four related to offences in 1970 against the first group of boys, and counts five to seven related to offences against the second group of boys in 1971. The defence was one of innocent association. The judge directed the jury that they would be entitled to take the uncorroborated evidence of the second group of boys, if they were satisfied that the boys were speaking the truth as to what the respondent had done to them, as supporting evidence given by the first group of boys. The Court of Appeal having quashed the convictions, the Crown appealed to the House of Lords.

LORD HAILSHAM LC: 'The Court of Appeal whose judgment was given by Lawton LJ approached the matter in three stages.

Lawton LJ said, at p. 1369:

> . . . we have to decide whether the evidence of one group of boys was admissible at all on the counts in which the other group of boys were named. If it was not, there was a misdirection as to the admissibility of evidence; but if it was admissible, the second and third stages have to be considered. The question at the second stage is whether such evidence if it had involved neither victims nor children could have been capable of being corroboration; and the third stage is whether, in the circumstances of this case in which child victims were involved, it was capable of being corroboration.

The Court of Appeal then held on the authority of *R* v *Sims* [1946] KB 531, *R* v *Chandor* [1959] 1 QB 545 and *R* v *Flack* [1969] 1 WLR 937 that the evidence was admissible, and admissible because it was relevant to the matters in dispute and implicated the accused in the criminal conduct alleged in the indictment. The nerve of their argument is contained in the following short passage in the judgment of the court [1972] 1 WLR 1365, 1369–1370:

> In the present case, with the exception of the penis touching incident involving the boy Kevin, each accusation bears a resemblance to the other and shows not merely that the appellant was a homosexual which would not have been enough to make the evidence admissible, but that he was one whose proclivities in that regard took a particular form. Further, the evidence of each boy went to rebut the defence of innocent association which the appellant put forward: this by itself made the similar fact evidence admissible: see *R* v *Chandor* [1959] 1 QB 545, 550 *per* Lord Parker CJ. We have had no doubt that the evidence of one group of boys could properly be taken into account by the jury when considering the counts relating to the other group. But for what purpose since only relevant evidence is admissible? What, for example, did Gary's evidence prove in relation to John's on count 1? The answer must be that his evidence, having the striking features of the resemblance between the acts committed on him and those alleged to have been committed on John, makes it more likely that

John was telling the truth when he said that the appellant had behaved in the same way to him.

The court went on to quote the passage of the judgment of the Court of Criminal Appeal in *R* v *Sims* [1946] KB 531, 539–540 when they say:

> The evidence of each man was that the accused invited him into the house and there committed the acts charged. The acts they describe bear a striking similarity. That is a special feature sufficient in itself to justify the admissibility of the evidence; . . . The probative force of all the acts together is much greater than one alone; for, whereas the jury might think that one man might be telling an untruth, three or four are hardly likely to tell the same untruth unless they were conspiring together. If there is nothing to suggest a conspiracy, their evidence would seem to be overwhelming.

In spite of this reasoning, the Court of Appeal went on to say that nonetheless there was nothing mutually corroborative in testimony of this kind. They felt themselves constrained to come to this conclusion because of the later passage in *R* v *Sims* which says, at p. 544: "We do not think that the evidence of the men can be considered as corroborating one another, because each may be said to be an accomplice in the act to which he speaks and his evidence is to be viewed with caution;" On this the Court of Appeal quoted with some relish, the comments of Professor Cross on *Evidence*, 3rd ed (1967), p. 182: " . . . it is difficult to see how admissible evidence of misconduct of the defendant or accused on other occasions could ever fail to corroborate the evidence relating to the question with which the court is concerned. If it is admissible at all on account of its relevance for some reason other than its tendency to show a propensity towards wrongdoing in general or wrongdoing of the kind into which the court is inquiring, the conduct must, it would seem, implicate the defendant or accused in a material particular in relation to the occasion into which the court is inquiring."

In quashing all the convictions on this ground the Court of Appeal went on to rely on the authority of *R* v *Campbell* [1956] 2 QB 432 where it is said, at p. 438:

> . . . we may perhaps endeavour to give some guidance to courts who have from time to time to deal with cases of sexual assaults on children where the evidence of each child deals only with the assault on himself or herself. In such cases it is right to tell a jury that because A says that the accused assaulted him, it is no corroboration of his evidence that B says that he also was the victim of a similar assault though both say it on oath. At the same time we think a jury may be told that a succession of these cases may help them to determine the truth of the matter provided they are satisfied that there is no collaboration between the children to put up a false story. And if the defence is one of innocent association by the accused with the children, *R* v *Sims*, subsequently approved on this point by the House of Lords in *Harris* v *Director of Public Prosecutions* [1952] AC 694, shows that such evidence can be given to rebut the defence.

On this particular passage the Court of Appeal comment [1972] 1 WLR 1365, 1371–1372:

> Here Lord Goddard CJ is apparently distinguishing between evidence which can be used as corroboration and evidence which may help the jury in some way to determine

the truth. A's evidence that the accused indecently assaulted him may not be used to corroborate B's evidence that B was indecently assaulted, but it may be used in some other way to help the jury to determine the truth of B's evidence; see *Cross on Evidence* at pp. 320 and 321, footnote 7, where he cites *Sims'* case as an authority for this difficult distinction.

Basing themselves on this state of the authorities, the Court of Appeal decided, at p. 1372: "Accordingly we must hold the direction to be defective, with whatever consequences may follow from this view." The consequences, of course, involved the quashing of all the convictions.

We now have to determine at the invitation of the Court of Appeal how "evidence which can be used as corroboration, and evidence which may help the jury in some other way to determine the truth" can be validly distinguished, and the distinction explained to a jury.

The question certified by the Court of Appeal in the present case as of general public importance is: "whether and in what circumstances the sworn evidence of a child victim as to an offence charged can be corroborated by the admissible but uncorroborated evidence of another child victim as to similar misconduct of the accused on a different occasion."

I may say at once that I regard the passage in *R* v *Campbell* [1956] 2 QB 432 which attempts to draw a distinction between evidence which helps the jury to arrive at a conclusion about evidence requiring corroboration and evidence which is confirmatory or corroborative of evidence requiring corroboration as a valiant, but wholly unsuccessful, attempt to reconcile the two quoted passages in *R* v *Sims* [1946] KB 531, 539, 544, the second of which I believe to be wholly inconsistent with the first. The second passage may be based on what I believe to be a false analogy with the use which can be made by the prosecution of complaints by the alleged victim of a rape as evidence of consistency, but not corroboration, since a witness requiring corroboration "cannot corroborate herself". It may also be based to some extent on the rule about joint accomplices stretching back to *R* v *Noakes* (1832) 5 C & P 326, 328 *per* Littledale J. But this also, as I shall endeavour to show, is a false analogy.

In my view, there is no magic or artificiality about the rule of practice concerning corroboration at all. In Scottish law, it seems, some corroboration is necessary in every criminal case. In contrast, by the English common law, the evidence of one competent witness is enough to support a verdict whether in civil or criminal proceedings except in cases of perjury (cf. *Hawkins' Pleas of the Crown*, vol. 4, c. 46, s. 2; *Foster's Crown Cases* (1762) 233). This is still the general rule, but there are now two main classes of exception to it. In the first place, there are a number of statutory exceptions. . . .

But side by side with the statutory exceptions is the rule of practice now under discussion by which judges have in fact warned juries in certain classes of case that it is dangerous to found a conviction on the evidence of particular witnesses or classes of witness unless that evidence is corroborated in a material particular implicating the accused, or confirming the disputed items in the case. The earliest of these classes to be recognised was probably the evidence of accomplices "approving" for the Crown, no doubt, partly because at that time the accused could not give evidence on his own behalf and was therefore peculiarly vulnerable to invented allegations by persons guilty of the same offence. By now the recognised categories also include children who give evidence under oath, the alleged victims, whether adults or children, in cases of sexual assault, and persons of admittedly bad character. I do not regard these categories as closed. A judge is almost certainly wise to give a similar warning about the evidence of any principal witness for the Crown where the witness can reasonably be suggested to have some purpose of his own to serve in giving false evidence (cf. *R* v *Prater* [1960] 2 QB 464, *R* v *Russell* (1968) 52 Cr App R 147). The Supreme Court of the Republic of Ireland has apparently decided that at least in some cases of disputed identity a similar warning is necessary (*People* v *Casey (No. 2)* [1963] IR 33, 39–40.) This question may still be open here (cf. *R* v *Williams* [1956] Crim LR 833; *Arthurs* v *Attorney-General for Northern Ireland* (1970) 55 Cr App R 161, 169).

Since the institution of the Court of Criminal Appeal in 1907, the rule, which was originally discretionary in the trial judge, has acquired the force of a rule of law in the sense that a conviction after a direction to the jury which does not contain the warning will be quashed, unless the proviso is applied: see *R* v *Baskerville* [1916] 2 KB 658; *Davies* v *Director of Public Prosecutions* [1954] AC 378, 398 *per* Lord Simonds LC.

However, it is open to a judge to discuss with the jury the nature of the danger to be apprehended in convicting without corroboration and the degree of such danger (cf. *R* v *Price (Herbert)* [1969] 1 QB 541, 546) and it is well established that a conviction after an appropriate warning may stand notwithstanding that the evidence is uncorroborated, unless, of course, the verdict is otherwise unsatisfactory: *R* v *Baskerville* [1916] 2 KB 658. There is, moreover, no magic formula to be used: *R* v *Price* [1969] 1 QB 541. I agree with the opinions expressed in this House in *R* v *Hester* [1973] AC 296 that it is wrong for a judge to confuse the jury with a general if learned disquisition on the law. His summing-up should be tailormade to suit the circumstances of the particular case. The word "corroboration" is not a technical term of art, but a dictionary word bearing its ordinary meaning; since it is slightly unusual in common speech the actual word need not be used, and in fact it may be better not to use it. Where it is used it needs to be explained.

The difficulty which has arisen in the present case was complicated by the fact that the witnesses requiring corroboration were said to be corroborated by witnesses not of the same incident, but of incidents of a similar character themselves all of the class requiring corroboration. A considerable part of the time taken up in argument was devoted to a consideration whether such evidence of similar incidents could be used against the accused to establish his guilt at all, and we examined the authorities in some depth from *Makin* v *Attorney-General for New South Wales* [1894] AC 57, through Lord Sumner's observations in *Thompson* v *The King* [1918] AC 221, to *Harris* v *Director of Public Prosecutions* [1952] AC 694. I do not myself feel that the point really arises in the present case. Counsel for the respondent was in the end constrained to agree that all the evidence in this case was both admissible and relevant, and that the Court of Appeal was right to draw attention [1972] 1 WLR 1365, 1370 to the "striking features of the resemblance" between the acts alleged to have been committed in one count and those alleged to have been committed in the others, and to say that this made it "more likely that John was telling the truth when he said that the appellant had behaved in the same way to him". In my view, this was wholly correct. With the exception of one incident "each accusation bears a resemblance to the other and shows not merely that [Kilbourne] was a homosexual, which would not have been enough to make the evidence admissible, but that he was one whose proclivities in that regard took a particular form" ([1972] 1 WLR 1365, 1369). I also agree with the Court of Appeal in saying that the evidence of each child went to contradict any possibility of innocent association. As such it was admissible as part of the prosecution case, and since, by the time the judge came to sum up, innocent association was the foundation of the defence put forward by the accused, the admissibility, relevance, and, indeed cogency of the evidence was beyond question. The word "corroboration" by itself means no more than evidence tending to confirm other evidence. In my opinion, evidence which is (a) admissible and (b) relevant to the evidence requiring corroboration, and, if believed, confirming it in the required particulars, is capable of being corroboration of that evidence and, when believed, is in fact such corroboration.

As Professor Cross well says in his book on *Evidence*, 3rd ed, p. 316: "The ground of the admissibility of this type of evidence was succinctly stated by Hallett J, when delivering the judgment by the Court of Criminal Appeal: 'If the jury are precluded by some rule of law from taking the view that something is a coincidence which is against all probabilities if the accused person is innocent, then it would seem to be a doctrine of law which prevents a jury from using what looks like common sense'." (*R* v *Robinson* (1953) 37 Cr App R 95, 106–107.)

That this is so in the law of Scotland seems beyond dispute, and it would be astonishing if the law of England were different in this respect, since one would hope that the same rules of logic and common sense are common to both. We were referred to the cases of *Moorov* v *HM Advocate*, 1930 JC 68 (an indecent assault case); *HM Advocate* v *AE* 1937 JC 96 (an incest case) and *Ogg* v *HM Advocate* 1938 JC 152, (a case of indecent conduct with male persons) . . .

In *HM Advocate* v *AE*, 1937 JC 96, 98–100, a case at first instance, the Lord Justice-Clerk (Lord Aitchison) summed up to the jury as follows:

> Now, I want finally to put before you one or two circumstances that you may think point in the direction of corroboration. First, I must give you a decision on this question—Can you take the evidence of the one girl as corroboration of the evidence of the other? Now, unless you believe both girls you need not consider whether you are going to take the evidence of the one as corroboration of the other. If you believe J and do not believe E, then, of course, E's evidence would be no use in the case of J, because you do not believe what E said. And J's evidence would be of no use in the case of E, for the same reason; but, if you believe both, I want you to consider anxiously whether you ought not to accept the evidence of the one as corroborating the evidence of the other. Now, it is a well-established rule in our criminal law that you do not prove one crime by proving another or by leading evidence tending to show that another crime has been committed. That is a good general rule. But then, when you are dealing with this class of crime there is some relaxation of the rule, otherwise you might never be able to bring the crime home at all. Let me give you an illustration that is not at all unfamiliar—there are many cases of it, especially in our large cities—you get a degraded man who finds some little girl in the street, and he gives her a penny, and gets her to go up a close, and there he does something immoral with her, and then he sends her away. Nobody sees what he has done; there is only the evidence of the child. And then the same thing happens with another child, and again nobody sees that; and then there is a third child, and the same thing happens again. Well, of course, if you had to have two witnesses to every one of these acts—they are all separate crimes—you would never prove anything at all. But that is not the law. The law is this, that, when you find a man doing the same kind of criminal thing in the same kind of way towards two or more people, you may be entitled to say that the man is pursuing a course of criminal conduct, and you may take the evidence on one charge as evidence on another. That is

a very sound rule, because a great many scoundrels would get off altogether if we had not some such rule in our law. Now, I give you this direction in law. If the conduct which is the subject of these charges is similar in character and circumstances, and substantially coincident in time, and you believe the evidence of both of these girls, then the evidence of the one may be taken as corroboration of the evidence of the other. This is in substance what was laid down in the High Court in the case of *Moorov* v *HM Advocate*, 1930 JC 68. That was a case where an employer in a Glasgow warehouse used to take one girl employee at a time up to his private office, and there commit an act of indecency, and then she was put out of the door. Nobody saw the act of indecency committed. There was only the girl's word for it. And then he would get another girl to go up, and the same thing would happen. Again nobody else was there, and there was just the girl's word for it. Now, no doubt there were in that case a number of these criminal assaults committed upon separate girls, whereas in this case we are only dealing with two, but I do not hesitate to tell you—and I take the responsibility of telling you—that if you believe the evidence of these two girls whom you have seen in the witness box, and accept it as the evidence of reliable witnesses, you may take the one as corroborating the other, and, therefore, as against the accused on each charge.

In addition to the valuable direction to the jury, this summing-up appears to me to contain a proposition which is central to the nature of corroboration, but which does not appear to date to have been emphasised in any reported English decision until the opinion delivered in *R* v *Hester* [1973] AC 296 by Lord Morris of Borth-y-Gest although it is implicit in them all. Corroboration is only required or afforded if the witness requiring corroboration or giving it is otherwise credible. If his evidence is not credible, a witness's testimony should be rejected and the accused acquitted, even if there could be found evidence capable of being corroboration in other testimony. Corroboration can only be afforded to or by a witness who is otherwise to be believed. If a witness's testimony falls of its own inanition the question of his needing, or being capable of giving, corroboration does not arise. It is for this reason that evidence of complaint is acceptable in rape cases to defeat any presumption of consent and to establish consistency of conduct, but not as corroboration. The jury is entitled to examine any evidence of complaint, in order to consider the question whether the witness is credible at all. It is not entitled to treat that evidence as corroboration because a witness, though otherwise credible, "cannot corroborate himself," i.e., the evidence is not "independent testimony" to satisfy the requirements of corroboration in *R* v *Baskerville* [1916] 2 KB 658, 667. Of course, the moment at which the jury must make up its mind is at the end of the case. They must look at the evidence as a whole before asking themselves whether the evidence of a given witness is credible in itself and whether, if otherwise credible, it is corroborated. Nevertheless, corroboration is a doctrine applying to otherwise credible testimony and not to testimony incredible in itself. In the present case Mark's evidence (count 3) was corroborated. But it was not credible and the conviction founded on it was rightly quashed.

It seems to me that the only way in which the doctrine upon which the decision of the Court of Appeal was founded can be supported, would be if there were some general rule of law to the effect that witnesses of a class requiring corroboration could not corroborate one another. For this rule of law counsel for the respondent expressly contended. I do not believe that such a rule of law exists . . ..

In *R* v *Hester* [1973] AC 296 this House has stigmatised this argument as fallacious. With respect, I wholly agree, and I hope no more will be heard of it.

The other ground upon which the general proposition may be defended is the bald proposition that one accomplice cannot corroborate another. In support of this proposition were cited *R* v *Noakes* (1832) 5 C & P 326 *per* Littledale J; *R* v *Gay* (1909) 2 Cr App R 327; *R* v *Prater* [1960] 2 QB 464, 465 *per* Edmund Davies J; *R* v *Baskerville* [1916] 2 KB 658, 664 citing *Noakes*; and *R* v *Cratchley* (1913) 9 Cr App R 232.

I believe these citations have been misunderstood. They all refer to fellow accomplices: see *per* Lord Diplock in *R* v *Hester* [1973] AC 296. Obviously where two or more fellow accomplices give evidence against an accused their evidence is equally tainted. The reason why accomplice evidence requires corroboration is the danger of a concocted story designed to throw the blame on the accused. The danger is not less, but may be greater, in the case of fellow accomplices. Their joint evidence is not "independent" in the sense required by *R* v *Baskerville* [1916] 2 KB 658, 667, and a jury must be warned not to treat it as a corroboration. But this illustrates the danger of mistaking the shadow for the substance. I feel quite sure that, for instance, where an unpopular officer in the army or the unpopular headmaster of a school could have been the victim of a conspiracy to give false evidence of this kind as the suggestion was in *R* v *Bailey* [1924] 2 KB 300 a similar warning should be given. As Lord Hewart CJ said in that case (which turned, however, on a wholly different point), at p. 305:

> The risk, the danger, the logical fallacy is indeed quite manifest to those who are in the habit of thinking about such matters. It is so easy to derive from a series of unsatisfactory accusations, if there are enough of them, an accusation which at least appears satisfactory. It is so easy to collect from a mass of ingredients, not one of which is sufficient, a totality which will appear to contain what is missing.

On the other hand, where the so-called accomplices are of the third class listed by Lord Simonds LC in *Davies* v *Director of Public Prosecutions* [1954] AC 378, 400 the danger is or may be nugatory. The real need is to warn the jury of the danger of a conspiracy to commit perjury in these cases, and, where there is the possibility of this, it is right to direct them not to treat as corroborative of one witness the evidence of another witness who may be part of the same conspiracy, but who cannot be an accomplice because if the evidence is untrue there has been no crime committed. This prompts me to point out that although the warning must be given in every appropriate case, the dangers to be guarded against may be quite different. Thus the evidence of accomplices is dangerous because it may be perjured. The evidence of Lady Wishfort complaining of rape may be dangerous because she may be indulging in undiluted sexual fantasy. A Mrs Frail making the same allegation may need corroboration because of the danger that she does not wish to admit the consensual intercourse of which she is ashamed. In another case the danger may be one of honestly mistaken identity as when the conviction of the accused depends on an identification by a single uncorroborated witness to whom he was previously unknown. These matters should, in suitable cases, be explored when the nature and degree of danger is being discussed, as suggested in *R* v *Price (Herbert)* [1969] 1 QB 541, 546. I do not, therefore, believe that there is a general rule that no persons who come within the definition of accomplice may be mutually corroborative. It applies to those in the first and second of Lord Simond LC's categories and to many other cases where witnesses are not or may not be accomplices. It does not necessarily apply to all witnesses in the same case who may deserve to be categorised as "accomplice". In particular it does not necessarily apply to accomplices of Lord Simonds LC's third class, where they give independent evidence of separate incidents, and where the circumstances are such as to exclude the danger of a jointly fabricated story.

Whatever else it is, the rule about fellow accomplices is not authority for the proposition that no witness who may himself require corroboration may afford corroboration for another to whom the same consideration applies, and this alone is what would help the respondent. When a small boy relates a sexual incident implicating a given man he may be indulging in fantasy. If another small boy relates such an incident it may be a coincidence if the detail is insufficient. If a large number of small boys relate similar incidents in enough detail about the same person, if it is not conspiracy it may well be that the stories are true. Once there is a sufficient nexus it must be for the jury to say what weight is given to the combined testimony of a number of witnesses.'

LORD REID: 'The main difficulty in the case is caused by observations in the case of *R* v *Manser* (1934) 25 Cr App R 18 to the effect that the evidence of one witness which required corroboration cannot be used as corroboration of that of another witness which also requires corroboration. For some unexplained reason it was held that there can be no mutual corroboration in such a case.

I do not see why that should be so. There is nothing technical in the idea of corroboration. When in the ordinary affairs of life one is doubtful whether or not to believe a particular statement one naturally looks to see whether it fits in with other statements or circumstances relating to the particular matter; the better it fits in, the more one is inclined to believe it. The doubted statement is corroborated to a greater or lesser extent by the other statements or circumstances with which it fits in.

In ordinary life we should be, and in law we are required to be, careful in applying this idea. We must be astute to see that the apparently corroborative statement is truly independent of the doubted statement. If there is any real chance that there has been collusion between the makers of the two statements we should not accept them as corroborative. And the law says that a witness cannot corroborate himself. In ordinary affairs we are often influenced by the fact that the maker of the doubted statement has consistently said the same thing ever since the event described happened. But the justification for the legal view must, I think, be that generally it would be too dangerous to take this into account and therefore it is best to have a universal rule.

So when we are considering whether there can be mutual corroboration between witnesses each of whom requires corroboration, the question must or at least ought to be whether it would be too dangerous to allow this. It might often be dangerous if there were only two children. But here we are dealing with cases where there is a "system", and I do not think that only two instances would be enough to establish a "system". Where several children, between whom there can have been no collaboration in concocting a story, all tell similar stories it appears to me that the conclusion that each is telling the truth is likely to be inescapable and the corroboration is very strong. So I can see no ground at all for the law refusing to recognise the obvious. Once there are enough children to show a "system" I can see no ground for refusing to recognise that they can corroborate each other.

Many of the authorities cited deal with accomplices where the rule as to the need of warning that there should be corroboration is similar to the rule with regard to children. I do not think it useful to regard children as accomplices; the rule with regard to children applies whether or not they are accomplices.

In most of the authorities the accomplices were accomplices to a single crime so the danger that they collaborated in concocting their story is obvious, and it is therefore quite right that there should be a general rule that accomplices cannot corroborate each other. Whether that should be a universal rule I greatly doubt, but I need not pursue that matter in this case.

Then there are indications of a special rule for homosexual crimes. If there ever was a time for that, that time is past, and on the view which I take of the law any such special rule is quite unnecessary . . .'

LORD SIMON OF GLAISDALE: 'The reason why corroboration is required in some types of case, and the nature of corroboration, were recently considered by your Lordships' House in *R* v *Hester* [1973] AC 296. It is required because experience has shown that there is a real risk that an innocent person may be convicted unless certain evidence against an accused (neatly called "suspect evidence" by my noble and learned friend, Lord Diplock, at p. 324) is confirmed by other evidence. Corroboration is therefore nothing other than evidence which "confirms" or "supports" or "strengthens" other evidence (Lord Morris of Borth-y-Gest, p. 315; Lord Pearson, p. 321; Lord Diplock pp. 323, 325). It is, in short, evidence which renders other evidence more probable. If so, there is no essential difference between, on the one hand, corroboration and, on the other, "supporting evidence" or "evidence which helps to determine the truth of the matter". Each is evidence which makes other evidence more probable. Once it is accepted that the direct evidence on one count is relevant to another by way of circumstantial evidence, it follows that it is available as corroboration if corroboration is required. Whether it operates as such depends on what weight the jury attaches to it, and what inferences the jury draws as to whether the offences demonstrate an underlying unity. For that purpose the jury will be directed in appropriate terms to take into account the proximity in time of the offences, their multiplicity, their similarity in detail and circumstance, whether such similarity has any unusual feature, what, if any, risk there is of collaboration in presenting a false case, and any other matter which tends to suggest or rebut an underlying unity—a system—something which would cause common sense to revolt at a hypothesis of mere coincidence.'

(LORDS MORRIS OF BORTH-Y-GEST and CROSS OF CHELSEA agreed.)

Appeal allowed.

• Is Lord Hailsham's statement in *DPP* v *Kilbourne* that 'corroboration is only required or afforded if the witness requiring corroboration or giving it is otherwise credible' open to criticism?

Attorney-General of Hong Kong v *Wong Muk Ping* [1987] 2 WLR 1033 (PC)

The defendant was charged with conspiracy to traffic in dangerous drugs in relation, *inter alia*, to the importation of opium into Hong Kong on a particular night. The prosecution case was that the defendant had attended a meeting at which the importation was planned and had supervised the transfer of the opium from a fishing vessel to a van, which he had then followed in order to ascertain its safe arrival at a warehouse. The police stopped the van containing the opium, and they also stopped the car driven by the defendant with two of the fishermen as passengers. The prosecution relied on the evidence of accomplices and the defendant's confession statement, which the judge admitted as a voluntary confession. The defendant gave no evidence before the jury. In his summing-up the judge warned the jury of the danger of convicting on the uncorroborated evidence of accomplices and he explained the meaning of corroboration. He directed them that they could convict on the uncorroborated testimony of accomplices if having regard to his warning they were satisfied beyond reasonable doubt that the accomplices' evidence was true, but he pointed out its unreliability. The defendant was convicted and appealed on the ground, *inter alia*, that the judge had erred in failing to direct the jury that the evidence of an accomplice had to be credible before any question of corroboration could arise. The Court of Appeal of Hong Kong allowed the defendant's appeal against conviction on that ground.

LORD BRIDGE OF HARWICH, delivering the judgment of their Lordships: 'The rule requiring a warning to be given to a jury of the danger of convicting on uncorroborated evidence applies to accomplices, victims of alleged sexual offences and children of tender years. It will be convenient to refer to these categories as "suspect witnesses". The submission made for the defendant is that, at least in some cases, it is essential for a judge to direct a jury with reference to the evidence of a suspect witness to consider whether the witness is credible *before* considering any other evidence capable of providing corroboration. The implication of this submission and the sense in which it must have been understood by the Court of Appeal of Hong Kong is that, in such a case, the jury must be directed first to assess the credibility of the evidence given by the suspect witness in isolation from any other evidence in the case. If at this stage they find the evidence not to be credible, they are to reject it in limine. Only if, at the first stage, they find that the evidence is credible, are they to proceed to the second stage, which will involve an examination of any material capable of providing corroboration, a decision whether it does so and finally a decision whether the evidence of the suspect witness is, in the event, to be accepted and relied on.

It is said that this two stage approach is implicitly indicated by passages from speeches in the House of Lords in two of the leading authorities. In *R* v *Hester* [1973] AC 296, 315, Lord Morris of Borth-y-Gest said:

> One of the elements supplied by corroborative evidence is that there are two witnesses rather than one. The weight of the evidence is for the jury—in cases where there is a trial by jury. It is for the jury to decide whether witnesses are creditworthy witness is not, then the testimony of the witness must be rejected. The essence of corroborative evidence is that one creditworthy witness confirms what another creditworthy witness has said. Any risk of the conviction of an innocent person is lessened if conviction is based upon the testimony of more than one acceptable witness. Corroborative evidence in the sense of some other material evidence in support implicating the accused furnishes a safeguard which makes a conclusion more sure than it would be without such evidence. But to rule it out on the basis that there is some mutuality between that which confirms and that which is confirmed would be to rule it out because of its essential nature and indeed because of its virtue. The purpose of corroboration is not to give validity or credence to evidence which is deficient or suspect or incredible but only to confirm and support that which as evidence is sufficient and satisfactory and credible: and corroborative evidence will only fill its role if it itself is completely credible evidence.

In *R* v *Kilbourne* [1973] AC 729, 746, Lord Hailsham of St Marylebone LC said:

> Corroboration is only required or afforded if the witness requiring corroboration or
> giving it is otherwise credible. If his evidence is not credible, a witness's testimony
> should be rejected and the accused acquitted, even if there could be found evidence
> capable of being corroboration in other testimony. Corroboration can only be
> afforded to or by a witness who is otherwise to be believed. If a witness's testimony
> falls of its own inanition the question of his needing, or being capable of giving
> corroboration does not arise. . . . Of course, the moment at which the jury must make
> up its mind is at the end of the case. They must look at the evidence as a whole before
> asking themselves whether the evidence of a given witness is credible in itself and
> whether, if otherwise credible, it is corroborated.

Before examining these passages further, their Lordships find it helpful first to consider
whether the suggested two stage approach is one which good sense or judicial experience
in assessing the credibility of evidence supports. There may, of course, be extreme cases
where a witness under cross-examination is driven to admit that his evidence-in-chief was
false. Such triumphs for the cross-examiner are more frequently seen in fictional
courtroom dramas than in real life. But in such an extreme case, if it should happen, there
would no longer be any question of credibility. Evidence which a witness first gives and
then admits to have been false is no longer his sworn testimony and, if a criminal
prosecution depends on it, the judge should direct an acquittal. But, apart from such
extremes, any tribunal of fact confronted with a conflict of testimony must evaluate the
credibility of evidence in deciding whether the party who bears the burden of proof has
discharged it. It is a commonplace of judicial experience that a witness who makes a poor
impression in the witness box may be found at the end of the day, when his evidence is
considered in the light of all the other evidence bearing upon the issue, to have been both
truthful and accurate. Conversely, the evidence of a witness who at first seemed
impressive and reliable may at the end of the day have to be rejected. Such experience
suggests that it is dangerous to assess the credibility of the evidence given by any witness
in isolation from other evidence in the case which is capable of throwing light on its
reliability; it would, to their Lordships' minds, be surprising if the law requiring juries to
be warned of the danger of convicting on the uncorroborated evidence of a witness in one
of the suspect categories should have developed to the point where, in some cases, the jury
must be directed to make such an assessment of credibility in isolation.

The concluding sentence in the passage which their Lordships have cited from the
speech of Lord Hailsham of St Marylebone LC in *R* v *Kilbourne* [1973] AC 729, 746,
seems to point directly against the suggested two stage process. The passage as a whole,
their Lordships think, is primarily emphasising what is plainly correct, viz., that the
evidence of a suspect witness, even though it receives some independent support in a form
capable of providing corroboration, cannot found a conviction unless itself accepted as
true.

More difficulty arises from the passage cited from the speech of Lord Morris of Borth-
y-Gest in *R* v *Hester* [1973] AC 296, 315, particularly the last sentence. It is possible to
read the sentence as supporting the proposition that corroborative evidence cannot "give
validity or credence to evidence which is . . . suspect". If this was indeed a proposition
which Lord Morris of Borth-y-Gest intended to enunciate, it is one from which their
Lordships feel constrained respectfully to dissent. It is precisely because the evidence of a

witness in one of the categories which their Lordships for convenience have called "suspect witnesses" may be of questionable reliability for a variety of reasons, familiar to generations of judges but not immediately apparent to jurors, that juries must be warned of the danger of convicting on that evidence if not corroborated; in short because it is suspect evidence. The corroborative evidence will not, of course, necessarily authenticate the evidence of the suspect witness. But it may at least allay some of the suspicion. In other words it may assist in establishing the reliability of the suspect evidence.

Their Lordships attach particular significance to the words of Lord Reid in *R v Kilbourne* [1973] AC 729, 750: "There is nothing technical in the idea of corroboration. When in the ordinary affairs of life one is doubtful whether or not to believe a particular statement one naturally looks to see whether it fits in with other statements or circumstances relating to the particular matter; the better it fits in, the more one is inclined to believe it. The doubted statement is corroborated to a greater or lesser extent by the other statements or circumstances with which it fits in".

This passage was relied on by Lord Hailsham of St Marylebone LC in *R v Boardman* [1975] AC 421, 454, to refute a misinterpretation of his own observations in *Kilbourne* which had been advanced in an argument which seems to have been not dissimilar from the argument advanced on behalf of the defendant in the instant case.

If, as Lord Reid's *dictum* in *R v Kilbourne* [1973] AC 729, 750, suggests, the presence or absence of corroborative evidence may assist a jury to resolve, one way or the other, their doubts as to whether or not to believe the evidence of a suspect witness, it must, in their Lordships' judgment, be wrong to direct them to approach the question of credibility in two stages as suggested in the submission made on behalf of the defendant.

A very familiar situation where directions as to corroboration are required is where the case for the prosecution cannot succeed unless an accomplice witness is believed, but where there is some evidence capable of providing corroboration. Just such a case was *R v Turner (Bryan)* (1975) 61 Cr App R 67. This was a case where the prosecution of a number of defendants charged with a series of bank robberies depended essentially on the evidence of a so called "supergrass" named Smalls. It was stated, at p. 83, that counsel for one of the defendants named Salmon "argued that the learned trial judge fell into error in his direction to the jury as to corroboration in that he failed to make it clear that the jury had to be satisfied that Smalls was a credible witness before they considered the question whether there was evidence which corroborated Smalls in a material particular implicating Salmon in the crime charged." James LJ delivering the judgment of the Court of Appeal (Criminal Division), after rehearsing this argument and referring to some of the passages from the speeches of Lord Morris of Borth-y-Gest in *R v Hester* [1973] AC 296 and Lord Hailsham of St Marylebone LC in *R v Kilbourne* [1973] AC 729 which have been quoted earlier in this judgment, said, 61 Cr App R 67, 84:

The credibility of the witness whose evidence requires corroboration is judged not on his evidence alone but on all the evidence in the case. In some cases that which adds credence to the evidence of the witness also serves to corroborate his evidence. In other cases evidence capable of providing corroboration is more clearly distinguishable from evidence which only goes to credibility. Some cases may call for a more emphatic or more elaborate direction than others. In the present case it must have been obvious to the jury from the start of the trial that, if they did not find Smalls to be a credible witness, that was the end of the case for the prosecution. This must have been even more obvious after the attack that was made upon the credibility of Smalls in the course of the trial.

Their Lordships can find no error in this passage. Where the prosecution relies on the evidence of an accomplice and where (in contrast with the instant case) the independent evidence capable of providing corroboration is not by itself sufficient to establish guilt, it will have become obvious to the jury in the course of the trial that the credibility of the accomplice is at the heart of the matter and that they can only convict if they believe him. The accomplice will inevitably have been cross-examined to suggest that his evidence is untrue. The jury will have been duly warned of the danger of relying on his evidence without corroboration. Their Lordships can see no sense in the proposition that the jury should be invited, in effect, to reject his evidence without first considering what, if any, support it derives from other evidence capable of providing corroboration.'

Appeal allowed. Conviction restored.

R v Reeves (1979) 68 Cr App R 331 (CA)

The appellant pleaded not guilty to handling stolen goods and his co-accused, M, pleaded guilty to theft of the same goods. M then proceeded to give evidence against the appellant who was convicted. The main ground of appeal was that the trial judge had failed to indicate to the jury what evidence was capable of corroborating M's evidence.

LORD WIDGERY CJ, giving the judgment of the court: 'The criticism of the learned judge's treatment of the whole question of corroboration is that, whereas on that page that I have just read the general direction is given certainly in adequate terms, what the judge fails to do is to indicate to the jury whether there was in the evidence in this case any matter which could be regarded as corroborative. It is becoming progressively more clearly recognised that this is a very important feature of the summing-up where the judge has to deal with such questions. The reason for that is that an identification of evidence which is capable of corroboration is not always easy. Even lawyers find it difficult sometimes, and it is, therefore, quite vital that the trial judge should not dispose of the matter as this judge did merely by describing the dangers of acting on uncorroborated evidence unless he produces the back-up direction which tells the jury what evidence can be regarded as corroborative for this purpose. I have said that the tendency of modern authority is to be more stringent in this regard, and that, I think, can be made out by one or two of the authorities which have been shown to us. First, there is the case of *Rance* (1975) 62 Cr App R 118. That was a decision of this Court, and it deals, amongst other things, with the argument in that case on the very subject with which I am seeking now to deal. The matters which were held in *Rance (supra)* were, first of all, whether the summing-up was at fault through not identifying the evidence capable of corroboration, and, secondly, in dealing with whether one accomplice could corroborate another. The report, in fairness to the prosecution in this case, does not indicate that in *Rance's* case *(supra)* the conviction was upset solely on the ground that the evidence capable of corroboration was not identified. That was taken as a point though it does not seem by itself to have been regarded as fatal to the success of the prosecution.

However, in a later decision in the case of *Charles and Others* [(1979) 68 Cr App R 334] where the presiding judge was Lawton LJ and where the date of the hearing was 29 June

1976, in that case this Court came out strongly with the proposition that items capable of corroborating should be identified.

I turn particularly to that part of the judgment in *Charles* where Lawton LJ said this, [at] p. 340: "There was a time some 20 years ago when the old Court of Criminal Appeal ruled that it was unnecessary for a judge to direct the jury as to what evidence was capable of being corroboration. Since that time the general practice has changed and it is now generally accepted, certainly in cases of any complication, that the judge should indicate to the jury what evidence is and what evidence is not capable of being corroboration".

That principle, reasserted by Lawton LJ at that point, is supported and confirmed by us sitting in this Court today.'
Appeal allowed. Conviction quashed.

C: EVIDENCE OF VISUAL IDENTIFICATION

(Suggested preliminary reading: *A Practical Approach to Evidence,* pp. 370–371, 425–426.)

R v Turnbull [1977] QB 224 (CA)

The Court of Appeal considered four separate appeals against conviction, all on the ground that the identification of the defendant was unsatisfactory.

LORD WIDGERY CJ, reading the judgment of the court: 'Each of these appeals raises problems relating to evidence of visual identification in criminal cases. Such evidence can bring about miscarriages of justice and has done so in a few cases in recent years. The number of such cases, although small compared with the number in which evidence of visual identification is known to be satisfactory, necessitates steps being taken by the courts, including this court, to reduce that number as far as is possible. In our judgment the danger of miscarriages of justice occurring can be much reduced if trial judges sum up to juries in the way indicated in this judgment.

First, whenever the case against an accused depends wholly or substantially on the correctness of one or more identifications of the accused which the defence alleges to be mistaken, the judge should warn the jury of the special need for caution before convicting the accused in reliance on the correctness of the identification or identifications. In addition he should instruct them as to the reason for the need for such a warning and should make some reference to the possibility that a mistaken witness can be a convincing one and that a number of such witnesses can all be mistaken. Provided this is done in clear terms the judge need not use any particular form of words.

Secondly, the judge should direct the jury to examine closely the circumstances in which the identification by each witness came to be made. How long did the witness have the accused under observation? At what distance? In what light? Was the observation impeded in any way, as for example by passing traffic or a press of people? Had the witness ever seen the accused before? How often? If only occasionally, had he any special reason for remembering the accused? How long elapsed between the original observation and the subsequent identification to the police? Was there any material discrepancy between the description of the accused given to the police by the witness when first seen by them and his actual appearance? If in any case, whether it is being dealt with summarily or on indictment, the prosecution have reason to believe that there is such a material discrepancy they should supply the accused or his legal advisers with particulars of the description the police were first given. In all cases if the accused asks to be given particulars of such descriptions, the prosecution should supply them. Finally, he should remind the jury of any specific weaknesses which had appeared in the identification evidence.

Recognition may be more reliable than identification of a stranger; but even when the witness is purporting to recognise someone whom he knows, the jury should be reminded that mistakes in recognition of close relatives and friends are sometimes made.

All these matters go to the quality of the identification evidence. If the quality is good and remains good at the close of the accused's case, the danger of a mistaken identification is lessened; but the poorer the quality, the greater the danger.

In our judgment when the quality is good, as for example when the identification is made after a long period of observation, or in satisfactory conditions by a relative, neighbour, a close friend, a workmate and the like, the jury can safely be left to assess the value of the identifying evidence even though there is no other evidence to support it: provided always, however, that an adequate warning has been given about the special need for caution. Were the courts to adjudge otherwise, affronts to justice would frequently occur. A few examples taken over the whole spectrum of criminal activity, will illustrate what the effects upon the maintenance of law and order would be if any law were enacted that no person could be convicted on evidence of visual identification alone.

Here are the examples. A had been kidnapped and held to ransom over many days. His captor stayed with him all the time. At last he was released but he did not know the identity of his kidnapper nor where he had been kept. Months later the police arrested X for robbery and as a result of what they had been told by an informer they suspected him of the kidnapping. They had no other evidence. They arranged for A to attend an identity parade. He picked out X without hesitation. At X's trial, is the trial judge to rule at the end of the prosecution's case that X must be acquitted?

This is another example. Over a period of a week two police officers, B and C, kept observation in turn on a house which was suspected of being a distribution centre for drugs. A suspected supplier, Y, visited it from time to time. On the last day of the observation B saw Y enter the house. He at once signalled to other waiting police officers, who had a search warrant to enter. They did so; but by the time they got in, Y had escaped by a back window. Six months later C saw Y in the street and arrested him. Y at once alleged that C had mistaken him for someone else. At an identity parade he was picked out by B. Would it really be right and in the interests of justice for a judge to direct Y's acquittal at the end of the prosecution's case?

A rule such as the one under consideration would gravely impede the police in their work and would make the conviction of street offenders such as pickpockets, car thieves and the disorderly very difficult. But it would not only be the police who might be aggrieved by such a rule. Take the case of a factory worker, D, who during the course of his work went to the locker room to get something from his jacket which he had forgotten. As he went in he saw a workmate, Z, whom he had known for years and who worked nearby him in the same shop, standing by D's open locker with his hand inside. He hailed the thief by name. Z turned round and faced D; he dropped D's wallet on the floor and ran out of the locker room by another door. D reported what he had seen to his chargehand. When the chargehand went to find Z, he saw him walking towards his machine. Z alleged that D had been mistaken. A directed acquittal might well be greatly resented not only by D but by many others in the same shop.

When, in the judgment of the trial judge, the quality of the identifying evidence is poor, as for example when it depends solely on a fleeting glance or on a longer observation made in difficult conditions, the situation is very different. The judge should then withdraw the case from the jury and direct an acquittal unless there is other evidence which goes to support the correctness of the identification. This may be corroboration in the sense lawyers use that word; but it need not be so if its effect is to make the jury sure that there has been no mistaken identification: for example, X sees the accused snatch a woman's handbag; he gets only a fleeting glance of the thief's face as he runs off but he does see him entering a nearby house. Later he picks out the accused on an identity parade. If there was no more evidence than this, the poor quality of the identification would require the judge to withdraw the case from the jury; but this would not be so if there was evidence that the house into which the accused was alleged by X to have run was his father's. Another example of supporting evidence not amounting to corroboration in a technical sense is to be found in *R* v *Long* (1973) 57 Cr App R 871. The accused, who was charged with robbery, had been identified by three witnesses in different places on different occasions but each had only a momentary opportunity for observation. Immediately after the robbery the accused had left his home and could not be found by the police. When later he was seen by them he claimed to know who had done the robbery and offered to help to find the robbers. At his trial he put forward an alibi which the jury rejected. It was an odd coincidence that the witnesses should have identified a man who had behaved in this way. In our judgment odd coincidences can, if unexplained, be supporting evidence.

The trial judge should identify to the jury the evidence which he adjudges is capable of supporting the evidence of identification. If there is any evidence or circumstances which the jury might think was supporting when it did not have this quality, the judge should say so. A jury, for example, might think that support for identification evidence could be found in the fact that the accused had not given evidence before them. An accused's absence from the witness box cannot provide evidence of anything and the judge should tell the jury so. But he would be entitled to tell them that when assessing the quality of the identification evidence they could take into consideration the fact it was uncontradicted by any evidence coming from the accused himself.

Care should be taken by the judge when directing the jury about the support for an identification which may be derived from the fact that they have rejected an alibi. False alibis may be put forward for many reasons: an accused, for example, who has only his own truthful evidence to rely on may stupidly fabricate an alibi and get lying witnesses to support it out of fear that his own evidence will not be enough. Further, alibi witnesses can make genuine mistakes about dates and occasions like any other witnesses can. It is only when the jury is satisfied that the sole reason for the fabrication was to deceive them and there is no other explanation for its being put forward can fabrication provide any support for identification evidence. The jury should be reminded that proving the accused has told lies about where he was at the material time does not by itself prove that he was where the identifying witness says he was.

In setting out these guidelines for trial judges, which involve only changes of practice, not law, we have tried to follow the recommendations set out in the Report which Lord Devlin's Committee made to the Secretary of State for the Home Department in April 1976. We have not followed that report in using the phrase "exceptional circumstances" to describe situations in which the risk of mistaken identification is reduced. In our judgment the use of such a phrase is likely to result in the build up of case law as to what circumstances can properly be described as exceptional and what cannot. Case law of this kind is likely to be a fetter on the administration of justice when so much depends upon the quality of the evidence in each case. Quality is what matters in the end. In many cases the exceptional circumstances to which the report refers will provide evidence of good quality, but they may not: the converse is also true.

A failure to follow these guidelines is likely to result in a conviction being quashed and will do so if in the judgment of this court on all the evidence the verdict is either unsatisfactory or unsafe.'

R v Weeder (1980) 71 Cr App R 228 (CA)

The appellant was charged with wounding with intent contrary to s. 18 of the Offences Against the Person Act 1861, following a street attack at night on T.T was struck on the back of the head from behind and fell to the ground underneath a lamp-post. The street lamp provided a bright light and he had a good look at the appellant. M looked out of a window during the attack and saw the appellant's face. She was acquainted with him. T identified the appellant in a street identification. The judge is summing-up told the jury that one identification could constitute support for the identification by another. The appellant was convicted and appealed.

LORD LANE CJ, giving the judgment of the court: 'Mr Locke suggested that the learned judge might have been wrong in law in suggesting that one identification can act as supporting evidence for another. The learned judge disagreed and after reference to *Turnbull's* case [[1977] QB 224] said that he accepted that Mr Locke was right to this extent, that the judge should warn the jury that because the identification is supported by another one it does not mean that the possibility of a mistake has disappeared. This satisfied Mr Locke and this point was then made by the learned judge when he resumed his summing-up.

Mr Locke, however, now returns to the charge and the main ground of his appeal is that the learned judge was wrong to direct the jury that an identification by one witness can constitute support for the identification by another. He submits that because a number of identifying witnesses can all be mistaken, the jury should be instructed to look at the evidence of each such witness separately in, so to speak, a hermetically sealed compartment and that they should be warned not to allow themselves to be affected by the accumulation of such evidence.

If this Court were to accept Mr Locke's submission, we would be imposing upon trial judges the obligation to pronounce a wholly useless incantation in the course of their summing-up. No jury, urged to use their common sense, could realistically be expected to follow, let alone understand, the reasoning of such direction. Take the simple case of violence at a football match. If a dozen witnesses, all of whom had in satisfactory conditions a good opportunity of observing who was committing the particular act of violence complained of, all identified the accused, is their evidence not to be viewed as capable of supporting each other?

In our judgment the position is a simple one and the guidance provided by this Court in *Turnbull (supra)* fully covers the position:

(1) When the quality of the identifying evidence is poor the judge should withdraw the case from the jury and direct an acquittal unless there is other evidence which goes to support the correctness of the identification. The identification evidence can be poor,

even though it is given by a number of witnesses. They may all have had only the opportunity of a fleeting glance or a longer observation made in difficult conditions, e.g., the occupants of a bus who observed the incident at night as they drove past.

(2) Where the quality of the identification evidence is such that the jury can be safely left to assess its value, even though there is no other evidence to support it, then the trial judge is fully entitled, if so minded, to direct the jury that an identification by one witness can constitute support for the identification by another, *provided* that he warns them in clear terms that even a number of honest witnesses can all be mistaken.'

Appeal dismissed.

R v Oakwell [1978] 1 WLR 32 (CA)

The defendant was one of a group of young people seen fighting by a police officer. The officer intervened and told the defendant that he was arresting him for breach of the peace. The police officer was then assaulted and he alleged that his assailant was the defendant. The defendant was charged with using threatening behaviour and assaulting a constable. He was convicted and appealed.

LORD WIDGERY CJ, giving the judgment of the court: 'It is alleged that the directions given in the recent case of *R v Turnbull* [1977] QB 224, were not applied to the identification problem which it is said arose in this case.

To start with, it was something of a surprise to the court to realise that any identification problem arose in this case at all. But further investigation shows that it amounts to this. There was a period when PC Tapson was on the ground when he had not got the defendant in his sight, and the suggestion is that there may have been confusion in PC Tapson's mind between the man who knocked him down and the defendant, who was standing up beside him when he got up again. This is not the sort of identity problem which *R v Turnbull* is really intended to cope with. *Turnbull* is intended primarily to deal with the ghastly risk run in cases of fleeting encounters. This certainly was not that kind of case.

Prompted by counsel doing their duty, the judge gave the jury a special passage in the summing-up on identification at the end, and we think it was perfectly adequate for the relatively minor identification problem which is eventually disclosed in this case, it being possible to say there might have been a mistake made.'

Appeal dismissed.

• Do you agree with Lord Widgery CJ's statement in *R v Oakwell* that *R v Turnbull* [1977] QB 224 is intended primarily to deal with the ghastly risk run in cases of fleeting encounters?

R v Penman (1986) 82 Cr App R 44 (CA)

The appellant was charged with burglary. The principal evidence on which the prosecution relied was scientific evidence which was not and could not sensibly have been challenged. The appellant's defence was an alibi. The judge's summing-up contained no suggestion that the jury should, if they concluded that the alibi was untrue, regard that as supporting or corroborating the forensic evidence, and he dealt in the most neutral terms with the discrepancies between what the appellant said to the police and what he said in evidence. The appellant was convicted and appealed.

HUTCHISON J, giving the judgment of the court: 'Mr Salmon relied on a passage in the judgment of this Court in the case of *Turnbull and Others* (1976) 63 Cr App R 132. That case, as is well known, is concerned with the way in which juries should be directed in cases where the evidence against the defendants depends wholly or substantially on the correctness of visual identification alleged by the defence to be mistaken. The passage on which Mr Salmon relies, at p. 139, is in the following terms: "Care should be taken by the judge when directing the jury about the support for an identification which may be derived from the fact that they have rejected an alibi. False alibis may be put forward for many reasons: an accused, for example, who has only his own truthful evidence to rely on may stupidly fabricate an alibi and get lying witnesses to support it out of fear that his own evidence will not be enough. Further, alibi witnesses can make genuine mistakes about dates and occasions like any other witnesses can. It is only when the jury is satisfied that the sole reason for the fabrication was to deceive them and there is no other explanation for its being put forward, that fabrication can provide any support for identification evidence. The jury should be reminded that proving the accused has told lies about where he was at the material time does not by itself prove that he was where the identifying witness says he was."

Basing himself upon this passage, Mr Salmon argued that it was incumbent upon the learned judge in the present case to warn the jury that a lying alibi was not necessarily indicative of guilt. As he originally developed it, his argument involved the contention that the present was in truth a case where identity was in issue. However, his argument finally came to this: that wherever an alibi was relied upon and there was a possibility that in rejecting the alibi evidence the jury might conclude that the defendant was lying, the judge was obliged to give a warning of the sort mentioned in *Turnbull (supra)*. While it was unnecessary for Mr Salmon in the present case to contend for any wider proposition, it is difficult to see why, if his argument in relation to cases where an alibi is relied on be correct, the judge should not be obliged to give a similar warning in any case where the jury are invited to conclude that the defendant had lied either to the police or in evidence.

Counsel were unable to refer us to any case which supported so wide a proposition and we know of none. There are, of course, many authorities dealing with the question whether lies by the defendant can constitute corroboration, in those cases where corroboration is either necessary or desirable. It appears to us that in the passage in *Turnbull (supra)* upon which Mr Salmon relies, this Court was dealing with an analogous situation. We draw attention, in particular, to the first and last sentences of the quoted passage. As we understand.it, the court was not there purporting to lay down any general proposition of the sort contended for by Mr Salmon. Still less do we think that the passage supports the wider proposition to which we have suggested his argument would logically lead.

It is, of course, true that the observations of this Court as to the reasons which may cause a defendant to put forward a false alibi must be of general application. It would be absurd to suggest that those reasons exist only in cases where the evidence against the defendant consists wholly or mainly of evidence of visual identification. However, as the first and last sentences of the quoted passage show, the particular question to which the Court, in making those observations was addressing itself was whether and in what circumstances a lying alibi could be regarded as providing support for a visual identification which was challenged. In such a case, it is the duty of the trial judge to identify evidence capable of supporting the evidence of identification and, in some such cases, the supporting evidence may take the form of a false alibi which has been fabricated by the defendant in order to deceive the jury. When the judge refers, in such a case, to lies by the defendant as being capable of constituting supporting evidence, he should remind the jury that the mere fact that the defendant has told lies about his whereabouts does not of itself prove that he was at the place where the identifying witness said he was. Similarly, in other cases in which a judge refers to lies by the defendant as being capable of constituting corroboration, his direction to the jury will indicate that the defendant's motive for lying must have been realisation of his guilt and fear of the truth.

It appears to us that the present case is wholly different. The principle evidence on which the prosecution relied was scientific evidence which was not and could not sensibly have been challenged. It was for the jury to decide whether they were prepared to infer from that evidence that the appellant was one of the burglars. In deciding whether to draw that inference they, of course, had to take into account what he had said to the police and what he had said in evidence as to his movements that night. Plainly, as their verdict shows, they did not believe his account, and they must have been prepared to draw the inference from the forensic evidence that he was one of the men involved. The learned judge's summing-up contains no suggestion that the jury should, if they concluded that the alibi was untrue, regard that as supporting or corroborating the forensic evidence. Indeed, as the passages we have cited from his summing up show, the learned judge dealt in the most neutral possible terms with the discrepancies between what the defendant said to the police and what he said in evidence. The present case was, as we have said, in no way comparable with those cases which have to do with lies as corroboration, or with the case of *Turnbull (supra)*.

In our judgment, there is no rule which, in a case such as the present, requires a warning in the terms contemplated by Mr Salmon's third ground of appeal. Of course, the circumstances of individual cases vary infinitely, and very often when a question arises as to whether a defendant has been lying, either to the police or in evidence, a judge will consider it appropriate to advise the jury that the mere fact that he has told lies does not prove guilt because there may be many reasons why a person will lie. However, as we have indicated, there is in our judgment no rule which requires that such a warning should invariably be given whenever the veracity of the defendant or the truth of an alibi defence is challenged, and we can well understand why the learned judge felt it unnecessary to give any such warning in the present case.'

Appeal dismissed.

Questions for discussion

R v Coke; R v Littleton

1 What requirements of corroboration arise in relation to the evidence of (a) Margaret, and (b) Angela Blackstone?

2 What evidence is to be found in the papers which would be capable in law of corroborating the evidence of each girl?

3 If either Coke or Littleton pleads guilty and gives evidence for the prosecution against the other, what requirements of corroboration may arise? How would the position differ from that where each pleaded not guilty and gave evidence in his defence implicating the other?

4 What are the respective functions of the judge and jury in relation to the requirements of corroboration?

5 The following is an extract from the summing-up of the trial judge in *R* v *Coke; R* v *Littleton*: 'Members of the jury, now that I have told you what corroboration means, you will naturally expect some guidance as to whether there is any evidence in this case which you could regard as corroborative of Margaret's evidence. Certainly there is. Whether you do find it corroborative in the circumstances is entirely a question of fact for you. But you may think that there was an abundance of evidence given which you could regard as corroborating her evidence. Let me give you two examples. You will recall that Margaret related to you a conversation she had with her mother on returning home from Coke's flat shortly after the commission of the alleged rape. That complaint was allowed to be given in evidence because it had the effect of confirming what Margaret said in evidence. Indeed, had it not possessed that confirming quality, it could not have been given in evidence at all because it would be what we lawyers call a mere self-serving statement. Or take another example. You heard evidence given that Dr Vesey took a vaginal swab from Margaret very shortly after the alleged offence, and that examination of that swab by Dr Espinasse showed that Margaret had had sexual intercourse within a recent time of its taking and definitely within forty-eight hours before. Now those are the sort of matters which you may think go to support Margaret's evidence and therefore corroborate it. But as I say, that is entirely a matter for you'.

Criticise this passage.

6 The following is a further extract from the summing-up: 'Members of the jury, you have heard argument from counsel and I have directed you to the effect that you should look for corroboration of Margaret's evidence, and that it would be dangerous, you may think, to convict unless that evidence was corroborated. In those circumstances, where can you find corroboration? It may occur to you to look at the evidence of the defendant Coke himself. He was not obliged to give evidence, but he elected to do so and you can consider that evidence. Bear in mind that on his own admission, he found himself sexually attracted to this girl and fully intended to have sexual relations with her. If you wish, you might regard that as some support for the account which Margaret has given you from the witness box. It may also be, though it is entirely a matter for you, that you do not accept what the defendant Coke says about his intentions, or about Margaret's consent. Well, if you disbelieve him, what better support could there be for Margaret's evidence? You would be entitled to regard that as corroborative, and you may well find that that removes some of the danger you would feel in acting on her unsupported evidence.'

Criticise this passage.

7 What considerations apply to the evidence of identification of Littleton?

Additional questions

1 Donald, a man in his twenties, is charged with raping Ethel, a schoolgirl, in a field at about 5 p.m. on the 1 June. The case has gone to trial, and the following evidence has been given:

(a) Ethel has said that Donald, who was a neighbour, met her at school, started to walk home with her, enticed her off the road, and pushed her over and had intercourse with her.

(b) Freda, Ethel's schoolfriend, has said that she saw Donald hanging around the school gates at about 4 p.m. on the 1 June, and that he and Ethel started to walk home together.

(c) Gertrude, Ethel's mother, has said that Ethel came home late on the 1 June: her clothes were dirty and dishevelled and Ethel told her that Donald had been very naughty.

(d) The police surgeon, who examined Ethel on the evening of the 1 June, has said that Ethel appeared to have had sexual intercourse recently.

(e) PC Harold has said that he interviewed Donald who told him that he was waiting outside the school to meet his niece, Jane, that he did speak to Ethel, but did not start to walk home with her.

Donald has not given evidence and has called no witnesses.
What direction should the judge give to the jury?

2 You are acting for Leonard, a man of about 30 with a record of burglary offences, who is charged with attempted burglary in Leeds in the following circumstances: At about 11 p.m. on Christmas Eve, Mary was just going to bed when she heard a sound of breaking glass; she switched on the light of her bathroom, saw the window was broken, and saw a man sliding down the drainpipe and running across the garden; she subsequently identified this man as Leonard at an identification parade but she admitted, under cross-examination, that she could not really be sure if it was the right man. Norman, her next door neighbour, was walking home from a party, and saw someone he thought was Leonard, whom he had known previously, pass him on the road at about 11.15 p.m.: he did not speak to him but noticed that he was dabbing his hand with a handkerchief. The police interviewed Leonard on Boxing Day: he said that he had spent Christmas in Lincoln with his mother; the police noticed a plaster on his hand; he volunteered to lend his clothes to the police for examination and the forensic scientist has found fragments of glass on his sleeve which were consistent with the glass in Mary's bathroom, but admits that the sample was very small. Leonard has given evidence himself: he told the court that he had cut his hand on a broken tumbler; he said he spent Christmas Eve with his sister in Nottingham (and she has given evidence to the same effect) and that when he said he was in Lincoln he had got confused over the dates. In his summing-up the judge said: 'You have to be pretty careful in this type of case, but you may think that there is ample evidence to show that Leonard was the man who broke Mary's window.'

Leonard has been convicted and wishes to appeal. Advise him.

Further reading

Carter, 'Corroboration requirements reconsidered: two comments' [1985] Crim LR 143.
Dennis, 'Corroboration requirements reconsidered: a postscript' [1985] Crim LR 146.
Dennis, 'Corroboration requirements reconsidered' [1984] Crim LR 316.
Grayson, 'Identifying Turnbull' [1977] Crim LR 509.
Heydon, 'Can lies corroborate' (1973) 89 LQR 552.
Jackson, 'The insufficiency of identification evidence based on personal impression' [1986] Crim LR 203.
Munday, 'Corroboration and the partial admission [1985] Crim LR 190.
Oughton, 'The distressing nature of corroboration' [1984] Crim LR 265.
Spencer, 'Child witnesses, corroboration and expert evidence' [1987] Crim LR 239.
Thorp, 'Cumulative corroboration' [1984] Crim LR 142.
Yates, 'Accomplice evidence' [1984] Crim LR 213.

Index